September 16-19, 2014
Fort Collins, CO

I0054708

**Association for Computing Machinery**

Advancing Computing as a Science & Profession

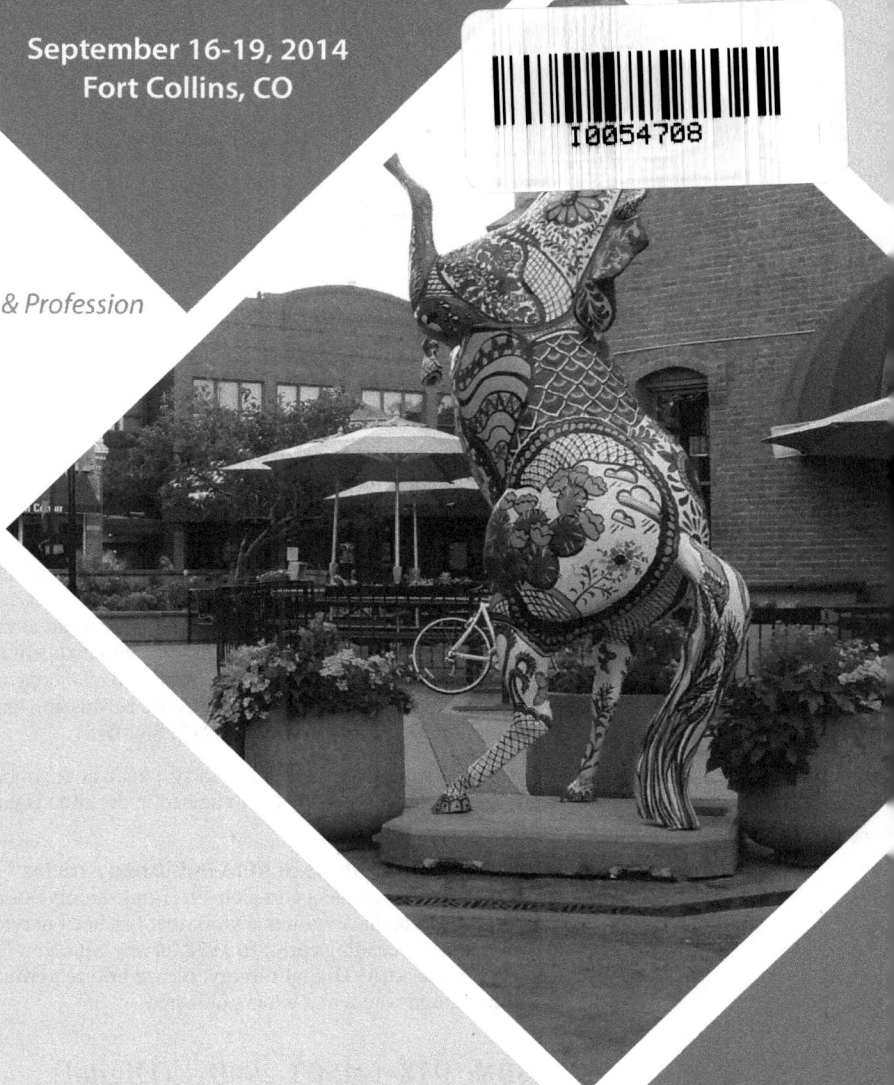

# DocEng'14

Proceedings of the 2014 ACM Symposium on
**Document Engineering**

Sponsored by:
*ACM SIGWEB*

Supported by:
*Adobe, FX Palo Alto Laboratory, HP & Xerox*

**ISBN:** 978-1-4503-2949-1 (Digital)

**ISBN:** 978-1-4503-3364-1 (Print)

Additional copies may be ordered prepaid from:

**ACM Order Department**
PO Box 30777
New York, NY  10087-0777, USA

Phone: 1-800-342-6626 (USA and Canada)
+1-212-626-0500 (Global)
Fax: +1-212-944-1318
E-mail: acmhelp@acm.org
Hours of Operation: 8:30 am – 4:30 pm ET

Printed in the USA

# Symposium and Program Chairs' Welcome

We are truly pleased to welcome you to the *2014 ACM Symposium on Document Engineering (DocEng14)*. DocEng14 is being held in Fort Collins, Colorado, USA, on 16-19 September, 2014. This year's DocEng Symposium continues and expands its tradition as the premier international forum for presentations, discussions, demonstrations and other sharing of the principles, technologies and processes for improving our capabilities in creating, managing and maintaining documents. This year's Symposium includes special focus on the digital humanities, document classification and clustering, document management and text similarity research. A highlight will be the two keynotes:

- The Evolving Scholarly Record: New Uses and New Forms, by Clifford Lynch (Coalition for Networked Information)

- Web-Intrinsic Interactive Documents, by Tony Wiley (HP Exstream R&D)

Building on events introduced in last year's Symposium, we have four accepted entries in this year's Doctoral Consortium (ProDoc@DocEng), aimed at providing expert advice to PhD-seeking students in the field of document engineering. We also have another "Birds of a Feather (BoF)" discussion group organized by Patrick Schmitz. This is also the sophomore year of the DocEng Best Student Paper Award. In addition, DocEng14 continues to provide an ACM SIGWEB DocEng Best Paper Award. The first day of the four-day conference is devoted to three workshops (DChanges 2014, SemADoc, and DH-CASE II), and one tutorial (PDF Tutorial): these are all-day events running in four parallel sessions.

A large and diverse set of submissions were received from all six inhabited continents. DocEng14 received 41 full paper submissions of which 15 were accepted (37%) and a further 41 short paper, application note and poster submissions of which 14 were accepted (34%). We want to thank all of those who contributed papers, ensuring a high-quality technical program and an exciting and interesting conference. We are very grateful to the assiduous and talented Program Committee and the additional reviewers who prepared more than 250 thoughtful and thorough reviews and then participated in the final selection discussions.

We also wish to thank ACM SIGWEB, Adobe, FXPAL, HP and Xerox for their generous support and the many people who have helped with organization including the Publicity Chair Tamir Hassan, the Local Arrangements Chair Margaret Sturgill, the Website Content Chair Marie Vans, the Workshop Chair Sonja Maier, the Doctoral Consortium Chair Cerstin Mahlow, the BoF Chair Patrick Schmitz and the workshop/tutorial organizers (Gioele Barabucci, Uwe M. Borghoff, Angelo Di Iorio, Sonja Maier, Ethan Munson, Carlotta Domeniconi, Evangelos Milios, Patrick Schmitz, Laurie Pearce, Quinn Dombrowski, Matthew Hardy, and Steven Bagley). Special thanks to Peter King, the Chair of the Steering Committee, and Ethan Munson, the liaison with SIGWEB, for their continued counsel, support and guidance. We are indebted to the other members of the Steering Committee and last year's Chairs, Simone Marinai and Kim Marriott, for their assistance and advice. Thanks very much to Lisa Tolles and her colleagues at Sheridan Communications for her flexibility with deadlines. We hope that you find the Symposium engaging and meaningful, and hope that you can join in sharing your ideas with other researchers and practitioners from around the world.

**Steven Simske**
*DocEng14 General Chair*
Hewlett-Packard Labs, USA

**Sebastian Rönnau**
*DocEng14 Program Chair*
Zalando, Berlin, Germany

# Table of Contents

## Session: Workshops & Tutorial
Session Chair: Sonja Maier *(UniBw München)*

# ACM DocEng 2014 Symposium Organization

**General Chair:** Steven Simske *(Hewlett-Packard, Fort Collins, USA)*

**Program Chair:** Sebastian Rönnau *(Zalando AG, Berlin, Germany)*

**Local Chair:** Margaret Sturgill *(Hewlett-Packard, Fort Collins, USA)*

**Publicity Chair:** Tamir Hassan *(Hewlett-Packard, Vienna, Austria)*

**Workshop Chair:** Sonja Maier *(University of the Federal Armed Forces, Munich, Germany)*

**Doctoral Symposium Chair:** Cerstin Mahlow *(University of Stuttgart, Germany)*

**Birds of a Feather Chair:** Patrick Schmitz *(University of California, Berkeley, USA)*

**Website Content Chair:** Marie Vans *(Hewlett-Packard, Fort Collins, USA)*

**Steering Committee Chair:** Peter King *(University of Manitoba, Winnipeg, Canada)*

**Steering Committee:**
David Brailsford *(University of Nottingham, UK)*
Dick Bulterman *(FX Palo Alto Laboratory, USA)*
Peter King (Chair) *(University of Manitoba, Canada)*
Kim Marriott *(Monash University, Australia)*
Ethan Munson *(University of Wisconsin-Milwaukee, USA)*
Charles Nicholas *(University of Maryland, Baltimore County, USA)*
Maria de Graca C. Pimentel *(Universidade de São Paulo, Brazil)*
Cecile Roisin *(Université Pierre Mendes-France and INRIA, France)*
Steven Simske *(Hewlett-Packard, USA)*
Jean-Yves Vion-Dury *(Xerox Research Centre Europe, France)*
Anthony Wiley *(HP Exstream, USA)*

**Program Committee:**

| | |
|---|---|
| Apostolos Antonacopoulos | Stefano Ferilli |
| Steven Bagley | Pierre Genevès |
| Helen Balinsky | Gersende Georg |
| Uwe Borghoff | Luiz Fernando Gomes Soares |
| David Brailsford | Michael Gormish |
| Dick Bulterman | Matthew Hardy |
| Pablo Cesar | Tamir Hassan |
| Boris Chidlovskii | Nathan Hurst |
| Paolo Ciccarese | Rolf Ingold |
| Michael Collard | Peter King |
| Cyril Concolato | Alberto Laender |
| Niranjan Damera-Venkata | Monica Landoni |

**Program Committee (continued):**

Nabil Layaïda
Baoli Li
John Lumley
Sonja Maier
Simone Marinai
Kim Marriott
Evangelos Milios
Mirella Moro
Ethan Munson
Charles Nicholas
Moira Norrie
Maria da Graça Pimentel
Stefan Pletschacher

Steve Probets
Cécile Roisin
Sebastian Rönnau
Patrick Schmitz
Ryan Shaw
Steven Simske
Margaret Sturgill
Frank Tompa
Jean-Yves Vion-Dury
Fabio Vitali
Anthony Wiley
Raymond Wong

**Sponsor:**

**Supporters:**

# The Evolving Scholarly Record: New Uses and New Forms

Clifford A. Lynch
Executive Director
Coalition for Networked Information
Washington, DC, USA
cliff@cni.org

## ABSTRACT

This presentation will take a very broad view of the emergence of literary corpora as objects of computation, with a particular focus on the various literatures and genres that form the scholarly record. The developments and implications here that I will explore include: the evolution of the scholarly literature into a semi-structured network of information used by both human readers and computational agents through the introduction of markup technologies; the interpenetration and interweaving of data and evidence with the literature; and the creation of an invisible infrastructure of names, taxonomies and ontologies, and the challenges this presents.

Primary forms of computation on this corpus include both comprehensive text mining and stream analysis (focused on what's new and what's changing as the base of literature and related factual databases expand with reports of new discoveries). I'll explore some of the developments in this area, including some practical considerations about platforms, licensing, and access.

As the use of the literature evolves, so do the individual genres that comprise it. Today's typical digital journal article looks almost identical to one half of a century old, except that it is viewed on screen and printed on demand. Yet there is a great deal of activity driven by the move to data and computationally intensive scholarship, demands for greater precision and replicability in scientific communication, and related sources to move journal articles "beyond the PDF," reconsidering relationships among traditional texts, software, workflows, data and the broad cultural record in its role as evidence. I'll look briefly at some of these developments, with particular focus on what this may mean for the management of the scholarly record as a whole, and also briefly discuss some parallel challenges emerging in scholarly monographs.

Finally, I will close with a very brief discussion of what might be called corpus-scale thinking with regard to the scholarly record at the disciplinary level. I'll briefly discuss the findings of a 2014 National Research Council study that I co-chaired dealing with the future of the mathematics literature and the possibility of creating a global digital mathematics library, as well as offering some comments on developments in the life sciences. I will also consider the emergence of new corpus-wide tools and standards, such as Web-scale annotation, and some of their implications.

**Categories and Subject Descriptors**
H.3.7 Digital Libraries

**Keywords**
scholarly communications; analysis of text corpora; digital journals

**Bio**
Clifford Lynch has led the Coalition for Networked Information (CNI) since 1997. CNI, jointly sponsored by the Association of Research Libraries and EDUCAUSE, includes about 200 member organizations concerned with the intelligent uses of information technology and networked information to enhance scholarship and intellectual life. CNI's wide-ranging agenda includes work in digital preservation, data intensive scholarship, teaching, learning and technology, and infrastructure and standards development.

Prior to joining CNI, Lynch spent 18 years at the University of California Office of the President, the last 10 as Director of Library Automation. Lynch, who holds a Ph.D. in Computer Science from the University of California, Berkeley, is an adjunct professor at Berkeley's School of Information. He is both a past president and recipient of the Award of Merit of the American Society for Information Science, and a fellow of the American Association for the Advancement of Science and the National Information Standards Organization.

In 2011, Lynch was appointed co-chair of the National Academies Board on Research Data and Information (BRDI); he serves on numerous advisory boards and visiting committees. His work has been recognized by the American Library Association's Lippincott Award, the EDUCAUSE Leadership Award in Public Policy and Practice, and the American Society for Engineering Education's Homer Bernhardt Award.

DocEng'14, September 16–19, 2014, Fort Collins, Colorado, USA.
ACM 978-1-4503-2949-1/14/09.
http://dx.doi.org/10.1145/2644866.2644900

# ActiveTimesheets: Extending Web-based Multimedia Documents with Dynamic Modification and Reuse Features

Diogo S. Martins[1,2]
[1]Universidade Federal do ABC, CMCC
Santo André, Brazil
santana.martins@ufabc.edu.br

Maria da Graça C. Pimentel[2]
[2]Universidade de São Paulo, ICMC
São Carlos, Brazil
mgp@icmc.usp.br

## ABSTRACT

Methods for authoring Web-based multimedia presentations have advanced considerably with the improvements provided by HTML5. However, authors of these multimedia presentations still lack expressive, declarative language constructs to encode synchronized multimedia scenarios. The SMIL Timesheets language is a serious contender to tackle this problem as it provides alternatives to associate a declarative timing specification to an HTML document. However, in its current form, the SMIL Timesheets language does not meet important requirements observed in Web-based multimedia applications. In order to tackle this problem, this paper presents the ActiveTimesheets engine, which extends the SMIL Timesheets language by providing dynamic client-side modifications, temporal linking and reuse of temporal constructs in fine granularity. All these contributions are demonstrated in the context of a Web-based annotation and extension tool for multimedia documents.

**Categories and Subject Descriptors:** H.5.1 Information Interfaces and Presentations: Multimedia Information Systems - Audio and Video

**Keywords:** interactive multimedia documents; web multimedia; dynamic modifications; document reuse.

## 1. INTRODUCTION

The adoption of multimedia technologies on the Web is highly dependent on how well user agents support them. Up until a few years ago, user agents have delegated most of the multimedia presentation functionalities to external, self-contained execution environments that could be embedded in a Web document via plugins. Tackling potential portability limitations and lack of open standards in these technologies, HTML5 [20] includes a number of extensions toward native multimedia functionalities on the Web, such as continuous media playback, inline vector-based graphics, state machine -based raster graphics, access to multimedia capture devices, just to name a few.

Despite these advances, HTML5 still lacks support for synchronized multimedia presentations. Even though continuous media streams can be included via specific tags, there are very limited resources to declaratively specify the temporal layout of a group of media elements. As an alternative to provide richer layouts, several authors have proposed the integration of multimedia authoring languages in the HTML5 technology stack [13, 6, 14, 18, 9, 12]. The SMIL Timesheets [21] (or simply Timesheets) language, a derivative of SMIL [19], stands out among these approaches since it includes an expressive temporal model and it provides reasonable decoupling between spatial and temporal layouts. Despite these advantages, Timesheets makes it harder to meet important requirements in Web-based multimedia authoring. In this paper, we emphasize two of such requirements: *dynamic modifications* and *reuse features*.

The first requirement, the modification of a document while it is being presented, is a recurrent design pattern in Web applications. The realization of such pattern in Timesheets documents, however, imposes some challenges. For all practical purposes, a typical multimedia document authored according to the Timesheets approach is composed of two subdocuments: the *spatial* document, in HTML; and the *temporal* document (or simply timesheet). The problem of modifying an HTML document is well understood and widely supported in user agents. Dynamically modifying a SMIL document, on the other hand, is not much understood [7], and this problem also affects its derivative languages. Being XML-based, a timesheet can be manipulated via DOM operations, but the practical implications of these operations on the data structures that govern the temporal layout are not well documented in the literature. Consequently, this language still lacks a concrete method to provide dynamic modifications in an active document.

Finally, the second requirement, reuse of authoring abstractions, is advocated not only to reduce authoring costs but also as means to improve the maintainability of a resulting document. SMIL Timesheets has reuse at its foundation, since it separates temporal and spatial models. Regarding reuse on its temporal model, some features are also present, for instance the nesting of timesheets. However, important patterns cannot be accomplished with this language, such as reuse of temporal relations (for instance to refer to an internal or external temporal composition) and reuse of fragments of temporal relations (for instance to refer to a fragment of a temporal composition). The impossibility of accomplishing such use cases demands solutions to incorporate additional reuse features in this language.

In order to tackle these requirements, this paper introduces the ActiveTimesheets engine, which provides a group of language extensions and temporal formatting mechanisms to enable dynamic document modifications, granular reuse of document elements and their fragments and seamless spatio-temporal linking. The remaining of this paper is organized as follows. First, Section 2 discusses work related to the most important contributions of ActiveTimesheets. Section 3 presents preliminary definitions on the timegraph model, which is used as a basis to realize the language extensions. After that, Section 4 introduces ActiveTimesheets core extensions, namely the model of dynamic modifications (Section 4.1), the strategy for linking (Section 4.2) and reuse features (Section 4.3). Then in Section 5, implementation issues of the engine are discussed, followed by an instantiation of the engine (Section 6) in the context of a tool for enriching and extending Web-based multimedia documents. At last, Section 7 concludes this paper.

## 2. RELATED WORK

In order to provide richer synchronization constructs in HTML5-based documents, some authors have proposed the integration of foreign multimedia authoring languages (e.g. NCL[1], SMIL, or non-standardized formats [11]) in a web document via scripting-based engines. One line of approaches (e.g. SmilingWeb [6], WebNCL [13] and NCL4Web [14]) consist in converting, statically or dynamically, a document completely authored in the foreign language to an equivalent representation in HTML, CSS and Javascript. Such strategy makes it easier to migrate documents in the foreign language to HTML, but they make it harder to apply synchronization constructs to documents originally authored in HTML. Another line of approaches consist in augmenting HTML with timing functionality (e.g. XHTML+SMIL [18], smilText-JS [9] and Timesheets.js [4]). An advantage of this approach is that an author can take full benefit of the HTML syntax, while applying a temporal model to the document.

Regarding dynamic modifications on multimedia documents, several authoring languages tackle this problem by mapping an editing operation into the data structures that guide the spatio-temporal layout. Editing operations can originate on client-side or on server-side; additionally, the resulting update in the temporal layout can be incremental or lead to a complete recomputation of it. In certain languages, editing operations occur directly in the layout data structures: this is the case of MPEG-4 BIFS[2] and LASeR[3], both of which define commands to incrementally manipulate the scene graph that is generated from a document specification. A different approach is taken by NCL, which provides both server-side and client-side live editing commands directly in the document syntax: consequently, the incremental effect of an operation is mapped, via predefined rules, into the HTG (Hypermedia Temporal Graph) that represents the document temporal layout.

In most SMIL rendering engines, the temporal layout is governed by a graph-based data structure called timegraph. The Timesheets.js [4] API provides an experimental opera-

tion to directly edit the timegraph, in this case restricted to addition (but not removal or updates) of time container nodes. Directly editing the rendering structures is also performed by the Ambulant Annotator tool [9], but the operations are restricted to those required for captioning single videos using smilText. A more robust and author-friendly approach consists of, similarly to NCL, providing every editing operation in the authoring syntax (e.g. via DOM methods) and properly map their effects into the timegraph. A general approach to this problem is analyzed by Jansen et al. [7], which propose an abstract taxonomy of editing operations and their expected costs regarding timegraph updates. Modification operations are organized in clusters, of which timegraph updates are expected only on the Media Item (in some cases) and the Structure (in all cases) clusters. As advocated by the authors [8], this classification is a starting model to be extended by other researchers: in this paper, we take this classification as a basis and report a group of concrete methods to realize incremental updates in the timegraph.

Regarding reuse features, previous research in hypermedia authoring languages [15, 2, 16] has established patterns that allow reuse of several aspects of a document, such as: templates, internal and external references, media content, style definitions, spatial and temporal relations and compositions, just to name a few. In HTML, more granular reuse of media content is possible once the user agent supports the Media Fragments scheme [10], which provides syntax for addressing elements in the spatial, temporal, track and id dimensions. In SVG [17], intra-document reuse of geometrical shapes is possible via def and use tags, as well as inter-document reuse is accomplished via namespaces. In NCL, reuse has been thoroughly studied, which leads this language to support an ample group of reuse constructs, either internally (e.g. media content, layout, structure, etc.) or externally (e.g. nested documents, imported objects, etc.).

In SMIL, reuse of media content is possible via the src attribute of media objects and, in the case of continuous media content, media objects can be constrained to a subinterval of its intrinsic timeline via the clipEnd and clipBegin attributes. The SMIL Timesheets language augment these possibilities by introducing the timesheet element whose src attribute can refer to an external document: consequently, several timesheets can be nested in interesting reuse schemes. Additionally, the method for binding temporal specifications to spatial fragments, via CSS expressions in the item element, allows reuse of a spatial fragment in multiple item elements. Besides these improvements, some useful reuse patterns are still not possible, such as reuse of individual elements in the temporal document. In this paper, we tackle this limitation by proposing a group of techniques to reuse fragments from internal and external documents and to reuse fragments of temporal compositions (e.g. clipping of time containers).

## 3. THE TIMEGRAPH MODEL

The semantics of the SMIL language has been described by various formalisms, for instance, automata [1], timed petri nets [3] and logic rules [5], just to name a few. In order to compute the temporal layout of a document, the SMIL recommendation promotes a graph-based model, called *timegraph*. However, the SMIL literature does not include a formal definition for it, being its semantics defined mostly via natural language and sometimes pseudocode. In order to establish a basis for the extensions reported in this paper,

---

[1]ITU-T H.761: Nested Context Language (NCL) and Ginga-NCL. http://www.itu.int/rec/T-REC-H.761

[2]ISO/IEC 14496-11:2005: http://www.iso.org/iso/iso_catalogue/catalogue_tc/catalogue_detail.htm?csnumber=38560

[3]ISO/IEC 14496-20:2008: http://www.iso.org/iso/iso_catalogue/catalogue_ics/catalogue_detail_ics.htm?csnumber=52454

hereafter it is provided a working definition of the timegraph model, with a focus on timegraphs generated from documents authored in the SMIL Timesheets language.

A timegraph is a directed acyclic graph $TG = (N, R)$, where: $N$ is a set of vertices, or nodes, representing time elements; and $R$ is a set of directed edges representing temporal relationships. A node is specialized into one of various types and, being SMIL a modular language, the total set of types will depend on the language profile being used. For the present discussion, it is enough to focus on the most important groups of nodes, which are time containers (*par*, *seq* and *excl*), media elements (continuous and discrete) and link anchors. Timegraph relationships can be: *i) hierarchical relationships*, which represent temporal composition between time elements, for example between time containers and media elements; or *ii) event relationships*, which can represent either predictable (internal) or unpredictable (external) synchronization relationships between time elements.

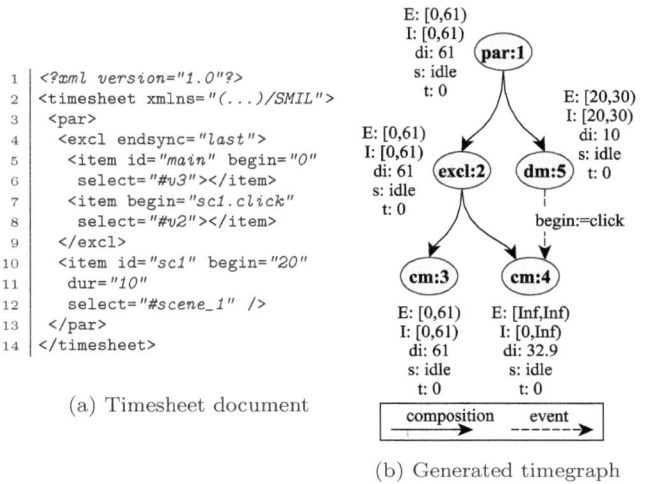

```
1   <?xml version="1.0"?>
2   <timesheet xmlns="(...)/SMIL">
3    <par>
4     <excl endsync="last">
5      <item id="main" begin="0"
6       select="#v3"></item>
7      <item begin="sc1.click"
8       select="#v2"></item>
9     </excl>
10    <item id="sc1" begin="20"
11     dur="10"
12     select="#scene_1" />
13   </par>
14  </timesheet>
```

(a) Timesheet document

(b) Generated timegraph

Figure 1: Example of a SMIL Timesheets document and the corresponding timegraph.

Figure 1 presents a multimedia document modeling the scenario of an interactive video: when a user clicks on an overlaid menu, an alternative video is played. Figure 1a represents an external timesheet which should be included in an HTML document (omitted here) that contains the spatial layout. The presentation will initially schedule the activation of the main video (line 5), which eventually will be interrupted by the activation of an alternative video (line 7). The alternative video is scheduled by a user interaction event (`sc1.click`) that can occur while the menu is active (line 10).

The timegraph generated from this temporal document is illustrated in Figure 1b. Each node in the timegraph is labeled by its type and identifier. In this example, a node was created for every time container (*par:1* and *excl:2*) and media element (either continuous media elements, e.g., *cm:3*, *cm:4*, or discrete media elements, e.g., *dm:5*). Notice that in this example, taking composition relationships alone, the timegraph structure is very similar to the document (timesheet) DOM, because every **item** element represents a single media object. In SMIL Timesheets, this correspondence does not always apply, given that an **item** element can represent (depending

on the expression given by **select** attribute) multiple media objects or it can be used as a composition (i.e. similarly to a time container). Every timegraph node contains a timeline, which represents its activation interval. Given that the SMIL temporal model is hierarchical, the subgraph formed only by the nodes and the composition relationships is a hierarchy, or tree, of timelines. Every node stores its scheduling information, which is composed of the following attributes: *i)* the external timeline ($E$), which is the synchronization constraint between the node and its parent (via a composition relationship); *ii)* the internal timeline ($I$), which is the reference to enforce the synchronization constraint of the node's children, if any; *iii)* the implicit duration ($di$), which can be intrinsic (e.g. for continuous media) or computed (e.g. for time containers); *iv)* the execution state ($s$), e.g. paused, playing, etc.; and *v)* the current time ($t$) of the node, which is hierarchically computed from the parent of each node.

A node can have unresolved timing because of an event relationship. In Figure 1b, event relationships are represented by a dashed line and an associated constraint, for instance the edge (*dm:5*, *cm:4*) in the figure. Additionally, an unresolved node have unresolved timelines, which in the figure is implied by the *Inf* (Infinity) value in the target node of the relationship. In the example, the relationship constraint states that when the event *click* occurs on the element abstracted by *dm:5*, the time of this occurrence resolves (or is assigned to) the begin attribute of the element abstracted by *cm:4*.

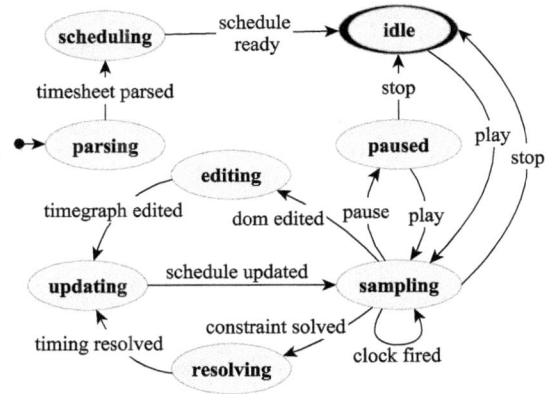

Figure 2: Timegraph lifecycle as a simplified state machine

The lifecycle of a timegraph is abstracted as a finite state machine, whose states and most important transitions are represented in Figure 2. Part of the states represent the following timegraph processes: *i) parsing*, in which the timegraph is built from document syntax; *ii) scheduling*, which consists in computing the internal and external timelines of each node; *iii) sampling*, which consists in updating the timing of the timegraph and activating/deactivating nodes according to the schedule; *iv) resolution*, which consists in updating the timegraph schedule when some event-based constraint is solved; *v) editing*, which consists in mapping DOM modifications into the timegraph; *vi) update*, which consists in updating the schedule of the timegraph in response to resolution or editing. The last two processes, in particular, are discussed in the next section.

# 4. ACTIVETIMESHEETS

ActiveTimesheets is an enhanced presentation engine for the SMIL Timesheets language. Of the three modules originally included in the Timesheets recommendation, only the ones related to Timing and Synchronization are directly implemented in ActiveTimesheets; the remaining ones, Animation and Prefetch, are not included in the engine, as document authors can resort to analogous functionality already present in HTML5 (e.g. CSS Animations and MediaElement preload). In addition, ActiveTimesheets is augmented by other SMIL modules, with adaptations to reflect the particularities of the Timesheets approach. These include the Linking module, which is adapted for a seamless integration with HTML linking; and the Media Clipping module, which is extended to allow clipping of time containers.

Table 1 compares ActiveTimesheets with other related languages and engines. As the table demonstrates, Active-Timesheets presents a set of extensions that potentially make it suitable for a greater range of use cases. Whereas it does not support the full range of SMIL 3.0 timing constructs, it extends the language in important ways. For instance, support for dynamic modifications, fine-grained reuse and media fragments are features fully provided only in Active-Timesheets. Additionally, in some cases, such as media clipping and linking, the original functionality is extended to make it more conforming to novel extensions or to the HTML5 environment. The remaining of this section concentrate on the techniques that realize these extensions.

## 4.1 Dynamic modifications

Editing a document while it is active has several implications in the processes of scheduling, sampling and resolution of the timegraph. From the standpoint of scheduling, manipulating document elements may require a structural or logical change in the timegraph in order to accommodate the modification. Such schedule changes also affect sampling, as some of them, for instance time manipulations, require that parameters used in the sampling process be adapted to reflect the changes. Additionally, other groups of changes may add or remove indeterminate timing attributes from the document, which also affects the occurrences of the resolution process. As a consequence, performing editing operations in the document requires some mechanism to control these processes: in ActiveTimesheets, this is achieved via the Timegraph Model, which also provides objects and methods to manipulate timegraph nodes. Even though this model suffices the needs of directly manipulating a timegraph, another complementary mechanism must be provided to edit the document in the authoring syntax and, more important, make sure that the document syntax and the corresponding timegraph specify equivalent scenarios.

From the standpoint of document editing, the usual mechanism for manipulating structured documents, in the Web platform, is via the DOM. Once a DOM-based editing operation is applied to a document, the rendering engine must keep the DOM and the rendering data structures in a consistent state. In ActiveTimesheets, a DOM inheritance strategy is adopted (Figure 3), which consists in extending the DOM by overloading a selection of methods that are guaranteed to affect the timegraph, i.e., those related to the MediaItem and Structure clusters [7]. In order that a DOM modification be properly mapped into the timegraph, procedural code in every DOM node manipulates this data structure using the

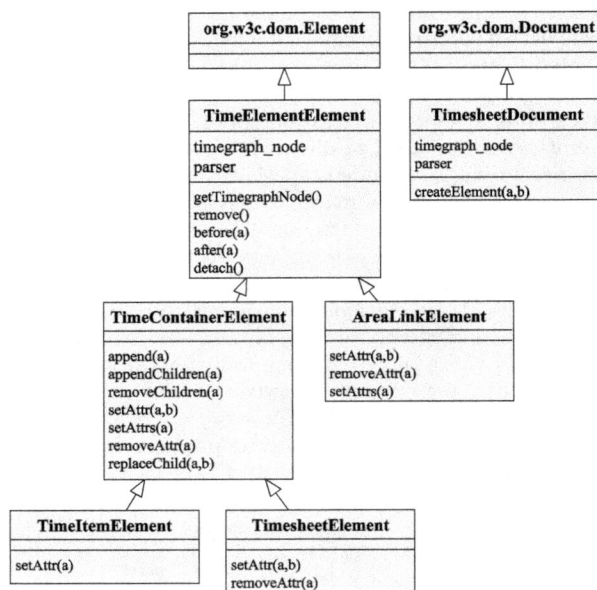

Figure 3: Excerpt of the ActiveTimesheets DOM API emphasizing methods that affect the timegraph

Timegraph Model. Only the DOM API is exposed to applications, being the use of the Timegraph Model restricted to the DOM API.

In Figure 3, the element *TimesheetDocument* extends a DOM document (*org.w3c.dom.Document*) and allows creation of new document nodes. Upon creation, not only a DOM node is generated, but also a new timegraph node corresponding to the DOM specification (attribute *timegraph_node*): this aggregation integrates the Timegraph Model to the DOM API. The nodes created by *Timesheet-Document* belong to a hierarchy of elements, all of which derive their functionality from *TimeElementElement*. This class also associates the DOM element to a corresponding timegraph node which, depending on the composition structure abstracted by the syntax, may be a single node or a sub-timegraph. The *TimeContainerElement* class has an important role: it not only allows manipulation of **par**, **seq**, and **excl** nodes, but also other elements which are composite structures: *TimeItemElement* and *TimesheetElement*. This is because, at the timegraph level, both **item** (in the composite case) and **timesheet** elements are represented as implicit time containers. The class *AreaLinkElement*, which represents **area** links in ActiveTimesheets (refer to Section 4.2), is not a composition structure, consequently it is derived directly from *TimeElementElement*.

### 4.1.1 Editing elements and attributes

In the ActiveTimesheets DOM API, modification of elements and attributes consists in, first, performing the modification in the extended DOM and, after, translating the modification to the timegraph. As the timegraph is updated, its schedule needs to be updated as well. All these steps are performed during a single atomic operation. Such atomicity is possible because, when an editing operation is performed, the timegraph state machine transitions to the *editing* state

6

Table 1: Comparison between ActiveTimesheets and other SMIL-based temporal languages and engines.

| Module/features | SMIL | XHTML+SMIL | SMIL Timesheets | Timesheets.js | ActiveTimesheets |
|---|---|---|---|---|---|
| **Media** | | | | | |
| MediaClipping | + | + | - | - | + + |
| **Timing** | | | | | |
| TimingAttr | + | + | + | + | + |
| RepeatTiming | + | + | + | + | + |
| EventTiming | + | + | + | + | + |
| SyncBaseTiming | + | + | + | + | + |
| SyncBehavior | + | - | - | - + | - |
| TimeContainerAttr | + | + | + | + | + |
| BasicTimeCont | + | + | + | + | + |
| BasicExclTimeCont | + | + | + | + | + |
| **Linking** | | | | | |
| FragmentIdentifier | + | - | - | + | + + |
| LinkingAttributes | + | - | - | - | + |
| BasicLinking | + | - | - | - | + |
| **Metainformation** | | | | | |
| Metadata | + | - | - | - | + |
| **Novel extensions** | | | | | |
| Dynamic modifications | - | - | - | - + | + |
| Reuse extended | - | - | - | - | + |
| Media fragments | - | - | - | - | + |

+ supported      - unsupported      -+ partially supported      ++ supported with extensions

(refer to Figure 2), which keeps all other processes suspended until it completes the modification; in case unpredictable conditions, such as user interaction events, occur during the update, they are queued and their resolution occurs only after the modification completes.

---

**Algorithm 1** Element addition on a time container

```
 1: function TIMECONTAINERELEMENT.APPEND(child)
 2:     super.APPENDCHILD(child)
 3:     if tag(child) is par|seq|excl|item|area then
 4:         P ← this.GETTIMEGRAPHNODE( )
 5:         C ← child.GETTIMEGRAPHNODE( )
 6:         P.APPENDCHILD(C)
 7:         C.UPDATEATTRIBUTES( )
 8:         C.COMPUTESCHEDULE( )
 9:         P.UPDATESCHEDULE(C)
10:     end if
11: end function
```

An example of this procedure is demonstrated in Algorithm 1, which adds a new element to the document. In ActiveTimesheets, addition of new elements occurs by manipulating a composite element via its **append** method. First, the new element is assigned to the extended DOM node (line 2). Then, the wrapped timegraph node has its scheduling updated in order to reflect the changes (lines 3-10). In fact, the schedule is updated only if the node that was added affects the timegraph: this is the case of a restricted set of elements, depicted in the condition in line 3. Other a-temporal elements, such as **meta** and **metadata**, do not affect the timegraph and, therefore, do not require an update.

Updating the timegraph consists in a number of steps. First, the timegraph node of the DOM child is appended to the timegraph. Second, a semantic verification of the node attributes is performed, to make sure that semantic restrictions from its parent are satisfied (for instance, to disallow indeterminate begin times in the children of a **seq** container), opting for default values in case such verification fails. Third, the schedule of the element is computed from its attributes. Finally, the timegraph schedule is updated in an incremental manner (details of this operation are discussed in Section 4.1.2). Removal and update of nodes follows a similar procedure, i.e., both the DOM and the timegraph are modified in a proper order.

Modification of attributes in the document is performed via the **setAttr** methods, which are overloaded by all concrete elements (refer to Figure 3), given that each element has particularities in their attributes. In general, the editing procedure consists basically of updating the attribute in the DOM and, if the attribute affects the timegraph, perform an incremental schedule update. An exception to this general procedure is the update of the **select** attribute in the **item** element, which can lead to significant structural and logical changes in the timegraph.

---

**Algorithm 2** Attribute modification on **item** element

```
 1: function TIMEITEMELEMENT.SETATTR(name, value)
 2:     super.SETATTRIBUTE(name, value)
 3:     if name is begin|dur|end|...|clipend then
 4:         T ← this.GETTIMEGRAPHNODE( )
 5:         A ← this.parser.PARSEATTR(name, value)
 6:         T.SETATTRIBUTE(A)
 7:         T.UPDATESCHEDULE( )
 8:     else if name is select then
 9:         T_old ← this.GETTIMEGRAPHNODE( )
10:         T_new ← parser.PARSETIMEELEMENT(this)
11:         P ← T_old.GETANCESTOR( )
12:         P.ADDCHILDAFTER(T_new, T_old)
13:         P.REMOVECHILD(T_old)
14:         T_new.UPDATESCHEDULE( )
15:     end if
16: end function
```

Algorithm 2 demonstrates this procedure. The first important action taken by the algorithm is updating the DOM by assigning a new attribute (line 2). In case the attribute affects the timegraph, but it is not **select**, it is parsed and assigned to the associated timegraph node (lines 3-7). After that, the timegraph schedule is incrementally updated. The other situation refers to the update of the **select** attribute: in this case, a new sub-timegraph, corresponding to selected elements, must be generated and replaced in the timegraph. The sub-timegraph can be a single media element or a time container, depending on the number of elements retrieved by the selection expression. After that, the schedule is incrementally updated, starting from the new sub-timegraph.

### 4.1.2 Incremental schedule updates

An important performance requirement for a schedule update is that only the subgraph affected by the operation must be recomputed. As depicted in Figure 2, schedule updates occur in two situations: *a)* when an event-based constraint is solved; and *b)* when the document is edited. In the first case, the process consists in hierarchically propagating the resolved timing to all ancestor nodes (via traversal of the composition relationships) of every node whose timing is affected by this constraint. This is required because, due to the hierarchical temporal model, when an element has an unresolved timeline, the whole chain of ancestors have unresolved timelines as well. A full schedule computation requires traversal of all composition relationships $C$ ($C \subseteq R$), acting only on the subgraph formed by these relationships, the *composition tree*. Whereas a full schedule computation requires $O(C)$ operations, the resolution process takes $O(h)$ operations, whereas $h$ is the height of the composition tree. Differently from the resolution process, dynamic modifications do not always require propagation of updates up to the topmost ancestor. In fact, only those ancestors who have their timelines modified by the editing operation need to be updated. This process, called incremental schedule update, is demonstrated in Figure 4.

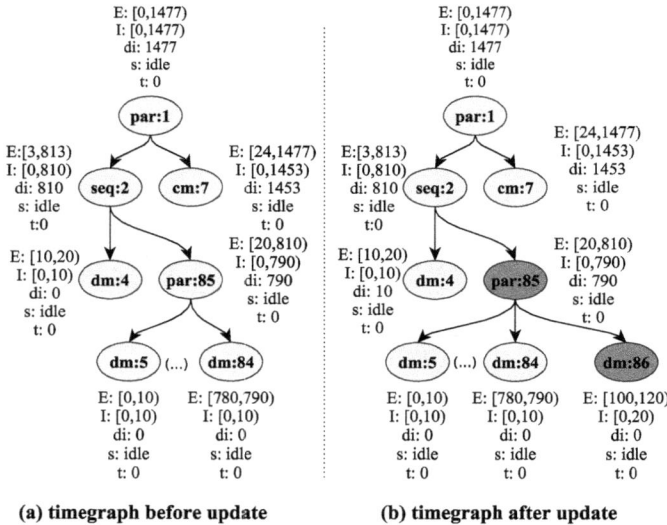

**(a) timegraph before update**    **(b) timegraph after update**

Figure 4: Example of an incremental timegraph schedule update due to dynamic modification

The relevant fragment of the timegraph in Figure 4a is the composition *par:85* which aggregates an arbitrary number of discrete media elements which are executed according to **par** semantics. Upon insertion of a new node (*dm:86*) as a child of *par:85*, the insertion procedure will attempt to incrementally update the timegraph, which will make *par:85* attempt to update its schedule (refer to Algorithm 1). But, as the external timeline of *dm:86* is already contained in the internal timeline of its ancestor ($[100, 120) \subset [0, 790)$), then no change in the schedule of *par:85* will be observed.

Consequently, no other update is expected in any further ancestor and the update procedure can stop at this point.

---

**Algorithm 3** Incremental schedule update
---

1: **function** TimeElement.updateSchedule( )
2:    Let $\beta$, $\varepsilon$, and $\delta$ be the **begin**, **end** and **dur** attributes
3:    $this.d_i \leftarrow$ computeImplicitDuration( )
4:    $b \leftarrow$ computeBegin($\beta$)
5:    $d \leftarrow$ computeDuration($\delta$, $\varepsilon$, $b$)
6:    Let $i_{new} \leftarrow [b, b + d)$
7:    **if** $this.E \neq i_{new}$ **then**
8:       $this.E \leftarrow i_{new}$
9:       $P \leftarrow this.$getAncestor( )
10:       **if** $P$ is defined **then**
11:          $P.$updateSchedule( )
12:       **end if**
13:    **end if**
14: **end function**

---

This optimization is demonstrated in Algorithm 3, which is part of the Timegraph Model. The algorithm is an adaptation of the full schedule computation algorithm with additional verifications. The algorithm starts with computation of the external timeline of the element ($E$), from its timing attributes (lines 2-6). Then, if the computed timeline has changed, the schedule update will propagate to the immediate ancestor (lines 7-13), otherwise the update stops at this point. The example in Figure 4 presents, in fact, a best case scenario, $O(1)$, i.e., the schedule propagation stops at the immediate ancestor of the newly inserted node, involving a constant number of operations. In the case of attribute modification, the best case scenario would occur when the edited attribute do not change the element interval: in this case, the change would not even be propagated to the ancestor. Thus, it is expected that the worst case for incremental scheduling is the same as that for resolution, i.e., $O(h)$.

Another relevant optimization is the batch execution of editing operations. When multiple modifications occur in the timegraph in sequence (for instance, adding multiple children in a time container), the naive method is to call the append operation for every element, which would lead to a schedule update for every operation. In order to avoid this behavior, the ActiveTimesheets DOM API provides a number of methods for modifying multiple elements or attributes at once: for instance *appendChildren()* in *TimeContainerElement* and *setAttrs()* in *AreaLinkElement*. The distinguishing characteristic of these methods is that they apply multiple modifications in the timegraph but call a single schedule update, in the immediate ancestor, only when all the modifications are finished, potentially leading to performance improvements.

## 4.2 Linking

The core linking features in ActiveTimesheets are based on a subset of the SMIL Linking modules, because some adaptations are necessary to sort out conflicts between constructs provided by SMIL and similar constructs provided by HTML. SMIL defines the following syntax for links: *i)* the **a** element, which is similar to the homonymous HTML element; and *ii)* the **area** element, which defines spatio-temporal anchors to fragments of media elements. In ActiveTimesheets, the **a** element is dropped in favor of the HTML counterpart[4]. The

---

[4]The SMIL **a** element has a temporal dimension that frames its sensitivity, which is not present in the HTML counterpart. Incorporating

**area** element is adapted to conform to the characteristics of a Timesheets-based approach.

The elaborate semantics of the **area** element allows the definition of both source anchors, in which spatio-temporal fragments can be defined, and target anchors, in which spatial fragments can be defined. In ActiveTimesheets, when **area** is used as a source anchor, spatial fragmentation is dropped, because this issue is out of the scope of the Timesheets language, whereas temporal fragmentation is supported. When used as a target anchor, ActiveTimesheets extends its semantics by allowing its application to any element with an internal timeline (e.g. including time containers and composite **item** elements) instead to only media objects.

## 4.3 Extended reuse features

ActiveTimesheets extends the reuse features in SMIL Timesheets by allowing reuse of document constructs in more granularities: *i)* named elements from external documents; *ii)* named internal elements; and *iii)* temporal fragments (clipping) of named internal or external elements. Realizing these contributions requires the development of language syntax extensions and timegraph construction patterns.

### 4.3.1 Element reuse

Reusing individual elements of an external document has several applications in authoring. In enrichment activities, for instance, an external fragment can be reused to be annotated in a separate document. This allows a granular versioning of a document using only references to the original content. In order to explore these opportunities, ActiveTimesheets allows that any element of a document, provided that it is addressable (i.e. its **id** attribute is non-empty), can be reused in other contexts. This feature is demonstrated in Figure 5.

In Figure 5a, an element from an external timesheet is reused. The general scenario modeled by this document is the bookmarking of external content by reference. But, instead of bookmarking the whole document content, only a fragment of it is included. This is achieved by taking advantage of a specific addressing syntax: a fragment identifier is used in the **src** attribute of the **timesheet** element (line 3). This fragment identifier refer to a **par** container, identified as "videos", in the external document (omitted in the example). Additionally, the timesheet includes a series of target anchors, via **area** elements, representing bookmarks (consequently, this example is also taking advantage of linking features).

The side effect of reusing an external element is, first, the retrieval and parsing of the element fragment and, only then, the inclusion of the corresponding subgraph in the presentation timegraph. Figure 5 demonstrates this effect: the subgraphs which were included by reuse are highlighted. For all practical purposes, these subgraphs are considered as regular timegraph elements. Nodes corresponding to link anchors are prefixed with "*lnk*". The solution discussed here also allows reuse of internal elements. For that purpose, the only requirement is to use an internal fragment identifier. In summary, reuse of external and internal elements allows some compelling use cases while enriching and extending content. Additionally, the possibility of reusing temporal structures

---

this temporal dimension in the HTML a element would require a syntactical extension to the language, which is out of scope of the Active-Timesheets engine. In newer versions of HTML, this limitation could be minimized via inline markup using, for instance, data-* attributes.

---

```
1  <timesheet xmlns="http://www.w3.org/ns/SMIL">
2    <par id="bookmarks">
3      <timesheet src="(...)/timesheet/1304.smil#videos" />
4      <area id="bk1" begin="235" />
5      (...)
6      <area id="bk45" begin="1238" />
7    </par>
8  </timesheet>
```

(a) Timesheet with a reused element.

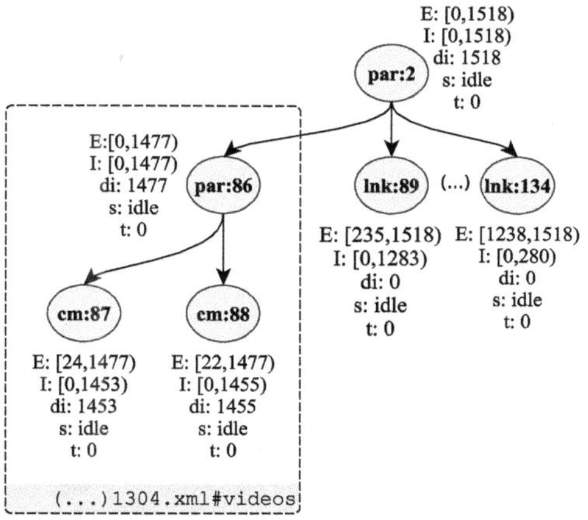

(b) Resulting timegraph emphasizing reused subgraph.

Figure 5: Example of element reuse via the **src** attribute of the **timesheet** element

potentially reduces duplication of declarative code, making the resulting document less verbose.

### 4.3.2 Element fragment reuse

One step further in reuse functionalities consists in reusing, instead of a whole element, only a fragment of it. In the video bookmarking use case, for instance, this would allow importing only a reduced clip of a group of potentially long videos. In SMIL, reuse of fragments of continuous media elements can be achieved via clipping attributes (**clipBegin** and **clipEnd**). In practice, media object clipping is a kind of non-destructive, virtual, editing operation in the temporal scope: once the media content is edited, it can be reused in different situations. The problem with clipping attributes is that they are originally applicable only to continuous media elements. In ActiveTimesheets, the semantics of these attributes are extended so that they can be applied to any element that has an internal timeline, intrinsic or not. Naturally, the usefulness of clipping temporal compositions is more appealing when an element is being reused, otherwise the same clipping result could be achieved by a proper timing scheme in the children of the composition. Figure 6 demonstrates how the timegraph is affected by clipping temporal compositions.

In Figure 6a, clipping occurs in the container **videos**, represented by node **par:1** in Figure 6b. This element is left-clipped at $15s$ and right-clipped at $55s$ (line 1), consequently its internal timeline ($I$), which unclipped would be $[0, 1477)$, becomes $[15, 55)$. Thus, the element implicit duration ($di$) becomes $40s$. Based only on this information, the element external timeline ($E$) is scheduled to the interval $[0, 40)$. The main effect of clipping is that the element, when activated,

```
1   <par clipBegin="15" clipEnd="55"
2    id="videos">
3    <item id="mevideo_82"
4     clipBegin="5"
5     clipEnd="15"
6     select="#video_82" />
7    <item begin="22" end="1477"
8     id="mevideo_83"
9     select="#video_83" />
10  </par>
```

```
              E: [0,40)
              I: [15,55)
              di: 40
     par:1    s: idle
              t: 0

    cm:2      cm:3

E: [0,10)     E: [0,1453)
I: [5,15]     I: [0,1453)
di: 10        di: 1453
s: idle       s: idle
t: 0          t: 0
```

(a) Timesheet with a reused element fragment

(b) Timegraph

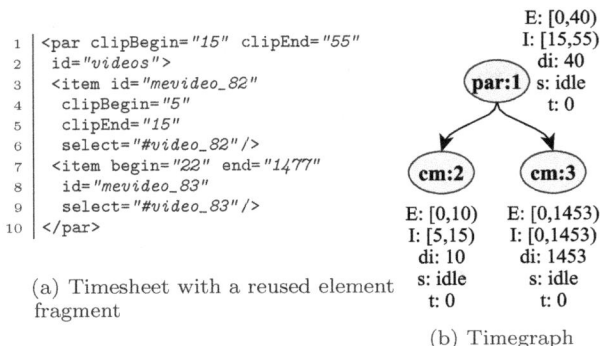

Figure 6: Example of combined clipping in `item` and time container

instead of starting *cm:2* at 0*s*, will seek to 15*s*, being later deactivated at 55*s*. As the element is a composite structure, clipping this element means that all its temporal relationships are affected by the clipping. This means that the time container, when activated, will start with its internal timeline at 15*s*. A consequence of this is that the element `cm:2` (also clipped) will never be activated, because the beginning of its active interval will occur in the past. The element cm:3 will be interrupted at 55*s*, before completing its original duration.

```
1   <timesheet xmlns="http://www.w3.org/ns/SMIL">
2    <par id="bookmarks">
3     <timesheet clipBegin="30" clipEnd="900"
4     src="(...)/timesheet/1304.smil#videos" />
5     <area id="bk1" begin="235" />
6     (...)
7     <area id="bk45" begin="1238" />
8    </par>
9   </timesheet>
```

Figure 7: Timesheet reusing a clipped external element

A compelling advantage of an extended clipping model is to reuse composite abstractions: Figure 7 illustrates this syntax by adapting the example of Figure 5. This can be done for instance by including clipping attributes in a `timesheet` element whose `src` attribute refers to a named external element (lines 3-4). For instance, if a time container aggregates a video track, an audio track, a subtitle and associated discrete annotations, clipping over this container would allow reuse of a fragment of the whole composition, sliced to the specified clip. One possible use case of this functionality is, for example, the extraction of a short fragment from a long presentation.

## 5. IMPLEMENTATION

The ActiveTimesheets language has been implemented in a Javascript-based engine[5] to be used in HTML5-compliant web browsers. The engine includes all the language extensions discussed in this paper. Figure 8 presents an overview of the most important components of this implementation.

The most important component is `PresentationWrapper`, which controls the whole lifecycle of the presentation, i.e., it manages the engine state machine discussed in Figure 2. This component is the main entry point of the engine, providing

---
[5]https://github.com/diogostmartins/activetimesheets

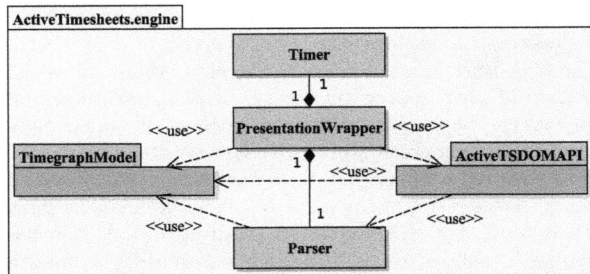

Figure 8: ActiveTimesheets: simplified package diagram

methods for most of the exposed functionalities. Regarding presentation setup, the wrapper, once started, commands parsing of the document and builds the DOM, using the ActiveTimesheets DOM API, and the timegraph, conforming to the Timegraph Model. The wrapper also triggers the first, full scheduling computation of the timegraph after constructing it. In addition, it uses a reference clock to control the sampling process, via a reference to the topmost timegraph node. Playback control of the presentation is also provided by the wrapper, which manages contextual conditions, such as buffering of media streams. Finally, the component exposes access methods the ActiveTimesheets DOM API so that a developer can perform dynamic modifications in the document.

## 6. CASE STUDY

The ActiveTimesheets engine has been integrated as a component of a Web-based enrichment and extension tool for multimedia documents. Depicted in Figure 9, the tool provides functionalities to import synchronized multimedia sessions obtained from capture environments (e.g. lectures, videoconferences, meeting recordings, etc.). An imported session is automatically transformed, at access time, in a multimedia document in HTML5 and SMIL Timesheets. Users accessing the presentation can apply textual annotations and editing commands to the multimedia document. In addition, a group of annotations can be used to generate new versions of the document containing only the fragments discriminated by the annotations. In the following discussion, it is emphasized how the extensions proposed in this paper support these activities.

### 6.1 Dynamic creation of annotations

A primary functionality of the tool is the creation of annotations indexed to the temporal scope of the multimedia session. From the document perspective, this involves: *i)* creating a media element to represent the annotation; and *ii)* a source anchor whose target is the interval the annotation is indexing. This is achieved using the dynamic modifications and linking features of ActiveTimesheets, consequently the user can immediately use the annotation to jump to the indexed interval, for instance.

The code excerpt in Figure 10 illustrates the use of the ActiveTimesheets DOM API to include a new annotation in the document. Annotations in the tool can have an associated editing behavior (e.g. play, pause, skip, loop, jump, etc.): in the example, an annotation with the "loop" behavior is being added to the document. First, a reference to the

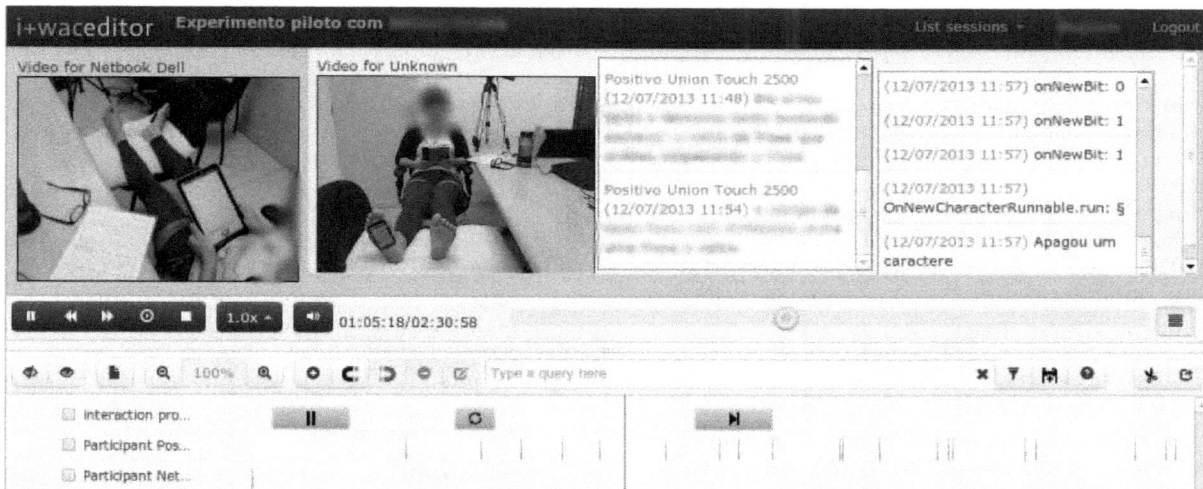

Figure 9: A Web-based enrichment and extension tool integrating ActiveTimesheets. The multimedia document corresponds to an annotated recording of a usability experiment.

```
1  function addLoopComment(annotation) {
2    var dom = ACTIVETIMESHEETS.engine.getExternalDOM();
3    var root = dom.findOne(annotation._timeline_id);
4    (...)
5    var node = dom.createElement('par', {id: annotation._id,
6      begin: annotation.begin, end: annotation.end + 1});
7    (...)
8    node.append(c1); node.append(c2); root.append(node);
9  };
```

Figure 10: Excerpt of code for dynamic modification using the ActiveTimesheets DOM API

ActiveTimesheets DOM API is obtained (line 2) and then the container of the annotation is retrieved (line 3). After this point, link anchors for the annotation are created (lines 5-7). After that, the fragment of the annotation is composed and added to the DOM using the *append* method (recall Algorithm 1). During the last *append* operation (line 8), the schedule of the presentation will be incrementally updated (as per Algorithm 3). As a consequence, the temporal and interactivity relationships defined in the annotation are immediately available in the tool.

```
1  <?xml version="1.0" encoding="UTF-8"?>
2  <timesheet xmlns="http://www.w3.org/ns/SMIL">
3    <par id="presentation">
4      <par id="group_me">
5        <item begin="236.18" end="9001.38" id="mevideo92537"
6          select="#video92537" />
7        (...)
8      </par>
9      <par id="group_1329">
10        <par begin="2375.16" end="2742.85" id="link46542">
11          <area begin="0.0" end="366.69" id="link46542l1" />
12          <area actuate="onload" begin="link46542l1.end" dur="1"
13            href="#link46542l1" id="link46542l2" />
14        </par>
15        (...)
16      </par>
17      (...)
18    </par>
19  </timesheet>
```

Figure 11: Result of a dynamic modification.

The result of this operation is demonstrated in Figure 11. A new time container (lines 9-16) is added to the document in order to represent the new annotation. The timing of the link anchors were specified in a way that, once the first anchor (line 11) is completely traversed, the second anchor (lines 12-13) automatically seek the presentation to the start of the annotation. This is possible via event relationships and the **actuate** attribute in the second anchor. As a consequence, the presentation will keep in a loop over the annotation interval until some other event interrupts it.

## 6.2 Versioning by reference

Another important functionality of the tool is the derivation of new versions of a multimedia document based on the annotations. A user can select a group of annotations applied in the document and generate a new document containing only the fragments indexed by the selected annotations (i.e., a "summary" of the document based on annotations). With the reuse features in ActiveTimesheets, instead of duplicating fragments of the base document, the derived document simply reuses fragments of it.

```
1   <timesheet xmlns="http://www.w3.org/ns/SMIL">
2     <par id="presentation">
3       <seq id="group_me">
4         <timesheet clip-begin="699.91" clip-end="1408.30"
5           src="(...)/1307.smil#group_me"/>
6         <timesheet clip-begin="2375.16" clip-end="2741.85"
7           src="(...)/1307.smil#group_me"/>
8         <timesheet clip-begin="4566.98" clip-end="5275.37"
9           src="(...)/1307.smil#group_me"/>
10       </seq>
11   </timesheet>
```

Figure 12: Result of a versioned document generated via reuse of external element fragments

Figure 12 demonstrates the layout of a derived document. Taking as a basis the document in Figure 11, a new document was generated containing three fragments. This is done by including in the new document a **timesheet** element (e.g. line 4) with the values of the clipping attributes assigned to the interval of the base annotation. Additionally, the `src` attribute refers to an element of an external timesheet (line 5), which is the one being versioned. As discussed in Section 4.3.2, at the timegraph level, this construct will lead to the inclusion of the nodes corresponding to the whole imported composition into the presentation timegraph. The same is done in the other fragments (lines 6-9), each framed to the temporal interval of the annotation that generated it. All the fragments are combined in a `seq` container that will execute them like a playlist. Using this versioning pattern, users can create customized versions with no modifications in the original document and without duplication of declarative code.

## 7. FINAL REMARKS

This paper presented the ActiveTimesheets engine, which provides important features to Web-based multimedia authoring: dynamic modifications, extended linking and reuse of elements and their fragments. These extensions have been presented considering their effects in the language syntax and in the timegraph model. Finally, a case study regarding enrichment and versioning of multimedia content have demonstrated the applicability of these extensions.

In document languages that support scripting, it is expected that procedural code can modify the host document: this is true for various Web languages, such as HTML and SVG. Consequently, realizing dynamic modifications in ActiveTimesheets brings contributions to make multimedia applications more conformant to current practices of Web development. Even though we have concentrated the discussion of dynamic modifications on SMIL Timesheets, much of the ActiveTimesheets model is applicable to SMIL as well. The core aspects of the approach, the Timegraph Model and the DOM API, can be extended to include the syntax and semantics of other elements and attributes of the SMIL language. From the standpoint of reuse features, referencing internal or external elements has several applications in authoring multimedia documents. On one hand, reuse enables non-destructive extension of external content, as enrichments can be applied in a decoupled manner over a document fragment. Additionally, reusing elements in fine granularity potentially reduces the verbosity of the document.

An important issue that is not tackled by ActiveTimesheets is that of spatio-temporal binding consistency. This problem consists in keeping the temporal layout updated if a change in the spatial document occurs. This is particularly important because a timesheet is binded to its host HTML document via CSS selectors: if the host document is modified (nodes are added or removed) in a way that affects the results retrieved by the selectors, then the temporal layout must be updated as well. A solution to this problem would require some change detection mechanism and an efficient expression evaluation procedure to keep the bindings updated. This also requires deeper investigation regarding the best alternative solutions and their trade-offs.

The expression power of SMIL can lead, in certain situations, to the specification of inconsistent presentations. This problem is particularly important with dynamic modifications, which can lead a document to immediately enter an inconsistent state. Given that verification of document consistency is a desirable feature in the context of dynamic modifications as well, live verification is an important theme for future improvements in ActiveTimesheets.

**Acknowledgments**. This work was supported by funding from CNPq (process no. 143144/2009-0) and FAPESP (process no. 2013/03337-6). We would like to thank Jack Jansen, Pablo Cesar and Dick Bulterman, for valuable insights of the SMIL language while the first author was visiting CWI, Amsterdam, Netherlands.

## 8. REFERENCES

[1] P. Bertolotti and O. Gaggi. A study on multimedia documents behavior: a notion of equivalence. *Multimedia Tools and Applications*, 33(3):301–324, 2007.

[2] S. Boll and W. Klas. ZYX-a multimedia document model for reuse and adaptation of multimedia content. *IEEE Transactions on Knowledge and Data Engineering*, 13(3):361–382, 2001.

[3] S. Bouyakoub and A. Belkhir. SMIL builder: An incremental authoring tool for SMIL documents. *ACM Trans. Multimedia Comput. Commun. Appl.*, 7(1):1–30, 2011.

[4] F. Cazenave, V. Quint, and C. Roisin. Timesheets.js: when SMIL meets HTML5 and CSS3. In *Proc. of the 11th ACM Symp. on Document Engineering*, pages 43–52, 2011.

[5] O. Gaggi and A. Bossi. Analysis and verification of SMIL documents. *Multimedia Systems*, 17(6):487–506, 2011.

[6] O. Gaggi and L. Danese. A SMIL player for any web browser. In *Proc. of the 17th Int. Conf. on Distrib. Multimedia Systems*, pages 114–119, 2011.

[7] J. Jansen, P. Cesar, and D. C. Bulterman. A model for editing operations on active temporal multimedia documents. In *Proc. of the 10th ACM Symp. on Document Engineering*, pages 87–96, 2010.

[8] J. Jansen, P. Cesar, R. L. Guimaraes, and D. C. A. Bulterman. Just-in-time personalized video presentations. In *Proc. of the 2012 ACM Symp. on Document Engineering*, pages 59–68, 2012.

[9] R. Laiola Guimarães, P. Cesar, and D. C. Bulterman. Creating and sharing personalized time-based annotations of videos on the web. *Proc. of the 10th ACM Symp. on Document Engineering*, pages 27–36, 2010.

[10] E. Mannens, D. Deursen, R. Troncy, S. Pfeiffer, C. Parker, Y. Lafon, J. Jansen, M. Hausenblas, and R. Walle. A URI-based approach for addressing fragments of media resources on the web. *Multimedia Tools and Applications*, 59(2):691–715, 2012.

[11] B. Meixner, K. Matusik, C. Grill, and H. Kosch. Towards an easy to use authoring tool for interactive non-linear video. *Multimedia Tools and Applications (Online first)*, pages 1–26, 2012.

[12] B. Meixner, B. Siegel, P. Schultes, F. Lehner, and H. Kosch. An HTML5 Player for Interactive Non-linear Video with Time-based Collaborative Annotations. In *Proc. of 2013 Int. Conf. on Advances in Mobile Computing & Multimedia*, pages 490–499, 2013.

[13] E. L. Melo, C. Viel, C. A. C. Teixeira, A. C. Rondon, D. P. Silva, D. G. Rodrigues, and E. C. Silva. WebNCL: a web-based presentation machine for multimedia documents. In *Proc. of the 18th Braz. Symp. on Multimedia and the Web*, pages 403–410, 2012.

[14] E. C. O. Silva, J. A. F. dos Santos, and D. C. Muchaluat-Saade. NCL4WEB: translating NCL applications to HTML5 web pages. In *Proc. of the 2013 ACM Symp. on Document engineering*, pages 253–262, 2013.

[15] C. S. Soares Neto, H. F. Pinto, and L. F. G. Soares. TAL processor for hypermedia applications. In *Proc. of the 2012 ACM Symp. on Document Engineering*, pages 69–78, 2012.

[16] C. S. Soares Neto, L. F. G. Soares, and C. S. Souza. The Nested Context Language reuse features. *Journal of the Brazilian Computer Society*, 16(4):229–245, 2010.

[17] Scalable Vector Graphics (SVG) 1.1 (Second Edition), W3C Recommendation, August 2011. Accessed April, 2014.

[18] W3C. XHTML+SMIL Profile (W3C Note), January 2002. Accessed April, 2014.

[19] W3C. Synchronized Multimedia Integration Language (SMIL 3.0), Recommendation, 2008. Accessed April, 2014.

[20] W3C. HTML5: A vocabulary and associated APIs for HTML and XHTML (Candidate Recommendation), November 2012. Accessed April, 2014.

[21] W3C. SMIL Timesheets 1.0, W3C Working Group Note, March 2012. Accessed April, 2014.

# Automated Refactoring for Size Reduction of CSS Style Sheets

Martí Bosch
UPC & Inria
marti.bosch-
padros@inria.fr

Pierre Genevès
CNRS
pierre.geneves@cnrs.fr

Nabil Layaïda[*]
Inria
nabil.layaida@inria.fr

## ABSTRACT

Cascading Style Sheets (CSS) is a standard language for stylizing and formatting web documents. Its role in web user experience becomes increasingly important. However, CSS files tend to be designed from a result-driven point of view, without much attention devoted to the CSS file structure as long as it produces the desired results. Furthermore, the rendering intended in the browser is often checked and debugged with a document instance. Style sheets normally apply to a set of documents, therefore modifications added while focusing on a particular instance might affect other documents of the set.

We present a first prototype of static CSS semantical analyzer and optimizer that is capable of automatically detecting and removing redundant property declarations and rules. We build on earlier work on tree logics to locate redundancies due to the semantics of selectors and properties. Existing purely syntactic CSS optimizers might be used in conjunction with our tool, for performing complementary (and orthogonal) size reduction, toward the common goal of providing smaller and cleaner CSS files.

## Categories and Subject Descriptors

1.7 [**Document and Text Processing**]: Document preparation; D.2 [**Software Engineering**]: Testing and Debugging

## Keywords

Web development; Style sheets; CSS; Debugging

## 1. INTRODUCTION

Cascading style sheets (CSS) is one of the main components of web development, used to describe the aspect and

---

[*] Detailed affiliation of authors: M. Bosch[1234], P. Genevès[213], N. Layaïda[123] with: [1]Inria; [2]CNRS, LIG; [3]Univ. Grenoble Alpes; [4]Universitat Politècnica de Catalunya. Work partly supported by ANR project Typex (ANR-11-BS02-007).

format of a markup document, most of the time an HTML web page. The simplicity of its syntax makes it attractive for designers and amateurs as it only requires assigning values to properties under certain elements of the document.

However CSS language presents a set of combinatorial features that empower its possibilities, while inevitably making it more complex. A single document might use several style sheets, include embedded CSS under the `style` HTML element, or even use inline styles set directly as attributes of the element concerned. Furthermore, the language used to write selectors is very expressive. The combination of these features might lead to a series of semantical errors and redundancies that make it difficult to spot the origin of problems when one does not get the desired output in the browser. The tool we propose is aimed to help web developers in that matter, as well as reducing the style sheet size.

## 2. RELATED WORKS

In sharp contrast with existing debugging tools [5, 6, 7, 4], we propose a method for automatically analysing and refactoring a CSS file, with the guarantee that the rendering in the browser will not be affected, *for any possible document* that might use the CSS. A highly novel aspect of our tool is that it is capable of performing CSS refactoring by a semantical analysis of a given CSS file, in the absence of any other information (such as a particular document instance). For this purpose, we build on our previous logical modeling of CSS selectors introduced in [2]. The main difference between the present work and [2] is that [2] focuses on the detection of rendering bugs, whereas the present work seeks to perform automatic CSS size reduction while preserving the rendering semantics.

## 3. CSS ANALYSIS AND REFACTORING

In CSS, rules are encapsulated by a selector, that points to the set of elements that will be affected by the rule's declarations. We borrow ideas from the fields of set theory and tree logics to analyze the sets of elements pointed by the different selectors present in a CSS file. Our tool is concerned with the detection of semantical relations between CSS selectors. When some of these relations are detected, our tool might determine that a property declaration is unnecessary and it will thus be deleted, based on the *specificity* of selectors. In CSS, a selector's *specificity* is a vector of four integers $(a, b, c, d)$, where $a = 1$ if the property is declared in a `style` attribute ($a = 0$ otherwise), $b$ is the number of `id` attributes (of the form "#␣") in the selector, $c$ is the number of other attributes and pseudo-classes in the selector, and $d$ is the number of element names and pseudo-elements in the selector. Our tool exploits the facts that: (1) if selectors of two different rules have the same specificity, then the last rule in the style sheet gains precedence; (2) when several selectors point to the same set of elements, then the declarations under the one with higher *specificity* gain precedence.

## 3.1 Containment of selectors

One fundamental relation between two CSS selectors is *containment*. For example we say that "ul > li" is *contained* into "li" since any "li" element with an "ul" parent is indeed a "li" element. The existence of containment relations is determined by the analysis of the nested structures of elements and the sets of attributes carried by elements. A selector such as "p.someclass" is contained into "p", since any "p" element with "class" attribute "someclass" is indeed a "p" element. These two kinds of containment can occur simultaneously as it is the case with "table td#someid" $\subset$ "td". More generally, containment relates sets of pointed elements that are associated with selectors.

Given two selectors $S_b$ and $S_p$, $S_b$ is contained in $S_p$ iff any element pointed by $S_b$ is also pointed by $S_p$. In this section we treat only *proper containment*, which means $S_b \subset S_p$ and not $S_b \subseteq S_p$. Under these circumstances, for each property declared under both selectors, there are two different procedures according to the selector's specificity:

**Refactoring 1.** *Subset more specific: delete the property declaration from $S_b$ only if it has the same value set under both $S_b$ and $S_p$.*

**Refactoring 2.** *Subset less specific: delete the property declaration from $S_b$, since the value set under $S_p$ will always override the one under $S_b$.*

For example, consider the following code snippet:

```
Listing 1: containment_input.css
1  table.foo { color: #333;
2              font-size: 12px;
3              font-weight: bold }
4
5  table { color: #666;
6          font-size: 12px }
```

Note that "table.foo" $\subset$ "table" and the subset has a higher specificity $(0,0,1,1)$ against $(0,0,0,1)$ from the superset, so we are in the case of *refactoring 1*. Consequently, we have to preserve the "color: #333" declaration as it will override the one from "table" when both rules apply. On the other hand, the "font-size" property statement can be removed from the subset as the same value is already pulled from the superset "table". The following code corresponds to the output of the analysis:

```
Listing 2: containment_output.css
1  table.foo { color: #333;
2              font-weight: bold }
3
4  table { color: #666;
5          font-size: 12px }
```

If "table" was more specific than "table.foo", *refactoring 2* would apply and the "color" property declaration could be erased from the subset too as its value would always be overridden by the dominant "#666" set in the superset.

## 3.2 Equivalence of selectors

Another relation between CSS selectors that can lead to some refactoring is *equivalence*. Two or more CSS selectors can be equivalent in several ways. Is not uncommon to find a rule $R_i$ with a selector such as "body", and later in the same file another rule $R_j$ with the same selector "body". Another case of equivalence could be a class selector ".classname" and the attribute selector "[class='classname']", or any similar case with the dual syntax for **id** attributes. These examples could be studied with basic string processing, but the logical and semantical analysis of selectors allows us to detect more complex equivalences too such as the one between selectors "p:nth-child(odd), p:nth-child(even)" and "p", as every paragraph is either odd or even.

Given two selectors $S_i$ and $S_j$, they are *equivalent* iff any element pointed by $S_i$ is also pointed by $S_j$ and vice-versa. In this context there is only one procedure over the bodies:

**Refactoring 3.** *For each property declared under both selectors, delete the statements under the less specific selector.*

To illustrate the analysis, let's look at the next listing:

```
Listing 3: equivalence_input.css
1  div#bar { font-style: italic;
2            border: none }
3
4  div[id='bar'] { color: #666;
5                  font-style: normal;
6                  border: none }
```

In this case we have two equivalent selectors, "div#bar" and "div[id='bar']" whose specificities are $(0,1,0,1)$ and $(0,0,1,1)$ respectively. For the properties declared under both rules, the values from "div#bar" will dominate, so the ones under "div[id='bar']" will never apply, as selectors point to the same set of elements. This means that for "font-style" and "border", the declarations can be safely erased from "div[id='bar']", resulting in the following output:

```
Listing 4: equivalence_output.css
1  div#bar { font-style: italic;
2            border: none }
3
4  div[id='bar'] { color: #666 }
```

## 3.3 Inheritance of properties

Whenever containment or equivalence relations are detected between selectors, several selectors point to the same elements, and specificity decides which declarations get precedence. In the context of inheritance, an element might be pointed by only one selector and yet be affected by declarations outside the concerning rule. This is because the declaration has been propagated from some ancestor through the inheritance mechanism. Consider a selector using a descendant combinator "$E_{anc} > E_{desc}$" with a inheritable property declaration $P_a : V_a$, and another selector "$E_{anc}$" with the same declaration. This statement might then be redundant as for $E_{desc}$ the property might inherited from $E_{anc}$.

However we do not know if some document using this CSS file, presents a structure in which there is a certain element $E_x$ placed in between $E_{anc}$ and $E_{desc}$, and the property declarations for $E_x$ alter the property inheritance among $E_{anc}$ and $E_{desc}$. For example, a selector concerning only an attribute, such as "[input]", is free to be applied to any element on the document. Only certain CSS properties are inherited by default. Therefore, in our analyses, the amount of refactoring due to inheritance is a priori limited.

## 4. IMPLEMENTATION TECHNIQUES

### 4.1 Reasoning over selectors

Given two selectors, we intend to automatically check whether some containment or equivalence relation holds between them. For this purpose, we use the translation of CSS selectors into the tree logic described in [2] and obtain logical formulas. We then formulate containment as logical implication, and test the formula for satisfiability using the logical solver of [3]. For two selectors $S_1$ and $S_2$, Table 1 summarizes the tests performed, the four possible scenarios obtained according to the results, and the corresponding actions performed, as explained in section 3.1 and 3.2.

| $S_1 \subseteq S_2$ | $S_1 \supseteq S_2$ | Relation | Action |
|---|---|---|---|
| 0 | 0 | None | None |
| 0 | 1 | $S_1 \supset S_2$ | Refactoring 1, 2 |
| 1 | 0 | $S_1 \subset S_2$ | Refactoring 1, 2 |
| 1 | 1 | $S_1 \Leftrightarrow S_2$ | Rafactoring 3 |

Table 1: Actions associated with detected relations.

### 4.2 Processing on declaration blocks

Once a relation between selectors $S_1$ and $S_2$ has been found, for each of the properties declared under both rules, we determine whether it is necessary or not, depending on three aspects: the relation between selectors, the selector's specificity, and whether the properties share the same value; as illustrated on examples in sections 3.1 and 3.2.

In some cases, the deletion of unnecessary property declarations results in an empty rule. In this case, the whole rule is (safely) erased from the style sheet.

### 4.3 Optimization of elapsed time

In a style sheet with $n$ rules, each rule can be tested against all rules but itself, adding up to a total of $n \times (n-1)$ possible tests. Given the diversity of elements in a HTML tree, tests concerning selector pairs such as "body" and "p" will not be uncommon. Only by adding a few basic pre checks, we will be able to determine the result of logical tests before actually processing it. We take advantage of two main observations for drastically reducing the number of pairwise tests:

**1.** *If two selectors point to elements with syntactically different names, they will never be contained in each other, in any of the two possible containment directions.*

**2.** *If a selector $S_1$ refers to one or more attributes that $S_2$ does not, $S_1$ will never contain $S_2$.*

### 4.4 Statistics tracking

The tool tracks some statistics about the analysis. First, while parsing it detects the total number of rules, the number of ignored ones, the number of possible tests, and the tests that were actually carried out. After all reasoning is done, the tool counts the number of relations between selectors, the modified rules, the number of deleted properties as well as the deleted bits. Finally, the time spent on each one of the analysis parts is also shown.

### 4.5 Room for improvements

Our prototype implements the aforementioned procedures for a significant CSS subset, sufficient for performing practical experiments with real-world style sheets. Our prototype can be improved in many respects, though. In particular, the library css-validator[1], that is used for parsing the CSS file and traversing the properties of the rules, could be improved. Some methods concerning comparisons of properties are not implemented, and thus some potential property deletions cannot be automatically carried out. It does not support browser specific properties yet.

Some CSS selectors' features are not supported yet, such as grouping, pseudo-classes, pseudo-elements, multiple class and id selectors and media queries. Consequently, the concerning selectors are ignored. With their implementation, additional refactoring might be performed.

## 5. EXPERIMENTAL RESULTS

In order to get a representative collection of results, three different groups have been defined. The first group involves CSS code provided by frameworks and CMS, and is represented by *Bootstrap*, *Joomla* and *JQuery*. The second group consists in style sheets from complex web applications, and features *Instagram*, *Twitter* and *The Times*. Finally, we have extracted CSS files from some random web sites of medium complexity, which are *ACM DL*, *DocEng*, and *Inovallée*. Table 2 provides detailed information about the corresponding CSS file sizes and complexity.

| Name | # bytes | # rules |
|---|---|---|
| Bootstrap (*Framework's CSS*) | 127343 | 805 |
| Joomla (*Template Beez20's CSS*) | 30158 | 325 |
| JQuery (*Framework's CSS*) | 32891 | 349 |
| Instagram (*www.instagram.com*) | 123815 | 791 |
| The Times (*www.thetimes.co.uk*) | 89362 | 469 |
| Twitter (*www.twitter.com*) | 245473 | 2402 |
| ACM DL (*dl.acm.org*) | 11151 | 97 |
| DocEng (*www.doceng2014.org*) | 204970 | 1571 |
| Inovallée (*www.inovallee.com*) | 29930 | 189 |

Table 2: Dataset for the experiments.

---

[1]see http://jigsaw.w3.org/css-validator/

## 5.1 CSS Size Reduction in Practice

After processing the aforementioned files, the tool has spotted on average $4.95\%^2$ of unnecessary property declarations, modifying $4.56\%$ of the total rules. Of the relations found, $83.38\%$ were containment ones, and the remaining $16.62\%$ correspond to equivalence between selectors.

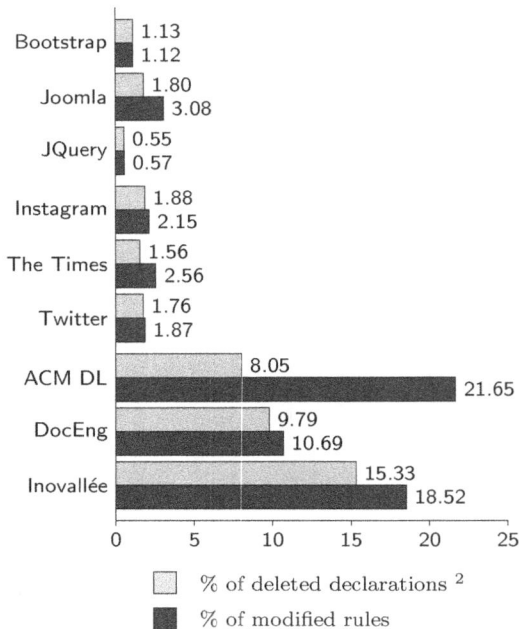

Figure 1: Refactoring performed.

It is clear that the style sheets from the first and second group present a low percentage of deleted property declarations (1.16% and 1.73% respectively). The same holds for the percentage of modified rules (1.59% for the first group and 2.19% for the second one). However, in the third group these numbers rise dramatically, reaching 11.05% of deleted declarations and 16.95% of modified rules. Although these latter sites might not have involved as much testing as the first ones, they are not amateur web sites either.

## 5.2 Performance of the tool

The time taken to analyze each file is shown in Figure 2. A 34.30% of the rules have been ignored due to unsupported selectors commented in Section 4.5, and an average of $99.88\%^3$ of the them has been discarded by the optimization mechanism described in Section 4.3. Each test between selectors requires a median of 156.71 ms, so without the optimization mechanism, each file analysis would have taken a median of 16.60 hours, in contraposition to the 78.16 seconds that were actually required, still guaranteeing the same results.

## 6. CONCLUSION

This paper presents a tool that automatically detects and removes unnecessary property declarations in CSS files, based on the analysis of semantical relations between selectors. We provide a first prototype implementation, with many perspectives for further development. Our method can constitute the core mechanism in several applications aimed to

---

$^2$calculated over the properties that the tool supports.
$^3$calculated over considered tests, discarding ignored ones.

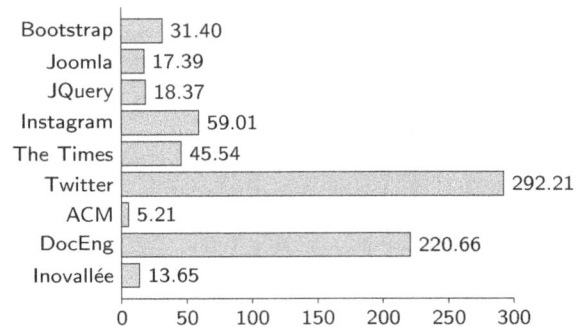

Figure 2: elapsed time (s)

help developers code higher quality style sheets. A basic example could be a file processor where the user inputs a CSS file and gets as output an equivalent lighter file. The tool could also be integrated into more powerful components such as context features for web IDEs. In any scenario, the benefit of our tool is to conduct precise semantical analyses, that go far beyond the capabilities of purely syntactic analyses done by current CSS optimizers. Generating equivalent but simpler CSS files not only improves the time spent in loading and formatting a web page, but might also facilitate the debugging process of style sheets.

Despite the large number of unsupported features, the results obtained in section 5 already validate our approach: we have been able to detect large numbers of unnecessary property declarations in non-amateur web pages; and we have also found mistakes in the style sheets of some of the most popular web sites. The number of safe modifications can easily grow as more components of CSS are supported and more features are implemented, such as property inheritance, translation of pseudo-classes into query languages, analysis of media queries, merging of equivalent selectors or containment involving grouped selectors.

A perspective for further work consists in extending the number and the precision of our analyses by supporting constraints on the document structure when they are available (as a DTD/Schema, or via another formalism such as [1]).

## 7. REFERENCES

[1] E. Benson and D. R. Karger. Cascading tree sheets and recombinant HTML: better encapsulation and retargeting of web content. In *WWW'13*, pages 107–118, 2013.

[2] P. Genevès, N. Layaïda, and V. Quint. On the analysis of cascading style sheets. In *WWW'12*, pages 809–818, 2012.

[3] P. Genevès, N. Layaïda, and A. Schmitt. Efficient static analysis of XML paths and types. In *PLDI '07*, pages 342–351, 2007.

[4] Google. Chrome developer tools, May 2014. https://developer.chrome.com/devtools/.

[5] H.-S. Liang, K.-H. Kuo, P.-W. Lee, Y.-C. Chan, Y.-C. Lin, and M. Y. Chen. SeeSS: Seeing what i broke – visualizing change impact of cascading style sheets (CSS). In *UIST'13*, pages 353–356, 2013.

[6] A. Mesbah and S. Mirshokraie. Automated analysis of CSS rules to support style maintenance. In *ICSE'12*, pages 408–418, 2012.

[7] Mozilla. Firebug, May 2014. https://getfirebug.com/.

# FlexiFont: A Flexible System to Generate Personal Font Libraries

Wanqiong Pan, Zhouhui Lian,* Rongju Sun, Yingmin Tang, Jianguo Xiao

Institute of Computer Science and Technology
Peking University
Beijing, China
{panwanqiong, lianzhouhui, sunrongju, tangyingmin, xiaojianguo}@pku.edu.cn

## ABSTRACT

This paper proposes FlexiFont, a system designed to generate personal font libraries from the camera-captured character images. Compared with existing methods, our system is able to process most kinds of languages and the generated font libraries can be extended by adding new characters based on the user's requirement. Moreover, digital cameras instead of scanners are chosen as the input devices, so that it is more convenient for common people to use the system. First of all, the users should choose a default template or define their own templates, then write the characters on the printed templates according to the certain instructions. After the users upload the photos of the templates with written characters, the system will automatically correct the perspective and split the whole photo into a set of individual character images. As the final step, FlexiFont will denoise, vectorize, and normalize each character image before storing it into a TrueType file. Experimental results demonstrate the robustness and efficiency of our system.

## Categories and Subject Descriptors

I.3.3 [**Computer Graphics**]: Picture/Image Generation—*Line and curve generation*; I.4.3 [**Image Processing and Computer Vision**]: Enhancement—*Geometric correction*

## Keywords

Camera-based image processing; document image rectification; character image vectorization; font library

## 1. INTRODUCTION

Since handwriting is a signature to each individual, it has become a novel way to show the characteristics and personalities by using personal font, such as writing emails and posting tweets in the personal handwriting.

---

*Corresponding author.

Currently, several web sites have started providing the service to generate personal font libraries consisting of English characters and common symbols, such as PilotHandwriting [2], FontsforPeas [1] and YourFonts [3]. The generation procedure usually contains the following steps: printing the template, writing the characters, uploading the scanned template images to the web site and then a font library will be generated within several minutes. However, in all the web sites mentioned above, the number of characters in the template is very small and the content of the template is not editable. Moreover, most of the web sites can only process scanned template images, while not most of the people have their own scanners.

Other than the web sites, a commercial software named ScanFont [7] and an open source software called FontForge [15] are also capable of turning images into fonts. The generation procedure is similar to the steps mentioned above. Beyond, such software yields many other advanced functions, such as they usually allow users to edit contour glyph, which make them more suitable for the professional users rather than common people.

In comparison with the western languages, Chinese has larger number of characters and more complicated shape information. A standard commercial font library usually contains more than 20,000 characters according to the G-BK specification. Furthermore, it is expensive and time-consuming to generate a Chinese personal font library with the aid from a commercial company. It usually takes several months for a font company to produce a complete and high-quality Chinese personal font library, which usually contains 6,763 Chinese characters according to the GB2312 specification. Therefore, it becomes necessary to develop a flexible system to generate personal font libraries efficiently.

In this paper, we present an outline of FlexiFont and show some examples of the generated font libraries. Furthermore, we will introduce the details of the algorithms applied for document image rectification and character image vectorization, as well as the techniques used to generate a practical and beautiful font library. In addition, to demonstrate the robustness and efficiency of our system, we will present the generated font libraries of four volunteers. In the end, we conclude this paper with some thoughts about the future work to further improve the service and extend the application of our system.

## 2. OVERVIEW

FlexiFont is a system designed to generate personal font libraries from camera-captured character images. As shown in Fig. 1, there are several steps of interactions between users and FlexiFont during the generation procedure.

1. *Users:* First of all, users should define the content in the template, by providing a text file which contains all the characters and symbols they want to include in the font library. Optionally, the users can simply choose one of our pre-defined templates. The generated templates are a serial of ordered images. The users should download and print these templates, then write each character in the corresponding blank space. Afterwards, the users should take photos of the template and upload them to the system.

2. *FlexiFont:* Once the template photos are uploaded, the system first splits the template images into single character images. Then each single character image is properly vectorized. Finally, a TrueType font library is automatically generated.

Compared with existing methods, FlexiFont has the following advantages:

1. *Flexible template:* The template in our system yields no restriction in terms of the language and quantity. The users can choose the pre-defined templates or create their own templates in most kinds of languages, and the templates may contain as many characters as they want.

2. *Extensible font library:* The number of Chinese characters is so large that it is hard for the users to write all the characters at one time. Our system provides users with the function to conveniently add new characters into existing font libraries they generated before.

3. *Easy to use:* Our system is designed to process camera-captured template images, due to the more widely used portable devices with cameras, such as mobile phones and tablet computers. In addition, the optimal size and position of each character are calculated automatically by the system to create the font library.

## 3. METHOD DESCRIPTION

The workflow of FlexiFont consists of the following four steps: 1) Generate Template, 2) Get Single Character Images, 3) Vectorize Character Images and 4) Generate/Merge Font Library, which are discussed in more details below.

### 3.1 Generate Template

An example of our designed template in FlexiFont is shown in Fig. 2 (a). The left side is the reference zone, and the right side is the writing zone. In the reference zone, the characters are generated according to the text file automatically and duplicate characters will be removed. While writing characters, the users can refer to the reference zone to avoid writing in the wrong position. After all the characters are written, the users just need to take photos of the writing zones, including the outer rectangle (shown in Fig. 2 (b)).

### 3.2 Get Single Character Images

Since the template photos are captured by cameras, and different cameras may vary in different resolutions. In addition, the lighting conditions and focus also significantly affect the quality of the template photos. In our system,

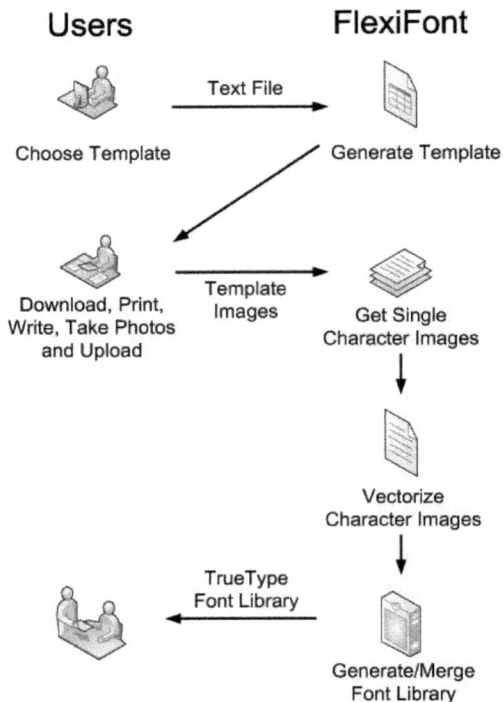

**Figure 1: The flowchart of interactions between users and FlexiFont to generate a font library.**

the template paper is assumed as flat as possible, so we do not need to de-warp the image. Furthermore, we assume that the template photo is in the right orientation and the quality of each character image is clear enough to be recognized. Otherwise, FlexiFont will return an error message to the users, and another photo of this template should be taken. Then the main task is to find the accurate boundary of the writing zone and rectify it (shown in Fig. 2 (c)).

The core algorithm in this step is the image rectification which involves perspective transformation. During the last decades, a lot of methods have been developed for document image rectification [8]. Those existing techniques could be classified into two types [13], the first one is based on 3-D document shape reconstruction and the second type involves 2-D document image processing. By detecting and analyzing the straight lines in the image, we can locate the largest quadrilateral in the template photo, then get four corner points of the writing zone. These four corner points are used to generate the homography matrix $H$, which relates the points on the template photo plane to the points on the destination image plane by the equations in [4].

Once the writing zone is identified and rectified into a $3000 \times 2100$ rectangle image, the single character images can be extracted automatically according to their positions. Thus the resolution of each single character image is $300 \times 300$.

### 3.3 Vectorize Character Images

Image vectorization is a raster-to-vector procedure, which approximates the image contours by curves and lines. It is required to truthfully preserve the writing style and remove the contour noises at the same time. In FlexiFont, median

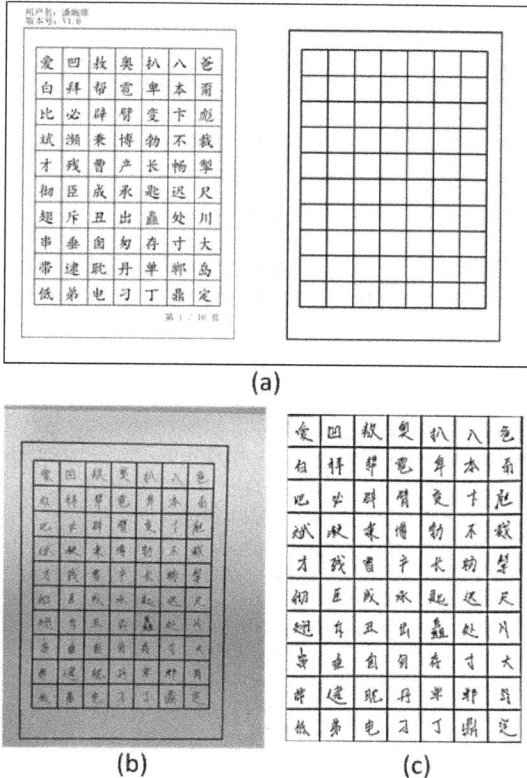

Figure 2: The template in FlexiFont. (a) is the generated template image, (b) is the template photo and (c) is the rectified writing zone.

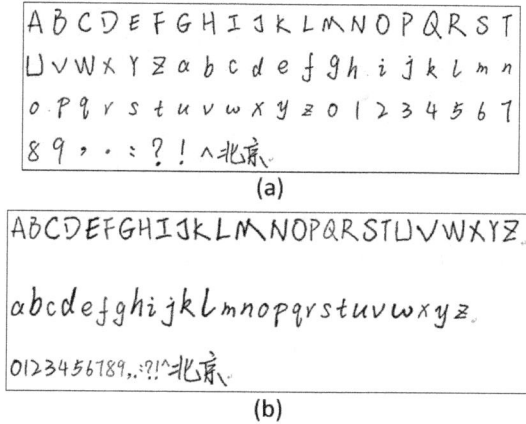

Figure 3: (a) shows the font library without adjustment where all characters are centered. (b) shows the font library with adjustment where all characters are normalized to its best size and position.

First of all, the average height $h_{avg}$ of all characters in the font library is calculated. FlexiFont defines a best height $h_{best}$ for Chinese characters. Afterwards, each character is scaled from $h_{old}^i$ to $h_{new}^i$ by the rate $s$ using the following functions

$$h_{new}^i = \frac{h_{old}^i * h_{best}}{h_{avg}}. \tag{1}$$

For the position adjustment, if all characters are handled in the same manner, the western characters will appear as the situation in Fig. 3 (a). Consequently, we built a rule-based technique to automatically adjust the position of each character. Chinese characters, western characters, numbers and symbols are classified into several categories in our system, and characters in each category are normalized to their best height and position (shown in Fig. 3 (b)).

After all the character images are vectorized and contours are represented by Bezier curves and lines, the fitting results are written into the TrueType file according to the official specifications [9]. Ten necessary tables are included in the TrueType file and the file can be directly installed and used in personal computers.

In addition, FlexiFont allows users to improve and extend their font libraries. If the user has generated a font library before, then the newly generated font library could be merged to the existing one by merging their font files.

## 4. EXPERIMENTS

FlexiFont has been implemented as a web site and a PC demo software, respectively. The web site is now available for simple test at http://59.108.48.27/flexifont. More functions will be added in the future.

In order to demonstrate the effectiveness and robustness of our system, four volunteers were invited to test FlexiFont. They followed the instructions on our web site to generate their own font libraries. We observe that it is easy for common people to use FlexiFont and through our system the users can get their font libraries within several minutes. As shown in Table 1, different input devices were utilized in our experiments, which demonstrates that FlexiFont is capable of processing images with different resolutions and qualities.

filter and bilateral filter [14] are used to remove the contour noise, and the adaptive threshold algorithm [5] is adapted for binarization.

Up to now, a lot of vectorization approaches have been developed [6, 10, 11]. For high-quality images, the vectorization techniques are very mature and there exist many open source projects such as Potrace [12]. For noisy character images, recently Zhang et al. [16] proposed a vectorization method that builds a database to store the best parameters of Gaussian kernel for each stroke of Chinese characters. However it is not practical to build the database for all these strokes in every font style.

In FlexiFont, the vectorization procedure consists of the following steps: First, the character contours are traced and the contour points with maxima curvature are chosen as the corner points. Secondly, the contour segments separated by corner points are approximated by quadratic Bezier curves. Least square method and Newton Raphson method are adopted for curve fitting. Finally, a dynamic programming algorithm is applied to minimize the fitting error by splitting or merging adjacent contour segments.

### 3.4 Generate or Merge Font Library

In order to generate a practical font library, the size and position of each character should be optimally adjusted. When we normalize the size of each character, its original ratio between height and width is not changed. Thus in our system, we only need to consider the calculation of height.

**Table 1: Generating font libraries by FlexiFont.**

| User Name | Input Device | Character Number | Processing Time (s) |
|-----------|--------------|------------------|---------------------|
| Biu | Digital camera | 129 | 16 |
| Meng | iPad mini 2 | 210 | 22 |
| Tai | Samsung i9308 | 347 | 48 |
| Hao | iPhone 5S | 419 | 59 |

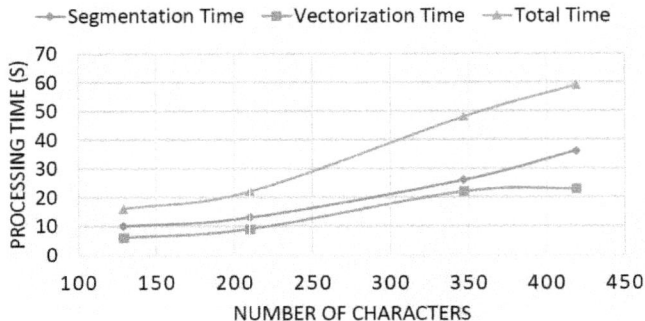

Figure 4: The processing time of generating the font library for each volunteer. The total time is equal to the sum of the Segmentation Time (time of Get Single Character Images) and the Vectorization Time (time of Vectorization Character Images and Generate Font Library).

As we can see in Fig.4, the total processing time for each font library is linearly proportion to the number of characters. For each character image, the total processing time is around 120 ms. Some results are shown in Fig.5, and more images and the generated font libraries can be found at http://59.108.48.27/exps.

## 5. CONCLUSIONS

In this paper, we introduce a flexible system to generate personal font libraries. Compared with existing approaches, FlexiFont has the following three advantages: flexible template, extensible font library, and easy to use. Rather than acquiring images from scanners, our system is designed for camera-based images. Moreover, the whole procedure of generating font libraries from template images is automatic and does not involve parameter tuning.

For future work, we will develop an Android application to realize our system in smart mobile devices. Also, we will try to investigate how to learn the font style merely from the input handwriting characters, so we can automatically generate all other characters in the font library, and the user does not need to write out all characters to get a complete font library in his/her personal style.

## 6. ACKNOWLEDGEMENTS

This work was supported by National Natural Science Foundation of China (Grant No.: 61202230), National Hi-Tech Research and Development Program (863 Program) of China (Grant No.: 2014AA015102) and China Postdoctoral Science Foundation (Grant No.: 2013T60038).

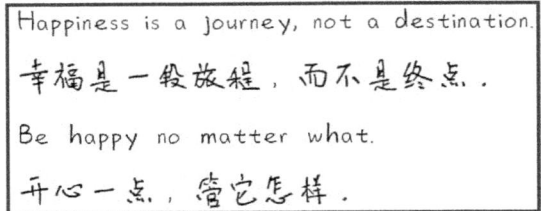

Figure 5: Demonstration of a paragraph consisting of characters in the font library generated by Flexi-Font.

## 7. REFERENCES

[1] Fonts for peas. http://kevinandamanda.com/fonts/fontsforpeas.

[2] Pilot handwriting. http://pilothandwriting.com.

[3] Your fonts. http://www.yourfonts.com.

[4] G. Bradski and A. Kaehler. *Learning OpenCV: Computer vision with the OpenCV library*. O'Reilly Media, Inc., 2008.

[5] A. K. Jain. *Fundamentals of digital image processing*. Prentice-Hall, Inc., 1989.

[6] A. Kolesnikov. Approximation of digitized curves with cubic bézier splines. In *ICIP*, pages 4285–4288. IEEE, 2010.

[7] F. Lab. Scan font. http://www.fontlab.com/font-converter/scanfont.

[8] J. Liang, D. Doermann, and H. Li. Camera-based analysis of text and documents: a survey. *IJDAR*, 7(2-3):84–104, 2005.

[9] Microsoft. Opentype specification. https://www.microsoft.com/typography/otspec/otff.htm.

[10] S. Pal, P. Ganguly, and P. Biswas. Cubic bézier approximation of a digitized curve. *Pattern recognition*, 40(10):2730–2741, 2007.

[11] M. Plass and M. Stone. Curve-fitting with piecewise parametric cubics. In *ACM SIGGRAPH*, volume 17, pages 229–239. ACM, 1983.

[12] P. Selinger. Potrace: a polygon-based tracing algorithm. *Potrace (online), http://potrace. sourceforge. net/potrace. pdf (2009-07-01)*, 2003.

[13] N. Stamatopoulos, B. Gatos, I. Pratikakis, and S. J. Perantonis. Goal-oriented rectification of camera-based document images. *Image Processing, IEEE Transactions on*, 20(4):910–920, 2011.

[14] C. Tomasi and R. Manduchi. Bilateral filtering for gray and color images. In *ICCV*, pages 839–846. IEEE, 1998.

[15] G. Williams. Fontforge. http://fontforge.sourceforge.net, 2004.

[16] J. Zhang, H. Lin, and J. Yu. A novel method for vectorizing historical documents of chinese calligraphy. In *ICCDCG*, pages 219–224. IEEE, 2007.

# Circular Coding with Interleaving Phase

Robert Ulichney
Hewlett-Packard Laboratories
165 Dascomb Road
Andover, MA 01810
+1-978-897-6223
u@hp.com

Matthew Gaubatz
Hewlett-Packard Laboratories
701 Pike Street, Suite 900
Seattle, WA 98101
+1-206-245-5766
matthew.gaubatz@hp.com

Steven Simske
Hewlett-Packard Laboratories
3404 E Harmony Rd.
Ft. Collins, CO 80528-9544
+1-970-898-1359
steve.simske@hp.com

## ABSTRACT

A general two-dimensional coding method is presented that allows recovery of data based on only a cropped portion of the code, and without knowledge of the carrier image. A description of both an encoding and recovery system is provided. Our solution involves repeating a payload with a fixed number of bits, assigning one bit to every symbol in the image –whether that symbol is data carrying or non-data carrying– with the goal of guaranteeing recovery of all the bits in the payload. Because the technique is applied to images, for aesthetic reasons we do not use fiducials, and do not employ any end-of-payload symbols. The beginning of the payload is determined by a phase code that is interleaved between groups of payload rows. The recovery system finds the phase row by evaluating candidate rows, and ranks confidence based on the sample variance. The target application is data-bearing clustered-dot halftones, so special consideration is given to the resulting checkerboard subsampling. This particular application is examined via exhaustive simulations to quantify the likelihood of unrecoverable bits and bit redundancy as a function of offset, crop window size, and phase code spacing.

## Categories and Subject Descriptors

I.7.5 [**Document and Text Processing**]: Graphics recognition and interpretation; E.4 [**Coding and Information Theory**]; H.3.2 [**Information Storage and Retrieval**]: Information Storage.

## Keywords

Data-bearing Hardcopy; Coding, Halftoning; Data Recovery.

## 1. INTRODUCTION

Embedding data in hardcopy is increasingly important for linking paper and electronic workflows, security and other applications. Data-bearing hardcopy is most often accomplished with various types of multidimensional barcodes, along with more aesthetically pleasing alternatives of encoding symbols in halftones [1][2]. We propose a new solution for recovering data when only a part of the data-bearing image can be captured, with no knowledge of the carrier image. The solution is designed to be robust in the presence of one or more of the many print-scan process degradations [3] that can hurt data integrity.

In this paper, we describe a coding scheme that allows complete recovery of a payload from an arbitrarily cropped version of a 2D array of symbols representing 1-bit values. The following notation is used to describe the approach:

| | |
|---|---|
| $B$ | Number of bits in the payload. |
| $P$ | Payload, representing a value between 0 and $2^B$-1. |
| $S$ | Payload in Standard form. |
| $C$ | Circular shift to get the payload from the standard form. |
| $c$ | Number of bits needed to represent $C$ |
| $U$ | Phase code representation of $C$. |
| $V$ | Phase code row interleave period. |
| $D$ | Row-to-row Offset of the payload in the image. |
| $P'$ | Candidate recovered payload. |
| $U'$ | Candidate recovered Phase code. |
| $D'$ | Candidate row-to-row offset. |
| $W$ | Width of the crop window. |

The coding scheme employs a circularly shifted payload. Before describing the encoder and decoder we define what we call the "standard form" of such a payload.

### 1.1 Circular Shifting and Standard Form

As a simple one-dimensional example, consider a $B$=5 bit payload $P=11001_2$ repeated continuously:

$$\ldots 1001110011100111001110011 \ldots$$

An arbitrary crop of 5 bits from that stream will yield one of 5 circularly shifted versions of that payload: $11100_2$, $11001_2$, $10011_2$, $00111_2$, or $01110_2$. To specify the correct payload from such a crop, we need one more piece of information: the circular shift to the right, $C$, (= 0,1,2,3, or 4) relative to some reference representation. We define that reference representation the "standard form", $S$, as the minimum value of all possible circularly shifted versions of the payload. In our example, $S=00111_2$. The circular shift to get the payload $P=11001_2$ from the standard form is $C$=2.

When the number of bits in the payload, $B$, can be segmented into parts of equal length it is possible that certain payloads can have more than one circular shift that maps the standard form back to the payload. Consider $B$=6 and $P=101101_2$, which repeats a series of 3 bits "101". The standard form is $S=011011_2$, and the payload can be resolved with a circular shift of both $C$=1 and $C$=4. Similarly $P=101010_2$ has standard form $S=010101_2$ with three equivalent circular shifts $C$=1,3, and 5.

In an earlier work, a 2D circular coding scheme [4] was presented that repeated the payload on each row but offset successive rows by an amount equal to the circular shift $C$, so that the payload could be recovered from the standard form $S$. Using that method, cases of equivalent circular shifts did not present an issue since all such shifts would correctly resolve the payload. The method herein demonstrates other advantages over the earlier method, but requires that the circular shift, C, be unique. For that reason we restrict the number of payload bits, B, to have no multiplicative factors, and so B must be prime. The reason for the need for a unique value of C will be made clear in the Recovery System section. If the desired payload size is not prime the next larger prime number can be used, with the extra bits used for error correction.

## 2. ENCODING SYSTEM

The goal of the encoder is to represent a payload, P, consisting of B bits in a two-dimensional array of one-bit symbols. Encoding is accomplished by repeating the payload across each line where each successive row is circularly shifted relative to the row above it by a fixed amount, D. The circular phase C is embedded in a "phase code", U, also of length B and interleaved between groups of payload rows. Every row of phase code, U, is followed by (V-1) rows of payload, P.

For a payload of B bits, the circular shift can have values $C \in \{0,1,2,...(B-1)\}$. The number of bits needed to represent C is denoted as $c = \lceil \log_2 B \rceil$, where $\lceil . \rceil$ is the ceiling function. As c is less than B, there are a number of ways to construct the phase code U. One approach is constructing an error correcting code to fill the B bits, but there are other strategies that can be better suited for the carrier of this data.

While the coding scheme can be used for any two-dimensional array that could include magnetic or optical media, the target use is for printed halftone images where individual halftone clusters carry a bit of data as indicated by single-pixel shifts [4]. We use monochrome classical $45^\circ$ screen clustered-dot halftones. One way to think of such a halftone screen is as a set of clusters in complementary checkerboard arrangements of highlight and shadow cells. Figure 1 illustrates an enlargement of a portion of an image with a transition from shadow to highlight area. The shadow cell positions are denoted by red dots. Half of the cells are incapable of carrying data: shadow cells in highlight areas are completely white, and highlight cells in shadow areas are completely black. This checkerboard subsampling of the code adds a challenge for preserving the data.

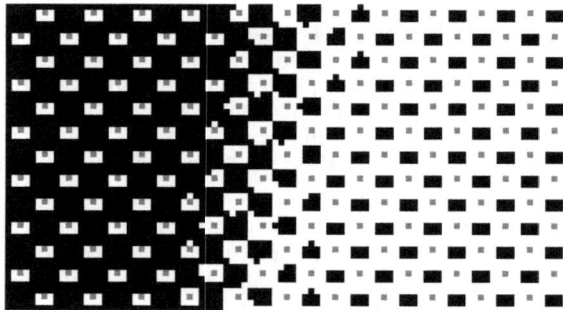

**Figure 1. Zoomed halftone image with shadow cells indicated by red dots.**

To protect the phase code, U, against the checkerboard decimation of halftone embedding, one approach is to duplicate every bit of C in succession, then repeat this "double" pattern until all B bits are filled. While there are many other possible representations, this is the method we use in this study. As an example, consider the case of B=17. The number of bits in C is c=5. The bit positions in the phase code U and C would be related as follows:

| U bit position | 16 | 15 | 14 | 13 | 12 | 11 | 10 | 9 | 8 | 7 | 6 | 5 | 4 | 3 | 2 | 1 | 0 |
|---|---|---|---|---|---|---|---|---|---|---|---|---|---|---|---|---|---|
| C bit position | 4 | 4 | 3 | 3 | 2 | 2 | 1 | 1 | 0 | 0 | 4 | 4 | 3 | 3 | 2 | 2 | 1 |

Encoding the 2D array of symbols is carried out as follows:

(1) Set the payload bit length B, row-to-row offset D, phase code representation method, and interleave period V. B, D, and V must be known to the recovery system.

(2) Determine the standard form S of the payload P, and the circular phase C between S and P.

(3) Generate the Phase Code, U.

(4) Repeatedly fill (V-1) rows of S, followed by one row of U, with each row circularly shifted by D more bits than the row above.

Consider the example were B=17, D=2, and V=3. This code represents a very short payload but illustrates the approach. Figure 2 depicts the top left corner of a code generated by this method. Black numbers represent bit positions of the payload in standard form S and red numbers represent bit positions of the phase code U. Note that each row is circularly shifted by D=2 more bit positions than the row above it regardless of payload or phase code.

| 16 | 15 | 14 | 13 | 12 | 11 | 10 | 9 | 8 | 7 | 6 | 5 | 4 | 3 | 2 | 1 | 0 | 16 | 15 | 14 | |
|---|---|---|---|---|---|---|---|---|---|---|---|---|---|---|---|---|---|---|---|---|
| 1 | 0 | 16 | 15 | 14 | 13 | 12 | 11 | 10 | 9 | 8 | 7 | 6 | 5 | 4 | 3 | 2 | 1 | 0 | 16 | ... |
| 3 | 2 | 1 | 0 | 16 | 15 | 14 | 13 | 12 | 11 | 10 | 9 | 8 | 7 | 6 | 5 | 4 | 3 | 2 | 1 | |
| 5 | 4 | 3 | 2 | 1 | 0 | 16 | 15 | 14 | 13 | 12 | 11 | 10 | 9 | 8 | 7 | 6 | 5 | 4 | 3 | |
| 7 | 6 | 5 | 4 | 3 | 2 | 1 | 0 | 16 | 15 | 14 | 13 | 12 | 11 | 10 | 9 | 8 | 7 | 6 | 5 | |
| 9 | 8 | 7 | 6 | 5 | 4 | 3 | 2 | 1 | 0 | 16 | 15 | 14 | 13 | 12 | 11 | 10 | 9 | 8 | 7 | |
| 11 | 10 | 9 | 8 | 7 | 6 | 5 | 4 | 3 | 2 | 1 | 0 | 16 | 15 | 14 | 13 | 12 | 11 | 10 | 9 | |
| 13 | 12 | 11 | 10 | 9 | 8 | 7 | 6 | 5 | 4 | 3 | 2 | 1 | 0 | 16 | 15 | 14 | 13 | 12 | 11 | |
| 15 | 14 | 13 | 12 | 11 | 10 | 9 | 8 | 7 | 6 | 5 | 4 | 3 | 2 | 1 | 0 | 16 | 15 | 14 | 13 | |
| 0 | 16 | 15 | 14 | 13 | 12 | 11 | 10 | 9 | 8 | 7 | 6 | 5 | 4 | 3 | 2 | 1 | 0 | 16 | 15 | |
| 2 | 1 | 0 | 16 | 15 | 14 | 13 | 12 | 11 | 10 | 9 | 8 | 7 | 6 | 5 | 4 | 3 | 2 | 1 | 0 | |
| 4 | 3 | 2 | 1 | 0 | 16 | 15 | 14 | 13 | 12 | 11 | 10 | 9 | 8 | 7 | 6 | 5 | 4 | 3 | 2 | |

...

**Figure 2. The top right corner of an example 2D code for B=17, D=2, and V=3.**

## 3. RECOVERY SYSTEM

The purpose of the recovery system is to find the payload P. The capture device only reads a cropped W by W subset of the array. The payload bit length B, row-to-row offset D, phase code representation method, and interleave period V are communicated from the encoder.

Recovery is achieved through the following steps:

(1) For each symbol in the 2D array, interpret its value as a 0, 1 or abstain. Abstains are assigned when the symbol is too ambiguous to decode and will not contribute to the averages. (At least half of the cells in an encoded halftone will be abstains as they are all black or all white.)

(2) Determine which rows contain the phase codes. For each of V possibilities, find an estimate of a shifted payload P', and the Confidence value associated with that estimate.

For each candidate phase code row position, eliminate the phase code rows and compute an average for each bit position from the remaining D-shifted rows. For each bit position $\{b_{B-1}, ... , b_1, b_0\}$ find an average of all non-abstained values and assign a value of 0 if that average is less than 0.5 and a value of 1 if that value is greater than or equal to 0.5. The uncertainty, $u_j$, for each bit position is then the absolute value of the difference between bit estimate and the average. The uncertainty of a bit will range from 0 to 0.5.

The Confidence associated with a candidate is then

$$\text{Confidence} = 1 - (2/B)\Sigma u_j, \text{ for } j=\{0, 1, 2, \ldots, (B-1)\}.$$

and ranges from 0 to 1.0.

(3) Select the candidate set where P' has the highest confidence.

(4) Find the corresponding phase code U'. For each bit position $\{b_{B-1}, \ldots, b_1, b_0\}$ find an average for of all non-abstained values and assign a value of 0 if that average is less than 0.5 and a value of 1 if that value is greater than or equal to 0.5.

(5) Convert P' into the standard form S by finding the minimum binary number value of the binary strings representing all B circular shifts of P'.

(6) Convert U' to U by circularly shifting it by the same amount as in step (5) to convert P' to S.

(7) Extract the Circular Phase C from the Phase Code U.

(8) Circularly shift S by C to get the payload P.

Because the unambiguous recovery of U is tied to the uniqueness of the standard form, it is clear why B must be prime to avoid multiple values of C. Otherwise one will be unable to find the phase of the phase code.

## 3.1 Recovery Example

To continue the example using the code from Figure 2 with B=17, D=2, and V=3, a 10x10 capture is shown in Figure 3. The correct bit positions of the payload in standard form are indicated in black, and the correct bit positions of the phase code rows are indicated in red. This information will not be known to the recovery system but is shown for reference. This sample is from an encoded halftone in an area of all highlight or all shadow, indicated by the gray and white cells in the figure; this is shown to indicate that only half of the bits will survive checkerboard subsampling.

**Figure 3. 10x10 capture of a portion of the code in Figure 2.**

Following the steps for recovery above:

(1) While not shown, the value of each symbol is recovered and stored as a 0, 1 or abstain.

(2) Since V=3, there are a total of 3 candidate sets of rows where the phase code is present. These three sets of rows are indicated in Figure 4. In each case the rows in-between the candidate phase code rows are assumed to be payload rows and evaluated. The corresponding bit positions are averaged and the uncertainties and confidence scores are generated.

(3) In this case, the correct set (in Figure 4(b)), results in the highest confidence score. Sets 1 and 3 will have payload bits combined with phase code bits, which will be different from payload bits, and thus will generate more uncertainty.

(4) The Figure 4(b) phase code rows are averaged to form a shifted U' code. The codes are 3 rows apart so the relative shifts are D*V = 2*3 = 6 bit positions.

With the correct shifted payload P' and phase code U', steps (5) through (8) can then be carried out to deliver the payload P.

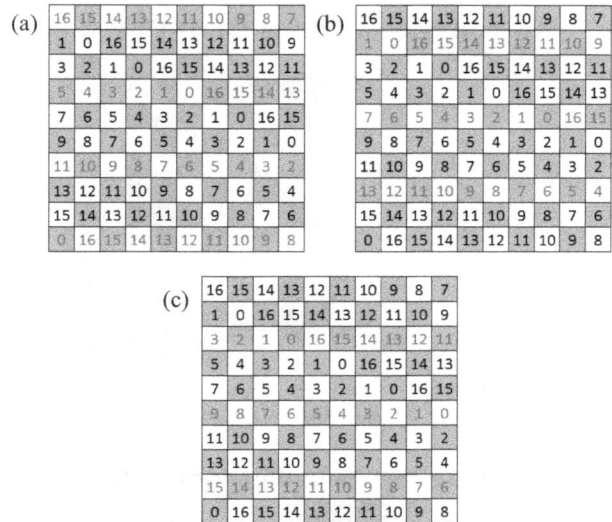

**Figure 4. The 3 candidate assignments of the phase code rows (bit positions shown in red).**

## 4. ANALYSIS

The circular coding method as described has the flexibility to select a number of parameters. Once a payload size B is chosen, there is some question as to what the optimal value of row-to-row offset D and phase code row interleave period V should be. An important consideration for robust recovery is first assuring that all bits for the payload P and circular shift C survive, then knowing the number of repeat instances of each bit – the higher the number the better to combat the uncertainties in the print-scan process. For a given square crop window of width W, the number of times a payload or phase code bit is repeated depends on the position of the crop window and the nature of the checkerboard subsampling. While sample tests can offer some insight, it is more useful to exhaustively simulate all possible crop positions within a halftone checkerboard subsampled array of codes.

The repeat count varies for each bit. For payload recovery, the average bit repeat count is not as important as a guaranteed repeat count of some high percentage of the all code bits. The value of 90% is used in this study. For the one 10x10 crop in our example in Figure 3, counting the highlight or shadow subsampled payload (black numbered) bits we find that 4 bits are repeated 3 times, 10 bits are repeated 2 times and 3 bits survive only once. The guaranteed repeat count for 90% of the bits is then only 1. The guaranteed repeat count for the bits of the phase code also be so analyzed.

Figure 5 plots the guaranteed 90% repeat counts for B=17 and V=3 for all row-to-row offsets D and a range of small crop window sizes for both the payload and phase code. Each point on the graph is the aggregate of an exhaustive set of all crop configurations for the specified values of D and W. The point circled indicates the example case in Figure 3, with a 10x10 crop window and D=2. This testing clearly reveals that some choices for D are better than others, and that D=0,1,6,11, and 16 in particular should be avoided.

The reason for this test is that in the presence of noise in the print and scan process, the accuracy of correctly recovering any single bit is not perfect; thus, redundancy is needed. It is not practical to rely on a guaranteed repeat count of 1, so a larger crop window is needed.

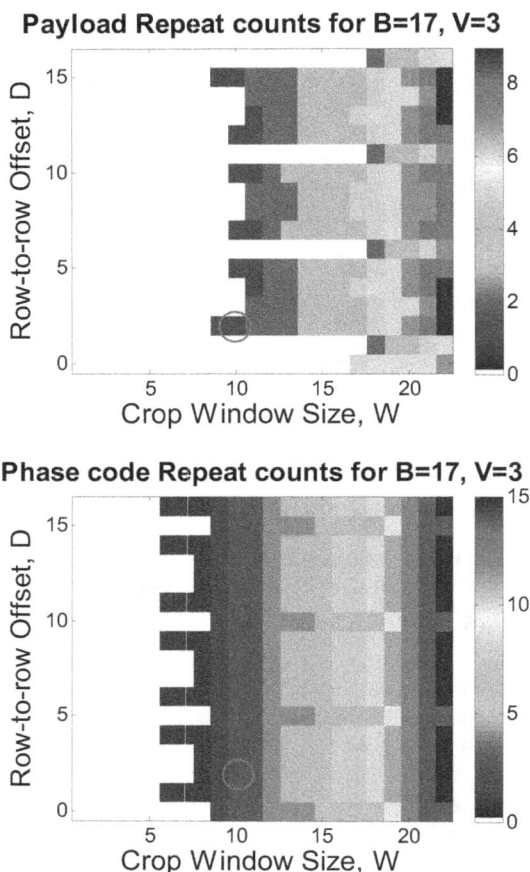

**Payload Repeat counts for B=17, V=3**

**Phase code Repeat counts for B=17, V=3**

**Figure 5. Minimum repeat counts for 90% of the bits in the payload and phase code as a function of crop window size and offset. Circled point corresponds to the example in Figure 3.**

As phase code interleave period V decreases phase code repeat values increase but payload repeat counts decrease. For the larger payload size of B=67, examining the results for several choices of V showed that V=9 offers a good balance between these tendencies. Analysis of this case is shown in Figure 6. The plot shows that D=4 would be a good choice for row-to-row offset. Cropped captures as small as 30x30 will still have 90% of the bits repeated at least 4 times for both the payload and the phase.

The raw recovery rates for data encoded in clustered-dot halftone cells (stegatones) have been measured for a wide variety of printers and resolutions [5]. Combining this data with the minimum repeat count analysis allows for an efficient and robust design of a reference-free steganographic halftone generation and recovery system. The key advantage over the earlier method [4] is the ability to select a fixed row-to-row offset to optimize performance. The method allows complete data payload recovery

from a cropped portion of the encoded image without the need for fiducial marks.

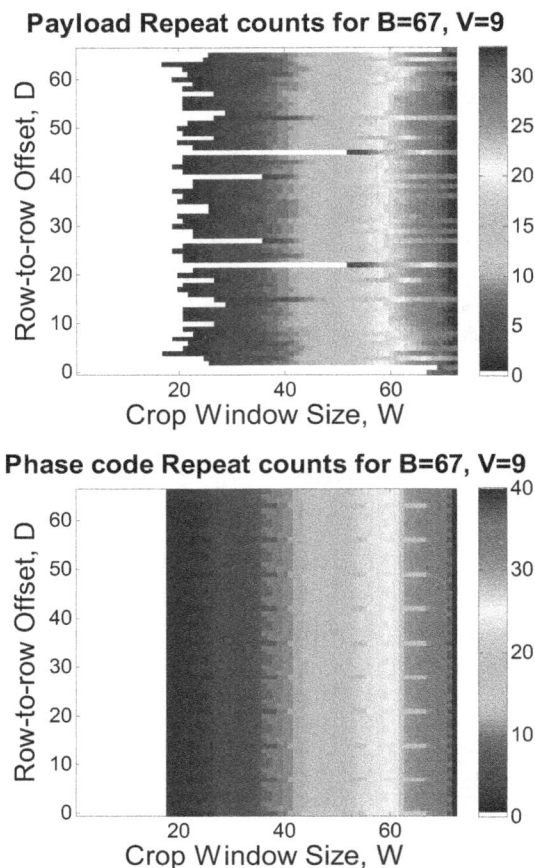

**Payload Repeat counts for B=67, V=9**

**Phase code Repeat counts for B=67, V=9**

**Figure 6. 90% repeat counts for B=67 and V=9.**

# 5. REFERENCES

[1] Ulichney, R., Gaubatz, M., Simske, S., "Encoding Information in Clustered-Dot Halftones", *IS&T NIP26 (26th Int. Conf. on Digital Printing Technologies)*, Austin, TX, 602-605, Sep 2010.

[2] Bulan, O., Sharma, G., and Monga, V., "Orientation Modulation for Data Hiding in Clustered-Dot Halftone Prints," *IEEE Transactions on Image Processing*, vol. 19, no. 8, pp. 2070-2084, Aug 2010.

[3] Solanki, K., Madhow, U., Manjanuath, B., Chandrasekaran,S., and El-Khalil, I., "'Print and Scan' Resilient Data Hiding in Images," *IEEE Transaction on Information Forensics and Security*, vol 1, pp 464-478, 2006.

[4] Ulichney, R., M. Gaubatz, S. Simske, "Circular Coding for Data Embedding", *IS&T NIP29 (29th Int. Conf. on Digital Printing Technologies)*, Seattle, WA, Sep 2013.

[5] Chen, Y., Ulichney, R., Gaubatz, M., Pollard, S., "Stegatone Performance Characterization", Media Watermarking, Security, and Forensics 2013, *IS&T/SPIE Electronic Imaging Symposium*, 8665-27, Feb 3-7, 2013.

# A New Sentence Similarity Assessment Measure based on a Three-Layer Sentence Representation

Rafael Ferreira
Federal University of
Pernambuco
Recife, Pernambuco, Brazil
rflm@cin.ufpe.br

Rafael Dueire Lins
Federal University of
Pernambuco
Recife, Pernambuco, Brazil
rdl@cin.ufpe.br

Fred Freitas
Federal University of
Pernambuco
Recife, Pernambuco, Brazil
fred@cin.ufpe.br

Steven J. Simske
Hewlett-Packard Labs
Fort Collins, CO 80528, USA
steven.simske@hp.com

Marcelo Riss
Hewlett-Packard Brazil
Porto Alegre, Rio Grande do
Sul, Brazil
marcelo.riss@hp.com

## ABSTRACT

Sentence similarity is used to measure the degree of likelihood between sentences. It is used in many natural language applications, such as text summarization, information retrieval, text categorization, and machine translation. The current methods for assessing sentence similarity represent sentences as vectors of bag of words or the syntactic information of the words in the sentence. The degree of likelihood between phrases is calculated by composing the similarity between the words in the sentences. Two important concerns in the area, the meaning problem and the word order, are not handled, however. This paper proposes a new sentence similarity assessment measure that largely improves and refines a recently published method that takes into account the lexical, syntactic and semantic components of sentences. The new method proposed here was benchmarked using a publically available standard dataset. The results obtained show that the new similarity assessment measure proposed outperforms the state of the art systems and achieve results comparable to the evaluation made by humans.

## Categories and Subject Descriptors

H.3.3 [**Information Search and Retrieval**]: Information gathering and extraction; I.2.6 [**Learning**]: Knowledge Acquisition.

## General Terms

Algorithms, Experimentation

## Keywords

Graph-based Model; Sentence Simplification; Relation Extraction; Inductive Logic Programming

## 1. INTRODUCTION

The degree of similarity between phrases is measured by sentence similarity, or short-text similarity methods. The similarity methods should also address problems of measuring sentences with partial information, such as when one sentence is split into two or more short texts and phrases that contain two or more sentences. Automatic text summarization [7], information retrieval [27], image retrieval [3], text categorization [15], and machine translation [22] are examples of applications rely or may benefit from sentence similarity methods.

The technical literature reports several efforts to address such problem [9, 12, 17, 21] by the syntactic information among words or representing sentences using vectors of bag of words. Sentences are modeled in such a way to allow the similarity methods to compute different measures to evaluate the degree of similarity between words. The overall sentence similarity is obtained as a function of those partial measures. Two important problems are not handled by using such approach:

**Word Order Problem[28]:** The order that the words appear in the text influences the meaning of texts. For example, in the sentences *A hires B* and *B hires A*, are built using the same words, but the order changes completely their meaning.

**Meaning Problem [2]:** Sentences with the same meaning, but with different words. For example, the sentences *Joe is an intelligent boy* and *Joe is a smart lad*, have similar meaning, if the context they appear does not change much.

The recent paper [24] addressed these problems by proposing a sentence representation and similarity measure based on lexical, syntactic and semantic analysis. The similarity measures proposed in [24] have some limitations, however. For example, they do not consider sentence sizes. Taking such problems into account, this paper presents (i) a new sentence representation that improves the one proposed in reference [24] to deal with meaning problem and word order problems, and (ii) a new sentence similarity measure based on a similarity matrix and a size penalization coefficient.

The lexical analysis is performed in the first layer, in which the similarity measure uses bag of word vectors, similarly to references [9, 12, 17, 21]. In addition to lexical analysis, this layer applies two preprocessing services [8]: *stopwords removal* and *stemming*. The syntactic layer uses relations to deal with word order problem. The semantic layer employs Semantic Role Annotation (SRA) [5] to handle both problems. The SRA analysis returns the meaning of the actions, the actor who performs the action, and the object/actor that suffers the action, among other information. Reference [24] was possibly the first to use SRA as a measure of the semantic similarity between sentences, while other methods employ only WordNet [6] or a corpus-based measure [17] in a classic bag of word vectors similarity.

The measure presented here was benchmarked using the dataset proposed by Li *et al* [12], which is reputed as the standard dataset for such problem. Pearson's correlation coefficient (PCC) and Spearman's rank correlation coefficient (SRCC), which are traditional measures for assessing sentence similarity, were compared with the results of the measure described in reference [24] and the new one proposed in this paper. A combination of the proposed measure achieves 0.92 for the PCC, which means that the proposed measure has the same accuracy of the best human assigned values to the similarities in such dataset. Compared with SRCC the measure proposed here achieved 0.94, which means an improvement of 3% in relation to the state of the art results reported in reference [24].

The rest of this paper is organized as follows. Section 2 presents the most relevant differences between the proposed method and the state of the art related work. The sentence representation method used here is described in Section 3. Section 4 details the proposed similarity measure. The benchmarking of the proposed and the best other similar methods is presented in Section 5. This paper ends drawing the conclusions and discussing lines for further work in Section 7.

## 2. RELATED WORK

This section presents the state of the art methods for the sentence similarity problem [9, 12, 17, 21, 24].

A similarity measure that translates each sentence in a semantic vector by using a lexical database and a word order vector is proposed by Li and his colleagues in reference [12]. They propose the creation of a ratio to weight the significance between semantic and syntactic information. A new word vector is created for each sentence using information from the lexical database that calculates the weight of significance of a word using information content obtained from a corpus-based method to measure similarities between words [11]. By combining the semantic vector with the information contents from the corpus-based method, a new semantic vector is built for each of the two sentences. The semantic similarity is measured taking into account the semantic vectors. At last, the sentence similarity is computed by combining semantic similarity and order similarity.

Islam and Inkpen, in reference[9], present an approach to measure the similarity of two texts that makes use of semantic and syntactic information. At first, they calculate

the string similarity, which is acquired applying the longest common subsequence measure, and the semantic word similarity, which is measured by a corpus-based measure. Such information helps the creation of an optional common-word order similarity function to incorporate the syntactic information. Then, the text similarity is calculated combining the string similarity, semantic similarity and common-word order similarity.

Reference [17] describes a similarity measure that works as follows: for each word in the first sentence (main sentence), it tries to identify the word in the second sentence that has the highest semantic similarity according to one of the word-to-word similarity measure. Then, the process is repeated using the second sentence as the main sentence. Finally, the resulting similarity scores are combined using the arithmetic average.

Oliva and collaborators in reference [21] propose the SyMSS method that assesses the influence of the syntactic structure of two compared sentences on the calculation of similarity. It relies on the idea that a sentence is made up of the meaning of its individual words and the syntactic connections among them. Using WordNet, the semantic information is obtained through a deep parsing process that finds the main phrases that compose the sentence.

The recent work by Ferreira and colleagues [24] presents a method similar to the one described in reference [17] to compare sentences, but here the approach use lexical, syntactic and semantic analysis. It proposed a word matching algorithm, using statistics and WordNet measures, to perform the similarity between sentences. The algorithm [24] has two drawbacks. The first one is that it does not take into consideration the similarities of all words, in general, only the words with high similarity value are used. The second deficiency is that the similarity measure in [24] does not take into consideration the size of sentences, and this represents a problem especially when there is a high difference between the size of the sentences.

Although the methods in this paper use similar ideas to reference [24] to compare sentences, the approach here uses different preprocessing services to represent the lexical, syntactic and semantic analysis and proposes a completely new sentence similarity algorithm based on a similarity matrix. Besides that, the similarity measure introduced in this paper also proposes a size penalization coefficient to reduce the similarity for sentences with different sizes. Thus, the approach proposed in this paper combines: (i) the three layer sentence representation, which encompasses different levels of sentence information. Previous works that claim to use semantic information, do not actually evaluate the sentence semantics. They use WordNet to evaluate the semantics of the words instead, yielding potential poor results. (ii) A similarity measure that uses a matrix to consider the similarities among all words in sentences and a size penalization coefficient to deal with sentences with different sizes.

## 3. THE NEW THREE-LAYER SENTENCE REPRESENTATION

This section presents the proposed sentence representation used for calculating the similarity measure encompassing three layers: lexical, syntactic and semantic. It is important to remark that these layers do not reflect exactly the

**Lexical Representation**

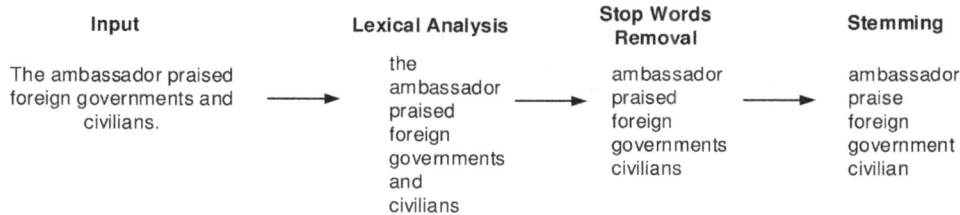

| Input | Lexical Analysis | Stop Words Removal | Stemming |
|---|---|---|---|
| The ambassador praised foreign governments and civilians. | the ambassador praised foreign governments and civilians | ambassador praised foreign governments civilians | ambassador praise foreign government civilian |

**Figure 1: Lexical layer for the sentence** *"The ambassador praised foreign governments and civilians".*

standard linguistic analysis as one assumes that the input text was preprocessed for stopword removal and stemming.

A single sentence is taken as input to build such representation. The output is a text and two RDF files that contain the lexical, syntactic and semantic layers, respectively. Each layer is detailed as follows.

## 3.1 The Lexical Layer

The lexical layer takes a sentence as input and yields as output a text file a list of the sentence tokens representing it. The steps performed in this layer are:

1. **Lexical analysis**: This step splits the sentence into a list of tokens, including punctuation.

2. **Stop word removal**: It rules out words with little representative value to the document, e.g. articles and pronouns, and the punctuation.

3. **Stemming**: This step applies the stemming preprocessing service, which translates the tokens in its basic form. For instance, plural words are made singular and all verb tenses and persons are exchanged by the verb infinitive.

Figure 1 depicts the operations performed in this layer for the sentence *"The ambassador praised foreign governments and civilians"*. It also displays the output of each step. The output of this layer is a text file containing the list of tokens.

This layer is important to improve the performance of simple text processing tasks. Although it does not convey much information about the sentence, it is widely employed in various traditional text mining tasks, such as, information retrieval and summarization.

## 3.2 The Syntactic Layer

This layer receives the sequence of tokens, generated in the lexical layer, and converts into a graph represented using RDF triples [25]. This transformation follows the steps of:

1. **Syntactic analysis**: In this step relations such as subject, direct object, adverbial modifier, among others, are represented as usual. Prepositions and conjunction relations are also extracted from the syntactic analysis.

2. **Graph creation**: A directed graph is used to store the entities with their relations. The vertices are the elements obtained from the shallow layer, while the edges denote the relations described in the previous steps.

Figure 2 deploys the syntactic layer for the sentence *"The ambassador praised foreign governments and civilians"*. The edges usually have one direction, following the direction of the syntactic relations. This is not always the case, however. The model also accommodates bi-directed edges, usually corresponding to conjunction relations. One should notice that all vertices from the example are listed in the output of the previous layer.

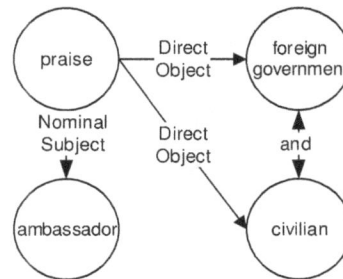

**Figure 2: Syntactic layer for** *"The ambassador praised foreign governments and civilians".*

The syntactic analysis step is important as it represents an order relation among the tokens of a sentence. It describes the possible or acceptable syntactic structures of the language; and decomposes the text into syntactic units in order to "understand" the way in which the syntactic elements are arranged in a sentence. Such kind of relations could be used in applications, as for instance, automatic text summarization, text categorization, information retrieval, etc.

RDF format was chosen to store the graph because: (i) it is a standard model for data interchange on the web; (ii) it provides a simple and clean format; (iii) inferences are easily summoned with the RDF triples; and (iv) there are several freely available tools to handle RDF.

## 3.3 The Semantic Layer

This layer decorates the RDF graph with entity roles and sense identification. It takes as input the sequence of groups of tokens, extracted in the lexical layer and applies SRA to define the roles of each of the entities and to identify their "meaning" in the sentence.

The semantic layer uses SRA to perform two different operations:

1. **Sense identification**: Sense identification is of paramount importance to this type of representation since

different words could denote the same meaning, particularly regarding to verbs. For instance, "accuse", "blame", "criticize", "deprecate", "praise" are words that could be associated with the sense of *"judgment"*.

2. **Role annotation**: Differently from in the syntactic layer, role annotation identifies the semantic function of each entity. For instance, in the same sentence of the previous example, the *ambassator* is the communicator of the action *praized*. Thus, the interpretation of the action is identified, not only its syntactic relation.

This layer deals with the problem of meaning using the output of the step of sense identification. The general meaning of the main entities of a sentence, not just the written words, is identified in this step. On the other hand, the role annotation extracts discourse information, as it deploys the order of the actions, the actors, etc, dealing with word order problem. Such information is relevant in extraction and summarization tasks, for instance.

Figure 3 presents a semantic layer example. Two different types of relations are identified in the figure: the sense relations, e.g. the triple foreign_government-sense-leadership, and the role annotation relations, e.g. praise-evaluee-civilian. The semantic layer uses a RDF graph representation, likewise the syntactic layer.

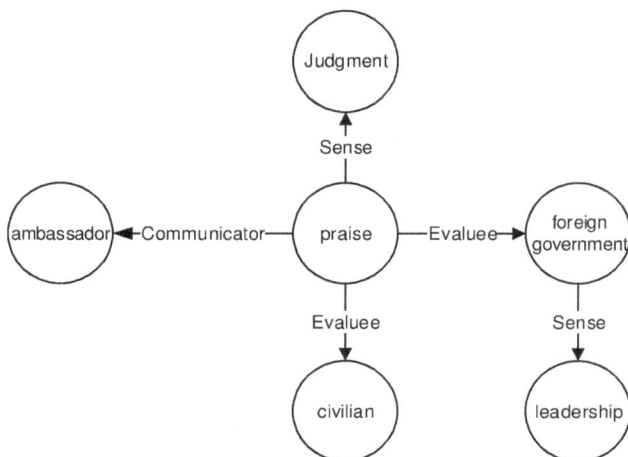

**Figure 3: Semantic layer for the phrase *"The ambassador praised foreign governments and civilians"*.**

## 4. ASSESSING SENTENCE SIMILARITY

This section introduces measure to assess the degree of sentence similarity based on the three-layer representation of sentences presented in Section 3. The proposed assessment makes use of the measure of similarity between words. The first part of this section describes six measures to evaluate the similarity between words, and the second one presents details of the proposed approach.

### 4.1 Word Similarity

The six measures used to calculate the similarity between words are presented. They cover the top five dictionary measures based on the results extracted from references [21] and [1]. In addition, the Levenshtein metric [18] is used to

provide a statistic evaluation because, in general, it is faster to calculate than dictionary based methods. The similarity measures are:

**Path measure** stands for the length of the path between two concepts to score their similarity.

**Resnik measure (Res)** attempts to quantify how much information content is common to two concepts. The information content is based on the lowest common subsumer (LCS) of the two concepts.

**Lin measure** is the ratio of the information contents of the LCS in the Resnik measure to the information contents of each of the concepts.

**Wu and Palmer measure (WP)** compares the global depth value of two concepts, using the WordNet taxonomy.

**Leacock and Chodorow measure (LC)** uses the length of the shortest path and the maximum depth of the taxonomy of two concepts to measure the similarity between them.

**Levenshtein metric (Lev)** between two strings calculates the minimum number of operations of insertion, deletion, or substitution of a single character needed to transform one string into the other.

In general one of the methods above is applied to measure the degree of similarity between words. They cover different aspects, however. WordNet based measures attempt to convey the semantic of the words, but they do not handle named entities, such as proper names of person and places. Thus, the approach proposed here applies the Algorithm 1 to measure the degree of similarity between two words, where *semanticSim* and *statisticSim* are the similarities measured using WordNet measures and levenshtein metric, respectively.

---

**Algorithm 1** Similarity Between Words
**Require:** $word1$ and $word2$
1: $similarity = 0$
2: $semanticSim = wordnetSimilarity(word1, word2)$
3: $statisticSim = levenshteinSimilarity(word1, word2)$
4: **if** $semanticSimilarity > 0$ **then**
5:     $similarity = semanticSim$
6: **else**
7:     $similarity = statisticSim$
8: **end if**
9: **return** $similarity$

---

From this point on, the similarity between concepts, tokens and words refers to the method presented in this section.

### 4.2 Sentence Similarity

Three different sentence similarity measures and a combination of them were developed based on the three-layer representation. Each of those measures model a different similarity relation that complete each other, as will be presented in Section 5. A detailed explanation of each measure is presented next.

### 4.2.1 The lexical measure

This measure accounts for the degree of lexical resemblance between sentences through the analysis of lexical similarity between the sentence tokens. This paper proposes the creation of a matrix with the similarities of all sentence tokens as a way to represent the similarity between the two sentences. It follows a detailed explanation of the calculation of this measure.

Let $A = \{a_1, a_2 ..., a_n\}$ and $B = \{b_1, b_2 ..., b_m\}$ be two sentences, such that, $a_i$ is a token of sentence $A$, $b_j$ is a token of sentence $B$, $n$ is the number of tokens of sentence $A$ and $m$ is the number of tokens of sentence $B$. The calculus of the lexical similarity is presented in Algorithm 2.

---

**Algorithm 2** Proposed Similarity Algorithm

**Require:** $A$ and $B$ {One BU set of sentences A and B}
1: $matrix = newmatrix(size(A)xsize(B))$
2: $total\_similarity = 0$
3: $iteration = 0$
4: **for** $bu_i \in A$ **do**
5:    **for** $bu'_j \in B$ **do**
6:       $matrix(i, j) = similarity(t_i, t'_j)$
7:    **end for**
8: **end for**
9: **for** $has\_line(matrix)$ and $has\_column(matrix)$ **do**
10:    $total\_similarity = total\_similarity + bigger\_similarity(matrix)$
11:    $remove\_line(matrix, bigger\_similarity(matrix))$
12:    $remove\_column(matrix, bigger\_similarity(matrix))$
13:    $iteration + +$
14: **end for**
15: **return** $total\_similarity/iteration$

---

The algorithm receives the set of tokens of sentence A and sentence B as input (Require). Then, it creates a matrix of dimension of $m \times n$ the dimension of the input tokens sets. The variables $total\_similarity$ and $iteration$ are initialized with values 0. The variable $total\_similarity$ adds up the values of the similarities in each step, while $iteration$ is used to transform the $total\_similarity$ into a value between 0-1(lines 1-3). The second step is the calculation of similarities for each pair $(a_i, b_j)$, where $a_i$ and $b_j$ are the tokens of sentence A and B respectively. The matrix stores the calculated similarities (lines 4-8). The last part of the algorithm is divided in three steps. First, it sums to $total\_similarity$ the high similarity value from $matrix$ (line 10). Then, it removes the line and column from the matrix that contains the high similarity (lines 11 and 12). To conclude, it updates the $iteration$ value (line 13). The output is the division of $total\_similarity$ and $iteration$ (line 15).

After the calculation of the $total\_similarity$, the system computes a Size Penalization Coefficient (SPC), that lowers the weight of the similarity between sentences with different number of tokens. The $SPC$ is proportional to the $total\_similarity$. Equation 1 shows how $SPC$ is calculated. It is important to notice that in case of sentences with the same number of tokens, $SPC$ is equal to zero.

$$SPC = \begin{cases} (|n - m| \times SMV)/n & \text{if } (n > m) \\ (|n - m| \times SMV)/m & otherwise \end{cases} \quad (1)$$

where: $n$ and $m$ are the number of tokens in sentence 1 and sentence 2, respectively; $SMV$ is the total similarity found in the $SMV$ process.

The system calculates the final similarity as present in Equation 2.

$$final\_similarity = total\_similarity - SPC \quad (2)$$

### 4.2.2 The syntactic measure

The syntactic similarity between sentences is measured using the relation of the syntactic layer calculated by matching the vertices of the RDF triples.

The process works similarly to the calculus of the lexical measure. Instead of comparing words, this measure compares RDF triples, however. The comparison is performed by checking the triples in two steps as presented in Figure 4. At each step, the similarity between vertices is measured by using the similarity between words (see section 4.1). The similarity is the arithmetic mean of the values. The overall syntactic similarity between the triples is the average of the values obtained in the two steps. In the case of the example presented, the final result for the syntactic similarity measure is 0.3.

### 4.2.3 The semantic measure

The last sentence similarity measure takes into account some semantic information. The calculus of the semantic similarity measure follows similar steps to the one for the syntactic measure. A different layer representation and way the comparison between RDF triples is made are used, however. The semantic measure compares the pairs (vertex, edge) as the basic similarity value. The analysis of the graphs generated by semantic layer showed that the pair (vertex, edge) conveys relevant information of the degree of similarity between phrases. For instance, the *sense* edges, introduced in Section 3, are connected with the token presented in the sentence and with its meaning. Thus, it is important to measure if two sentences contain related tokens and meaning. The calculus of the semantic similarity is illustrated in Figure 5.

### 4.2.4 Combining the measures

As presented in section 3, each representation conveys a different outlook of the sentences analyzed. Thus, the similarity measures proposed give a value for each one of these perspective. It is necessary to combine the three similarity measures in order to have a global view of the degree of similarity between the sentences under analysis. Formula 3 presents the combination of the lexical, syntactic and semantic measures adopted here to provide the overall measure of sentence similarity.

$$similarity = \frac{(lex_n \times lex_s) + (syn_n \times syn_s) + (sem_n \times sem_s)}{lex_n + syn_n + sem_n} \quad (3)$$

where: $lex_n$ is the number of words in the lexical file, $syn_n$ and $sem_n$ are the number of triples in syntactic and semantic rdf, respectively. $lex_s$, $syn_s$ and $sem_s$ are the values of the similarities obtained using lexical, syntactic and semantic layers, respectively

## 5. EXPERIMENTAL RESULTS

The proposed quantitative measure of sentence similarity was comparatively assessed with the state of the art methods in the area. The benchmarks used here was a subset of

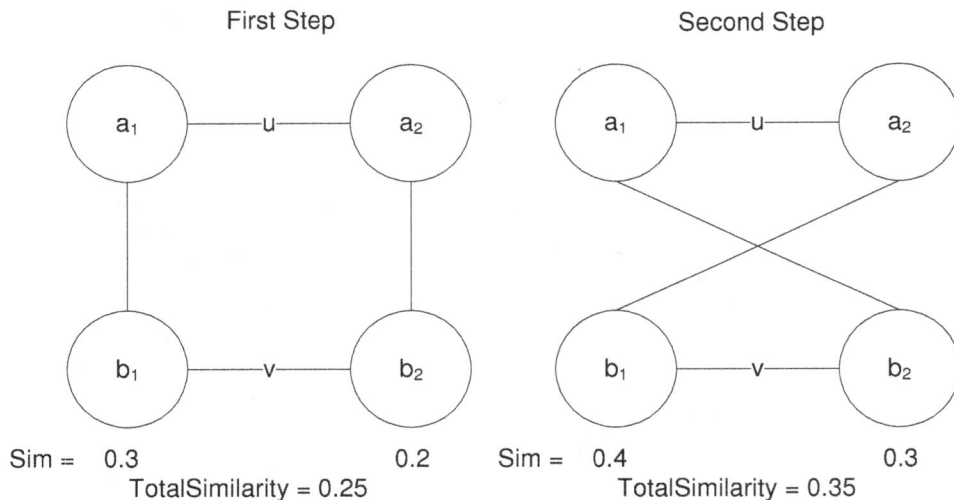

**Figure 4: Example of syntactic similarity between triples, where** *Sim* **is the similarity between two tokens or two edges,** *TotalSimilarity* **is the total similarity of one triple,** $u$ **and** $v$ **are edges and** $a_1$, $a_2$, $b_1$ **and** $b_2$ **are the tokens associated with the nodes of the graph.**

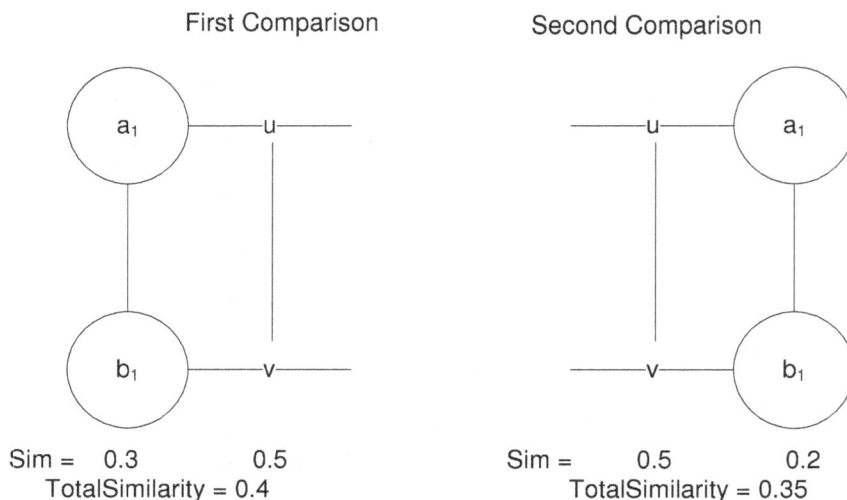

**Figure 5: Example of Similarity Between Pairs (vertex, edge), where** *Sim* **is the similarity between two tokens or two edges,** *TotalSimilarity* **is the total similarity of one triple,** $u$ **and** $v$ **are edges and** $a_1$ **and** $b_1$ **are the tokens associated with the nodes of the graph.**

the dataset proposed by Li and his collaborators [12], which encompass of 65 pairs of sentences extracted from word definitions in the Collins Cobuild dictionary. The dataset contains the average similarity scores given to each pair of sentence by 32 human judges. Only 30 of those 65 pairs of sentences were considered relevant for similarity assessment purposes by McLean and his colleagues [12]. Such relevant subset is used here for comparison purposes.

The Pearson's correlation coefficient (PCC) and the Spearman's rank correlation coefficient (SRCC) are used to evaluate the proposed similarity measure. The PCC measures the strength and direction of the linear relationship between two variables. It provides the relation between human similarity and the similarity obtained with the proposed measure. The SRCC calculates the correlation between the ranks of two

variables. In this experiment, the sentences are ranked from the highest to the lowest similarity.

Table 1 presents the results of each proposed measures in terms of Pearson's and Spearman's coefficients. The measures are described as the pair (similarity between words, similarity between sentences), defined in Sections 4.1 and 4.2, respectively.

As one may observe, the similarity measure based on the lexical layer provided the best results. This demonstrates that the preprocessing applied to the lexical layer combining word similarities (see section 4.1) improves the accuracy of lexical similarity measure. The best result achieved is the combination of Path and Lexical measures (Path-Lexical), which achieve 0.87 and 0.90 of PCC and SCC, respectively.

**Table 1:** *Pearson's and Spearman's coefficients of the sentences similarities given by proposed measure.*

| Measure | PCC | SRCC |
|---|---|---|
| Path-Lexical | 0.87 | 0.90 |
| Lin-Lexical | 0.87 | 0.86 |
| LC-Lexical | 0.79 | 0.78 |
| Res-Lexical | 0.85 | 0.87 |
| WP-Lexical | 0.76 | 0.65 |
| Path-Syntactic | 0.66 | 0.62 |
| Lin-Syntactic | 0.75 | 0.68 |
| LC-Syntactic | 0.65 | 0.53 |
| Res-Syntactic | 0.70 | 0.53 |
| WP-Syntactic | 0.52 | 0.34 |
| Path-Semantic | 0.76 | 0.75 |
| Lin-Semantic | 0.76 | 0.72 |
| LC-Semantic | 0.71 | 0.68 |
| Res-Semantic | 0.78 | 0.71 |
| WP-Semantic | 0.62 | 0.58 |

Another conclusion one may draw is about the measure of similarity between words (Section 4.1). The Path, Lin and Resnik measure achieves better results compared to other measures (see Table 1). This behavior corroborates the results reported in reference [24] that the best results were provided by Lin, Resnik and the Path measure [21]. This happens because the three-layer representation proposed here uses more general terms, mainly in the semantic layer, and the path, lin and resnik measures achieve better results in such case.

Although the syntactic and semantic measures do not achieve good results on their own, they incorporate information that refines the results provided by lexical layer. Table 2 presents the results of the combination of the lexical, syntactical and semantic layers proposed in this paper.

**Table 2:** *Pearson's and Spearman's coefficients of the sentences similarities combination.*

| Measure | PCC | SRCC |
|---|---|---|
| Path-Combination | 0.92 | 0.94 |
| Lin-Combination | 0.88 | 0.89 |
| LC-Combination | 0.86 | 0.89 |
| Res-Combination | 0.86 | 0.89 |
| WP-Combination | 0.82 | 0.86 |

The results provided in Table 2 confirm the hypothesis rose in this work that dealing with the meaning and word order problems by using syntactic and semantic analyses improves the results of sentence similarity. Every measure was improved after the incorporation of syntactic and semantic measures by combining them with lexical one.

Table 3 presents a comparison between the measure proposed here, the other state of the art related measures [12, 9, 21, 10, 24] and the human similarity ratings.

Besides averaging the similarity mark given by all human Li and colleagues [12] also calculated the correlation coefficient for the score given by each participant against the rest of the group. The best human participant obtained a correlation coefficient of 0.92, the worst was a correlation of 0.59 and the average of all participants was a correlation of 0.82, the value taken as the expected solution for the task. The system proposed here outperforms the related

**Table 3:** *Comparing the proposed measure against the related work and human similarity ratings in terms of PCC.*

| Measure | PCC |
|---|---|
| Worst Human Participant | 0.59 |
| Mean of all Human Participants | 0.82 |
| SyMSS[21] | 0.79 |
| Li-McLean[12] | 0.81 |
| Islam-Inkpen[9] | 0.85 |
| Path-Lexical | 0.87 |
| Islam *et al.*[10] | 0.91 |
| Ferreira *et al.*[24] | 0.92 |
| Proposed combination | 0.92 |
| Best Human Participant | 0.92 |

works and achieved the same PCC as the best human performance. Thus, the performance of the proposed similarity measure in the dataset analyzed was as good as the human evaluation provided in reference [12].

To conclude the experiments, Table 4 presents a comparison between the similarity measure proposed here and the best other related measure in the literature [9, 12, 21, 24] in terms of SRCC. The combined version of the proposed measure, attained results 3% better with regard to SRCC. The Path-Lexical measure achieved results comparable to the state of the art, mainly in relation to the SRCC. For some applications, such as, information retrieval, the rank of more relevant sentences is more important than the similarity itself. An information retrieval system does not need to reach good similarity; it only needs to retrieve the most relevant sentences (based on their ranks) for a specific query. Therefore, it is important to stress that SRCC is more important than PCC for some applications. Unfortunately, reference [12] does not provide figures for the SRCC evaluation of the similarity assessment made by the human judges.

**Table 4:** *Comparing the proposed measure against the best related work in terms of SRCC.*

| Measure | SRCC |
|---|---|
| Li-McLean[12] | 0.81 |
| Islam-Inkpen[9] | 0.83 |
| SyMSS[21] | 0.85 |
| Path-Lexical | 0.90 |
| Ferreira *et al.*[24] | 0.91 |
| Proposed Combination | 0.94 |

## 6. FURTHER EXPERIMENTS

The measure proposed for assessing sentence similarity was also used in analyzing the quality of extractive summaries. A summary is a shorter version of one or more text document that attempts to get their "meaning". Extractive summarization collects the most "important" sentences of the original document(s) without altering it. In this experiment the similarity between summaries is taken as the average of the values of the measure of the similarities between each of the sentences from the summary and the sentences in the *gold standard*. The CNN corpus developed by Lins and colleagues [14] was used in such evaluation.

The CNN corpus encompasses news articles from all over the world. The current version of this corpus presents 400 texts in the following categories: Africa, Asia, business, Europe, Latin America, Middle East, US, sports, tech, travel, and world news. The texts were selected from the news articles of CNN website (www.cnn.com). Besides the very high quality, conciseness, general interest, up-to-date subject, clarity, and linguistic correctness, one of the advantages of this new corpus is that a good-quality summary for each text, called the "*highlights*", is also provided. The highlights are three or four sentences long and are of paramount importance for evaluation purposes, as they may be taken as a summary of reference. The highlights were the basis for the development of two *gold standards*, the summaries taken as reference for new evaluation purposes. The first one was obtained by mapping each of the sentences in the highlights onto the original sentences of the text. The second gold standard was generated by three persons blindly reading the texts and selecting $n$ sentences that one thought better described each text. The value of $n$ was chosen depending on the text size, but in general it was equal to the number of sentences in the highlight plus two. The most voted sentences were chosen and a very high sentence selection coincidence was observed. A consistency check between the chosen sentences was performed. The second gold standard encompassed the first one in all cases.

In this assessment of summary similarity the first set of gold standard sentences is used to check the degree of similarity in relation to the original sentences in the highlights. In other words, the current test analyzes the similarity between the sentences in the highlights and the sentences from original text that three human evaluators considered the best match to the highlights. The final result is the arithmetic mean of the measure of the degree of similarity in the 400 texts from the CNN dataset. If the similarity measure proposed in this paper performs well, then one should expect a high score in the proposed test.

Table 5 presents the results of the proposed measure in terms similarity using CNN dataset. The lexical measure achieved the best results, comparing to the other proposed measures. This corroborates the result obtained in the previous experiment reported in the section 5. The main difference between the evaluation of the measure in summary and sentence similarity is the similarity between words that achieved the best results. Differently from the experimentation with sentence similarity, which Path achieve better results, in this experiment the Leacock and Chodorow (LC) provided the best results.

The results using the measures in isolation did not achieve expressive values. However, the combination of all measures proposed in this paper improves the results as presented in Table 6. This is indicative that the proposed combination could be efficiently applied in the context of summary evaluation.

There are several methods to evaluate a summarization output [16] in the literature. The relative utility [23] and the Pyramid method [20], are instances of some of them. However, the traditional information retrieval measures of *precision, recall* and *F-measure* are still the most popular evaluation method for such a task. Recall represents the number of sentences selected by humans that are also identified by a system, while precision is the fraction of those sentences identified by a system that are correct [19]. The F-measure is a combination of both precision and recall.

**Table 5:** *Similarity measures applied to summaries.*

| Measure | Similarity |
|---------|------------|
| Path-Lexical | 0.51 |
| Res-Lexical | 0.55 |
| Lin-Lexical | 0.55 |
| WP-Lexical | 0.53 |
| LC-Lexical | 0.58 |
| Path-Syntactic | 0.26 |
| Res-Syntactic | 0.28 |
| Lin-Syntactic | 0.31 |
| WP-Syntactic | 0.27 |
| LC-Syntactic | 0.36 |
| Path-Semantic | 0.36 |
| Res-Semantic | 0.38 |
| Lin-Semantic | 0.40 |
| WP-Semantic | 0.37 |
| LC-Semantic | 0.45 |

**Table 6:** *Similarity combinations applied to summaries.*

| Measure | Similarity |
|---------|------------|
| Path-Combination | 0.70 |
| Res-Combination | 0.73 |
| Lin-Combination | 0.75 |
| WP-Combination | 0.72 |
| LC-Combination | 0.80 |

Lin [13] proposed an evaluation system called ROUGE (Recall-Oriented Understudy for Gisting Evaluation). It provides a set of measures used in automatically evaluating summarization and machine translation using n-gram co-occurrence. The central idea in ROUGE is to compare a summary or translation against a reference or a set of references, and counting the number of n-grams of words they have in common. The ROUGE library provides different evaluation methods, such as:

**ROUGE-1** : N-gram based co-occurrence statistics from unigram scores.

**ROUGE-2** : N-gram based co-occurrence statistics from bigram scores.

**ROUGE-L** : Longest Common Subsequence based statistics. The longest common subsequence problem takes into account sentence level structure similarity naturally and identifies the longest co-occurring in sequence n-grams automatically.

**ROUGE-SU4** : Skip-bigram plus unigram-based co-occurrence statistics.

Since 2004, ROUGE has become of widespread use for the automatic evaluation of summaries [4, 26]. Now, the proposed assessment method is compared to ROUGE-1, ROUGE-2, ROUGE-L and ROUGE-SU4.

Table 7 presents the results obtained by the similarity measure proposed here against ROUGE in the task of summary evaluation. The best combination of proposed measures achieved an outcome 16% better than ROUGE. This brings some evidence of the importance of combine lexical, syntactic and semantic analysis information in order to evaluate similarities between texts. This experiment empirically demonstrates that the measures used to evaluate the similarity between sentences may also be used to evaluate similarity between summaries.

**Table 7:** *Comparing the proposed similarity measure against ROUGE for summary evaluation.*

| Measure | Similarity |
|---|---|
| Proposed Measure | **0.80** |
| ROUGE-1 | 0.64 |
| ROUGE-2 | 0.64 |
| ROUGE-L | 0.59 |
| ROUGE-SU4 | 0.44 |

## 7. CONCLUSIONS AND LINES FOR FURTHER WORK

This paper presents a three-layer sentence representation and different measures to compute the similarity between two sentences. The three layers are: (i) the lexical layer, which encompasses lexical analysis, stop words removal and stemming; (ii) the syntactic layer, which performs syntactic; and (iii) the semantic layer, that mainly describes the annotations that play semantic role. These three layers handle the two major problems in measuring sentence similarity: the meaning and word order problems.

The main contribution of this work is to propose the integration of lexical, syntactic and semantic analysis to further improve the results in automatically assessing sentence similarity better incorporating the different levels of information in the sentence. The semantics of the text is extracted using SRA. Previous works, that claim to use semantic information, do not actually take that sort of information into account. Instead, they use WordNet to evaluate the semantic of the words, which could provide poor results.

A series of benchmarks is presented here using the dataset proposed in reference [12] and the two most widely accepted sentence similarity measures: Pearson's correlation coefficient (PCC) and Spearman's rank correlation coefficient (SRCC). The combinations of proposed measures obtained 0.92 of PCC, achieving a result equal to the best human evaluation reported in [12]. In addition, the best measure in the literature reports reaching 0.91 of SRCC, while the combination measure proposed here achieved 0.94, an enhancement of 3% to SRCC.

The sentence similarity measure proposed here was also used to assess the quality of sentences in automatic extractive summarization, by comparing the degree of similarity between the sentences of an automatically generated extractive summary and the text provided by the original author of the text known as the highlights. The experiments performed showed that the proposed measure better describes the degree of similarity between the two summaries than any other assessment method in the literature.

There are new developments of this work already in progress, which include: (i) the evaluation of the proposed measure in paraphrase detection; (ii) the analysis of different combinations of the proposed measure; and (iii) applying the sentence similarity measure presented to improve text summarization systems.

## 8. ACKNOWLEDGMENTS

The research results reported in this paper have been partly funded by a R&D project between Hewlett-Packard do Brazil and UFPE originated from tax exemption (IPI - Law number 8.248, of 1991 and later updates).

## 9. REFERENCES

[1] A. Budanitsky and G. Hirst. Evaluating wordnet-based measures of lexical semantic relatedness. *Comput. Linguist.*, 32(1):13–47, Mar. 2006.

[2] B. Choudhary and P. Bhattacharyya. Text clustering using semantics. In *Proceedings of WORLD WIDE WEB CONFERENCE 2002*, WWW '02, 2002.

[3] T. A. S. Coelho, P. Calado, L. V. Souza, B. A. Ribeiro-Neto, and R. R. Muntz. Image retrieval using multiple evidence ranking. *IEEE Transactions on Knowledge and Data Engineering*, 16(4):408–417, 2004.

[4] D. Das and A. F. T. Martins. A survey on automatic text summarization. Technical report, Literature Survey for the Language and Statistics II course at Carnegie Mellon University, 2007.

[5] D. Das, N. Schneider, D. Chen, and N. A. Smith. Probabilistic frame-semantic parsing. In *Human Language Technologies: The 2010 Annual Conference of the North American Chapter of the Association for Computational Linguistics*, HLT '10, pages 948–956, Stroudsburg, PA, USA, 2010. Association for Computational Linguistics.

[6] C. Fellbaum, editor. *WordNet: an electronic lexical database.* MIT Press, 1998.

[7] R. Ferreira, L. de Souza Cabral, R. D. Lins, G. de Franca Silva, F. Freitas, G. D. C. Cavalcanti, R. Lima, S. J. Simske, and L. Favaro. Assessing sentence scoring techniques for extractive text summarization. *Expert Systems with Applications*, 40(14):5755–5764, 2013.

[8] A. Hotho, A. Nurnberger, and G. Paas. A brief survey of text mining. *LDV Forum - GLDV Journal for Computational Linguistics and Language Technology*, 20(1):19–62, May 2005.

[9] A. Islam and D. Inkpen. Semantic text similarity using corpus-based word similarity and string similarity. *ACM Transactions on Knowledge Discovery from Data*, 2(2):10:1–10:25, July 2008.

[10] A. Islam, E. E. Milios, and V. Keselj. Text similarity using google tri-grams. In L. Kosseim and D. Inkpen, editors, *Canadian Conference on AI*, volume 7310 of *Lecture Notes in Computer Science*, pages 312–317. Springer, 2012.

[11] Y. Li, Z. A. Bandar, and D. McLean. An approach for measuring semantic similarity between words using multiple information sources. *IEEE Trans. on Knowl. and Data Eng.*, 15(4):871–882, July 2003.

[12] Y. Li, D. McLean, Z. Bandar, J. O'Shea, and K. A. Crockett. Sentence similarity based on semantic nets and corpus statistics. *IEEE Trans. Knowl. Data Eng.*, 18(8):1138–1150, 2006.

[13] C.-Y. Lin. Rouge: A package for automatic evaluation of summaries. In M.-F. Moens and S. Szpakowicz, editors, *Text Summarization Branches Out:*

*Proceedings of the ACL-04 Workshop*, pages 74–81, Barcelona, Spain, July 2004. Association for Computational Linguistics.

[14] R. D. Lins, S. J. Simske, L. de Souza Cabral, G. de Silva, R. Lima, R. F. Mello, and L. Favaro. A multi-tool scheme for summarizing textual documents. In *Proc. of 11st IADIS International Conference WWW/INTERNET 2012*, pages 1–8, July 2012.

[15] T. Liu and J. Guo. Text similarity computing based on standard deviation. In *Proceedings of the 2005 International Conference on Advances in Intelligent Computing - Volume Part I*, ICIC'05, pages 456–464, Berlin, Heidelberg, 2005. Springer-Verlag.

[16] E. Lloret and M. Palomar. Text summarisation in progress: a literature review. *Artif. Intell. Rev.*, 37(1):1–41, Jan. 2012.

[17] R. Mihalcea, C. Corley, and C. Strapparava. Corpus-based and knowledge-based measures of text semantic similarity. In *Proceedings of the 21st National Conference on Artificial Intelligence - Volume 1*, AAAI'06, pages 775–780. AAAI Press, 2006.

[18] F. P. Miller, A. F. Vandome, and J. McBrewster. *Levenshtein Distance: Information theory, Computer science, String (computer science), String metric, Damerau? Levenshtein distance, Spell checker, Hamming distance.* Alpha Press, 2009.

[19] A. Nenkova. Summarization evaluation for text and speech: issues andapproaches. In *NTERSPEECH*, 2006.

[20] A. Nenkova, R. Passonneau, and K. McKeown. The pyramid method: Incorporating human content selection variation in summarization evaluation. *ACM Trans. Speech Lang. Process.*, 4(2), May 2007.

[21] J. Oliva, J. I. Serrano, M. D. del Castillo, and A. Iglesias. Symss: A syntax-based measure for short-text semantic similarity. *Data Knowl. Eng.*, 70(4):390–405, Apr. 2011.

[22] K. Papineni, S. Roukos, T. Ward, and W.-J. Zhu. Bleu: A method for automatic evaluation of machine translation. In *Proceedings of the 40th Annual Meeting on Association for Computational Linguistics*, ACL '02, pages 311–318, Stroudsburg, PA, USA, 2002. Association for Computational Linguistics.

[23] D. R. Radev and D. Tam. Summarization evaluation using relative utility. In *Proceedings of the twelfth international conference on Information and knowledge management*, CIKM '03, pages 508–511, New York, NY, USA, 2003. ACM.

[24] F. F. B. A. S. J. S. Rafael Ferreira, Rafael Lins and M. Riss. A new sentence similarity method based on a three-layer sentence representation. In *IEEE/WIC/ACM International Conference on Web Intelligence*, 2014.

[25] W3C. Resource description framework. http://www.w3.org/RDF/, 2004. Last Access March 2014.

[26] F. Wei, W. Li, Q. Lu, and Y. He. A document-sensitive graph model for multi-document summarization. *Knowledge and Information Systems*, 22(2):245–259, 2010.

[27] L.-C. Yu, C.-H. Wu, and F.-L. Jang. Psychiatric document retrieval using a discourse-aware model. *Artificial Intelligence*, 173(7-8):817–829, May 2009.

[28] F. Zhou, F. Zhang, and B. Yang. Graph-based text representation model and its realization. In *Natural Language Processing and Knowledge Engineering (NLP-KE), 2010 International Conference on*, pages 1–8, 2010.

# Paper Stitching using Maximum Tolerant Seam under Local Distortions

Wei Liu, Wei Fan, Jun Sun, Naoi Satoshi [†]
Fujitsu R&D Center, No. 56 Dong Si Huan Zhong Rd, Beijing, P.R. China
{willie,fanwei,sunjun}@cn.fujitsu.com
[†] naoi.satoshi@jp.fujitsu.com

## ABSTRACT

Paper stitching technology can reconstruct a whole paper page from two sub-images separately scanned from a camera with limited vision field.

Traditional technology usually chooses a global optimal seam, and the two sub-images are stitched along it. These methods perform well on the rigid object, but when distortion exists caused by the uneven placement of paper, local contents of two sub-images may be upside-down and their positions are misaligned. Although some methods choose two matching seams on each sub-image, they use either the local patch similarity or the global consistent constraint to get two matching seams. However, only the local matching may lead to stitching failure when wrong matching occurs at the local patch, while only the global constraint usually suffers from inaccuracy of the stitching result. After the two seams are obtained, the traditional methods usually construct the whole image through global transformation along the seams, and image deformation usually occurs in this stage.

In this paper, we proposed a robust estimation algorithm to get the matched seams in the sub-images, and stitched the sub-images with a maximum tolerance to conquer the image deformation. Finally a whole image with a smooth stitching seam and the minimum deformation is generated. Experimental results show that this new paper stitching method can produce better results than state-of-arts methods even under challenging scenarios such as large distortion and large contrast difference.

## Categories and Subject Descriptors

I.4.0 [**Image Processing and Computer Vision**]: General—*Image processing software*; I.5.4 [**Pattern Recognition**]: Applications—*Computer vision*

## General Terms

Algorithm

## Keywords

Dynamic Programming;Viterbi;Image Stitching;In-painting

## 1. INTRODUCTION

Paper stitching technology can reconstruct a whole paper page from two separately scanned images. When the camera has a limited vision range, by the stitching technology, a panorama can be built up. Many applications have requirements on this technology, for example, scene restoration, autonomous navigation, remote sensing image reconstruction and panoramic map generation, etc. The complete process on paper stitching contains two parts: image stitching and image blending. Next, detailed discussion is given.

### 1.1 Image Stitching

Difficulties on this technology mainly lie on the following aspects: **1)** how to find the optimal stitching seam; **2)** how to amend the stitched image with minimum deformation to keep the high-fidelity of the image. If the object to be stitched is not a rigid one such as maps, magazines and papers, there is another important problem: **3)** how to stitch images with the minimum artifacts or content loss.

Traditional stitching methods can be summarized into the following two categories: the first is to stitch images using a global optimal seam, and the second is to search corresponding seams in each image, and stitch images using the seams. The general processing procedure of the first category is to roughly align the two images by estimating a global transformation [1, 2, 3, 4] between them, and then a panorama is constructed by stitching the two parts along an optimal seam. For example, V. Kwatra et.al [5] selected the optimal seam by minimizing the intensity or texture difference in the overlapped area of the two images, similar methods include [6]. C.V.Veena et.al [7] proposed a method which attempted to minimize the image artifacts along the stitching seam, reducing both photometric inconsistencies and geometric misalignments between the two sub-images.

However, in non-rigid paper stitching, local distortions exist, and it would lead to misalignment of the image structures such as characters or figures. F. Isgro et.al[8] proposed a registration based method, but the local content of the sub-images is not well stitched. It is because in the above methods, the content near the seam of the two images are always misaligned, and only one seam could produce content loss. For example, Figure 1 shows the separately scanned sub-images with local distortion. The horizonal line shows the content of the two images are misaligned.

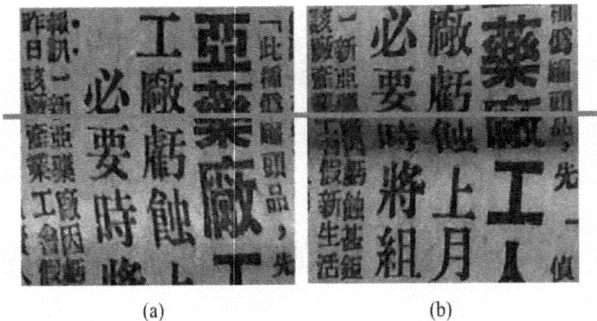

**Figure 1: Large distortions in two sub-images. (a): one of the sub-images; (b): the other sub-image.**

Current popular tools include ICE[1], which is included in the first category of the stitching methods. An example is given in Figure 2 to compare the performance of the results. Figure 2 (a) and Figure 2 (b) are the stitching results of ICE and our proposed method respectively.

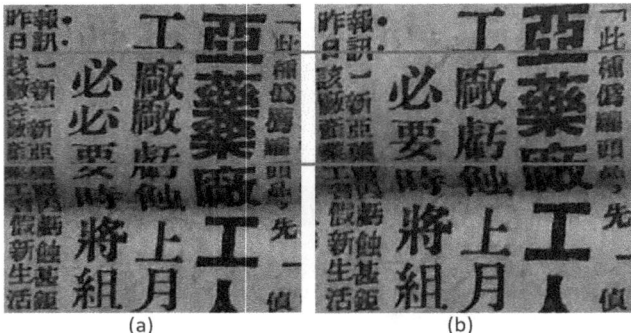

**Figure 2: Comparison between ICE and ours.**

To solve this problem, many researches begin to focus on the stitching technology to find corresponding seams on the sub-images using image features. With the features matching, a transform matrix is calculated to describe the transform between the local structure of the two image, or a Delaunay triangulation [9] is operated on each image, and the desired correspondence between the local structure of the two images can be obtained. With accurate feature correspondence, local misalignment and local distortion can be conquered. Then the whole image can be acquired by stitching at the same structure of the two sub-images. For example, J. Jia, et.al [10] estimate two corresponding seams in each sub-image, and propagate the content of each sub-image to form a sub-part of the whole image. J. Gao et.al [11] proposed a seam-driven method using perspective transformations to stitch two images. These methods always use KNN [12], bundled features [13], or the RANSAC [14] algorithm to select the features satisfying a fixed model. However, two problems exist: **1)** how to extract enough useful features when the image content is rare; **2)** how to filter the outliers. For the first problem, there are still no perfect solution. For the second, KNN just considered the global geometric

_____
[1]ICE (Image Composite Editor) is a tool provided by Microsoft Co., LTD. used for image stitching

similarity between two clusters of features, while the inner distribution in each cluster is not considered, so outliers is not filtered efficiently. Bundled features rely on the prior division of bundle, and RANSAC is limited to the application using only a single model. The above stitching methods can handle the image content with misalignment. However, if wrong feature matching occurs, a wrong seam would be determined. It is because the above stitching methods depend heavily on the precision of local feature matching, and they do not consider the global attribute of the seam points.

## 1.2 Image Blending

Subsequently, after the corresponding seams on the two sub-images are obtained, the content of the two sub-images at the opposite sides of seams are deformed and stitched at the seam. Some methods use elastic registration [15, 16] to register images, but complex local structures and misalignment are still difficult to deal with. J. Jia [10] uses a global deformation to assure the consistence of the image intensity and the image structure of the two images by searching for the solution of an optimization function. However, the deformation would lead to image blurring and abnormal change. Besides, the contrast of the two sub-images may be not same, so the contrast at the two sides of the stitching seam would be not same, and it would give unnatural stitching result.

To summarize the state of arts methods for image stitching, Table 1 gives a brief demonstration. In which, several typical methods are used for comparison.

**Table 1: State of Art**

| Method | Seam | Feature matching | Blending |
|--------|------|------------------|----------|
| Kwatra[5] | One | No | Add |
| Jia[10] | Two | Traditional | Global deformation |
| Ours | Two | Local matching in adaptive window & global constraint | Tolerance compensation |

In this paper, enough useful features are extracted through an adaptive window decided by the image content, and multiple models are utilized to describe the features matching. With robust features matching, robust correspondence between two sub-images can be obtained. Even if when the features matching fails, a global optimization algorithm is proposed to refine the correspondence between two sub-images. Then the two sub-images are stitched with a maximum tolerance to conquer the global deformation, and a contrast normalization method is used to balance the contrast near the stitching seam. Finally a whole image with a smooth stitching seam and a minimum deformation is generated.

The rest of this paper is organized as following: Section 2 explains the proposed paper stitching method, in which the corresponding seams are estimated and the two sub-images are stitched to form a whole image, Section 3 shows the experimental results. Conclusions and acknowledgements are given in Section 4 and Section 5.

## 2. PAPER STITCHING ALGORITHM

The diagram of the proposed method is given in Figure 3. Detailed illustration is given in the following sections.

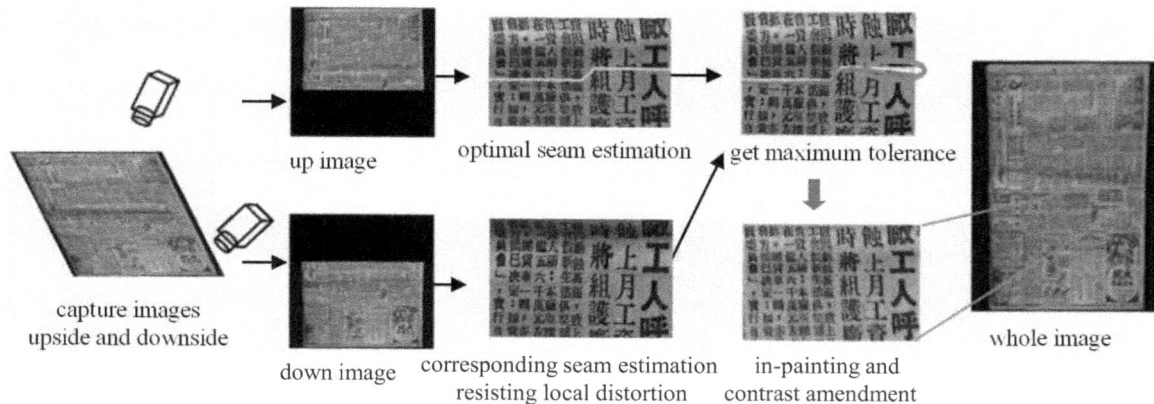

Figure 3: Overview of our proposed paper stitching algorithm.

**Problem Statement:**

Paper stitching algorithm aims to stitch two sub-images together. Suppose the two sub-images are captured with two cameras placed upside and downside respectively. The up image is denoted as $I_1$, and the down image is denoted as $I_2$. By searching for a optimal seam $S_1$ in $I_1$ and the corresponding seam $S_2$ in $I_2$, the image content at the upside of $S_1$ and that at the downside of $S_2$ are stitched together to form a final whole image.

The main steps of the proposed paper stitching method are shown in Table 2.

**Table 2: Main Steps of Proposed Method**

1.Rough alignment with layout analysis
  $I_1$ and $I_2$ are aligned according to the layout.
2.Optimal seam estimation
  get the optimal seam $S_1$ in $I_1$.
3.Corresponding seam estimation resisting local distortion
  1): landmark seam points selection in $S_1$;
  2): coarse seam points matching in sub-windows;
  3): global optimization to get seam $S_2$ in $I_2$;
4.Maximum tolerance stitching and image amendment
  1): compensate the tolerance between two seams;
  2): amend the illumination difference;

## 2.1 Rough Alignment with Layout Analysis

With the image deskewing technology [17], each sub-image will has a vertical direction. Then the overlapping area of the two sub-images is obtained through a correlation matching.

By now, two sub-images are roughly aligned. Figure 4 shows the roughly aligned sub-images $I_1$ and $I_2$, in the next sections, the seams $S_1$ and $S_2$ are estimated.

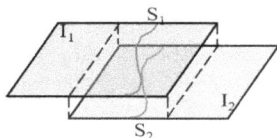

Figure 4: Roughly aligned sub-images.

## 2.2 Optimal Seam Estimation

The optimal seam should go across the smooth region where texture changes little, and be able to avoid cutting the foreground such as characters, figures and so on. So first, a initial row with little texture change is selected, and then a path which inclines to go through the background is searched near the initial row.

Suppose $I_1$ and $I_2$ are first binarized through Otsu [18] algorithm, the binary images of $I_1$ is denoted as $B_1$, and its background pixels and foreground pixels are set as 0 and 255 respectively. The pixel value along a certain row $i$ of $B_1$ is defined as $B_1(i,1), ..., B_1(i,w)$, where $1 \leq i \leq h$, $h$ and $w$ are the height and width of the up image respectively. The row with minimum number of texture change is defined as:

$$i^* = \arg\min_{1 \leq i \leq h} \sum_{j=1}^{w-1} |B_1(i, j+1) - B_1(i,j)| \qquad (1)$$

where $i^*$ is the optimal row with minimum number of texture change, and it is shown in red in Figure 5, while the seam with maximum number of texture change is shown in blue.

Figure 5: Texture analysis to get initial position of the seam.

The above procedure provides a candidate row of the optimal seam, but there may still be local crossings through the characters. To avoid these cases, a method of 3 Neighborhood Dynamic Programming attempts to find a continuously traversing near the rough seam with minimum crossings is proposed. Compared with the traditional Dynamic Programming [19], the proposed method works on a binary image, and just use a 3 nearest neighbor search, so it can not only assure the minimum crossing and also the minimum vibration.

Supposing $(i,j)$ is a pixel in the image $B_1$, $(i^*,1)$ and $(i^*,w)$ are the starting point and the end point of the rough seam, and $P$ is a traversing path connecting them. To assure $P$ travels through the maximum number of background pixels, the following function is minimized to get the temporary optimal position at the $j$ column:

$$P(j) = \underset{1 \leq i \leq h}{\arg \min}(B(i-1,j-1)+c, B(i,j-1), B(i+1,j-1)+c) \tag{2}$$

where $c$ is an empirical cost from the upper left pixel and the down left pixel to the current pixel which aims at a smooth connection between nearby pixels. With each temporary optimal position obtained above, the whole connecting seam $S_1$ is obtained by connecting the temporary optimal positions.

Figure 6 shows the refined seam (in green) in $I_1$, we can see that the seam can effectively avoid crossing the characters. In the following sections, a corresponding seam $S_2$ in the down image $I_2$ is estimated.

Figure 6: Refined seam.

## 2.3 Corresponding Seam Estimation Resisting Local Distortion

To realize seamless stitching, a seam ( also referred as the corresponding seam $S_2$ ) which represents a perfect matching with the $S_1$ is searched in this section. As the paper is always arbitrarily placed, and some parts of the paper may have large curly distortions. So the matching is performed in several sub-windows surrounding the point in $S_1$.

### 2.3.1 Landmark Seam Points Selection

To get the matched seam, several landmark points on the seam $S_1$ are selected and corresponding points are searched in image $I_2$. The example of landmark of seam points are shown in Figure 7.

1. $S_1$ is verified through its concavity, and the points with large concavity are chosen. (Solid points)

2. An equal length $l$ sampling is also used to assure the equal distribution of sample points. (Circle points)

3. As small zigzag would lead to computational complexity, a distance threshold is used to avoid too near sampling points. (Rectangle)

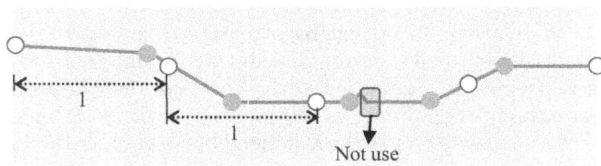

Figure 7: Landmark seam points.

The corresponding points in $S_2$ are searched individually at the nearby areas of the landmarks in $S_1$.

### 2.3.2 Coarse Seam Points Matching in Sub-windows

The strip area along seam $S_1$ is divided into several sub-windows equally. After the sub-windows are obtained, feature extraction and matching (shown in Figure 8(a)) are performed to get the affine transformation between the two sub-windows. Popular feature extraction methods include the FAST detector [20], SIFT detector [21], et.al, and the feature description methods include the SURF [22], FREAK [23], et.al. In this paper, FAST detector and SURF descriptor are utilized. Figure 8(b) shows a sub-window in the up image, the white circles denote the sampling points, and Figure 8(c) shows the candidate sub-window of $I_2$. With the affine transform estimated, the matched seam points are shown in Figure 8(c) in white circles.

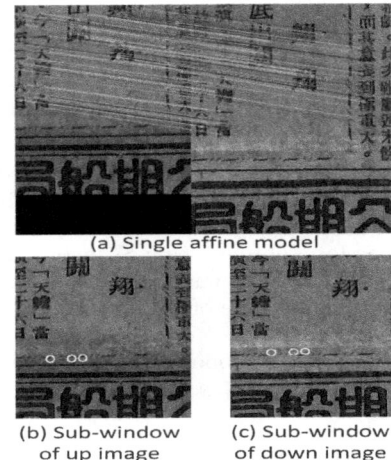

(a) Single affine model

(b) Sub-window of up image  (c) Sub-window of down image

Figure 8: Matched seam points with an affine model.

However, the positions of the matched seam points are not accurate. It is because there is little content in the sub-window as the seam is selected with minimum texture, and the transform between the two sub-windows can not be described by a single affine transform.

To get a robust estimation with more features, we use an adaptive sub-window, and then use multiple models to describe the transform between the sub-windows, and finally choose the close features to estimate the final affine matrix.

1. **Adaptive Sub-window**
   Two conditions are used to decide how to extend the sub-window in a proper range:
   *a.pixels should have an uniform distribution:*

$$E = [E_x, E_y] = [-p_x \log p_x, -p_y \log p_y]$$
$$E_i \geq E_{th}, \forall E_i \in \{E_x, E_y\} \tag{3}$$

   where $E$ is the entropy [24] of the foreground pixels, $E_{th}$ is a certain threshold, $E_x$ and $E_y$ denote the entropy along the horizontal and vertical directions, and $p_x$ and $p_y$ are the normalized histograms of the foreground pixels along the two directions, which also denote the probability of pixels lying in each bin of the histograms.

   If the entropy $E_x$ or $E_y$ do not satisfy the above condition, the sub-window should be extended accordingly, and the entropy is recalculated until the condition is satisfied.

*b.features should distribute surrounding $S_1$:*

$$h_i \geq \alpha \sum_{k=1}^{4} h_k, \forall i \in \{1, ...4\} \qquad (4)$$

where $\alpha$ is a constant coefficient. Suppose the center point of the seam points in the sub-window is $C(x_0, y_0)$, and four sets which represent the pixels in the four quadrants are defined as: $Q_1 : \{(x,y)|x \geq x_0, y \leq y_0\}$, $Q_2 : \{(x,y)|x \leq x_0, y \leq y_0\}$, $Q_3 : \{(x,y)|x \leq x_0, y \geq y_0\}$, $Q_4 : \{(x,y)|x \geq x_0, y \geq y_0\}$. We can define $h_k$ as the histograms in the four quadrants as:

$$h_k = \sum_{(x,y) \in Q_k} B_1(x,y), k \in \{1, ...4\} \qquad (5)$$

where $B_1$ is the binary images of $I_1$. If $h_k$ does not satisfy the above condition, the sub-window should be extended in the according quadrant, and the histogram $h_k$ is recalculated until the condition is satisfied. The sub-windows are extended to meet the two conditions.

2. **Multiple Models**

Usually, a single affine model is assumed in the sub-window. However, in Figure 8(a), only the features above the seam points are used to estimate the affine transform. As the deformations above and below the seam points are different, so only a single affine model is not appropriate to represent the transformation between the sub-windows of the up and down image.

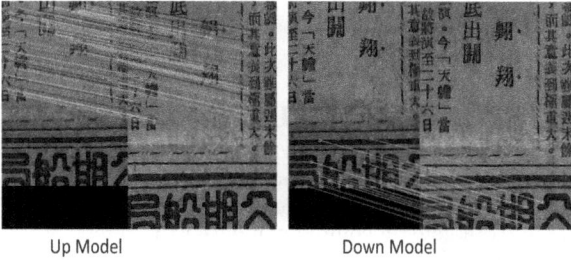

Up Model          Down Model

**Figure 9: Multiple models.**

So we prompt a method to represent the transforms above and below the seam points with multiple models. In this method, an individual affine model is built with the upside (or downside) features.

Figure 9 gives the two models. This method can express more detailed deformations. Meanwhile, sometimes, wrong matchings are considered as right matching when the features have a reasonable geometric position. This method can also solve this wrong matching problem.

3. **Close Feature Selection**

Moreover, after the multiple models are obtained, to get the accurate affine transform model, the features which are used in the estimation of the multiple affine transforms are further filtered. Only the close ones of the seam points are reserved to fit a final transform matrix.

In Figure 10, a proper range (areas in dashed lines) is set to choose the close features, and the final selected

features are shown in Figure 10 too. With their fitted model (shown in Figure 10(a)), the matched seam points in the down image is shown in Figure 10(c) in white circles.

Compared with one single model, of which the result (shown in Figure 8) has large errors, this new fused model can get more accurate result.

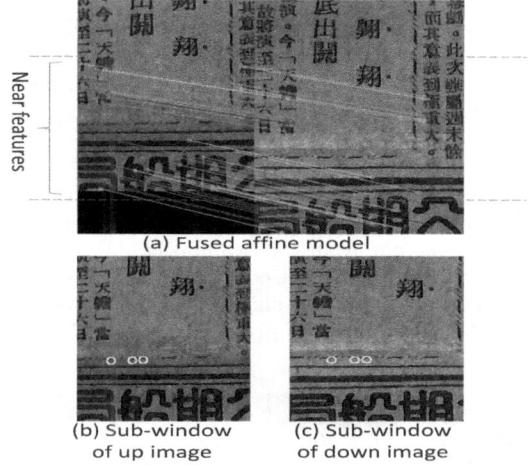

(a) Fused affine model

(b) Sub-window of up image    (c) Sub-window of down image

**Figure 10: Matched seam points with fused model.**

### 2.3.3 Global Optimization to Get Seam in Down Image

To further increase the precision of matched seam points, or even to correct the wrong estimation of the affine transform in some sub-windows, we proposed the following method. As there is geometric consistence of the seam points between the up and down images, we can utilize this attribute as a global constraint to avoid the outliers.

From Figure 11, we can see that distortion occurs at the sub-window, the curve in the up image has a different convexity with that of the down image. However, the trend and the length of the two paper are similar as they are from the same paper. In Figure 11, an example is given. $P$ is an outlier which is intended to be avoided.

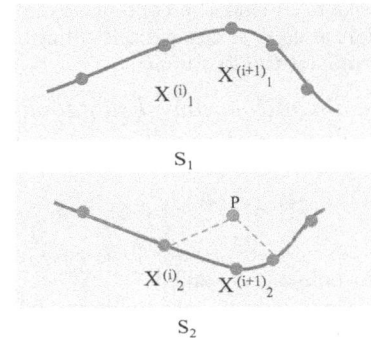

**Figure 11: Geometric consistence constraint.**

So we utilize this to prompt an energy function, which not only considers the one order position change of the roughly estimated seam points, but also considers the two orders consistence constraints to assure the similar trends of the two curves. The optimal positions of the seam points in $I_2$ is estimated by minimizing the following energy function:

$$\arg\min_{\delta y_2^{(i)}} \sum_{i=1}^{n-1} |\delta y_2^{(i)}| + \lambda \left| \frac{\|X_2^{(i+1)} - X_2^{(i)}\|}{\|X_1^{(i+1)} - X_1^{(i)}\|} \right| \qquad (6)$$

where the superscript $i$ denotes the index of the seam point, the subscript 1 and 2 denotes the index of the images, which means that 1 and 2 denotes the up and down images respectively. $\lambda$ is a weight coefficient, and $\delta y_2^{(i)}$ is the desired offset of $y_2^{(i)}$. $X_1^i = [x_1^{(i)}, y_1^{(i)}]$ is the vector representation of the $i$th pixel's coordinates in $I_1$, and $X_2$ is defined as:

$$X_2^{(i)} = [x_2^{(i)}, y_2^{(i)} + \delta y_2^{(i)}] \qquad (7)$$

The above equation attempts to both minimize the changes in y direction of the seam points $S_2$, and the difference of the trends of the two curves in the two images. With the above energy function being minimized, the outlier $P$ in Figure 11 can be removed. A Viterbi algorithm [25] can be used to solve the above optimization problem. Figure 12 shows the estimated seam $S_2$.

Figure 12: $S_2$ obtained by global optimization.

## 2.4 Maximum Tolerance Stitching and Image Amendment

As there are distortions in the seam region, the roughly aligned images $I_1$ and $I_2$ may have misalignment. For example, $I_2$ is on the up side of $I_1$ even if it should be at the down side of $I_1$. To rectify this, the gap or the maximum tolerance between two images is estimated.

Besides, As the area in the gap between two seams contains no content, so to fill the area, the in-painting technology is used to amend the content. Finally, the contrast normalization is used to amend the illumination difference along the seams of the two images.

### 2.4.1 Maximum Tolerance Estimation

To assure the content in $I_2$ is below that of $I_1$, a condition is required:

$$s_1^{(k)} \leq s_2^{(k)}, \forall k \in \{1, ..., w\} \qquad (8)$$

where $S_1 = \{s_1^{(1)}, ..., s_1^{(k)}, ..., s_1^{(w)}\}$, $S_2 = \{s_2^{(1)}, ..., s_2^{(k)}, ..., s_2^{(w)}\}$ are the seam points in $I_1$ and $I_2$.

To satisfy this condition, the minimum offset between the two images is calculated as the gap, which is also defined as the maximum tolerance between the two images. Then $S_2$ can be compensated to move down a distance to satisfy the tolerance (shown as the arrow in Figure 13).

Compared with the traditional methods with global deformation of the images [10], this method can avoid the transformation of the content of images, so the deformation is

avoided. Besides, without the global deformation, the time of the whole stitching process is shortened.

### 2.4.2 Image Amendment

The shadow area between $S_1$ and $S_2$ has no content, so an image in-painting [26] is used to amend the loss of content. Meanwhile, as there may be illumination differences along the two seams, we use a contrast normalization method to solve this problem:

$$I_1'(i,j) = (I_1(i,j) - b_1)\frac{f_2 - b_2}{f_1 - b_1} + b_2 \qquad (9)$$

where $I_1(i,j)$ and $I_1'(i,j)$ are the pixel value in $I_1$ before and after the contrast normalization, $b_1$ and $f_1$ denote the average value of background and foreground pixels values of $I_1$, and $b_2$ and $f_2$ denote the average value of background and foreground pixels values of $I_2$.

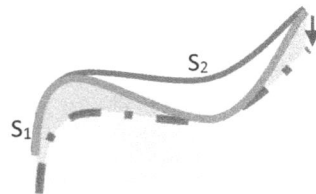

Figure 13: Maximum tolerance estimation.

Through the above steps, the final stitched image is obtained. Multiple images can also be stitched together through each coupled stitching.

## 3. EXPERIMENTAL RESULTS

In this section, the performance of the proposed method on several data sets is given. Comparison with the other kinds of methods is also given.

Firstly, a general comparison with other kinds of methods is shown in Figure 14, Figure 15, Figure 16. Figure 14 is the comparative result between the PhotoStitch [2] and our method, Figure 15 is that between the hard stitch and ours (hard stitch means that one sub-image is directly combined with the other sub-image to form a whole image at an arbitrary seam in the overlap area), and Figure 16 is the result between ICE and ours. The results show that our method can well handle the content loss problem.

Three data sets are used for evaluate the performance of the proposed method. 56 ancient Chinese papers constitute the data set 1, 16 English papers constitute the data set 2, and 31 modern Chinese papers constitute data set 3. The criteria for judging the good stitching is by whether the stitched image has content loss or content misalignment. Comparative result is given in Table 3.

Table 3: Performance on 3 data sets

| Data set | ICE | PhotoStitch | Hard | Ours |
|---|---|---|---|---|
| Ancient | 66.7% | 3.6% | 1.8% | 100.0% |
| English | 81.3% | 6.3% | 6.3% | 100.0% |
| Modern Chinese | 57.1% | 3.2% | 0.0% | 71.0% |

[2]PhotoStitch is a tool provided by Canon Co., LTD. used for image stitching

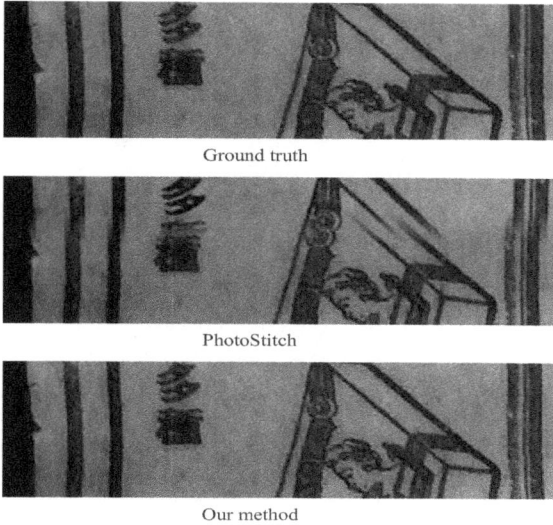
Figure 14: Results of PhotoStitch and ours.

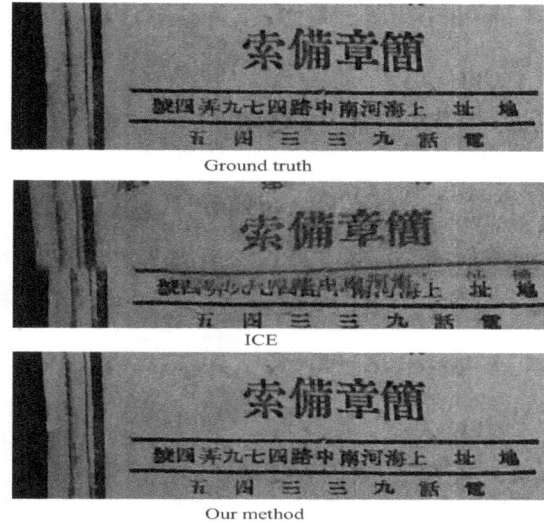
Figure 16: Results of ICE and ours.

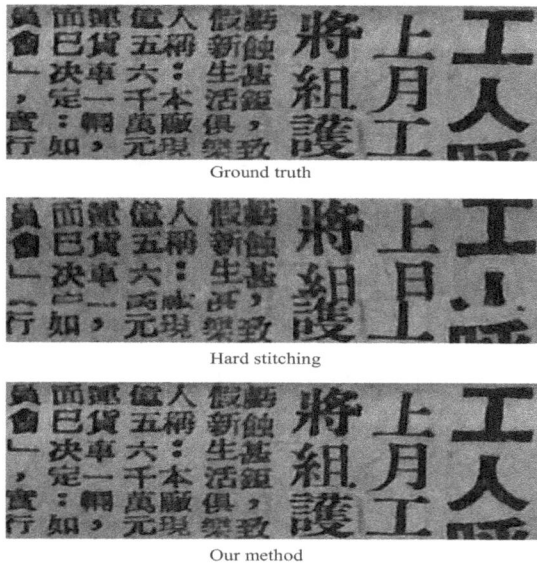
Figure 15: Results of hard stitch and ours.

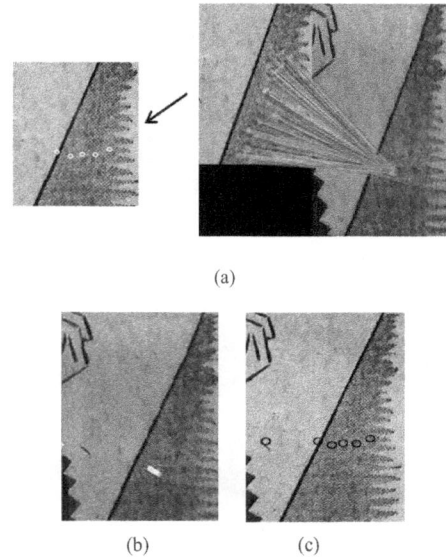
Figure 17: Corrected results by global optimization. (a): feature matching between two sub-images, and the white circles in the left part denote the original seam points in one sub-image; (b): the estimated seam points (white circles) in other sub-image without global optimization; (c): the estimated seam points (black circles) in other sub-image using the global optimization.

In the next, the results on the corresponding seam estimation before and after the global optimization in Section 2.3.3 are given in Figure 17. It shows that the global optimization can correct the local wrong estimation of the seams. Then the results obtained by the implementation of global deformation [10] by ourself and the proposed maximum tolerance correction method are given in Figure 18. It shows that the proposed method can preserve the content of the original image without deforming any part of it, while the global deformation method changes the positions of the original image content.

For the contrast normalization, the original brightness values in $I_1$ and $I_2$, the brightness values without and with contrast normalization are shown in Figure 19. It shows that with the proposed contrast normalization method, the con-

trast difference between the two sub-images is eliminated.

Figure 20 shows an example of the error which occurs on the data set of modern Chinese papers. The error is caused by the crease at the paper. In the future, we will try to solve this problem.

Finally, some stitching results on different datasets are shown in Figure 21. The seams are shown in green.

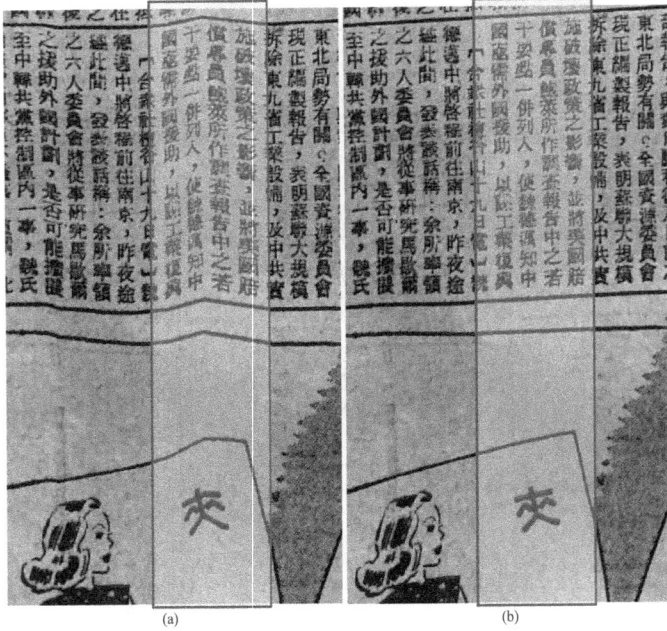

Figure 18: Results between Jia's global deformation [10] and ours. (a):Jia's method; (b):ours.

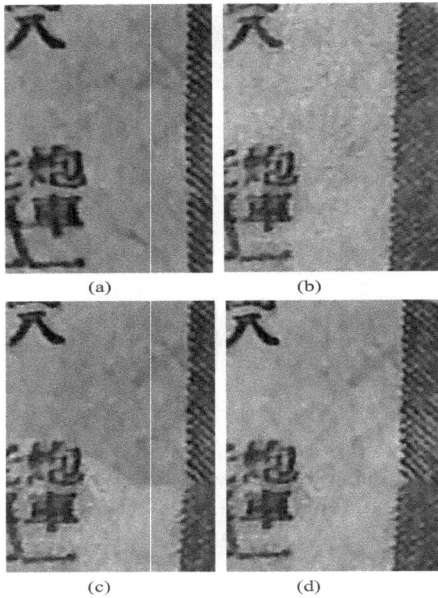

Figure 19: Contrast normalization. (a): part of $I_1$; (b): part of $I_2$; (c): no contrast normalization is used; (d): contrast normalization is used.

## 4. CONCLUSIONS

In this paper, we proposed a paper stitching method using maximum tolerant seam under local distortions. First a dynamic programming algorithm is employed to find the smooth seam which has minimum texture change in one sub-image, and then a local feature matching method with an adaptive window is utilized to get a robust corresponding

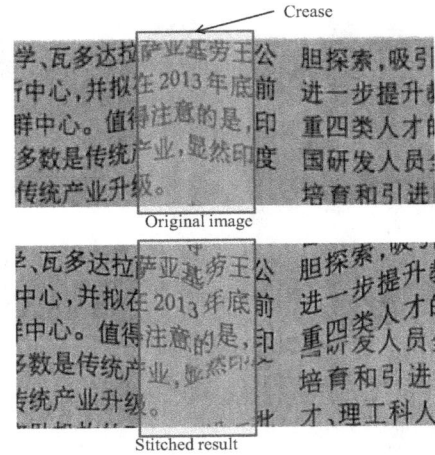

Figure 20: Error caused by crease. Green line denotes the seam.

seam in the other sub-image. In the next, a global optimization algorithm is proposed to refine the matched seams. Then we stitched the two sub-images with a maximum tolerance to avoid the global deformation, and the contrast normalization is used to assure the area near the seam looks natural. With the proposed method, a whole image with a smooth stitching seam and a minimum deformation is generated.

The existing problem of the proposed method mainly lies on the crease cases along the vertical direction. It is because the crease would lead to wrong estimation of the affine transform matrix between two sub-images. So in future, we intend to adopt a Optical Character Recognition (OCR) method to solve the correspondence between two sub-images.

## 5. ACKNOWLEDGMENTS

The author wants to thank Dr. He yuan for his useful suggestions and valuable work on the implementation of the proposed method. The author also would like to thank Dr. Pan pan for his initial exploration efforts on this paper, and Dr. Zheng yun for his valuable suggestions on the draft of this paper.

## 6. REFERENCES

[1] Luis GB Mirisola and Jorge MM Dias. Exploiting inertial sensing in mosaicing and visual navigation. In *Intelligent Autonomous Vehicles*, volume 6, pages 306–311, 2007.

[2] Matthew Brown and David G Lowe. Automatic panoramic image stitching using invariant features. *International Journal of Computer Vision*, 74(1):59–73, 2007.

[3] David Hasler and Sabine E Susstrunk. Color handling in panoramic photography. In *Photonics West 2001-Electronic Imaging*, pages 62–72. International Society for Optics and Photonics, 2000.

[4] Jiaya Jia and Chi-Keung Tang. Image registration with global and local luminance alignment. In *Computer Vision, 2003. Proceedings of The Ninth IEEE International Conference on*, pages 156–163. IEEE, 2003.

[5] Vivek Kwatra, Arno Schödl, Irfan Essa, Greg Turk, and Aaron Bobick. Graphcut textures: image and video synthesis using graph cuts. In *ACM Transactions on Graphics (ToG)*, volume 22, pages 277–286. ACM, 2003.

[6] Alexei A Efros and William T Freeman. Image quilting for texture synthesis and transfer. In *Proceedings of the 28th annual conference on Computer graphics and interactive techniques*, pages 341–346. ACM, 2001.

[7] CV Veena. Minimizing seam artifacts in image stitching. *Asian Journal of Information Technology*, 6(2):209–214, 2007.

[8] Francesco Isgrò and Maurizio Pilu. A fast and robust image registration method based on an early consensus paradigm. *Pattern Recognition Letters*, 25(8):943–954, 2004.

[9] David Eppstein. The farthest point delaunay triangulation minimizes angles. *Computational Geometry*, 1(3):143–148, 1992.

[10] Jiaya Jia and Chi-Keung Tang. Image stitching using structure deformation. *Pattern Analysis and Machine Intelligence, IEEE Transactions on*, 30(4):617–631, 2008.

[11] Junhong Gao, Yu Li, Tat-Jun Chin, and Michael S Brown. Seam-driven image stitching. In *Eurographics 2013-Short Papers*, pages 45–48. The Eurographics Association, 2013.

[12] Gongde Guo, Daniel Neagu, and Mark TD Cronin. Using knn model for automatic feature selection. In *Pattern Recognition and Data Mining*, pages 410–419. Springer, 2005.

[13] Zhong Wu, Qifa Ke, Michael Isard, and Jian Sun. Bundling features for large scale partial-duplicate web image search. In *Computer Vision and Pattern Recognition, 2009. CVPR 2009. IEEE Conference on*, pages 25–32. IEEE, 2009.

[14] Martin A Fischler and Robert C Bolles. Random sample consensus: a paradigm for model fitting with applications to image analysis and automated cartography. *Communications of the ACM*, 24(6):381–395, 1981.

[15] Ruzena Bajcsy and Stane Kovačič. Multiresolution elastic matching. *Computer vision, graphics, and image processing*, 46(1):1–21, 1989.

[16] Karl Rohr, H Siegfried Stiehl, Rainer Sprengel, Thorsten M Buzug, Jürgen Weese, and MH Kuhn. Landmark-based elastic registration using approximating thin-plate splines. *Medical Imaging, IEEE Transactions on*, 20(6):526–534, 2001.

[17] Maurizio Pilu. Deskewing perspectively distorted documents: An approach based on perceptual organization. *HP LABORATORIES TECHNICAL REPORT HPL*, (100), 2001.

[18] Nobuyuki Otsu. A threshold selection method from gray-level histograms. *Automatica*, 11(285-296):23–27, 1975.

[19] Dimitri P Bertsekas, Dimitri P Bertsekas, Dimitri P Bertsekas, and Dimitri P Bertsekas. *Dynamic programming and optimal control*, volume 1. Athena Scientific Belmont, MA, 1995.

[20] Edward Rosten and Tom Drummond. Machine learning for high-speed corner detection. In *Computer Vision–ECCV 2006*, pages 430–443. Springer, 2006.

[21] David G Lowe. Object recognition from local scale-invariant features. In *Computer vision, 1999. The proceedings of the seventh IEEE international conference on*, volume 2, pages 1150–1157. Ieee, 1999.

[22] Herbert Bay, Tinne Tuytelaars, and Luc Van Gool. Surf: Speeded up robust features. In *Computer Vision–ECCV 2006*, pages 404–417. Springer, 2006.

[23] Alexandre Alahi, Raphael Ortiz, and Pierre Vandergheynst. Freak: Fast retina keypoint. In *Computer Vision and Pattern Recognition (CVPR), 2012 IEEE Conference on*, pages 510–517. IEEE, 2012.

[24] Jagat Narain Kapur and Hiremaglur K Kesavan. *Entropy optimization principles with applications*. Academic Pr, 1992.

[25] G David Forney Jr. The viterbi algorithm. *Proceedings of the IEEE*, 61(3):268–278, 1973.

[26] Marcelo Bertalmio, Guillermo Sapiro, Vincent Caselles, and Coloma Ballester. Image inpainting. In *Proceedings of the 27th annual conference on Computer graphics and interactive techniques*, pages 417–424. ACM Press/Addison-Wesley Publishing Co., 2000.

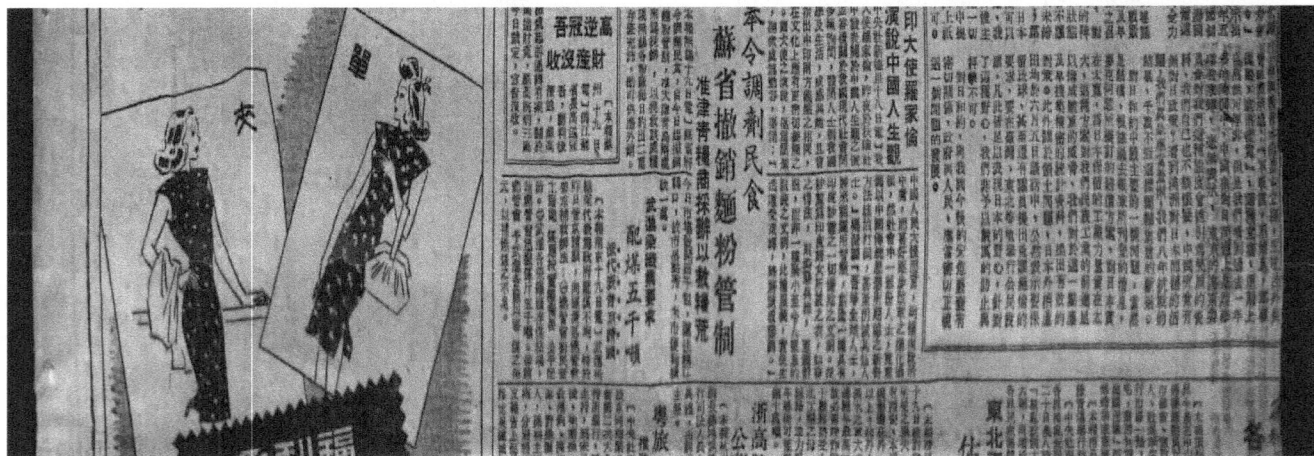

Figure 21: Performance on 3 data sets.

# Abstract Argumentation for Reading Order Detection

Stefano Ferilli[*]
University of Bari
Bari, Italy
stefano.ferilli@uniba.it

Domenico Grieco
University of Bari
Bari, Italy
domenico.grieco@hotmail.it

Domenico Redavid
Artificial Brain S.r.l.
Bari, Italy
redavid@abrain.it

Floriana Esposito[†]
University of Bari
Bari, Italy
floriana.esposito@uniba.it

## ABSTRACT

Detecting the reading order among the layout components of a document's page is fundamental to ensure effectiveness or even applicability of subsequent content extraction steps. While in single-column documents the reading flow can be straightforwardly determined, in more complex documents the task may become very hard. This paper proposes an automatic strategy for identifying the correct reading order of a document page's components based on abstract argumentation. The technique is unsupervised, and works on any kind of document based only on general assumptions about how humans behave when reading documents. Experimental results show that it is effective in more complex cases, and requires less background knowledge, than previous solutions that have been proposed in the literature.

## Categories and Subject Descriptors

I.2.6 [**Artificial Intelligence**]: Learning—*Knowledge Acquisition*; I.7.5 [**Document and Text Processing**]: Document Capture—*Document analysis*

## General Terms

Algorithms, Experimentation

## Keywords

Reading Order Detection; Document Understanding; Abstract Argumentation

---

[*]Department of Computer Science & Inter-departmental Center for Logics and Applications (CILA).

[†]Department of Computer Science & Inter-departmental Center for Logics and Applications (CILA).

*DocEng'14*, September 16–19, 2014, Fort Collins, Colorado, USA.
Copyright 2014 ACM 978-1-4503-2949-1/14/09 ...$15.00.
http://dx.doi.org/10.1145/2644866.2644883.

## 1. INTRODUCTION

While today most documents are generated, stored and exchanged in a digital format, the typing conventions of classical *paper* documents are still in use. Moreover, many *legacy* documents are used in their digitized version. The huge amount of material requires automatic techniques for understanding, organizing and managing single documents or entire collections. *Document Image Understanding* is in charge of extracting semantic information from the document structure. One of its tasks is to determine the correct reading order of components in a document. While in some classes of documents (e.g., single- or multi-column scientific articles) the reading order is quite stable, and hence might in principle be learned if suitable examples for that class are provided, in other cases it might be totally out of reach of supervised learning techniques. E.g., a newspaper's page includes several articles, that can be read independently of each other, but whose constituent components have a well-defined reading order. The articles are composed in the page in several unpredictable combinations, and have different size and number of components. A simple top-down, left-to-right reading order of the pages would return a text flow that interleaves components from different unrelated articles. In such cases, Reading Order Detection in a document is a hot problem, requiring new approaches that can provide general and flexible solutions.

This paper proposes to solve this problem using an abstract argumentation framework, based on a representation that is totally general and applicable to any kind of document. The proposed solution does not need any learning and complies with an incremental extension of the document base. After discussing related work in the next section, Section 3 describes the solution, and Section 4 reports experimental results showing its effectiveness. Finally, Section 5 concludes the paper.

## 2. RELATED WORK

Many approaches to the reading order detection problem have been proposed in the literature. Some [7, 11] are based on the XY-cuts segmentation algorithm [12]. However, XY-cuts cannot deal with blocks organized in L-like shapes, and it needs to know the minimum required width of the horizontal/vertical stripes for the cutting strategy. Knowledge-based approaches use rules to identify a reading order in the pages [2, 9, 13, 6]. Typically the rules encode general criteria concerning reading order, and are manually written by experts. The approach in [1, 5, 8] uses Natural Language Processing (NLP) techniques to improve reading order detection. The approach in [10] uses only visual information, casting the reading order problem as a learning problem where the goal is to find a First-Order Logic theory that is complete and consistent with respect to all training examples. Approaches based on XY-cuts work reasonably well only on simple layouts. Rule-based approaches may overcome this limit, but generally use hand-coded rules. Good rules make the approach more general and domain-independent, but their generation is a difficult, costly and error-prone activity, in which mistakes are highly probable. On the other hand, solving this problem by trying to automatically learn the rules makes the approach domain-dependent, because inductive learning allows to correctly identify the reading order only for the classes of documents used in the training set. The use of linguistic information may overcome some limitations of the approaches that use only geometric information [5], but requires the availability of NLP techniques and linguistic resources, which makes the approaches more complex and language-dependent. While many approaches assume that there is a single correct reading order for each page, this assumption is clearly wrong in newspapers or magazines, where many articles are present in each page and can be read in any order. To the best of our knowledge, only [10] and [5] explicitly support layouts where different valid reading orders exist, and allow to identify multiple reading chains over the set of logical components in the same page.

## 3. ARGUMENTATION-BASED APPROACH

In this work, we want to reflect the usual human strategy for determining the reading order of a document page. First of all, the procedure must take into account only the layout organization of the document blocks. Indeed, using the textual content would require the exploitation of Natural Language Processing techniques, that are language-dependent and are not available for all languages, or at least not with the same quality. In facts, humans usually determine the reading order without actually reading the document. Also, we are interested in a generic approach that is able to deal with the widest possible range of document classes, including those having complex layouts (e.g., newspapers), where techniques based on a partition of the page according to its background are not applicable. Third, we want the technique to be based on very simple layout information, that can be easily and reliably extracted by an automatic procedure and is independent of the specific kind of document. Having such a low-level input clearly places most burden on the reading order detection technique. While this complexity is often tackled using knowledge-based approaches, we want to avoid this setting, because hand-written rules are costly, error-prone and typically depend on the kind of document. We want to avoid also the Machine Learning-based solution to this problem, by which such rules are automatically obtained by the system starting from examples of manually labeled documents. Indeed, a manual intervention is anyway required, and the learned knowledge is in any case dependent on the kind of documents, and on the specific documents, used for training the system. Finally, often the reading order in a document page does not determine a total order, but the components can be partitioned into independent subgroups, each characterized by its own reading order,

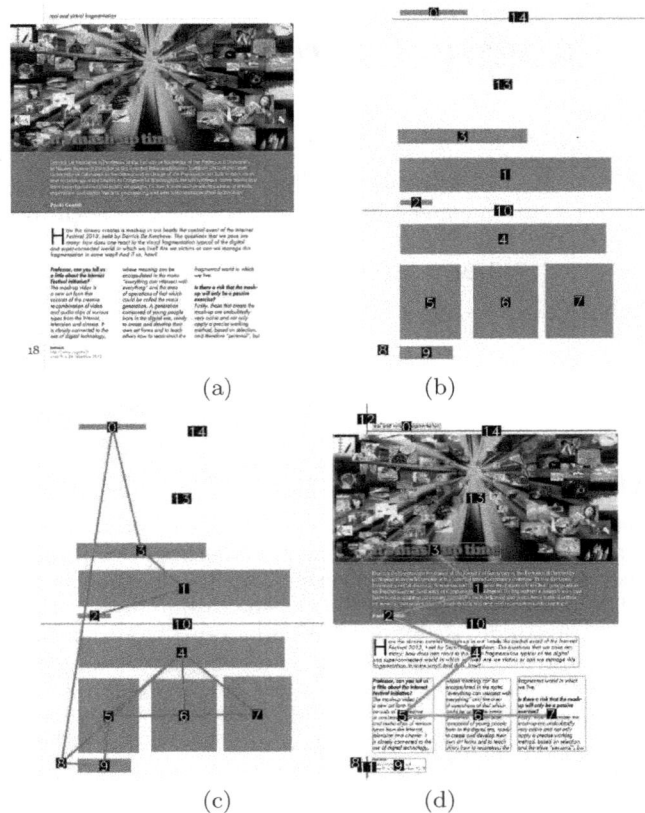

Figure 1: Sample document (a), corresponding layout structure extracted by DoMInUS (b), arguments (c) and correct reading order (d)

leaving the reader free to decide an order among groups. For these reasons, we do not assume a unique reading order for a page, but we consider all consistent independent orders.

Abstract argumentation provides a general approach to model defeasible and non-monotonic reasoning, to help make decisions about conflicting information. It is a suitable inference technique to deal with all of the above requirements. Indeed, one might just express possible (even trivial) partial reading orderings and identify pairs of these partial solutions that are mutually inconsistent. According to [3], an *argumentation framework* consists of a set of arguments and an *attack relation* on these arguments. Different semantics (called *extensions*) may be defined for an argumentation framework, that involve different degrees of skepticism in evaluating the arguments. E.g., *preferred* extensions select as reliable any maximal (w.r.t. set inclusion) set of arguments $S$ that is conflict-free (i.e., no element of $S$ attacks another element of $S$) and that defends itself (i.e., for each argument $a$ outside $S$ that attacks an element of $S$, there is an element of $S$ that attacks $a$).

As a first step, given a document page, we obtain its layout structure, consisting of layout blocks labeled with their type of content, using the document processing and management system DoMInUS (DOcument Management INtelligent Universal System) [4]. Fig. 1 shows a document (a) and the corresponding output of DoMInUS (b). For the reading order detection purposes, image blocks are simply ignored. Moreover, horizontal or vertical lines are considered as natural separators when their projection spans more than one content (i.e., image or text) block. The presence of these separators allows to partition the page into independent portions in which the reading order can be determined separately, which slightly simplifies the problem.

Given the text blocks in a page, we consider only the following quite trivial and document-independent rules for providing the input to our technique: (**1**) horizontally or vertically adjacent components are candidates to be read consequently; (**2**) a component at the bottom of the (portion of) page might be followed by a component at the top of an adjacent column, and (**3**) a rightmost (resp., leftmost) component might be followed by a leftmost (resp., rightmost) component in an adjacent row. Each pair of blocks $(A, B)$ that fulfills any of these requirements generates an argument. Note that this argument does not imply any direction in the relationship between $A$ and $B$, and hence it applies both to languages in which the reading order proceeds left-to-right and to those in which it proceeds right-to-left. As said, no argument is generated for pairs of blocks having a separator in between. Due to the linearity of reading order, two arguments $(A, B)$ and $(A, C)$ are mutually exclusive because if $B$ is to be read immediately after $A$, then $C$ cannot be read immediately after $A$ as well, and *vice-versa*. Thus, we say that arguments $(A, B)$ and $(A, C)$ attack each other. The same holds for arguments $(A, C)$ and $(B, C)$. Based on these attacks, our argumentation engine identifies all the alternative consistent groups of partial orderings according to the preferred extension. This is the core of our approach.

For instance, the document in Fig. 1b yields the following formal description, corresponding to the segments in Fig. 1c:

$$(0,3), (1,2), (3,1), (4,5), (4,6), (4,7), (5,6), (5,9), (6,7), (8,0), (8,4), (8,9)$$

for which the following attacks are automatically derived:

$$(4,5)\text{-}(4,6), (4,6)\text{-}(4,5), (4,6)\text{-}(4,7), (4,7)\text{-}(4,6), (4,5)\text{-}(4,7), \\ (4,7)\text{-}(4,5), (5,6)\text{-}(5,9), (5,9)\text{-}(5,6), (8,0)\text{-}(8,4), (8,4)\text{-}(8,0), \\ (8,0)\text{-}(8,9), (8,9)\text{-}(8,0), (8,4)\text{-}(8,9), (8,9)\text{-}(8,4), (4,6)\text{-}(5,6), \\ (5,6)\text{-}(4,6), (4,7)\text{-}(6,7), (6,7)\text{-}(4,7), (5,9)\text{-}(8,9), (8,9)\text{-}(5,9)$$

The correct reading order is (see Fig. 1d):

$$(3,1), (1,2), (2,4), (4,5), (5,6), (6,7)$$

Our technique returned exactly this reading order, except for $(2,4)$, due to the ruling line between the paper heading and its body. This is acceptable, since the heading and the body may indeed be read independently: some might read the heading and decide the paper is not interesting to them, while others might know what the paper is about and want to read directly its content.

## 4. EVALUATION

The proposed technique was tested on a dataset including 103 document pages of different layout complexity, taken from newspapers, magazines and (scientific) papers. Trivial cases of single-column documents were not included. Some samples are shown in Figure 2. Statistics about the dataset are reported in Table 1, both for single classes and for the whole dataset. Table cells report average values, with minimum-maximum range in parentheses. The last column reports both the micro- and (in parentheses) the macro-averages. The top and middle rows describe the dataset: it involved

**Figure 2: Examples of documents in dataset**

on average 20.73 blocks, 22.98 arguments and 63.17 attacks per document. As expected, the simplest class is 'Magazine', while the most complex one is 'Newspaper', both for the number of involved components and for the reading order-related relationships. The most complex document in the dataset is a newspaper page involving 106 blocks, 137 arguments and 1020 attacks. The last rows in Table 1 report experimental results. Interestingly, the number of partial orderings for 'Magazine' and 'Paper' are very close to each other. While the maximum is still higher for papers, on average magazines turn out to have slightly more partial orderings. However, the gap between these classes and 'Newspaper' is huge (the latter is 3 orders of magnitude larger). This is because pages with complex layout arrangement are often partitioned so that reading order is relevant for blocks within the same element of the partition, but reading order of partition elements is independent. Newspaper pages have a significant impact on the overall complexity of the dataset, as shown by the averages in the last column.

For each outcome, the recall was evaluated as the ratio of correct pairs retrieved over pairs in the correct order sequence (the gold standard was defined manually). Since a page may admit several alternative correct reading orders, the recall of a given page was determined as the average recall over all alternative outcomes for that page. 77.94% average recall was reached on the entire dataset (79.73% considering the macro-average). The worst recall, occurred on the most complex class (newspapers), is still quite satisfactory (70.74%) for such a difficult class. Interestingly, the best recall was reached on papers (91.32%), even if they have a more complex structure than magazines. Conversely,

**Table 1: Dataset and experimental statistics**

|  | Paper | Magazine | Newspaper | Overall |
|---|---|---|---|---|
| #Docs | 43 | 40 | 20 | 103 |
| Text blocks | 15.18 (5-14) | 8.13 (5-13) | 26.35 (16-66) | 14.61 (16.55) |
| Image blocks | 1.05 (0-6) | 0.70 (0-1) | 5.35 (3-11) | 1.75 (2.37) |
| Rule lines | 0.37 (0-3) | 2.60 (0-5) | 16.50 (8-50) | 4.37 (6.49) |
| #Blocks | 16.60 (3-27) | 11.42 (7-18) | 48.20 (29-106) | 20.73 (25.41) |
| #Args | 24.13 (2-42) | 9.20 (3-19) | 44.45 (21-137) | 22.98 (25.93) |
| #Attacks | 61.67 (0-180) | 14.20 (0-62) | 164.3 (42-1020) | 63.17 (80.06) |
| #Partial orderings | 6.65 (1-120) | 6.83 (1-108) | 5 053.85 (14-59 916) | 986.76 (1 689.11) |
| Recall(%) | 91.32 (62.50-100) | 71.75 (0-100) | 70.74 (10.80-100) | 77.94 (79.73) |

the performance on magazines is very close to that for newspapers (71.75%), despite its much less complex structure.

We could not run a direct comparison with competitor systems, since they, and/or the datasets on which they were run, are not available. However, our performance is comparable to those reported in the literature, in spite of our dataset including very complex cases. This is a success, since we take a trivial input that does not require high-level interpretation, and we use a few and very general background knowledge compared to other rule-based systems. As regards handling many possible reading orders, we are better than [10]. We are worse than [5], but [5] uses linguistic information, which we deliberately avoided in our approach.

A qualitative evaluation revealed that most errors are due to fancy reading orders that, due to stylistic choices, deviate from the general 'top-down, left-to-right' rule, found mainly in magazines and newspapers. These cases are difficult also for humans, who must read the text in the candidate next blocks to understand which is the correct one. In these cases linguistic informations may help. To keep our approach language-independent, we accepted this limitation. Other minor problems concerned page segmentation. In some papers, header and footer are not separated by lines, so they are considered as parts of the body by our technique, which produces wrong arguments. In newspapers, arguments are not generated when columns of the same article are separated by lines. In magazines, the text of multi-line titles is split when they cross frames with different backgrounds, and no argument is created because the boundaries of the frames are seen as lines. All these problems might be tackled by refining the rules to consider additional layout information, such as spacing and font size.

## 5. CONCLUSIONS

Determining the reading order among text components in a document page is an important task in document processing. While this may be trivial in some documents, there are tricky cases in which different layout components in a document page contain different portions of a single discourse. This paper proposed an automatic unsupervised strategy for identifying the correct reading order of a document page's components based on abstract argumentation. It works on any kind of document, leveraging only general assumptions about how humans behave when reading documents. Experimental results show that it is very effective, also compared to previous solutions that have been proposed in the literature. Qualitative analysis of the results suggested possible directions for further improvement of the approach. Also, the predicted reading order might be compared to the actual one of human readers as sensed by eye tracking.

## 6. ACKNOWLEDGMENTS

This work was partially funded by the Italian PON 2007-2013 project PON02_00563_3489339 'Puglia@Service'.

## 7. REFERENCES

[1] M. Aiello, C. Monz, and L. Todoran. Document understanding for a broad class of documents. *IJDAR*, 5(1):1–16, 2002.

[2] T. M. Breuel. High performance document layout analysis. In *Proc. Symp. Document Image Understanding Technology*, 2003.

[3] P. M. Dung. On the acceptability of arguments and its fundamental role in nonmonotonic reasoning, logic programming and n-person games. *Artif. Intell.*, 77(2):321–358, 1995.

[4] F. Esposito, S. Ferilli, T. Basile, and N. D. Mauro. Machine learning for digital document processing: From layout analysis to metadata extraction. In S. Marinai and H. Fujisawa, editors, *Machine Learning in Document Analysis and Recognition*, volume 90 of *Studies in Computational Intelligence*, pages 79–112. Springer, 2008.

[5] L. Gao, Z. Tang, X. Lin, and Y. Wang. A graph-based method of newspaper article reconstruction. In *ICPR*, pages 1566–1569, 2012.

[6] I. Hasan, J. Parapar, and A. Barreiro. Improving the extraction of text in pdfs by simulating the human reading order. *J. UCS*, 18(5):623–649, 2012.

[7] Y. Ishitani. Document transformation system from papers to xml data based on pivot xml document method. In *ICDAR*, volume 1, pages 250–255, 2003.

[8] S. Klampfl and R. Kern. An unsupervised machine learning approach to body text and table of contents extraction from digital scientific articles. In *TPDL*, pages 144–155, 2013.

[9] P. Liang, M. Narasimhan, M. Shilman, and P. A. Viola. Efficient geometric algorithms for parsing in two dimensions. In *ICDAR*, pages 1172–1177. IEEE Computer Society, 2005.

[10] D. Malerba, M. Ceci, and M. Berardi. Machine learning for reading order detection in document image understanding. In S. Marinai and H. Fujisawa, editors, *Machine Learning in Document Analysis and Recognition*, volume 90 of *Studies in Computational Intelligence*, pages 45–69. Springer, 2008.

[11] J.-L. Meunier. Optimized xy-cut for determining a page reading order. In *ICDAR*, pages 347–351. IEEE Computer Society, 2005.

[12] G. Nagy and S. C. Seth. Hierarchical representation of optically scanned documents. In *ICPR*, pages 347–349, 1984.

[13] R. Smith. Hybrid page layout analysis via tab-stop detection. In *ICDAR*, pages 241–245, July 2009.

# Generating Summary Documents for a Variable-Quality PDF Document Collection

Jacob Hughes
School of Computer Science
University of Nottingham
NOTTINGHAM NG8 1BB, UK
jxh00u@cs.nott.ac.uk

David F. Brailsford
School of Computer Science
University of Nottingham
NOTTINGHAM NG8 1BB, UK
dfb@cs.nott.ac.uk

Steven R. Bagley
School of Computer Science
University of Nottingham
NOTTINGHAM NG8 1BB, UK
srb@cs.nott.ac.uk

Clive E. Adams
Institute of Mental Health
University of Nottingham
NOTTINGHAM NG7 2TU, UK
clive.adams@nottingham.ac.uk

## ABSTRACT

The Cochrane Schizophrenia Group's Register of studies details all aspects of the effects of treating people with schizophrenia. It has been gathered over the last 20 years and consists of around 20,000 documents, overwhelmingly in PDF. Document collections of this sort – on a given theme but gathered from a wide range of sources – will generally have huge variability in the quality of the PDF, particularly with respect to the key property of text searchability.

Summarising the results from the best of these papers, to allow evidence-based health care decision making, has so far been done by manually creating a summary document, starting from a visual inspection of the relevant PDF file. This labour-intensive process has resulted, to date, in only 4,000 of the papers being summarised – with enormous duplication of effort and with many issues around the validity and reliability of the data extraction.

This paper describes a pilot project to provide a computer-assisted framework in which any of the PDF documents could be searched for the occurrence of some 8,000 keywords and key phrases. Once keyword tagging has been completed the framework assists in the generation of a standard summary document, thereby greatly speeding up the production of these summaries. Early examples of the framework are described and its capabilities illustrated.

## Categories and Subject Descriptors

H.3.3 [**Information Search and Retrieval**]: Search Process, Selection Process; I.7.5 [**Document Capture**]: Optical Character Recognition (OCR)

## General Terms

Algorithms, Documentation, Languages

## Keywords

Schizophrenia; PDF; OCR; document collections

## 1. INTRODUCTION

In the field of medicine it is rarely the case that a single set of trials can give a definitive answer about the efficacy of the treatment, or treatments, under evaluation. A UK epidemiologist called Archie Cochrane was one of the first to call for collecting all controlled trials of health care and for combining results from similar, suitably rigorous, trials, In this way one can deliver the most accurate estimate of the effects of care.

Cochrane's influence led to the Cochrane Database of Systematic Reviews and, in the case of schizophrenia, a repository collated over 20 years, comprising six decades of published evidence – now held at the Institute of Mental Health at the University of Nottingham [1]. A problem with combining several studies, however well conducted they may have been, is that there is little chance that results are recorded in a standard way, let alone any possibility of access to a project's internal documentation to acquire results directly. The 20,000 documents of the Cochrane Schizophrenia Group's Register of Trials is overwhelmingly in the form of published papers archived in Adobe's PDF. This format is far from ideal in terms of easy data extraction but, being ubiquitous, it is in reality 'the only show in town'.

To make full use of these PDF files it is necessary to manually extract all quantitative and qualitative data on methods, participants, interventions and outcomes into a standardized format. Until now this has required the effort of experienced researchers, often with a suitable medical background. Only 20% of the total number of trials have been data extracted – most data remain unused and potentially useful evidence of the effects of care are not fully utilized. Furthermore those data that have been extracted are often impossible to verify, since their exact origin within the original document is not transparent.

This paper describes a pilot project, representing the first stages of a concerted effort to provide a computer-assisted framework for tagging key phrases within this variable-quality PDF document collection, followed by automated extraction and assemblage of the tagged phrases into standardised summary documents.

## 2. OVERVIEW OF PDF

In October 1993 Adobe Systems Inc. introduced the Portable Document Format (PDF) and released viewer software for that format called Acrobat, initially for Macintosh and MS-Windows systems. PDF is an optimized development, (with document portability in mind) of the earlier PostScript format that had revolutionized typesetting in the 1980s.

The acceptance of PDF for providing distributable 'electronic page masters' was very rapid in the technical publication field.

Publishers soon became used to turning their PostScript files (used for creating the hard-copy form of their journals) into the equivalent PDF files, using Adobe's own Distiller conversion program. Acceptance of PDF took rather longer to happen in fields such as law, business and medicine. Here the problems included the legal acceptability of PDF master files (as opposed to traditional 'hard copy') coupled with waiting patiently for software such as word processors and spreadsheets to be able to export output to PDF swiftly and efficiently. However, by 2005, the status of PDF as an archival medium was becoming sufficiently clear for ISO to begin work on making PDF be an archival standard (PDF/A).

## 2.1 Varieties of PDF

PDF offers a convenient way of making high-quality documents be readily exchangeable. Ideally all the running text will be formatted in the chosen body-text typefaces; lettering within diagrams may be set in some different face. Line diagrams will be drawn using the correct line-drawing primitives, while bitmapped material such as photographs (either lossily or losslessly compressed) is catered for by the PostScript/PDF **image** operator. PDF files of this quality are referred to as PDF-FTG (i.e. 'PDF, Formatted Text and Graphics')[1]. The key advantage of this format is that text strings can usually be located within the PDF of the body text.

It would be comforting to hope that all collected corpora of PDF documents would be of PDF-FTG quality. More often than not this fails to be achieved because the 'umbrella' nature of PDF allows scanned-page documentation to be stored in PDF **image** (PDF-I) format which can replicate, inside a PDF wrapper, widely accepted image formats such as JPG or TIFF. However, this PDF-I format, just like JPG and TIFF, is not text-searchable.

In 1994 Adobe introduced an OCR-based product called Acrobat Capture. When applied to a PDF-I file it went beyond mere OCR by creating an invisible, searchable, text overlay, using what was technically called 'Text Mode 3' (see [2] page 306). By suitably adjusting the point sizes and the inter-word spacing in this hidden textual layer it was possible to make it be in exact registration with the perceived words in the page image. Adobe named this new hybrid format 'PDF Image plus Hidden Text' (PDF-IT). It has the great virtue that searched-for words are highlighted via the correct bounding box in the textual layer but they show up as highlights in the exactly superposed image layer, thereby creating the illusion of a textually searchable image.

For more than ten years the technology from Acrobat Capture has been deployed in the full releases of Acrobat itself to satisfy a demand for making potentially huge document-bases of scanned material (e.g. in legal work) be text searchable.

## 3. FIRST STEPS

The long-term aim of this work is to fully realize the potential of the schizophrenia register of trials in terms of extracting 'best practice' procedures from sets of separate, but related, trials. In moving from a fully manual scheme to a computer assisted one it was immediately clear that it was vital to assess the relative proportions of PDF-FTG, PDF-I and PDF-IT files within the schizophrenia document-base

---

[1] In earlier documentation Adobe referred to PDF files of this sort as 'PDF Normal'

## 3.1 Analyzing the documents

An analysis took place in early December 2013 of 17,990 documents available to us from the document set. The analysis program was written in Objective C and used the Quartzcore Framework to provide PDF analysis functionality. The analysis algorithm relies on a function called getPageType which tests to see if there is a whole-page image layer on the current page but with no associated textual content stream; if so then the page is Image Only. The second per-page test is to see if the word count for invisibly-rendered text exceeds that for visibly rendered. If the majority of the text is invisible, in most of the pages, then the document is PDF-IT. Otherwise it is a PDF-FTG file.

Having applied the above algorithm to the full set of 17,990 PDF files the following breakdown of the document set was obtained (actual numbers of files are in parentheses)

- PDF-FTG        62.8%        (11,296)
- PDF-I          32.2%        (5,796)
- PDF-IT         5.0%         (898)

## 3.2 Converting PDF-I to PDF-IT

By applying the OCR functionality of the Acrobat Capture plugin, with the batch processing capability contained in the full Acrobat product, from Acrobat 7.0 onwards, it was possible to automate the conversion of the 5796 PDF-I files into the PDF-IT format. Details of the required procedure are given on an Adobe Web site [3]. Preliminary tests showed that, on average, each of these file conversions took just over 2 minutes using Acrobat X Pro running on a 2.4 GHz Pentium system. This led to an estimate of 8 days to complete the conversion task — an estimate which turned out to be remarkably accurate.

Given that almost a third of the document collection was PDF-I, and hence not text-searchable, it was a vital first step, in contemplating automated keyword recognition for the whole document collection, to establish that this retrofitting of searchability was indeed feasible.

## 4. SYSTEMATIC REVIEWS

The Cochrane Group currently organises a large number of medical professionals to undertake systematic reviews of health care topics based on reports of trials. A systematic review attempts to identify, appraise and incorporate all relevant evidence that meets pre-specified criteria, in order to answer a given research question. Data harvested from the trials, as recorded in the PDF, are manually entered into a separate system called RevMan [4]. This software – a writing and analysis tool – helps prepare data for meta-analysis and publication.

The current process of data input for systematic reviewing is as follows:

1. Read through the PDF for the chosen clinical trial.

2. Identify a piece of data (quantitative or qualitative) within the PDF, that is relevant for extraction.

3. Manually input this data into RevMan

An important requirement here is for total accuracy in identifying and transferring information in steps 2 and 3. Furthermore, for data-checking at a later stage, the page number and location of all data items should be logged as part of stage 3. It is precisely these two activities that could benefit most from an automated system.

Note also that the conversion of PDF-I files to PDF-IT, described in the previous section, is yet another big bonus for transferring

data into RevMan, because cut-and-paste of text from a PDF file is not possible for PDF-I – in this case the reviewer would have to manually type all of the relevant data into RevMan.

## 5. HIGHLIGHTS AND LINKS IN PDF FILES

PDF itself defines various ways in which selected objects such as images, text, section headings and so on can be highlighted or made the target of hyperlinks either internally (e.g. from a table of contents) or externally from an incoming link. This latter often originates in HTML but can finish on a fixed destination page within the PDF file using the so-called Named Destinations facility.

These features are challenging indeed to add, programmatically, into arbitrary PDF material of variable quality, as encountered in the current studies. Nevertheless Adobe's (very costly) Acrobat SDK will enable a JavaScript programmer to add exactly these features, thereby enhancing the original PDF. We shall call this a *direct* editing system because it alters the original PDF file.

For all the above reasons of technical difficulty, third-party PDF analysis and augmentation systems commonly display page images of the PDF and create the illusion of genuine PDF highlights by holding the PDF's text, in HTML, alongside the page image. Any requested annotations or highlighting are superposed on the page image using a variety of ingenious methods, often known generically as *standoff markup* [5], for cross linking the HTML to the image. This is an example of an *indirect* editing system, where the PDF file itself is not altered.

In wanting to create an environment for automating the highlighting of key phrases, and for extracting data from our schizophrenia documents, we looked at a few indirect systems already available, such as Document Cloud and ExaCT. Both of these provided some aspects of the facilities we were seeking but neither of them provided all we wanted. For this reason we chose to implement our own system.

## 6. A PROTOTYPE SYSTEM IN PDF.js

Part of the core functionality required for our text highlighting and extraction system (PET) was the ability to interact with a PDF document;. An Open Source library called *PDF.js* [6] has been found that provides this functionality by creating a platform on which an interaction API can be developed.

Our prototype PDF extraction tool (PET) was implemented within the PDF.js library, initially created by Mozilla (and which is still in the early stages of development). PDF.js renders PDF files to a native HTML format using Javascript.

A large proportion of this HTML version of the PDF is constructed of HTML DIV tags, which are used to denote a division or section within an HTML file. Each DIV contains a text area that has been transformed to align with the original PDF's text. In this sense it resembles the approach taken by the hidden text layer within a PDF-IT file.

Below is an example of what a small segment of this HTML code looks like when displaying a few lines of text in a PDF file, using the PDF.js library.

```
<div data-canvas-width="381.48" data-font-name="g_font_4_0"
data-angle="0" dir="ltr" style="font-size:
13.333333333333332px; font-family: serif; left:
433.2181333333333px; top: 311.9842665666663px; -webkit-
transform: rotate(0deg) scale(0.9852287581699347, 1); -
webkit-transform-origin: 0% 0%;">impracticality of blinding
the patients to their allocation</div>
```

**Figure 1. PDF text as an HTML <DIV> within PDF.js**

One of the problems posed by PDF.js is that it does not support the display of some extra objects, optionally present in a PDF file, such as Named Destinations, Article Threads and highlighted text. It also does not provide the ability to 'write back' data into the PDF source file, to enhance the richness of the original document.

Despite the fact that PET had to be prototyped as an indirect editing system we were fully aware that any such system has the huge drawback that any enhancements to the PDF file are visible only within the indirect framework (DocumentCloud, ExaCT, PET etc.). Ultimately this means that anyone wanting to see the PDF enhancements has to install a copy of the indirect system.

The first requirement of the PET functionality was to identify, and link back to, the page on which a particular keyword occurred. It was already known that this could be achieved in PDF itself by a facility known as Named Destinations, held within the root node of the PDF tree. Equally, PDF itself implements its own highlighting facility (located on the actual PDF pages) which can easily reproduce any indirect highlights added within PET.

If we could find a way to make PET be a more direct system and to overwrite the source PDF file with Named Destinations and highlights then we would achieve the goal of making the summary XML document, and its corresponding enhanced PDF, be a free-standing pair of documents – not at all dependent on the PET framework for visual display, nor for acting as an independent resource for further research.

### 6.1 Text highlighting in PET

So far we have described how an experienced researcher might transfer tagged phrases from a PDF file into RevMan either by cut-and-paste or via direct text input. The PET environment provides automated assistance by allowing a researcher to highlight key phrases in the PDF image, by simply dragging the mouse over them. Further assistance is at hand in the shape of a dataset of 8,000 keywords and key phrases (painstakingly built up over 20 years). This keyword dataset takes the form of row entries in a spreadsheet file that can readily be converted into database entries in some suitable format.

The architecture of PET is based around communicating client and server processes. The front-end client allows for the display of highlighted tagged phrases either manually or automatically generated and for later editing, or even complete removal, of the highlighted phrase. The server process handles the generation of a suitable subset of keywords from the keyword database and it also copes with writing out the final XML summary document, together with a revised version of the input PDF. This revised version of the PDF uses Named Destinations to implement a bounding box and a page number for each highlighted keyword.

### 6.2 Auto-generation of highlighted tags

The main driver for generating highlighted tags for keywords was the dataset of keywords and key phrases. To speed up the tagging process this dataset was used, first of all, to search the PDF file under analysis, very quickly, for whether any of these words or phrases actually occurred. At this stage no attempt was made to find the page number, or page position, of each occurrence. Once the 'used subset' of the 8,000 keywords had been found, the second pass of the tagging process could start to create tags that include page position and page number.

We should note, at this stage, that problems sometimes occurred with the PDF file's textual content, which is contained within HTML DIV markers inside the PET/PDF.js environment. The text blocks on a PDF page are not always rendered to the screen in what the user might think of as "correct reading order". For this reason, when PDF.js converts the text streams of the PDF into HTML DIVs, the reading order may not look correct and this can be particularly problematical if a key phrase straddles more than one DIV. The problem is neatly solved by being prepared to shuffle the DIVs around into a correct reading order, as determined by their textual placement co-ordinates.

A sample of highlighted text, as it appears in PET, and corresponding to the coding in Figure 1, is shown below

> follow-up rates between the intervention and control groups deserves comment. The local ethics committee did not allow access to the case-notes of the non-respondents so data on the non-respondents is missing. A possible reason for this differential response rate arises from impracticality of blinding the patients to their allocation to either intervention or control groups. Those patients

**Figure 2. Highlighting and tagging of keywords**

At the end of the tagging process (which may involve a mixture of auto-generated and manually added tags) an XML-structured file of these tags is handed back from client to server as shown in the sample below.

```
▼<PDF>
  ▶<interventions>...</interventions>
  ▼<participants>
    ▼<setting>
        <element link="id1400685880982">UK.</element>
      </setting>
    ▼<diagnosis>
        <element link="id1400685881214">schizophrenia</element>
      </diagnosis>
    </participants>
  ▼<methods>
    ▼<blinding>
        <element link="id1400685881127">blinding</element>
      </blinding>
    </methods>
  </PDF>
```

**Figure 3. A portion of the XML summary document**

Each individual data tag was assigned its own unique ID, generated using the exact date and time of its creation,. Using this ID it is possible to edit and remove tags either individually or in groups. The unique ID was also ideally suited for the generation of a unique name when each of the tags was converted into a Named Destination.

## 6.3 Implementation of Named Destinations

In addition to making the XML summary file of Figure 3 available as one of the standard outputs from PET there was also a need to write back an enhanced PDF file, ideally with a Named Destination for each tag and with PDF highlighting of those same tags. Given that we have used PDF.js and Python hosted on the cloud compute platform provided by Google, specifically GAE (the Google App Engine), to create an 'indirect' system, it comes as no surprise that it lacks the ability to alter the input PDF file by writing back an enhanced version of it. For this reason the server side of the PET system calls on a separate module, written in C, to perform this task. It takes as its input a comma-separated variable (CSV) list denoting each of the desired Named Destinations This module was written by one of us (SRB) using technology from the COGs [7] project.

A glance at page 82 of the PDF reference manual [2] shows that Named Destinations are located at the root of the PDF tree and are therefore relatively easy to insert. However, the related desire to make all these places be PDF highlights, to mirror those highlights we created in the PET environment (see Figure 2), is a much harder task. Highlights in PDF are located on the actual PDF pages. Some very careful calculations have to be performed to convert the bounding boxes of the PET highlights into PDF format, followed by equally careful tree traversal, inside the PDF, to plant the highlights in the correct format on the correct page.

## 7. DISCUSSION AND CONCLUSIONS

The work described here was a pilot project to try out an editing and creation environment (PET) for use by researchers when tagging and highlighting key words and phrases in a database of randomized trials. An important issue was whether, when tagging was complete, other medical sub-specialties could get benefit from this markup in the form of an enhanced PDF file and an XML summary document i.e. without having to install the entire PET environment.

The results we obtained are very encouraging. Much work remains to be done in reducing the number of 'hits' that result when the dataset of keywords is processed against the content of the target paper. A greater degree of context sensitivity is needed possibly coupled with a learning mechanism connected to gathering data about which of the auto-inserted key phrases the researcher chooses to accept or discard. As noted in the previous section there is also a large amount of work to be done in writing back the corrected highlights into the PDF file.

Encouraged by what has been achieved already a consortium of enthusiastic medical-informatics professionals has now submitted a major bid for European funding so that the full potential of the schizophrenia register of trials can be exploited.

## 8. REFERENCES

[1] C. E. Adams, The Cochrane Schizophrenia Group's Specialised Register of trials, 2014. http://szg.cochrane.org/cszg-specialised-register

[2] Adobe Systems Inc, *PDF Reference (Third Edition; PDF 1.4)*, Addison Wesley, 2002.

[3] Rick Borstein, *Batch Processing using Acrobat Professional*, 2005. http://blogs.adobe.com/acrolaw/2005/10

[4] Cochrane Informatics and Knowledge Management Dept., *RevMan*,. http://tech.cochrane.org/Revman

[5] Peter L. Thomas and David F. Brailsford, "Enhancing Digital Documents using XML-based Standoff Markup", *Proceedings ACM Document Engineering Symposium (DocEng05)*, pp. 177–186, Nov. 2005.

[6] Mozilla (Open Source), *PDF.js*. https://wiki.mozilla.org/PDF.js

[7] Steven Bagley, David Brailsford, and Matthew Hardy, "Creating well-structured PDF as a sequence of Component Object Graphic (COG) elements", *Proceedings ACM Document Engineering Symposium (DocEng03)*, pp. 58–67, Nov. 2003.

# Transforming Graph-based Sentence Representations to Alleviate Overfitting in Relation Extraction

Rinaldo Lima, Jamilson Batista, Rafael Ferreira,
Fred Freitas, Rafael Lins
Federal University of Pernambuco, Recife, Brazil
{rjl4, jba, rflm, fred, rdl}@cin.ufpe.br

Steven Simske, Marcelo Riss
Hewlett-Packard Labs
Fort Collins, USA/Porto Alegre, Brazil
{steven.simske, marcelo.riss}@hp.com

## ABSTRACT

Relation extraction (RE) aims at finding the way entities, such as person, location, organization, date, etc., depend upon each other in a text document. Ontology Population, Automatic Summarization, and Question Answering are fields in which relation extraction offers valuable solutions. A relation extraction method based on inductive logic programming that induces extraction rules suitable to identify semantic relations between entities was proposed by the authors in a previous work. This paper proposes a method to simplify graph-based representations of sentences that replaces dependency graphs of sentences by simpler ones, keeping the target entities in it. The goal is to speed up the learning phase in a RE framework, by applying several rules for graph simplification that constrain the hypothesis space for generating extraction rules. Moreover, the direct impact on the extraction performance results is also investigated. The proposed techniques outperformed some other state-of-the-art systems when assessed on two standard datasets for relation extraction in the biomedical domain.

## Categories and Subject Descriptors

H.3.1 [**Content Analysis and Indexing**]: Linguistic Processing - I.2.6 [**Learning**]: Induction.

## General Terms

Algorithms, Experimentation

## Keywords

Graph-based Model; Sentence Simplification; Relation Extraction; Inductive Logic Programming

## 1. INTRODUCTION

Relation Extraction (RE) aims at finding predefined relationships between target entities in a text. It has lately drawn the attention of the community of information extraction as offering potential solutions to a number of problems in that area. The typical target entities in RE consists of real world named objects, or named entities, such as people, organizations, geographical locations, among others. In the domain of molecular biology, for instance, the focus has largely been on the investigation of protein-protein interactions (PPI) [1] [3] [8]. For that purpose, biomedical NLP communities have made available several annotated corpora on PPI.

Most of the state-of-the-art RE approaches proposed so far on

news [11] [14][6] and biomedical domain [1], [3] has relied on the exploitation of the full constituent and dependency parsing trees [14] without any form of simplification or filtering. Thus, the syntactic structures, as they directly result from natural language parsing tools, may not always be adequate for relation extraction [3].

The path connecting a pair of entities in a parsed sentence was extensively used to construct feature vectors or kernel functions to identify relations [1] [11] [23]. However, some problems were reported: the tree-like structures derived from parsed sentences usually contain unnecessary sub-paths that, although quite useful, may also have misleading information [12]. This paper hypothesizes that filtering and simplification operations which prune non-essential nodes and edges of a graph-based model for sentence representation can improve overall accuracy of RE. Previous work introduced an Inductive Logic Programming-based method [13] that induces symbolic extraction rules suitable to identify semantic relations between entities. Such approach to RE is grounded on a graph-based model of sentences as a hypothesis space for generating candidate extraction rules.

This paper proposes a method to simplify graph-based representations of sentences that replaces dependency graphs of sentences by simpler ones, keeping the target entities in it. The key idea is to speed up the learning phase in the proposed RE framework, by applying several rules for graph simplification that constrain the hypothesis space for generating extraction rules. Additionally, this paper investigates the effects of the simplified graph-based representations on the relation extraction performance. In particular, the effect of such simplification operations as a means to alleviate overfitting in our relation extraction rules is investigated. As a "proof-of-concept", the relation extraction task on protein–protein interactions was chosen to validate the proposed method to simplify the graph-based representations of sentences. Other contributions of this work are:

- the proposal of several rules for syntactic and non-syntactic transformations of a dependency-based graph model for sentence representation;
- an intrinsic evaluation of the proposed rules showing promising results on trimming graph-based representations of sentences;
- a further assessment of the effectiveness of the simplification rules on the performance of relation extraction tasks;
- the development of a tool for visualization of graph-based representations of sentences.

The experimental results show that the proposed approach outperforms other state-of-the-art systems on two PPI corpora test-set, and competitive performance results on a third PPI corpus.

## 2. RELATED WORK

Automatic simplification of sentences was first proposed for improving the performance of parsing tools [5]. Later on, researchers have found other applications for sentence simplification. One of them consists in creating sentences that are shorter, grammatically correct, and information preserving to help people with reading problems [4]. Another application of the technique is related to the automatic text summarization systems [22]. The focus in that work was to preserve only the important content in the final summaries.

Reference [12] presents an application for sentence simplification that is closer related to the one proposed in this paper, since the authors in [9] also describes a sentence simplification method, called "BioSimplify", which was evaluated on relation extraction. The main goal of their method is to improve the performance of biomedical extraction systems by reducing the complexity of sentences that could be hiding protein-protein interactions (relations). Their method can also remove noun phrases that are important for a given relation of interest.

The method presented in this paper differs from that attempt to remove all information outside the target verb and arguments as presented in reference [21]. It also differs from the method proposed in [12] in which the authors attempted to keep all information in a sentence aiming at improving a parser. The approach presented here generates canonical graphs for representing sentences.

## 3. A FRAMEWORK FOR EXTRACTING RELATIONS

The objective of this section is to place the proposed method for transforming graph-based representation of sentences into the context of the main goal of this study. A brief view of the proposed framework for RE and its graph-based model for sentence representation are presented here.

### 3.1 An ILP-based Framework for RE

Reference [13] introduced the main underlying ideas of the method for RE proposed here, called *ILPER (Inductive Logic Programming-based Approach to Entity and Relation Extraction)*, which relies on Inductive Logic Programming (ILP) [16][9], a supervised machine learning technique able to induce *theories*, or a set of logical extraction rules [16]. This set of extraction rules expressed in Prolog is used to classify relation mentions (instances) in textual data. In other words, the ILP framework constitutes the core component for building classification models in ILPER. Furthermore, ILPER takes advantages of ontologies [10] in its RE process. Such ontologies capture the knowledge about a given domain that can be converted as *background knowledge* (BK) by ILPER [13].

An overview of the processing flow performed by ILPER is shown in Fig. 1. After the *Text Preprocessing* step, the annotated documents in XML format are given as input to the step that performs *Graph-based Representation* of *Sentences* integrating several features (lexical, syntactic, and semantic) into a graph (see Section. 3.2). Next, the *Transformation of Graph-based Representation* step (in gray in Fig. 1), the focus of this paper, aims at transforming the graph-based representations of sentences, either by simplifying (reducing) or transforming the graphs. Then, the reduced graphs representing the sentences containing positive and negative examples of relation pairs, e.g., *rel(arg1, arg2)* are passed to the *Background Knowledge Generation* step which exploits a given domain ontology. This ontology provides valuable information (by means of *TBox* and *ABox* axioms [10]) as background knowledge that guides the entire information extraction process. Next, in the *Extraction Rule Learning* step, a general ILP system, provided with the previous BK in the form of *logic programs* as well as custom parameters, induces symbolic extraction rules also expressed as a set of logical programs, or a *theory*, in ILP terms. Using such set of extraction rules, the *Extraction Rule Application* step applies them on examples that had not been used in previous steps, finally resulting in extracted instances of relations that are used for populating a domain ontology.

### 3.2 A Graph-based Model for Sentence Representation

Reference [13] proposed a RE method which employs a rich *relational (graph-based) model* of sentences based on both *structural* and *properties* features that describe mentions of entities and relations. Such features are considered as *logical predicates* that can be exploited by a supervised machine learning technique which induces symbolic extraction rules from examples. This method is based on the principle that the establishment of a relationship between two entities in the same sentence can be obtained, for instance, by a path between them in the graph which that encodes both morpho-syntactical attributes of individual words, and semantic relations between constituent phrases [14].

The representation supporting the proposed RE approach consists of a *graph-based model* of sentences. In this model, a relationship can be specified between *conceptual entities* (instances of classes and relations): each major phrasal constituent (nominal and verbal chunk) in a sentence is considered as a candidate instance for extraction. In other words, all phrases that express tokens or chunking constituents are either potentially referencing real-world concepts or semantic relations defined by a domain ontology of interest. Thus, such relational representation of the syntactic structure of a sentence *S* provided by this graph-based model can be defined as the mapping function $G: S \rightarrow relations\ tuples$.

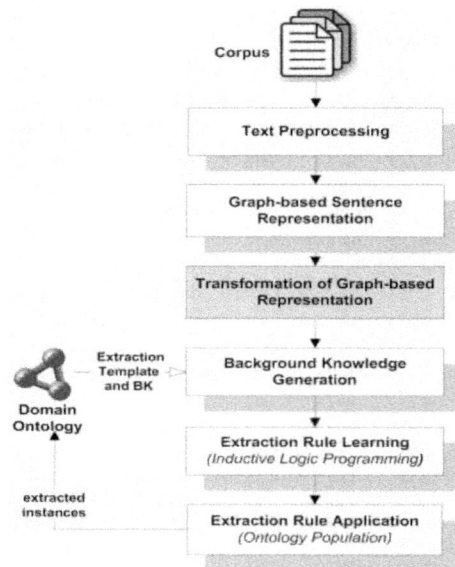

**Figure 1.** Main processing steps of the ILPER approach.

This model integrates a dependency grammar analysis which generates typed dependencies parses of sentences, and finally produces a *dependency graph* [14]. This directed graph is the result of an all-path parsing algorithm based on a dependency grammar [3] in which the resulting syntactic structures are expressed in terms of dependency relations between pairs of words, a *head* and a *modifier*. All derived dependencies of a sentence, define a dependency graph whose root is a word that does not depend on any word. A dependency graph constitutes a very useful data structure for syntactic structuring and subsequent knowledge elicitation from texts.

The typed dependencies proposed in [14] also known as *Stanford dependencies,* were adopted mainly because their advantage as a mean for sentence representation that, when applying simplification rules, one can iteratively apply multiple transformations on the same set of dependency relations [18]. Different variants of the Stanford typed dependency representation are generated by the Stanford parser[1]. The *collapsed tree* representation was adopted, where dependencies involving prepositions, conjunctions, as well as information about the referent of relative clauses, are collapsed to get direct dependencies between content words. Such collapsed representation can simplify the relation extraction process [14]. Fig. 2 depicts an example of a dependency graph of a sentence.

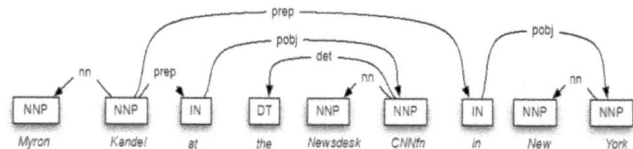

**Figure 2.** Dependency graph of the sentence

In addition, the proposed graph-based model exploits *chunking analysis*, which is useful to define entity boundaries, and the head constituents of nominal, verbal and prepositional phrases. For example, consider the sentence *"Myron Kandel at CNNfn Newsdesk in New York"*. Fig. 3 shows the head tokens of this sentence obtained after a previous chunking analysis. Usually verb phrases are possible candidates for relations, and noun phrases may represent an entity or an instance of a class.

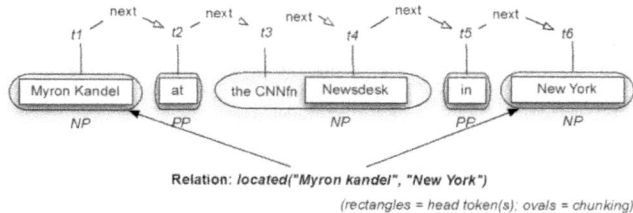

**Figure 3.** Chunking analysis and head tokens of the sentence

In this graph-based model, edges denote *relational features* that can be exploited in the automatic induction of symbolic extraction rules from sentences. In addition, the proposed approach is based on the premise that, when learning about properties of objects in relational domains, feature construction can be guided by the structure of individual objects, which can be used for asserting relationships between two class instances in the same sentence.

An illustrative example of a sentence represented according to the aforementioned graph-based model is depicted in Fig. 4.

---
[1] http://nlp.stanford.edu/software/corenlp.shtml

This graph-based representation of the sentence combines the following elements:

- a *dependency analysis* with collapsed dependencies (e.g. prep_on) according to the Stanford dependency parser;
- a *chunking analysis* (head tokens in bold);
- the *sequencing* of tokens in a sentence (NextToken edges);
- *morpho-syntactic features* as nodes attributes (arrows in gray color); and
- *semantic attributes*, obtained by mapping ontological classes to instances found in text.

Thus, the graph-based model is characterized by a set of binary relations or *predicates*. For the same sentence in Fig. 3, one can recognize several binary relations in it, including *det(Newsdesk, the)*, *nn(Newsdesk,CNNfn)*, *prep_at(Myron-Kandel,Newsdesk)*, and *prep_in(Myron-Kandel, New-York)*.

## 4. TRANFORMING GRAPH-BASED REPRESENTATIONS OF SENTENCES

Syntactic parsing, as performed by state-of-the art NLP tools, commonly constitute one of the first steps (preprocessing) in information extraction systems. However, such tools often neglect the characteristic complexity of long sentences found in biomedical literature. As a result, the syntactic structures as they come directly from such parsers may not always be suitable for relation extraction, mainly for two reasons: they contain a lot of apparently irrelevant lexical nodes and the distracting structural noisy information, as it might occur in the original dependency graphs, may cause overfitting in the classifier learning phase. It is well known that overfitting prevents classifiers of finding more general extraction patterns.

To alleviate this problem, a set of simplification rules to be applied on the sentences represented by the graph-based model introduced in Section 3 is proposed. Such simplification rules attempt to reduce the complexity of the dependency graph-based component employed in ILPER, by eliminating both spurious nodes and relations.

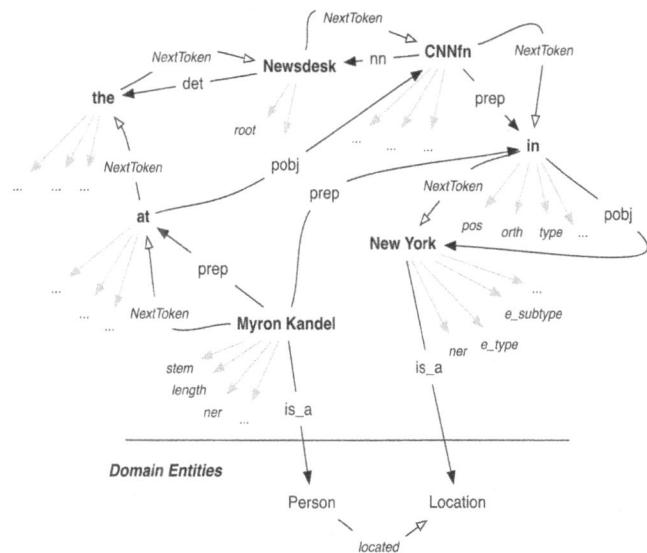

**Figure 4.** The graph-based model of the sentence: "Myron Kandel at the Newsdesk CNNfn in New York".

Therefore, the ultimate goal here is reducing and rearranging the final representation of sentences in ILPER in order to avoid over-fitting of the relational feature space caused by overly specific syntactic and lexical information. One may argue that all proposed trimming/ transformation operations are well-motivated by linguistic aspects, and they should guarantee minimal information loss. On the other hand, one assumes that the meaning of the target sentences itself is less important than keeping the truth-value of the relations, i.e., whether or not there exists a semantic relation between two entities.

In the remainder of this section, the proposed method for simplification of graph-based representation of sentences is introduced.

## 4.1 Method Implementation

The approach to simplify graph-based representation of sentences was implemented as a separate module in the ILPER functional architecture. The decision to decouple the simplification process from the preprocessing step was motivated by the fact that it allows it to be performed separately, taking advantage of previous preprocessed datasets from other domains besides the biomedical domain.

The prototype implemented for validating the proposed approach provides to the user the following options:

**Graph-based model visualization:** It offers the convenient visualization of each sentence in the input corpora according to the graph-based model for sentence representation in ILPER. In addition, the user interface shows the original sentence as well as the simplified version of it.

For graph visualization and manipulation, the software library JUNG[2] (Java Universal Network/Graph Framework) was used. It provides a common and extendible language for the modeling, and visualization of data that can be represented as directed and undirected graphs, among others. Fig. 5 shows a dependency graph generated by the proposed tool.

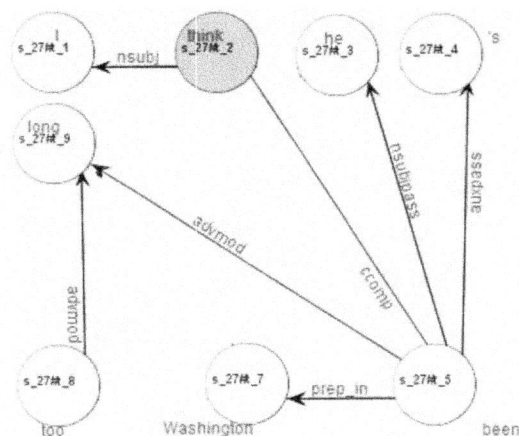

**Figure 5.** Visual dependency parsing representation of the sentence: "I think he´s been in Washington too long". Nodes and edges denote tokens and typed dependency relations, respectively. The gray node is the root (the main verb of the sentence). Node content "s_id#t_id" means: *s_id* denotes the sentence order in the corpus; and *t_id* is the token order in the sentence.

**Basic reduction statistical information**: after choosing the desired set of rules, this module generates, in a .csv file, basic statistics about the simplification process in terms of reduction ratios of tokens, chunks, typed dependencies, entities, etc.

**Ground predicates about nodes (entities) and edges (relations)**: It provides the automatic generation of background knowledge in ILPER framework, in which relational predicates (or features in ILPER) are converted from the previous preprocessing and simplification steps.

## 4.2 Transformation Rules

The graph-based model used in ILPER is used here as the hypothesis space for generating symbolic extraction rules. The proposed simplification rules introduced in this section, only concerns the dependency graph and the chunk sequencing, both constituting the structural predicates in the hypothesis space here.

The term "simplification" must be understood as something which is closer to the *canonical form* of sentences. Therefore, given an input sentence, the aim is to produce a shorter sentence which contains as much information as possible from the original one.

Since the primary objective here is to perform relation extraction on the canonical sentences, the approach adopted to sentence simplification is rather *entity-oriented*, in the sense that it seeks to preserve the minimal relevant contextual information around entities in a dependency graph. This favors the discovery of more general patterns (extraction rules), as they proved to be very useful in improving the overall performance in all biomedical datasets tested here. Furthermore, not only the resulting simplified graphs further constrain the original hypothesis space, but also impacts in less learning time required.

In the proposed simplification approach, a rule transforms a dependency graph (or dependency tree) of a sentence in the sense that some nodes and its outgoing edges, if there are any, can be completely removed from the graph. Another trimming operation on graphs targets the incoming and/or outgoing edges of a given token, which can be reassigned to another different node, or nodes in the same graph.

All rules were defined after a careful study of typical grammatical types of sentences or phrases, and how they are represented in a dependency graph output by the Stanford parser.

The rules have the form: $R_i : \{C_i\} \rightarrow \{A_i\}$, where $C_i$ denotes the *conditional part* which is mainly defined by constraints on nodes POS tags, type of outgoing/incoming edges, parents of nodes, etc; and $A_i$ is just a series of simple actions that are applied on the matched nodes. For instance, most of the rules play the role of *filters* that, given a dependency relation between two nodes e.g., *rel(A, B)*, it removes the $B$ node and the corresponding relation *rel*, leaving the $A$ node unaltered.

One should emphasize that any node not matched by the condition part of the rules remains as they were in the original dependency graph, i.e., no transformation is performed on them.

For convenience, Tab. 1 provides the meaning of the typed dependencies, according to [14], mentioned in the rule descriptions to follow.

---

[2] http://jung.sourceforge.net/

## Table 1. Typed dependency acronyms with related words in italics.

| Dependency | Meaning: Example. |
|---|---|
| det | a noun determiner: "*the* boys..." |
| aux | modal or auxiliary verb: "it *should* appear now." |
| auxpass | a non-main verb of the clause which contains the passive information: "He has done the job: Kennedy has *been* killed". |
| {a\|adv\|part\|t} mod | a noun modifier, such as adverbs, adjective, quantified modifier: "I do not eat *red* meat". |
| predet | it modifies the meaning of a noun determiner: "*All* the boys are here". |
| mark | a subordinate conjunction such as "that", "which": "This is the man *that* I mentioned". |
| ccomp | clausal complement: : *I am certain that* he did it. |
| rcmod | relative clause modifier: "I saw the *man* you *love*". |

Two kinds of rules are addressed: (i) *clause-level* rules, and (ii) *entity-level* rules. In the following, each rule with some illustrated examples[3] is described.

### 4.2.1 Clause-Level Rules

This kind of rule deals with *compound* or more complex sentences, where it is assumed that one of the clauses (main clause) have both entities participating in a relation. Usually the main clause contains the main verb of the sentence, or the root of the dependency graph. The subordinate clauses may contain non-crucial information, and thereby, may be discarded. In fact, before removing a clause, including initial and final adverbial phrases, one checks for the existence of important entities in it. In the case of finding such entities, the option made here was not to exclude them from the graph.

The intuition behind the proposed rules is to try to identify independent clauses from complex sentences. Thus, in order to properly apply the clause-level rules, one needs to first identify whether the sentence is simple, i.e., with just one main verb, or compound. A compound sentence may have or not a relative clause. Thus, to be classified as simple, there should be only one verb sentence and no clausal complement dependency from the set {*comp, csubj, csubjpass, rcmod}. Otherwise, the sentence is complex, or compound. The test whether a compound sentence has the *rcmod* dependency characterizes a relative or subordinate clause.

**R1. Removal of Non-Informative Clauses**

There are three possible positions where subordinate clauses can be embedded in a compound sentence: start, middle, and end. This rule checks for the existence of non-informative clauses in any of these positions. This rule for sentence simplification selects the more important of the two compound clauses in a compound sentence.

A first look at Fig. 6 reveals that the most informative clause is the second one: "the costs will rise". Thus, in order to remove the first sentence, the following rule (pseudo code) removes the first non-informative clause.

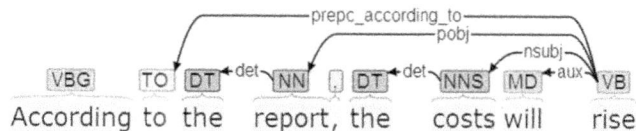

**Figure 6.** Example of a adverbial clause in a sentence: "According to the report"

The pseudo code given below:

```
for each (token tkA of the sentence) do
    if (tkA contains a dep in {prepc_*| dep} with a token tkB ) then
        if ((tkA has POS in{VB*}) and (tkB has POS in
            {DT|JJ|IN|TO}))
        then
            remove {prep_*(tkA, tkB) | dep(tkA, tkB)} from the graph
        end if
    end if
```

**R2. Removal of Attribution Clauses**

This rule is in charge of swapping the role of the main verb, i.e., the root element of the dependency graph in a compound sentence between clauses, as illustrated in Fig. 7. In this example, the verb of the attribution clause is the root of the dependency graph, but the more relevant clause is the other one. Thus, one should swap the roles between the two verbs, accordingly.

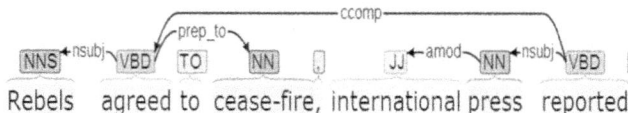

**Figure 7.** Dependency graph of a compound sentence with the attribution clause "international press reported".

The rule that performs that transformation is given below.

```
if (tkA is root) and
    ( tkA POS is in {JJ | VB*} and (tkA dep is not in {dobj|pobj})
        and ( tkA has the dep {ccomp(tkA, tkB)}) and (tkB POS is
            in{VB*} )
    ) then
        tkB is the new root of the sentence S
        remove {ccomp(tkA, tkB)} from the graph
    end if
```

**R3. Subject-Verb-Object Rearrangement**

Particularly in biomedical texts, complex coordinated syntactic structures that link together two or more conjuncts of the same type abound. Such structures pose several problems to dependency parsers. Fig. 8 displays an example where two coordinated verbs (with the *CC* coordinating conjuncts) share the same object. However, just the first verb has a direct link to its object CC via its *dobj* dependency relation. This may also difficult the generation of extraction rules in our framework for relation extraction in the sense that only the first verb has the (*subject-verb-object*) path as a typical pattern used in extraction. Accordingly, this rule looks for such configuration, by checking if chunk sequences (verbal and nominal) appear before and after the conjunction that link similar types of words. The task here consists in propagating the *obj* dependency relation of the first verb by creating a new *obj*

---

[3] The corpus is assumed in the English language.

dependency for the second one, pointing to the same target object (see Fig. 9). Indeed, this rule is generalized by taking into account up to 3 verbs with 3 respective objects in the same sentence. One must be aware that, although this rule does not actually simplify the graph in terms of removing nodes as it was done in other rules presented so far, it was often used in the biomedical corpus tested here.

Tab. 2 provides additional sentences matching the clause-level rules described above.

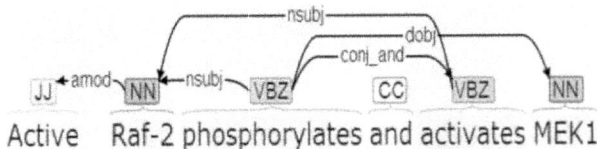

**Figure 8.** Sentence with a coordinating conjunct between verbs.

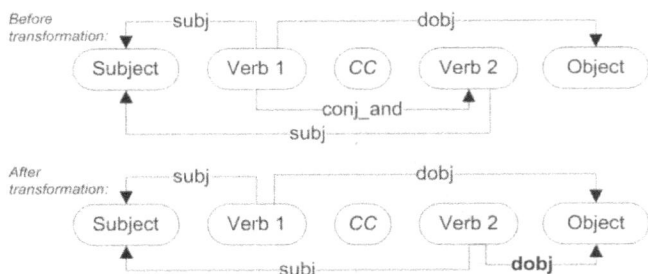

**Figure 9.** *verb-dobj* missing dependency before transformation and its inclusion after transformation (in bold).

**Table 2.** Examples of simplified sentences by clause-level rules. Removed tokens are underlined.

| Rule | Original/Simplified Sentences |
|------|-------------------------------|
| R1 | As a matter of fact, John came into the room while you were talking about him. |
| R2 | On the assumption that mothers stay home with children. |
| R2 | Rebels agreed to talk with government officials, international observers said Tuesday. |
| R2 | It was suggested that Yak1 phosphorylates Crf1 to promote its nuclear entry. |

### 4.2.2 Entity-Level Rules

This kind of rule makes a small change in the graph by acting on one or two nodes.

#### R4. Replacement of Protein/Genes Names

Single terms or noun in a sentence are stemmed, i.e., we keep its *lemma* or *root*. Thus, plurals and verb tenses are reduced to singular and infinitive form, respectively. Although this rule does not reduce the sentence in number of tokens, it helps generalization over specific protein/genes names.

#### R5. Treatment of Multi-word Entities

This rule deals with the *nn* dependencies or *noun compound modifiers* of another noun node. For instance, the dependency graph in Fig. 10 shows two multi-words terms, or noun chunks: "Nevada Corporation" and "United States" (Fig. 10). There are two *nn* dependencies (labeled edges) with the same governor term "Corporation", which is also identified as the head noun of the noun

chunk. Thus, this rule checks for head tokens with *nn* edges outgoing from them, and concatenate these words in a multi-word term by a hyphen, but keeping a reference to its head noun.

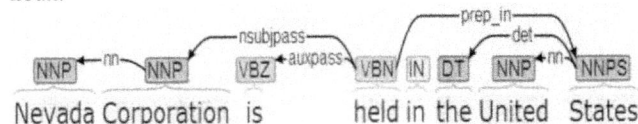

**Figure 10.** Parsed sentence with two *nn* dependencies.

#### R6. Removal of Distracting Dependencies

Aiming at pruning syntactic determiners, auxiliaries, modals, and all the tokens other than the head noun, this rule removes from a given sentence, any of the dependency relations belonging to the set: {*det, aux, auxpass, amod, predet, advmod, partmod, tmod, mark*}. However, before removing such dependencies, one needs to verify if the node candidate to deletion is a leaf in the graph. Examples of sentences containing such types of dependencies are shown in Tab. 3.

**Table 3.** Examples of sentences simplified by entity-level rules. Removed or modified tokens are underlined.

| Rule | Original/Simplified Sentences |
|------|-------------------------------|
| R2+R6 | I think he´s been in Washington too long. |
| R6 | However, cytokines, in particular IL-2 and IL4, ... |
| R5 | Nevada-Corporation is held in the United-States. |
| R5+R6 | Mutations in CBP have recently been identified in RTS-patients. |
| R6 | You are the girl that I am looking for. |

### 4.2.3 A Minimal Example

Fig. 11 presents the reduced dependency graph of the sentence introduced in subsection 4.1. It should be highlighted that this graph minimally retains the core information for the relation *located_in(he, Washington)*.

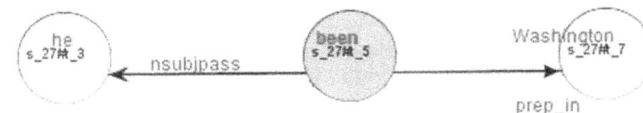

**Figure 11.** Reduced dependency graph of the sentence "I think he´s been in Washington too long" in the visual graph reduction and representation tool developed.

**Rule Application Order.** The application order of rules in the approach proposed must be considered with special attention due to the "loss of information" that is achieved after each individual rule has taken place. Thus, in order to avoid misleading results, the rules are applied in the following order: *R4, R5, R1, R2, R3,* and *R6*.

## 5. EMPIRICAL EVALUATION

This section details the experiments and results related to the PPI extraction task using several combinations of the simplification rules. In what follows, after introducing the PPI corpora, the evaluation methodology is described.

## 5.1 Datasets

The proposed transformation rules of graph-based representations of sentences were evaluated in two distinct scenarios:

(i) *intrinsic assessment*, in which the basis statistics on the reduction ratios of the simplification rules were investigated (Section 5.3); and,

(ii) *extrinsic assessment*, which takes the simplified graphs as input into ILPER framework (Section 5.4).

For both aforementioned evaluation scenarios, three standard PPI datasets on biomedical domain were selected. The following PPI datasets are considered more complex than normal English texts:

- *Learning Language in Logic (LLL)* [17]. This dataset was proposed to the genic interaction task from a set of sentences concerning Bacillus subtilis transcription.
- *HPRD50* [8]. It consists of a randomly selected subset of 50 abstracts referenced by the Human Protein Reference Database (HPRD).
- *Interaction Extraction Performance Assessment (IEPA)*[7] It consists of a corpus containing 303 abstracts from PubMed, each containing a specific pair of co-occurring chemicals.

Tab. 4 summarizes the basic statistics on these datasets.

**Table 4.** Basic statistics of three corpora for RE

| Corpus | #Sentences | #E+ | #E- |
|--------|-----------|-----|-----|
| LLL | 77 | 164 | 166 |
| HPRD50 | 145 | 163 | 270 |
| IEPA | 486 | 335 | 482 |

## 5.2 Evaluation Metrics and ILPER Setting

*Evaluation Metrics.* Several experiments were conducted aiming at assessing the effectiveness of the proposed approach on the 3 PPI corpora. The performance evaluation is based on the IR classical measures, i.e., Precision $P$, Recall $R$, and $F1$-measure [2]. The Area Under the Receiver Operating Characteristics (*AUC*) as suggested in [1] was also used in the evaluations.

*Cross-Validation (CV).* All models reported here were created using 10-fold cross validation. This allows for both the maximal use of the available training data, and the comparison with related work.

*ILPER Setting.* The main goal of the learning component in ILPER consists of building models from a training set of examples. However, for building models with high classification accuracy and good generalization power, it is necessary to find optimal parameters in the first place. Accordingly, several preliminary experiments for determining the best parameters for this particular RE scenario were conducted.

As a result, the best setting for the ILP parameters was selected, according to following criteria: maximizing accuracy performance and avoiding model *overfitting*. These parameters were obtained using a separate test dataset, i.e., a dataset with no previously used examples. The parameter setting in all experiments reported in this section were: *theory_construction = global, evaluation_function = coverage, i = 3, and minimum _positive_examples = 3*.

## 5.3 Results on Graph Transformations

Four different combinations of simplification rules (see Section 4), or *Filters* were used in all experiments reported in this section. The set of rules that compose each filter is shown in Tab. 5. As it can be noticed, they gradually become more restrictive, i.e., the filter in the last row of the table is composed of the preceding

filters. Besides the *baseline filter* (*No Filter* in Tab. 5), denoting the case where no transformation rule is applied, four different combinations of simplification rules (see Section 4), or simply *filters*, were provided.

**Table 5.** Filters used in the experiments.

| Filter | Rules composing the filter |
|--------|---------------------------|
| *No Filter* | No rule application |
| *Filter 1* | R4 + R5 + R6 on dependencies in {*det, aux, auxpass*} |
| *Filter 2* | R4 + R5 + R6 on dependencies in {*det, aux, auxpass, amod, predet, advmod, partmod, tmod, mark* } |
| *Filter 3* | Filter 2 + R1 + R2 |
| *Filter 4* | Filter 3 + R3 |

The analysis here starts with the overall results of the transformation/simplification process itself with its basic statistics taken into consideration that are reported in Tab. 6. The average number of tokens and dependencies per sentence, compared to the original version of the dataset (with no reduction) and the final version applying all simplification rules are shown in Tab. 6. As expected, for all datasets, the number of nodes or tokens in the graph-based representation of sentences, and dependencies, the edges in this same graph are considerably reduced by the proposed simplification rules. One should note that the average number of nodes is always slightly less than the number of the edges in our representation graphs. This can be explained by the fact that several tokens or nodes of the sentences are removed, e.g., determiners and prepositions, contrarily to the dependencies (edges) that still remains in the simplified version of the graph. For instance, if one considers the following prepositional phrase "tears in heaven", where the token denoting the preposition is removed from the graph and it is created the edge *prep_in(tears, heaven)* in the graph.

Tab. 7 shows the simplification ratio, in terms of the number of edges, for all datasets and all filters. Again, the more restrictive filters further reduce the number of edges in the graphs. According to the results reported in this table, the minimum (12%) and the maximum reduction ratio (35%) for the IEPA and the LLL datasets were obtained, respectively.

**Table 6.** Average number of nodes and dependencies per sentence before/after transformation

| | LLL | | HPDR50 | | IEPA | |
|---|---|---|---|---|---|---|
| | **No filter** | **All filters** | **No filter** | **All filters** | **No filter** | **All filters** |
| Average #nodes/sent | 20.3 | 13.3 | 18.4 | 13.1 | 22.0 | 15.4 |
| Average #depend/sent | 20.4 | 13.2 | 18.8 | 13.4 | 22.9 | 16.0 |

**Table 7.** Reduction of the number of dependencies per filter in percentage points (%)

| | LLL | HPDR | IEP |
|---|-----|------|-----|
| Filter 1 | 17.31 | 12.50 | 12.08 |
| Filter 2 | 19.29 | 14.74 | 14.20 |
| Filter 3 | 28.26 | 24.01 | 25.03 |
| Filter 4 | 35.07 | 28.75 | 29.91 |

Besides the direct effect on the extraction results, the reduced version of the graphs also has a significant impact on reducing the training time. In reality, a reduction up to 15% in training time was obtained using the simplified versions for the datasets in all experiments in this section. The experiments were performed on an Intel Core 2 Duo, 2.30 GHz with 6 GB of RAM on Linux. GILPS[4] was executed on YAP Prolog 6.2.2[5].

Going deeper into the types of the dependencies reduced from the IEPA dataset using Filter 4, i.e., the more restrict, it is obtained the results shown in Tab. 8. This filter removes all of the determiners, verb auxiliaries and markers (like "that") from the IEPA corpus. The modifiers including adjective, temporal, and quantifiers are severely reduced from the original version of the dataset. The same occurs to some dependencies representing the subject and clausal complement of the sentences, due to the clausal-level simplification rules defined in Section 4, which only removes the non-informational clauses in sentences, leaving untouched the other more informational ones.

**Table 8.** Number of the typed dependencies removed from the IEPA corpus using the Filter 4

| Dep. | det | aux | mark | *mod | advcl | nsubj | ccomp |
|------|-----|-----|------|------|-------|-------|-------|
| No filter | 956 | 593 | 169 | 1632 | 79 | 919 | 179 |
| Filter 4 | 0 | 0 | 0 | 113 | 72 | 829 | 60 |

## 5.4 Performance on PPI Extraction

The ILPER framework presented in Section 3.1 was used in the experiments to evaluate the proposed method for simplifying the graph-based representations of sentences. In the experiments on PPI extraction, the filters showed in Tab. 5 were applied on the original version of each dataset described in Section 5.1. The resulting simplified versions of the PPI were used by ILPER for training. Table 9 reports on the results obtained for each modified versions of the datasets. The baseline for comparisons in this experiment was established as indicated by "No Filter".

A first look at Tab. 9 reveals that the overall average result in terms of *P*, *R*, and consequently *F1*, was consistently higher than the baseline score for all datasets. On the other hand, taking the filters individually, one can see that the only case where a filter hampered a little bit the recall score was for the *Filter 2* of the HPRD50 dataset, but for all the filters in the other datasets, the simplified versions of the dataset achieved better results. Such results suggest that all evaluated corpora may profit from the application of the transformation/simplification rules proposed in the present work.

The best filter seems to be *Filter 2* on the LLL dataset and *Filter 1* for the other datasets. Interestingly, *Filters 3* and *Filter 4* practically had the same performance in terms of *P/R/F1* on the LLL dataset. An explanation for such results is probably due to the size of such dataset. Indeed, the LLL dataset has less than 100 sentences, and the system could not found any sentence for applying the *R3* rule using this dataset. On the contrary, with the other larger datasets, especially for the IEPA dataset which contains 480 sentences, the difference between the results of *Filter 3* and *Filter 4* is more noticeable.

The last row of Tab. 9 shows the difference in performance in percentage points between the average F1 score of the filters, and its related baseline score. According to the results reported in Tab. 9, we can expect a improvement in terms of both precision and recall, since the difference between the average of all filters and the baseline performance (*No Filter*) is always positive. In fact, the extraction rules that were induced using the simplified versions of the graphs were slightly more precise (in average 2.9 points) than the same rules induced without any simplification. In particular to the IEPA dataset, the same line of this table shows a significant improvement in precision of 4.8 percentage points.

**Table 9.** Performance results on PPI extraction using the filters.

| Filter | LLL | | | HPRD50 | | |
|--------|-----|-----|-----|--------|-----|-----|
| | P | R | F | P | R | F |
| *No Filter* | 80.9 | 67.9 | 73.8 | 68.4 | 68.4 | 68.4 |
| Filter 1 | 80.8 | 74.0 | 77.3 | **72.6** | **78.2** | **75.3** |
| Filter 2 | **84.2** | **76.1** | **79.9** | 69.3 | 66.9 | 68.1 |
| Filter 3 | 82.8 | 75.3 | 78.9 | 70.2 | 73.7 | 71.9 |
| Filter 4 | 82.8 | 75.3 | 78.9 | 69.9 | 73.2 | 71.5 |
| *Avg. all filters* | 82.7 | 75.2 | 78.8 | 70.5 | 73.0 | 71.7 |
| *Diff. to base-* | 1.8 | **7.3** | 5.0 | 2.1 | **4.6** | 3.3 |

| Filter | IEPA | | |
|--------|------|-----|-----|
| | P | R | F |
| *No Filter* | 64.1 | 75.5 | 69.3 |
| Filter 1 | **71.7** | **81.0** | **76.1** |
| Filter 2 | 68.7 | 76.2 | 72.3 |
| Filter 3 | 68.6 | 71.7 | 70.1 |
| Filter 4 | 66.6 | 77.5 | 71.6 |
| *Average of all filters* | 68.9 | 76.6 | 72.5 |
| *Diff. to baseline* | **4.8** | 1.1 | 3.2 |

Considering the difference between averaged recall scores and their corresponding baseline performance scores shown in the last line of Tab. 9, the results were even more promising (up to 7% to on the LLL dataset). Indeed, the improvement in recall on all datasets in this experiment supports the working hypothesis raised here that a previous transformation step, carried out before the relation extraction task, can improve overall extraction results, mainly alleviating overfitting of the extraction rules automatically induced by ILPER. In other words, the rules induced using the simplified versions of the graphs were able to generalize more examples, as demonstrated by the consistent higher recall values for all dataset, and notably for the LLL and HPRD50 datasets. However, contrarily to what was expected, it was on precision, instead of recall, that the filters contributed more for the IEPA dataset.

Tab. 10 summarizes the detailed results of the Tab. 9 showing the percentage gain relative to the baseline performance of each filter.

**Table 10.** Relative gain (in F1) of the filters to the baseline.

| Relative Gain | LLL | HPRD50 | IEPA |
|---------------|-----|--------|------|
| Filter 1 | 3.50 | **6.90** | **6.80** |
| Filter 2 | **6.10** | -0.30 | 3.00 |
| Filter 3 | 5.10 | 3.50 | 0.80 |
| Filter 4 | 5.10 | 3.10 | 2.30 |
| *Average rel. gain* | 4.95 | 3.30 | 3.23 |

---

[4] General Inductive Logic Programming System (GILPS). http://www.doc.ic.ac.uk/~jcs06/GILPS
[5] Yet Another Prolog. http://www.dcc.fc.up.pt/~vsc/Yap

The highest relative gain in terms of *F1* was obtained on the LLL dataset. Interestingly, the only case in which the *Filter 2* was not good for the PPI extraction occurred on the dataset HPRD50. By contrast, *Filter 1* achieved the best *F1* score on the HPRD50 and IEPA datasets.

One can draw to the conclusion that, the proposed filters fit well to relation extraction as they significantly improve the relation extraction results in both precision (2.9 in average) and recall (4.36 in average) when evaluated on three PPI corpora used in this study. In addition, *Filter 1* is the best filter to choose in future applications, as they do not remove too many nodes from the graphs, while improving the overall extraction results. However, if one wants to reduce the size of the training data to a minimum possible, while keeping the overall accuracy of the extraction rules, *Filter 4* seems to be the right choice.

### 5.4.1 Comparative Evaluation

A comparative assessment was conducted with the aim of positioning our contribution against related work. For these experiments, the same PPI datasets evaluated in the previous section were used. All compared classification models, excluding the ones proposed by us, are based on Support Vector Machines [6], a state-of-the-art in ML research community. The evaluation is carried out using 10-fold cross-validation.

Besides the traditional evaluation measures of *precision P*, recall *R*, and F1-measure, and the results in terms of AUC are also reported. AUC is as alternative to *F1* score, which is invariant to the class distribution of the test dataset. In other words, AUC is not biased in the case of unbalanced dataset a major difference in positive/negative ratio in the test set [1]. In addition, all comparative test to determine whether an improvement of performance is statistically significant or not is based on the t-Student paired test in which null hypothesis is rejected for values of $p <= 0.005$. These comparative results are reported in Tab. 11, where the highest scores for *F1* are in bold, whereas the best AUC score are in italics.

The original models without any filter and the best filtered models discussed in the previous section are indicated by the column entitled *New Model (no simplification)* and New *Simple Model* in Tab. 11, respectively. As already discussed in the previous section, the former statistically outperforms the latter. Table 11 also indicates that the model proposed here ("Simplified Model") is the best on the HPRD50 dataset. On the other hand, the PPI extraction method recently introduced by Quian & Zhou [19] achieved the best performance on the LLL corpus.

On the IEPA dataset, the simplified model takes the second position in the rank of the best models (*F1*) assessed on the IEPA dataset, being the first position occupied by the model proposed in reference [15]. It worth stressing that the boost in performance was due to the transformation rules that significantly contributed to the overall second position. Actually, that is the only system analyzed that performs a simplification step somewhat similar to the one proposed in this paper.

Reference [15] proposes a set of sentence simplification rules focuses on entities. Their method for sentence simplification consists of two groups of rules: clause-selection which constructs a simpler sentence by removing noisy information before the relevant clause; and the entity-phrase rules that simplifies an entity-containing region. More concretely, the clause-selection rules remove some marker of relative clauses, copula phrases, and some non-information clauses, while the entity-phrase rules removes coordination, parenthesis involving entities, and appositions.

The work presented here differs from the proposed by Miwa and colleagues [15] mainly with respect to the type of rules, and the target syntactical constructions of the sentences to be simplified. Furthermore, the method presented here is based on the typed-dependencies given by a dependency parser, while in [15] a constituent parser was used. As a result, the rules presented here tend to be simpler in the sense that the graphs derived by a dependency par. Besides that, they tend also to be more robust to the order of the target entities and clauses in the sentence. It is a well-known fact that contrarily to dependency parsers, rules based on the output of constituent parsers have to consider the exact position of the target elements in a sentence [3]. To the best of the knowledge of the authors of this paper, this work is the first to propose simplification rules for relation extraction purposes relying on the output of a dependency parser.

## 6. CONCLUSIONS AND FUTHER WORK

This paper introduced a method for simplifying graph-based representations of sentences using transformation rules applied on typed dependency graphs. Such graphs consist of one of the elements that constitute the graph-based model of sentence representation in ILPER, an ILP-based framework for extracting relation instances from textual data. ILPER was used in two important tasks in this study: (i) for performing PPI extraction tasks from three standard biomedical datasets; (ii) and to verify our working hypothesis that a previous transformation step, carried out before the relation extraction task, can improve overall extraction results, specially alleviating over fitting of the extraction rules automatically induced by ILPER.

The overall results on the simplified sentence representations achieved an average increase of almost 4%, in terms of recall, compared to their original versions. The proposed simplification rules also proved very effective in the sense that they allowed for a statistically significant boost in performance when tested using three biomedical corpora. The obtained results also outperformed other state-of-the-art systems evaluated using the same datasets.

Despite the encouraging results achieved by this study, there is still room for further work and improvements in different aspects. First, the evaluation of the simplification rules on other biomedical datasets is an important issue. Second, the inclusion of additional rules to deal with other sentence constructions, including the removal of irrelevant noun appositive, gerundive, and nonrestrictive clauses is also planned. The application or adaptation of the underlying ideas of the proposed simplification method on other text mining tasks, especially automatic text summarization [24] [25] is also part of the work plan. Finally, functional experiments will be performed in order to analyze the possible improvements brought to the search behavior of the sentence representation and simplifications introduced in this paper.

## ACKNOWLEDGEMENTS
The research results reported in this paper have been partly funded by a R&D project between Hewlett-Packard Brazil and UFPE originated from tax exemption (IPI Law no 8.248 of 1991 and later updates).

Table 11. Comparative evaluation of the systems tested in three different corpora.

| Corpus | New Model (no simplif.) | | New Simple Model | | Miwa et al. (2010) [15] | | Quian/Zhou (2012) [19] | | Tikk et al. (2010) [20] | | Airola et al. (2008) [1] | |
|---|---|---|---|---|---|---|---|---|---|---|---|---|
| | F1 | AUC | F1 | AUC | F1 | AUC | F1 | AUC | F1 | AUC | F1 | AUC |
| LLL | 73. | 82.0 | 79.9 | 85.2 | 82.9 | *90.5* | **84.6** | 89.9 | 79.1 | 86.8 | 76.8 | 83.4 |
| HPRD50 | 68. | 86.8 | **75.3** | *87.6* | 75.0 | 86.6 | 68.8 | 83.7 | 69.7 | 84.0 | 63.4 | 79.7 |
| IEPA | 69. | 84.9 | 76.1 | 87.2 | **77.8** | *88.7* | 69.8 | 82.8 | 70.7 | 81.0 | 75.1 | 85.1 |

# REFERENCES

[1] Airola, A., Pyysalo, S., Björne, J., Pahikkala, T., Ginter, F. , and Salakoski, T. 2008. All-paths graph kernel for protein–protein interaction extraction with evaluation of cross corpus learning, *BMC Bioinformatics* 9:S2.

[2] Baeza-Yates, R. A., and Ribeiro-Neto, B. 1999. *Modern Information Retrieval*. Addison-Wesley Longman Publishing, USA.

[3] Buyko, E., Faessler, E., Wermter, J., and Hahn, U. 2011. Syntactic Simplification and Semantic Enrichment: Trimming Dependency Graphs for Event Extraction. *Computational Intelligence*, 27(4): 610-644.

[4] Carroll, J., Minnen, G., Canning, Y., Devlin, S., and Tait, J. 1998. Practical simplification of English newspaper text to assist aphasic readers. In *Proceedings. of AAAI*, 7–10.

[5] Chandrasekar, R., and Srinivas, B. 1997. Automatic induction rules for text simplification. *Knowledge-Based Systems*, vol. 10, 183–190.

[6] Choi, S.-P., Lee. S., Jung, H., Song, S. 2013. An intensive case study on kernel-based relation extraction. *Proc. Multimedia Tools and Applications*, Springer, US, 1-27.

[7] Ding J., Berleant, D., Nettleton, D., and Wurtele, E. 2002. Mining MEDLINE: abstracts, sentences, or phrases? *Proc. of the Pacific Symposium on Biocomputing*, 326-337

[8] Fundel, K., Kuffner, R., and Zimmer, R. 2007. RelEx-Relation extraction using dependency parse trees. *Bioinformatics*, 23(3), 365-371.

[9] Fürnkranz, J., Gamberger, D., and Lavrac, N. 2012. *Foundations of Rule Learning*, Springer-Verlag.

[10] Hitzler, P., Krötzsch, M., and Rudolph, S. 2009. *Foundations of Semantic Web Technologies*. Chapman & Hall/CRC.

[11] Jiang, J., and Zhai, C. 2007. A systematic exploration of the feature space for relation extraction. In *NAACL HLT*.

[12] Jonnalagadda, S. and Gonzalez, G. 2009. Sentence Simplification Aids Protein-Protein Interaction Extraction. In *Proc. of the 3rd International Symposium on Languages in Biology and Medicine (LBM'09)*, (November), 8-10.

[13] Lima, R. J., Espinasse, B., Oliveira, H. T. A., Pentagrossa, L., and Freitas, F. 2013. Information Extraction from the Web: An Ontology-based Method using Inductive Logic Programming. *Int. Conf. on Tools for Artificial Intelligence (ICTAI)*, 741-748.

[14] Marneffe, C. D., and Manning, C. D. 2008. Stanford Dependencies Manual. Stanford University.

[15] Miwa, M., Saetre R., Miyao, Y., and Tsujii, J. 2010. Entity-Focused Sentence Simplification for Relation Extraction. In *23rd Int. Conf. on Computational Linguistics*, 788-796.

[16] Muggleton, S. 2001. *Inductive Logic Programming*. New Generation Computing. Tokyo, Japan.

[17] Nédellec, C. 2005. Learning language in logic – genic interaction extraction challenge. In *Proceedings of the 4th Learning Language in Logic Workshop*, 31-37.

[18] Siddharthan, A. 2011. Text simplification using typed dependencies: a comparison of the robustness of different generation strategies. In Proc. of the 13th European Workshop on Natural Language Generation (ENLG '11). Association for Comp. Linguistics, Stroudsburg, PA, USA, 2-11.

[19] Qian, L., and Zhou, G. 2012. Tree kernel-based protein-protein interaction extraction from biomedical literature. *Journal of Biomedical Informatics,* 45(3), 535-543.

[20] Tikk, D., Thomas, P. E., Palaga, P., Hakenberg, J., Leser, U. 2010. A Comprehensive Benchmark of Kernel Methods to Extract Protein-Protein Interactions from Literature., *PLoS Computational Biology,* 6 (7).

[21] Vickrey, D., and Koller, D. 2008. Sentence simplification for semantic role labeling. In *Proceedings of ACL-08: HLT*, 344–352. Association for Computational Linguistics.

[22] Zajic D., Dorr J., Lin J., and Schwartz, R. 2007. Multi-candidate reduction: Sentence compression as a tool for document summarization tasks. In *Information Processing and Management Special Issue on Summarization*, Vol. 43, No. 6, 1549-1570.

[23] Zhou, G. D., and Zhang, M. 2007. Extracting relation information from text documents by exploring various types of knowledge. Inf. *Process. Management.* 43, 969–982.

[24] Ferreira. R., Cabral, L. S., Freitas, F., Lins, R. D., Silva, G. F., Simske, S. J., Favaro, L. 2014. A multi-document summarization system based on statistics and linguistic treatment, *Expert Systems with Applications*, Volume 41, Issue 13, (October), 5780-5787.

[25] Ferreira, R., Cabral, L. S., Lins, R. D., Silva, G. F., Freitas, F., Cavalcanti, G. C., Lima, R., Simske, S. J., Favaro, L. 2013. Assessing sentence scoring techniques for extractive text summarization, Expert Systems with Applications, Volume 40, Issue 14, (October), 5755-5764

# Ruling Analysis and Classification of Torn Documents

Markus Diem
Computer Vision Lab
Vienna University of
Technology
Vienna, Austria
diem@caa.tuwien.ac.at

Florian Kleber
Computer Vision Lab
Vienna University of
Technology
Vienna, Austria
kleber@caa.tuwien.ac.at

Robert Sablatnig
Computer Vision Lab
Vienna University of
Technology
Vienna, Austria
sab@caa.tuwien.ac.at

## ABSTRACT

A ruling classification is presented in this paper. In contrast to state-of-the-art methods which focus on ruling line removal, ruling lines are analyzed for document clustering in the context of document snippet reassembling. First, a background patch is extracted from a snippet at a position which minimizes the inscribed content. A novel Fourier feature is then computed on the image patch. The classification into *void*, *lined* and *checked* is carried out using Support Vector Machines. Finally, an accurate line localization is performed by means of projection profiles and robust line fitting. The ruling classification achieves an F-score of 0.987 evaluated on a dataset comprising real world document snippets. In addition the line removal was evaluated on a synthetically generated dataset where an F-score of 0.931 is achieved. This dataset is made publicly available so as to allow for benchmarking.

## Categories and Subject Descriptors

I.4 [**Image Processing and Computer Vision**]: Miscellaneous; I.7.4 [**Document and Text Processing**]: Document Capture—*Document Analysis*

## General Terms

Document Analysis; Ruling Analysis; Ruling Classification

## 1. INTRODUCTION

Ruling analysis is proposed for applications such as music score analysis [10], form analysis [18, 17] or handwriting processing [9, 3]. The former two applications detect ruling for further analysis or segmentation tasks while in the latter ruling is assumed to be noise, needed to be removed in a pre-processing step [1, 9]. If ruling lines in handwritten documents are considered, a few properties can be derived as presented by D. Lopresti and E. Kavallieratou [9]. Ruling lines have a uniform contrast, thickness, orientation and spacing within a page. They are – on purpose – brighter than the writing which overlaps with ruling.

*DocEng'14,* September 16–19, 2014, Fort Collins, Colorado, USA.
Copyright 2014 ACM 978-1-4503-2949-1/14/09 ...$15.00.
http://dx.doi.org/10.1145/2644866.2644876

Y. Zheng et al. [18] extract ruling lines in forms using Directional Single-Connected Chains (DSCC). They analyze white runs in binary images in order to detect lines. *Abnormal* run-lengths and crossings are removed so that lines which are merged with other foreground elements (e.g. text) get isolated. A dynamic length threshold, which is estimated based on the character size, rejects short lines such that lines of characters are not removed. This methodology is fast and able to extract clean lines present in document images without degrading foreground elements. However, broken ruling lines that occur due to the properties previously mentioned cannot be extracted using the DSCC. In order to overcome this drawback, Y. Zheng et al. [17] extend the algorithm. In this approach they again detect lines in the binary image using DSCCs. Then, a Hidden Markov Model HMM is trained on the document's Projection Profiles (PP) for accurate line positioning. Finally, lines are represented by polylines which account for non-rigid distortions present due to bad storage or digitization conditions.

W. Abd-Almageed et al. [1] present a ruling line removal for handwritten documents. For each pixel in the binary image features are computed within a local neighborhood based on central and statistical moments (standard deviation and kurtosis). The pixels are then classified into *line* or *non-line* pixels using a linear subspace. Though this algorithm has a potential for general line detection scenarios (no assumption about line parallelism or uniform spacing is incorporated), it tends to classify stroke endings of characters, ruling lines close to text, and noisy lines falsely.

D. Lopresti and E. Kavallieratou [9] present a ruling line removal based on a scanning approach. Lines are initialized in the left and right area of a page and the mean line slope and thickness are derived. Then, each column is scanned for pixel groups that have a similar thickness and are potentially on a line that was detected during initialization. The line slope and position is iteratively updated to account for quantization errors. Recently, J. Chen and D. Lopresti [3] present a ruling line detection for handwritten documents. A rough estimation of potential ruling lines is made by a simplified Hough transform. Then, broken line segments are clustered using Sequential Clustering. A multi-line linear regression finds a global optimum in the sense of Least Square Error (LSE) of ruling lines.

In contrast to state-of-the-art methods, this work focuses on ruling analysis for document clustering. The subjects of investigation are manually torn Stasi records. Due to the number of snippets ($\approx$ 600 million), documents need to be grouped before reassembling so as to minimize the number of comparisons [11]. Beside text analysis [6], the ruling is analyzed for document grouping and – if present – accurate snippet alignment. The ruling analysis classifies snippets into *void*, *lined* and *checked*. In addition, it performs a line localization that can subsequently be used for snippet alignment and removal if ruling is present.

Figure 1 shows an example of each ruling class. For both ruled classes (*lined*, *checked*), the ruling is clearly visible and in c) the text does not cover the entire snippet which improves the ruling classification. In contrast to this, Figure 2 shows challenging examples. The first example (a,b) is *lined* but the horizontal lines have hardly any recognizable contrast. In b) the contrast is stretched for an improved illustration. Note that the histogram stretching additionally increases the noise and renders extruded pen strokes from other pages visible. The last two images (c,d) show a similar example with *checked* paper. Here, the histogram stretching d) shows scanning artifacts that can be traced back to the low contrast.

**Figure 1: A snippet of each ruling class** *void* **a),** *lined* **b) and** *checked* **c).**

In addition to the methodology proposed in this paper, a synthetic dataset is presented that can be used to empirically evaluate the performance of ruling line removal and compare different approaches. The dataset is based on images from the ICDAR 2013 Handwriting Segmentation Contest [12] and contains in total 600 handwritten images. The dataset together with an evaluation script can be downloaded from: `http://caa.tuwien.ac.at/cvl/research/ruling-database/`.

The remainder of the paper is organized as follows. Section 2 outlines the approach proposed including background localization, feature extraction, classification and ruling line localization. The method presented is evaluated in Section 3 with respect to the classification performance and the line localization. Finally, the paper is concluded in Section 4.

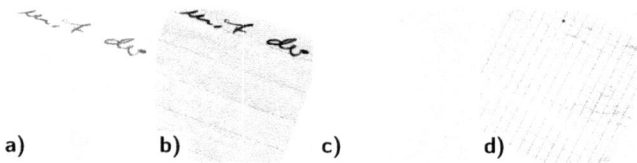

**Figure 2: Challenging ruling examples. Low contrast ruling lines in a) and c). After a manual histogram stretch in b) and d) the ruling lines are visible with the ancillary effect of amplified noise.**

## 2. METHODOLOGY

The ruling analysis can be divided into four modules (see Figure 3). First, a rectangle which maximizes background pixels, and thus minimizes the inscribed content, is estimated. Then, features are extracted from this patch. A classifier labels documents in one of the three classes mentioned previously. If ruling is present, an accurate ruling line estimation is performed. Depending on the application, ruling lines can be removed after this processing stage.

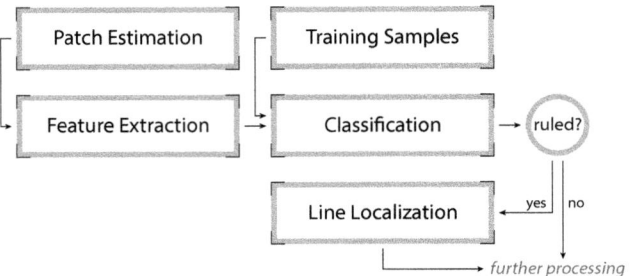

**Figure 3: Ruling analysis processing pipeline proposed in this paper.**

### 2.1 Patch Extraction

Ruling lines are repeated with a fixed line frequency. For classification, a homogeneous frequency is assumed for a whole snippet. In real world scenarios local frequency changes might occur because of scanning artifacts (paper is moved while scanning) or documents imperfectly pieced together. In order to speed up the computation, a patch of maximal $512 \times 512$ px is extracted. The reason for the patch size being 512 px is discussed in Section 3. An area filter is applied so that a patch with maximal background is detected in a page. The maximum of the filtered image indicates the region which contains most background pixels. Figure 4 shows a sample document a), its filtering result b) and the resulting image patch (blue rectangle). The area filter is visualized using pseudo color to increase its contrast.

A convolution using large kernels is slow if it is computed in the spatial domain (for area filtering a $512 \times 512$ px kernel is needed). Since an area filter is symmetric, two convolutions can be applied successively with a row and a column filter to speed up the computation. According to the convolution theorem [2], a convolution in the spatial domain is equal to a multiplication in the Discrete Fourier Transform (DFT) domain and vice versa. Hence, transforming an image to the DFT and back is faster than convolving it in the spatial domain if large kernels ($M > 256$) are used.

Because we are dealing with an area filter – which is a box filter – the convolution speed can be further improved using integral images which were first introduced for texture mapping in computer graphics [5] and later extended for general filtering tasks [15]. Hence, filtering using integral images is constant with respect to the kernel size. In order to filter images with this method, an integral image is first computed by summing each pixel with its left and lower pixel:

$$I_i(x,y) = I(x,y) + I(x,y-1) + I(x-1,y) \qquad (1)$$

where $I_i(x,y)$ is the resulting integral image of an image $I(x,y)$. In this way, each pixel value represents the area

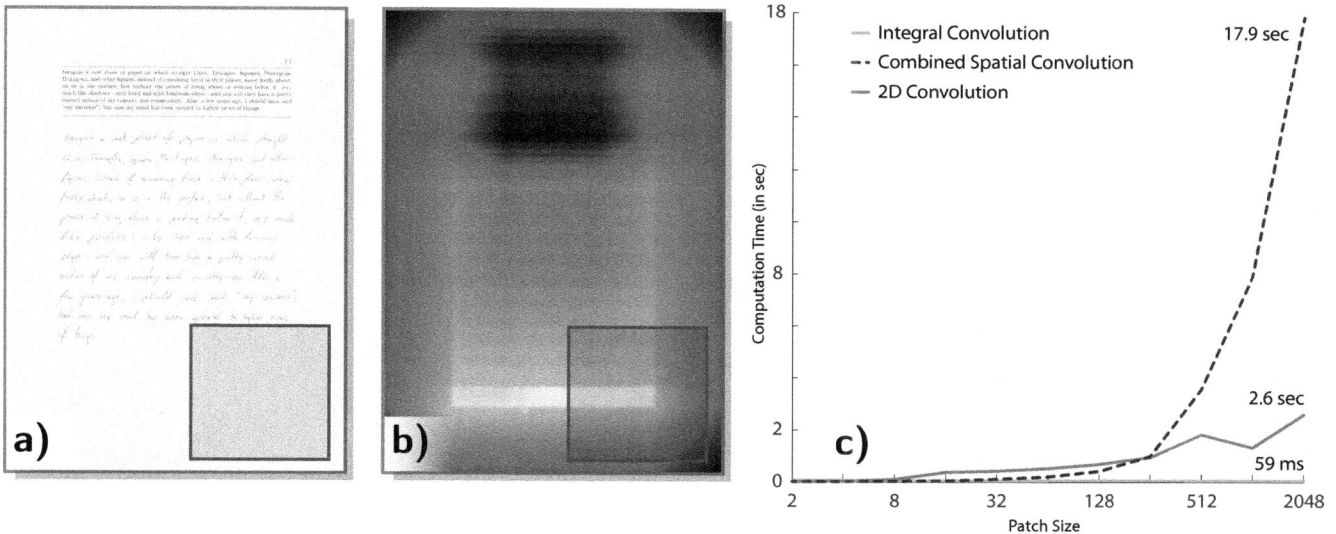

**Figure 4: Sample from the CVL Database [8] with the resulting background patch a). Corresponding area filter b). Computation time of the three convolution techniques discussed c).**

with respect to the coordinate origin. A drawback of this method is the memory usage, since the integral image needs to be allocated using 64 bit integers or floating points for 8 bit $N \times N$ images larger than $N = 2^{12} = 4096$. Having computed the integral images, box filter operations such as the mean or area filter are computed with 4 operations:

$$I_a(x, y) = p_3 - p_1 - p_2 + p_0 \qquad (2)$$

where $p_i = I_i(x \pm \frac{M}{2}, y \pm \frac{M}{2})$

Figure 4 c) illustrates the computation time of the three convolution techniques presented. It was evaluated in a C++ environment on an Intel i7-3520M @2.9 GHz running Windows 8.1. Each operation was carried out 10 times as a trade off between total testing time and stability of the results. The integral image convolution takes 59 ms for a $2548 \times 3510$ px image independent to the kernel size. The spatial convolution with two 1D kernels is faster than the DFT convolution up to a kernel size of $M = 256$. The 2D filtering is performed in the spatial domain until a kernel size of $M = 16$. Then, the convolution is computed using the DFT transform. Though, the theoretical complexity is lower for integral images, the implementation is slower for small kernels $M < 8$ where the 1D convolution takes 32 ms.

## 2.2 Pre-Processing

The subsequent feature computations are carried out on the patch extracted previously. As the contrast between lines and background is low for some images (see Figure 2), the gradient magnitude is computed which emphasizes edges:

$$I_x(x, y) = I_g(x - 1, y) - I_g(x + 1, y)$$
$$I_y(x, y) = I_g(x, y - 1) - I_g(x, y + 1)$$
$$M(x, y) = \sqrt{(I_x(x, y))^2 + (I_y(x, y))^2}$$

with $M(x, y)$ being the resulting magnitude image and $I_g$ the image patch smoothed by a Gaussian with $\sigma = 3$ (see Section 3.2). Foreground elements are removed by means of

a local threshold [7] so that ruling lines are enhanced. A histogram stretch that maps values below the $Q_{99.5}$ Quantile linearly to [0 1] and sets values $x > Q_{99.5}$ to 1 further improves the ruling contrast. Figure 5 shows this enhancement for two documents a) and d). First, the gradients are computed in b) and e). Then, the foreground is removed and the histogram stretch is applied in c) and f). Especially f) shows the enhancement though the lines are noisy.

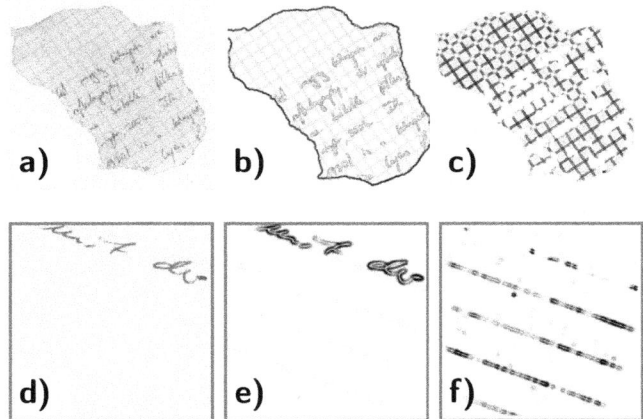

**Figure 5: Two samples of *checked* a) and *lined* d) snippets. The gradient magnitude b), e) and the enhanced version c), f).**

## 2.3 Texture Feature Extraction

Lines in the enhanced patches could be extracted using e.g. the Hough transform. However, ruling – compared to other lines present in documents – has two additional properties. First, ruling lines are parallel. Second, they have a fixed distance to their nearest neighbor. Since features with fixed (known) frequency and orientation can be easily extracted from the DFT, the patch is transformed to the DFT domain.

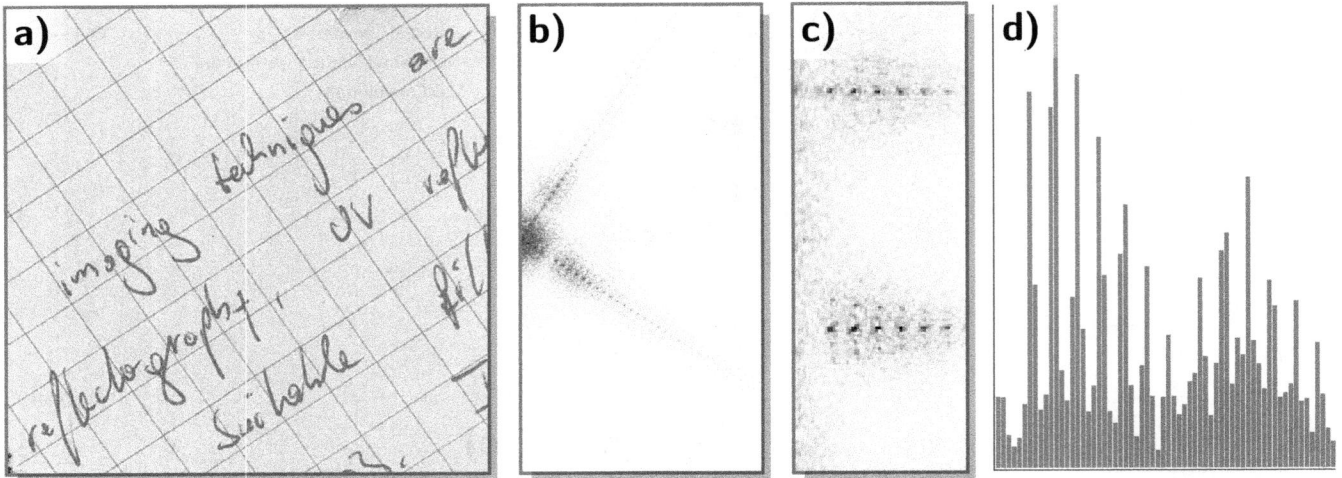

Figure 6: Feature extraction of a *checked* image patch. Power spectrum of the cleaned patch in b), polar transformed feature space c) and the final feature vector d).

The DFT is symmetric for real-valued inputs. Hence, solely half of the DFT image is used for subsequent computations. In addition, it is shifted by $N/2$ so that low frequencies are at the vertical center of the Fourier image rather than the border. The power spectrum combining real and imaginary part is computed for the texture features:

$$\mathcal{P}(x,y) = \sqrt{Re(I_{\mathcal{F}}(x,y))^2 + Im(I_{\mathcal{F}}(x,y))^2} \qquad (3)$$

where $I_{\mathcal{F}}(x,y)$ is the Fourier transformed image and $\mathcal{P}(x,y)$ the resulting power spectrum (see Figure 6 b)). The ruling orientation is unknown up to this processing stage. However, the features should be extracted rotationally invariant. That is why, the power spectrum is transformed using a polar transformation with a center located at the DFT's lowest frequencies $c = (0, N/2)$. By these means, the rows represent the changing angle $\theta$ and columns stand for the frequency. As can be seen in Figure 6 b), high frequencies (at the right image border) do not carry much information for these images. Thus, solely 64 columns are considered for the feature computation. By these means a polar-power spectrum (see Figure 6 c)) is extracted from the image patch. The dotted rows in c) show the features we are interested in. The horizontal distance between the peaks is $1/f$ of the ruling frequency $f$ in the spatial domain.

Having extracted the polar-power spectrum, the ruling orientation is extracted using PPs. Since frequent peaks indicate the ruling, the maximum in the vertical PP is the ruling's main orientation. Skew issues of the PP do not apply for the polar-power spectrum, as the features are – by definition – perpendicular to the ordinate. The row at the global maximum $max(p)$ and the corresponding perpendicular row $mod(max(p) + 90, 180)$ are extracted for the final feature vector. Concatenating both rows results in a 128 dimensional feature vector which is normalized to [0 1] for robustness with respect to luminance changes. Instead of solely taking one row at each location, five rows are accumulated which improves the feature's profile if the ruling lines have a non-integer angle (e.g. 12.5°). Figure 6 d) shows a concatenated feature vector. This vector has random peaks

if *void* paper is regarded, solely the first 64 dimensions have recurring peaks for *lined* paper and all 128 dimensions have peaks for *checked* paper.

## 2.4 Classification

The features are classified using Support Vector Machines (SVM) (the OpenCV[1] implementation is used) with a Radial Basis Function (RBF) kernel [13, 4]. The classifier and kernel selection is based on tests with empirical data which are presented in Section 3. The training set is comparatively small with 54 training images (18 per class). The training samples were randomly chosen from an annotated data set which consists in total of 436 document snippets. The advantage of a small training set is on the one hand that training is fast[2] and on the other hand a low manual effort which includes ground truth tagging. In contrast to the evaluation presented in this paper, the SVM is trained on all images of the dataset for real world recognition scenarios.

Since the SVM is – by definition – a binary classifier, the multi-class problem is reduced to three binary class decisions using a *one-versus-all* scheme. Therefore, three kernels are used where each corresponds to a class label *void*, *lined* or *checked*. Hence, the classifiers are trained with all 54 sample features where the labels of the currently observed class are set to 1 and all others are set to -1. Having trained the SVMs, the prediction value for a newly observed feature vector is computed for each kernel. A negative prediction value indicates that the feature does not belong to the class of the respective kernel while features with a positive value belong to the respective class. In addition to the class label, the prediction value which is the normalized distance between the observed feature vector and the hyperplane is used. Thus, features with low values are close to the hyperplane and therefore more likely to be wrong. The final class decision is the maximum of all three prediction values. Note that the class decision is made even if all kernels classify

---

[1] http://opencv.org
[2] training takes $\approx 23.1$ seconds including the feature computation and cross validation

a feature as not belonging to their class. The $3 \times 1$ prediction value histogram is further used during re-assembling where a decision is made if the ruling feature is disregarded (depending on the likelihood of other features such as text classification labels).

In order to train the SVMs, a 3-fold cross validation is carried out for each kernel. Therefore, the training set is split into three data sets of equal size where two are used for training and one is used for testing. This procedure is repeated until each set was once used for testing. The SVM – if an RBF kernel is used – has two parameters $(C, \gamma)$ which need to be optimized for new training sets. The cost $C > 0$ is the penalty of a falsely classified feature vector. Low cost values result in a low penalty. The second parameter $\gamma > 0$ controls the flexibility of the RBF kernel. Here, high values allow the hyperplane to be more *flexible*. Where *flexible* means that the hyperplane better fits the training data. The parameters are tuned for specific data using a parameter grid where each parameter is varied. The bounds are chosen to be $\exp(-5) \le C \le \exp(14)$ and $\exp(-14) \le \gamma \le \exp(1)$ which covers all variations present in the training set. The SVM is trained for each parameter tuple in the grid and evaluated using the 3-fold cross validation. The parameters which maximize the cross validation are chosen for training. Figure 7 shows the cross validation for each kernel. The gray dot indicates the final parameter tupel that maximizes the cross validation while minimizing the parameter values. Note that the a-priori class probability is the same for all classes since the number of samples is chosen to be equally distributed.

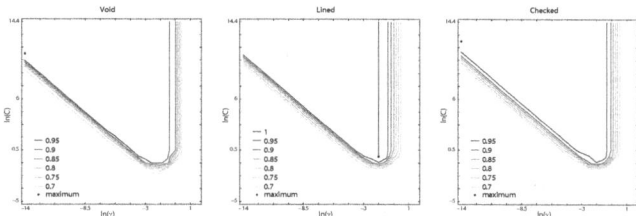

**Figure 7: Cross validation on the training set having 18 samples per class.**

## 2.5 Ruling Line Estimation

After classifying the document image into *void*, *lined* and *checked*, lines are extracted for images classified as *lined* or *checked*. The ruling lines are enhanced and writing is removed as described in Section 2.1. Then, the image is rotated according to the ruling angle which was detected in the polar-power spectrum. A vertical PP (for documents classified as *checked* a vertical and horizontal PP) is used in order to determine the accurate position of ruling lines. Local maxima $p$ in the PP which have a stronger peak than 0.2 of the global maximum ($p \ge 0.2 \max(\text{PP})$) are used as initial guess.

It was previously mentioned, that ruling has a fixed frequency. Hence, the ruling frequency $f_r$ is estimated by the $Q_{0.75}$ quartile of the distance between each line and its closest neighbor. Lines whose distance between the preceding or succeeding neighbor is not in the range of $\pm 10\ px$ with respected to the frequency $f_r$ are removed. Finally, missing

lines are added with respect to the frequency. Figure 8 shows the ruling lines found of two sample snippets. Green lines are those detected in the PP while blue lines illustrate *virtual* lines that are estimated based on the ruling frequency.

The skew estimation in the polar transformed power spectrum is accurate enough for the initial line localization. However, slight deviations ($\pm 0.3°$) result in a degraded line removal. In order to overcome this, an image patch is extracted in the de-skewed background image. The height is set to 40 px while the width is the width of the currently observed line. All pixels whose vertical derivation is larger than 0.2 and horizontal deviation is below 0.2 are marked as line candidates. A robust line fitting using the Welsch distance [16] is performed on these pixels. If less than 40 line candidates are detected the line gets rejected. In addition, lines whose angle difference is larger than $0.8°$ with respect to the global line angle, are replaced with the initial guess.

Cleaning lines is performed by a logical AND operation of the lines found and the binary image. Overlapping text elements are then removed by means of Local Projection Profiles (LPP) which are perpendicular to the lines detected. An empirical evaluation of the LPP size showed that a kernel size of 9 px performs best.

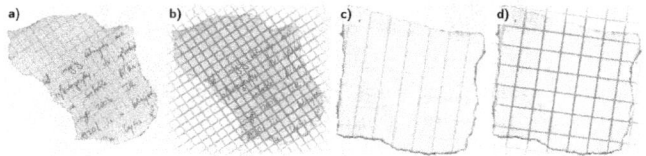

**Figure 8: Ruling estimation of two sample snippets (a, c). Green lines are found in the PP while the location of blue lines is estimated using the ruling frequency.**

## 3. EVALUATION

The ruling estimation was evaluated on a data set which has a total of 434 images. The data set is real world data from fragmented Stasi files scanned at 300 *dpi*. The data is particularly challenging because of its great variety. Thus, it comprises snippets with varying area, background and background clutter. The paper fragments have a mean area of 42.4 $cm^2$ with a standard deviation of $\pm 37.1\ cm^2$ where a DIN A4 page has 623.7 $cm^2$. The data set has an equal class distribution.

## 3.1 Classifier Evaluation

The SVM proposed previously for classification is compared with three frequently used classifiers, namely Naïve Bayes, Linear Discriminant Analysis (LDA) and $k$-NN. It can be seen in Figure 9 that the Bayes and the LDA perform significantly worse compared to e.g. SVMs. This can be attributed to the curse of dimensionality. As previously discussed, the training is carried out on solely 18 samples per class while the feature dimension is set to 128. The LDA and the Bayes classifier are both *generative models*. Hence, the model parameters – whose number depends on the dimension – need to be estimated from the training samples. In contrast, the VC theory, which is the basis of SVMs, utilizes the entropy of training samples rather than their dimension [14]. Thus,

SVMs can find good classification boundaries even if the feature space is sparse. The same applies to $k$-NN which is a *predictive model* and therefore an empirical loss is minimized rather than finding the model that generates the data.

Besides, evaluating different classifiers, three popular SVM kernels were tested. Figure 9 (left) shows the results. It can be seen that the polynomial kernel of $2^{nd}$ degree has the worst performance being 92.4%. The linear SVM kernel has a lower precision by 1.05% compared to the RBF. Hence, this is the best choice if speed is of importance as the classification can be carried out with one vector multiplication. Note that the classification is carried out once per document snippet and that the whole ruling estimation presented (including feature extraction) takes 141 $ms$ to compute if a $2512 \times 3510$ px document is observed. That is why, the higher precision of the RBF kernel is chosen rather than the linear SVM.

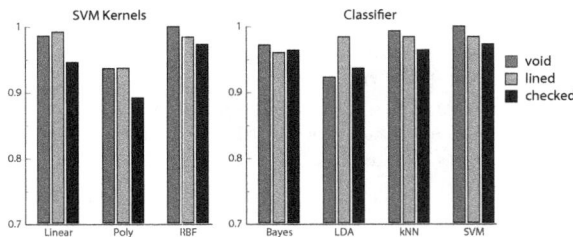

**Figure 9: Evaluation with different SVM kernels (left) and classifiers (right).**

Furthermore the classifier's weights are evaluated to show their use for subsequent processing steps such as the re-assembling. Figure 10 shows a plot of the precision versus classification weights. The precision is accumulated for all classes with respect to the classification weights $w$. For small weights, the precisions are bending because of the small number of samples. As the number of samples increases ($w \approx 0.4$), the plot gets more stable and therefore more reliable. The bins represent the underlying sample distribution. Most snippets classified have a classification weight around one which hints at a reliable decision. The plot allows for choosing thresholds on which classification results are rejected when combining different features. In more detail, if someone would need a precision of at least 0.9, a classification weight $w \geq 0.43$ has to be chosen.

## 3.2 Empirical Parameter Evaluation

The previously discussed ruling estimation has four parameters which influence its behavior:

- **Sigma** $\sigma$ the filter size of the Gaussian which is applied before computing the gradient magnitude.

- **Patch Size** of the patch with most background pixels where the DFT is applied.

- **Feature Dimension** of the features classified.

- **Interpolation Interval** for extracting the feature from the polar-power spectrum.

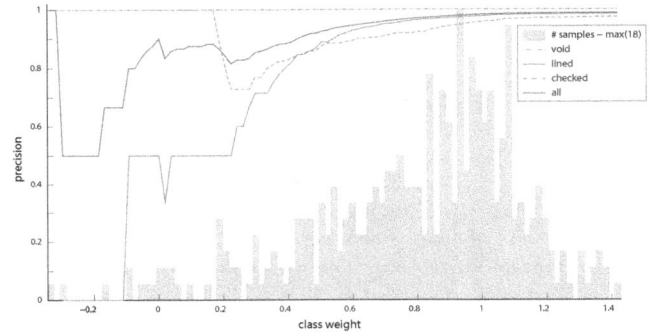

**Figure 10: Classification weights versus precision. The precision is accumulated for each class with respect to the maximal class weight. It can be seen that the precision increases with increasing weights.**

In order to find optimal values for these parameters, they are empirically evaluated. The Gaussian kernel size $\sigma$ was evaluated with $1.5, 3$ and $4.5$. Figure 11 (left) shows the evaluation. The best performance is achieved if it is set to $\sigma = 3$ which is a trade-off between removing too few noise but keeping the relevant line information. It can be seen additionally, that *lined* paper is hardly affected by $\sigma$. This can be traced back to the fact that *checked* paper has a higher frequency (lower distance between lines) and therefore peaks are merged if $\sigma$ is too large. Choosing $\sigma$ too low on the other hand leaves too much noise which results in a lower accuracy.

The *patch size* controls the window size which is used for observation. The maximum performance is achieved if it is set to 512 px as can be seen in Figure 11 (right). A too small patch (e.g. $128 \times 128$) has a negative effect on the recognition of *lined* paper because the mean line frequency is $\approx 106$ px if documents are scanned at 300 $dpi$. Hence, a small patch captures solely one line which is too few for an accurate recognition. Large patch sizes on the other hand capture more foreground information and therefore increase the risk of an erroneous binarization.

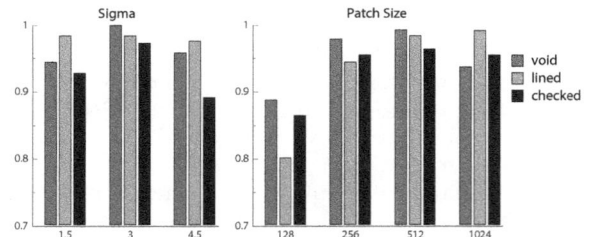

**Figure 11: Evaluation of $\sigma$ (left) and *patch size* (right).**

A low *feature dimension* (see Figure 12 (left)) has a stronger effect on the ruling estimation (−4.7%) than a higher dimension (0.1%). Hence, the classifiers are capable of dealing with high dimensional features although the size of the training set is not increased. In addition, it can be argued from this test that a feature dimension of 64 is too low if the ruling is extracted from the DFT.

In contrast to the previously evaluated parameters, the *interpolation interval* has a comparatively low impact on the ruling estimation performance. Figure 12 (right) illustrates the test with varying parameters for the interpolation. An interval $\geq 1$ removes noise that might be present in the line of the polar-power spectrum. Additionally, it improves the feature vector if the ruling orientation is not integer valued as it reduces interpolation artifacts from the polar transform.

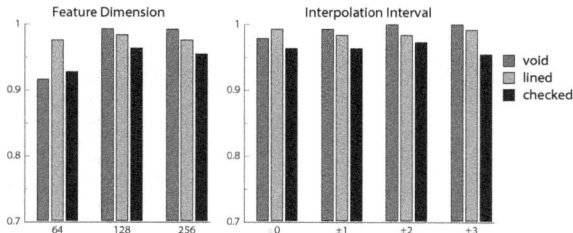

**Figure 12:** Evaluation of *feature dimension* and *interpolation interval*.

## 3.3 Dataset Evaluation

The performance of the ruling analysis presented is empirically evaluated on the data set previously introduced (SET A) and a second dataset SET B which is also presented in [6]. The first dataset SET A contains clean data with no class ambiguity while the second one contains ambiguous real world examples including e.g. tables or underlined text. The groundtruth of both datasets was manually annotated and saved to an XML file. For each image, the ruling class (*void, lined, checked*) and the dominant orientation were annotated. First, a confusion matrix is given which shows the class confusion numerically. Table 1 shows how the confusion matrix can be interpreted. The rows indicate predictions while the columns represent the ground truth. Hence, diagonal elements are documents predicted as $i^{th}$ class which are actually class $i$ (true positives **tp**). All other values are false positives (**fp**) for the predicted class and false negatives (**fn**) for the true class. Table 2 shows the evaluation

**Table 1: Confusion matrix with $n = 2$; $a_i$ are predictions of class $i$, and $c_i$ are the true class labels.**

|  | $a_0$ | $a_1$ | $\cdots$ | $\mathbf{a_i}$ | $\cdots$ | $a_n$ |
|---|---|---|---|---|---|---|
| $c_0$ |  |  |  | $fp$ |  |  |
| $c_1$ |  |  |  | $fp$ |  |  |
| $\vdots$ |  |  |  | $\vdots$ |  |  |
| $\mathbf{c_i}$ | $fn$ | $fn$ | $\cdots$ | $tp$ | $\cdots$ | $fn$ |
| $\vdots$ |  |  |  | $\vdots$ |  |  |
| $c_n$ |  |  |  | $fp$ |  |  |

results. It can be seen that using the methodology proposed with the previously evaluated parameters, all *void* classes are classified correctly. Two *lined* documents are falsely predicted as *void* and three *checked* documents are falsely classified as *lined*. Four out of the five errors can be attributed to a flawed foreground extraction. The error either arises from colored ink that is not binarized or binarized lines (see Figure 13 a),b)) that are removed in the magnitude image. Again, the magnitude images are inverted for

illustration and therefore dark areas represent high gradient magnitudes. Figure 13 c), d) show a scanning artifact. In this scenario, the snippet was moved during scanning. Since the ruling lines are not parallel anymore, the proposed methodology cannot correctly classify this snippet.

**Table 2: The rows of the confusion matrix show the groundtruth labels, while the columns represent predicted labels (e.g. 1.6% of the *lined* paper is falsely classified as *void*).**

|  | predicted | | | |
|---|---|---|---|---|
|  | void | lined | checked | # |
| void | **1.0** | · | · | 143 |
| lined | 0.016 | **0.984** | · | 126 |
| checked | · | 0.027 | **0.973** | 111 |
|  | 145 | 127 | 108 | 380 |

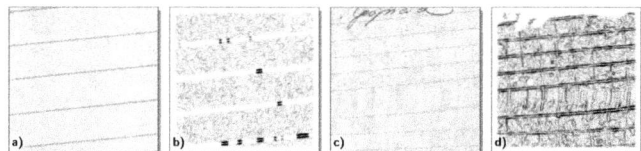

**Figure 13: Two falsely classified examples.**

In Table 3 the confusion matrix for SET B is given which was presented in [6]. In this dataset *void* document snippets have a precision of 92.4%. This can be traced back to the fact that tables such as table of contents are present which have recurring horizontal and vertical lines. The comparatively low precision of *lined* documents results from empty carbon copies where lines are – similarly to the example given in Figure 13 a) – falsely binarized as foreground elements and therefore removed from the magnitude image.

**Table 3: The rows of the confusion matrix show the groundtruth labels of SET B, while the columns represent predicted labels.**

|  | predicted | | | |
|---|---|---|---|---|
|  | void | lined | checked | # |
| void | **0.924** | 0.029 | 0.048 | 314 |
| lined | 0.116 | **0.884** | · | 103 |
| checked | 0.049 | · | **0.951** | 41 |
|  | 304 | 100 | 54 | 458 |

Furthermore, F-score, precision, and recall are calculated for each class in order to allow for drawing conclusions about the nature of errors and class confusions. For these error measures, true positives $tp_i$, false positives $fp_i$, and false negatives $fn_i$ of a given class $i$ are defined by:

$$tp_i \ldots \langle a_i, c_i \rangle$$
$$fp_i \ldots \langle a_i, c_{j \neq i} \rangle$$
$$fn_i \ldots \langle a_{j \neq i}, c_i \rangle$$

where $i, j \in 0...n$ and $n = 2$ with $0 = void$, $1 = lined$ and $2 = checked$. The precision $p_i$, recall $r_i$, and F-score $F_i$ of a class $i$ are thus defined as:

$$p_i = \frac{tp_i}{tp_i + fp_i}$$

$$r_i = \frac{tp_i}{tp_i + fn_i}$$

$$F_i = \frac{tp_i}{2tp_i + fp_i + fn_i}$$

Figure 14 shows the precision and recall for each class on SET A and SET B respectively. The recall is low for *checked* paper in SET B being 0.722. This can be attributed to the priors in SET B where *checked* paper has a prior of solely 8.9%. This prior reflects a small subset of the real world data where printed documents are more common than handwritten. However, the true a-priori probability of all classes is unknown. That is why a second test set (SET A) was created with similar priors for all classes that reduce the bias. The recall of *checked* paper is 1 in SET A since no other class is falsely predicted as *checked*. The F-score of SET A is 0.987 and 0.919 for SET B.

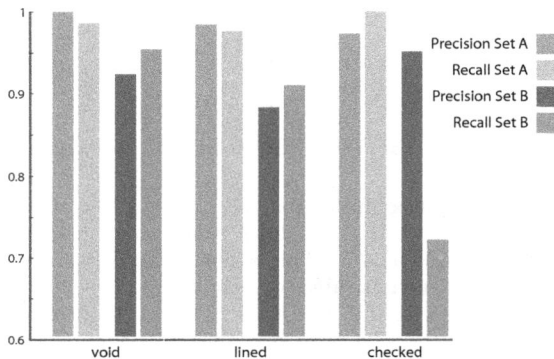

**Figure 14: Precision recall plot of SET A and SET B.**

## 3.4 Line Removal Evaluation

In addition to the classification evaluation, a line removal evaluation is performed. The evaluation is performed similar to that presented in [1, 9]. Therefore, a dataset is created by synthetically merging handwriting images from the IC-DAR 2013 Handwriting Segmentation Contest [12] with four different ruling masks. Figure 15 shows four examples of the ruling images created synthetically. The masks are extracted from scanned images and exhibit typical degradations such as broken lines. The CVL ruling dataset is made publicly available[3] and consists of 150 images written in English, Greek and Bangla. This results in a total of 600 test images.

Figure 16 shows a sample page of the dataset. Green pixels indicate true positives (line pixels detected that are actually line pixels), red pixels illustrate false positives (line pixels detected that are actually text pixels) and black pixels are false negatives (true line pixels that are not detected). The gray pixels are for illustration reasons, they correspond – similar to white pixels – to the true negative class (pixels

---

[3]http://caa.tuwien.ac.at/cvl/research/ruling-database/

that are not line pixels and were not detected as such). Figure 16 shows that the LPP is good at removing false line detections if strokes are perpendicular to the currently observed line (e.g. upper text in the zoomed area). However, it is not capable of correctly removing false positives if text strokes are parallel to a line (e.g. lower right text). It can be seen that the methodology presented is able to detected broken and noisy ruling lines.

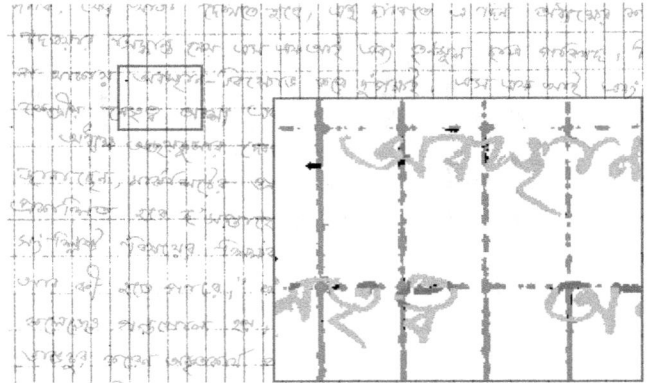

**Figure 16: A sample page of the dataset presented. Green pixels are true positives, red pixels are false positives and black pixels are false negatives. Gray and white pixels correspond to true negatives.**

The sole parameter that influences the quality of ruling line removal is the kernel size of the LPP. The Receiver Operator curve (ROC) is given in Figure 17 when varying the kernel size between 0 (text restoration) and 15 with a step size of 2 px. The blue line shows the median recall versus precision when varying the kernel size. In addition the area within the $Q_{0.25}$ and $Q_{0.75}$ Quartiles is illustrated in gray. The maximal F-score of 0.93 is achieved with a kernel size of 9.

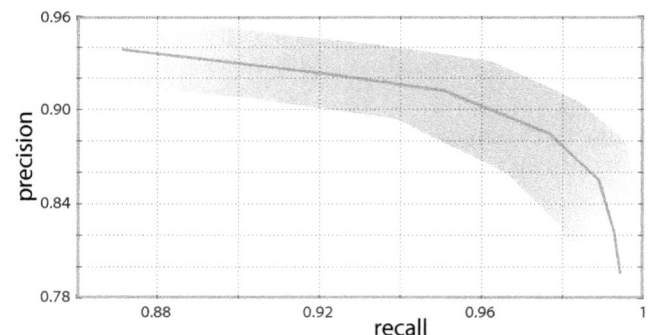

**Figure 17: ROC curve when varying the kernel size of the LPP.**

Since solely 9% of an image are line pixels (for checked paper), true negatives are not considered in the evaluation as this would bias the results. Abd-Amageed et al. [1] and Lopresti et al. [9] create synthetic datasets similar to the one proposed with 50 and 100 sample images respectively. Although, the dataset generation is similar and the error measurements are the same, the results presented in Table 4 cannot be directly compared since their datasets are not published.

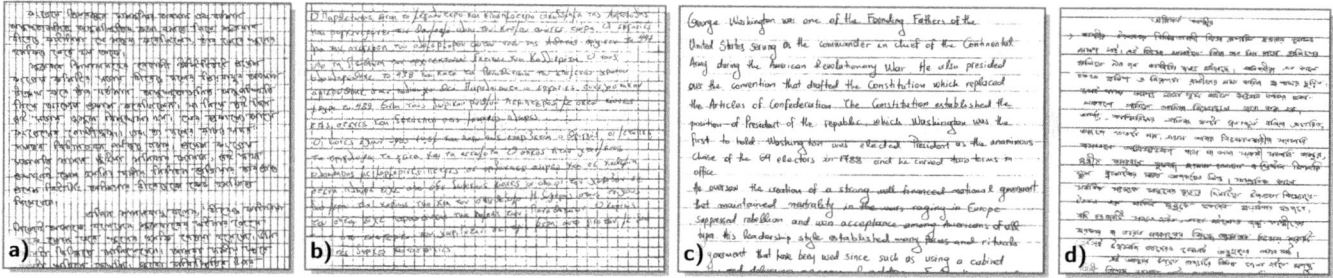

Figure 15: Four different samples of the synthetically generated line removal database.

Table 4: Line removal comparison. #I number of images, p precision, r recall and F F-score.

|  | #I | P | R | F |
|---|---|---|---|---|
| W. Abd-Amageed et al. [1] | 50 | 0.88 | 0.88 | 0.88 |
| D. Lopresti et al. [9] | 100 | 0.76 | 0.91 | 0.81 |
| proposed | 600 | 0.91 | 0.95 | 0.93 |

## 4. CONCLUSION

A ruling analysis which is applicable for torn documents was presented in this paper. The ruling analysis first extracts a background patch which is enhanced by means of gradient magnitudes and histogram stretching. Furthermore, foreground elements are removed for an improved frequency signature in the DFT. A polar power spectrum allows for feature extraction invariant with respect to rotation. Changing ruling frequencies are trained by means of SVMs with a one-versus-all classification scheme. The evaluation showed that the designed workflow is capable of recognizing different paper types including *void*, *lined* and *checked* paper. Since the features are able to separate all classes cleanly, training can be carried out on a relatively small training set (18 samples per class) which reduces the human effort. The evaluation set presented include small document snippets which shows the method's robustness with respect to reduced information (e.g. short lines). The evaluation showed, that the foreground extraction (binarization) is crucial with respect to the precision. Hence, foreground elements missed degrade the contrast enhancement and therefore reduce the feature's signature. In addition, the binarization detects strong ruling lines if a snippet has no written content. As shown in Figure 13 c), the method fails if ruling lines in the patch are not parallel to each other. This is inherent with the design of the method, as snippets might be composed of several lines that are not equidistant or parallel to each other. By definition these snippets must not be classified as *lined* or *checked*. In addition, the ruling line removal quality was evaluated on a synthetically generated dataset which is freely available[4]. The precision was increased if the overlapping of text and ruling lines was modeled rather than applying LPPs on the cleaned text image. The second dataset SET B pointed out that ruling is ambiguous if formal criteria are considered. Structured elements such as tables have the same properties as ruling if they are composed of equidistant parallel lines.

---

[4]http://caa.tuwien.ac.at/cvl/research/ruling-database/

## Acknowledgment
The authors would like to thank Dirk Pöhler, Jan Schneider and the Fraunhofer-Institute for Production Systems and Design Technology (IPK), Berlin for supporting the work.

## 5. REFERENCES

[1] Wael Abd-Almageed, Jayant Kumar, and David S. Doermann. Page Rule-Line Removal Using Linear Subspaces in Monochromatic Handwritten Arabic Documents. In *Proceedings of the 10th International Conference on Document Analysis and Recognition*, pages 768–772. IEEE Computer Society, 2009.

[2] George B. Arfken, Hans J. Weber, and Frank E. Harris. *Mathematical Methods for Physicists, Sixth Edition: A Comprehensive Guide*. Academic Press, 6 edition, July 2005.

[3] Jin Chen and Daniel P. Lopresti. Model-based ruling line detection in noisy handwritten documents. *Pattern Recognition Letters*, 35:34–45, 2014.

[4] Corinna Cortes and Vladimir Vapnik. Support-vector networks. *Machine Learning*, 20(3):273–297, 1995.

[5] Franklin C. Crow. Summed-area Tables for Texture Mapping. *SIGGRAPH Comput. Graph.*, 18(3):207–212, January 1984.

[6] Markus Diem, Florian Kleber, Stefan Fiel, and Robert Sablatnig. Semi-Automated Document Image Clustering and Retrie. In *Document Recognition and Retrieval*, 2014.

[7] Florian Kleber, Markus Diem, and Robert Sablatnig. Scale Space Binarization Using Edge Information Weighted by a Foreground Estimation. In *Proceedings of the 11th International Conference on Document Analysis and Reconstruction (ICDAR 2011)*, pages 854–858, Beijing, China, 2011. IEEE Computer Society CPS.

[8] Florian Kleber, Stefan Fiel, Markus Diem, and Robert Sablatnig. CVL-DataBase: An Off-Line Database for Writer Retrieval, Writer Identification and Word Spotting. In *Proceedings of the 12th International Conference on Document Analysis and Recognition*, pages 560–564, 2013.

[9] Daniel P. Lopresti and Ergina Kavallieratou. Ruling Line Removal in Handwritten Page Images. In *Proceedings of the 20th International Conference on Pattern Recognition*, pages 2704–2707, 2010.

[10] Ana Rebelo and Jaime S. Cardoso. Staff Line Detection and Removal in the Grayscale Domain. In *Proceedings of the 12th International Conference on*

*Document Analysis and Recognition*, pages 57–61, 2013.

[11] Jan Schneider and Bertram Nickolay. The Stasi puzzle. *Fraunhofer Magazine, Special Issue*, 1:32–33, 2008.

[12] Nikolaos Stamatopoulos, Basilis Gatos, Georgios Louloudis, Umapada Pal, and Alireza Alaei. ICDAR 2013 Handwriting Segmentation Contest. In *Proceedings of the 12th International Conference on Document Analysis and Recognition*, pages 1402–1406, 2013.

[13] Vladimir Vapnik. *Estimation of Dependences Based on Empirical Data: Springer Series in Statistics (Springer Series in Statistics)*. Springer-Verlag New York, Inc., Secaucus, NJ, USA, 1982.

[14] Vladimir Vapnik. *Estimation of Dependences Based on Empirical Data*. Springer Science and Business Media, Inc., New York, USA, 2006.

[15] Paul A. Viola and Michael J. Jones. Robust Real-Time Face Detection. *International Journal of Computer Vision*, 57(2):137–154, 2004.

[16] Roy E. Welsch and Edwin Kuh. Linear Regression Diagnostics. Technical Report 923-77, Massachusetts Institute of Technology, April 1977.

[17] Yefeng Zheng, Huiping Li, and David S. Doermann. A Parallel-Line Detection Algorithm Based on HMM Decoding. *IEEE Trans. Pattern Anal. Mach. Intell.*, 27(5):777–792, 2005.

[18] Yefeng Zheng, Changsong Liu, Xiaoqing Ding, and Shiyan Pan. Form Frame Line Detection with Directional Single-Connected Chain. In *Proceedings of the 6th International Conference on Document*

# On Automatic Text Segmentation

**Boris Dadachev**
Cardiff School of Mathematics
Cardiff University
Cardiff CF24 4AG, UK
DadachevBK@cf.ac.uk

**Alexander Balinsky**
Cardiff School of Mathematics
Cardiff University
Cardiff CF24 4AG, UK
BalinskyA@cf.ac.uk

**Helen Balinsky**
Hewlett-Packard Laboratories
Long Down Avenue
Bristol BS34 8QZ, UK
helen.balinsky@hp.com

## ABSTRACT

Automatic text segmentation, which is the task of breaking a text into topically-consistent segments, is a fundamental problem in Natural Language Processing, Document Classification and Information Retrieval. Text segmentation can significantly improve the performance of various text mining algorithms, by splitting heterogeneous documents into homogeneous fragments and thus facilitating subsequent processing. Applications range from screening of radio communication transcripts to document summarization, from automatic document classification to information visualization, from automatic filtering to security policy enforcement - all rely on, or can largely benefit from, automatic document segmentation. In this article, a novel approach for automatic text and data stream segmentation is presented and studied. The proposed automatic segmentation algorithm takes advantage of feature extraction and unusual behaviour detection algorithms developed in [4, 5]. It is entirely unsupervised and flexible to allow segmentation at different scales, such as short paragraphs and large sections. We also briefly review the most popular and important algorithms for automatic text segmentation and present detailed comparisons of our approach with several of those state-of-the-art algorithms.

## Categories and Subject Descriptors

I.2.7 [**Natural Language Processing**]: Text Analysis; I.5.4 [**Pattern Recognition**]: Applications—*text processing*; I.7 [**Document and Text Processing**]: Miscellaneous

## Keywords

Natural Language Processing; Automatic Text Segmentation; Weighted Feature Extraction; Unusual Behavior Detection; Scale-Space Theory

## 1. INTRODUCTION

Automatic text and data stream segmentation into topically consistent segments is a fundamental problem in text and stream data mining. Even a moderately long document may consist of several relatively independent topics and parts. Such heterogeneity in documents can seriously affect the performance of classification and other mining algorithms. Depending on the needs, a textual document could be required to be automatically partitioned into relatively small paragraphs or large sections.

The vast majority of text segmentation algorithms rely on the same underlying idea: the quantification of lexical cohesion between different parts of a document. Lexical cohesion can be defined as "the cohesive effect achieved by the selection of vocabulary" (see page 274 of [10]) which intuitively means that changes in the vocabulary signal topic changes. A number of linguistic structures create lexical cohesion, such as word repetitions, synonyms, pronouns and more generally related vocabulary. However, many of these structures can be difficult to detect due to language ambiguities and variabilities. This is why, even if more sophisticated alternatives exist [16], many popular and effective approaches to the quantification of lexical cohesion are solely based on some measure of word repetitions. From the point of view of image processing this is similar to histogram-based segmentation.

In this paper, a novel approach for automatic text and data stream segmentation is proposed and studied. The proposed automatic segmentation algorithm takes advantage of the Helmholtz-based feature extraction and unusual behaviour detection developed in [4, 5]. The weighted feature extraction algorithms from [4, 5] are based on principles from image processing and especially on the Gestalt Theory of human perception. There are many similarities between the text segmentation and the image segmentation problems. The main idea behind using the Gestalt Theory for text analysis is that humans actively use visual sensors when reading and writing documents. The human brain has evolved to work with images and as such, visual perception dominates our way of thinking.

The present article is organized as follows. We start by reviewing previous work on text segmentation in Section 2. In Section 3, we present our new approach to automatic text segmentation. An evaluation and comparison of our approach with the state-of-the-art algorithms are presented in Section 4. Finally, conclusion and future work are discussed in Section 5.

## 2. PREVIOUS WORK

Text segmentation has been a large research area in the past twenty years and many different techniques have been proposed. Let us review the most popular and influential approaches.

In one of the earliest algorithm *TextTiling* [11], Hearst uses two adjacent blocks of length 120 words (see Figure 1) and calculates the cosine similarity between these two blocks as:

$$sim(b_1, b_2) = \frac{\sum_w f(w, b_1) f(w, b_2)}{\sqrt{\sum_w f(w, b_1)^2 \sum_w f(w, b_2)^2}} \tag{1}$$

where $f(w, b)$ is the frequency of the word $w$ in the block $b$. This similarity is attached to the gaps between the blocks; here, a gap corresponds to a space between two consecutive words.

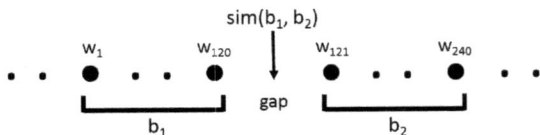

**Figure 1: Cosine similarity computation between adjacent blocks of 120 words, in the TextTiling algorithm [11]**

By moving the two blocks along the document (shifting the blocks to the right by 20 words at a time), we can graphically represent the calculated cosine similarity as a function of gaps. The author then introduces a depth score, defined as the average of the relative depths between the gap value and the two closest local maxima, one on the left and one on the right. The gaps with the biggest depth scores are selected using some automatic threshold and those gaps are used to divide the document into segments. Let us point out that those gaps are between words and not between sentences, so additional adjustments need to be done.

Choi applies methods and ideas from image processing in his algorithm *C99* [7]. If a text document consists of $n$ sentences, then a $n \times n$ gray image is constructed with "pixel" values at $(i, j)$ equal to the similarity $sim(s_i, s_j)$ between sentences $s_i$ and $s_j$ (see Equation (1)). The resulting image has several light patches around the diagonal which correspond to groups of consecutive sentences with high cosine similarities between them. To extract such disjoint objects, the image of similarity scores is first filtered using a $11 \times 11$ rank mask. Then coherent square regions near the diagonal of the image (i.e., segments) are extracted using a divisive clustering procedure that maximizes their density. As in TextTiling [11], the number of segments is determined by some empirical threshold.

A more rigorous approach to automatic segmentation, using a Bayesian statistical model, was developed by Utiyama and Isahara in [19]. Their algorithm, *TextSeg*, subsequently influenced many new developments and generalizations. Let us denote a text document by $D$ and the set of all possible segmentations by $\mathcal{F}$. The optimal segmentation is defined as the segmentation $\hat{S} \in \mathcal{F}$ that has maximum probability given the document $D$, i.e.,

$$\hat{S} = \underset{S \in \mathcal{F}}{\operatorname{argmax}} \, P(S|D). \tag{2}$$

Using Bayes formula, we can rewrite Equation (2) as:

$$\hat{S} = \underset{S \in \mathcal{F}}{\operatorname{argmax}} \, P(D|S) P(S) \tag{3}$$

$$= \underset{S \in \mathcal{F}}{\operatorname{argmin}} - \log \Big( P(D|S) P(S) \Big). \tag{4}$$

The authors in [19] impose strong independence assumptions and present the following models for the likelihood $P(D|S)$ and the prior $P(S)$:

$$P(D|S) = \prod_{i=1}^{m} \prod_{j=1}^{n_i} \frac{f(w_j, S_i) + 1}{n_i + V} \tag{5}$$

$$P(S) = n^{-m} \tag{6}$$

where:

- $m$ is the number of segments in $S$,
- $n$ is the number of words in $D$,
- $n_i$ is the number of words in segment $S_i$,
- $f(w_j, S_i)$ is the frequency of the word $w_j$ in $S_i$, and
- $V$ is the vocabulary size (i.e., the number of different words in $D$).

To find the optimal segmentation, the following complete graph $G$ is constructed: the vertex set is the set of all gaps between sentences $\{g_i : i = 1, \ldots, n - 1\}$ plus two additional vertices START and END corresponding respectively to the beginning and end of $D$, as illustrated on Figure 2. From Equations (4), (5) and (6), the weight $c_i$ of the edge corresponding to the segment $S_i$, between the two vertices encompassing all words in the segment, is defined as:

$$c_i = \log n + \sum_{j=1}^{n_i} \log \frac{n_i + V}{f(w_j, S_i) + 1}. \tag{7}$$

Then, the solution of Equation (2) corresponds to the shortest path between START and END in the weighted graph $G$, which can be found efficiently using dynamic programming.

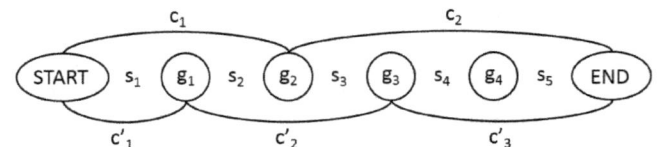

**Figure 2: The graph $G$ for an example document of 5 sentences in *TextSeg* [19]; for clarity, some edges are omitted. Two paths between START and END, corresponding to two possible segmentations, are shown.**

Eisenstein and Barzilay [8] introduced *BayesSeg*, an extension of *TextSeg* [19], in which they developed a more general model for $P(D|S)$ based on Latent Dirichlet allocation (LDA) [6]. LDA is a very natural approach to text segmentation since we can think of segments as types of topics inside a document. This makes *TextSeg* more general and flexible at the expense of a more difficult analysis.

A few other influential approaches are worth mentioning. Galley et al.'s *LCSeg* algorithm [9] weights lexical chains with a variant of TF-IDF and then computes a cosine similarity score for each gap, based on the weights of chains overlapping two adjacent moving windows.

Malioutov and Barzilay [15] build a fully connected graph and use a Minimum Cut algorithm to find the optimal segmentation. The edge weights are pairwise sentence cosine similarities, similarly to C99 [7], but also take into account neighboring sentences to get smoother similarities.

Finally, Yamron et al. [20] compare text segmentation to speech segmentation, a necessary step in speech recognition. Indeed, segmenting a text document into topics is, in some respects, similar to segmenting a sound signal into a sequence of phonemes. Therefore, speech segmentation algorithms can be adapted to text segmentation and the authors develop a topic modeling approach based on Hidden Markov models. However, contrary to the approaches introduced so far, the topic models need to be learned on training data.

Even though this is not the focus of this article, one should also add for completeness that supervised learning techniques are often used to improve the algorithms' performance in practical systems. Those techniques also allow to incorporate domain knowledge and specialize the system for the task at hand. For example, cue phrases, silences and speaker changes are effective features for speech segmentation [14, 9].

## 3. OUR ALGORITHM

In this section, we present our new approach to automatic text segmentation based on a weighted feature extraction algorithm developed in [4].

We will assume in our work that segment boundaries need to be placed at the location of gaps (i.e., breaks) between consecutive sentences. Depending on the application, one could need to place boundaries between clauses, sentences, paragraphs or even changes of speaker when working with human conversations. Our algorithm can be trivially extended to all these cases.

Inspired by previous work, the main idea of our algorithm is to calculate, for each gap in the document to segment, a measure of lexical cohesion between the sentences around that gap. After that, the gaps where the biggest drops in cohesion occur will be selected to segment the document.

### 3.1 Preprocessing

Let $D$ denote a text document. We start by preprocessing the document $D$ by splitting each sentence into a list of words, using all non-alphabetical characters as delimiters. Then we downcase all words and apply the Porter stemming algorithm [18]. Only stems of length at least two are considered. Stop-words removal is optional and is most of the time detrimental as will be seen in Section 4. After this preprocessing the document D is the sequence of $n$ sentences $s_1, s_2, \ldots, s_n$.

### 3.2 Weighted feature extraction

A general approach for unusual behaviour detection in texts and data streams was developed in [4]. For the reader's convenience, we present here a brief summary of this approach to calculating weighted features.

Let us consider a block $P$, consisting of $p$ consecutive sentences of the document $D$: $P = s_{j+1}, \ldots, s_{j+p}$. For any word $w$ from $P$, we would like to decide if $w$ appears "unusually" frequently in $P$, compared to the rest of the document. If this is the case, we would also like to have some numerical measure of this unusual behavior.

To this end, let us denote by:

- $B$ the length of the block $P$ in number of words, and

- $L$ the total length of the document $D$, also in number of words.

Let us imagine that we have divided $D$ into equally-sized blocks of $B$ words. As illustrated on Figure 3, there are $N = [L/B]$ such blocks, where $[x]$ denotes the integer part of $x$.

**Figure 3: Division of the document $D$ into $N$ equally-sized blocks of $B$ words. One of these blocks is the block $P$.**

Let us also introduce the following notations:

- $k = f(w, P)$ is the frequency of the word $w$ in $P$,

- $K = f(w, D)$ is the frequency of the word $w$ in the entire document $D$, and

- $S_w = \{w_1, w_2, ..., w_K\}$ is the set of all $K$ occurrences of $w$ inside $D$.

Finally, let us call $C_k$ the random variable that counts how many times a $k$-tuple of the elements of $S_w$ appears in the same block from the collection of blocks $D_1, D_2, \ldots, D_N$.

Now we would like to calculate the expected value of the random variable $C_k$ under the assumption that elements from $S_w$ are randomly and independently placed into $D_1, D_2, \ldots, D_N$. This expected value $E(C_k)$ is equal to (see [4] for details):

$$E(C_k) = \binom{K}{k} \cdot \frac{1}{N^{k-1}}, \qquad (8)$$

where $\binom{K}{k} = {K!}/{k!(K-k)!}$ is a binomial coefficient.

We are now ready to answer the previous question: if the word $w$ appears $k$ times in the block $P$ but $E(C_k) < 1$, then this is an *unexpected event*. In other words, we observe $k$ copies of $w$ inside the block $P$, but the expectation of having that many copies inside any of the $N$ blocks is less than 1. Therefore, the frequency of $w$ inside $P$ is unexpectedly, or unusually, high.

We define a *measure of meaningfulness* of the word $w$ in $P$ as follows:

$$Meaning(w, P) = -\frac{1}{k} \log E(C_k). \qquad (9)$$

So, when $E(C_k) < 1$, i.e., in the case of an unexpected event, $Meaning(w, P)$ is strictly positive. Furthermore, the unexpectedness of the event increases as $E(C_k)$ decreases, so an increase in meaningfulness corresponds to an increase in unexpectedness.

It should be noted that this feature extraction algorithm does not require stop-words removal, as most stop-words will not be meaningful (equivalently, they will have a negative *Meaning* score). This is important for applications where a good set of stop-words is not known or where such a set needs to be manually constructed. Also, in the case of text segmentation, removing stop-words is equivalent to assuming that stop-words do not contribute to the lexical cohesion effect, which may be untrue.

## 3.3  Automatic text segmentation

Text documents typically contain several weakly related or unrelated topics, or parts. Our main goal in this article is to identify topically-coherent segments in a document with $n$ sentences. From the $n - 1$ gaps between the document sentences, we are looking for the gaps which best separate the different topics inside the document (see Figure 4).

**Figure 4: Segmenting is finding which of the $n -$ 1 gaps between sentences best separate the topics inside the documents.**

In most documents topics have a hierarchical structure. Indeed, a book is divided into chapters, each chapter being divided into sections, themselves divided into paragraphs. The desired segment size will depend on the applications and requirements, so we believe a generic segmentation algorithm should not prefer a level of segmentation over another. This is why our algorithm takes a single input parameter: the number of segments desired. We denote this parameter by $m$.

Let us now present the main steps of the proposed algorithm for text segmentation. First of all, the document to be segmented is tokenized into sentences and words, and all words are stemmed (see Section 3.1 for more preprocessing details). Our algorithm then works by quantifying lexical cohesion between several consecutive sentences using *gap scores* that are attached to each one of the $n - 1$ gaps. Those gap scores are computed using sliding windows and the weighted measure of meaningfulness from Equation (9), as follows.

The $n - 1$ gap scores are initialized to 0. The window size is set to the average segment size desired, which is simply computed as $round(n/m)$ since the desired number of segments, $m$, is given.

Then, for each window, the weighted meaningfulness scores of all words inside the window are computed; words with a *strictly positive* score are declared meaningful inside that window. It is important to note that some meaningful words may be present only in a small portion of the window; therefore, such a word should only have an influence in the part of

the window where it appears. We call this "part" the *activity stretch* of the word inside the window. Formally, the activity stretch of a word $w$ inside a window $W_i$ is the group of consecutive sentences between the *first* and *last* occurrence of $w$ in the sentences inside $W_i$.

For each meaningful word in each window, the gap scores corresponding to gaps in the current window are updated by adding the meaningfulness score to all gap scores encompassed by the activity stretch of the current word. Thus, larger gap scores indicate stronger lexical cohesion between the sentences before and after the corresponding gaps.

Note that since there are more windows in the middle of a document than in its beginning or end, we use periodic boundary conditions for defining sliding windows, assuming the document sentences are arranged in a circular fashion. The exact algorithm for gap scores calculations is summarized in Listing 1.

**Listing 1: Algorithm for gap scores calculation**

```
Initialize all gap scores to 0.
For all possible sliding windows W_i (using
periodic boundary conditions) :
    For each word w appearing in W_i :
        Compute Meaning(w, W_i) [ see Eqn. (9)].
        If Meaning(w, W_i) > 0 :
            * Determine the activity stretch
              of w inside W_i.
            * Add Meaning(w, W_i) to the gap
              score of each gap encompassed by
              the computed activity stretch.
```

This moving windows approach allows us to compare the local word frequencies, in each window, to the frequencies in the whole document. Also, combining a large window size (set to the expected segment size) together with words' activity stretches allows us to capture the lexical cohesion created by both short-range and long-range word repetitions (i.e., from words repeated very locally in a few sentences to word repetitions spanning entire segments).

Intuitively, a small gap score indicates that a small number of meaningful words have their activity stretch encompassing the associated gap, and/or that those words are less meaningful (i.e., have smaller weighted scores) than in other parts of the document. Thus, a small gap score indicates low lexical cohesion between sentences before and after the gap, making it a good candidate for placing a segment boundary.

Figure 5 shows the typical shape of the gap scores curve for test documents. Sharp drops in gap scores can be observed at the location of ground truth cuts. The simplest approach to identify the best cuts (i.e., segment boundaries) is to look for the smallest gap scores. Unfortunately, as we can see from the figure, the gap scores function is typically very irregular and noisy. Indeed, it is a highly variable function with a lot of local minima, even in the vicinity of the global minimum. So, to identify gaps with sharp drops, some regularization of the gap scores function is required.

To regularize the gap scores function we shall follow the well-known approach from image processing to similar problems. We use the *diffusion equation* (or the one-dimensional *scale-space* theory):

$$u_t = \frac{1}{2} u_{xx} \qquad (10)$$

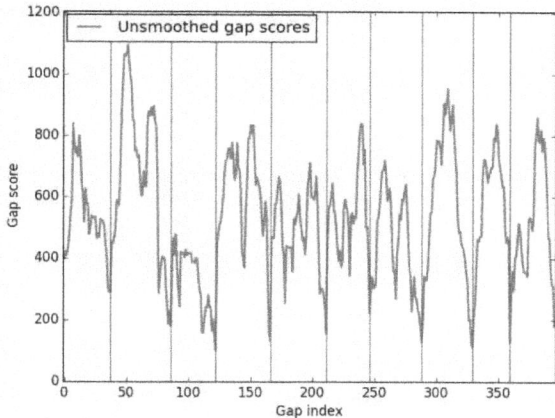

Figure 5: Unsmoothed gap scores and ground truth boundaries. The ground truth boundaries coincide, as expected, with sharp drops in gap scores.

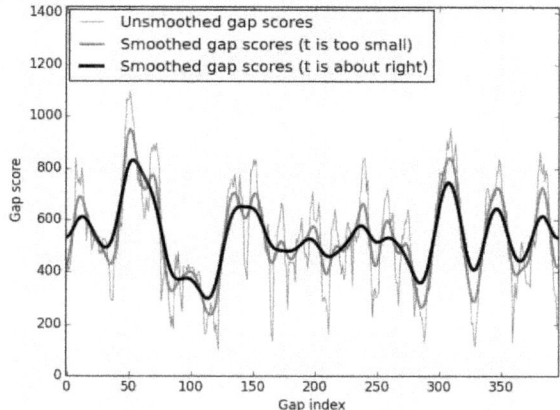

Figure 6: Effect of the parameter $\sigma$ for smoothing the gap score curve. $\sigma$ is gradually increased until the desired number of local minima is obtained.

to smooth the gap score curve (i.e., $u|_{t=0}$ is the gap scores function), and find stable and reliable critical points. In our case, the crucial property of the one-dimensional scale-space theory is that *increasing the smoothing parameter (or diffusion time) results in the decrease of the number of critical points* (see [13] for details). Note that this property is valid only in one dimension and not in any other dimensions.

From the numerical point of view, the evolution of the gap scores function under the diffusion equation is just a convolution of this function with a Gaussian filter:

$$G(x; \sigma) = \frac{1}{\sqrt{2\pi}\sigma} e^{x^2/2\sigma^2}, \qquad (11)$$

where $\sigma^2 = t$. Using the three-sigma rule (i.e., so that 0.9973 probability under the normal distribution is concentrated in a neighborhood of size $3\sigma$ around the mean value), we convolve the filter only in a neighborhood of size $3\sigma$ around every gap. Figure 6 illustrates gap scores smoothing with different values for the parameter $\sigma$. Since increasing the smoothing parameter decreases the number of local minima, our strategy is to increase $\sigma$ with small steps until the number of minima reaches the desired number of cuts. Alternatively, for faster computations, one can start from a large value of $\sigma$, giving too few local minima, and refine it using dichotomy.

An undesirable effect of this diffusion process is that each point shifts, on average, by a distance less than or equal to $\sigma$. This is a well-known property of the Brownian motion. This phenomenon can be observed on Figure 7. We are only interested in the locations of the critical points but one cannot predict the exact shift of any given point. Some points will shift by a small distance only from their original location, while some others will go much farther (i.e., at a distance greater than $\sigma$ from their original location).

In our algorithm, we consider that a critical point can shift at a distance up to $1.5\sigma$. So, we first calculate the shifted critical points (i.e., the local minima computed from the smoothed curve). After that we find the "true" local minima in the *original* noisy curve in the $1.5\sigma$ vicinity of the shifted critical points. The segment boundaries output by

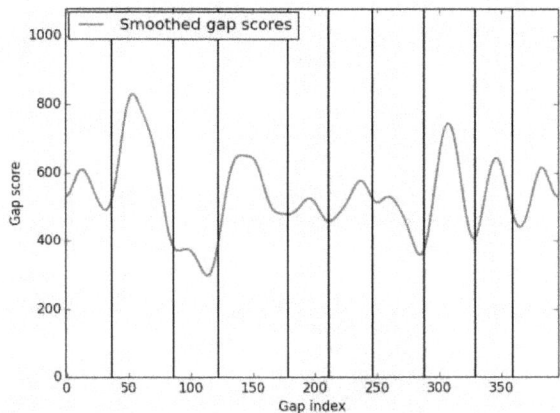

Figure 7: Smoothed gap scores and final boundaries identified by our algorithm. These boundaries are placed in local minima from the *unsmoothed* signal. We can clearly see that most boundaries are slightly away from the *smooth* local minima.

our automatic text segmentation algorithm are those "true" local minima.

Figure 8 shows a comparison of the algorithm output with the ground truth segmentation of the example document used for Figures 5, 6 and 7.

## 4. EVALUATION

### 4.1 Evaluation measures

Let us explain the general approach to evaluating the performance of text segmentation algorithms.

For each document from the evaluation dataset, we need to estimate how different the reference segmentation is from a candidate segmentation obtained with an automatic segmentation algorithm. A rigorous mathematical approach would proceed as follows. If a document $D$ is a sequence

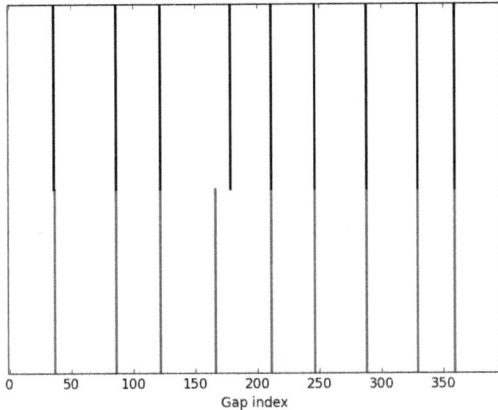

**Figure 8: Comparison of the boundaries from the ground truth segmentation (bottom) and from the output of our algorithm (top). Most boundaries are identified precisely, except the first and fourth ones that are off by 1 and 12 sentences respectively.**

of sentences $s_1, s_2, \ldots, s_n$, then any segmentation is a subset of the space of gaps: $Gaps = \{g_1, g_2, \ldots, g_{n-1}\}$ (see Figure 4).

This space of gaps can be turned into a metric space by introducing a distance $d(g_i, g_j)$ between any pair of gaps $g_i$ and $g_j$. A simple choice for $d(g_i, g_j)$ is $|j - i|$, i.e., the number of sentences between the two gaps. Alternatively, if we also want to take into account the number of words in the sentences, $d(g_i, g_j)$ can be defined as the sum of the sentence lengths (in number of words) between the two gaps. To take into account the document length, this distance can be normalized by scaling the diameter of gaps to one.

Now, the segmentations $S$ and $S'$ are subsets of the metric space $Gaps$. Therefore, the Hausdorff distance between subsets [1] can be used to evaluate the distance between the two segmentations. Unfortunately, the Hausdorff distance is very sensitive to outliers, so some averaging is needed.

Currently, the most popular distance between segmentations is the WindowDiff distance ($WD$) [17]. It computes the distance between a reference segmentation $R$ and a candidate segmentation $C$ as follows:

$$WD(R, C) = \frac{1}{n - k} \sum_{i=1}^{n-k} \mathbb{1}\Big[B_R(i, i+k) \neq B_C(i, i+k)\Big]$$
(12)

where:

- $n$ is the number of sentences in the document,

- $k$ is the window size, in number of sentences, set to half the average segment size in the reference segmentation,

- $B_S(i, j)$ is the number of boundaries between sentences $s_i$ and $s_j$ in the segmentation $S$, and

- $\mathbb{1}$ is an "indicator" function:

$$\mathbb{1}[c] = \begin{cases} 1 & \text{if c is true,} \\ 0 & \text{otherwise.} \end{cases}$$
(13)

In words, the WindowDiff distance works by moving a window of size $k$ along the document. It adds a penalty of 1 for each window where the number of segment boundaries differs between the reference and candidate segmentations. The sum of penalties is then divided by the total number of windows to get a normalized score with values between 0 and 1.

Lamprier et al., in [12], noticed that errors at the beginning and end of a document are less penalized than errors in the middle of the document. This is corrected by adding $k - 1$ fictitious sentences at both ends of the document.

For evaluation, in this article, we shall be using the WindowDiff distance, with the Lamprier et al.'s correction [12].

## 4.2 Datasets

Evaluating and comparing segmentation algorithms can be tricky as it is often difficult to define what the reference (i.e., ground-truth) segmentation of a document should be. This is why most evaluation datasets are synthetic and contain documents created by concatenating segments of varying sizes and from different sources. However, a drawback of such synthetic datasets is that transitions between segments are more abrupt than in some natural documents.

In this article, we use Choi's synthetic dataset [7] which is commonly used for evaluation and contains 700 documents made of 10 segments[1]. Each segment consists of the beginning of a randomly sampled document from the Brown corpus. The segment sizes are chosen randomly and range between 3 and 11 sentences. The exact composition of the dataset is given in Table 1; the reader may refer to [7] for more details on this corpus.

**Table 1: Composition of Choi's dataset [7]**

| Range of segment sizes (in nb of sentences) | 3-5 | 3-11 | 6-8 | 9-11 |
|---|---|---|---|---|
| Nb of documents | 100 | 400 | 100 | 100 |

Segment with lengths ranging between 3 and 11 sentences are quite short and practical problems may require to deal with much longer segment sizes and much larger volumes of data. For this reason, we created another dataset containing 100 documents. Each document consists, again, of 10 segments, with segment sizes ranging between 30 to 50 sentences. We will refer to this dataset as "30-50". Similarly to Choi's methodology, we use articles sampled from the *News* and *Learned* categories of the Brown corpus.

## 4.3 Evaluation procedure

In this article, we compare our algorithm to *C99* [7] and *BayesSeg* [8]. We use the public domain implementations released by their respective authors. Two baseline algorithms are also used. The *Uniform* algorithm creates segments of equal size, while *Random* places segment boundaries randomly.

In all experiments, we consider the number of segments in each document known and given. This is a common assumption used for evaluation and comparison; the reasons are two-fold.

First, topics have inherently a hierarchical nature and segmentation can usually be done at different scales. Indeed, a

---

[1]These documents can be found in the folders $data/\{1,2,3\}/$ in package made publicly available by the author.

**Table 2: WindowDiff scores (using Lamprier et al.'s correction) of algorithms *with* stop-words removal.**

|            | C99   | BayesSeg | Our algorithm | Uniform | Random |
|------------|-------|----------|---------------|---------|--------|
| Choi 3-5   | 0.129 | **0.106** | 0.168        | 0.380   | 0.532  |
| Choi 3-11  | 0.140 | **0.108** | 0.191        | 0.456   | 0.531  |
| Choi 6-8   | 0.110 | **0.069** | 0.160        | 0.223   | 0.548  |
| Choi 9-11  | 0.093 | **0.057** | 0.128        | 0.189   | 0.537  |
| 30-50      | 0.078 | **0.014** | 0.050        | 0.274   | 0.522  |

**Table 3: WindowDiff scores (using Lamprier et al.'s correction) of algorithms *without* stop-words removal.**

|            | C99   | BayesSeg | Our algorithm | Uniform | Random |
|------------|-------|----------|---------------|---------|--------|
| Choi 3-5   | 0.340 | 0.189    | **0.141**     | 0.380   | 0.532  |
| Choi 3-11  | 0.378 | 0.182    | **0.176**     | 0.456   | 0.531  |
| Choi 6-8   | 0.356 | 0.178    | **0.143**     | 0.223   | 0.548  |
| Choi 9-11  | 0.385 | 0.141    | **0.109**     | 0.189   | 0.537  |
| 30-50      | 0.466 | 0.074    | **0.052**     | 0.274   | 0.522  |

long segment that discusses a broad topic is likely to discuss several sub-topics. For example, the chapter dedicated to the standard library of a C++ book may describe, in turn, basic containers, strings, streams and numeric tools. Therefore, the scale of segmentation (or, similarly, the number of segments desired) should be an input of the segmentation algorithm.

Second, inter-agreement between human annotators is generally very low. Even when receiving similar instructions, annotators tend to select widely different segment sizes on the same data. In [15], four annotators were asked to manually segment physics lecture transcripts; the average number of segments created by the different annotators ranged between 6.6 and 18.4. Naturally, algorithms face the same problem. The problem is even exacerbated as automatic procedures for determining the number of segments in a document are likely to be domain dependent, making comparisons difficult. As an illustration, we experimented with the *TextTiling* algorithm [11] (Choi's implementation with default parameters) and the 3-5 subset of Choi's dataset. The average number of segments produced by *TextTiling* is 23, when each document actually contains 10 segments. Inevitably *TextTiling* would score poorly; however, such a poor performance reflects an inadequate automatic selection of the number of segments but does not allow to fairly judge the intrinsic qualities of *TextTiling*.

We will also experiment with the effect of stop-words filtering on the results and, to this end, we modified both *C99* and *BayesSeg* implementations to make stop-words filtering optional. Indeed, stop-words removal is an extremely common preprocessing step across all Natural Language Processing techniques and algorithms, but it does create undesirable effects. Furthermore, there is not any universal list of stop-words. In the case of text segmentation, we argue that stop-words may contribute to the creation of lexical cohesion in a document and that, in most cases, stop-words can be helpful features for segmentation. Documents where each part has been written by a different author are clear examples; such documents include streams of news stories, specialized books where each chapter is written by a different expert, documents written collaboratively, etc. It is then reasonable to assume that each author will have his own writing style

and will use a slightly different set of stop-words. Filtering them inevitably means discarding useful information.

## 4.4 Experimental results and Discussion

Table 2 shows the evaluation results when stop-words are removed during preprocessing. The default list of stop-words for each algorithm was used. Choi's implementation of *C99* uses a list of 327 words while Eisenstein's implementation of *BayesSeg* uses 329 stop-words. In our algorithm, we used the default list provided by the Natural Language ToolKit library (NLTK) [3], consisting of 127 words. In this setting, *BayesSeg* consistently outperforms both *C99* and our algorithm, in most cases by a relatively wide margin. On short documents, *C99* performs slightly better than our algorithm while we outperform *C99* on longer documents.

However, all three algorithms behave quite differently when stop-words are not removed, as shown in Table 3. Our algorithm now gives better results than both *C99* and *BayesSeg*. The performance of *C99* is much worse in this case. The most likely explanation is that the pairwise sentence similarities are now completely dominated by insignificant words. The performance of *BayesSeg* is also degraded in this setting. On the contrary, our algorithm performs in most cases best when stop-words are not filtered.

Table 4 shows the influence of the stop-words list on the results. Each algorithm was tested using two different lists: the first one is a list of 127 words (the default for our algorithm, from NLTK) and the second one a common list of 571 words [2]. As can be seen from the table, the chosen stop-words list can have a significant impact on the performance of the algorithms. Furthermore, apart from *C99* where larger lists are preferable for reasons already explained, the list giving the best results is dependent on the dataset.

Summarizing the data from all three results tables, *BayesSeg* gives the best performance whenever a well-defined list of stop-words is available. This is not surprising: the algorithm looks for the best segmentation from all possible segmentations. However, such an analysis, as well as Bayesian inference techniques, are computationally expensive. Precise comparisons are not possible due to different programming languages. However, to give the reader an

Table 4: WindowDiff scores (using Lamprier et al.'s correction) of algorithms with different stop-words list. In each cell, the first score is obtained using a list of 127 words and the second using a list of 571 words.

| | C99 | BayesSeg | Our algorithm | Uniform | Random |
|---|---|---|---|---|---|
| Choi 3-5 | 0.138 / 0.122 | **0.109 / 0.110** | 0.168 / 0.180 | 0.380 | 0.532 |
| Choi 3-11 | 0.146 / 0.144 | **0.113 / 0.108** | 0.191 / 0.195 | 0.456 | 0.531 |
| Choi 6-8 | 0.117 / 0.105 | **0.072 / 0.078** | 0.160 / 0.176 | 0.223 | 0.548 |
| Choi 9-11 | 0.097 / 0.094 | **0.054 / 0.057** | 0.128 / 0.127 | 0.189 | 0.537 |
| 30-50 | 0.077 / 0.077 | **0.014 / 0.017** | 0.050 / 0.058 | 0.274 | 0.522 |

idea, the average running times of our algorithm (Python) and *C99* (Java) are about 0.5 seconds per document on the 30-50 dataset; *BayesSeg* (Java) requires on average 5.5 seconds per document on the same dataset. Furthermore, *BayesSeg* performs significantly worse when stop-words are not removed and this can be problematic since there is no canonical list. Therefore, adapting the algorithm to different domains (emails, tweets, IM, speech transcripts, etc.) or languages will require manual adaptation. On the other hand, our algorithm proves extremely robust to stop-words. It even performs best when stop-words are not removed. Furthermore, its relative performance compared to other algorithms improve as documents get longer. Those two facts can be explained by the statistical nature of the meaningulness scores used for feature extraction. Indeed, these scores seem to get more reliable as more data becomes available.

## 5. CONCLUSION

Automatic text segmentation algorithms can be used to improve the performance of many text mining tasks. In this article, we introduced a novel text segmentation algorithm that is completely unsupervised. This algorithm takes a single input parameter, the desired number of segments, allowing to segment a document at different scales, from small paragraphs to large sections. We evaluated and compared our algorithm with several state-of-the-art approaches. We showed that our algorithm has excellent accuracy and that it is both fast and extremely robust to stop-words, making it much more generic than other algorithms.

As part of future work, we would like to confirm the performance and genericity of our algorithm by evaluating it on different domains and languages.

## 6. REFERENCES

[1] Hausdorff distance. en.wikipedia.org/wiki/Hausdorff_distance. Accessed: 2014-07-21.

[2] List of stop-words. jmlr.org/papers/volume5/lewis04a/a11-smart-stop-list/english.stop. Accessed: 2014-07-21.

[3] Natural Language ToolKit (NLTK). nltk.org. Accessed: 2014-07-21.

[4] A. Balinsky, H. Balinsky, and S. Simske. On the Helmholtz principle for documents processing. *Proceedings of the 10th ACM DocEng*, 2010.

[5] H. Balinsky, A. Balinsky, and S. Simske. Automatic text summarization and small-world networks. *Proceedings of the 11th ACM DocEng*, 2011.

[6] D. Blei, A. Ng, and M. Jordan. Latent Dirichlet allocation. *ML Research*, 3:993–1022, 2003.

[7] F. Choi. Advances in domain independent linear text segmentation. In *Proceedings of the North American Chapter of the Association for Comp. Ling. Conference*, pages 26–33, 2000.

[8] J. Eisenstein and R. Barzilay. Bayesian unsupervised topic segmentation. In *Proceedings of the Conference on Empirical Methods in NLP*, pages 334–343, 2008.

[9] M. Galley, K. McKeown, E. Fosler-Lussier, and H. Jing. Discourse segmentation of multi-party conversation. In *Proceedings of the Annual Meeting on Association for Comp. Ling.*, pages 562–569, 2003.

[10] M. A. Halliday and R. Hasan. *Cohesion in English*. Longman, 1976.

[11] M. Hearst. TextTiling: segmenting text into multi-paragraph subtopic passages. *Comp. Ling.*, 23(1):33–64, 1997.

[12] S. Lamprier, T. Amghar, B. Levrat, and F. Saubion. On evaluation methodologies for text segmentation algorithms. In *Proceedings of the Conference on Tools with AI*, volume 2, pages 19–26, 2007.

[13] T. Lindeberg. *Scale-Space Theory in Computer Vision*. Springer, 1993.

[14] D. Litman and R. Passonneau. Combining multiple knowledge sources for discourse segmentation. In *Proceedings of the Annual Meeting of the Association for Comp. Ling.*, pages 108–115, 1995.

[15] I. Malioutov and R. Barzilay. Minimum cut model for spoken lecture segmentation. In *Proceedings of the International Conference on Comp. Ling.*, pages 25–32, 2006.

[16] J. Morris and G. Hirst. Lexical cohesion computed by thesaural relations as an indicator of the structure of text. *Comp. Ling.*, 17(1):21–48, 1991.

[17] L. Pevzner and M. Hearst. A critique and improvement of an evaluation metric for text segmentation. *Comp. Ling.*, 28(1):19–36, 2002.

[18] M. F. Porter. An algorithm for suffix stripping. *Program*, 14(3):130–137, 1980.

[19] M. Utiyama and H. Isahara. A statistical model for domain-independent text segmentation. In *Proceedings of the Annual Meeting on Association for Comp. Ling.*, pages 499–506, 2001.

[20] J. Yamron, I. Carp, L. Gillick, S. Lowe, and P. Van Mulbregt. A Hidden Markov model approach to text segmentation and event tracking. In *Proceedings of the Conference on Acoustics, Speech and Signal Processing*, pages 333–336, 1998.

# P-GTM: Privacy-Preserving Google Tri-gram Method for Semantic Text Similarity

Owen Davison        Abidalrahman Moh'd        Evangelos E. Milios

{odavison, amohd, eem}@cs.dal.ca
Faculty of Computer Science
Dalhousie University
6050 University Avenue
Halifax, NS, Canada, B3H 1W5

## ABSTRACT

This paper presents P-GTM, a privacy-preserving text similarity algorithm that extends the Google Tri-gram Method (GTM). The Google Tri-gram Method is a high-performance unsupervised semantic text similarity method based on the use of context from the Google Web 1T n-gram dataset. P-GTM computes the *semantic similarity* between two input bag-of-words documents on public cloud hardware, without disclosing the documents' contents. Like the GTM, P-GTM requires the uni-gram and tri-gram lists from the Google Web 1T n-gram dataset as additional inputs. The need for these additional lists makes private computation of GTM text similarities a challenging problem. P-GTM uses a combination of pre-computation, encryption, and randomized preprocessing to enable private computation of text similarities using the GTM. We discuss the security of the algorithm and quantify its privacy using standard and real life corpora.

## Categories and Subject Descriptors

K.4.1 [**Computers and Society**]: Public Policy Issues—*Privacy*; I.5.4 [**Pattern Recognition**]: Applications—*Text processing*

## Keywords

Data Privacy;Google Tri-gram Method;Text Similarity

## 1. INTRODUCTION

Data privacy is important to industry and end-users. Both have datasets whose contents they want to keep private, while at the same time being able to mine the data for useful insights.

The calculation of document similarity is a basic method in text-mining. It enables applications like document classification, clustering, and document-based queries. The Google

Tri-gram Method[1] is a recently-proposed[5] unsupervised semantic document similarity method that can be applied to any of these tasks. While the GTM has attractive similarity performance for an unsupervised method, it is a computationally expensive process.

Our work is motivated by the following scenario from industry. A company is implementing a document-similarity-based clustering method for automatic categorization of documents. Their corpora consist of sensitive documents, whose content must remain private. The GTM will be used because of its good text-similarity performance, but it proves to be too computationally expensive for the company's private hardware. We are therefore tasked with developing a privacy-preserving version of the GTM, to allow computation to take place on rented public cloud infrastructure, while maintaining the documents' privacy.

We propose P-GTM, an extension of the Google Tri-gram Method that allows the semantic similarity between texts to be computed while maintaining privacy. To achieve this, we add four pre-processing steps: computation of word-pair similarities, removal from the word-similarity list of lines with uni-grams that are not in the corpus, encryption of tokens in the word-similarity list and corpus, and an alphabetical sort of the encrypted text to randomize line orderings. After preprocessing, these files may be sent to un-trusted third-party hardware to perform the GTM computation. Since the similarity computation is extremely parallelizable, this allows us to take advantage of high-performance parallel machines or public cloud infrastructure, such as Amazon's EC2. In addition, the methods used for privacy of the GTM could be applied to other co-occurrence similarity techniques that require a shared resource accessible to an adversary.

## 2. RELATED WORK

Many different privacy-preserving techniques for document similarity have been explored, for applications in private document clustering and Secure Similar Document Detection (SSDD). P-GTM may be applied to the same problems, as well as allowing potentially expensive pair-wise similarity computations to take place on public cloud hardware.

Set-based approaches to the problem include techniques based on the Jaccard similarity index that allow two entities to maintain privacy while determining if their corpora contain any similar documents. This type of technique has

---

[1] http://ares.research.cs.dal.ca/gtm/

been extended by using MinHash to produce an approximation to the Jaccard similarity index, reducing computational cost[1]. Document fingerprints, unique document digests, can be used in place of entire documents to reduce the computational complexity of the SSDD problem. The SimHash method has been applied to produce these document fingerprints for application to SSDD[3].

Researchers have also evaluated vector-space approaches to SSDD. Special-purpose homomorphic encryptions have been used to allow the secure comparison of vector-space representations to find similar documents[6, 9]. As an alternative approach, the vectors used to calculate cosine-similarity may be permuted in a way that maintains privacy of the original data, without changing the angle computed for any pair of vectors[7].

Most methods compute the similarity between one document at a side with a corpus on the other side, and many are based on computationally expensive cryptographic operations like asymmetric and partially homomorphic encryption. P-GTM provides a suitable approach to both the SSDD and privacy-preserving clustering problems, while minimizing overhead to a few low-cost preprocessing steps.

## 3. GOOGLE TRI-GRAM METHOD

The Google Tri-gram Method (GTM) is an unsupervised method for calculating the semantic similarity between two texts[5]. Word n-grams from the Google Web 1T dataset[2] are used as context to compute similarities between two words, $w_a$ and $w_b$. If the words are the same, then their similarity is equal to 1.0. Otherwise, it is a function of the number and frequency of Google tri-grams that begin with $w_a$ and end with $w_b$ or vice versa.

To calculate the similarity between a pair of documents, the GTM considers a few of the words from the longer document which are most similar to each of the words in the shorter document. Word similarities are summed and then normalized to the length of the document, producing a similarity in $[0, 1]$. The document similarities may then be used as an input for machine learning algorithms.

| Uni-gram | Freq. | Tri-gram | Freq. |
|---|---|---|---|
| ... | ... | ... | ... |
| academic | 384 | academic and testing | 232 |
| also | 23422 | also need comprehensive | 145 |
| auctions | 123 | auctions are intended | 71 |
| ceramics | 4712 | ceramics chlorine free | 207 |
| driveway | 49 | driveway is plowed | 49 |
| ... | ... | ... | ... |

Table 1: Example uni-gram (left) and tri-gram (right) file format. Each line contains a uni-gram or tri-gram and its frequency in the Google dataset.

To compute document similarity, the algorithm requires bag-of-words representations of the documents and lists of uni-gram and tri-gram frequencies from the Google Web 1T dataset for the documents vocabulary. An example of each of these lists is shown in Table 1. To maintain privacy on the machine computing text similarity, we must conceal the tokens in the corpus and the n-gram lists while ensuring that the frequencies can still be used to compute similarities.

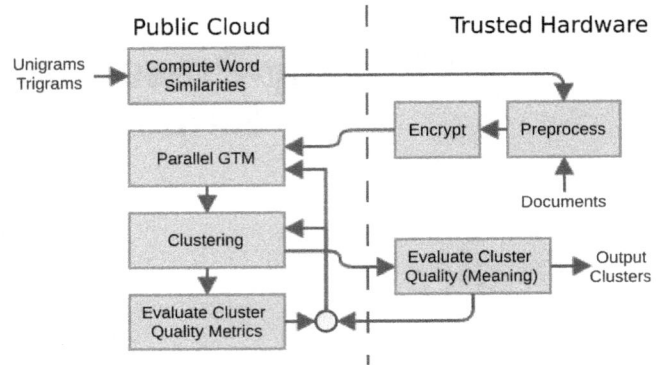

Figure 1: An overview of the scenario addressed by P-GTM. The work is divided into pre-processing steps that must be run on the trusted hardware, and text-similarity computation and clustering that takes place on the public cloud once the input data is made private.

## 4. PRIVATE GTM (P-GTM)

We show an overview of the security scenario in Figure 1, and summarize the algorithm in Algorithm 1. The public cloud is the third-party parallel hardware on which all of the GTM computation and the clustering is performed, and is assumed to be accessible to an adversary. The trusted hardware is the machine controlled by the owner of the private corpus that will be processed, and we assume it to be fully secure.

---

On the trusted hardware:
1. **Pre-compute word-pair similarities from unigrams and tri-grams**
2. Tokenize the corpus using Penn-Treebank tokenizer
3. Remove stop-words
4. **Remove all tokens that do not appear in the corpus from the similarity list**
5. **Encrypt each token in the corpus and word-similarity list with AES-128 in ECB mode**
6. **Sort encrypted word-similarity list alphabetically**

On the public cloud:
7. Perform the GTM text-similarity computation and return the results

---

Algorithm 1: High-level description of P-GTM. Bolded lines indicate the additions made to the GTM.

**Steps 2, 3, and 7** in Algorithm 1 are common to both P-GTM and GTM. Both methods operate on bag-of-words representations of the input documents, produced through a Penn-Treebank tokenization, and both remove stopwords to reduce noise in computed document similarities. The remaining steps are added in P-GTM to ensure document privacy.

| List | $k$-anonymity | |
|---|---|---|
| | Minimum | Average |
| Uni-gram | 1 | 29 |
| Tri-gram | 1 | 397 |
| Word-Similarity | 1696 | 97202 |

**Table 2: $k$-anonymity of tokens in the Google uni-gram list, tri-gram list, and the pre-computed word-similarity list.**

| Quantity | Value |
|---|---|
| Average | $9.7 \times 10^{-6}$ |
| Standard Deviation | $8.1 \times 10^{-5}$ |
| One-Sample $t(29)$ | 0.7 |
| p-value | 0.5 |

**Table 3: Differences between text-similarity values calculated with and without word-similarity rounding.**

## 4.1 Development of P-GTM

The main obstacle to privacy for the GTM is the required frequency information in the uni-gram and tri-gram lists. An adversary may use the frequencies in his own downloaded copy of the Google n-gram dataset to match encrypted tokens to their cleartext equivalents. This relates to a concept in privacy known as $k$-anonymity[10]. If an entity has a unique value for an attribute, then given the value of that attribute, an adversary can identify the entity. Modifying the dataset so that $k$ entities share that attribute-value means that the adversary can only know the entity is one of those $k$, and cannot identify the specific entity. There are many trigrams with unique frequencies ($k$-anonymity of 1), as shown in Table 2.

This issue motivates a search for a way to increase the $k$-anonymity of the tokens. By pre-computing word-pair similarities, we reduce the range of values from $[40, \sim 9 \times 10^6)$ in the case of tri-gram frequencies to a similarity in $[0, 1]$. Because the number of word pairs with similarities is large ($\sim 1 \times 10^7$) and well-distributed in $[0, 1]$, rounding similarities to a finite precision causes the similarities for many word-pairs to be the same. Now, given a similarity value, an adversary only knows that it is connected to one of these $k$ word pairs. Rounding to three decimal places guarantees that every similarity value is repeated at least 1000 times ($k > 1000$). This pre-computation need only be done once for any version of the Google n-gram dataset, and becomes **Step 1** of P-GTM.

To ensure this process does not significantly impact the text-similarity results of the method, we evaluate the effect of rounding similarities to three decimal places. We use the 30-sentences dataset[8] from the original evaluation of the tri-gram similarity method[5]. We compute the similarity for each sentence pair with the rounding, and subtract the similarity calculate with no rounding. The text similarities computed with rounding were not significantly different from those calculated with all the available word-similarity precision (Table 3).

The requirement for the shared word-similarity lists enables another kind of frequency attack on the GTM. An adversary could traverse the cleartext and ciphertext word-similarity lists, counting the number of lines on which each token appears. For each token, these counts will be the same for both lists, allowing the adversary to find the unencrypted token for many of the encrypted tokens. In a related process, the adversary could read through both lists, summing the similarity values for each token. This value is also correlated between the encrypted and cleartext lists. We call these two attacks *line-counts* and *similarity-sums*.

To mitigate this type of attack, the word-similarity list is processed on the trusted hardware to remove all similarity pairs containing tokens not in the corpus. These removals change computed line-counts and similarity-sums in an unpredictable way, and produce a re-ordering of the words' totals for these values. This becomes **Step 4** of P-GTM.

In **Step 5**, tokens in both the word-similarity list and corpus are encrypted using AES-128 in Electronic Code Book (ECB) mode. This conceals the meaning of each token, while still allowing us to correlate tokens between the corpus and word-similarity list to perform the GTM computation. We then sort the lists alphabetically based on the ciphertext, randomizing line order (**Step 6**). Finally, with document privacy protected, the GTM similarity computation can be run on the public cloud.

## 5. QUANTIFICATION OF PRIVACY

To determine the level of privacy offered by P-GTM, we evaluate the computational cost of correlating a single word between the clear- and cypher-texts, and of doing the same for an entire document from the corpus.

As described in Section 4.1, an adversary can compute line-counts or similarity-sums for each token in a word similarity list he precomputes from the Google n-gram dataset. He can do the same for the encrypted word-similarity list. If he then ranks the two lists by, for example, the line-counts for each token, the two lists will have a similar ordering. The adversary can assume that a token found in his cleartext list will be in approximately the same position in the encrypted list, and attempt to recover the cleartext tokens for each encrypted token.

To evaluate this possibility, we performed the preprocessing steps for three datasets: Reuters 21578, and two industry corpora. We pre-computed word similarities and removed words not in the corpus from the similarity list. To allow us to measure rank differences between tokens, we did not encrypt the processed list. We computed the line-counts and similarity-sums for all datasets, and ranked the resulting lists by line count and by similarity sum. We recorded the difference between each token's rank on the unprocessed and processed lists. We show the resulting rank differences for similarity sums, the worse of the two cases, in Figure 2.

At the top of the list (highest line-counts or similarity-sums), the same token appears in both lists with nearly the same rank, but this rank difference increases rapidly as we move down the list to less-common words. The words near the top of the list are the most common English words in the corpus, and are less informative than those found lower in the list. Preprocessing the similarity-list to remove words that do not appear in the corpus is effective for protecting single informative words from an adversary who has access to both the Google n-gram dataset and the encrypted word-similarity list.

At the document level, an adversary would need to generate and check the different possible cleartext bag-of-word representations, a combinatorial problem. Assuming that

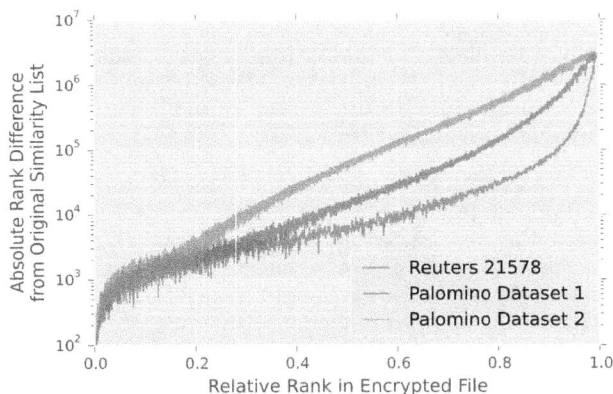

**Figure 2: Absolute rank differences between similarity-sums for encrypted and unencrypted lists as a function of rank in the encrypted list for the Reuters 21578, and two real-world datasets.**

he can make an educated guess for $d$, the rank difference between word in the original and processed similarity-sum lists, he will still need to search $2 * d$ tokens, $d$ on average, to find the cleartext corresponding to an encrypted token.

For a document with $n$ encrypted tokens, $N_{avg}$, the number of possible decryptions the adversary will need to check will be given by Equation 1, where $d_i$ is the maximum rank difference for word $i$. Each decryption will need to be evaluated, a difficult task in itself, given that all structural information about the document is removed in the preprocessing step. Even with successful decryption, the adversary can only recover a bag-of-words representation of the original document.

$$N_{avg} = \prod_{i=1}^{n} d_i \qquad (1)$$

We performed an empirical evaluation of this computational cost using the Reuters 21578 dataset. For this dataset, the shortest document has a length of 17 tokens, and could be recovered in $2^{159}$ attempts on average.

## 6. CONCLUSIONS AND FUTURE WORK

We evaluated P-GTM in terms of the computational cost to an adversary of discovering the contents of the input documents. The method is very effective at protecting the contents of entire documents, due to the combinatorial problem produced by the high $k$-anonymity for each word-pair. By removing words that do not appear in the corpus from the pre-computed word-similarity list, P-GTM also becomes resistant to more sophisticated frequency attacks such as line-counts and similarity sums.

There are several avenues of future work that could further improve P-GTM. The first is to incorporate tri-grams collected from the corpus into the calculation of the word-similarity list, before sending it to the public cloud. This will produce word-pair similarities that an adversary would be unable to calculate using only the public Google n-gram dataset.

A second option is to remove more of the common words from the word-similarity list and preprocessed corpus. Words

in the corpus could be weighted by some measure of their informativeness, such as term frequency-inverse document frequency (*tf-idf*). Words below some threshold weight would then be discarded. Since these unimportant words are likely to be common in the Google n-Gram dataset, they will interact with many other words. Removing them will introduce a strong random element to the line-counts and similarity-sums mentioned in Section 4.1.

Finally, should homomorphic encryption[4] become computationally practical, it could immediately be applied to ensure complete privacy of the method.

## 7. ACKNOWLEDGEMENTS

We gratefully acknowledge funding from the Natural Sciences and Engineering Research Council of Canada (NSERC) and the Boeing Company, and technical advice by Dr. Bryan Kramer of Palomino System Innovations Inc.

## 8. REFERENCES

[1] C. Blundo, E. De Cristofaro, and P. Gasti. EsPRESSo: efficient privacy-preserving evaluation of sample set similarity. *Data Privacy Management and Autonomous Spontaneous Security Lecture Notes in Computer Science*, 7731:89–103, 2013.

[2] T. Brants and A. Franz. Web 1T 5-gram corpus version 1.1. Technical report, Google Research, 2006.

[3] S. Buyrukbilen and S. Bakiras. Secure similar document detection with simhash. In W. Jonker and M. Petkovi, editors, *Secure Data Management*, Lecture Notes in Computer Science, pages 61–75. Springer International Publishing, 2014.

[4] C. Gentry. *A fully homomorphic encryption scheme.* PhD thesis, Stanford University, 2009. crypto.stanford.edu/craig.

[5] A. Islam, E. Milios, and V. Keselj. Text similarity using google tri-grams. In L. Kosseim and D. Inkpen, editors, *Advances in Artificial Intelligence*, volume 7310 of *Lecture Notes in Computer Science*, pages 312–317. Springer Berlin Heidelberg, 2012.

[6] W. Jiang and B. Samanthula. N-gram based secure similar document detection. *Data and Applications Security and Privacy XXV Lecture Notes in Computer Science*, 6818:239–246, 2011.

[7] I. Leontiadis, M. Onen, R. Molva, M. Chorley, and G. Colombo. Privacy preserving similarity detection for data analysis. *2013 IEEE Third International Conference on Cloud and Green Computing*, pages 547–552, Sept. 2013.

[8] Y. Li, D. McLean, Z. A. Bandar, J. D. O'shea, and K. Crockett. Sentence similarity based on semantic nets and corpus statistics. *IEEE Transactions on Knowledge and Data Engineering*, 18(8):1138–1150, 2006.

[9] M. Murugesan, W. Jiang, C. Clifton, L. Si, and J. Vaidya. Efficient privacy-preserving similar document detection. *The International Journal on Very Large Data Bases*, 7731(4):457–475, Aug. 2010.

[10] L. Sweeney. K-anonymity: A model for protecting privacy. *International Journal of Uncertainty, Fuzziness and Knowledge-Based Systems*, 10(5):557–570, Oct. 2002.

# Web-Intrinsic Interactive Documents

Anthony Wiley
HP Exstream
810 Bull Lea Run
Lexington, KY 40511 USA
anthony.wiley@hp.com

## ABSTRACT

Modern interactive documents are complex applications that give the user the editing experience of editing a document as it will look in its final visual form. Sections of the document can be either editable, or read-only, and can dynamically conform artifacts like images to specific users. The components underlying interactive documents are dynamically bound variables and a complex rule engine for adapting the document as the user edits.

Web interactive documents deliver the dynamic editing experience through the web by using a web browser for deploying the editor. Document editors *built-in* the web browser as a native application provide a higher quality editing experience because the editor's look and feel is consistent with the web browser's innate controls and navigation.

The majority of traditional interactive documents have been developed using proprietary formats which are not compatible with today's web browser implementations because they were originally intended as desk-top applications. As a consequence, traditional interactive documents are not inherently web applications.

This talk will provide an overview of the technical challenges faced in developing a web-intrinsic interactive document solution that simultaneously addresses the need for simple, yet rich, user editing features combined with the scalability, and ease of deployment, demanded by enterprises today.

By way of example, I will introduce, and demonstrate, a new interactive document representation and deployment model. A prerequisite for such representations is that they enable documents to account for traditional document roles and still behave as intrinsic web content for document interaction. Another is that they are also able to support conventional enterprise workflows and complex processes, e.g. approvals, audit, versioning, storage and archival.

## Categories and Subject Descriptors

I.7.1 [**Document and Text Processing**]: Document and Text Editing; H.3.4 [**Information Storage and Retrieval**]: Systems and Software – *Distributed Systems.*

## General Terms

Design, Standardization, Languages

## Keywords

Interactive documents

*DocEng'14*, September 16–19, 2014, Fort Collins, Colorado, USA.
ACM 978-1-4503-2949-1/14/09.
http://dx.doi.org/10.1145/2644866.2644901

## Short Bio

Anthony (Tony) Wiley is the R&D Director for HP Exstream. A leader in Customer Communications Management (CCM) HP Exstream develops and sells automated customized document production and distribution software and services.

Tony joined Hewlett-Packard Laboratories in 1989 where his research was centred on High Performance Networks and Communications. His early work lead to advances in areas including high performance protocol testing and packet/frame switching architectures. After forming, and leading, the Custom Publishing Systems group in HP Labs in 2002 he went on to build the Web Services & Systems Laboratory in 2007 before taking on the role of Director, HP Exstream R&D in 2009. Key aspects of his current role are to identify, develop and deliver, key innovations that lead to significant product and service differentiation; an example of which is HP Relate: a cloud deployed document composition service.

# Fine-grained Change Detection in Structured Text Documents

Hannes Dohrn
Friedrich-Alexander-University
Erlangen-Nürnberg
Martensstr. 3, 91058 Erlangen, Germany
+49 9131 85 27621
hannes.dohrn@fau.de

Dirk Riehle
Friedrich-Alexander-University
Erlangen-Nürnberg
Martensstr. 3, 91058 Erlangen, Germany
+49 9131 85 27621
dirk@riehle.org

## ABSTRACT

Detecting and understanding changes between document revisions is an important task. The acquired knowledge can be used to classify the nature of a new document revision or to support a human editor in the review process. While purely textual change detection algorithms offer fine-grained results, they do not understand the syntactic meaning of a change. By representing structured text documents as XML documents we can apply tree-to-tree correction algorithms to identify the syntactic nature of a change.

Many algorithms for change detection in XML documents have been propsed but most of them focus on the intricacies of generic XML data and emphasize speed over the quality of the result. Structured text requires a change detection algorithm to pay close attention to the content in text nodes, however, recent algorithms treat text nodes as black boxes.

We present an algorithm that combines the advantages of the purely textual approach with the advantages of tree-to-tree change detection by redistributing text from non-overlapping common substrings to the nodes of the trees. This allows us to not only spot changes in the structure but also in the text itself, thus achieving higher quality and a fine-grained result in linear time on average. The algorithm is evaluated by applying it to the corpus of structured text documents that can be found in the English Wikipedia.

## Categories and Subject Descriptors

I.7.1 [**Computing Methodologies**]: Document and Text Editing; F.2.2 [**Theory of Computation**]: Nonnumerical Algorithms and Problems; E.1 [**Data**]: Data Structures

## General Terms

Algorithms, Design, Performance

## Keywords

XML; WOM; structured text; change detection; tree matching; tree differencing; tree similarity; tree-to-tree correction; diff

## 1. INTRODUCTION

Change detection is important in many applications. It can be used for temporal queries (when did a certain change occur in an article) or to maintain an index (just update what we know has changed, don't re-index). It can be used for merging documents that have diverged from a common ancestor or to visualize the changes between two revisions of a document (in version control systems). By only storing differences between revisions, change detection algorithms can be used to compress data, and in classification it can help to understand the intent of an author or identify unwanted contributions like spam.

We focus on change detection in structured text documents as generated by word processors or markup languages like HTML, in order to help authors understand the nature of changes by visualization and to automatically classify changes. Structured text documents are composed of mainly text interspersed with formatting elements (e.g. bold font, hyperlink, section heading) that we refer to as syntactic markup. To detect changes between two revisions of a document textual differencing algorithms are commonly used. However, these tools treat structured text as a sequence of characters, without paying special attention to its syntactic markup. This leads to misalignment of content between the revisions under comparison and makes it difficult to discover the syntactic nature of changes.

These problems can be avoided by using tree-to-tree correction algorithms that are applied to the syntax tree representation of structured text documents. However, unlike textual differencing tools, which generate fine-grained information on the character level, available tree differencing algorithms treat continuous blocks of text as atomic entities. Assume a sentence in which bold formatting is applied to a word. If the sentence was stored in a single text node previously, the text node will be split in the new revision and in between the two halves of the text the bold formatting node is inserted, with the formatted word as its only child node. This and similar changes are common in structured text, however, current tree differencing algorithms are unable to properly address this situation since they can only perform a one-to-one mapping between the nodes of the old and new tree.

Another problem we face when applying tree differencing tools to structured text is the focus on speed and greedy matching behavior and in some cases the reliance on XML intricacies like IDs or keys to find matching nodes. Since we aim to support humans and automatic text classification the quality of the generated change set is important and overly greedy behavior for the sake of speed is not constructive.

Our main contribution is the novel treatment of text leaves. As detailed in the following chapters we analyze unmatched text and subdivide text nodes to achieve a fine-grained matching where other algorithms report the removal and insertion of whole text nodes. We further modify existing differencing algorithms to perform less greedy and emphasize ancestor relationships between nodes when searching for a matching.

Our algorithm has the following features:

- It operates on an XML representation of structured text called WOM [6]. That is, it operates on rooted, ordered labeled trees in which only attributes and leaves can have values.

- It does not assume the presence of IDs or other unique identifiers that would otherwise simplify the matching process.

- It produces an edit script that features the operations insert, delete, move and update.

- It computes an edit script in near linear time and space on average.

The remainder of the paper is structured as follows. In section 2 we discuss related work. We then introduce terms and definitions and define the input data that our algorithm operates on in section 3. Afterwards we present and analyze our algorithm in section 4. Finally, we evaluate the algorithm in section 5 and conclude in section 6.

## 2. RELATED WORK

Often software for describing and visualizing differences between two versions of the same document relies on a purely textual, line-based representation of the document. A prominent example is the GNU diffutils[1] package which uses an algorithm described by Myers in [11]. Myers presents an algorithm that solves the *longest common subsequence* (LCS) problem in $O(nd)$ time, where $n$ is the combined lengths of two strings $A$ and $B$ and $d$ is the size of the minimum edit script that transforms $A$ into $B$.

The textual approach is appealing for its simplicity and its broad applicability. Any document that has a textual, line-based representation (which also includes almost any kind of XML document) can be efficiently compared using this algorithm. On the other hand, such a generic algorithm does not consider syntactic subtleties of the document. Many document formats in use today, however, exhibit a rich syntactic structure either implicitly or explicitly.

Many algorithms have been devised to calculate the differences between two trees, also called the tree-to-tree correction problem [17]. One way to classify existing tree differencing algorithms is by the type of tree they operate on (ordered/unordered). Another way is to ask whether the algorithm strictly minimizes a cost function to produce a minimal edit script or if it uses a heuristic approach that orientates itself on a cost metric but is not guaranteed to produce a minimal edit script for that metric. Although we want to operate on ordered trees exclusively, it is instructive to see what algorithms exist for unordered trees as well. In the following discussion $n_i$ denotes the number of nodes, $d_{max,i}$ the maximum depth and $l_i$ the number leaves of tree $T_i$. If no index is given, the quantities are summed up from both trees.

[1] http://www.gnu.org/software/diffutils/

In [17] Tai defines the distance $d(T_1, T_2)$ between two trees as the cost of the minimum cost edit sequence $s$, according to a restricted cost function $c(s)$ and presents an algorithm that solves this minimization problem in time $O(n_1 \cdot n_2 \cdot d_{max,1}^2 \cdot d_{max,2}^2)$. The algorithm generates the edit operations update, delete and change label.

In [20] Zhang and Shasha improve on Tai's algorithm with sequential time in $O(n_1 \cdot n_2 \cdot \min(d_{max,1}, l_1) \cdot \min(d_{max,2}, l_2))$, while supporting the same edit operations.

Chawathe et al. are the first to introduce a heuristic algorithm called *LaDiff* in [3]. Instead of only considering labeled trees they also take node values into account to deal with LaTeX documents. The finest level of subdivision that Chawathe et al. use are sentences; the leaf nodes are therefore large text nodes. They are also the first to propose approximate text node matching using an edit cost function to calculate the similarity of two text nodes. After first matching the leaf nodes of a document using the LCS algorithm by Myers they then propagate matches to the inner nodes, again using the LCS algorithm.

Their heuristic assumes that input documents contain only few identical nodes. The produced edit script is always correct, however, if the assumption does not hold the result may be sub-optimal. They try to compensate for identical nodes with a post-processing step and achieve an overall run time complexity in $O(ne + e^2)$, where $e$ is the weighted edit distance and typically $e \ll n$. The algorithm generates the edit operations insert, delete, update and move.

In [2] Chawathe et al. assert that the change detection problem for unordered labeled tress that considers move and copy operations is $\mathcal{NP}$-hard. They propose a heuristic algorithm, called *MH-DIFF*, that transforms the tree-to-tree correction problem to the problem of finding the minimum cost edge cover of a bipartite graph. Its worst case performance is in $O(n^3)$ but most often requires time in $O(n^2)$.

Cobéna and Marian [4] focus on performance in terms of speed and space. Their heuristic algorithm *XyDiff* makes use of node IDs and first matches nodes that have the same ID. Then identical subtrees are matched by computing hash values for subtrees to allow fast look-ups, always matching the next biggest subtree first. The remaining nodes are matched by propagating matches bottom-up similar to [3], followed by an additional lazy-down pass. The matching rules during the propagation pass are kept simple but greedy which can lead to bad mappings as observed by [18], especially if there are many small identical subtrees. The algorithm generates the edit operations insert, delete, update and move and runs in $O(n \log(n))$ time. It therefore does not slow down when faced with lots of changes.

Xu et al. [19] transform the problem of finding a match between trees to finding a match between so-called key trees. In a key tree each node is a label and all paths from the root to a leaf generate a unique sequence of labels. If a label is not unique among its siblings, it is replaced by a value from the original node's subtree that is expected to be unique. Their algorithm *KF-Diff+* supports the edit operations insert, delete and update and runs in $O(n)$. It can be extended to support node moves among siblings (called alignment).

Wang et al. [18] implement an XML change detection algorithm called *X-Diff* that assumes that left-to-right order among siblings is not important and instead focuses on ancestor relationship. They drastically reduce the search space by only matching nodes whose parents match as well and who have the same signature, where signature$(x)$ = label$(p_1)$/ label$(p_2)$/.../label$(p_{i-1})$/type$(x)$ and $(p_1, ..., p_{i-1}, x)$ is a path from the root node $p_1$ to node $x$. They achieve a run time complexity in $O(n)$ and support the edit operations insert, delete and update.

Lindholm et al. [10] transform both trees into sequences of nodes. To match the trees they slide windows of decreasing size over the sequences and search for matches using a rolling hash function. They achieve worst case performance in $O(n^2)$ if both documents have nothing in common and $O(n)$ if both documents are identical. The supported edit operations are insert, delete, update and move. We refer to their algorithm under the name *FcDiff*.

Fluri et al. [7] apply various improvements to the *LaDiff* algorithm [3] to adapt it for detecting and classifying changes in source code. Their algorithm *change distilling* produces the same edit operations as the original.

Rönnau et al. [13] present the algorithm *DocTreeDiff* which, similar to the *LaDiff* algorithm [3], uses a leaf-based LCS to compute an initial matching. Unlike *LaDiff* they operate on hash values of leaf nodes which also incorporate the node's depth. Using the initial matching, structural changes among the parent nodes are encoded as updates while all remaining un-matched nodes are recorded as deletes and inserts. Their algorithm performs in $O(lD+n)$, where $D$ denotes the number of edit operations required.

Rönnau et al. analyzed requirements for version control of XML documents produced by word processors or spreadsheets in [14]. For a broader selection of algorithms and more in-depth information on the individual algorithms one can consult the survey from Peters [12] on change detection in XML trees or the survey by Bille [1] on solutions for the general tree edit distance problem.

## 3. PRELIMINARIES

In the following chapters variable names $a_i$, $s, t, u$ and $x$ refer to nodes in $T_1$, $b_i$, $s', t', u'$ and $y$ refer to nodes in $T_2$, where $T_1$ and $T_2$ refer to the tree representation of the old and new document respectively.

### 3.1 Edit Script and Tree Format

An edit script generated from two documents $A$ and $B$ is a list of operations that when applied to document $A$ transforms it into document $B$. Which edit operations an algorithm uses in an edit script depends on its design. We are not aware of a standardized format for presenting edit scripts and rely on the operations introduced by Chawathe in [3].

The design of tree nodes differs between implementations. Our algorithm is designed to expect trees similar to XML documents that consist of two types of nodes: elements and text nodes. An element node $n$ has a label $l(n)$ (called tag in XML), a set of attributes, where an attribute is a (name, value) pair and an ordered list of children. Elements can be leaf nodes if their list of children is empty. Text nodes, on the other hand, cannot have children and are therefore always leaf nodes. They have a value $v(n)$ but no label or attributes. It is possible to map other tree designs onto XML trees.

### 3.2 Input Data Format

We use wiki articles as test corpus for our algorithm. Articles in wikis are usually written in a markup language called wiki markup. For the wiki markup dialect used in MediaWiki we have implemented a parser in [5] that produces

an Abstract Syntax Tree (AST). This representation is further converted into a wiki independent exchange format called Wiki Object Model (WOM) [6], which we will use as input data in our evaluation.

A distinctive feature of the WOM is the optional support of so-called Round Trip Data (RTD) tags. These tags preserve the syntactic markup from the original source and guarantee that the formatting of the original source can be restored from WOM trees after a transformation. For illustration consider the following piece of wiki markup:

```
'''Tree''' differencing
```

which translates to the following WOM document:

```
<article><body><p>
  <b><rtd>'''</rtd><text>Tree</text><rtd>'''</rtd>
  </b><text> differencing</text>
</p></body></article>
```

Three ticks denote the use of bold font and the ticks themselves are stored as RTD information. As this short example shows, the WOM format has some idiosyncrasies that require special attention. Our differencing algorithm does not operate on the WOM directly but uses an adapter mechanism that allows processing of various data structure designs. In the case of the WOM the adapter hides `<rtd>` elements when the algorithm asks for text nodes explicitly, however, they are reported in a traversal of the tree. When traversing the tree, the adapter reports `<rtd>` and `<text>` nodes as leaf text nodes instead of elements that contain XML text nodes. Finally, it also represents certain element attributes (e.g. the target attribute of a link) as child nodes.

The reason for presenting attributes as elements is that our algorithm does not consider attributes when evaluating the similarity of nodes. This adjustment therefore guarantees that important information that is stored in attributes is considered by the algorithm while keeping the algorithm itself simple. The reasons for the other adjustments are explained when the algorithm is described. All of the mentioned variations are reversible and other document formats may not require any adaptions at all.

### 3.3 Challenges of Structured Text Documents

In the English Wikipedia we find the following text in the article "Danish pastry" [2]:

```
Danish pastry is formed of flour, milk,
eggs, and butter -- especially butter.
```

In the next revision an editor has turned the words "flour", "milk", "eggs" and "butter" into links so that they point to the respective articles in Wikipedia:

```
Danish pastry is formed of [[flour]], [[milk]],
[[egg]]s, and [[butter]] -- especially butter.
```

Removing or adding styles happens frequently in structured documents as [13] note as well, and line-based diff algorithms can cope with this change well and report only the insertion of square brackets, however, they are unaware of the syntactic implications.

Another common practice is the rearrangement of text within a sentence or paragraph. Line-based diff algorithms report the movement of text as insertion and deletion since they often don't support move operations. However, they usually only report the text span that has actually changed. They don't report the removal or insertion of a whole sentence if only part of it has changed.

---

[2]Revision 657740 and 1019401

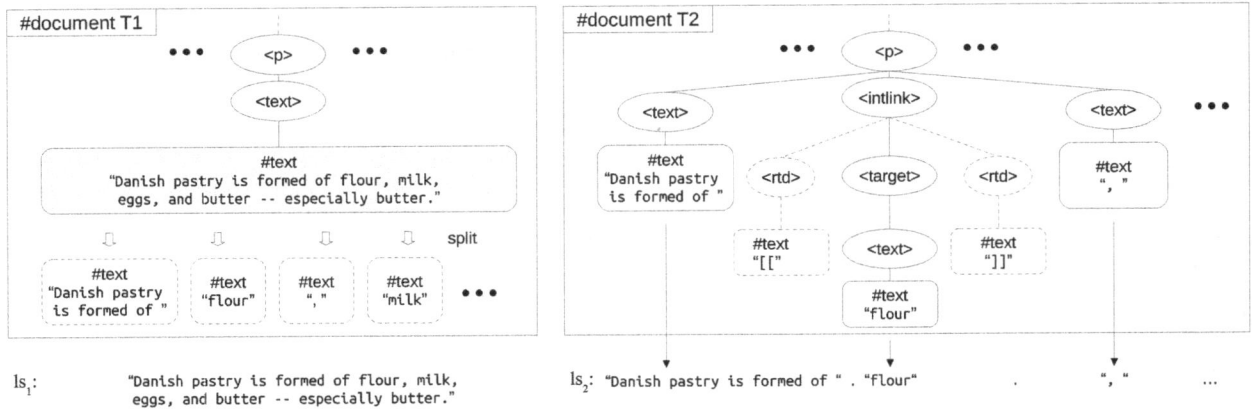

**Figure 1:** Distribution of text over nodes in the old and new revision of an article and the corresponding leaf strings. Only a part of the new tree ($T_2$) is shown for clarity. Both trees have more paragraphs than those depicted. In $T_1$ the dashed nodes indicate the possible splits of the text leaf.

In both of the above cases tree differencing algorithms behave differently. An excerpt of the corresponding WOM trees for both revisions is shown in figure 1. The article "Danish pastry" has more than just one paragraph (<p>) but we do not show them for reasons of clarity. In the old revision the whole text was contained within one text node. In the new revision text nodes are interspersed with internal links (<intlink>) which contain a target node (that is also the title) and two <rtd> tags that store the syntactic markup.

If we only extract and concatenate the <text> nodes and not the <rtd> nodes from these trees, we obtain the same string for both documents. In other words: No changes with regard to textual content have occurred between the two revisions. Tree differencing algorithms, however, can only match nodes one-to-one. Algorithms that perform approximate text node matching might associate the initial "Danish pastry is formed of" text node in the new revision with the entire <text> node in the old revision, because it yields the smallest edit distance between all candidates. Still all other nodes in the new tree remain unmatched and the algorithms usually report the complete removal of the whole paragraph and new node insertions. While [13] identify this challenge as well, they do not present a solution to this particular problem.

The same problem occurs when text is moved within a text node, as shown in figure 2. In that case the number of text nodes stays the same, however, the old and new text nodes don't match any more and an insertion and a removal is reported. In the case of approximate matching the result depends on the nature of the change within the text node. If the edit distance between old and new text stays below a preconfigured threshold, an update is reported. Otherwise, insertion and removal is reported. In the following section we describe how we address these challenges.

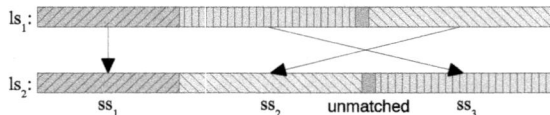

**Figure 2:** Two leaf strings $ls_1$ and $ls_2$, that are possibly spread over multiple text nodes, were concatenated. The NOCS algorithm found three common substrings $s_1$, $s_2$ and $s_3$ that have been rearranged by the edit. A small part of the leaf strings is not part of a common substring and the corresponding text node splits will not be matched.

## 4. CHANGE DETECTION WITH HDDiff

Most tree differencing algorithms run through a sequence of processing phases. First a matching between the two trees is computed. It pairs a node from the old tree with exactly one and only one partner node from the new tree. Nodes in the old tree that do not have a partner are reported as deleted nodes. Nodes in the new tree that do not have a partner are reported as inserted nodes. Nodes that are partners but have different parent nodes (according to the matching) are reported as moved nodes. If nodes have the same parents but have changed position among their siblings, they are reported as moved nodes as well, however, the process of finding those cases is called *alignment*. Except for one exception ([2]) we are not aware of heuristic algorithms that support copy operations (one-to-many mappings). Once a mapping is computed, a list of operations called an edit script is generated that transforms the old tree into the new tree.

### 4.1 Matching Substrings of Text Nodes

In section 3.3 we have illustrated what happens if editors mark up words or move text around among paragraphs. While the textual content stays the same (the order may change) the atomic treatment of text nodes does not allow existing differencing algorithms to properly address the situation. As solution we introduce the **split** operation. This operation is an auxiliary edit script operation. It is not reported to the user since it doesn't change the content of a document, however, it allows us to internally operate on substrings that originally were part of a bigger text node.

When looking at the example in figure 1 again it becomes clear that by splitting the original and only text node into a sequence of smaller text nodes we can match the complete original document. We only have to report the newly inserted links and their RTD information in the new document, but no text will be reported as deleted or inserted. By concatenating the splits we can restore the text from the original text node, which is why we regard this operation as effectless.

If we have found a good splitting of text nodes that allows us to match a greater portion of old and new content, we apply the operation to the trees and add the necessary operations to the edit script. The relevance of the split operations in the edit script depends on the purpose of the edit script. If the edit script is used to report information about changes to the user, splits can be ignored. If the edit script is used to transform a document to its new revision, splits have to be applied since other edit operations will depend on the already split nodes.

The split operation is also the reason why the WOM tree adapter presents `<rtd>` and `<text>` elements as text leaves and not as XML elements that contain XML text. If our algorithm would split the XML text nodes and not the combination of XML element and XML text, the XML text splits would become the children of only one `<text>` element. However, in a WOM tree every XML text needs its own `<text>` parent element.

### 4.1.1 Finding a Good Split

Our goal is therefore to find those text leaves in both documents that, when split, will allow us to precisely match unchanged textual content in both revisions. A naive approach is to split all text nodes into individual words. This, however, is difficult when dealing with languages that do not support simple word segmentation (e.g. they don't require spaces between words) and it would also force matches by aligning words from arbitrary locations in the document.

Instead we search for continuous substrings that are shared by both documents and satisfy certain requirements (e.g. are of sufficient length or contain enough words). To this end we concatenate the text from all text leaves into the leaf strings $ls_1$ for $T_1$ and $ls_2$ for $T_2$ as illustrated in figure 1. Between these strings we search for *non-overlapping common substrings* (NOCSs) [16]. Once we have a set of NOCSs, we examine the text leaves from which a NOCS originates and split the nodes in such a way that the tree-to-tree correction algorithm can build a one-to-one mapping between the text leaves.

### 4.1.2 Finding all Common Substrings

To find all common substrings from which we compute the NOCSs we use *Suffix Arrays* (SA) and *Longest Common Prefix* (LCP) information. A suffix array $sa$ for a string $s$ is an array of indices, where each index $sa_i$ points to the first character of a suffix $s_{sa_i...n}$ in $s$ with $n = \text{len}(s)$. The array is ordered in such a way that it refers to suffixes in lexicographical order. Kärkkäinen et al. show in [8] how to compute a suffix array in $O(n)$.

Suffix arrays can be augmented with longest common prefix (LCP) information. LCP information assigns a pair of consecutive suffix array indices $(sa_{i-1}, sa_i)$ an additional number $lcp_i$ that indicates the length of the longest common prefix $s_{sa_{i-1}...sa_{i-1}+lcp_i}$ or $s_{sa_i...sa_i+lcp_i}$ that both consecutive suffixes share. When a suffix array has been computed, LCP information can be added in $O(n)$ as shown by Kasai et al. in [9]. By iterating through the suffix array by decreasing LCP length, we obtain a list of substrings ordered from longest to shortest.

Using this tool set we can compute the longest common substrings within one string [15]. To compute the longest common substrings between two strings $s_1$ and $s_2$, we concatenate both strings:

$$s_{1,2} = s_1 . "\$_1" . s_2 . "\$_0"$$

where "." is the concatenation operator and "$\$_0$" and "$\$_1$" are unique terminator characters. The terminator character $\$_0$ is required by the SA algorithm. Terminator $\$_1$ is used to separate the two strings. Since $\$_1$ cannot be part of one of the strings it is unique within the concatenated string and assures no substrings cross the terminator. To guarantee that a substring is shared by both strings $s_1$ and $s_2$ we have to make sure that the two associated suffixes are located to the left and right of the separator character. This part of the algorithm is implemented in *saLcpBucketSort* in listing 3. For

```
findNOCSs(ls1, ls2):
    n1 = len(ls1); n2 = len(ls2)
    input = ls1 + '$1' + ls2 + '$0'
    sa = computeSuffixArray(input)
    lcp = computeLcp(sa, input)
    buckets = saLcpBucketSort(sa, lcp, n1)
    return greedyCover(buckets, n1, n2)

saLcpBucketSort(sa[], lcp[], n1):
    L1: for i = 1 to len(lcp):
        len = lcp[i]
        # Only accept long enough substrings
        if len < minLen: continue L1
        start1 = sa[i-1]
        start2 = sa[i]
        # Skip duplicates
        j = i + 1
        while (j < lcp.length) and
            (lcp[j] == len): ++j
        if j > i + 1:
            continue L1 with i = j
        # Only accept substrings from both strings
        if (start1 < n1) == (start2 < n1):
            continue L1
        # Correct start1 and start2
        if (start2 < start1):
            (start1, start2) = (start2, start1)
        start2 -= n1 + 1
        # Bucket sort by len
        buckets[len].add(new CS(start1, start2, len))
    return buckets

greedyCover(buckets, n1, n2):
    # Initialize cover arrays
    for i in (0, n1]: covered1[i] = false
    for i in (0, n2]: covered2[i] = false
    # From longest to shortest substring
    for bucket in reverse(buckets):
        # For every common substring
        L2: for cs in bucket:
            # Substring alreay covered?
            if covered1[cs.start1] or
                covered2[cs.start2]: continue L2
            if not isValid(cs.start1, cs.len):
                continue L2
            L3: for j in (0, cs.len]:
                k1 = cs.start1 + j
                k2 = cs.start2 + j
                # Substrings already partially covered?
                if covered[k1] or covered[k2]:
                    cs.len = j
                    break L3
                covered1[k1] = covered2[k2] = true
            # Add NOCS
            result.add(cs)
    return result
```

**Figure 3:** Finding all non-overlapping common substrings.

computing the suffix array and LCP information please refer to [8] and [9].

Now we found all common substrings shared by $ls_1$ and $ls_2$, including substrings of substrings. Finding an optimal set of non-overlapping common substrings for $ls_1$ and $ls_2$ is $\mathcal{NP}$-hard [15]. Instead we use a greedy approach. In `greedyCover` in listing 3 we first accept the longest common substring. Then we accept the next longest substring unless it overlaps. If the next substring should overlap with an already accepted substring, we shrink the substring until it no longer overlaps. This process continues until no more appropriate substrings remain. Substrings are only considered appropriate above a certain length and structure which is checked by `isValid`.

### 4.1.3 Splitting Nodes

Once we have obtained a non-overlapping set of substrings we can split the nodes in both trees as required. This step is facilitated by another data structure that was built when the two leaf strings were concatenated from the leaf nodes. In order to locate a substring within one of the trees, we construct two arrays that for every character in the leaf strings $ls_1$ and $ls_2$ contain the information from which node and from which position in the node's text the character came. With this information at hand we split nodes as detailed in *splitNodesWithNocs* in listing 4.

```
splitNodesWithNocs(nocs):
    # Split nodes if nocs doesn't start at node boundary
    curNode1 = node in which nocs starts in T1
    if nocs does not start at node boundary in T1:
        split(curNode1, at position where substring starts)
        curNode1 = right node of split
    curNode2 = node in which nocs starts in T2
    if nocs does not start at node boundary in T2:
        split(curNode2, at position where substring starts)
        curNode2 = right node of split

    # Find node discontinuities in nocs
    endNocs = false
L1: while not endNocs:
        i = search for next position where the nocs crosses
            a node boundary in T1 or T2 or where the nocs ends

        # Find out which nodes we have to split
        endNocs = end of nocs reached?
        if endNocs:
            break1 = node continues in T1 at end of nocs
            break2 = node continues in T2 at end of nocs
        else:
            break1 = nocs crosses node boundary in T2 (!)
            break2 = nocs crosses node boundary in T1 (!)

        # Split nodes
        leftNode1 = curNode1
        if (break2 and not break1 and not endNocs) or
           (break1 and endNocs):
            split(curNode1, at position where string crosses
                node boundary in T2 or where nocs ends)
            curNode1 = right node of split
        leftNode2 = curNode2
        if (break1 and not break2 and not endNocs) or
           (break2 and endNocs):
            split(curNode2, at position where string crosses
                node boundary in T1 or where nocs ends)
            curNode2 = right node of split
        if break1:curNode1=node in which nocs continues in T1
        if break2:curNode2=node in which nocs continues in T2

        # Match left parts of split
        if break1 or break2 or endNocs:
            match(leftNode1, leftNode2)
```

**Figure 4:** Splitting nodes after a non-overlapping common substring (NOCS) is found. The parameter *nocs* contains information about the starting positions in the leaf strings and the length of the NOCS.

Every time a node is split into a left and a right part within the loop L1, the left part is matched to its partner node in the other tree. An implementation has to make sure that the boundary splits to the left and to the right of the substring retain their partners, if any. This procedure guarantees that all nodes and split nodes that are part of the common substring are matched after this phase is over. To speed up the search for the next discontinuity position $i$ one can use a binary search.

**Complexity analysis:** Let $n$ be the length of the input to the respective algorithm. The SA and LCP algorithms are shown to require time in $O(n)$ in [8] and [9]. *saLcpBucketSort* has one loop that runs over the length of the LCP array and requires time in $O(n)$. In *greedyCover* the innermost loop runs at most twice for every character in the shorter leaf string and therefore runs in time $O(n)$. Finally, in *splitNodesWithNocs* the search for the next discontinuity examines at most every character in the leaf string and runs in time $O(n)$. Hence the whole splitting process runs in time $O(n)$, where $n$ is the length of the two leaf strings combined.

## 4.2 Embedding the Split Algorithm into a Tree Differencing Algorithm

While matching substrings of nodes can be done in linear time, it still is expensive since it is a character based process with high constant costs and documents usually have considerably more characters than leaf nodes. On the other hand, big portions of the old and new document usually remain unchanged between revisions. Therefore we can drastically reduce the search space before we start looking for substrings by identifying the unchanged portions of the documents.

By computing a mapping between old and new tree every differencing algorithm identifies the unchanged portions of the documents. A first outline of the complete algorithm therefore starts by computing a mapping with an existing differencing algorithm in phase one. In phase two we concatenate yet unmatched text leaves to leaf strings for which we compute NOCSs. Using the NOCSs, nodes are split and matched. If nodes were not matched in phase one, their parents and siblings often cannot be matched in phase one either. This requires us to complete the mapping in phase three and four by propagating the matches found in phase one and two to parents and siblings.

Most algorithms we are aware of are not suitable for this task because they are computationally too expensive [2, 3, 7] or not applicable since they make assumptions that do not hold for our data [3, 18, 19]. The *XyDiff* algorithm [4] is a good candidate since its phases two to four map well to phases one, three and four of our outline. In the next sections we will describe how we adapted the *XyDiff* algorithm to finalize the mapping between the old and the new tree and how we integrated the edit script building from *LaDiff* into our own algorithm.

### 4.2.1 Phase 1 - Reducing the Search Space

In a precomputation step the *XyDiff* algorithm computes weights and hash values for subtrees in both $T_1$ and $T_2$. We adopt this step and compute a hash value $h_n$ for every subtree that is rooted at node $n$. Text leaves compute their hash value from the text they store. All other nodes compute a hash value from their label and then combine this value with the hash values of their children. The weight of a text leaf is a function of the length $l$ of its text. Inner nodes compute their weight by summing up the weights of their children and adding a constant $w_{inner}$ for themselves. While this is subject to tuning, we use the text length $l$ directly as weight function and set $w_{inner} = 3$.

Next *XyDiff* matches subtrees by comparing the hash values from $T_1$ with the hash values from $T_2$, starting with the heaviest subtree. If there is more than one candidate to match a subtree, simple and greedy heuristics help to decide which two subtrees are matched or the subtrees remain unmatched at this point. After matching a subtree *XyDiff* immediately tries to propagate the match to the ancestor nodes of the subtree. How many ancestor nodes are matched depends on the subtree's weight.

Greedy matching and propagation heuristics can easily lead to mismatched node, as [18] note and as our own observations confirm. Especially when dealing with many small subtrees or with many small identical subtrees. On the other hand we already reach our primary goal of reducing the search space by only considering big subtrees without duplicates, that can be matched unambiguously. Hence we modify Cobena's algorithm and only consider subtrees without duplicates that are above a certain weight (we use a minimum

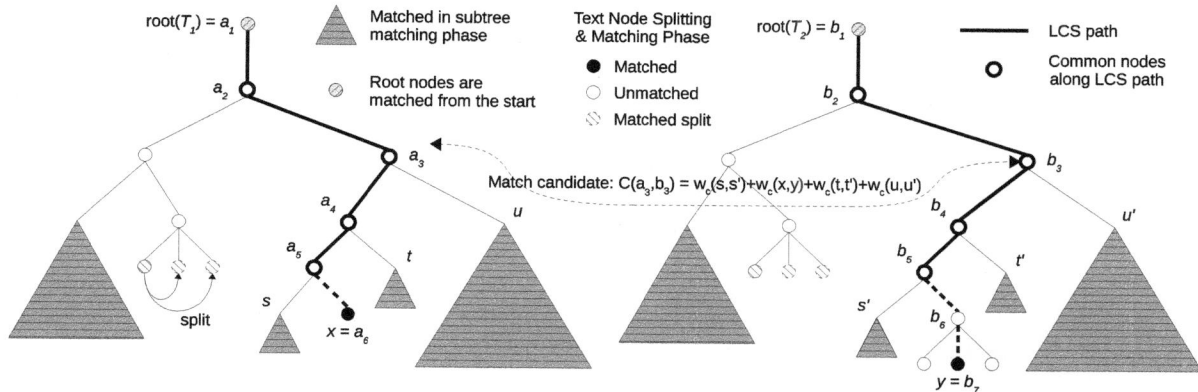

**Figure 5:** Two document trees $T_1$ and $T_2$ during step 3 (propagating matches to ancestors). Large subtrees have already been matched in step 1, and in step 2 a text node has been split into 3 smaller text nodes that were immediately matched. The algorithm is currently examining node $y$, distributing the common weight $w_c(x, y)$ to all ancestors that are part of the LCS of the paths $[root(T_1) \ldots x]$ and $[root(T_2) \ldots y]$. After all candidates have been gathered, match candidates $C(a_2, b_2)$, $C(a_3, b_3)$, $C(a_4, b_4)$ and $C(a_5, b_5)$ are assigned the combined weight of all of their respective descendant shared subtress.

weight of 12) and we do not match ancestors based on subtree matches.

Since element attributes do not feature in the subtree hash computation we have to check node attributes for changes which we report as node updates in the edit script. After checking subtrees for real equality, to deal with the possibility of hash collisions, and after recording node updates, our algorithm will not revisit matched subtrees.

**Complexity analysis:** The precomputation of weights and subtree hashes requires time in $O(|T_1| + |T_2|)$. Actually matching subtrees using hash maps for fast look ups requires time in $O(|T_2|)$. Sorting by weight requires time in $O(n_s \cdot \log(n_s))$, where $n_s$ is the number of shared heavy subtrees (excluding subtrees of subtrees). Since usually $n_s \ll |T_2|$, phase one requires $O(|T_1| + |T_2|)$.

### 4.2.2   Phase 3 - Propagating Matches to Ancestors

In figure 5 we illustrate the situation in an exemplary pair of documents after phase one and phase two have run. The largest subtrees have been matched in phase one and in phase two the text in unmatched leaves was concatenated and the search for NOCSs has led to splits and matches between leaves. At this point, two kinds of nodes remain unmatched: ancestor nodes of matched subtrees and text leaves, and subtrees that could not be matched in phase one because they have duplicates or their weight is too small.

This leads us back to *XyDiff*'s propagation rules to match ancestors from step one and their BULD (Bottom-Up Lazy-Down) matching phase. To avoid mismatching nodes and generating needless move operations we propose the following procedure. It is motivated by *XyDiff*'s propagation rules combined with *LaDiff*'s LCS breadth-first matching of inner nodes with the same label.

**Step 3.1)** Assume we found two matching nodes $x$ and $y$ from both trees. All pairs of ancestor nodes from $T_1$ and $T_2$ along the paths from the root nodes to $x$ and $y$ are potential candidates for a match. In order for a pair of ancestor nodes to be considered as partners their labels have to be equal. Furthermore, if children have been moved between revisions, a parent node in one tree can have multiple potential partners in the other tree. In order to decide which pair of candidates is matched we accumulate the weight of the already matched descendant subtrees that the candidates share.

Let $C(x, y) \rightarrow w_c$ be a map of candidate tuples $(x, y) \in (T_1, T_2)$ onto a weight $w_c \in \mathbb{N}_{\geq 0}$. Such a mapping implies that the two mapped candidate nodes $x$ and $y$ share common descendant subtrees that have at least a combined weight of $w_c$ in each tree. We can see in figure 5 that after step two, if an inner node is matched, all its descendants are matched as well down to the leaves. Consequently the new tree $T_2$ is traversed pre-order until we reach a matched node $y \in T_2$ and the path $p_2 = (b_2, b_3, \ldots, b_{j-1})$ from node $root(T_2) = b_1$ to $y = b_j$ is stored as a sequence of nodes. For the old tree $T_1$ we also build a path $p_1 = (a_2, a_3, \ldots, a_{i-1})$ from $root(T_1) = a_1$ to $x = a_i$, where $x \in T_1$ is the matched partner of $y$. Myers LCS algorithm is applied to both sequences and two nodes are considered equal by the LCS algorithm if their labels match. We get $s = \text{lcs}(p_1, p_2), s_i \in (T_1, T_2)$ for $1 \leq i \leq |s|$, the longest sequence of nodes from both paths that share the same label. Let $w_c$ be the weight shared by the subtrees rooted at $x$ and $y$. For each $s_i \in s$, if $s_i \in C$ then update the mapping $C(s_i) \rightarrow C(s_i) + w_c$. Otherwise add $C(s_i) \rightarrow w_c$ to the mappping.

After we have processed node $y$ in the described way we do not descend into its subtree but continue with the traversal until we reach the next matched node.

**Step 3.2)** Once the traversal is complete we have a mapping of node pairs with an associated common weight. Each pair is a candidate to be matched. We sort the candidates by descending common weight $w_c$ and match the heaviest pair first. We then continue with the next heaviest pair and match its two nodes unless one or both of the nodes have already been matched by a previous candidate.

By now we have propagated the matches from step one and two to ancestor nodes. We use a greedy strategy as well, however, we make sure that it considers the weights of all matched children of a pair of nodes instead of making a decision by looking only at the heaviest child.

**Complexity analysis:** Let $n = \max(|T_1|, |T_2|)$. If we assume that the trees are balanced, their maximum height can be approximated by $h = \log(n)$. The cost for $\text{lcs}(s_1, s_2)$ is $O(ld)$, where $l = |s_1| + |s_2|$ and $d \in (1 \ldots l)$ is the edit distance between both sequences. In the worst case the LCS computation requires $O(l^2)$, in the best case the algorithm finishes in $O(l)$. The bigger the subtrees are that were matched in step one, the shorter the paths from the root to a subtree become and the LCS effort approaches $O(1)$. Sorting partner candidates by weight requires $n_s \cdot \log(n_s)$, where $n_s$ is the number of subtree candidates. Thus the ancestor pass requires time in $O(n)$ to $O(n_s \cdot h^2)$.

### 4.2.3 Phase 4 - Building an Edit Script

When looking at figure 6 we can see that some nodes and subtrees are still not matched. Furthermore, we also have not discussed the generation of an edit script yet. In this section we explain how we match the remaining nodes and at the same time build an edit script. We adapt the algorithm by Chawathe et al. [3] and use absolute child node indices computed from the new document instead of a context dependent index that Chawathe et al. call $k$. This allows us to match remaining nodes and subtrees and generate edit script operations in the same traversal of the tree since it doesn't require a finished mapping of both trees up front.

The types of nodes and subtrees that remain unmatched and the reasons therefor are explained in figure 6. The details of the algorithm are explained in listing 7. We proceed by traversing $T_2$ pre-order, where $n_2$ is the current node in $T_2$ and $n_1$ is its partner, if it has been matched. We then build sequences of unmatched children for $n_1$ and $n_2$ and compute the LCS according to subtree hash equality (subtreeLCS). Pairs of subtrees in the LCS are then matched in the same way as in phase one. The subtree LCS step is optional, however, it improves edit script quality since it prevents the following step from matching a subtree root node with a single unmatched node by label although a better match between two complete subtrees would have been possible.

In the next step we test the children of $n_1$ and $n_2$ for proper alignment. This can be expensive if both nodes have many misaligned children. However, since we have to perform this step anyway, it presents a good opportunity to also match nodes that are aligned by label. To this end we compute the LCS of all children of $n_1$ and $n_2$, where two nodes are considered equal if they are already partners or have the same label (matchedOrLabelLCS). In the following loop we generate move operations for matched but misaligned nodes and match yet unmatched nodes that occur in order and have the same label.

Now we visit all children of $n_2$. If a child has still no partner in $T_1$, an insert operation is generated. Otherwise we check each pair of matched children for changed attributes or text content and generate update operations accordingly. Then we descend to the child of $n_2$ that was just processed.

Finally, after the traversal of $T_2$ is complete, we traverse $T_1$ and for every node that does not have a partner in $T_2$ we generate a delete operation (traverseAndDelete). This step concludes the *HDDiff* algorithm.

**Complexity analysis:** The most expensive step is the LCS computation over all children of both nodes. In the worst case the majority of all nodes are children of a single parent and have been completely replaced between old and new revision. In this case phase four requires time in $O(n^2)$, where $n = |T_1| + |T_2|$. In the best case the trees are well balanced and we can assume a constant number of children per inner node and no alignments. Then phase four requires time in $O(n)$.

## 5. EVALUATION

Our focus is better support of change detection in structured text documents and a fine-grained analysis of changes between two document revisions in reasonable time. To validate that our algorithm meets these goals, we use a sample

```
topDown(root1, root2):
  checkUpdate(root1, root2)
  topDownRec(root1, root2)
  traverseAndDelete(root1) # not elaborated

topDownRec(n1, n2):
  if n2 is leaf: return
  # We don't have to process matched subtrees
  if n2 is matched subtree: return

  if n1 != None:
    # Match duplicate subtrees below n1 and n2
    s1, s2 = unmatched children of n1, n2
    s = subtreeLCS(s1, s2)
    for c in s: matchSubtree(c)

    # Match by label and generate align ops
    s1, s2 = all children of n1, n2
    s = matchedOrLabelLCS(s1, s2)
    i = 1
    for b in s2:
      if (b has partner) and (b != s[i][2]):
        a = partner(b)
        if (parent(a) == partner(parent(b))):
          # Nodes a and b are misaligned
          generate move op for (a, b)
        else:
          i += 1
      else if (b has no partner) and (b == s[i][2]):
        # Match children with same label
        matchNodes(s[i][1], s[i][2])
        i += 1

  # Generate update, insert and move ops
  for c2 in children(n2):
    if c2 has partner:
      c1 = partner(c2):
      checkUpdate(c1, c2)
      if parent(c1) != n1:
        # Node was moved and is now child of n2
        generate move op for (c1, c2)
    else:
      # Node in n2 still has no partner
      c1 = None
      generate insert op

    # Descend
    topDownRec(c1, c2)
```

**Figure 7:** Phase 4 - Building an Edit Script.

of articles from the English Wikipedia. Initially we have randomly selected $400,000$ revisions from the English Wikipedia that have a predecessor revision. Since the parser software sometimes fails to parse a revision $371,451$ pairs of revisions remain after conversion to the WOM XML format.

We have applied our *HDDiff* algorithm as well as the *XyDiff* [4] and the *FcDiff* [10] algorithm to the data, and called the algorithms "HDDiff", "XyDiff" and "FcDiff" in the charts respectively. In order to compare the algorithms' results we parse in the edit scripts and analyze them for the number of character insertions and deletions they require. Sometimes *XyDiff* timed out and sometimes our parser was not able to understand *FcDiff*'s edit script format. If we failed to obtain an edit script analysis from any of the algorithms we removed the sample for all algorithms. After this step $360,246$ pairs of revisions remain. Furthermore our sample contains various kinds of content from Wikipedia. We tell apart articles from other content by only selecting revisions from the *main namespace*, after which $266,233$ pairs of revisions remain.

First we examine the quality of *HDDiff*'s edit script in figure 8. If mostly textual changes are performed, character-based diff algorithms outperform conventional tree diff algorithms in the number of character insertions and deletions that the edit script requires to transform the old into the new revision. This is due to the fact that conventional tree diff al-

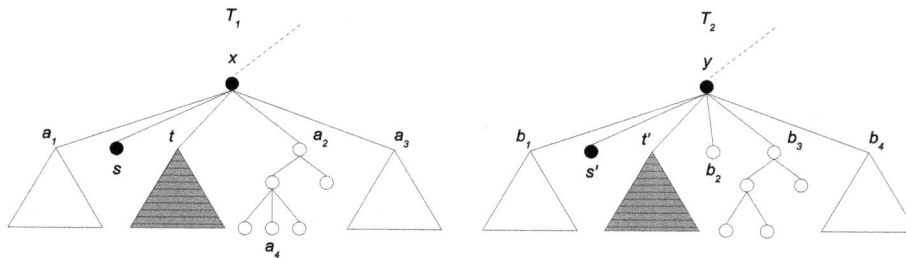

**Figure 6:** Two document trees $T_1$ and $T_2$ after step 3.2 (propagating matches to ancestors). $(s, s')$ and $(t, t')$ caused the match of ancestors $(x, y)$. $a_1, a_3, b_1$ and $b_4$ are all identical but were not matched earlier due to the exclusion of duplicates. $b_2$ is inserted in $T_2$ and the subtrees at $a_2$ and $b_3$ are identical except for the deleted node $a_4$. Since the individual nodes of the subtrees have not enough weight none of them were matched.

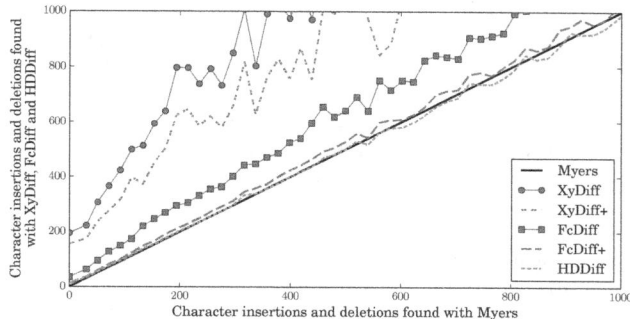

**Figure 8:** The number of character insertions and deletions generated by each algorithm compared to the number of insertions and deletions required by Myers LCS algorithm. The data is spread over 50 bins. The lines indicate the mean number of operations in each bin per algorithm.

gorithms cannot deal with situations in which text from one node is spread over multiple text nodes in the new revision, even though the textual content does not change. However, if content is moved inside a document, tree diff algorithms can outperform a character-based algorithm that does not support move operations and which instead has to report the movement of content as deletion in the old and insertion in the new revision. Since *HDDiff* combines features from both worlds, we expect it to not only outperform other tree diff algorithms in the number of character insertions and deletions, but also to outperform Myers textual diff algorithm for some documents, which is confirmed by figure 8.

By applying the three algorithms to pairs of revisions stored in the WOM XML format we can compare the change detection performance of the algorithms as a whole. As shown in figure 8 our algorithm (green, finely dashed) requires significantly less character insertions and deletions than *XyDiff* (brown circles) and *FcDiff* (red squares) on average. This is especially remarkable since our algorithm is specifically designed to avoid move and align operations if it is not clear whether such an operation conforms with the modification that was actually applied to the old revision. *HDDiff* rather issues insertions and deletions in such a situation, a restriction that does not apply to *XyDiff* and *FcDiff*.

We further want to evaluate how well our phases three and four, which are the part of our algorithm that solves the tree-to-tree-correction problem, perform, compared to other tree diff algorithms. To this end we use *HDDiff* to split text nodes in each pair of revisions as required for a one-to-one mapping of text nodes. We also attach XML IDs to pairs of

split text nodes since this mapping information is available to our algorithm in step three as well, however, only *XyDiff* can make use of this information. The algorithms *XyDiff* and *FcDiff* are then applied to the modified WOM XML and are called "XyDiff+" and "FcDiff+" in figure 8. While both algorithms can improve with the split text nodes and *FcDiff* almost draws even with the textual LCS algorithm, *HDDiff* still outperforms the other algorithms. This supports our claim that phase three and four of our algorithm are well chosen.

Next we examine the performance of *HDDiff* in terms of speed[3]. The upper chart in figure 9 gives an impression of *HDDiff*'s speed depending on the size of the input documents. However, since the speed depends on multiple factors, a clear trend is not discernible. To confirm that *HDDiff* requires nearly linear time on average, we have computed a least squares fit of a linear model that depends on (a) the combined number of nodes from both documents, (b) the minimum number of nodes from both documents, (c) the number of nodes that were initially matched in phase one $n_{st}$ and which are a coarse measurement of the similarity of both documents and (d) the combined lengths of the leaf strings from unmatched nodes $n_{ls}$ that are used to compute the NOCSs. The result is plotted in the lower chart of figure 9.

The $R^2$ measure of the fit is 0.78 and our model therefore confirms, that our algorithm works in linear time on average. When analyzing the phases individually, precomputation, greedy subtree matching and NOCSs computation behave strictly linear and are well predictable. Phase three and four are difficult to predict with the variables from our model and are responsible for almost all the remaining variance. When confronted with degenerated trees (e.g. long lists of items that are all children of a single parent and many alignment operations have taken place) phase four can lead to superlinear behavior.

## 6. CONCLUSION AND FUTURE WORK

We have presented a tree-to-tree correction algorithm that is specifically tailored to structured text documents. The algorithm pays special attention to the fact that text documents tend to feature large text leaves in which many of the modifications occur. Existing algorithms that treat text nodes as atomic elements therefore can only report removal or insertion of whole text nodes where purely textual differencing tools can report changes on the character level. We introduce an algorithm that offers the advantages of both approaches,

---

[3]All tests were run on an Intel Xeon Processor E5-2630 (15M Cache, 2.30 GHz) with the Oracle Java HotSpot VM 1.7.0_51

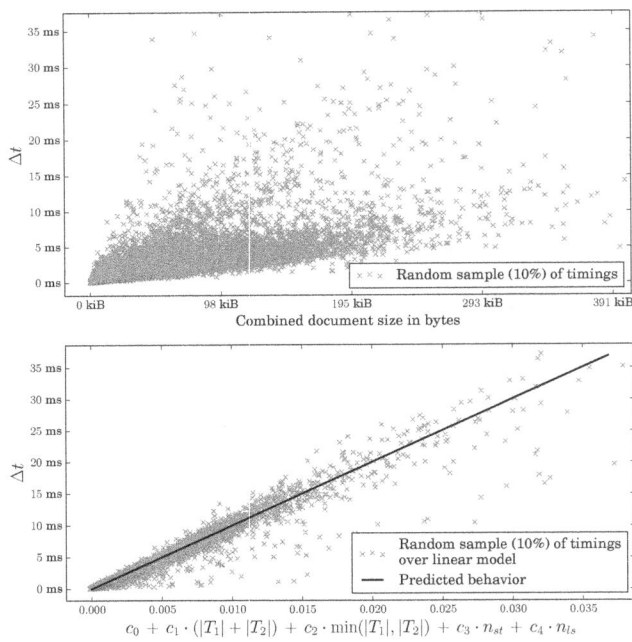

**Figure 9:** Scatter plot of timings of *HDDiff* over the combined length of two documents (upper chart) and a least squares fit of a linear model of the timings (lower chart).

by adding a novel node splitting step which allows the subsequent tree-to-tree correction algorithm to perform a fine-grained analysis and indication of the differences.

Since we focus our efforts on the support of users in understanding changes and in the automatic classification of changes, we take special care to avoid needless move operations by emphasizing ancestor relationships in the matching algorithm. We prefer that insertions and deletions of minor subtrees are reported instead of spurious moves. Unlike other works in this domain speed is not our primary concern. Still our algorithm delivers solid performance in near linear time on average.

In future work we want to investigate other tree-to-tree correction algorithms that follow the text splitting phase. Another direction of research is the simplification of the algorithm and the reduction of processing passes. To improve classification performance we would like to investigate support for copy operations and duplicates.

The implementation of *HDDiff* will be made available upon publication at http://sweble.org/projects/hddiff.

# 7. ACKNOWLEDGEMENT

We would like to thank Georg Dotzler for getting us started with his implementation of the *Change Distilling* algorithm.

# 8. REFERENCES

[1] P. Bille. A survey on tree edit distance and related problems. *Theoretical computer science*, 337(1):217–239, 2005.

[2] S. S. Chawathe and H. Garcia-Molina. Meaningful change detection in structured data. In *ACM SIGMOD Record*, volume 26, pages 26–37. ACM, 1997.

[3] S. S. Chawathe, A. Rajaraman, H. Garcia-Molina, and J. Widom. Change detection in hierarchically structured information. In *ACM SIGMOD Record*, volume 25, pages 493–504. ACM, 1996.

[4] G. Cobena, S. Abiteboul, and A. Marian. Detecting changes in xml documents. In *Data Engineering, 2002. Proceedings. 18th International Conference on*, pages 41–52. IEEE, 2002.

[5] H. Dohrn and D. Riehle. Design and implementation of the sweble wikitext parser: unlocking the structured data of wikipedia. In *Proceedings of the 7th International Symposium on Wikis and Open Collaboration*, pages 72–81. ACM, 2011.

[6] H. Dohrn and D. Riehle. Wom: An object model for wikitext. Technical report, Technical Report CS-2011-05, University of Erlangen, Dept. of Computer Science, 2011.

[7] B. Fluri, M. Wursch, M. Pinzger, and H. C. Gall. Change distilling: Tree differencing for fine-grained source code change extraction. *Software Engineering, IEEE Transactions on*, 33(11):725–743, 2007.

[8] J. Kärkkäinen and P. Sanders. Simple linear work suffix array construction. In *Automata, Languages and Programming*, pages 943–955. Springer, 2003.

[9] T. Kasai, G. Lee, H. Arimura, S. Arikawa, and K. Park. Linear-time longest-common-prefix computation in suffix arrays and its applications. In *Combinatorial Pattern Matching*, pages 181–192. Springer, 2001.

[10] T. Lindholm, J. Kangasharju, and S. Tarkoma. Fast and simple xml tree differencing by sequence alignment. In *Proceedings of the 2006 ACM symposium on Document engineering*, pages 75–84. ACM, 2006.

[11] E. W. Myers. An O(ND) difference algorithm and its variations. *Algorithmica*, 1(1-4):251–266, 1986.

[12] L. Peters. Change detection in xml trees: a survey. In *3rd Twente Student Conference on IT*, 2005.

[13] S. Rönnau, G. Philipp, and U. M. Borghoff. Efficient change control of xml documents. In *Proceedings of the 9th ACM symposium on Document engineering*, pages 3–12. ACM, 2009.

[14] S. Rönnau, J. Scheffczyk, and U. M. Borghoff. Towards xml version control of office documents. In *Proceedings of the 2005 ACM symposium on Document engineering*, pages 10–19. ACM, 2005.

[15] D. Shapira and J. A. Storer. Edit distance with move operations. In *Combinatorial Pattern Matching*, pages 85–98. Springer, 2002.

[16] D. Shapira and J. A. Storer. In place differential file compression. *The Computer Journal*, 48(6):677–691, 2005.

[17] K.-C. Tai. The tree-to-tree correction problem. *Journal of the ACM (JACM)*, 26(3):422–433, 1979.

[18] Y. Wang, D. J. DeWitt, and J.-Y. Cai. X-diff: An effective change detection algorithm for xml documents. In *Data Engineering, 2003. Proceedings. 19th International Conference on*, pages 519–530. IEEE, 2003.

[19] H. Xu, Q. Wu, H. Wang, G. Yang, and Y. Jia. Kf-diff+: Highly efficient change detection algorithm for xml documents. In *On the Move to Meaningful Internet Systems 2002: CoopIS, DOA, and ODBASE*, pages 1273–1286. Springer, 2002.

[20] K. Zhang and D. Shasha. Simple fast algorithms for the editing distance between trees and related problems. *SIAM journal on computing*, 18(6):1245–1262, 1989.

# Classifying and Ranking Search Engine Results as Potential Sources of Plagiarism

Kyle Williams‡, Hung-Hsuan Chen†, C. Lee Giles†‡
‡Information Sciences and Technology, †Computer Science and Engineering
Pennsylvania State University, University Park, PA 16802, USA
kwilliams@psu.edu, hhchen@psu.edu, giles@ist.psu.edu

## ABSTRACT

Source retrieval for plagiarism detection involves using a search engine to retrieve candidate sources of plagiarism for a given suspicious document so that more accurate comparisons can be made. An important consideration is that only documents that are likely to be sources of plagiarism should be retrieved so as to minimize the number of unnecessary comparisons made. A supervised strategy for source retrieval is described whereby search results are classified and ranked as potential sources of plagiarism without retrieving the search result documents and using only the information available at search time. The performance of the supervised method is compared to a baseline method and shown to improve precision by up to 3.28%, recall by up to 2.6% and the $F_1$ score by up to 3.37%. Furthermore, features are analyzed to determine which of them are most important for search result classification with features based on document and search result similarity appearing to be the most important.

## Categories and Subject Descriptors

I.2.6 [**Artificial Intelligence**]: Learning; I.7.5 [**Document and Text Processing**]: Document Capture—*Document Analysis*; H.3.3 [**Information Storage And Retrieval**]: Information Search and Retrieval

## General Terms

Experimentation, Measurement, Performance

## Keywords

Source retrieval; plagiarism detection; search result ranking; query generation

*DocEng'14,* September 16–19, 2014, Fort Collins, Colorado, USA.
Copyright is held by the owner/author(s). Publication rights licensed to ACM.
ACM 978-1-4503-2949-1/14/09 ...$15.00.
http://dx.doi.org/10.1145/2644866.2644879.

## 1. INTRODUCTION

The advent of the Web has led to an exponential increase in the amount of information that is publicly available and accessible. This increase in information has had a number of benefits in important domains, such as healthcare, education, disaster management and community involvement. Search engines have become an important tool in dealing with the exponentially increasing amount of information available on the Web by allowing people to construct queries that describe their information needs and effectively retrieving search results that may satisfy those information needs. However, in addition to the many positive effects search engines have had, they have also made it increasingly easy to plagiarize information from the Web. For instance, a study conducted over the years 2002-2005 found that 36% of undergraduate college students admitted to plagiarizing information from the Web without proper citation [18] and a study in 2010 found that 1 in 3 American high school students admitted to plagiarizing from the Internet[1].

Given the negative impact that plagiarism has on education and society, a number of techniques have been developed for identifying cases of plagiarism [17]. Generally, the plagiarism detection problem is framed as:

***Problem 1:*** *Given a suspicious document and a potential source document for plagiarism, find all areas of overlapping text, which may have been subjected to obfuscation.*

A number of approaches have been developed for addressing Problem 1. For instance, a method based on citation pattern matching has been developed for detecting plagiarism among scholarly documents [7] and many software tools have been developed for identifying plagiarism [17]

There is an inherent assumption in the definition of Problem 1 that potential source documents for plagiarism have been identified. For small collections of documents one might just assume that all documents in the collection are potential sources of plagiarism and perform a comparison between the suspicious document and each document in the collection. However, this approach is infeasible for all but the smallest collections. Another task in plagiarism detection that does not make this assumption is known as source retrieval. In source retrieval, the goal is to use a search engine to retrieve a subset of documents in a collection that are likely to be sources of plagiarism by constructing queries from the suspicious document that can be used to query the search engine. The source retrieval problem can be described as:

---

[1] http://charactercounts.org/programs/reportcard/2010/installment02_report-card_honesty-integrity.html

***Problem 2:*** *Given a suspicious document and a search engine, use the search engine to retrieve candidate documents that may be sources of plagiarism.*

To address *Problem 2*, a function $\Phi(\cdot)$ must be designed such that, for a suspicious document $D$, $\Phi(D) \to \mathbb{Q}$, where $\mathbb{Q}$ is a set of queries that can be submitted to the search engine. Once the set of queries is submitted to the search engine, the search result documents can then be retrieved and more accurate matching performed in order to check if they are sources of plagiarism. One way of doing this is to download the results in the order that they are ranked by the search engine; however, there is no guarantee that the search engine ranking reflects the probability of a result being a source of plagiarism. Thus, documents that are not sources of plagiarism may be downloaded and unnecessary attempts at solving *Problem 1* may take place.

This paper describes a strategy for solving *Problem 2* that attempts to minimize the number of unnecessary comparisons made as described above. This is done by classifying each result returned by the queries in $\mathbb{Q}$ as either being a candidate source of plagiarism or not using only the information that is available at search time, i.e., without retrieving the documents themselves. Furthermore, attempts are made at ranking those results that are classified as being candidate sources of plagiarism in order to improve the order in which they are retrieved. In order to do this, various features are extracted and various methods for search engine result classification and ranking are analyzed and compared to a baseline method that achieved the highest $F_1$ score in the 2013 PAN Source Retrieval Task [23]. In summary, this work makes two main contributions:

- It presents a novel supervised source retrieval strategy for finding potential sources of plagiarism on the Web.

- It compares various methods for search engine result classification for source retrieval and evaluates the features used for this classification.

In making these contribution, the rest of this paper is structured as follows. We first begin by discussing work related to source retrieval in Section 2. Section 3 describes the supervised source retrieval strategy and algorithm and Section 4 describes the creation of a data set for source retrieval evaluation as well as set of features that can be used for supervised search result classification. Section 5 describes a set of supervised methods that were used for classifying and ranking search results. Section 6 then presents a set of experiments comparing these methods to a baseline and also provides an evaluation of the features used for classification. Lastly, conclusions and future work are discussed in Section 7.

## 2. RELATED WORK

To our knowledge, there has been no previous work on supervised classification of search results as potential sources of plagiarism; however, there has been previous research on classifying search results in other ways. For instance, it has been noted that the order of results returned by search engines is based on relevance scores alone and may not take the topic of documents into consideration [35]. As a result, some efforts have been made to group search engine results into categories or clusters. For instance, [33] describe

a probabilistic ranking model that includes document categories and [26] describe an approach to presenting search results in user defined hierarchies by classifying documents into concepts from an ontology.

The *Learning to rank* machine learning framework has been used to learn a function for re-ranking the search results returned by a search engine for a specific query [16]. For instance, the ranking may be based on user clickthrough data [13] which can be used to infer which results are relevant for a specific queries. Learning to rank has been applied in a number of domains, such as learning a ranking of sponsored search results [34] and for ranking answers in Q&A systems [27]. [32] argue that many approaches for learning to rank in information retrieval attempt to optimize scores such as accuracy and ROCArea, rather than the mean average precision (MAP) score often used to evaluate information retrieval systems. They thus propose a method for optimizing MAP and show how it performs better than other methods when it comes to maximizing MAP. Supervised ensemble ranking methods have been used to combine the ranking outputs from multiple ranking algorithms; however, it has been noted that the drawback of this approach is that the learned weights are query independent and thus semi-supervised solutions for ensemble ranking have been proposed [12]. In [6], a set of candidate answers in a bibliographic Q&A system are re-ranked after being retrieved. This is similar to this work where search results are retrieved, classified and then re-ranked.

The Query By Document (QBD) search methodology is similar to the source retrieval problem. In QBD, a user submits a whole document as a query and the QBD system returns a list of documents ranked using some pre-determined similarity function [29]. Several systems have been designed for similar document retrieval. For instance, systems have been developed that make use of standard search engines and different query formulation strategies [21, 9, 3]. In each case, queries are formulated from the input document and submitted to a search engine and the results are ranked based on some similarity metric. QBD systems have been designed for use with full documents, passages of text [14], books [20] and blog posts [31]. The main difference between QBD and the source retrieval strategy described in this paper is that QBD systems return documents that are similar to a query document whereas we specifically focus on classifying search results as being potential sources of plagiarism for a given suspicious document. Furthermore, QBD systems usually perform ranking based on the full text similarity of documents whereas we instead focus on classifying search results based only on information that is available at search time without retrieving the actual documents.

Commercial systems for plagiarism detection generally focus on finding the overlap among texts; however, some systems do consult external sources. For instance, the Essay Verification Engine[2] automatically constructs queries from an input document and conducts a Web-based search to retrieve similar documents.

The work most similar to that described in this paper would be the approaches used in the Source Retrieval task at PAN 2013 [8]. In that task, the approach that achieved the highest $F_1$ score used a naive method for determining whether or not a search engine result is a source of plagia-

---

[2]http://www.canexus.com/eve/abouteve.shtml

rism based on a measure of similarity between the snippet of text associated with the result and the original suspicious document. Other approaches were similar in that they often compared the similarity of some part of the search result snippet with the original suspicious document and used that to determine whether to download a document or not [23].

This work differs from existing work in that it specifically attempts to classify and rank the search results returned by a search engine as being sources of plagiarism using a supervised approach and using only features that are available at search time.

## 3. SOURCE RETRIEVAL STRATEGY

Having introduced the problem and described related work, we now describe an online source retrieval strategy that can be used for real interaction with a search engine for retrieving potential sources of plagiarism. This strategy is similar to existing source retrieval strategies [23]; however, the main difference is that it makes use of a supervised method for determining which results are potential candidate sources of retrieval. Algorithm 1 shows the source retrieval strategy employed in this study.

---

**Algorithm 1** General overview of source retrieval strategy

---

1: **procedure** SOURCERETRIEVAL($doc$)
2:   $paragraphs \leftarrow$ SPLITINTOPARAGRAPHS($doc$)
3:   **for all** $p \in paragraphs$ **do**
4:     $p \leftarrow$ PREPROCESS($p$)
5:     $queries \leftarrow$ EXTRACTQUERIES($p$)
6:     **for** $i = 0 \rightarrow n$ **do**      ▷ n is the top n queries
7:       $results \leftarrow$ SUBMITQUERIES($queries[i]$)
8:     **end for**
9:     $results \leftarrow$ CLASSIFYANDRANK($results$)
10:     **for all** $result \in results$ **do**
11:       **if** $result$ is True **then**
12:         **if** PREVIOUSSOURCE($result$) = false **then**
13:           $source \leftarrow$ DOWNLOAD($result$)
14:           **if** ISSOURCE($source$) **then**
15:             print $source$
16:             PreviousSource $\leftarrow source$
17:             break
18:           **end if**
19:         **end if**
20:       **end if**
21:     **end for**
22:   **end for**
23: **end procedure**

---

First the input document is split into paragraphs made up of sentences (line 2). Then the text of each paragraph is preprocessed to remove stop words, etc., (line 4) and queries are extracted from the paragraph using the process described in Section 4.2.1 (line 5). The top $n$ queries are submitted to the search engine and results are returned for each query resulting in a set of search results per paragraph, which are then classified as potential sources of plagiarism and possibly ranked (line 9; described later). The intuition behind submitting multiple queries and combining their search results before classifying them as sources of plagiarism is that the probability of the union of the search results of all queries containing a source of plagiarism is at least as high as the

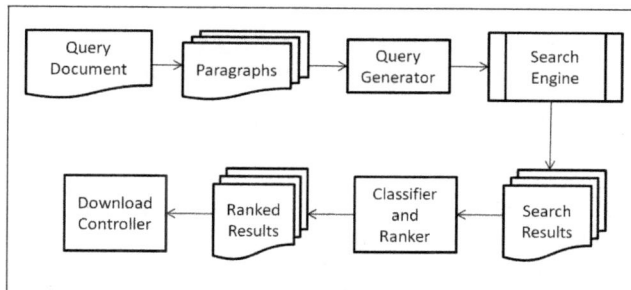

**Figure 1: Flow chart representation of source retrieval strategy**

probability of the results for a single query containing a source of plagiarism and likely higher.

If a result is classified as a source of plagiarism (line 11) and if the result has previously not been downloaded and identified as a source of plagiarism (based on the URL; line 12) then it is retrieved (line 13). The reason for checking whether or not a result has previously been downloaded and identified as a potential source of plagiarism is to prevent redundant retrieval. When a document is retrieved, an Oracle (described in the next section) is consulted to determine if it is a source of plagiarism (line 14). If it is, then the result is added to the set of previous successful results (line 16) and processing for the paragraph stops (line 17), otherwise the loop continues and the next result is processed. The reason for stopping the loop after a positive result has been retrieved is based on the previous intuition that a paragraph is likely to be plagiarized from a single source and thus retrieving additional results will not improve performance.

Figure 1 provides a high level visualization of Algorithm 1 showing the steps involving query generation and result submission, result classification and ranking, and the controlling of downloads.

## 4. DATA AND FEATURES

### 4.1 Original Dataset

The data used in this study is based on the training data provided as part of the Source Retrieval task at PAN 2013 [8]. The way in which this data was originally collected is described in detail in [25] and involved crowdsourcing whereby people were asked to write plagiarized documents on specific topics. Two batches of plagiarized documents were created in this way: for *Batch 1* people were allowed to freely search the ChatNoir Search Engine[3] [24] to find sources for plagiarism whereas for *Batch 2* people were provided with 20 search results on a specific topic and asked to use those results for plagiarism. The data used in this study is based on the *Batch 2*, which was the only data available at the time this study was conducted.

A total of 40 documents from *Batch 2* were provided as training data for the Source Retrieval task at PAN 2013 and those 40 documents were used in this study. Table 1 shows the descriptive statistics for the number of words in these documents.

As can be seen from these statistics, the documents are relatively long (i.e. around 5-10 pages). Twenty documents

---

[3]http://chatnoir.webis.de/

**Table 1: Descriptive statistics for number of words**

| Min | Max | Mode | Median | Mean |
|-----|-----|------|--------|------|
| 1873 | 7335 | 5383 | 5104 | 5152 |

were randomly sampled from this collection for classification and model training, 10 were used for validation and the remaining 10 documents were retained for testing. From these documents, a search result dataset was created.

## 4.2 Search Result Dataset

A search result dataset was constructed by extracting a set of queries from each document, submitting them to the ChatNoir search engine, downloading the results, and labelling each result as being a source of plagiarism or not.

### 4.2.1 Query Generation

To generate queries from a given document, the text of each document was first partitioned in paragraphs, with each paragraph containing 5 sentences that were tagged by the Stanford Tagger [28]. The words in each paragraph extracted this way were then POS-tagged using the Stanford POS Tagger and, following [15], only nouns, verbs and adjectives were retained while all words were filtered out. Queries were then constructed from the remaining nouns, verbs and adjectives by combining every non-overlapping sequence of 10 words, which resulted in a set of queries for each paragraph, of which only the first three were retained while the others were discarded. The intuition behind this is that a paragraph is likely to be plagiarized from a single source and that the first 3 queries from a paragraph are likely to sufficiently capture enough information about the paragraph.

### 4.2.2 Query Submission and Result Labeling

The queries generated for each paragraph were submitted to the ChatNoir search engine [24] and the first three results returned by each query were retrieved. This number was selected since it was empirically found to lead to good results [30]. ChatNoir contains an *Oracle* that can be consulted to determine whether or not a search result is a source of plagiarism for a given suspicious document ID. The Oracle is a service provided by the PAN plagiarism detection competition organizers that provides a binary output of whether a document is a source of plagiarism for a given suspicious document. This label is not provided by prediction but is stated as a fact and is meant to be used for evaluating retrieval methods. We use the Oracle to label each search result appropriately.

### 4.2.3 Training Data

In total 2737 queries were constructed from the 20 training documents and 5740 search results were returned when querying the search engine with these queries with each search result being labelled based on the feedback from the ChatNoir Oracle. Of the 5740 search results, 4240 were labelled as negative (i.e., not sources of plagiarism) and the remaining 1500 being labelled as sources of plagiarism. Thus, the data was heavily skewed towards negative samples, which made up 73.87% of the data.

### 4.2.4 Validation Data

In total 1331 queries were constructed from the 10 validation documents and 2940 search results were returned and labelled when querying the search engine. 2365 of these were negative samples and the remaining 575 were positive. Negative samples made up 80.44% of the validation data.

### 4.2.5 Testing Dataset

A total of 1303 queries were constructed from the 10 testing documents and 2991 search results were returned. 2174 of these were negative samples and the remaining 817 were positive. Thus, the distribution of the testing data follows a similar ratio to the training data with negative samples making up 72.68% of the data.

## 4.3 Features

For each labelled search result the following features were extracted (some of which were provided by the ChatNoir search engine). All of these features are available at search result time and do not require the search result to be retrieved, which allows for classification to be performed as the search results become available.

1. **Readability.** The readability of the result document as measured by the Flesh-Kincaid grade level formula [22] (ChatNoir).

2. **Weight.** A weight assigned to the result by the search engine (ChatNoir).

3. **Proximity.** A proximity factor [24] (ChatNoir).

4. **PageRank.** The PageRank of the result (ChatNoir).

5. **BM25.** The BM25 score of the result (ChatNoir).

6. **Sentences.** The number of sentences in the result (ChatNoir).

7. **Words.** The number of words in the result (ChatNoir).

8. **Characters.** The number of characters in the result (ChatNoir).

9. **Syllables.** The number of syllables in the result (ChatNoir).

10. **Rank.** The rank of the result, i.e. the rank at which it appeared in the search results.

11. **Document-snippet 5-gram Intersection.** The set of 5-grams from the suspicious document are extracted as well as the set of 5 grams from each search result snippet, where the snippet is the small sample of text that appears under each search result. A document-snippet 5-gram intersection score is then calculated as:

$$Sim(s, d) = S(s) \cap S(d), \qquad (1)$$

where $s$ is the snippet, $d$ is the suspicious document and $S(\cdot)$ is a set of 5-grams.

12. **Snippet-document Cosine Similarity.** The cosine similarity between the snippet and the suspicious document, which is given by:

$$Cosine(s, d) = \cos(\theta) = \frac{V_s \cdot V_d}{||V_s||||V_d||}, \qquad (2)$$

where $V.$ is a term vector.

13. **Title-document Cosine Similarity.** The cosine similarity between the result title and the suspicious document (Eq. 2).

14. **Query-snippet Cosine Similarity.** The cosine similarity between the query and the snippet (Eq. 2).

15. **Query-title Cosine Similarity.** The cosine similarity between the query and the result title (Eq. 2) [13].

16. **Title length.** The number of words in the result title.

17. **Wikipedia source.** Boolean value for whether or not the source was a Wikipedia article (based on the existence of the word "Wikipedia in title).

18. **#Nouns.** Number of nouns in the title as tagged by the Stanford POS Tagger [28].

19. **#Verbs.** Number of verbs in the title as tagged by the Stanford POS Tagger.

20. **#Adjectives** Number of adjectives in the title as tagged by the Stanford POS Tagger.

# 5. SEARCH RESULT CLASSIFICATION AND RANKING

A number of different supervised classification methods using the features and data described in the previous section were compared. These supervised methods were also compared to a baseline method. The baseline method achieved the highest $F_1$ score in the source retrieval task at PAN 2013 [23]. The supervised methods include: linear discriminant analysis, logistic regression, random forests, AdaBoosting with decision trees and ensembles of these classifiers. Ranking involves determining the order in which to retrieve results that have been classified as being candidate sources of plagiarism.

## 5.1 Baseline

The baseline method classifies each search result as being a potential source of plagiarism based on the document-snippet 5-gram intersection (feature 11). Documents for which $Sim(s, d) = S(s) \cap S(d) \geq 5$, are classified as candidate sources of plagiarism and documents are ranked by $Sim(s, d)$ in descending order. This method achieved the highest $F_1$ score in the source retrieval task at PAN 2013 [23].

## 5.2 Supervised Methods

### 5.2.1 Linear Discriminant Analysis

A Linear Discriminant Analysis (LDA) classifier attempts to find a linear combination of features for classification. For LDA, two different ranking cases are considered for LDA: no ranking where positive results are retrieved in the order they were classified; and *ProbRank* where results are ranked by their probability of being a source of plagiarism. This probability value is output by the classifier.

### 5.2.2 Logistic Regression

Logistic regression is a form of binary classification where the classification decision is made based on:

$$p(\vec{x}) = \frac{1}{1 + e^{\beta_0 + \beta_1 \vec{x}}}, \qquad (3)$$

where $Y = 1$ is predicted when $p(\vec{x}) \geq 0.5$ and $Y = 0$ otherwise. In this study, we use L-1 regularization when learning the logistic regression model and, as with LDA, both no ranking and the *ProbRank* ranking method are both considered.

### 5.2.3 Random Forest

A random forest is an ensemble classifier made up of a set of decision trees [1]. Each tree is built with a bootstrap sample from the dataset and splitting in the decision tree is based on a random subset of the features rather than the full feature set [5]. In this study, the number of trees in the ensemble is set to 10 since this was empirically found to perform well and the number of features randomly selected is equal to $\sqrt{n\_features}$. At each level in the decision trees, variables are selected for splitting with the Gini index being used as a splitting criterion. The Gini index is defined as follows:

$$I_G(i) = \sum_{j=1}^{K} p_j(1 - p_j) = 1 - \sum_{j=1}^{K} p_j^2, \qquad (4)$$

where $K$ is the number of classes and $p_j$ is the proportion of instances belonging to class $j$ in node $i$. If a node $i$ is pure (only contains one type of class), then $I_G(i) = 0$. The Gini index is used in decision tree learning for selecting the variable to split on at each node, with the split that leads to the largest reduction in the Gini index being selected.

The other parameters for the decision trees in the random forest were found using a grid search over the training set with the validation set used for testing. The parameters were:

- Maximum tree depth, $d = None, 1, 2, 3, 4$
- Minimum samples to split a node, $s = 1, 2, 3, 4$
- Minimum samples per leaf, $l = 1, 2, 3, 4$

Once the grid search was performed, the parameters that resulted in the highest $F_1$ score on the validation set were used for training the final model.

As with other methods, two ranking options were considered for the random forest: the baseline ranking method (i.e., no ranking) and *ProbRank*.

### 5.2.4 AdaBoosting with Decision Trees

AdaBoost is another ensemble method that iteratively fits modified versions of data to a set of weak classifiers. For a set of weak classifiers $G_m(x), m = 1, 2, ...M$, the prediction, $G(x)$, for the target value of a sample is based on a weighted majority vote as [10]:

$$G(x) = \text{sign}(\sum_{m=1}^{M} \alpha_m G_m(x)), \qquad (5)$$

where $\alpha_m$ weighs the contribution of each classifier with more accurate classifiers being assigned more weight. During training, the data is modified at each iteration. Initially, the weight of each sample $w_1, w_2, ..., w_n$ is set to $\frac{1}{N}$; however, with each iteration these weights are modified with the weight being increased for samples incorrectly classified and decreased for samples correctly classified. This has the effect of making each successive classifier focus on the incorrectly classified examples since the error for a classifier is calculated based on these weights [10]. At the end of a training iteration, the weight $\alpha_m$ of a classifier $G_m(x)$ is based on this error rate.

The weak learners used are decision trees and the same parameters as in the random forest were used. Similarly, the same ranking options (no ranking and *ProbRank*) were used.

### 5.2.5 *Majority Voting Ensemble*

We also experiment with a voting ensemble of the four supervised and baseline classifiers described above. A necessary condition for an ensemble of classifiers to perform better than the individual classifiers is that the individual classifiers are accurate and diverse [4]. In this case, the ensemble can reduce the risk of selecting a bad classifier for a given problem, reduce the impact of local optima, and expand the number of possible hypothesis representations [4]. In this study, we use a simple voting ensemble. In a voting ensemble, each classifier in the ensemble individually classifies a result and then casts a vote, which may or may not be weighted. The final decision as to the class of a result can then be based on the majority vote. We define the majority vote $M(x)$ among classifiers as:

$$M(x) = \sum_{i=1}^{n} w_i C_i(x), \qquad (6)$$

where $n$ is the number of classifiers in the ensemble, $w_i$ is the weight assigned to the $i$-th classifier and $C_i(x)$ is the classification produced by the $i$-th classifier. When $M(x) > 0$, the weighted majority vote is positive and thus result is classified as a source of plagiarism. Similarity, when $M(x) < 0$, the result is classified as a non-source of plagiarism. In this study, we include the top $n = 3$ and $n = 5$ classifiers in ensembles based on their $F_1$ score (Equation 9) and all classifiers are weighted equally, i.e. $w_i = 1, i \in 1, 2, ...n$. Given the fact that an odd number of classifiers are used, $M(x)$ is guaranteed to be non-zero since the output of each classifier is either 1 (source of plagiarism) or $-1$ (non-source of plagiarism).

## 6. EXPERIMENTS

### 6.1 Experiment Methodology

The source retrieval strategy as described in Algorithm 1 was executed on the test set without classification and ranking (line 9), i.e., all results were retrieved for every query, and an interaction log was generated. The interaction log recorded each document name, paragraph number and results for each query. This allowed for different classification and ranking strategies to be compared without needing to re-submit the queries to the search engine. Performance was measured using precision, recall and the $F_1$ score, which are defined as follows:

$$Precision = \frac{tp}{tp + fp}, \qquad (7)$$

$$Recall = \frac{tp}{tp + fn}, \qquad (8)$$

$$F_1 = \frac{2 \cdot Precision \cdot Recall}{Precision + Recall}, \qquad (9)$$

where $tp, fp$ and $fn$ refer to true positives, false positives and false negatives respectively.

Precision measures the proportion of results that were retrieved that were actually sources of plagiarism and thus measures how good the algorithm is at correctly identifying true sources of plagiarism. Recall measures the proportion of the total number of plagiarized results that were retrieved when the known set of plagiarized results is known. To calculate recall, the set of all retrieved URLs was maintained and once all retrieval had completed this set was compared to the set of URLs that were known to be sources of plagiarism.

There is a tradeoff between precision and recall since high precision can be achieved by only retrieving documents for which there is high confidence that they may be sources of plagiarism, though this comes at the cost of recall. Similarly, high recall can be achieved by retrieving a large set of documents with low precision. The tradeoff between these two metrics is given by the $F_1$ score, which is the harmonic mean of the two measures.

From the perspective of plagiarism detection, it could be argued that recall is more important than precision since one may not mind examining a few extra documents in order to increase the chances of retrieving a source of plagiarism. However, at a large scale such as that of the Web, it is important to maintain good precision so that the number of documents that need to be analyzed in detail does not become prohibitive.

### 6.2 Data Sampling

As discussed, the training data was imbalanced with negative samples making up 73.87% of the data and it has been noted that most learning algorithms expect an equal class distribution and do not work well on imbalanced data [11]. Over sampling the minority class has successfully been used to address the imbalanced data problem and the SMOTE method for oversampling [2] is used in this study. The SMOTE method creates synthetic or artificial examples of the minority class based on existing samples. For each sample $x_i$, the $K$ nearest neighbors are identified and one of those nearest neighbors $\hat{x}_i$ is randomly selected. The difference between $x_i$ and $\hat{x}_i$ is then multiplied by a random number $r \in [0, 1]$ and this value is added to $x_i$ to create a new point that falls on the line segment joining $x_i$ and $\hat{x}_i$ [11]:

$$x_{new} = x_i + (\hat{x}_i - x_i) \times r. \qquad (10)$$

In this study, we set the number of nearest neighbors to consider $k = 3$ and increase the number of positive training samples by 200%. Since the SMOTE method randomly selects nearest neighbors, we train 5 models and the results reported are the average of the 5 models.

### 6.3 Results

Experimental results are shown for 3 cases: when no ranking is used; when the probabilistic outputs of the classifiers are used for ranking; and when the ensemble method is used.

### 6.3.1 *No Ranking*

Table 2 shows the performance when no ranking is used for the supervised methods. In this case, the results are retrieved in the order that they were classified as being sources of plagiarism, which is based on the ordering produced by

**Table 2:** Precision, recall and the $F_1$ score for the baseline method and different supervised methods. No ranking of results is used, i.e. they are retrieved in the order they were classified.

| Method | Precision | Recall | $F_1$ Score |
|---|---|---|---|
| Baseline | 0.3735 | 0.8543 | 0.5198 |
| LDA | **0.3894** | **0.8803** | **0.5399** |
| Logistic | 0.3848 | 0.8629 | 0.5322 |
| Random Forests (RF) | 0.3625 | 0.8725 | 0.5122 |
| AdaBoost | 0.3811 | 0.8414 | 0.5246 |

**Table 3:** Precision, recall and the $F_1$ score for the baseline and different supervised methods. The search results were ranked by the probabilistic output of the classifiers.

| Method | Precision | Recall | $F_1$ Score |
|---|---|---|---|
| Baseline | 0.3735 | 0.8543 | 0.5198 |
| LDA+ProbRank | **0.4063** | **0.8681** | **0.5535** |
| Logistic+ProbRank | 0.4019 | 0.8553 | 0.5469 |
| RF+ProbRank | 0.3833 | 0.8651 | 0.5311 |
| AdaBoost+ProbRank | 0.4018 | 0.8367 | 0.5429 |

**Table 4:** Precision, recall and the $F_1$ score for the baseline and ensemble classifiers.

| Method | Precision | Recall | $F_1$ Score |
|---|---|---|---|
| Baseline | 0.3735 | 0.8543 | 0.5198 |
| Ensemble-Top3 | **0.3874** | 0.8681 | 0.5357 |
| Ensemble-Top5 | 0.3868 | **0.8825** | **0.5379** |

the search engine. For the baseline method, the results are ranked and ordered by the value of their snippet-document 5-gram intersection (feature 11).

As can be seen from Table 2, the highest precision is achieved by the LDA classifier, which is about 0.5% higher than the second highest precision achieved by the Logistic Regression classifier and about 1.6% higher than the precision achieved by the baseline. The highest recall is also achieved by the LDA classifier, which beats the baseline method by 2.6%. In fact, all of the supervised methods, except the AdaBoost classifier achieve higher recall than the baseline method. Similarly, all classifiers except the random forest classifier achieve higher precision than the baseline method. The highest $F_1$ score, which measures the trade-off between precision and recall, was achieved by the LDA classifier and was just above 2% higher than the baseline. In fact, all of the supervised method except random forests achieve a better $F_1$ score than the baseline method. This comparison shows that using supervised methods to classify results as potential sources of plagiarism leads to an improvement in performance over the baseline even though the baseline makes use of an implicit ranking method based on the snippet-document similarity. The next experiment repeats this experiment with a ranking based on the probabilistic outputs of the classifiers.

### 6.3.2  Ranking by Probabilistic Output of Classifiers

Table 3 shows the performance when ProbRank is used. With *ProbRank*, the probabilistic outputs of the classifiers are used to infer a ranking or ordering of the search results for each paragraph, with results being ranked in terms of their probability of being a source of plagiarism. Once again, the baseline results are ranked and ordered by the value of their snippet-document 5-gram intersection (feature 11) for the baseline method.

As can be seen from Table 3, the use of ProbRank leads to an improvement in the performance of all of the supervised

methods. The highest precision is achieved by LDA, and represents an almost 2% improvement over LDA without ProbRank and an improvement of 3.28% over the baseline. However, this improvement in precision comes at the cost of recall, which drops by over 1% compared to LDA with no ProbRank, though it still performs better than the baseline method. The $F_1$ score is higher with ProbRank than it is without and is an improvement on the baseline of 3.37%. The same pattern is observed for all supervised classifiers when ProbRank is used: ProbRank leads to an improvement in precision at the cost of recall, though the final $F_1$ measure is higher. Furthermore, all supervised methods outperform the baseline when ProbRank is used. From these results it can be argued that ProbRank is useful for improving the overall performance of the source retrieval strategy since it leads to a relatively large improvement in precision. Furthermore, ProbRank is a relatively simple ranking strategy and thus it could be possible to improve the results further with more advanced ranking strategies.

### 6.3.3  Voting Ensemble

Table 4 shows the performance of the majority voting ensemble classifiers and the baseline method. The majority voting ensembles are built with the top 3 and 5 performing classifiers as measured by their $F_1$ score without ranking.

As can be seen from Table 4, the use of the ensembles leads to an improvement in precision and recall over the baseline method. Furthermore, the ensemble consisting of all 5 classifiers leads to a slight improvement in the recall achieved by any classifier individually both with and without ProbRank. However, this comes at the cost of a decrease in precision. The performance of the ensemble consisting of all 5 classifiers performs similarly overall to the LDA classifier without ranking though not better than LDA with ProbRank. Given that the ensemble classifier does not lead to a large improvement in performance suggests that the classifiers are not sufficiently diverse to benefit from being combined in an ensemble.

### 6.3.4  Discussion

Overall it was found that the supervised classification of search results leads to an improvement in performance compared to the baseline method. Classifying search results without applying any ranking leads to similar precision while leading to an improvement in recall. Applying ProbRank to those results in general led to an improvement in precision, though at a slight cost in recall. It could be argued that recall is more important than precision for source retrieval and that the cost of missing a true source of plagiarism exceeds the cost of mistakenly retrieving a false source. The difference in recall between the baseline method and best performing supervised method was 2.6%. In the testing set, a total of 817 results were sources of plagiarism and a 2.6% increase in recall translates into potentially retrieving 21 additional sources of plagiarism while also improving precision. Given the importance of plagiarism detection, an increase in recall of only a few percent can be considered significant since it increases the chances of identifying plagiarism. Furthermore, at large scale, such as on the Web, a small increase in recall may translate into a significant increase in the number of sources of plagiarism retrieved.

## 6.4 Feature Analysis

Feature analysis was performed to gain insight into which features are important for source retrieval. This analysis provides insight into which of these features may be important not only in classifying search results, but also in understanding what plagiarizers may consider when choosing from which documents to plagiarize. This insight can be of practical use in constraining the plagiarism detection search space.

LDA was the best performing model; however, since LDA performs dimensionality reduction, its output is difficult to interpret. Thus, feature analysis is performed based on the random forest model where the importance of each feature is estimated based on the depth at which it occurs in the decision trees. This calculation is done using a built in method for calculating feature importance in the *scikit-learn* machine learning toolkit [19]. The feature importances are averaged for the 5 random forest models that were trained with different synthetic data generated by the SMOTE algorithm and are shown in ranked order in Table 5.

**Table 5: Importance of different features in the random forest**

| Rank | No. | Feature | Importance |
|------|-----|---------|------------|
| 1 | Doc-snippet intersection | 11 | 0.39 |
| 2 | Title-doc cosine | 13 | 0.16 |
| 3 | Wikipedia source | 17 | 0.09 |
| 4 | Snippet-doc cosine | 12 | 0.07 |
| 5 | #Adjectives | 20 | 0.07 |
| 6 | Proximity | 3 | 0.06 |
| 7 | Query-snippet cosine | 14 | 0.03 |
| 8 | Syllables | 9 | 0.02 |
| 9 | Sentences | 6 | 0.01 |
| 10 | BM25 | 5 | 0.01 |
| 11 | Words | 7 | 0.01 |
| 12 | Title length | 16 | 0.01 |
| 13 | Query-title cosine | 15 | 0.01 |
| 14 | Characters | 8 | 0.01 |
| 15 | Weight | 2 | 0.01 |
| 16 | Readability | 1 | 0.01 |
| 17 | Rank | 10 | 0.00 |
| 18 | #Nouns | 18 | 0.00 |
| 19 | #Verbs | 19 | 0.00 |
| 20 | PageRank | 4 | 0.00 |

An interesting observation from Table 5 is that the most important feature in the random forest is the exact same feature as used in the baseline method. This feature, which measures the intersection between the 5-grams in the suspicious document and the snippet contributes the largest amount to the final classification of the samples. The cosine similarity between the title of a result and the suspicious document is also a relatively important feature, suggesting

that the titles of plagiarized sources may be strongly related to whether or not it is used as a source of plagiarism. This is intuitive since the title of a document is likely to be the first thing a user considers in judging whether a Web page is relevant to their query or not. The fact that the Wikipedia feature is the third most important feature suggests that whether or not a page is a Wikipedia page may have an impact on whether or not it is used as a source of plagiarism. This is intuitive since Wikipedia provides a general and easily accessible description of many topics and is often ranked highly in many public search engines. Interestingly, the number of adjectives in a search result title is a relatively important feature and is ranked much higher than the number of nouns. One possible reason for this is that nouns provide high level descriptions of the concepts of documents whereas adjectives help to better refine those concepts, which can be useful in deciding which among several documents on the same high level topic.

Other insights can be gained from the less important features. For instance, the BM25 ranking method used by the ChatNoir search engine (rank 10, feature 5) and where among the top 3 results a result is ranked (rank 17, feature 10) do not seem to be important features. This finding supports the hypothesis in the introduction that the order of results returned by a search engine does not necessarily reflect the probability of them being sources of plagiarism. Similarly, the properties of the result document in terms of length, readability, etc., do not seem to be important for classification which seems to mostly rely on similarity-based features.

Overall, this analysis provides some insight into which features may be important to improve the performance of the supervised methods and that can be used to inform the design of new features, i.e. the similarity between a result snippet and the suspicious document (rank 1 & rank 4) and the relationship between a result title and the suspicious document. Given these findings, it may be useful to design new similarity features that can be used to better improve performance.

## 7. CONCLUSIONS

Source retrieval involves using a search engine to retrieve potential sources of plagiarism for a given suspicious document and can be considered as a first step in a plagiarism detection pipeline. In this study, we investigated the use of a supervised source retrieval strategy for classifying search engine results as candidate sources of plagiarism using only information available at search time. For a given suspicious document, queries were generated automatically and were used to query a search engine for plagiarism sources. Using this method, a search result dataset was created with a set of features available at search time. Several different supervised methods and ranking options were compared to a baseline method for classifying and ranking these results. The performance of the best performing supervised methods were shown to improve precision by up to 3.28%, recall by up to 2.6% and the $F_1$ score by up to 3.37% compared to the baseline method.

An analysis of features showed that the feature used in the baseline was in fact the most important feature for supervised classification followed by the cosine similarity between the title of a result and the suspicious document itself. Interestingly, the search engine ranking of the results did not seem to be important feature for classification, thereby suggesting that retrieving search results in the ordering produced by a search engine is not a good strategy for source retrieval and plagiarism detection.

A large number of the features used in this study were provided by the search engine; however, it generally cannot be assumed that a search engine will return a set of features that can be used for classification. Thus, an important consideration for future work would be the creation of new features for classification. Furthermore, as is currently the case, these features would need to be derivable without retrieving the search results so as to allow for real-time results classification.

Generally, the focus in Web search is on precision since it is desirable that relevant search results appear on the first page. However, we argue that recall is more important for plagiarism detection since even a small improvement in recall is significant. This is especially the case at Web scale since a small increase in recall could potentially translate into a significant number of additional sources of plagiarism being retrieved. However, it is still important to maintain precision so as to reduce the number of unnecessary comparisons made. The supervised method described in this paper is able to achieve both better precision and recall than the baseline method thus satisfying both of these goals.

Future work seeks to investigate how we can improve the supervised methods by investigating additional query generation strategies and new features for supervised classification.

## Acknowledgments

We gratefully acknowledge partial support by the National Science Foundation under Grant No. 1143921.

## 8. REFERENCES

[1] L. Breiman. Random Forests. *Machine learning*, 45(1):5–32, 2001.

[2] N. Chawla, K. Bowyer, L. Hall, and W. Kegelmeyer. SMOTE: synthetic minority over-sampling technique. *Journal of Artificial Intelligence Research*, 16:321–357, 2002.

[3] A. Dasdan, P. D'Alberto, S. Kolay, and C. Drome. Automatic retrieval of similar content using search engine query interface. In *Proceeding of the 18th ACM conference on Information and knowledge management - CIKM '09*, pages 701–710, 2009.

[4] T. G. Dietterich. Ensemble Methods in Machine Learning. In *Proceedings of the First International Workshop on Multiple Classifier Systems*, pages 1–15. Springer-Verlag, 2000.

[5] W. Fan. On the optimality of probability estimation by random decision trees. In *Proceedings of the AAAI Conference on Artificial Intelligence*, pages 336–341, 2004.

[6] D. Feng, D. Ravichandran, and E. Hovy. Mining and re-ranking for answering biographical queries on the web. In *Proceedings of the AAAI Conference on Artificial Intelligence*, pages 1283–1288, 2006.

[7] B. Gipp and N. Meuschke. Citation pattern matching algorithms for citation-based plagiarism detection. In *Proceedings of the 11th ACM symposium on Document engineering - DocEng '11*, pages 249–258, 2011.

[8] T. Gollub, M. Potthast, A. Beyer, M. Busse, F. Rangel, P. Rosso, E. Stamatatos, and B. Stein. Recent Trends in Digital Text Forensics and Its Evaluation Plagiarism Detection, Author Identification, and Author Profiling. In *Information Access Evaluation. Multilinguality, Multimodality, and Visualization*, pages 282–302, 2013.

[9] V. Govindaraju and K. Ramanathan. Similar Document Search and Recommendation. *Journal of Emerging Technologies in Web Intelligence*, 4(1):84–93, 2012.

[10] T. Hastie, R. J. Tibshirani, and J. J. H. Friedman. *The Elements of Statistical Learning: Data Mining, Inference, and Prediction*. Springer, 2009.

[11] H. He and E. Garcia. Learning from Imbalanced Data. *IEEE Transactions on Knowledge and Data Engineering*, 21(9):1263–1284, 2009.

[12] S. Hoi and R. Jin. Semi-Supervised Ensemble Ranking. *Proceedings of the AAAI Conference on Artificial Intelligence*, pages 634–639, 2008.

[13] T. Joachims. Optimizing search engines using clickthrough data. In *Proceedings of the eighth ACM SIGKDD international conference on Knowledge discovery and data mining - KDD '02*, pages 133–142, 2002.

[14] C.-J. Lee and W. B. Croft. Generating queries from user-selected text. *Proceedings of the 4th Information Interaction in Context Symposium*, pages 100–109, 2012.

[15] F. Liu, D. Pennell, F. Liu, and Y. Liu. Unsupervised Approaches for Automatic Keyword Extraction Using Meeting Transcripts. In *Proceedings of Human Language Technologies: The 2009 Annual Conference of the North American Chapter of the Association for Computational Linguistics*, pages 620–628, 2009.

[16] T.-Y. Liu. *Learning to Rank for Information Retrieval*. Springer Berlin Heidelberg, Berlin, Heidelberg, 2011.

[17] H. Maurer, C. Media, F. Kappe, and B. Zaka. Plagiarism - A Survey. *Journal of Universal Computer Science*, 12(8):1050–1084, 2006.

[18] D. L. Mccabe. Cheating among college and university students : A North American perspective. *International Journal for Educational Integrity*, 1(1):1–11, 2004.

[19] F. Pedregosa, G. Varoquaux, A. Gramfort, V. Michel, B. Thirion, O. Grisel, M. Blondel, P. Prettenhofer, R. Weiss, V. Dubourg, J. Vanderplas, A. Passos, D. Cournapear, M. Brucher, M. Perrot, and E. Duchesnay. Scikit-learn: Machine learning in Python. *Journal of Machine Learning Research*, 12:2825–2830, 2011.

[20] M. Pera and Y. Ng. Brek12: A book recommender for k-12 users. In *Proceedings of the 35th international ACM SIGIR conference on Research and development in information retrieval*, pages 1037–1038, 2012.

[21] A. Pereira and N. Ziviani. Retrieving similar documents from the web. *Journal of Web Engineering*, 2(4):247–261, 2004.

[22] M. Potthast, T. Gollub, M. Hagen, J. Graß egger, J. Kiesel, M. Michel, A. Oberländer, M. Tippmann, A. Barrón-cedeño, P. Gupta, P. Rosso, and B. Stein.

Overview of the 4th International Competition on Plagiarism Detection. pages 17–20, 2012.

[23] M. Potthast, M. Hagen, T. Gollub, M. Tippmann, J. Kiesel, P. Rosso, E. Stamatatos, and B. Stein. Overview of the 5th International Competition on Plagiarism Detection. In *CLEF 2013 Evaluation Labs and Workshop Working Notes Papers*, 2013.

[24] M. Potthast, M. Hagen, B. Stein, J. Graß egger, M. Michel, M. Tippmann, and C. Welsch. ChatNoir: A Search Engine for the ClueWeb09 Corpus. In *Proceedings of the 35th international ACM SIGIR conference on Research and development in information retrieval - SIGIR '12*, page 1004, 2012.

[25] M. Potthast, M. Hagen, M. Völske, and B. Stein. Crowdsourcing Interaction Logs to Understand Text Reuse from the Web. In *51st Annual Meeting of the Association of Computational Linguistics (ACL 13)*, pages 1212–1221, 2013.

[26] A. Singh and K. Nakata. Hierarchical Classification of Web Search Results Using Personalized Ontologies Background Document Organization. In *Proceedings of the 3rd International Conference on Universal Access in Human-Computer Interaction*, 2005.

[27] M. Surdeanu and M. Ciaramita. Learning to rank answers on large online QA collections. In *46th Annual Meeting of the Association for Computational Linguistics: Human Language Technologies*, pages 719–727, 2008.

[28] K. Toutanova, D. Klein, C. D. Manning, and Y. Singer. Feature-rich part-of-speech tagging with a cyclic dependency network. In *Proceedings of the 2003 Conference of the North American Chapter of the Association for Computational Linguistics on Human Language Technology - NAACL '03*, volume 1, pages 173–180, 2003.

[29] L. Weng, Z. Li, R. Cai, Y. Zhang, Y. Zhou, L. T. Yang, and L. Zhang. Query by document via a decomposition-based two-level retrieval approach. In *Proceedings of the 34th international ACM SIGIR conference on Research and development in Information - SIGIR '11*, pages 505–514, 2011.

[30] K. Williams, H. Chen, S. Choudhury, and C. Giles. Unsupervised Ranking for Plagiarism Source Retrieval - Notebook for PAN at CLEF 2013. In *CLEF 2013 Evaluation Labs and Workshop Working Notes Papers*, 2013.

[31] Y. Yang, N. Bansal, W. Dakka, P. Ipeirotis, N. Koudas, and D. Papadias. Query by document. In *Proceedings of the Second ACM International Conference on Web Search and Data Mining*, pages 34–43, 2009.

[32] Y. Yue, T. Finley, F. Radlinski, and T. Joachims. A support vector method for optimizing average precision. In *Proceedings of the 30th annual international ACM SIGIR conference on Research and development in information retrieval - SIGIR '07*, 2007.

[33] Q. Zhang, Y. Zhang, H. Yu, and X. Huang. Efficient partial-duplicate detection based on sequence matching. In *Proceeding of the 33rd international ACM SIGIR conference on Research and development in information retrieval - SIGIR '10*, page 675, 2010.

[34] Y. Zhu, G. Wang, J. Yang, D. Wang, J. Yan, J. Hu, and Z. Chen. Optimizing search engine revenue in sponsored search. In *Proceedings of the 32nd international ACM SIGIR conference on Research and development in information retrieval - SIGIR '09*, pages 588–596, 2009.

[35] Z. Zhu, M. Levene, and I. Cox. Ranking Classes of Search Engine Results. In *KDIR*, pages 294–301, 2010.

# An Ensemble Approach for Text Document Clustering using Wikipedia Concepts

Seyednaser
Nourashrafeddin
Faculty of Computer Science
Dalhousie University
Halifax, Nova Scotia
Canada B3H 4R2
nourashr@cs.dal.ca

Evangelos Milios
Faculty of Computer Science
Dalhousie University
Halifax, Nova Scotia
Canada B3H 4R2
eem@cs.dal.ca

Dirk V. Arnold
Faculty of Computer Science
Dalhousie University
Halifax, Nova Scotia
Canada B3H 4R2
dirk@cs.dal.ca

## ABSTRACT

Most text clustering algorithms represent a corpus as a document-term matrix in the bag of words model. The feature values are computed based on term frequencies in documents and no semantic relatedness between terms is considered. Therefore, two semantically similar documents may sit in different clusters if they do not share any terms. One solution to this problem is to enrich the document representation using an external resource like Wikipedia. We propose a new way to integrate Wikipedia concepts in partitional text document clustering in this work. A text corpus is first represented as a document-term matrix and a document-concept matrix. Terms that exist in the corpus are then clustered based on the document-term representation. Given the term clusters, we propose two methods, one based on the document-term representation and the other one based on the document-concept representation, to find two sets of seed documents. The two sets are then used in our text clustering algorithm in an ensemble approach to cluster documents. The experimental results show that even though the document-concept representations do not result in good document clusters per se, integrating them in our ensemble approach improves the quality of document clusters significantly.

## Categories and Subject Descriptors

I.5.3 [**Clustering**]: Algorithms

## Keywords

Text Clustering; Ensemble Clustering; Wikipedia; Semantic Relatedness

## 1. INTRODUCTION

Clustering is an important step preceding browsing in a document collection. The problem of clustering is widely

studied in the data mining literature and numerous algorithms have been proposed [1]. Grouping similar documents brings forward precious information about the text topics in many applications. For instance, the output of search engines is clustered in order to help users in query refinement and knowledge extraction [8, 19]. Or it is used in grouping similar sentences in mining customer opinions [9].

Traditional text clustering algorithms usually represent a document collection as a document-term matrix in the bag of words (*BOW*) model [1]. The model is based on the idea that related documents have common terms, while unrelated documents are formed by different vocabulary barely share any terms. The representation is limited to the term frequencies in documents and no semantic relation among terms is considered. For instance, two documents with the same topic would sit in two different clusters if they are formed by different but semantically related terms. One solution to this problem is to enrich the document representation by using the external resources like WordNet and Wikipedia.

Several research works have exploited Wikipedia in text clustering. The document representation of *BOW* is augmented in [2] utilizing top relevant Wikipedia articles. The title of selected articles are appended to the content of documents and the best performance is obtained by doubling the weights of terms appearing in the titles. A framework is proposed in [11] to enhance the traditional document similarity measures using the semantic relations extracted from Wikipedia. Different combinations of the semantic relations (synonyms, hypernyms, and associated relations) with traditional similarity measures are evaluated in experimental results. A linear combination of cosine similarities based on document-term representation and document-concept representation is also proposed in [14] to enhance the document similarity measure. A similar approach is proposed in [12] to enhance the document similarity measure. Document contents are first mapped to Wikipedia concepts and categories. The document cosine similarity measure is then combined with cosine similarities of document concepts and categories. No significant improvement is obtained for the partitional text clustering and the approach is more effective in hierarchical text clustering.

Wikipedia categories are also used in [21] to enrich document representation. Experimental results demonstrate that document-category representation is not as good as document-term representation in partitional text clustering. Some improvements are obtained only when a combination of document contents and Wikipedia categories are used.

Wikipedia concepts are used in [13] to actively find pairwise constraints for a semi-supervised clustering algorithm. A document-concept representation is first created for the collection. All the extracted concepts are then clustered. Those documents with higher weights in concept clusters are then submitted to a noise-free oracle to form *must-link* and *cannot-link* constraints.

A framework to label document clusters is proposed in [6]. The application of the framework is in interactive text clustering, where an interface is provided for users. Instead of representing a document cluster by its top keyterms, the framework exploits categories and titles of the relevant Wikipedia articles to assign a label.

A graph based distance among Wikipedia articles is presented in [24]. Nodes of the graph are articles and edges are weighted by their content or link similarity. The documents are mapped to the nodes based on the cosine similarity among their contents and articles' text. A random walk model is then proposed to measure node distance. Node distance is then used to measure document distance.

The *BOW* document representation is replaced by a concept model using the features extracted from Wikipedia articles in [22]. The concept model is then used in a hierarchical algorithm to cluster the documents.

Document representation is also enriched by using WordNet. Synonyms and hypernyms extracted from WordNet are used in [10] to represent documents instead of (or in combination with) their contents. However, the coverage of WordNet is limited and it is not comprehensive enough to find all the concepts mentioned in a document collection [12].

Overall, there are three approaches to enrich document representation of the *BOW* model:

1. The *BOW* model is completely replaced by a conceptual model.

2. The *BOW* model is enriched by the information extracted from an external source, like relevant concepts added to the content of documents.

3. The document similarity measure based on *BOW* is enhanced by a similarity measure based on a conceptual model.

To the best of our knowledge, no one has proposed an ensemble clustering algorithm to combine the clusterings generated based on document contents and on document concepts. Most research works have spent more effort on extracting semantic relatedness or enhancing the document similarity measures, while we have focused on designing a document clusterer by using Wikipedia concepts in this work.

We propose a new framework in order to integrate the Wikipedia concepts in partitional document clustering. Using the Wikipedia concepts, we propose a method to find the seed documents later used for document clustering. We also introduce another method to find the seed documents based on document contents. Our ensemble clustering algorithm combines the clusters generated by these seed documents. To evaluate the performance of our method, we performed empirical experiments on some real text datasets. Our experimental results show that the quality of clusters is significantly improved by utilizing Wikipedia concepts.

The remainder of this paper is organized as follows. Section 2 reviews some methods in enriching document representation. Section 3 describes our partitional clustering algorithm. Section 4 explains our ensemble clustering algorithm. Experimental results on some real text datasets are reported in Section 5. Section 6 presents conclusions and future work.

## 2. RELATED WORK

In this section, we review some methods proposed to enrich document representation in text clustering.

Traditional document content similarity is leveraged by integrating Wikipedia based semantic relations in [11]. A concept thesaurus is first created from Wikipedia articles. It includes semantic relations like synonym, polysemy, hypernym, and associative relations extracted from anchor texts, disambiguation pages, categories, and hyperlinks in Wikipedia, respectively. Given a document, its text content is mapped to the most relevant Wikipedia articles. The category graph of those articles is then used to form a category vector. A concept vector is also created based on the concepts mentioned in the relevant articles using the thesaurus synonym and associative relations. The document similarity measure is then defined as:

$$\text{sim}_{\text{combination}} = (1-\alpha-\beta)\text{sim}_{content}+\alpha\text{sim}_{\text{cat}}+\beta\text{sim}_{\text{conc}} \quad (1)$$

where, $\text{sim}_{content}$ is the cosine similarity based on content vectors, $\text{sim}_{\text{cat}}$ is based on the category vectors, and $\text{sim}_{\text{conc}}$ is based on the concept vectors. Equal weights ($\alpha = \beta = 1/3$) are considered in empirical experiments. Given a few labeled documents, a parameter optimization is also performed to find the optimal values for $\alpha$ and $\beta$. The optimal weights could improve the clustering performance further.

A similar approach is proposed to enrich the document representation using Wikipedia concepts in [12]. A document collection is represented as a document-term matrix, a document-concept matrix, and a document-category matrix. The traditional document cosine similarity is then enhanced by using the concept and category matrices as:

$$\text{sim}(d_i, d_j) = \text{sim}(d_i, d_j)^{\text{term}} + \alpha\text{sim}(d_i, d_j)^{\text{concept}} + \beta\text{sim}(d_i, d_j)^{\text{category}} \quad (2)$$

No optimization method is proposed to find the optimal values for $\alpha$ and $\beta$. After using different values, the best improvement is reported in experimental results. Compared to the method proposed in [11], lower weights are considered for concepts and categories. An interesting observation in experimental results is that document-concept and document-category representations used alone never outperform the document-term representation in partitional document clustering.

A new concept based similarity measure is proposed in [14], which considers the semantic relatedness among concepts. The semantic similarity between two documents $d_i$ and $d_j$ is defined as:

$$\text{sim}(d_i, d_j)^{\text{sem}} = \frac{\sum_{c_k, c_l} w(c_k, d_i)w(c_l, d_j)SIM(c_k, c_l)}{\sum_{c_k, c_l} w(c_k, d_i)w(c_l, d_j)} \quad (3)$$

where $SIM(c_k, c_l)$ is the semantic relatedness between two concepts $c_k$ and $c_l$ extracted from Wikipedia articles regardless of the documents referred, and $w(c_k, d_i)$ is the weight of concept $c_k$ in vector $d_i$ in document-concept representation. The overall document similarity is then defined as the linear combination of the semantic similarity and the cosine similarity based on document contents. Lower weights are considered for semantic similarity compared to content similarity. The main contribution of the work is in Eq. (3), where the semantic similarity between documents is enhanced by using the semantic relatedness between concepts ($SIM(c_k, c_l)$).

Four different document representation techniques are evaluated for document clustering in [21]:

1. A document is represented in the $BOW$ model

2. A document is represented using Wikipedia categories

3. A document is represented only by the top 20 keyterms with the highest weight values

4. A document is represented as a combination of the categories and the top 20 keyterms.

The worst results are obtained when documents are only represented by Wikipedia categories. The $BOW$ model and the combined representation result in the same clusters and no significant improvement is achieved by integrating Wikipedia categories.

The titles of relevant Wikipedia articles are appended to the content of documents in [2]. The $BOW$ model is then used to represent documents with doubling the weights of the terms appearing in the titles. The proposed clustering method is applied on short texts and significant improvement is obtained by integrating the Wikipedia articles. An interesting observation is that the weight of Wikipedia title terms is double, while a lower or at most equal weights are considered in the other methods reviewed so far. The work demonstrated that integrating Wikipedia in document representation can be very effective, when documents are in the form of short texts like tweets or snippets.

A random walk model is proposed in [24] to measure the semantic relatedness among documents. Wikipedia articles are first mapped to a graph, where nodes correspond to articles and edges derived from either hyperlinks among articles or the cosine similarity among the articles' text. The content of a document is then mapped to the 10 closest nodes (articles) based on the cosine similarity of the content of the document and the articles' text. The semantic relatedness among documents is then computed as a Visiting probability of a random walk on the graph. The Visiting probability is computed using the probability of transition $t_{ij}$ between nodes $s_i$ and $s_j$ and is defined as:

$$P(t_{ij}) = \frac{W(i,j)}{\sum_{k=1}^{n} W(i,k)} \qquad (4)$$

where $n$ is the number of nodes in the article graph, and $W(i,j)$ is the weight of the edge between $s_i$ and $s_j$. A document similarity matrix is then formed by using the Visiting probability computed on the graph. The matrix is fed into a relational $k$-means algorithm to cluster documents. The best improvement is obtained by computing the Visiting probability over a combination of the hyperlinks and the lexical similarity among the articles' text.

A conceptual hierarchical clustering using the relevant concepts extracted from Wikipedia is proposed in [22]. Given a document, its noun-phrases are initially mapped to the relevant Wikipedia concepts. Besides concepts, relevant Wikipedia articles are also extracted in order to define the following conceptual features:

- The frequency of a concept in a document.

- The number of common links presented in the article of a relevant concept and in the articles of all relevant concepts.

- The cosine similarity between the document content and the article text.

- The position of a relevant concept in the document.

- The importance of a concept in Wikipedia regardless of the document referred to.

A linear combination of the above features is then used to measure the importance of a particular concept in the respective document. Given the conceptual representation, a hierarchical clustering algorithm is used to cluster documents.

We propose an ensemble approach to integrate Wikipedia concepts in document clustering. We first describe our partitional document clustering algorithm, which lexically finds seed documents. The seed extraction is based on the document-term representation. We then show another method to extract seed documents semantically, which is based on document-concept representation. The two sets of seed documents are then used separately to cluster documents. The documents with consensus labels in these two clusterings are found and treated as a training set to learn a classifier. The final clustering is then formed by classifying the remaining documents.

Our experimental results show the effectiveness of our consensus method even when the quality of clusters generated by the concepts is much worse than that generated by the document contents.

## 3. PARTITIONAL CLUSTERING

In this section, we describe our partitional document clustering algorithm proposed in [18]. We will present our ensemble algorithm, which integrates Wikipedia concepts in document clustering in Section 4.

We represent a text corpus as a document-term matrix in the $BOW$ model. Documents and terms are represented as row and column vectors in this matrix. Each entry of the matrix is the term frequency–inverse document frequency ($TFIDF$) that indicates the importance of a term in the respective document.

Since the number of terms in a text dataset is often large, it has been proposed to first focus on term clusters [7]. Following the same approach, our clustering algorithm is based on the idea that before finding document clusters, it is better to focus on term clustering and the keyterms that represent topics. Our clustering algorithm consists of three phases:

1. Term clustering

2. Finding lexical seed documents

3. Document clustering

The structure of the algorithm is depicted in Fig. 1. In Phase 1, fuzzy $c$-means is used to cluster terms (columns of the document-term matrix). Fuzzy $c$-means groups the terms into $k$ term clusters. We then remove general terms from the term clusters since these terms deteriorate the performance of our clustering algorithm [18]. We consider the remaining terms in term clusters as topic keyterms.

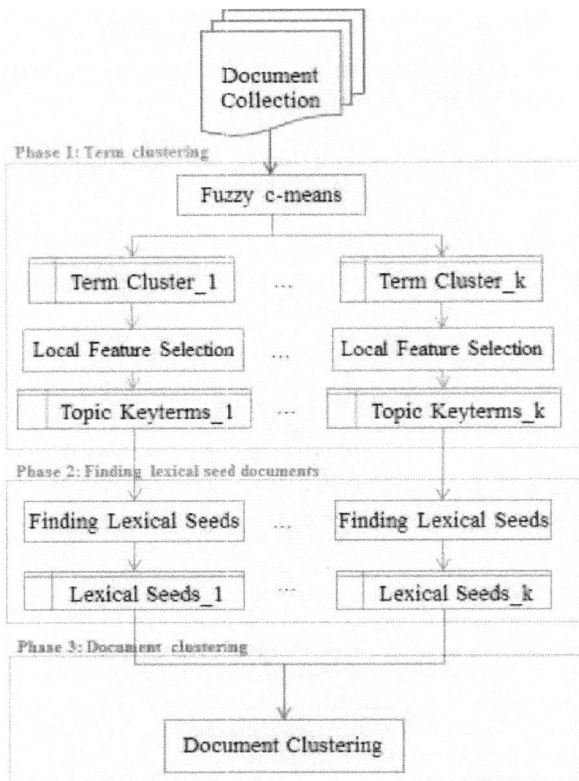

**Figure 1: The structure of the lexical document clustering algorithm, Algorithm 1. Fuzzy $c$-means is used for term clustering. A greedy approach distills the term clusters through feature selection in order to remove non-discriminative terms. Representative documents associated with each term cluster are then extracted and used as seeds to cluster all documents.**

Given the topic keyterms as the input in Phase 2, we extract the representative documents, which are used as seeds to cluster all documents later.

In Phase 3, a document centroid is computed based on the seed documents of each term cluster. The distances among documents and the centroids are then used to cluster documents. The main steps of this lexical document clustering ($LDC$) algorithm are shown in Algorithm 1.

## 3.1 Term Clustering

The presence of similar topics is a common case in text clustering. Similar topics share common terms and each term usually belongs to multiple topics with different degrees of relevance.

The integration of the fuzzy paradigm with the simplicity and efficiency of $k$-means, make fuzzy $c$-means a good candidate for term clustering. Given a document-term matrix, we apply fuzzy $c$-means on the term vectors to generate $k$ term clusters. For a matrix with $M$ term vectors $\{t_1, t_2, ..., t_M\}$, fuzzy $c$-means generates $k$ term clusters $\{TC_p\}_{p=1}^k$ such that

---

**Algorithm 1** Lexical Document Clustering ($LDC$)

**Input:** a document-term matrix, $k$
**Output:** $k$ document clusters
1: use fuzzy c-means to generate $k$ term clusters
2: remove non-discriminative terms from the term clusters
3: **for** each distilled term cluster **do**
4:     extract representative (seed) documents
5:     compute a document centroid for the representative documents
6: **end for**
7: **for** each document in the dataset **do**
8:     measure its distances to the document centroids
9:     assign the document to each document centroid with a membership value
10: **end for**

---

the following objective function is locally minimized [3]:

$$F_z = \sum_{i=1}^{M} \sum_{p=1}^{k} u_{ip}^z dist^2(t_i, \mu_p) \qquad (5)$$

where $z$ is a real number larger than 1, $u_{ip}$ is the degree of membership of $t_i$ in $TC_p$, and $\mu_p$ is the centroid of $TC_p$.

Each term cluster includes only terms whose memberships are greater than $1/k$ at the end. This method of defuzzification results in a soft clustering.

We assume that only a few terms represent topics and the other terms are non-discriminative [15]. We use a greedy approach to extract these topic keyterms. Our greedy approach consists of the following steps:

1. For each term, we first compute its score using the *Var-TFIDF* feature selection method [18].

2. We then compute an average score for each term cluster. The average score is the mean of all term scores included in a term cluster.

3. In each term cluster, those terms whose scores are smaller than the cluster average score are removed. The remaining terms are considered as topic keyterms and used in the next phase.

The output of this phase are $k$ term clusters distilled by the greedy approach.

## 3.2 Finding Lexical Seed Documents

The input of this phase consists of $k$ distilled term clusters, each including a set of topic keyterms. Each set characterizes a set of seed documents. The seed documents are those documents that are close to each other in the subspace spanned by topic keyterms. We extract the seed documents of each term cluster using the method proposed in [18]. The method consists of the following steps:

1. A term-centroid is first generated using the document-term representation. The term-centroid is the column average of the term vectors corresponding to the terms included in a term cluster. It is a vector with dimensionality equal to the number of documents.

2. The $k$-means algorithm with $k = 2$ is then applied on the term-centroid (in a one dimensional space) to partition its elements into two clusters. One cluster includes

110

elements with near-zero values and the other cluster includes elements with larger non-zero values. The near-zero values correspond to the documents in which the terms of a term cluster have low feature values. The elements with larger non-zero values correspond to the seed documents.

It is noteworthy to mention that a seed document can be linked with more than one term cluster in this phase. However, the *TFIDF* value of the document in a term-centroid indicates the weight of document in each term cluster. We use these weight values in computing document centroids. The extracted seed documents are called lexical seeds in the rest of the paper.

## 3.3 Document Clustering

The input of this phase is the lexical seed documents of the term clusters. Given the lexical seeds, we use the following steps to cluster documents:

1. For each term cluster, we compute a document centroid over its seed documents. A document centroid is the row average of the document vectors corresponding to the seed documents:

$$\text{lexical\_centroid}_p = \frac{\sum_{d_i \in \text{lexical\_seeds}(TC_p)} w_i * d_i}{|\text{lexical\_seeds}(TC_p)|} \quad (6)$$

where $w_i$ is the averaged *TFIDF* value of $d_i$ in the term-centroid of $TC_p$, and $||$ indicates the cardinality of a set.

2. The distances of each document to the lexical centroids are then computed. The memberships of documents in document clusters are then measured as the inverse of these distances. In this way, each document has a membership value in each document cluster.

A hard partitioning of a collection can be generated by assigning each document to the closest centroid.

The *LDC* algorithm described in this section can also be applied on the document-concept representation. Given a document-concept matrix, fuzzy *c*-means is used to cluster concepts (columns of the document-concept matrix). Fuzzy *c*-means groups the concepts into $k$ concept clusters. We remove general concepts from the concept clusters using the greedy approach of Section 3.1. The seed documents of the distilled concept clusters are then extracted and used to cluster documents based on the document-concept representation. The main steps of this semantic document clustering (*SDC*) algorithm are shown in Algorithm 2.

## 4. ENSEMBLE CLUSTERING

Besides the document-term representation, we represent a document as a bag of concepts (*BOC*) extracted from Wikipedia. The wikified concepts are the titles of the relevant articles. Given the documents in the *BOW* and *BOC* models, our ensemble algorithm clusters a document collection in the following phases:

1. Term clustering and topic keyterm selection

2. Finding lexical seed documents

3. Finding semantic seed documents

4. Document clustering using the consensus method

Phases 1 and 2 are the same as Phases 1 and 2 of our partitional algorithm, Section 3.1 and Section 3.2. Fuzzy c-means clusters terms (columns of the document-term matrix) into $k$ groups. The *Var-TFIDF* feature selection method distills term clusters by removing non-discriminative terms. The lexical seed documents are then extracted based on the document-term representations. Given the lexical seeds, we compute the lexical document centroids using Eq. (6).

In Phase 3, we present a method to semantically find seed documents. We first extract the relevant Wikipedia concepts of each term cluster by wikifying its topic keyterms. Any document which has a common concept with the concepts of a term cluster is considered as a semantic seed document. The number of common concepts is also considered as the weight of the semantic seed documents. Document centroids are then computed as the weighted mean of the semantic seed documents. We call these document centroids, semantic centroids in the rest of paper. Hence, the output of Phases 2 and 3 are two document centroids, lexical and semantic, for each term cluster.

Given the lexical and semantic centroids, we generate two clusterings of the documents in Phase 4. The first clustering is generated by only using the lexical centroids and the second one is generated by using the semantic centroids.

Reconciling the generated clusters reveals that some documents have the same labels in these two clusterings. It means that these documents belong to the same clusters based on the lexical and conceptual relatedness. We treat these documents and their labels as a training set to learn a text classifier. After training the classifier, the remaining documents are classified. The main steps of this ensemble lexical-semantic document clustering (*ELSDC*) algorithm are shown in Algorithm 3 and Fig. 2.

---

**Algorithm 2** Semantic Document Clustering (*SDC*)

---

**Input:** *a document-concept matrix, k*
**Output:** *k document clusters*
1: *use fuzzy c-means to generate k concept clusters*
2: *remove non-discriminative concepts from the concept clusters*
3: **for** *each distilled concept cluster* **do**
4:    *extract representative documents*
5:    *compute a document centroid for the representative documents*
6: **end for**
7: **for** *each document in the dataset* **do**
8:    *measure its distances to the document centroids*
9:    *assign the document to each document centroid with a membership value*
10: **end for**

---

## 4.1 Finding Semantic Seed Documents

The input of this phase are $k$ distilled term clusters. We extract semantic seed documents based on the concepts extracted for documents and for distilled term clusters. The idea is that the semantic seed documents share common concepts with the distilled term clusters. The semantic seed documents of term cluster $TC_p$ are extracted using the following equation:

$$\text{semantic\_seeds}(TC_p) = \{(d_i, w_i)| \quad w_i = |\text{wikify}(d_i) \cap \text{wikify}(TC_p)| \quad \text{AND} \quad w_i > 0\} \quad (7)$$

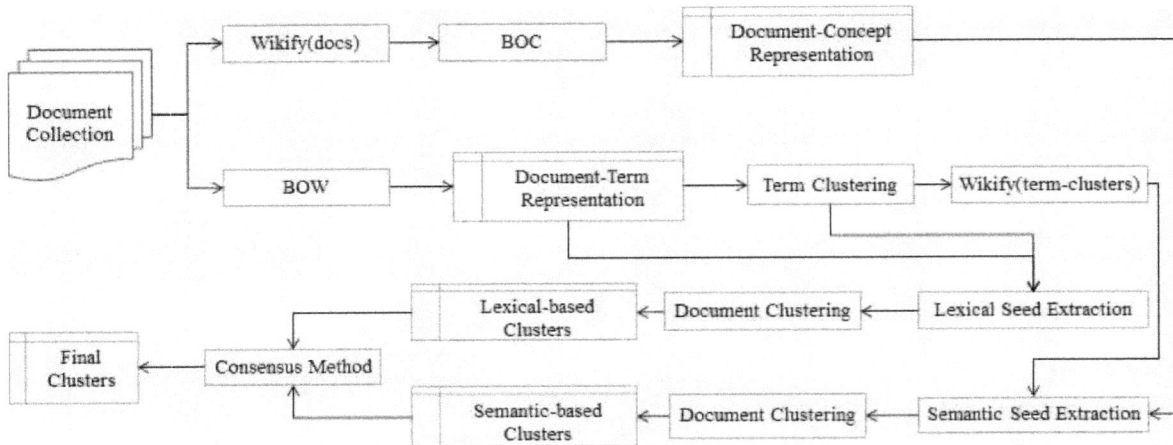

**Figure 2: The structure of the ensemble lexical-semantic document clustering algorithm, Algorithm 3. *BOW* and *BOC* are used to represent documents. The wikify module extracts relevant concepts from Wikipedia. The consensus method consists of a Naive Bayes classifier, which is trained by using the documents that belong to the same clusters in both clusterings. The final clustering is generated by classifying the remaining documents.**

where $w_i$ is the weight of seed document $d_i$. The semantic centroid of $TC_p$ is then computed using the following equation:

$$semantic\_centroid_p = \frac{\sum_{d_i \in semantic\_seeds(TC_p)} w_i * d_i}{|semantic\_seeds(TC_p)|} \quad (8)$$

where $d_i$ is the vector of the $i^{th}$ document in *BOW*.

## 4.2 Consensus Method

The input of this phase are two document centroids for each term cluster, a lexical centroid and a semantic centroid. We cluster documents once based on the lexical centroids and once based on the semantic centroids using the method of Section 3.3. We then combine the generated clusters to form the final clusters.

The idea behind our aggregation is that if the label of a document in both clusterings is the same, it is more likely that the label is correct. In other words, there are some documents that sit in the same clusters in both lexical-based and semantic-based clusterings. We find all these documents and treat them as a training set to learn a classifier. After training the classifier, the remaining documents are classified. The algorithm of this phase has the following steps:

- Cluster documents using the lexical centroids

- Cluster documents using the semantic centroids

- Find the documents with the same labels in both clusterings

- Treat these documents as a training set to learn a classifier

- Classify the remaining documents

We used the Naive Bayes classifier available in the Matlab[1] statistical toolbox as the text classifier in our experiments.

---
[1]http://www.mathworks.com/

---

**Algorithm 3** Ensemble Lexical-Semantic Document Clustering (*ELSDC*)

**Input:** *a document collection, k*
**Output:** *k document clusters*
1: **for** *each document* **do**
2:     *Extract relevant Wikipedia concepts*
3: **end for**
4: *use fuzzy c-means to generate k term clusters*
5: *remove non-discriminative terms from the term clusters*
6: **for** *each distilled term cluster* **do**
7:     *Extract relevant Wikipedia concepts*
8: **end for**
9: **for** *each distilled term cluster* **do**
10:     *Find the seed documents based on the BOW model*
11:     *Compute the lexical document centroids*
12:     *Find the seed documents based on the BOC model*
13:     *Compute the semantic document centroids*
14: **end for**
15: *Cluster the document collection using the lexical centroids*
16: *Cluster the document collection using the semantic centroids*
17: *Aggregate the clusterings by finding the documents with the same labels in both clusterings*
18: *Treat those documents as a training set and learn a classifier*
19: *Classify the remaining documents using the classifier*

# 5. EXPERIMENTAL RESULTS

In the first round of experiments, we compare the lexical document clustering (*LDC*) algorithm to the *LDA* model proposed in [4]. The idea behind *LDA* is that a document can be viewed as a probability distribution over latent topics and each topic in turn is viewed as a probability distribution over terms. We used a C++ implementation[2] of the *LDA* model in this round. We will show that *LDC* can generate comparable results to the *LDA* model on some real text datasets based on the document-term representation.

In the second round of experiments, we compare *LDC* to the proposed ensemble algorithm (*ELSDC*). We will show the benefits of integrating Wikipedia concepts in document clustering.

## 5.1 Datasets and Implementation

In our experiments, we used eight standard datasets whose characteristics are summarized in Table 1. The second last column of the table shows the percentage of zero values that exists in the document-term matrices of the datasets.

1. *20Newsgroups*: This dataset consists of approximately 20000 news articles grouped into 20 different topics[3]. We removed all articles duplicated in multiple groups. We then created three datasets from this collection. Each dataset is created by selecting a subset of the whole collection:

   - *News-sim3* includes all articles from three similar topics (classes) *comp.graphics*, *comp.os.ms-windows.misc*, and *comp.windows.x*.

   - *News-rel3* includes all articles from three related topics *talk-politics-misc*, *talk-politics-guns*, and *talk-politics-mideast*.

   - *20ng-whole* includes all the documents in all topics.

2. *Reuters-21578*: The documents in the *Reuters-21578*[4] dataset appeared on the *Reuters* newswire in 1987 and have been labeled manually. We selected a subset of topics in the collection to make a dataset. *Reuters8-whole* is a subset of *Reuters-21578* dataset consisting of documents in eight categories including *acq*, *crude*, *earn*, *grain*, *interest*, *money-fx*, *ship*, and *trade*. All the documents in these eight categories are included in the dataset.

3. *Classic4* is created from *SMART* data repository[5]. The repository contains paper abstracts in medical, information retrieval, aerodynamics, and computing algorithms. All abstracts are included in *Classic4*. We have stemmed and non-stemmed versions of this dataset in our experiments. The stemmed version is used in the first round and the non-stemmed version is used in the second round of our experiments.

4. *WebKB* consists of webpages collected from four computer science departments in *Cornell*, *Texas*, *Washington*, *Wisconsin* universities. The collection is created

## Table 1: Summary of the text datasets used in our experiments

| Dataset Name | No. of Docs | No. of Terms | $k$ | Sparsity | Stemmed |
|---|---|---|---|---|---|
| News-sim3 | 2924 | 20753 | 3 | 99.7% | ✓ |
| News-rel3 | 2624 | 21659 | 3 | 98.2% | ✓ |
| 20ng-whole | 18821 | 92587 | 20 | 99.1% | ✗ |
| Reuters8-whole | 7674 | 22750 | 8 | 99.4% | ✗ |
| Classic4 | 7095 | 41681 | 4 | 99.5% | ✗✓ |
| WebKB | 4168 | 7675 | 4 | 99.4% | ✓ |
| SMS | 5479 | 7288 | 2 | 99.3% | ✗ |
| Cade | 4069 | 36746 | 5 | 98% | ✓ |

in the World Wide Knowledge Base (Web-Kb) project of the *CMU* text learning group[6]. The webpages are manually labeled into seven categories: student, faculty, staff, departments, course, project, other. We used only four categories of student, faculty, course, and project which have more documents than the other categories.

5. *SMS Spam Collection* consists of a public set of text messages labeled as *spam* and *non-spam*. The collection is used in [23] and is publicly available[7].

6. *Cade* is gathered from the content of Brazilian web pages. The web pages are in Portuguese language. A pre-processed version of the dataset[8] has been generated in *Universidade Federal de Minas Gerais* in Brazil and is used in [5]. The dataset is labeled by human experts.

Stop-word removal, and removing low-variance terms [18] are applied to the datasets in a pre-processing step. Porter stemmer [20] is applied on some datasets. Each dataset is then represented as a document-term matrix in the *BOW* model. The effect of document length is reduced by using the *L2* norm to normalize the length of document vectors to one.

We used Euclidean distance to cluster document vectors since their length is normalized to one and Cosine similarity to cluster term vectors. To extract the Wikipedia concepts, we used the wikify method proposed in [17].

## 5.2 Evaluation Measure

We used the true labels of documents to evaluate clusterings. We consider the hard partitioning of documents in our experiments since our benchmark datasets are single-labeled. A confusion matrix is formed after each clustering. Each element of this matrix indicates the number of common documents between the corresponding cluster and class. The dimensionality of this matrix is $k$ by $k$. This confusion matrix is subsequently used to compute *Normalized Mutual Information* (*NMI*) [16].

*NMI* measures the amount of information we get about classes given a set of clusters [16]. It has a maximum value

---

[2]http://gibbslda.sourceforge.net/

[3]http://qwone.com/~jason/20Newsgroups/

[4]http://www.daviddlewis.com/resources/testcollections-/reuters21578/

[5]ftp://ftp.cs.cornell.edu/pub/smart/

[6]http://www.cs.cmu.edu/afs/cs.cmu.edu/project/theo-20/www/data/

[7]http://www.dt.fee.unicamp.br/~tiago/smsspamcollection/

[8]http://web.ist.utl.pt/~acardoso/datasets/

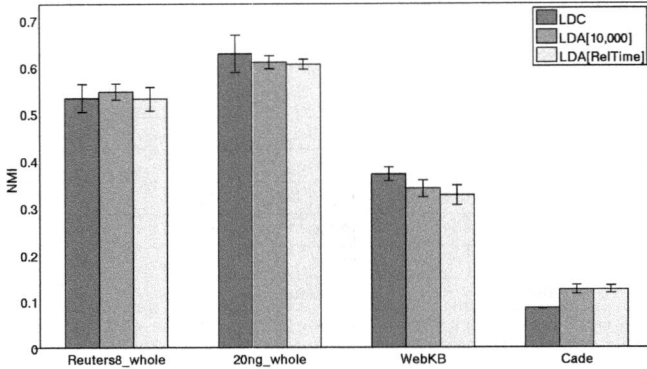

**Figure 3: The quality of clusters obtained from the lexical document clustering (*LDC*) algorithm and the *LDA* model in 50 runs. The *LDA* models outperform *LDC* on the *Cade* dataset. Otherwise, *LDC* and the *LDA* models generate similar results.**

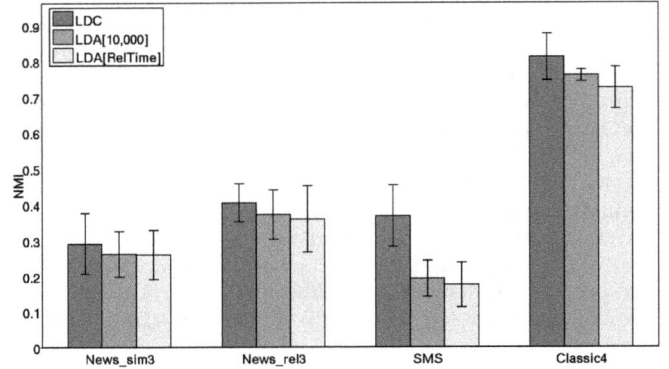

**Figure 4: The quality of clusters obtained from the lexical document clustering (*LDC*) algorithm and the *LDA* model in 50 runs. *LDC* outperforms both *LDAs* on the *SMS* dataset, where documents are short. Otherwise, they generate similar clusters.**

of one when the clustering process recreates classes perfectly and its minimum is zero:

$$\text{NMI} = \frac{2I(W,C)}{[H(W) + H(C)]}$$

$$I(W,C) = \sum_k \sum_j P(w_k \cap c_j) \log \frac{P(w_k \cap c_j)}{P(w_k)P(c_j)} \quad (9)$$

$$H(W) = -\sum_k P(w_k) \log(P(w_k))$$

where $W = \{w_1, w_2, .., w_k\}$ and $C = \{c_1, c_2, ..., c_k\}$ denote classes and clusters respectively.

### 5.3 Comparison to the LDA Model

In this round of experiments, we compare *LDC* algorithm to the *LDA* model using only the document-term representation. In *LDC*, the maximum number of iterations for fuzzy *c*-means is set to 50. The number of iterations for the LDA model is set to 10,000 and the number of topics is set to $k$. The value of $k$ is user-defined. After 10,000 iterations, we assign each document to the topic (cluster) with maximum probability. Similarly, we assign each document to the closest cluster in *LDC* algorithm (hard partitioning).

We also measured the running time of *LDC* for each dataset in the worst case when fuzzy *c*-means is run for all 50 iterations. We then let the *LDA* model run for these running times instead of 10,000 iterations. We call this algorithm *LDA*[RelTime] in experimental results. By running both algorithms for the same time on the same machine, we provided a more fair performance comparison. We have run these algorithms 50 times. The average and the standard deviation of *NMI* in these 50 runs are depicted in Fig. 3 and Fig. 4.

Based on the empirical results obtained in this round of experiments, we can conclude that *LDC* and the *LDA* model generate similar results using document-term representation, if they run for the same time.

**Table 2: Comparing the *BOW* and *BOC* models by using the lexical document clustering (*LDC*) and the semantic document clustering (*SDC*) algorithms. Each algorithm is run 50 times and the average *NMIs* are shown. The document representation in *BOW* generates significantly better results in our experiments. This observation is consistent with the results obtained in [12].**

| Datasets | LDC | SDC |
|---|---|---|
| 20ng-whole | **0.6328*** | 0.4143 |
| Reuters8-whole | **0.5381*** | 0.2663 |
| Classic4 | **0.8145*** | 0.4695 |

### 5.4 Integrating Wikipedia Concepts

In the second round of experiments, we show the benefit of integrating Wikipedia concepts in *BOW*. We first show that *BOW* is much better than *BOC* in our experiments. For this purpose, we compare *LDC* to *SDC* using the document-term and the document-concept matrices. We ran the algorithms 50 times on three non-stemmed datasets *Reuters8-whole*, *20ng-whole*, and *Classic4*. Non-stemmed datasets are used in this round since the Wikipedia articles are not stemmed. The average *NMIs* of these 50 runs are shown in Table 2. Significant improvements according to paired-sample T-test with $p \leqslant 0.05$ are indicated by "*".

We then show that combining the *BOW* and *BOC* models in the ensemble algorithm (*ELSDC*) generates better results than using *BOW* alone. For this purpose, we compared *LDC* to the proposed *ELSDC* algorithm. The average of *NMIs* obtained in 50 runs of these algorithms are shown in Table 3.

Based on the empirical results obtained in this experiment, we observed that:

1. We cannot ignore document terms from the clustering process. The comparison between the *BOW* and *BOC* models reveals that the quality of clusters deteriorates significantly if document contents are replaced by Wikipedia concepts. The first cause originates from term

**Table 3: Comparison between the proposed ensemble algorithm (*ELSDC*) and the lexical document clustering algorithm (*LDC*). *LDC* is based on the *BOW* model, while a consensus method is used in *ELSDC* to combine the results obtained from *BOW* and *BOC*. Each algorithm is run 50 times and the average *NMIs* are shown. Integrating document concepts extracted from Wikipedia improves the quality of clusters significantly.**

| Datasets | *LDC* | *ELSDC* |
|---|---|---|
| 20ng-whole | 0.6328 | **0.6695\*** |
| Reuters8-whole | 0.5381 | **0.5861\*** |
| Classic4 | 0.8145 | **0.8370\*** |

polysemy. A term like "tree" has different meanings in different contexts. Finding the best sense of the disambiguated terms is still a challenging task in extracting semantic relatedness. The second reason is that there are many discriminative terms in the content of documents that are not shown in the output of wikify modules. Eliminating those terms was not compensated for by adding Wikipedia concepts in our experiments.

2. The proposed ensemble algorithm (*ELSDC*) has successfully integrated concepts in document clustering. Significant improvements have been obtained even though the *BOC* model alone resulted in poor clusters in our experiments.

Overall, we conclude that the *ELSDC* algorithm is an effective way to integrate Wikipedia concepts in our partitional clustering algorithm. Besides, no parameter setting is needed in *ELSDC*, compared to the algorithms reviewed in Section 2. The proposed consensus method can be used with any partitional clustering algorithm and with other wikify approaches.

# 6. CONCLUSION AND FUTURE WORK

We proposed a new framework for partitional document clustering to integrate Wikipedia concepts in the *BOW* model. Our framework consists of an ensemble algorithm which combines the clusterings generated from *BOW* and *BOC*. The documents with the same labels in the clusterings are used as a training set to learn a text classifier. The trained classifier clusters the remaining documents.

We proposed two methods in the framework to extract seed documents. Lexical seed documents are extracted from the document-term representation and semantic seed documents are extracted from term clusters and Wikipedia concepts.

Our experimental results demonstrate that the proposed ensemble algorithm can improve the quality of document clusters even if the clusters obtained from the document-concept representation alone are inferior to those obtained from the document-term representation.

We also demonstrate that our partitional document clustering algorithm can generate comparable results to the *LDA* model. Based on our experiments, it can also outperform *LDA* on some real text datasets.

As future work, we plan to extend our work to integrate other information like the Wikipedia categories or the semantic relatedness among Wikipedia articles.

## Acknowledgment

This research was supported by the NSERC (Natural Sciences and Engineering Research Council of Canada) Business Intelligence Network.

# 7. REFERENCES

[1] C. Aggarwal and C. Zhai. A survey of text clustering algorithms. In *Mining Text Data*, pages 77–128. Springer US, 2012.

[2] S. Banerjee, K. Ramanathan, and A. Gupta. Clustering short texts using Wikipedia. In *Proceedings of the 30th Annual International ACM SIGIR Conference on Research and Development in Information Retrieval*, SIGIR '07, pages 787–788, New York, NY, USA, 2007. ACM.

[3] J. Bezdek. *Pattern recognition with fuzzy objective functions*. Kluwer Academic Publishers, Norwell, MA, USA, 1981.

[4] D. M. Blei, A. Y. Ng, and M. I. Jordan. Latent Dirichlet allocation. *Journal of Machine Learning Research*, 3:993–1022, 2003.

[5] A. Cardoso-Cachopo. Improving Methods for Single-label Text Categorization. PhD Thesis, Instituto Superior Tecnico, Universidade Tecnica de Lisboa, 2007.

[6] D. Carmel, H. Roitman, and N. Zwerdling. Enhancing cluster labeling using Wikipedia. In *Proceedings of the 32nd International ACM SIGIR Conference on Research and Development in Information Retrieval*, SIGIR '09, pages 139–146. ACM, New York, NY, USA, 2009.

[7] I. S. Dhillon, S. Mallela, and D. S. Modha. Information-theoretic co-clustering. In *Proceedings of the ninth ACM SIGKDD International Conference on Knowledge Discovery and Data Mining*, KDD '03, pages 89–98, New York, NY, USA, 2003. ACM.

[8] P. Ferragina and A. Gulli. A personalized search engine based on web-snippet hierarchical clustering. *Software: Practice and Experience*, 38(2):189–225, 2008.

[9] M. Gamon, A. Aue, S. Corston-Oliver, and E. Ringger. Pulse: Mining customer opinions from free text. In *Proceedings of the 6th International Conference on Advances in Intelligent Data Analysis*, IDA'05, pages 121–132, Berlin, Heidelberg, 2005. Springer-Verlag.

[10] A. Hotho, S. Staab, and G. Stumme. Ontologies improve text document clustering. In *Third IEEE International Conference on Data Mining (ICDM 2003)*, pages 541–544, Nov 2003.

[11] J. Hu, L. Fang, Y. Cao, H.-J. Zeng, H. Li, Q. Yang, and Z. Chen. Enhancing text clustering by leveraging Wikipedia semantics. In *Proceedings of the 31st Annual International ACM SIGIR Conference on Research and Development in Information Retrieval*, SIGIR '08, pages 179–186. ACM, New York, NY, USA, 2008.

[12] X. Hu, X. Zhang, C. Lu, E. K. Park, and X. Zhou. Exploiting Wikipedia as external knowledge for document clustering. In *Proceedings of the 15th ACM*

*SIGKDD International Conference on Knowledge Discovery and Data Mining*, KDD '09, pages 389–396. ACM, New York, NY, USA, 2009.

[13] A. Huang, D. Milne, E. Frank, and I. H. Witten. Clustering documents with active learning using Wikipedia. In *Eighth IEEE International Conference on Data Mining (ICDM '08)*, pages 839–844, Dec 2008.

[14] A. Huang, D. Milne, E. Frank, and I. H. Witten. Clustering documents using a Wikipedia-based concept representation. In *Proceedings of the 13th Pacific-Asia Conference on Advances in Knowledge Discovery and Data Mining*, PAKDD '09, pages 628–636, Berlin, Heidelberg, 2009. Springer-Verlag.

[15] J. Kogan, C. Nicholas, and V. Volkovich. Text mining with information-theoretic clustering. *Computing in Science and Engineering*, 5(6):52–59, Nov. 2003.

[16] C. D. Manning, P. Raghavan, and H. Schütze. *Introduction to Information Retrieval*, chapter 13, pages 253–287. Cambridge University Press, New York, NY, USA, 2008.

[17] D. Milne and I. H. Witten. Learning to link with Wikipedia. In *Proceedings of the 17th ACM Conference on Information and Knowledge Management*, CIKM '08, pages 509–518. ACM, New York, NY, USA, 2008.

[18] S. N. Nourashrafeddin, E. Milios, and D. V. Arnold. Interactive text document clustering using feature labeling. In *Proceedings of the 2013 ACM Symposium on Document Engineering*, DocEng '13, pages 61–70. ACM, New York, NY, USA, 2013.

[19] S. Osinski and D. Weiss. A concept-driven algorithm for clustering search results. *IEEE Intelligent Systems*, 20(3):48–54, May 2005.

[20] M. F. Porter. An algorithm for suffix stripping. In *Readings in Information Retrieval*, pages 313–316. Morgan Kaufmann Publishers Inc., San Francisco, CA, USA, 1997.

[21] P. Schonhofen. Identifying document topics using the Wikipedia category network. In *Proceedings of the 2006 IEEE/WIC/ACM International Conference on Web Intelligence*, WI '06, pages 456–462, Washington, DC, USA, 2006. IEEE Computer Society.

[22] G. Spanakis, G. Siolas, and A. Stafylopatis. Exploiting Wikipedia knowledge for conceptual hierarchical clustering of documents. *Comput. J.*, 55(3):299–312, Mar. 2012.

[23] J. H. V. Cormack and E. Sánz. Feature engineering for mobile (SMS) spam filtering. In *Proceedings of the 30th Annual International ACM SIGIR Conference on Research and Development in Information Retrieval*, SIGIR '07, pages 871–872. ACM, New York, NY, USA, 2007.

[24] M. Yazdani and A. Popescu-Belis. Using a Wikipedia-based semantic relatedness measure for document clustering. In *Proceedings of TextGraphs-6: Graph-based Methods for Natural Language Processing*, TextGraphs-6, pages 29–36, Stroudsburg, PA, USA, 2011. Association for Computational Linguistics.

# Image-Based Document Management: Aggregating Collections of Handwritten Forms

John W. Barrus
Ricoh Innovations, Corp.
2882 Sand Hill Road, Suite 115
Menlo Park, CA 94025
barrus@ric.ricoh.com

Edward L. Schwartz
Ricoh Innovations, Corp.
2882 Sand Hill Road, Suite 115
Menlo Park, CA 94025
schwartz@ric.ricoh.com

## ABSTRACT

Many companies still operate critical business processes using paper-based forms, including customer surveys, inspections, contracts and invoices. Converting those handwritten forms to symbolic data is expensive and complicated. This paper presents an overview of the Image-Based Document Management (IBDM) system for analyzing handwritten forms without requiring conversion to symbolic data. Strokes captured in a questionnaire on a tablet are separated into fields that are then displayed in a spreadsheet. Rows represent documents while columns represent corresponding fields across all documents. IBDM allows a process owner to capture and analyze large collections of documents with minimal IT support. IBDM supports the creation of filters and queries on the data. IBDM also allows the user to request symbolic conversion of individual columns of data and permits the user to create custom views by reordering and sorting the columns. In other words, IBDM provides a "writing on paper" experience for the data collector and a web-based database experience for the analyst.

## Categories and Subject Descriptors

I.7.5 Document Capture---Document analysis
J.1 ADMINISTRATIVE DATA PROCESSING---Business
H.3.5 Online Information Services---Web-based services
H.2.8 Database Applications---Image databases

## Keywords

Forms; handwriting; data capture; document management; tables

## 1. INTRODUCTION

According to a 2012 survey[1], even with the implementation of electronic health records, over 80% of healthcare organizations still relied on paper records and 10% of those organizations used paper as the primary method for recording information.

Converting to electronic records usually requires the development of complicated systems along with transcription of data collected on paper, both of which are expensive. We have created a system called Image-based Document Management (IBDM) that generically supports the capture of electronic strokes on forms

displayed on a tablet and presents the results of the data collection using a spreadsheet view. The need for IT support is greatly reduced and in some cases eliminated, giving the owner of the business process the ability to design forms, collect data and analyze it independently.

### 1.1 Example Use

Home health care providers (over 33,000 agencies and 1.3 million workers in the US[2]) typically have dozens of forms that must be filled out and signed by patients. For example, in the U.S., home health care providers are required by law to get a privacy (HIPAA) notice signed by the patient. Even large agencies use paper forms for these activities and home care nurses deliver those forms by hand to the office.

Using IBDM, the patient writes on an image of the form, which is displayed on a commercially available stylus-based tablet. The strokes are captured and sent over a wireless network back to the server. An administrator can access and review the forms over the web using special client software. The administrator has access to each individual document as well as an overview of all the documents (Figure 1). The overview displays the captured strokes from each document in a row. Each column represents a specific field for a form. For instance, the administrator can confirm that all HIPAA forms have been signed by reviewing the signature column of the HIPAA form collection.

### 1.2 Related work

A number of approaches have been taken to capture data from paper sources but most of those efforts have focused on complete conversion from handwritten strokes to symbolic data. The system most like IBDM grew out of a Berkeley Ph.D. thesis by Chen [1]. Chen's system uses probabilistic models for supporting automated data conversion combined with crowd sourcing. The system is built as a web service, accepting images of completed forms and providing an interface for human workers to either convert or verify conversions on the web and a dashboard for exploring the results. All conversion results are symbolic, although the original handwritten data is available. Hansen, et al. describe the *FamilySearch™* indexing effort [2] which used hundreds of thousands of volunteers to transcribe billions of records, including census, birth, death, and marriage records from around the world.

A survey of techniques for handwriting recognition and conversion was published in 2000 [3]. A number of researchers have worked on the automatic recognition of handwritten data

---

[1] http://anoto.com/trade-news-2.aspx?cid=anoto-survey-finds-healthcare-industry-buried-in-paperwork (visited Sep 19, 2012)
[2] U.S. Department of Labor, Bureau of Labor Statistics, Current Employment Statistics (National), data for May 2104.
http://www.bls.gov/web/empsit/ceseeb1a.htm

**Figure 1.** Analyst interface for viewing and analyzing data captured on a tablet using the IBDM system.

[4,5] or systems for separating handwritten data from a completed form [6]. The *Anoto™* system captures strokes electronically using a unique pen containing a camera and processor but works only with specially printed paper. The *Anoto™* pen is used in the ButterflyNet system developed at Stanford [7]. In ButterflyNet, the system goal was to integrate notes with digital data, including photos, audio recordings and video, but not necessarily to convert handwriting to a symbolic representation (although it supports transcription).

Another area with a focus on accurately converting handwriting to symbolic information is bank checks, 18.3 billion of which were processed in the US in 2012. Palacios et al. describe a system [8] that uses neural networks to convert digits written on checks and a context-aware post-processor to enhance the accuracy of the results.

## 2. SYSTEM ARCHITECTURE

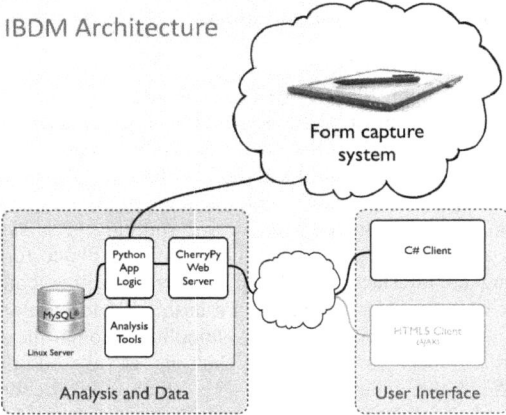

**Figure 2.** IBDM system architecture.

IBDM consists of a web-based service along with three applications. The form preparation application (FPA) allows a user to specify the location of handwritten fields on a picture of a form. The form capture application (FCA) runs on a tablet and is used for capturing strokes on electronic forms and uploading the forms and strokes to the server. The third application is a data analysis client (DAC) and runs on a PC. The DAC is used by administrators to access and analyze processed form data.

A *MySQL®* database and CherryPy web server were installed on an *Ubuntu®* virtual machine. *Python®* software is used to provide web services and application logic. The open source Lipi toolkit[3] is used for stroke classification and the *Python®* Boto library is used for integration with the *Amazon Mechanical Turk®* web service. A proprietary file format was adopted for capturing strokes and importing strokes into the server. Strokes can also be extracted from certain types of PDF files.

### 2.1 Workflow

Imagine that a retail company wants to conduct a survey with its customers. The company can scan in an existing blank paper survey or create an electronic document containing the questions leaving blank spaces for written responses.

The system administrator prepares an electronic version of the form by importing a PDF file of the survey into the form preparation application (FPA). Fields are marked on the form to indicate expected locations of handwritten responses. If desired, the administrator is able to add "widgets" to capture checkboxes, radio buttons, photos from the camera and text input from a soft keyboard. The document is pushed to the form capture application on the tablet.

A customer uses a stylus to fill out the form on the tablet. The customer can write anywhere on the form, including on photos captured by the camera. When complete, the form is pushed back to the form management server.

Each set of forms is stored as a "collection" on the server. The server extracts the strokes and symbolic data, including symbolic data and photos from the widgets and adds it to the collection. Additional metadata is captured, including stroke timing information and the form submission time and date.

Strokes are categorized and assigned to the predefined fields. Images of the strokes are created. Where widgets have been defined, images of the widgets are captured along with symbolic data. For instance, if a checkbox widget is checked, an image of the check is created and a "true" symbolic value is stored in the database.

When the data analysis client (DAC) connects to the server and selects a collection, the client can request the images representing the stroke and widget data for all or for a subset of the forms. The DAC constructs a table view of the data. Each row contains the

---

[3] http://lipitk.sourceforge.net/

stroke and widget data from a single survey and each column represents the strokes from corresponding fields across all documents. For instance, a "Name" column can contain the handwritten name data from every HIPAA form in the system.

## 3. CREATING FORMS

Forms can be based on any scanned paper document or electronic form. Dense forms are difficult to fill out on a tablet because handwriting tends to be larger on an electronic display than on paper. A typical 10.1" LCD is only half the size of an 8.5 x 11 sheet of paper. Users may choose to redesign their form to fit on multiple pages since there is no need to save paper.

The IBDM system accepts multi-page PDF files as input. After opening the document with the FPA, the user places rectangles on each page of the form indicating a "field" where handwriting is expected. For instance, if a form has a name field, the field rectangle will surround the location where the name is expected to be written.

The FPA also provides widgets like radio buttons, check boxes, text fields and image fields. Text fields pop up a soft keyboard when activated and image fields allow a photo taken using the camera on the tablet to be inserted into the form.

## 4. ASSIGNING STROKES TO FIELDS

After the form is filled out and the IBDM server receives a document, all of the strokes from the document are identified and assigned either to a specific field or identified as non-field strokes.

To assign strokes to fields, the server looks at "runs" of stroke assignments and minimizes the number of transitions between fields in a given run of strokes as described below.

If the bounding box of a single stroke is completely contained in a single field rectangle as defined above, the stroke is assigned to that field. If a bounding box of a stroke overlaps multiple fields, those fields are listed as alternatives for the stroke. Once all of the strokes are categorized, "runs" of strokes are created—sets of strokes where two adjacent strokes overlap the same fields. Each run is analyzed to minimize transitions between fields and maximize the overlap between the bounding boxes of the strokes and the field.

Once all of the strokes are assigned to fields, a bounding box for the strokes assigned to a field is calculated and an image the size of that bounding box is created containing just the strokes. Since the stroke image is typically smaller than the field's bounding box, the amount of data transferred to the client is reduced substantially. For one collection of documents, the original documents used 500 Mbytes of storage space, but the cropped images only required 5 Mbytes. We experimented using vector representations of strokes instead of semi-transparent PNG images and found almost no difference in storage requirements.

## 5. CREATING A TABLE

At launch, the data analysis client (DAC) requests the data for a collection, which is returned in JSON format, including information about every form and all of the strokes in those forms. The client also requests the stroke image data for the collection. The stroke image data is cached locally to minimize bandwidth usage. The client constructs a table (Figure 1) that displays the stroke images and other data. The height of each row depends on the height of the stroke images and other data displayed in the row. The original width of each column is equal to the stroke image width.

## 6. DAC INTERFACE

The user interface of the DAC application appears somewhat like a spreadsheet but there are some important differences.

Like a spreadsheet, columns can be hidden and column widths and row heights adjusted. The column names can be modified and individual documents (rows) can be deleted.

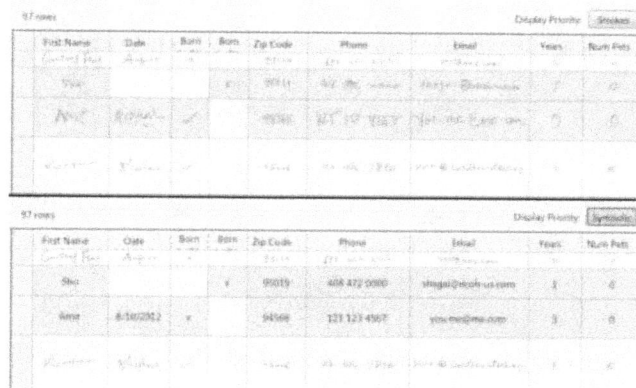

**Figure 3.** Cells containing both strokes and symbolic data are highlighted and the user can easily switch between them.

There are a few operations that are significantly different than a spreadsheet or database. Each non-empty cell in the table can contain either symbolic or image data or both. The cells containing both are highlighted by the application as shown in the Figure 3. The "Display Priority" button lets the user choose whether they prefer to see symbolic data or image data if both are available.

The "Single Form – Edit" tab shown in Figure 4 allows the user to add or update symbolic data for a selected document.

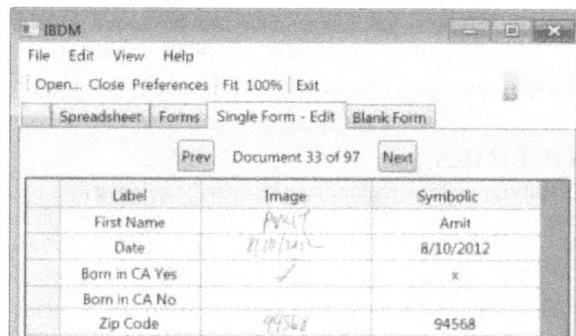

**Figure 4.** The "Single Form – Edit" tab allows the user to add symbolic data to individual cells.

The DAC automatically updates the table when new data is arrives from the server. The user can review and download a blank version of the form or any selected form in PDF format.

## 7. TRANSCRIPTION

Even though IBDM does not require transcription, it may be convenient to transcribe some portion of the data to make the collection of documents searchable. For instance, if HIPAA forms are filtered symbolically by last name, an administrator can quickly narrow the search for a specific patient's form.

The *Amazon Mechanical Turk*® web service (AMT) is integrated with IBDM to support automated conversion by human workers. IBDM is a "requestor" of crowd-sourced jobs. A DAC user can indicate that a specific column should be automatically converted to symbolic data. When a server receives a document with strokes for that column, the stroke image is created and a Human Intelligence Task (HIT) is created on AMT. An example HIT is shown in Figure 5 for the zip code field of a survey. As images are converted, the data is fed back to the server. In our experience, most of our zip code HITs were completed within 60 seconds.

**Figure 5.** An example HIT for a zip code field from a form.

## 8. SORTING

In the data analysis client, a user can click on the column heading to initiate a sort. If the column has been supplemented with symbolic data, by default the column is sorted in alphabetic order. When cells only contain stroke images or contain a combination of strokes and data, more information is required from the user. Each cell can be in one of four states: empty (E), symbolic data (S), image/stroke data (I) or both symbolic and image data (B). The user selects a sort priority—which types of cells come first, E, S, or I. Cells that have both (B) are always lumped with the higher priority cells S or I.

Symbolic data can be sorted alphanumerically, alphabetically or numerically. Strokes and image data can be sorted by image metadata: width, height, image file size or number of pixels.

An example sort would be 1) symbolic first in alphabetic order, 2) image by classification and then 3) empty cells.

## 9. QUERIES

As in sorting, queries require special handling depending on the column type. In the lower right part of the client application window (Figure 1), the user can select a date filter, which is always applied directly to submission timestamp.

Additional column filters can be created based on symbolic or image information. For instance, it is possible to filter using a regular expression on symbolic data or by the existence of an image. For instance, the user may want to review all HIPAA forms that have no signature. Filters can be applied to any column by using the column filter interface not described here.

## 10. RESULTS

The full system, including the applications and server were completed early in 2013 and the system was used for an electronic visitor log at Ricoh Innovations. The administrator responsible for the visitor log created the form, marked the stroke regions, added an email widget and photo widget and deployed the form to several tablets. The DAC application was installed on the PCs of several administrators at RIC. During the 3 month deployment, 65 visitors signed in using the tablets. In a separate experiment, over 100 surveys were administered to gather handwriting samples and provide a sample database for experimentation.

## 11. CONCLUSION

We implemented and demonstrated a system that allows people to fill out forms on an electronic tablet in a manner that feels like working with a paper and pen with a web-based backend that supports review and analysis. The simple interface allowed a non-technical administrator to develop, deploy and query a complete handwriting-based visitor log system.

## 12. ACKNOWLEDGMENTS

FamilySearch is a trademark of Intellectual Reserve, Inc. Anoto is a registered trademark of Anoto. MySQL is a registered trademark of Oracle and/or its affiliates. Ubuntu is a registered trademark of Canonical Ltd. Python is a registered trademark of Python Software Foundation. Amazon Mechanical Turk is a registered trademark of Amazon Technologies, Inc. in the United States and/or other countries.

## 13. REFERENCES

[1]  Kuang Chen. 2011. *Data-Driven Techniques for Improving Data Collection in Low-Resource Environments*. Ph.D. Dissertation. University of California at Berkeley, Berkeley, CA, USA. Advisors J. M. Hellerstein & T. S. Parikh.

[2]  Derek L. Hansen et al. 2013. Quality control mechanisms for crowdsourcing: peer review, arbitration, & expertise at familysearch indexing. In *Proceedings of the 2013 conference on Computer supported cooperative work* (CSCW '13). ACM, New York, NY, USA, 649-660.

[3]  Réjean Plamondon & Sargur N. Srihari. 2000. On-Line and Off-Line Handwriting Recognition: A Comprehensive Survey. *IEEE Trans. Pattern Anal. Mach. Intell.* 22, 1 (January 2000), 63-84.

[4]  M. D. Garris et al. NIST Form-Based Handprint recognition System (Release 2.0). NIST Internal. Report 5959, 1997.

[5]  R. Zanibbi & D. Blostein. "Recognition and retrieval of mathematical expressions." *International Journal on Document Analysis and Recognition (IJDAR)* 15, no. 4 (2012): 331-357.

[6]  D. Deodhare et al. "Preprocessing and Image Enhancement Algorithms for a Form-based Intelligent Character Recognition System." IJCSA 2, no. 2 (2005): 131-144.

[7]  R. Yeh et al. "ButterflyNet: a mobile capture and access system for field biology research." In Proceedings of the SIGCHI conference on Human Factors in computing systems, pp. 571-580. ACM, 2006.

[8]  R. Palacios et al. "Handwritten bank check recognition of courtesy amounts." International Journal of Image and Graphics 4, no. 02 (2004): 203-22

# ARTIC: Metadata Extraction from Scientific Papers using a Two-Layer CRF Model

Alan Souza, Viviane Moreira, Carlos Heuser
Instituto de Informática – Universidade Federal do Rio Grande do Sul (UFRGS)
Postal Code 15.064 – 91.501-970 – Porto Alegre – RS – Brazil
{apsouza,viviane,heuser}@inf.ufrgs.br

## ABSTRACT

Most scientific articles are available in PDF format. The PDF standard allows the generation of metadata that is included within the document. However, many authors do not define this information, making this feature unreliable or incomplete. This fact has been motivating research which aims to extract metadata automatically. Automatic metadata extraction has been identified as one of the most challenging tasks in document engineering. This work proposes Artic, a method for metadata extraction from scientific papers which employs a two-layer probabilistic framework based on Conditional Random Fields. The first layer aims at identifying the main sections with metadata information, and the second layer finds, for each section, the corresponding metadata. Given a PDF file containing a scientific paper, Artic extracts the title, author names, emails, affiliations, and venue information. We report on experiments using 100 real papers from a variety of publishers. Our results outperformed the state-of-the-art system used as the baseline, achieving a precision of over 99%.

## Categories and Subject Descriptors

H.3.1 [**Information Storage and Retrieval**]: Content Analysis and Indexing – Indexing methods; I.7.3 [**Document And Text Processing**]: Index Generation; I.2.6 [**Artificial Intelligence**]: Learning – Induction

## Keywords

Metadata Extraction; PDF; Machine Learning; CRF

## 1. INTRODUCTION

The metadata of a document are all the information describing the document itself. In scientific articles, this data usually includes: title, author, affiliation, date of publication, place of publication, etc. Collecting metadata is a crucial step for assembling a document repository, which in turn is very important in the document engineering area.

The Portable Document Format (PDF) is a file format that was created with the initial goal of being independent of application,

hardware, and operating system [10]. This format was developed in the '90s and is widely used in the scientific literature as the standard format for publications. PDF allows the generation of the aforementioned metadata which is directly included within the document. Therefore, it is not necessary to use an additional file containing the metadata for PDF-based articles.

With the popularization of Internet, many scientific articles have been made available on the Web. While in the beginning, the articles were scanned and provided as image-based PDFs, more recently, documents are directly created as text-based PDFs. The biggest limitation is the lack of metadata or, even when present, it does not provide complete and reliable information. As a result, many information retrieval and document engineering systems have difficulties in indexing these files. These facts have been motivating research that aims at automatically identifying metadata. Councill *et al.* [2] rated automatic metadata extraction as one of the most difficult tasks in document engineering. Research in this topic typically applies one of these three methods: template matching, web-based lookup (knowledge base), and machine learning techniques. A comparison of these methods with an evaluation of existing tools is presented in [7].

Recent techniques are increasingly using machine learning algorithms to try to achieve better results. They usually deal with the problem of metadata extraction as a sequence labeling task. In [11, 13], the authors address the metadata extraction problem using Hidden Markov Models (HMM). Luong *et al.* [8] created SectLabel, a metadata extraction tool that defines a single CRF model to identify 23 different classes, such as: address, affiliation, author, email, equation, figure, title, etc. SectLabel defines a set of features that allows the CRF model to identify each of the aforementioned classes. Having a single layer model may affect the metadata identification process since all features are naturally generic.

In this work we propose Artic, a two-layer CRF model that allows features to be metadata-specific. The first layer aims at identifying the main sections that may contain metadata information. For each of the given sections, a second layer will extract the desired metadata with a more granular level. Experiments yielded an overall precision of 99.84%, which represents a F1 improvement of 6.92% compared to the state-of-the-art baseline. We summarize our contributions as follows:

- Artic employs a two-layer CRF model. We believe that having an additional layer will improve the metadata extraction process as it allows the use of line-level features (first layer) and word-level features (second layer).

- Artic is able to identify the relationship between authors, emails, and affiliations. This functionality is not provided by the classification model, which is limited to identify the classes only (e.g Author Name, Affiliation).

- As opposed to a single classification tool, Artic provides the metadata output in a well-defined format (JSON). This allows anyone to use the metadata as it is, without the need for extra components to organize the classification results.

The remainder of this work is organized as follows: Section 2 reviews the existing solutions for metadata extraction. Section 3 explains Artic, the two-layer CRF approach proposed in this work. Section 4 evaluates Artic against a baseline and the expected JSON output. Section 5 discusses the limitations and future work that might be applicable to this work. Section 6 concludes the work with a summary of the contributions and results.

## 2. RELATED WORK

According to [7], existing solutions are divided into three different approaches: template matching, web-based lookup, and machine learning. Next, we review each approach.

Solutions that use **template matching** try to build an apriori structure (template) for the metadata candidates based on known properties of the desired content. With the defined template, a post-processing step is applied to identify the metadata that matches each template. For example, to identify the title of a given article, a simple template would be the biggest font with bold style on the first page. Then, the post-processing procedure would load an article, get the first page and look for the line that matches the title template [4, 5].

Techniques that use **web-based lookup** try to identify the smallest unit of information from the document itself, usually by template matching, and then retrieve the complete information from a universal database, such as Google Scholar, IEEE, or ACM [1]. The main limitation here is if the database does not contain the given paper, the web-based lookup strategy cannot give an adequate solution.

**Machine Learning** techniques build statistical frameworks, usually based on training examples, to avoid creating undesired assumptions about the document layout and content. The algorithms learn from the given examples to automatically identify metadata from real-instance documents. Solutions usually apply sequence labeling problems to the task of metadata extraction where the labels are the metadata of interest (e.g. title, author, affiliation) and the observations are the document entries with their given features (e.g. font size, weight, etc...).

Seymore *et al.* [11] focused on the task of extracting information from the headers of computer science research articles using a single HMM model. The authors automatically created a model using the training examples. Unlike their work, other systems use either one state per class or hand-built models assembled by manually inspecting the training examples. The header of the research article consists of title, author names, affiliations, and addresses.

Yin *et al.* [13] use a bigram HMM for automatic metadata extraction from bibliographies with various styles. Different from the traditional HMM, which uses only the word frequency, this model also considers information about the sequential relation and positions of the words in text fields.

CRF is a probabilistic framework commonly applied in pattern recognition. There are some advantages in using CRF as a replacement for HMM, especially for the task of sequence labeling. The first limitation of HMM is that it requires the enumeration of all possible observations. For most real-world applications, enumerating all possible observations is impossible [12]. Another important limitation of HMM is the assumption that the observed element, at any given instant of time, may only directly depend on the state or label at that time. This observation independence constraint is not valid in most cases, and it is not different in sequence labeling. When labeling sequence data, the previous observation (e.g. a word) has strong influence in the label of the next observation. CRF overcomes both aforementioned issues and studies have shown that CRF outperformed HMM [6].

Luong *et al.* [8] propose SectLabel, a method to detect the logical structure of a document in PDF using CRF. Also, the authors made use of a richer representation of the document that includes features from an Optical Character Recognition (OCR) tool. The proposed algorithm identifies metadata such as title, authors, abstract, and it also extracts the logical structure of the document (sections, subsections, figures, tables, equations footnotes, and captions). The system is composed of two main components: Logical Structure (LS), and Generic Section (GS). The LS classifier labels each line with the corresponding categories, such as title, author, etc. Labels that are classified as "headers" are passed on to the GS classifier that performs section labeling. For the LS component, each line of text can be assigned to one category from a set of 23 possibles values: address, affiliation, author, bodyText, categories, construct, copyright, email, equation, figure, figureCaption, footnote, keywords, liteItem, note, page, reference, sectionHeader, subsectionHeader, subsubsectionHeader, table, tableCaption, and title. For the GS component, the authors have defined a set of 13 categories to characterize the sections of scholarly documents: abstract, categories, general terms, keywords, introduction, background, related work, methodology, evaluation, discussion, conclusions acknowledgements, and references. Regarding the defined features, they are divided into two main areas: raw text and OCR-based. Raw text are the minimum set of features used to classify the lines of a document when no rich OCR features are provided. The LS classifier features have two levels: token and line. The token-level has the feature for the first $n$ tokens in each line (set to 4 experimentally). The line-level features have been defined as follows: (*i*) location: relative position of each line within a document; (*ii*) number: detects the occurrence of patterns specific to hierarchies ("1.1" and "1.1.1"); (*iii*) punctuation: checks if the line contains email addresses or web links; and (*iv*) length: the length of each line in terms of tokens. OCR-based features have been divided into two groups: stationary and differential. Stationary features are extracted directly from the OCR output, as opposed to differential features that model state changes between two consecutive lines. The stationary features have been defined as follows: (*i*) location: position of the text line within the page. More broadly, raw text location feature measures the position of the line with respect to the whole document. (*ii*) format: font information such as font size, bold and italic. (*iii*) object: models special line attributes, such as bullet, picture and table. With the defined stationary features, there is no direct information to the CRF engine to infer if two consecutive lines are of the same format. Hence, differential features have been defined as follows: (*i*) format: to explicitly mark if the current line has the same format as the previous line. The defined properties are: font size, bold, italic, font face and alignment; and (*ii*) paragraph: to detect blocks of text lines belonging to the same paragraph.

While existing solutions provide good results when using Machine Learning techniques, we believe that applying a two-layer strategy can still lead to improvements. Also, the assumption that each line in the article contains only one metadata is not valid as there can be multiple information in a given line (specially in the footnote). For example, this footnote line "DocEng'14 Fort Collins, Colorado USA" has two types of metadata: venue name (DocEng) and venue location (Fort Collins, Colorado USA). A two-layer CRF model allows detecting this line as Footnote (first-level), but it also provides a more granular analysis over the words (second-level) to extract the actual metadata (venue name and venue location).

# 3. ARTIC

Artic employs a two-layer CRF model so as to allow the creation of metadata-specific features. The first layer identifies larger components (sections) that may contain metadata information. These sections are defined as classes in the CRF engine with five possible values: Header, Title, Author Information, Body, and Footnote. The Header usually holds important information about the conference/journal in which the paper has been published. The Title class represents the title of the paper. Author information contains data about the authors, such as: name, affiliation, and email. The Body class does not include useful data for the task of metadata extraction. We do not perform any analysis over this class. Footnote usually contains information about the publisher, conference, and possibly some additional information about the authors (e.g. email and affiliation). For some of these sections, a second CRF layer was created. This extra layer allows us to extract the actual metadata and define features specific for the section. The second layer of the CRF model will be executed for the Header, Author Information, and Footnote. The Title class does not require another CRF level because it contains only one semantic value, which is the title of the paper.

For each layer, we need to provide the probabilistic framework with evidences that will help identify the class that maximizes the result of the model. These evidences are called *features* (e.g. font size, format, and alignment). The features of a given section do not affect other sections, and if the feature is present in one section that does not mean that that same feature will appear in another section. To implement the CRF model, we used CRF++[1]. These features need to be structured in a way that they can be interpreted by the CRF++ engine. The training and test files should be of the form "$value_1, value_2, ..., value_m \ class_i$", where $class_i$ is assigned to one of the aforementioned classes. This framework also requires a template file which describes the semantics of these columns and, also, enables the creation of the *context windows*. These windows allow the CRF engine to look at the previous/next occurrences to infer about the current state. The template file works like a matrix, each single column in the test and/or training file receives its definition in the template, which comes in the form of "$U_i : \%x[0, j]$", where $i$ is the feature identifier, 0 is the current line being observed (use -1,-2,+1,+2 to refer to previous/next lines), and, $j$ is the column index.

```
1  line_0 centered ... header new TITLE
2  line_1 centered ... header same TITLE
3  line_2 left...header new AUTHOR INFORMATION
4  line_3 left...header same AUTHOR_INFORMATION
5  line_4 left...header same AUTHOR_INFORMATION
6  line_5 left...header same AUTHOR_INFORMATION
7  line_6 left... new new BODY
8  line_7 justified...new new BODY
9  line_9 justified... same same BODY
10 line_10 justified... same same BODY
11 line_11 justified... same same BODY
12 line_14 justified... same same BODY
13 line_15 left true... new new BODY
14 line_16 justified... new new BODY
```

**Figure 1: The CRF++ train/test file.**

[1] http://crfpp.googlecode.com/svn/trunk/doc/index.html

Figure 1 shows an example of the train/test file, and, Figure 2 shows an example of the corresponding template file definition. Let us assume that the current line being considered is "line_6". Then, in the template engine, 0 represents the current line. When analyzing U19:%x[-2,1], for example, -2 represents "line_4" and 1 represents the feature (alignment). In "line_4" (Figure 1), alignment has the value set to "left".

```
1  #identifier
2  U0:%x[0,0]
3  #alignment
4  U1:%x[0,1]
5  ...
6  #alignment window
7  U18:%x[-1,1]
8  U19:%x[-2,1]
9  U20:%x[1,1]
10 U21:%x[2,1]
11 ...
12 # alignment and font size
13 U30:%x[0,1]/%x[0,5]
14 ...
```

**Figure 2: The CRF++ template file.**

After the CRF model labels the input with the corresponding classes, post-processing algorithms are applied in order to group the data that belong to the same class. The CRF model is able to classify all author names, but it is not able to group the names that belong to the same author. For example, a common representation for the authors of a paper is given in Figure 3.

Hang Li, Yunbo Cao
Microsoft Research Asia
5F Sigma Center
No.49 Zhichun Road,
Haidian, Beijing, China, 100080
{hangli, yucao}@microsoft.com

Jun Xu
College of Software
Nankai University
No.94 Weijin Road,
Tianjin, China, 300071
nkxj@yahoo.com.cn

**Figure 3: A sample representation of the author information of a given paper.**

In this scenario, the CRF engine is able to identify all the words that are likely to make up an author name. In Figure 3, these words are: Hang, Li, Yunbo, Cao, Jun, and Xu. One of the tasks of the post-processing component is to execute an algorithm that will group the words that belong to the same author. The expected result after executing this algorithm is: Hang Li, Yunbo Cao, and Jun Xu. Similar algorithms are required to group the affiliations and emails. Details of all the algorithms applied in the post-processing component are given in Section 3.3. Figure 4 illustrates the whole process performed in this work.

The following sections are divided as follows. Section 3.1 explains the details of the first-level layer. Similarly, Section 3.2 explains the details of the second-level layer. Finally, Section 3.3 describes the post-processing algorithms applied to the CRF results in order to provide the metadata output in a well-defined data structure (JSON).

## 3.1 First-level CRF

When dealing with metadata extraction, the important information is usually present only in the first page. Due to this reason, this work considers only the first page for analysis. The first-level of the model classifies each line into the five classes decribed as follows:

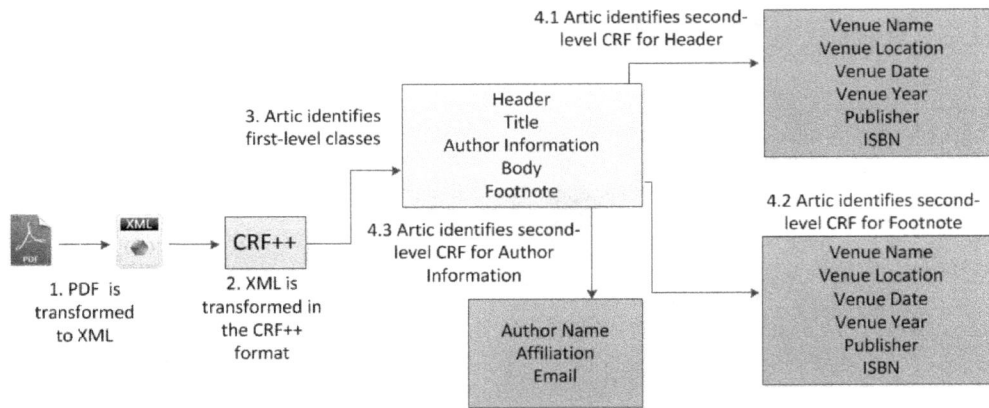

**Figure 4: The two-layer CRF generation process proposed in this work.**

- **Header:** usually is located at the top of the page and contains information regarding the paper itself, such as: venue, publication year, pages, among others.

- **Title:** contains the title of the paper. Papers which has the title spreading over two or more lines, each line should be assigned to this class. The location is usually at the top of the page with the largest font size.

- **Author Information:** contains information about the author, such as: first name, last name, email, affiliation, and address. This class, in most of the cases, appears after the title.

- **Body:** represents non-relevant information for the task of metadata extraction. In this work, abstract, keywords, and other structural components (e.g. section headers, body text, etc...) are not extracted.

- **Footnote:** contains information regarding copyright, conference, pages, publication year, authors' affiliation, address, etc. The location is usually at the bottom-left of the page with a small font size.

In order to distinguish among classes, features must be defined. These features will give the CRF engine evidences to help decide, for a given line $L_{i,j}$, its corresponding class $C_{i,j}$, where $i$ represents the line and $j$ represents the page. Some of the first-level features are: Alignment, Bold, Underline, Italic, and Font Size. The detailed description of each feature is given in Appendix A.

## 3.2 Second-level CRF

The second-level of the CRF model extracts the metadata for the Header, Author Information, and Footnote. Body and Title classes do not require a second layer.

The **Header CRF** model identifies the metadata for the Header section which is usually at the top of the first page of the paper. This model explores the words in the lines that have been identified as belonging to the Header class in the first-level of Artic. Each word is classified into the five different classes below:

- **Conference Name:** if the word belongs to the list of conference/journal name.

- **Conference Year:** if the word represents the conference year.

- **Conference Date:** if the word belongs to the conference date which is usually at the form "Month DAY_START-DAY_ENDS" (e.g. Jan 5-10).

- **Conference Location:** if the word belongs to the conference location which is usually at the form "City, Country" (e.g. Florence, Italy).

- **Publisher:** if the word represents the publisher. Currently, Artic has been tested with papers from ACM, IEEE, Springer and Elsevier.

- **Other:** if the word does not represent any useful information for the task of metadata extraction (e.g. copyright). We do not perform any further analysis over this class.

In order to distinguish one class from another, features were defined in a similar fashion to the ones implemented in the first-layer. These features will help identify for a given word $W_{i,j}$, its corresponding class $C_{i,j}$, where $i$ is the current word in line $j$. Some of the Header CRF features are: Word Content, Character Length, Month, Year, and Country. The detailed description of each feature is given in Appendix B.1.

The **Author Information CRF** model identifies the metadata for the Author Information section which usually follows the Title section. This model explores the words of the lines that have been identified as Author Information class in the first-level of Artic. Each word is classified into the four classes below:

- **Author Name:** if the word represents an author name. At this point, we do not identify individual authors. The post-processing algorithms will be responsible for grouping the authors by their names.

- **Affiliation:** if the word is part of the author's affiliation. The metadata that is usually contained in this section are: university, company, department, address, and telephone. At this point we do not assign affiliation to their corresponding authors. The post-processing will be responsible for matching affiliations and authors.

- **Email:** if the word is an email. At this point, we do not assign any email to any author. The post-processing algorithms will be responsible to match the given authors with their corresponding email.

- **Other:** if the word does not represent any useful information for the task of metadata extraction (e.g. "and" word, special characters, and superscript). We do not perform any further analysis over this class.

The Author Information CRF features include `Word Content`, `Possible Affiliation`, and `Possible Email`. The detailed description of each feature is given in Appendix B.2.

The **Footnote CRF** model deals with identifying metadata for the `Footnote` section which is usually at the bottom left of the first page of the paper. This model will explore the words of the lines that have been identified as `Footnote` class in the first-level of Artic. Each word is classified into the classes below:

- **Conference Name:** if the word belongs to the list of conference/journal name.

- **Conference Year:** if the word represents a conference year.

- **Conference Date:** if the word belongs to the conference date which is usually at the form `"Month DAY_START-DAY_ENDS"` (e.g. Jan 5-10).

- **Conference Location:** if the word belongs to the list of conference locations which is usually in the form `"City, Country"` (e.g. Florence, Italy).

- **Publisher:** if the word represents the publisher. Currently, Artic supports ACM, IEEE, and Elsevier.

- **ISBN:** if the word is represents an ISBN number (e.g. 978-1-60558-01/08/04).

- **Email:** if the word represents an email.

- **Other:** if the word does not represent any useful information for the task of metadata extraction (e.g. copyright). We do not perform any further analysis over this class.

`Word Content`, `Possible Email`, and `ISBN` are among the Footnote CRF features. The detailed description of all features is given in Appendix B.3.

## 3.3 Post-processing

The last step in Artic is to get the results from the CRF model and apply algorithms that output the metadata in a well-defined format. The CRF provides the classes for the given lines and words. The task of the post-processing step is to use that information to build the output data. The output format is JSON [2].

The first algorithm is for **entity grouping**. The goal of this algorithm is to group all the words that belong to the same class, i.e., authors names and affiliation. Algorithm 1 shows the logic applied for such grouping. The first step is to create an empty map with the group index as the key and an array of words as the map value (Line 1). Every new entry in this map holds a different entity. For example, if the map has four entries while identifying authors, this means that the algorithm has identified four different authors. The core step of this method is in lines 4 and 6. The method $getGroupIndex$ takes the group map and the current word to return the group index that this word belongs to. The calculation is based on the $HORIZONTAL\_BOUNDARY$ and $VERTICAL\_BOUNDARY$ parameters. Those parameters were experimentally set to 20% and 30%, respectively. If $groupIndex$ is $null$ (line 8), it means that the current word does not have any group to be attached to. As a result, a new index has

---

[2]http://json.org.

to be created in the group map (line 9 to 11). If $groupxIndex$ is found, the current word is added to the array of words of the group with $groupIndex$ key (lines 13 and 14).

---

**Algorithm 1** Algorithm for entity grouping

**Require:** List of words identified as Author Name or Affiliation.
1: $groupMap = new\ Map(int,\ Words[\ ]);$
2:
3: **for** all the words **do**
4:     $groupIndex = getGroupIndex(groupMap, word,$
5:         $HORIZONTAL\_BOUNDARY,$
6:         $VERTICAL\_BOUNDARY);$
7:
8:     **if** $groupIndex == null$ **then**
9:         $wordsOfIndex = new\ Array(\ );$
10:         $wordsOfIndex.add(word);$
11:         $groupMap(groupMap.size(\ ), wordsOfIndex);$
12:     **else**
13:         $wordsOfIndex = groupMap.get(groupIndex);$
14:         $wordsOfIndex.add(word);$
15:     **end if**
16: **end for**
17: **return** $groupMap$

---

**Algorithm 2** The Email Matching algorithm

**Require:** the list of authors and list of emails.
1:
2: **for** each $email$ in $emails$ **do**
3:     **for** each $author$ in $authors$ that does not have email **do**
4:         $distance = DynamicProgramming.distance($
5:                 $email, author.name);$
6:         **if** $distance <= MAX\_DISTANCE$ **then**
7:         $author.email = email;$
8:         $break;$
9:         **else**
10:         $names[] = author.name.split("");$
11:         **for** each $name$ in $names$ **do**
12:         $distance = DynamicProgramming.distance($
13:                 $email, name);$
14:         **if** $distance <= MAX\_DISTANCE$ **then**
15:         $author.email = email;$
16:         $break;$
17:         **end if**
18:         **end for**
19:         **end if**
20:     **end for**
21: **end for**

---

The second algorithm is the **email matching**. The purpose of this algorithm is to match the identified emails to their corresponding authors.

Algorithm 2 performs the logic required to match authors and emails. From line 2 to 21 the matching is done by calculating the edit distance between the email and the author name using Dynamic Programming. If the edit distance is smaller than or equal to $MAX\_DISTANCE$, we found the author for the current email (lines 6 and 7). $MAX\_DISTANCE$ has been experimentally set to 20%. If this is still not satisfactory, we try to use each token in the name of the author instead of the full name (from line 10 to 18). Emails that do not match any author are ignored.

**Algorithm 3** The Affiliation Matching Algorithm
---
**Require:** Affiliation and Authors Name map.
1:
2: **for** each *author* in *authorsMap* **do**
3:     *index = getGroupIndex(affiliationMap, author,*
4:                   *HORIZONTAL_BOUNDARY,*
5:                   *VERTICAL_BOUNDARY);*
6:     **if** *index* ! = *null* **then**
7:         *author.affiliation = affiliationList[index];*
8:     **end if**
9: **end for**
---

The last algorithm is the **affiliation matching**. The goal of this algorithm is to match the identified affiliations with the corresponding authors. Algorithm 3 shows the logic applied to match affiliations and authors. The logic is very similar to the author name grouping (Algorithm 1). The *getGroupIndex* function is also used, the map is *affiliationMap* and, for each author, we identify the best matching affiliation index. The values for *HORIZONTAL_BOUNDARY* and *VERTICAL_BOUNDARY* have been experimentally set to 17% and 70%, respectively. If the *index* is found, we assign this affiliation to the current author. We do not use any affiliation that we could not match to an author, thus being completely ignored from the final output.

## 4. EXPERIMENTS

The purpose of the experiments presented here is to answer the following questions: (*i*) Can the two-layer CRF model improve the classification results compared to using a single-layer? (*ii*) Can the results hold for a larger dataset? And, finally, (*iii*) Can the post-processing algorithms properly identify the relationship between authors, emails, and affiliations?

The following sections are divided as follows. Section 4.1 explains how the experiments were structured, providing data and metrics to support our evaluations. Section 4.2 compares the proposed approach against the baseline. Section 4.3 validates the proposed solution against the JSON gold-standard.

### 4.1 Experimental setup

We have selected SectLabel as our baseline due to their good results reported in [8]. Also, SectLabel has an open-source tool[3] that allowed us to have easy access to the dataset that was used to validate their proposed solution. Please refer to Section 2, for more details on how SectLabel works.

The dataset used in our experiments consists of of 100 scientific papers from IEEE, Elsevier, Springer and ACM. This set of papers already includes the 40 papers used by SectLabel. The remaining 60 papers were selected by eight postgraduate students from our institution. In addition to the papers, the students also provided the expected output, in JSON format, for each metadata identified by them in the papers. We refer to that as *JSON gold-standard*. In order to extract richer information from the PDF we convert the pages into images and run an OCR engine. The information provided by the OCR engine includes: coordinates, format, font size, font type, etc. The output of the OCR is a XML file. Based on the XML document we build the CRF components using the CRF++ format. OmniPage Professional Version 18[4] was used to perform all OCR-

related operations. The choice for this tool was made based on their usage in the academic area and their good reported results. Also, we have manually annotated the corresponding classes for each of the CRF levels using the CRF++ format. We refer to that as *Classes gold-standard*. When selecting the papers, we advised the participants to cover as many different formats as possible. We believe this helps ensuring that the proposed method is not restricted to a specific article format.

For the validation procedure, we applied the same strategy as SectLabel. We used 10-fold cross validation for all the experiments performed in this work. K-fold validation is a commonly used strategy. The systems were evaluated based on the $F_1$ measure, which is defined as follows. Let us assume that TP denotes the number of correctly assigned classes (true positives), FP denotes the number of incorrect classification (false positives), and FN denotes the number of incorrect classifications in reverse order (false negatives). For example, assuming that we are evaluating the `Title` class. TP would be the correct hits. FP would be the wrong hits, the actual class would be `Author Information`, for example, and it was classified as `Title`. FN would be the misses, e.g. if the actual class was `Title`, and was classified as `Author Information`. Then, precision ($P$), recall ($R$) and $F_1$ are calculated as follows:

$$P = \frac{TP}{TP + FP}, R = \frac{TP}{TP + FN}, F_1 = \frac{2 \times P \times R}{P + R}$$

In other words, precision can be thought as "from what the method classified as `Title`, what was actually `Title`". In a similar way, recall can be thought as "from what should have been assigned as `Title`, how many were classified as such by the method".

### 4.2 Evaluation against the baseline

The goal of the **first experiment** is to test whether the two-layer CRF model improves the classification results compared to SectLabel single-layer strategy. For this test we used the same 40 papers which have been used by the baseline in the experiments reported in [8]. The comparison is done using the *Classes gold-standard*. The set of metadata identified by Artic differs from the set of metadata identified by SectLabel. As a result, for this experiment, we compared just the classes that both systems provide. SectLabel results were extracted from the original paper [8], but we had to combine some of their classes to match ours. For example, Artic Affiliation class already includes the address as part of the metadata. So, we have combined SectLabel Address and Affiliation classes by taking the average over their $F_1$ results.

Table 1 presents the results for both methods using a total of five classes (`Title`, `Author Name`, `Email`, `Affiliation`, and `Footnote`). Artic's average $F_1$ is 99.84%, which represents a relative gain of 6.92% compared to SectLabel. Also, the classes `Affiliation` and `Footnote` presented the biggest improvements when applying the two-layer CRF model.

**Table 1: Can the two-layer CRF model improve the classification results compared to using a single-layer?**

| Class | SectLabel (Single-layer) | Artic (Two-Layer) |
|---|---|---|
| Title | 100.00 % | 100.00 % |
| Author Name | 97.74 % | 99.41 % |
| Email | 97.64 % | 100.00 % |
| Affiliation | 89.15 % | 99.83 % |
| Footnote | 82.34 % | 100.00 % |
| **Average ($F_1$)** | **93.37 %** | **99.84 %** |

[3]https://github.com/knmnyn/ParsCit/tree/master/bin/sectLabel
[4]http://www.nuance.com/for-individuals/by-product/omnipage/index.htm.

**Table 2: Can the results hold for a larger dataset?**

| Class | Artic (40 papers) | Artic (100 papers) |
|---|---|---|
| Title | 100.00 % | 100.00 % |
| Author Name | 99.41 % | 98.91 % |
| Email | 100.00 % | 100.00 % |
| Affiliation | 99.83 % | 99.64 % |
| Venue Name | 85.20 % | 85.94 % |
| Venue Year | 100.00 % | 100.00 % |
| Venue Date | 100.00 % | 98.89 % |
| Venue Publisher | 100.00 % | 100.00 % |
| Venue Location | 93.86 % | 96.60 % |
| ISBN | 100.00 % | 98.82 % |
| **Average ($F_1$)** | **97.83 %** | **97.88 %** |

## 4.3 Evaluation using a larger dataset

The **second experiment** performed in this work was to evaluate the behavior of the system with a larger dataset. The test used 100 papers, as described in Section 4.1. This time, we have included all 10 classes that Artic identifies. The comparison here is still in the classification level, meaning the *Classes gold-standard*. Table 2 summarizes the results of this experiment. The average $F_1$ with 40 papers was 97.83%, and, for 100 papers, it was 97.88%. These numbers demonstrate that the results hold while for a larger number of papers. Venue name presented the lowest $F_1$ among all the classes that Artic identifies. We have analyzed the cases in which Artic failed and most of them occurred when the name of the venue is in full (e.g. International Conference on Machine Learning) rather than abbreviated (e.g. ICML).

The **last experiment** aims at verifying if the post-processing algorithms can properly identify the relationship between authors, emails, and affiliations. We have run Artic with the 100 paper dataset and compared the generated JSON against the gold-standard provided by the annotators (*JSON gold-standard*). One problem that occurred during this experiment was the comparison between the generated output and gold-standard JSONs. For instance, Listing 1 shows an example of a gold-standard JSON element for author information. Similarly, Listing 2 shows a hypothetical automatically generated JSON for this author element. One may observe that the author's last name has been erroneously identified as another author. Similarly, the author's first name was appended by a number 2 (i.e., an undesired superscript). Also, the University name has been divided in two. The challenge here is how to calculate precision, recall, and $F_1$ for this comparison. In other words, how close these two JSONs are from each other? To the best of our knowledge, there is no tool that can compare two JSONs. As a result, we developed a method that does just that. We resorted to similar comparisons made in another area, i.e. Plagiarism Detection, to develop this assessment. In [9], an evaluation framework provides a model to calculate precision and recall for plagiarism detection systems. We have implemented a similar approach which is explained as follows.

Let $C$ be the set of classes that Artic provides. Let $W_c$ be the set of words of a class $c \in C$ from the gold-standard JSON. Similarly, let $G_c$ be the set of words of a class $c \in C$ from the generated JSON. Precision, Recall and $F_1$ for a given class $c$ is given as follows:

$$P_c = \frac{\sum_{g \in G_c} g \cap W_c}{|G_c|}$$

$$R_c = \frac{\sum_{w \in W_c} w \cap G_c}{|W_c|},$$

$$F_{1_c} = \frac{2 \times P_c \times R_c}{P_c + R_c}$$

where $\cap$ means the number of matching characters from the best match in $W_c$ or $G_c$.

```
{
    "authors": [{
        "name": "Alan Souza",
        "email": "apsouza@inf.ufrgs.br",
        "affiliation": "Cal University"
    }]
}
```

Listing 1– The gold-standard JSON element.

For example, precision, recall and $F_1$ for the Author Name are calculated as follows:

$$P_{name} = \frac{4}{5}, R_{name} = \frac{4}{9}, F_{1_{name}} = \frac{2 \times 0.8 \times 0.44}{1.24} = 0.57$$

```
{
    "authors": [{
        "name": "Alan2",
        "email": "apsouza@inf.ufrgs.br",
        "affiliation": "Cal"
    }, {
        "name": "Souza",
        "affiliation": "University"
    }
    ]
}
```

Listing 2– The possible generated JSON element.

Table 3 compares the post-processing results against the classification step. The post-processing results were extracted by applying the above formula for each of the 10 classes in Artic. After executing the post-processing algorithms, the average $F_1$ presented a relative loss of 5.34%. The results for author name and email are still below our expectations, while affiliation had itself a relative loss of 11.30%. During our experiments, we observed different affiliations that are positioned very close too each other, thus not allowing the heuristic framework to detect that those are actually distinct entities. Figure 5 shows an example of this problem.

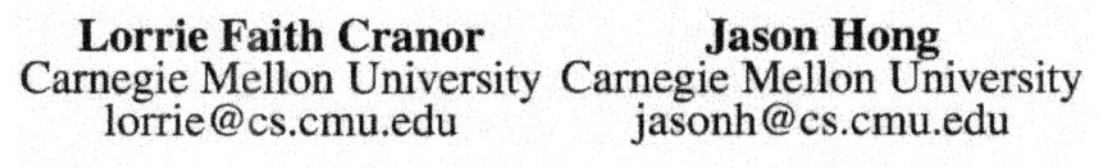

**Lorrie Faith Cranor**
Carnegie Mellon University
lorrie@cs.cmu.edu

**Jason Hong**
Carnegie Mellon University
jasonh@cs.cmu.edu

**Figure 5: Distinct Affiliations problem (too close)**

## 5. DISCUSSION AND LIMITATIONS

The first step of Artic is to extract information (evidences) from the PDF in order to build the features that will be further used by the CRF model. We tried a set of tools to extract data such as: font size, alignment, font family. To the best of our knowledge, the most effective way is to use an OCR engine that will convert the PDF into image and output a XML with all rich text features inside. Among all the OCR engines available, we chose OmniPage 18 Professional

**Table 3: Can the post-processing algorithms properly identify the relationship between authors, emails, and affiliations?**

| Class | Artic (Classification) | Artic (Post-Processing) |
|---|---|---|
| Title | 100.00 % | 100.00 % |
| Author Name | 98.91 % | 95.78 % |
| Email | 100.00 % | 92.57 % |
| Affiliation | 99.64 % | 88.38 % |
| Venue Name | 85.94 % | 77.40 % |
| Venue Year | 100.00 % | 97.94 % |
| Venue Date | 98.89 % | 95.27 % |
| Venue Publisher | 100.00 % | 97.22 % |
| Venue Location | 96.60 % | 83.86 % |
| ISBN | 98.82 % | 98.14 % |
| **Average ($F_1$)** | **97.88** % | **92.65** % |

due to its good reported results in the academic area. The limitation here is that OmniPage is for Windows only, which restrains our pre-processor to run in a specific operating system. Another issue is that if the OCR fails to recognize some words, this may lead to classification errors. One benefit of using an OCR tool is that we can basically support any format that the tool provides, not only PDF. We tried to run Artic using a paper with Microsoft Word format and the results were promising. The Artic dataset includes 100 papers. While the number is more than double the size of the state-of-the-art solution, we still consider 100 papers a small set as compared to the number of different paper styles available online. Also, manually annotating these papers took us considerable time. Another possible future work is to evaluate the possibility of leveraging this set of papers and build a broader dataset minimizing human intervention.

The post-processing algorithms try to identify the relationship between authors, emails, and affiliation. At this level, we do not introduce any machine learning, but, in contrast, we apply some heuristics to identify the components that should be grouped together. The main limitation is when we do not find the group index for a specific element (e.g. author name is off the boundaries for existing authors in the index). In this scenario, some information may be completely ignored in the JSON output. Do *et al.* [3] presents a method to match author and affiliations using Support Vector Machines (SVM). A possible future work is to evaluate the use of machine learning techniques also at the post-processing level.

## 6. CONCLUSION

This paper presented Artic, a metadata extraction approach based on a two-layer CRF model. The first-layer focuses on identifying the line-level structural components that may contain metadata information: `Title`, `Author Information`, `Header`, and `Footnote`. The second-layer analyzes, for each structural component, the words that may belong to a specific metadata element. Artic identifies a total of 10 metadata elements: Title, Author Name, Author Email, Author Affiliation, Venue Name, Venue Year, Venue Date, Venue Publisher, Venue Location, and ISBN. Author data can be found at the `Author Information` layer. Similarly, Venue data can be found either at `Header` or `Footnote` levels. Additionally, Artic provides a post-processing component that links authors, emails, and affiliation based on pre-defined heuristics.

We carried out an evaluation composed of three experiments. Artic was compared against our baseline (SectLabel) and against a

gold-standard with the expected JSON output. A total of 100 real PDF articles were used as test and training set in a 10-fold cross-validation setting. Artic presented a relative gain of 6.92% compared to SectLabel. The post-processing algorithms represented a relative loss of 5.34% compared to Artic classification step. A possible future work would consider using Machine Learning techniques also at the post-processing level.

Artic has been released as an open-source tool for anyone interested in re-using the components developed during this work. Links to all 100 papers used in our experiments together with their annotations and JSON output set can be found in the website `https://github.com/alansouzati/artic-poc`.

## Acknowledgments

We thank A. Kauer, B. Laranjeira, S. Pertile, E. Manica, D. Tumitan, M. Cadori, G. Kantorski, and E. Weren for their help in generating the JSON gold-standard. This work has been partially supported by CNPq-Brazil (project 478979/2012-6).

## 7. REFERENCES

[1] AUMÜLLER, D. Retrieving metadata for your local scholarly papers. In *BTW* (2009), pp. 577–583.

[2] COUNCILL, I. G., GILES, C. L., AND YEN KAN, M. Parscit: An open-source crf reference string parsing package. In *LREC* (2008).

[3] DO, H. H. N., CHANDRASEKARAN, M. K., CHO, P. S., AND KAN, M. Y. Extracting and matching authors and affiliations in scholarly documents. In *JCDL* (2013), pp. 219–228.

[4] FLYNN, P., ZHOU, L., MALY, K., ZEIL, S., AND ZUBAIR, M. Automated template-based metadata extraction architecture. In *Intl Conf. on Asian digital libraries* (2007), pp. 327–336.

[5] HUANG, Z., JIN, H., YUAN, P., AND HAN, Z. Header metadata extraction from semi-structured documents using template matching. In *Proc. Intel Conf. On the Move to Meaningful Internet Systems: AWeSOMe, CAMS, COMINF, IS, KSinBIT, MIOS-CIAO, MONET - Volume Part II* (2006), pp. 1776–1785.

[6] JOHN LAFFERTY, ANDREW MCCALLUM, F. P. Conditional random fields: Probabilistic models for segmenting and labeling sequence data. *ScholarlyCommons* (2001).

[7] LIPINSKI, M., YAO, K., BREITINGER, C., BEEL, J., AND GIPP, B. Evaluation of header metadata extraction approaches and tools for scientific PDF documents. In *JCDL* (2013), pp. 385–386.

[8] LUONG, M.-T., NGUYEN, T. D., AND KAN, M.-Y. Logical structure recovery in scholarly articles with rich document features. *IJDLS 1*, 4 (2010), 1–23.

[9] POTTHAST, M., STEIN, B., BARRÓN-CEDEÑO, A., AND ROSSO, P. An evaluation framework for plagiarism detection. In *COLING* (2010), pp. 997–1005.

[10] ROSENTHOL, L. *Developing with PDF: Dive Into the Portable Document Format*, 1 ed. O'REILLY, October 2013.

[11] SEYMORE, K., MCCALLUM, A., AND ROSENFELD, R. Learning hidden markov model structure for information extraction. In *AAAI Workshop on Machine Learning for Information Extraction* (1999), pp. 37–42.

[12] WALLACH, H. M. Conditional random fields: An introduction. *ScholarlyCommons* (2004).

[13] YIN, P., ZHANG, M., DENG, Z., AND YANG, D. Metadata extraction from bibliographies using bigram HMM. In *Intl Conf. on Asian digital libraries* (2004).

# APPENDIX

## A.   DETAILED FIRST-LEVEL FEATURES

- **Identifier:**   the line identifier, starts with "line_0" and goes until "line_n", where $n$ is the last line of the page. This could be a good indicator for the classes as their location usually does not change.

- **Alignment:**   the line alignment with four possible values: left, center, right, or justified. We expect this feature to be very useful for the identification of the `Title` (usually centered).

- **Bold:**   boolean that represents whether the line is bold (true) or not (false). This feature could be a good evidence for identifying `Title` which usually are in bold.

- **Underline:**   boolean that represents if the line contains any underlined words. This could be important to the `Footnote` that usually represents information with underline.

- **Italic:**   boolean that represents if the line contains any word in italic. This feature could be useful to identify `Footnote` as this class usually contains the elements in italic.

- **Font Size:**   the font size normalized into four different values: small, normal, medium, or large. The normalization process calculates the average font size for the given page, and, for each line, it assigns a value depending on the distance to the average font size. The values can be: *small* if it is more than 10% smaller than the average; *normal* if its difference in relation to the average size is less than 10%; *medium* if the size is from 10% to 45% larger than the average; and *big* if the size is over 45% larger than the average font size. All values have been set based on empirical observations of the training data. This feature could be very useful to identify `Title`, `Author Information`, and `Footnote`. `Title` usually has the biggest font size, `Author Information` usually has medium, and `Footnote` usually has small.

- **Top position:**   the normalized line location with respect to the top position. The normalization process retrieves the largest top position and creates buckets of 8 bits, which means that each bucket will have a size of $biggestTop/8$. Then, for each line, the current top position will be set depending on the bucket it belongs to. For example, if the current top location fits into the first bucket, its top position will be 0, if it fits into the second bucket, its top position will be 1, and so on. This could be very useful to identify `Header` which most probably have their top position set to 0.

- **Left position:**   the normalized line location with respect to the left position. The normalization process is almost the same as for the top position, the only difference is that it considers the left location instead of the top one. This feature could help to identify `Footnote` which usually has the left position set to 0.

- **Possible Email:**   boolean that indicates whether the current line has any "@" sign. This feature is important to identify `Author Information`. If the line contains an email it is a good indication to belong to the `Author Information` class.

- **Number of Words:**   the normalized number of words for the current line with four possible values: zero, few, medium, or many. The normalization process first extracts the words for the given line. Zero represents an empty line. Few if the line has between 1 and 4 words. Medium if the line between 5 and 9 words. Many if the line has more than 9 words. All values have been experimentally set based on the training data. The number of words could help to identify `Body` class, which usually has many words.

- **Paragraph Information:**   represents information about the paragraph. There are three possible values: header, new, or same. The header paragraph represents all lines before Abstract or Introduction. "New" represents a new paragraph, and "same" means that the line belongs to the same paragraph as the previous line. This feature has been implemented based on [8]. This feature could help identify the transitions between classes. When we have a different class, it is likely for it to have different paragraph information.

- **Formatting Information:**   represents information about the line format and can take two different values: new or same. "New" represents that the current line has a different format than the previous one. "Same" represents that the line has exact the same format as the previous one. The format has been defined as a concatenation of: font size, bold, italic, font face, and alignment. This feature has been implemented based on [8]. This feature could help to identify the transitions between classes. A new format could be a good indication of a new class.

## B.   DETAILED SECOND-LEVEL FEATURES

### B.1   Header CRF Features

- **Word Content:**   the original text of the word without spacing. This feature is very useful for identifying the `Publisher` (e.g. ACM, IEEE) and `Conference Names` (e.g. DocEng, WWW). These words tend not to vary (i.e. the same words are used in most papers), thus allowing us to use the word as a feature for the CRF engine. In the first-level of our CRF model, we did not use the value of the line because it is not useful for that level.

- **Word Identifier:**   the word identifier, starts with 0 and goes till $n$, where $n$ is the last word of the line. We believe that the location of the word within the line is relevant for the detection of classes. For example, `Conference Name` is usually one of the first words of the line.

- **Line Identifier:**   the line identifier, starts with 0 and goes till $n$, where $n$ is the last line of the page. This feature could be relevant because `Header` class usually is found in one of the first lines of the page.

- **Character length:**   the normalized number of characters for the current word with four possible values: zero, few, medium, or many. The normalization process first extracts the characters for the given word. *Zero* represents an empty word. *Few* if the word between 1 and 4 characters. *Medium* if the word has between 5 and 9 characters. *Many* if the word has more than 9 characters. All values have been experimentally set based on the training data. The number of characters could help identify the `Other` class, which usually has lines full of characters.

- **Numeral:**   boolean that represents if the word content is composed only by numbers. This feature is very useful when identifying days and years for the conference/journal. We remove all special characters from the word before checking for the pattern. For example, the word "$5,00" is considered a valid numeral entry in our method because we remove "$" and "," from the character sequence before applying the pattern.

- **Possible Conference:** boolean that represents if the word is a possible conference name by having the substring "conference" or "conf" (e.g. "International Conference on Database Systems"). Also, we currently maintain a list of about 1700 CS conferences around the world. If the given word is found in the conference list, we also classify this word as a possible conference. Before applying the filter, we convert the word to lowercase.

- **Month:** boolean that identifies if the word represents a month. We keep a list with all possible months in lowercase format. Also, we add the short and full value for the month (e.g. Jun and June). Before performing any checks, we remove all special characters from the word and apply the lowercase function. For example, the word "JuNe," is considered a valid month.

- **Year:** boolean that identifies if the word holds the conference/journal year.

- **Country:** boolean that represents if the word is part of a country name. We keep a list of country names in lowercase format. Again, we remove all special characters and convert to lowercase. For example, the word "StaTes..." is a valid country feature. The word "States" is part of the country name "United States of America". This is very important to detect `Conference Location`.

- **Special Character:** boolean that represents if the word contains any special character. This feature is important when identifying the conference location and conference dates. These classes usually include special characters like comma, dots, and colons. This feature could be useful to identify `Conference Name`, `Conference Location`, and `Conference Date`, as they usually include special characters as part of their data.

- **Website:** boolean that identifies if the word represents a URL (e.g. www.google.com). This feature is useful for `Other` class, if we find a website pattern we currently classify them as `Other`.

## B.2 Author Information CRF Features

- **Word Content, Word Identifier, Line Identifier, Character Size, Website:** The same implementation as the Header CRF.

- **Font Size, Possible Email:** implemented following the same algorithm as the one implemented in Appendix A.

- **Possible Affiliation:** boolean that indicates whether the current word is likely to belong to the affiliation block. In order for this feature to be valid, it has to match at least one of these criteria: be a possible university, or a possible country, or a possible department, or a possible continent. To be a possible university, the word should be equal to "University" or "Faculty". The logic for the country is the same that the one executed in the Header CRF. A possible department is a word that matches at least one of these cases: department, dept, center, laboratory, division, school, group, community, or academic. We keep a list of all continents, if the given word matches any of these values it will be classified as a possible affiliation too.

- **Word Format:** represents information about the word formatting. Same implementation as the one describe in A, but for the word-level.

## B.3 Footnote CRF Features

- **Word Content, Word Identifier, Line Identifier, Character Size, Month, Possible Conference, Country, Year, Website, Publisher, Numeral:** the same implementation as described in Header CRF.

- **Possible Email, Possible Affiliation:** the same implementation as described in Author Information CRF.

- **Day:** boolean that indicates if the word matches the following pattern DAY-DAY (e.g. 05-10).

- **ISBN:** boolean that indicates whether the word matches the following ISBN format XXX-X-XXXXX-XX/XX/XX (e.g. 978-1-60558-01/08/04). For some papers, the ISBN comes immediately followed by the fee, like 978-1-60558-01/08/04$5.00. The regular expression applied for this feature also supports ISBN with this particular scenario.

# Connecting Content and Annotations with LiveStroke

Michael J. Gormish        John W. Barrus
Ricoh Innovations, Corp.
2882 Sand Hill Rd. Ste. #115
Menlo Park, CA 94063 USA
{gormish,barrus}@ric.ricoh.com

## ABSTRACT

One common use for interactive whiteboards (IWBs) is to mark up content provided from a connected laptop. Typically a marking layer is provided which is independent of the laptop content. This leads to problems when the laptop content changes while the strokes in the mark up layer do not. The LiveStroke prototype described in this document uses computer vision techniques to associate the marks with the image of the underlying content from the laptop. For instance, if marks are made on the first page of a document, those marks disappear when the laptop user scrolls to a different page. The marks reappear in the right location on the page when the user returns to the first page. While we have integrated these techniques with interactive whiteboards the techniques are also applicable to screen sharing with mobile touch devices and projectors.

## Categories and Subject Descriptors

I.4.0 [**Image Processing and Computer Vision**]: General–*Image processing software;* I.5.4 [**Pattern Recognition**]: Applications–*Computer vision;*

## Keywords

Interactive Whiteboard; Screen Sharing; Video Conference

## 1. INTRODUCTION

One of the significant advantages of interactive whiteboards over non-interactive whiteboards and projectors is the ability to mark up any content displayed from a laptop, PC, or tablet. If a PC screen is displayed on a regular whiteboard and marked up with physical pens the result will be as shown in Figure 1. Namely, there will be no connection between the strokes and images. Each time the displayed information changes, the strokes must be manually erased and if the content appears again at the same or a different location the strokes must be redrawn. This physical operation is emulated in most electronic whiteboards with an "ink" layer and a content layer, even though both are being rendered by the same system. The object in this paper is to provide the experience shown in Figure 2; when the content moves the strokes should move with the content, when the content changes the strokes should disappear, and when the content returns the strokes should return.

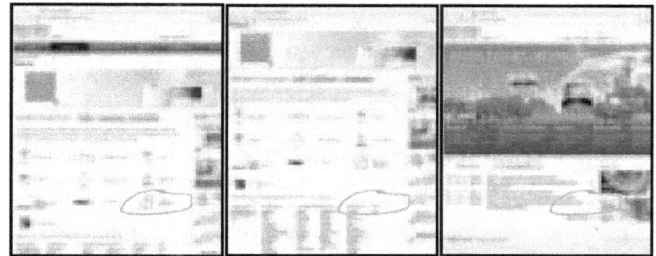

**Figure 1. Three shared screens. Left - green stroke is drawn around one product, Middle - stroke is in wrong place when window is scrolled, Right - stroke continues to remain when content changes.**

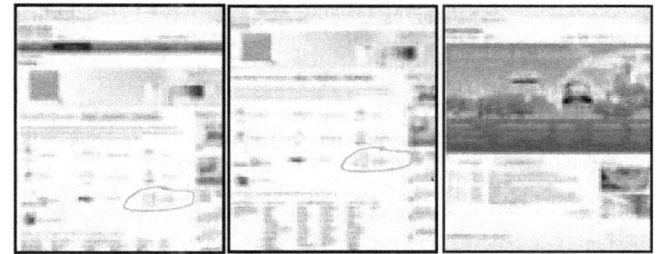

**Figure 2. Three shared screens with LiveStroke. Left - green stroke is drawn around one product, Middle - stroke is automatically moved when window scrolls, Right - stroke is removed when content changes.**

## 2. BACKGROUND

Historically, documents were marked up on paper using a pen. Today, documents are often marked up electronically using the "track changes" mode of modern word processors. Web-based solutions like "Third Voice" (external text comments) and "Markup.io" (stroke-based) used to provide solutions for annotating web pages within the web browser, but those services are no longer available. Many popular office productivity programs, including word processing and presentation programs support adding handwritten strokes to a document. Major PC operating systems provide "ink" support which allows the conversion of handwritten words to symbolic text for insertion in a program that expects text input. For some applications the ink can be inserted directly into a document as a stroke.

Bargeron integrated stroke-based annotation with a word processor [2]. Direct integration allowed the application to reflow highlight marks, text underlines and circles as the text was edited and reflowed. Norrie, Signer, and Weibel did extensive work connecting paper and electronic documents e.g. [7]. However, their work involves deciding in advance which presentation slides or documents are going to be marked up and printing them. We wish to markup any image connected without pre-printing.

IWBs are sold as computer peripherals and are usually set up to look like a mouse to the connected computer. Typically, software is provided that allows the user to mark up whatever appears on the screen. This software provides an independent transparent layer above and separate from the screen content. If users want to save the marked up content, they must remember to capture the strokes + content before the content changes. Infrequent use leads to the common mistake of scrolling the document or switching applications before capture. Some systems freeze the screen during markup to prevent this mistake. The implementation options for IWB systems are limited because they only have access to the video stream. While users can run special whiteboard applications on the attached PC, connecting any stroke with any content would require integration with every possible application. Also, running special software on the attached PC limits the ability for sharing content from multiple computers.

Computer vision techniques allow image-based recognition of screen content as it appears and disappears, even when transformed (i.e. moved or resized). The system reported in this paper was developed to associate strokes captured on a transparent layer with the underlying screen image. This system automatically removes strokes when the associated content disappears and reapplies the strokes when the content returns.

## 3. CHALLENGES

Matching strokes to document content based only on the image of the document is challenging because of the variety of content that might be shared, the real time update requirement, and user expectations for performance.

### 3.1. Content Variety

LiveStroke is intended to facilitate markup during meetings and one of the most useful operations is annotating presentations. This might be done in a practice session where the markup consists of corrections to be made to the slides or in a presentation where the markup consists of brainstorming ideas or design decisions. PowerPoint and other presentations tend to have repeated elements, such as company logos, headers and footers. Furthermore presentations often have "builds" where most of the content is repeated and a new element is added. All of these situations raise questions about annotations: If a stroke is written on a logo, should it always appear with the logo? If a stroke is written in white space and then a build adds material in the white space should the stroke be removed? The upper part of Figure 3 shows two slides of a presentation where a build has been added going from one slide to the other.

A common piece of content to be marked up on interactive whiteboards are web pages. In particular, people designing web pages can meet and make notes about changes to the design and content of the page by projecting it to everyone. Web pages often feature repeated sections (as with presentations), but web pages also commonly have dynamic content, especially large images that change every few seconds. What should happen with strokes written on dynamic content when the content changes? The lower part of Figure 3 shows this situation where the header remains the same, but a large image changes in the middle of the web page.

Word processing documents, spreadsheets, project plans, and source code are all document types that might be displayed and annotated. On a PC, these types of documents typically have a header or sidebar used for controls and scrolling which creates a challenge for connecting strokes and image content. Since our

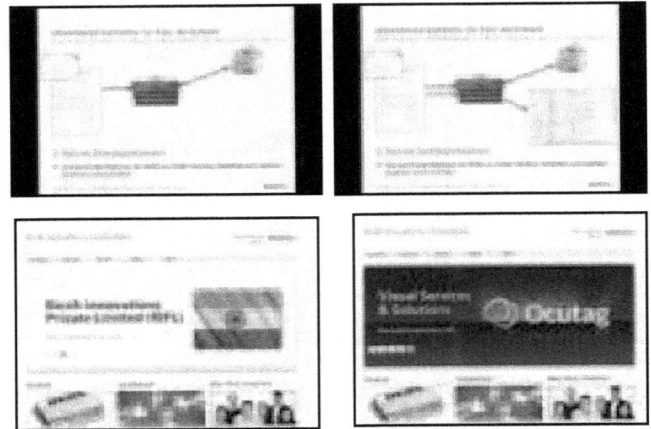

**Figure 3. Content to be marked up. Top: a presentation slide with common logos and an added build element on the right. Bottom: a web page with a static masthead but a large image that changes every few seconds.**

system does not assume access to the window manager on the PC, we must decide when strokes are on the "controls" or "body" of the document without knowing where the controls are.

### 3.2. Speed Requirements

When a user changes slides of a presentation or changes from one document to another the strokes associated with the new document must appear almost immediately. Finding all strokes associated with the new document and computing the position in case the document is in a different location should take far less than one second. At the same time the database of strokes must also be updated multiple times per second because users write very quickly. There is a trade-off between maintaining fast indices for search and being able to update the database quickly.

### 3.3. User Expectation

Perhaps the most difficult issue with matching strokes to content is that not all users have the same expectation of what should happen. As an extreme example, a PC might display a translucent window. A user could draw on the board to annotate something seen through the window. The user might later draw on the translucent window to make a "to do" list which is expected to move with the window regardless of the content beneath the window.

### 4. CONNECTING STROKES TO CONTENT

LiveStroke has two basic operations: creating an association between a stroke and the underlying content, and finding all strokes associated with a query image. The actual format for the stroke does not matter, all that matters is the location of the stroke on the content. LiveStroke has been implemented to allow storage of strokes either as images with transparency, or as an ID number with a bounding box relying on the application to store the strokes. This allows LiveStroke to be used to connect other types of annotations, e.g. text from a keypad, or images from a camera.

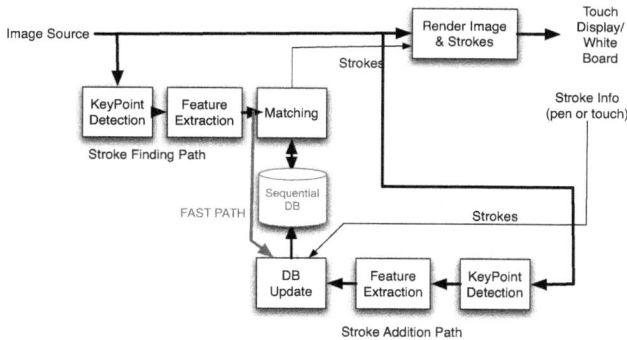

**Figure 4. Block diagram of stroke matching data path.**

Figure 4 shows the LiveStroke data flow. Images are provided from an independent source via VGA, or HDMI cable. No special software is run by the provider of the images, and indeed the cable could be switched between multiple laptops during a single session without an issue. The top path of Figure 4 shows the input image being rendered to the display, along with any strokes retrieved from the database of strokes associated with content for the session. The strokes to display with an image are determined by the upper three boxes (detection, extraction, and matching). This process repeats constantly. At the same time, when strokes are written on an image at the display these must be associated with the current image. This is done by the bottom path in the detection, extraction, and update boxes. It is possible to avoid the detection and extraction phases in most cases because these features have already been computed for a given image by the upper path in the block diagram for the finding operation. This possibility is indicated by the arrow labeled "FAST PATH" in the figure.

## 4.1. Creating Associations

Given an input background image and a stroke bounding box, an association is created by finding feature points of the background image, computing descriptors at each of the feature point locations, and storing those points and descriptors with a reference to the stroke id and the bounding box. Some portion of the background image is saved for match verification and testing. The OpenCV library [5] makes it easy to test multiple keypoint detectors, feature extractors and matching algorithms. We investigated several feature detectors and found that the feature detector Good Features to Track (GFTT) was overall the best [6] for the content we tested. Our source material did not require the illumination and scale invariance and other capabilities of newer detectors. We do handle changes of scale but because the content typically contains very strong edges e.g. from text and window boundaries, frequently the same keypoints are identified even after scaling. Several different feature extractors were usable but the speed and matching from Oriented Brief (ORB) worked well [4].

## 4.2. Finding the Correct Strokes

As each image is received by LiveStroke, feature points are detected and feature descriptors are created just as they are when an association is created. Then the feature descriptors (not the locations) are matched against points in the database. Good matches are then tested to see if a set of feature points have matching geometry. This is especially important with computer screens as features due to corners of window elements or common portions of text are likely to have numerous good matches. The Random Sample Consensus (RANSAC) algorithm is used to provide a consistent set of matches.

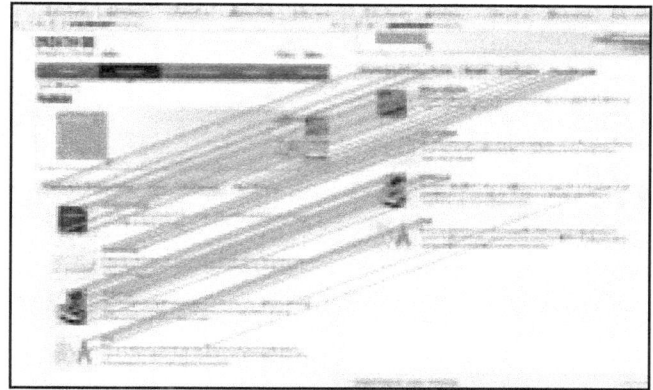

**Figure 5. Left and right images show different scroll positions. Thin green lines show matching feature points between images. Blue circles show feature points not part of the dominate homography. Once the correspondence has been determined a stroke can be redrawn at the new location.**

If a sufficient number of features have a geometric match, then the original image is transformed and compared with the current image to make sure the content where the stroke will be drawn is consistent. This is important because large portions of the screen might match but the stroke might be drawn in a region that has been scrolled, or has an overlapping window.

This process is repeated possibly matching many strokes. Typical operation is shown in Figure 5. Some of the features on the left have a consistent relationship with the features they are matched to on the right indicated by the thin lines. Therefore a homography can be computed for this transformation from one image to another, and the stroke written on the original image can be reproduced in the correct location on the right. Although we compute full perspective transformations we improve matching accuracy by eliminating matches that are uncommon with computer displays e.g. shear.

## 4.3. Session oriented stroke matching

Adding and retrieving every stroke independently did not provide sufficient speed for a viable system. Strokes would be matched, but as more strokes were indexed performance slowed, until there was a noticeable delay between a change in the background and the appearance of new content. Additional slowing would lead to seemingly random strokes appearing as the retrieval operations was completely out of sync with the background.

### 4.3.1. Sequential Stroke Retrieval

Content displayed in a meeting is not random. The most common image is the previous image, the second most common image is a scrolled version of the previous image. It is also likely that an image is either a new image or a repeat of a full screen.

In the case of a digital image source like an HDMI cable, it might be possible to uniquely identify each frame with a hash value of the content. However, our primary image source was VGA which is an analog transmission and thus even unchanging images from a computer have noise that changes and slightly different digital images are received. It is possible to do matches against single images very quickly thus when the image is unchanged or mostly unchanged we are able to do one match operation against the previously displayed image and the set of strokes that were shown on that image. Subsequently, the rest of the database can be searched for possibly matching images. This allows the strokes that were already visible to be quickly moved. A slightly longer delay for strokes from newly appearing regions is tolerable.

### 4.3.2. Sequential Stroke Addition
Typically feature matching is done either via brute force or by building structures to allow for fast searching e.g. nearest neighbor trees, or approximate nearest neighbor hashing solutions. In our case rebuilding an index with the addition of every stroke was impossible. However, because of the sequential nature of markup many strokes are written on the same image. We were able to create stroke groups that appeared together on an image at some point in time. These strokes could be indexed and retrieved together.

### 4.3.1. Area Matches
Groups of strokes sometimes crossed window boundaries making it impossible to keep the group of strokes together if the windows were moved independently. The stroke groups had to contain information about the background they were drawn on to insure that if the windows were moved they would still show up in the correct location. We computed multiple possible matches between the source image and the stroke groups and then checked each stroke to see which if any of the matches was appropriate based on the content underneath the stroke.

## 5. PERFORMANCE
Table 1 shows the initial time required to add strokes to the database, and to find all the strokes associated with an image using a brute force search with completely independent strokes in the second and third columns. Stroke addition time is very low because only append operations must be done. However, the time to perform a find operation is growing in proportion to the number of strokes and fairly quickly starts to require more than one second per operation.

**Table 1. Brute force matching operations**

| No. of Strokes | time per add (sec) | time per find (sec) | grouped strokes time per add (sec) | grouped strokes time per find (sec) |
|---|---|---|---|---|
| 1 | 0.052 | 0.064 | 0.057 | 0.050 |
| 5 | 0.032 | 0.206 | 0.038 | 0.094 |
| 25 | 0.031 | 1.359 | 0.041 | 0.481 |

The last two columns of Table 1 show the initial time required for adding strokes and finding strokes after the sequential nature of both operations has been considered and strokes are collected into stroke groups. Adding strokes takes a little longer in order to maintain data structures but finding operations happen much more quickly and slow down at a lower rate. These tables do not show the full performance improvement however. In testing, a fixed sequence of images and strokes are considered and time is only measured with complete image changes. Thus performance when scrolling or moving windows is much much better than the 0.481 seconds per update would indicate.

Performance depends both on speed and quality of matches. Although we created several sequences of images and strokes for testing purposes there is no standard data set of shared meetings

with strokes, and even the notion of ground truth is problematic. When shown a demo dozens of users appreciated the magical quality of having the strokes attach to whatever the image content shown from the PC was. Those users that had previously used stroke overlay solutions were especially enthusiastic. The match quality worked quite well when limited to the task of reviewing power points slides or web pages.

However, when general desktop windows where shown and users drew dashed lines over semi-transparent windows, the matches were often unpredictable. With the overlay method users know the method will fail, but it fails in predictable ways, while when LiveStroke did fail it was unexpected and harder to recover from. For example, one user drew a dash line to "circle" part of a window frame. When the window was moved, those parts of the dashed line inside the windows moved with the window and those outside remained on the background window. This is exactly what would happen if such a circle was drawn on a physical piece of paper on a physical desktop but the user was quite surprised and the interface did not provide an easy way to erase only those strokes left on the virtual desktop.

LiveStroke is also able to provide a record of all marked up video frames in a meeting. This requires saving images with strokes on them. But the benefit is that a PDF document can be created and provided to the participants of the meeting, even if they don't have access to the source content that was being discussed and marked up.

## 6. CONCLUSION
Keypoint detection and feature matching provide a way to annotate documents without access to anything but shared images. Realtime operation is possible by considering the sequential nature of annotation and the experience is viewed in some cases as delightful. However, some level of user control or expectation setting is needed for the system to be useful with the complete range of imagery that might be captured from a personal computer or tablet.

## 7. REFERENCES

1. Bargeron, David and Moscovich, Tomer, Reflowing Digital Ink Annotations, CHI 2003, April 5–10, 2003, Ft. Lauderdale, Florida, USA. (ACM 1-58113-630-7/03/0004)

2. Chen, Nicholas, Francois Guimbretiere, and Abigail Sellen. 2012. Designing a multi-slate reading environment to support active reading activities. ACM Trans. Comput.-Hum. Interact. 19, 3, Article 18 (October 2012), 35 pages. DOI=10.1145/2362364.2362366

3. Forsyth, D. and J. Ponce, Computer Vision a Modern Approach Second Edition, 2nd ed. Boston: Pearson, 2012.

4. Rublee, Ethan and Vincent Rabaud, Kurt Konolige, Gary R. Bradski: ORB: An efficient alternative to SIFT or SURF. ICCV 2011: 2564-2571.

5. Bradski, Gary, and Adrian Kaehler. Learning OpenCV: Computer vision with the OpenCV library. O'Reilly Media, Inc., 2008.

6. Shi, J. and C. Tomasi. Good Features to Track. Proceedings of the IEEE Conference on Computer Vision and Pattern Recognition, pages 593-600, June 1994.

7. Norrie, Moira C., Beat Signer, and Nadir Weibel. Print-n-link: weaving the paper web. Proceedings of the 2006 ACM symposium on Document engineering. ACM, 2006.

# Building Digital Project Rooms for Web Meetings

Laurent Denoue, Scott Carter, Andreas Girgensohn, Matthew Cooper
FX Palo Alto Laboratory
3174 Porter Dr.
Palo Alto, CA, 94304 USA
{denoue, carter, andreasg, cooper} @fxpal.com

## ABSTRACT

Distributed teams must co-ordinate a variety of tasks. To do so they need to be able to create, share, and annotate documents as well as discuss plans and goals. Many work-flow tools support document sharing, while other tools support videoconferencing. However, there exists little support for connecting the two. In this work, we describe a system that allows users to share and markup content during web meetings. This shared content can provide important conversational props within the context of a meeting; it can also help users review archived meetings. Users can also extract content from meetings directly into their personal notes or other workflow tools.

## Categories and Subject Descriptors

H.4 [**Information Systems Applications**]: Miscellaneous

## Keywords

Web meeting; video; annotation

## 1. INTRODUCTION

Project rooms are dedicated spaces that allow participants to revisit content in a series of meetings over weeks or months [1]. They involve the "creation, editing, and persistence of flexible documents" to support long-term collaboration around complex tasks. Physical project rooms typically include large shared spaces that a collocated design team can visually scan and utilize with ease. While aspects of the physical design space are invaluable, they increasingly do not align with the reality of modern knowledge work in which participants are distributed. Furthermore many smaller organizations do not have enough real estate to allow them to devote an entire room to a single project for weeks on end.

In this work, we are interested in supporting purely *digital* project rooms – online spaces that allow a group of participants to create, view, annotate and edit documents in a

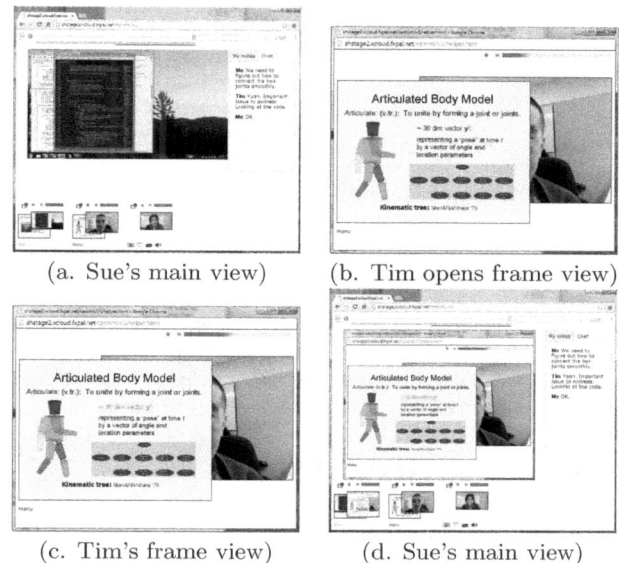

(a. Sue's main view)

(b. Tim opens frame view)

(c. Tim's frame view)

(d. Sue's main view)

**Figure 1: An interactive web meeting. (a) The current user (Sue) is looking at Tim's currently active stream in the main view. She can also see Tim's and Manu's frame archive along the bottom. (b) Tim clicks on Manu's icon to open his frame archive in a new window. (c) Tim annotates a frame from Manu's archive and shares his annotation with the rest of the meeting participants. (d) Sue sees Tim's view updated in the main view.**

flexible and persistent way. As described in [1], key components of such a room include shared, editable spaces, co-ordination documents (such as flow charts, todo lists, and other workflow tools), as well as co-working space. Online tools already exist that focus on editable digital spaces and coordination documents. For example, Trello[1] allows users to create a variety of workflow documents and to populate them with multimedia information. Other videoconferencing tools allow users to share, and discuss documents in a meeting environment (e.g., WebEx[2]). However, project rooms should support both *synchronous* and *asynchronous* collaboration. Additionally, they should allow documents to flow seamlessly from synchronous use (e.g., showing slides in

---

[1]http://trello.com/
[2]http://www.webex.com/

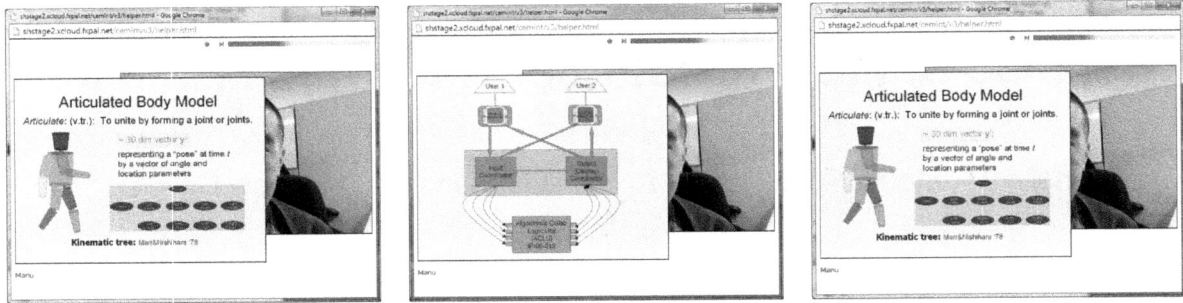

**Figure 2:** Annotations in our system are linked to underlying content. Here, Tim cycles through Manu's frame archive in a pop-up window (Manu is currently sharing his webcam, which appears in the background in the upper-right). Tim first views a slide he previously annotated (left) and then swipes to view the next slide in the deck (center). Next he swipes back to the first slide (right).

a meeting) to asynchronous use (e.g., perusing slides from a past meeting or extracting a photo of a slide so others can refer to it later). Current tools fail to bridge this gap.

We are building a digital project room environment that allows users to collaborate synchronously via web-based meetings as well as asynchronously via a shared document environment. With our system, users can annotate and extract content from live meetings both to improve *in situ* communication as well as to guide others as they explore documents later. In this paper we focus in particular on the aspects of our system that allow users to mark-up, extract, and archive live content.

## 2. INTERACTION DESIGN

### 2.1 Meeting support

Our system is a pure HTML5[3] solution that utilizes Web-RTC[4] to connect clients. It relies on WebRTC media capture and streaming[5] to gain access to a user's webcam and microphone. We use the WebSocket API[6] for communication between the clients and for signaling for the WebRTC connections. Any number of clients may participate in a meeting, limited only by the available network bandwidth and the screen real-estate for displaying content from remote participants. We also utilize the Desktop Capture API[7] to allow participants to stream arbitrary screen regions. Crucially, our system makes no other demands on the end user system. This allows users to share arbitrary documents without forcing other users in a meeting to install third-party applications. Several of those technologies are still under development and are only supported by few web browsers. Still, we expect more mature and widespread support in the near future.

A key feature of our system is that it automatically detects and indexes changes in shared content. When a user changes their content stream, e.g., from their webcam to a screen region, or from one screen region to another, our system records the change event and captures a representative frame of the new content. Furthermore, our system can determine

that the webcam has shifted focus from one participant to another via live face detection. This is particularly useful for connecting groups of users who have access to pan-tilt camera systems (e.g., Jarvis[8]). These content frames are archived immediately to an interactive stack that anyone in the meeting can peruse. Also, any user can re-share content from any other users' stack in the same meeting. Captured frames can also be extracted from the meeting and posted to a shared project page.

Figure 1 shows an example meeting with three participants. Stacks for each participant show both the currently shared content (on top of the stack) as well as previously captured frames from other content shared in the meeting. In this case, the two remote users (Tim and Manu) have shared a variety of different content types. The local user (Sue) has only shared her webcam and therefore does not have any archived frames. Note that the local user also has extra controls allowing her to switch her shared content from an arbitrary screen region or her webcam (similar to other web-conferencing tools she can also mute her audio stream). Sue is looking at Tim's stream, which is currently an image of one region of his screen. In Figure 1b,c, we see that Tim has opened Manu's history, has found a slide Manu shared previously, and has annotated it. The annotation snaps to the underlying content which is detected via real-time image analysis. At this point, only Tim sees these actions. However, he can choose to share this popup window (Figure 1d) so that everyone else can see his annotation while he makes a new remark.

In Figure 2, Tim continues to look through Manu's previously shared content and then returns to the slide he annotated. Note that the annotation remains via content matching algorithms we describe below.

### 2.2 Archiving meetings

Frames from each user are continuously captured at regular intervals. A keyframe is archived to the user's history whenever a screen change event is detected, while other frames are discarded. Also, users can optionally record their complete streams (both audio and video) during a meeting. In our system, recorded content is collected on the client browser and sent to the server opportunistically. The server maintains a database of all recorded meetings and makes archived content available via a web server.

---

[3]http://www.w3.org/TR/html5/

[4]http://www.w3.org/TR/webrtc/

[5]http://www.w3.org/TR/mediacapture-streams/

[6]http://www.w3.org/TR/websockets/

[7]http://developer.chrome.com/extensions/desktopCapture

[8]http://www.fxpal.com/research-projects/jarvis/

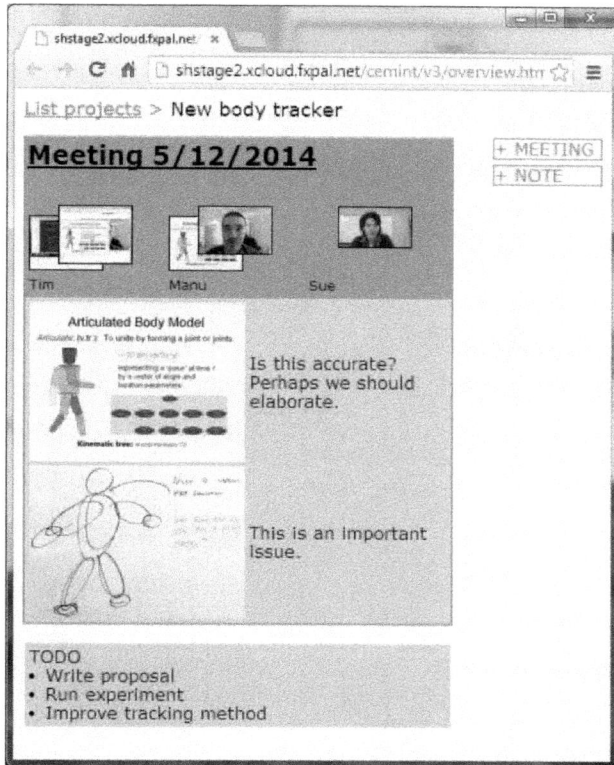

Figure 3: An example project page. Participants can view archived meetings, and notes and media can be attached to archived meeting or directly to the project. Participants can continue an archived meeting or start a new one at any time.

Users can manipulate a slider (Figure 1a, top) to peruse archived meeting content. As the user moves the slider back, each user's stack is updated to show the archived frame corresponding to that time. During a meeting the ability to peruse past content can be useful both for participants just joining the conference to catch up [5] as well as for ongoing participants who might want to revisit previously discussed topics. When no participants are actively streaming content the user can click a play button to watch the conference. This will play through the video in the main video view. If video streams from multiple participants were recorded, the playback switches among the streams based on voice activity detection. Alternatively, the viewer can select one of the participants to keep the focus there.

Note that users can join or rejoin a meeting at any time. Color-coded timelines just below the slider represent the periods of the meeting during which each user was present. If a portion of a client's stream was not recorded, either because they were not in the meeting at that time or because they switched off recording, the user's stack shows their last archived frame.

## 2.3 Projects

Our goal is for meetings to be integrated into a higher level project page that includes links to a set of related meetings as well as other multimedia and workflow tools. For example, a working group could archive a series of development meetings, design meetings, and HR meetings as well as a shared to-do list on the same page.

We are currently exploring integrating our web meeting tool into open-source organization frameworks (e.g., Redmine[9]). Simultaneously we are building a lightweight project page that allows us to experiment with representing and organizing meetings as well as content extracted from meetings. Figure 3 shows an example project page in which a meeting is represented by the history stacks of each participant. Users can drag arbitrary media into the project page either from their own laptop or from a meeting.

The fact that our annotation approach operates directly on shared screen content, rather than any specific document format, means that users can markup any content, including, for example, photos of sketches. Here, one user has extracted an annotated slide from the meeting, while another has uploaded and annotated a photo of a sketch.

Users can start a new meeting that will be associated with this project by clicking the "+ MEETING" button. They can also add multimedia notes directly to the project page ("TODO..." in the example). Furthermore, users can return to archived meetings at any time to peruse past content or continue the meeting.

## 3. ENHANCING ANNOTATION USING REAL-TIME ANALYSIS

It is common for one user to annotate the screen content shared by another conference participant. The keyframe history in our interface provides additional opportunities for users to review and optionally markup previously shared content throughout ongoing meetings.

### 3.1 Creating annotations

Remote participants do not have a way to easily markup content. Previous work on video-based annotation has focused on transient traces or enhanced remote pointers; in other cases markup is not linked to the underlying content and is usually freeform [3]. We utilize real time image processing to detect and segment underlying content in the shared screen. When users elect to annotate (e.g., highlight) underlying content, we integrate the results of the analysis to interpret their interaction.

To segment underlying content we compute a binary version of new frames as they are captured. Content streams such as screens and webcams are rendered into an HTML5 canvas element and we binarize and compute boxes using the canvas pixel data. Connected components [2] are then extracted and their bounding boxes are sorted and grouped to approximate word boundaries. We set a spacing threshold of six pixels for word groups and also filter out boxes that are less than ten pixels wide or high.

Users are shown this canvas element, refreshed in realtime as new video frames arrive. When a user starts a drag operation over the canvas, the system collects the underlying bounding boxes and draws a yellow filled rectangle over the canvas, giving users the impression that they are highlighting the text underneath. Because the rectangle snaps to the connected component boxes, users can create orderly marks as if they were working with an original document, i.e., their highlight follows the content.

---

[9]http://www.redmine.org/

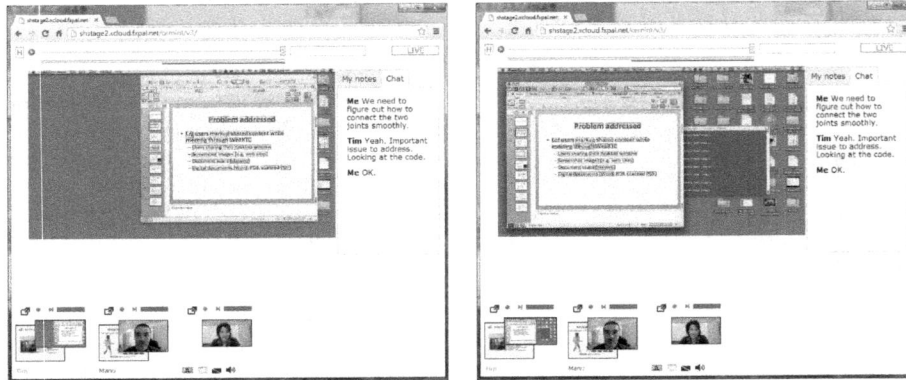

**Figure 4: Tracking annotations: word bounding boxes are shown in blue. The user has highlighted 2 words (left). Then the user shifts the window to the left, and the system finds these 2 word boxes in the new frames and repositions the highlight correctly (right).**

## 3.2 Tracking annotations

We are also developing algorithms that allow real-time repositioning of marks created by users. During the natural progression of a meeting, a user may move or scroll a window that has been previously annotated as in Figure 2. The system stores the word bounding boxes that are found under the highlight, and now needs to find where this highlight should be repositioned as new frames arrive.

Our implementation finds a match between the new bounding boxes and the boxes of the highlight based on their dimensions. While this algorithm is simple, we have found it to be fairly robust to the natural translations that occur in meetings. There are a number of extensions to this basic approach that could further improve accuracy such as processing boxes' content, or using spatial context to guide the matching. Document image processing includes a number of methods for word shape analysis that are relevant [6]. When a match is found, the system repositions the highlight(s) at the estimated new location, as shown in Figure 4.

This approach works well when the highlights are long enough (e.g., span more than 3 word boxes). It allowed us to test the usefulness of a system that can reposition marks in real-time: users do not have to worry about moving windows or scrolling documents during a web conference. Marks created by peers are automatically moved and reappear when the same content is shown again, even if at different positions. In a typical scenario, Sue shares her screen to request feedback about a slide deck she is writing for the team. Team members can highlight parts of the slide and when Sue moves her PowerPoint window on her screen or flips back and forth through slides, any previous marks are automatically redrawn.

## 4. CONCLUSIONS AND FUTURE WORK

In this work, we introduced a system designed to help remote users conduct and archive web-based meeting content such that it can be organized and extracted to digital project rooms. Our solution is novel in that it 1) automatically and in real time detects and bookmarks different content types from each user's stream (different faces, screens, etc.); and 2) allows users to add annotations linked to content in real time. In this way, users can share and annotate arbitrary content types without forcing others to use any third-party software. Furthermore, because content is archived in real time, users can quickly recover any previously shared content from the current meeting or another archived meeting.

We plan to continue building our web-based conferencing and meeting archive system with particular focus on the design of interfaces for exploring archived meetings. We aim to exploit meetings' persistence in a digital project room to support the types of collaboration that physical project rooms afford. Archived meetings can be reviewed and augmented by additional meeting participants subsequent to the original synchronous meeting, via interaction with the meeting's archived content. We will specifically explore the usefulness of the system's markup and multimedia annotation tools to support this mode of collaboration.

## 5. REFERENCES

[1] Covi, L. M., Olson, J. S., Rocco, E., Miller, W. J. and Allie, P. A Room of Your Own: What Do We Learn about Support of Teamwork from Assessing Teams in Dedicated Project Rooms? *Proc. of Cooperative Buildings: Integrating Information, Organization and Architecture.* 53–65. 1998.

[2] Chang, F., Chen, C-J. and Lu, C-J. A linear-time component-labeling algorithm using contour tracing technique. *Computer Vision and Image Understanding.* **93**(2):206-220. 2004.

[3] Fagá, Jr., F., Motti, V. G., Cattelan, R. G., Teixeira, C. A. C. and Pimentel, M. da G. C. A social approach to authoring media annotations. *Proc. of the ACM symposium on Document Engineering.* 17–26. 2010.

[4] Gutwin, C. and Penner, R. Improving interpretation of remote gestures with telepointer traces. *Proc. of the ACM conference on Computer Supported cooperative Work.* 49–57. 2002.

[5] Junuzovic, S., Inkpen, K., Hegde, R., Zhang, Z., Tang, J. and Brooks, C. What Did I Miss?: In-meeting Review Using Multimodal Accelerated Instant Replay (Air) Conferencing. *Proc. of the SIGCHI conference on Human Factors in Computing Systems.* 513–522. 2011.

[6] Lu, S., Li, L. and Tan, C.L. Document Image Retrieval through Word Shape Coding. *IEEE Transactions on Pattern Analysis and Machine Intelligence.* **30**(11):1913–18. 2008.

# The Virtual Splitter: Refactoring Web Applications for the Multiscreen Environment

Mira Sarkis, Cyril Concolato, Jean-Claude Dufourd
Telecom ParisTech; Institut Mines-Telecom; CNRS LTCI
{sarkis, concolato, dufourd}@telecom-paristech.fr

## ABSTRACT

Creating web applications for the multiscreen environment is still a challenge. One approach is to transform existing single-screen applications but this has not been done yet automatically or generically. This paper proposes a refactoring system. It consists of a generic and extensible mapping phase that automatically analyzes the application content based on a semantic or a visual criterion determined by the author or the user, and prepares it for the splitting process. The system then splits the application and as a result delivers two instrumented applications ready for distribution across devices. During runtime, the system uses a mirroring phase to maintain the functionality of the distributed application and to support a dynamic splitting process. Developed as a Chrome extension, our approach is validated on several web applications, including a YouTube page and a video application from Mozilla.

## Categories and Subject Descriptors

C.2.4 [**Distributed Systems**]: Distributed Applications; D.2.11 [**Software Engineering**]: [Software Architecture]

## Keywords

Application Distribution; Authoring; Multiscreen; Web Application

## 1. INTRODUCTION

Recently, intense research activity has been focused on multi-screen scenarios [4][6] inside home environment where cooperation between heterogeneous devices is leveraged. In such a cooperative environment, a "Multi-Screen Application" (MSA) is an application distributed across multiple connected devices, each having a screen, and designed to offer a convivial experience. Examples of MSA are: using a tablet to display additional information synchronized with a TV program, or using the interaction capabilities of smartphones (e.g., touch screen) jointly with the large screen and processing power of a PC or a TV to display media elements.

Multi-screen applications impose multiple challenges to the application developers. First, they have to design an application that leverages the multi-screen environment and copes with the diversity of devices. Then, they have to determine how the application content will be distributed across devices based on their specific capabilities, to manage the distributed content and to maintain the synchronization and consistency of the distributed content. The use of web technologies helps reducing the complexity of these tasks and increasing the possibility of deploying a ubiquitous application. In this paper, the term application refers to a web application. Many applications were created before the development of the multi-screen concept. Many of them are actually made of different components that could benefit from being distributed. However, few of them were designed in a modular manner that facilitates code distribution.

With such a motivation and focusing on challenges related to authoring MSAs, this paper aims to meet one principal objective: *To propose a new approach that reuses existing single-screen applications and refactors them for the multi-screen environment.* In contrast to existing works, our approach is based on mapping the application content onto available devices by automatically analyzing the content following the author or the user choices, on splitting the application into two sub-applications and synchronizing them while maintaining the overall application functionality and supporting a dynamic splitting process. The ability for the user to guide this splitting process is novel and opens up many usage scenarios.

This paper is organized as follows. Section 2 compares our approach with related work. Section 3 describes the virtual splitter architecture, including the mapping, annotation, splitting and mirroring phases. An implementation of the solution, an evaluation and a survey of its limitations are given in Section 4. Finally perspectives and conclusions are drawn in Section 5.

## 2. STATE OF THE ART

In prior works, a 'WebSplitter' [5] was proposed to split XML-based applications, based on a metadata file. This file is unique for each application and determines which application portions, i.e., which XML elements can be seen on each user device. The splitter requires a middleware proxy that splits the application content into partial views and a client-side component that receives data pushed by the server. The XML splitter architecture is centralized and requires a man-

*DocEng '14*, September 16 - 19 2014, Fort Collins, CO, USA
Copyright 2014 ACM 978-1-4503-2949-1/14/09 ...$15.00.
http://dx.doi.org/10.1145/2644866.2644893.

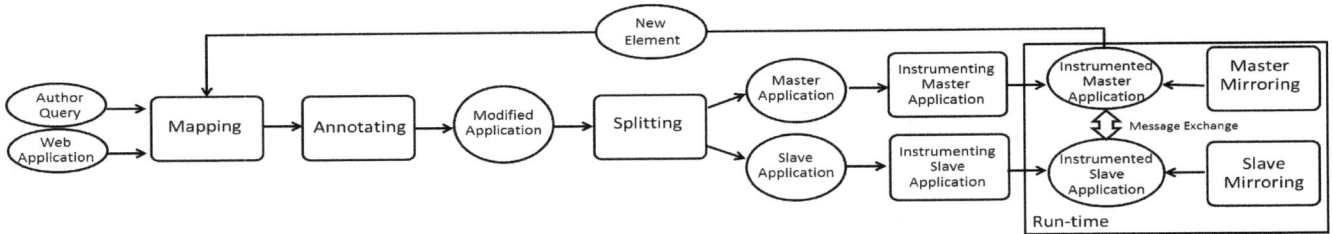

Figure 1: Virtual Splitter Architecture

ual mapping for each XML element of the application. In his research, Cheng [3] proposed a virtual browser capable of separating the application logic from its rendering. The logic is kept within a virtual web page. Automatically the virtual browser splits the main DOM tree into multiple DOM trees and maps these trees to corresponding devices as denoted in a hint file that is specific to each application and manually created by the developer. Cross-device operations are executed in a centralized manner depending ultimately on the browser. Bassbouss et al.[2] outlined how to enable traditional applications to become multi-screen-ready. The application is developed as a single-screen application and requires a multi-screen enabled browser. Based on metadata information provided manually by the developer, specific elements are assigned to a remote device while always being shown on the main device.

In contrast to [3] and [5] our system has a decentralized architecture. Similar to [2] it delivers master-slave applications. The common part for the three previous works is that each application is analyzed and mapped separately and manually by the author (via a hint file or metadata). This means there is no generic analysis method that can be applied to a set of applications. On the contrary, we propose an extensible system that is capable of automatically analyzing the application and mapping its elements, thus simplifying the author's task and involving the end user in mapping her application. The author only has to determine the analysis criterion.

## 3. THE VIRTUAL SPLITTER

### 3.1 Overview

A web application consists mainly of HTML, CSS and JavaScript (JS) resources, that are tightly linked. Links exist between elements in the DOM tree (e.g., parent-child, siblings), between the DOM and JS when the JS accesses elements by specific attributes (e.g., id) or by document navigation, between the DOM and the CSS via selectors, etc. In such a context, splitting an application will break some links and cause a failure in the application look and functionality.

In addition, an application presents two dynamic aspects that make the splitting approach more complicated. On one side, splitting a web application requires support for its dynamism since elements are continuously modified, created, moved or removed during runtime. Supporting this dynamism during run-time is essential to ensure the coherence between elements in each of the distributed application. On the other side, automatic partitioning of the application script is a hard task since JS is a flexible and dynamic language characterized by high-order functions, closures, 'eval' function which dynamically evaluates a string expression,

etc. In this paper, we take care of the links and dynamicity of the application by focusing on splitting only the HTML document, maintaining links and providing a dynamic splitting phase during run-time while keeping the JS code as a whole running on one device. The following subsections present a detailed description of the virtual splitter architecture as illustrated in Figure 1.

### 3.2 HTML Elements Mapping

The mapping phase is the first phase in our system. Its purpose is to determine which of the application elements map to the devices involved in the multi-screen experience. In any multiscreen scenario, at least two devices are cooperating. The literature refers to the smartTV as the first screen and assigns the expression 'companion screen' [1] or 'second screen' [8] to a device providing a means of interaction with the smartTV services. In this work, the 'principal device' is responsible of processing the main application logic, while the 'secondary device' receives processing results only if it is concerned. As depicted in Figure 1, the mapping phase takes as input a query from the application author, when the application is pre-processed offline; or from the user, when the whole process of splitting the application is done at run-time. In our approach, we have envisaged several possible mapping techniques: based on the analysis of HTML elements, their associated semantics and roles, discussed in Section 3.2.1; or based on the visual rendering of elements, discussed in Section 3.2.2. These techniques could be also combined. For instance, mapping only interactive elements placed in a certain region of the screen to the secondary device. This phase is extensible and other analysis techniques could be used here. The query can therefore be either a simple query indicating which mapping technique should be used along with its specific parameters (e.g., element category or position); or a combined query using boolean logic. The output of the mapping phase is two lists of elements, one for each device.

#### 3.2.1 Semantic Mapping

As a possible mapping criterion, we describe here a semantic based approach. It is fully automatic, selected by either the author or the user. In the context of multi-screen applications, we analyzed the HTML5 elements defined in the standard to determine their roles and how they could be classified for the purpose of application splitting. We identified four relevant classes: **interactive** elements (i.e., a, area, button, datalist, form, input, keygen, textarea, nav, optgroup, option, output, select), **multimedia** elements (i.e., video, audio, source, track), **non-interactive, non-multimedia visual** elements (i.e., caption, dialog, figcaption, h1 to h6, hgroup, img, kbd, label, legend, object, p, progress) and **other** elements. As part of the query parameters, the author indicates one or more class of elements to be moved to the secondary device depending on the characteristics of the available devices. For instance, if a smartTV is present, the system or the user may decide to move only multimedia elements on that device. As another example, if a touch screen is present, the interactive elements may be moved onto that device. This mapping technique produces the lists of elements as follows. First, for each element of the application, the algorithm compares it to the tag names present in the classes indicated in the author query. If the element falls within the indicated classes, it is added to the secondary device list. If the element is a composite element (i.e., div, table, iframe) the algorithm iterates over the its children first. If there is no match and if the element does not belong to the 'other' class, it is added to the primary device list. Then, the algorithm detects any change in the element basic role by checking its attributes, mainly declarative event listeners (e.g., 'onclick') since they are responsible of making elements interactive. A non-interactive element which role is only displaying content i.e., image, becomes interactive if it has an event listener that lets users interact with it. In addition, we exploit the semantic links that are created between HTML elements (e.g., 'for' attribute) by keeping these elements together in the same list.

### 3.2.2  Screen Region Mapping

We also investigated a region-based approach as a mapping criterion. It is fully automatic but this time based on the application visual rendering. It is selected during runtime by the end-user in her browser. Once the user selects a screen region, the system detects elements within that rectangular region to produce the secondary device list. All other elements are placed in the primary device list.

## 3.3  Annotating Elements

As depicted in Figure 1, the second phase is the annotation. It prepares the application for the splitting phase and takes as input the lists of elements produced by the mapping phase. The annotation algorithm starts by processing each DOM leaf element and sets the value of the 'data-device' attribute to 'device2' for elements in the secondary device list and 'device1' for elements in the primary device list. It should be noted that the previous mapping phase may have populated those lists with only some DOM elements, and not all elements in the tree, for instance only interactive elements or only the elements located in a given region. Thus, each remaining leaf element (resp. parent element) in the DOM tree is annotated with the value of its siblings (resp. its children), if the annotation is the same across siblings (resp. children), or with the value 'dev1&dev2' if they differ, meaning that the element will be present on both devices. As a result, the application is totally annotated: each element contains metadata information, in a 'data-device' attribute, reflecting its target device(s).

## 3.4  Splitting Application Content

After the annotation phase, during run-time, the splitting phase relies on the element metadata information to form two separated applications: a master and a slave application as Figure 1 shows. From the original application, elements annotated with 'device1' or 'dev1&dev2' values are kept visible on the screen of the primary device. Elements annotated with 'device2' value are hidden on the primary device. This

forms the master application. These hidden elements serves as a shortcut whenever the application main logic requires reading or modifying elements of the remote application on the secondary device, thus the term 'virtual splitter'. Elements annotated with 'device2' and 'dev1&dev2' values are extracted from the original application and imported to the new slave application running on the secondary device. On the master application, in addition to the retained original application logic, JS code is added in an instrumentation phase and aims at making the master application capable of working synchronously with its slave (see Section 3.5). This code also supports the application dynamism and ensures a dynamic mapping and splitting at run-time. On the slave application, the JS code makes the application capable of collecting user interactions, redirecting them to the master, receiving and integrating changes made to its DOM tree.

## 3.5  Mirroring Application Contents

The virtual splitting phase described in Section 3.4 duplicates some content between the master and slave applications. The role of the mirroring phase is to ensure that the slave application has a DOM tree that is an accurate mirror of the hidden DOM tree in the master application. It is performed as follows: On the 'primary device', any dynamic change affecting elements of the 'secondary device' (e.g., node modification, removal or creation) is mirrored to that device through change messages. Upon receiving a message, the application running on the 'secondary device' updates its DOM tree and integrates this change. On the 'secondary device', any user interaction (e.g., clicks, data inputs) is captured and propagated to the 'principal device' where the interaction handler is processed.

## 4.  IMPLEMENTATION AND RESULTS

## 4.1  Implementation

We decided to implement the virtual splitter as a Google Chrome extension, first to enable on-the-fly instrumentation of the application without having to change the application itself, and second for the better debugging environment compared to the situation on devices. Master and slave applications are rendered as tabs in the browser and communication between them is done using the postMessage API that is similar to the communication mechanism in COLTRAM[4].

As discussed in Section 3.5, to detect relevant changes in the DOM we use the Mutation Summary library[1] which is based on the working draft of the Mutation Observer API [2]. A Mutation-Summary object is configured to watch changes made to elements with 'device2' annotation. If any change happens to these elements, their descendants or attributes, the extension sends a message to the 'secondary device'. The message contains a list of changes. Each change object consists of the type of change, the concerned node, its position in the DOM tree (i.e., parent and previous sibling node), the concerned attribute(s) and the new value of a text node. However, the Mutation Summary library suffers from some limitations. For instance, it cannot detect changes made to HTML elements using JS functions especially if they are not reflected on the DOM tree. To overcome this limitation, as well as supporting dynamism, we use the Monkey Patching

---

[1]see http://code.google.com/p/mutation-summary
[2]see http://www.w3.org/TR/domcore

(a) Main Application      (b) Master Application      (c) Slave Application

Figure 2: Splitting The Semantic Video Application Based On The Screen-Region Criterion

technique [7], to extend in JS some native browser functions with custom code, in particular: the 'createElement' function is extended to detect the creation of new elements and to trigger dynamically the mapping, annotation and splitting of these elements; the 'setAttribute' function to update the Mutation Summary configuration, to enable the mirroring of newly created attributes; and the 'addEventListener' function to overcome the limitation of the Mutation Summary library, and to replace an event handler triggered on the slave application to a call to the master application.

## 4.2 Results and Discussion

We tested our system on different applications from simple static pages to dynamic applications, among them: a semantic video application[3], relying on the Popcorn and JQuery libraries and showing various information (e.g., map, text, images) synchronized with a video. We first used the region-based mapping. On the video application, we separated the video and Flick'r images from the additional information as Figure 2 shows. This experiment verified the performance of the mirroring phase by maintaining a reliable mirror and the synchronization between both master and slave applications. In addition, no compatibility issues were reported between our instrumented code and the JS libraries. We then used the semantic mapping to split a YouTube page and to separate the interactive class of elements from the other classes (i.e., non-interactive and multimedia). As a result, the video runs on the master with all the comments of users while all buttons, anchors, guide container that proposes additional videos to watch later are moved to the secondary device.

Based on this, we identified a few areas for future improvement. This includes mainly the re-organization of application layout based on devices screen characteristics, the solving of some problems related to the use of relative URLs, the handing of HTML elements such as Canvas that have no inner DOM representation but are controlled by JS code. We will also conduct more systematic testing and validation.

## 5. PERSPECTIVES AND CONCLUSIONS

In the multi-screen context, this paper proposed a system to transform existing applications from single-screen to multi-screen applications based on author or user choices. The system consists of an automatic and extensible mapping phase that analyzes the application semantically, visually or a combination of these two, an annotation and a virtual splitting phase that result in master-slave appli-

cations. A mirroring phase ensures the correct functionality and synchronization between both parts and a dynamic splitting process. We validated our system on two existing applications: YouTube and semantic-video, and we verified the correct content mapping, synchronization and application functionality. As a future step, we aim at implementing our system in the COLTRAM multi-screen platform and extending this system with a context driven splitting technique that collects information concerning involved devices and creates dynamically adaptive mapping criteria.

## 6. REFERENCES

[1] S. Basapur, H. Mandalia, S. Chaysinh, Y. Lee, N. Venkitaraman, and C. Matcalf. FANFEEDS: Evaluation of socially generated information feed on second screen as a tv show companion. In *EuroiTV '12 Proceedings of the 10th European Conference on Interactive TV and Video*, pages 87–96, Berlin, 2012.

[2] L. Bassbouss, M. Tritschler, S. Steglich, K. Tanaka, and Y. Miyazaki. Towards a multi-screen application model for the web. In *IEEE 37th Annual Computer Software and Applications Conference Workshops*, pages 528–533, Japan, July 2013.

[3] B. Cheng. Virtual browser for enabling multi-device web applications. In *Proceedings of the Workshop on Multi-device App Middleware*, Montreal, Quebec, December 2012.

[4] J.C. Dufourd, M. Tritschler, L. Bassbouss, R. Bouazizi, and S. Steglich. An open platform for multiscreen services. In *In the 11th European Interactive TV conference EuroITV*, Como, Italy, 2013.

[5] R. Han, V. Perret, and M. Naghshineh. Websplitter: A unifed xml framework for multi-device collaborative web browsing. In *Proceedings of the 2000 ACM Conference on Computer Supported Cooperative Work*, pages 221–230, Philadelphia, USA, December 2000.

[6] J. Jang, H. Nam, and Y. Kim. Mobile device-controlled live streaming traffic transfer for multi-screen services. In *IEEE International Conference on Information Networking*, pages 415 – 420, Bali, February 2012.

[7] B.S. Lerner, H. Venter, and D. Grossman. Supporting dynamic, third-party code customizations in javascript using aspects. *SIGPLAN Not.*, 45(10):361–376, 2010.

[8] E. Tsekleves, L. Cruickshank, A. Hill, K. Kondo, and R. Whitham. Interacting with digital media at home via a second screen. In *9th IEEE International Symposium on Multimedia*, pages 201–206, December 2007.

---

[3]see http://popcornjs.org/demo/semantic-video

# SimSeerX: A Similar Document Search Engine

Kyle Williams‡, Jian Wu‡, C. Lee Giles†‡
‡Information Sciences and Technology, †Computer Science and Engineering
The Pennsylvania State University, University Park, PA 16802, USA
kwilliams@psu.edu, jxw394@ist.psu.edu, giles@ist.psu.edu

## ABSTRACT

The need to find similar documents occurs in many settings, such as in plagiarism detection or research paper recommendation. Manually constructing queries to find similar documents may be overly complex, thus motivating the use of whole documents as queries. This paper introduces SimSeerX, a search engine for similar document retrieval that receives whole documents as queries and returns a ranked list of similar documents. Key to the design of SimSeerX is that is able to work with multiple similarity functions and document collections. We present the architecture and interface of SimSeerX, show its applicability with 3 different similarity functions and demonstrate its scalability on a collection of 3.5 million academic documents.

## Categories and Subject Descriptors

H.3.3 [**Information Storage And Retrieval**]: Information Search and Retrieval; I.7.5 [**Document and Text Processing**]: Document Capture—*Document Analysis*

## General Terms

Design, Experimentation

## Keywords

Similarity search; document similarity; query by document

## 1. INTRODUCTION

Search engines have simplified the way in which information is discovered. By submitting queries that capture an information need, relevant information can efficiently be found on the Web and in document collections. In the majority of cases, these queries are constructed based on keywords that are related to a topic of interest; however, a difficulty often arises in constructing queries for complex information needs. To address this problem, search methodologies such as content-based information retrieval have been developed where the queries are based on the *content* of digital objects.

Similar document search is a type of content-based information retrieval where the goal is to find documents that are *similar* to a query document. The definition of document similarity depends on the application. For instance, document similarity might be defined as documents that are about related topics or have overlapping text.

Traditionally, to find similar files, users construct queries that are submitted to an information retrieval system; however, as already mentioned, in many cases it may not be obvious to the user how they should construct queries from a document in order to retrieve the type of similar documents that they are looking for or, when the user does know how to construct the query, the complexity of actually constructing the query may be a limiting factor. A content-based search method known as *Query by Document (QBD)* attempts to overcome these problems by allowing users to submit whole documents as queries to an information retrieval system which then returns a ranked list of similar documents based on a pre-defined similarity function [12].

In this paper, we present SimSeerX[1], a similar document search engine framework. SimSeerX can be used to find similar files in a collection of documents and can support many different types of similarity scoring functions and document collections. SimSeerX incorporates a pseudo relevance feedback mechanism in the form of recursive search whereby the results of a search are used to formulate queries for additional searches. The recursive search may return additional results that were not retrieved by the original query and all results can be combined and ranked. SimSeerX has applications in a number of domains, such as plagiarism detection [4], near duplicate detection [13] and research paper recommendation. It can also be used to compare and evaluate new similarity functions that can be plugged into the system.

## 2. RELATED WORK

There have been many systems designed to retrieve similar documents with most focusing on specific use cases. An early system involved retrieving similar documents from the Web [10]. Signatures based on representative sentences of query documents are submitted to a search engine and the returned results are labelled as candidate documents. The documents are then compared to the query document using shingles and Patricia trees. Govindaraju et al. [5] extract key phrases from documents and submit them as queries to a search engine. The extracted key phrases are based on co-occurrences of words and the results that are returned are

---

[1]http://simseerx.ist.psu.edu

scored based on the Jaccard similarity of the keywords and key phrases of the query document and the returned results. Dasdan et al. [3] designed a similarity system based on querying a search engine interface. Queries are constructed based on the least frequent terms in the document and the similarity of the returned documents is calculated based on shingle similarity.

Similar document search can also be applied to different types of documents. For instance, Pera et al. developed a book recommender for K-12 users [9]. In addition to traditional content similarity, Pera et al. also considered the readability of books. Weng et al [12] formalize query by document as a document decomposition problem where the representation of a document is based on decomposing it into a feature vector as well as other information. Topics are used as features, which are supplemented with keywords that are used for the ranking. While SimSeerX does not use the same features as this approach, it does make use of the document representation for indexing and retrieval.

# 3. THE SIMSEERX SYSTEM

The SimSeerX system is made up of the user interface, the index subsystem and the query subsystem.

## 3.1 User Interface

As previously stated, SimSeerX supports multiple similarity functions and thus the first decision a user can make when using SimSeerX is which similarity function they wish to use when searching. Currently, SimSeerX supports three different similarity functions but it is possible to add more. When a similarity function has been selected, options specific to that similarity function appear. These options include search parameters as well as the ranking method that should be used. The user also has the option to select the recursive depth at which to search, which is referred to as the number of hops. Lastly, the user submits a file.

Figure 1 shows the results page that is displayed after the user conducts the search. The results show metadata that is automatically extracted from the query document, options to re-run the search with different options and a ranked list of results.

## 3.2 Document Representation

The ability of SimSeerX to work with multiple similarity signatures is based on the document representation. In SimSeerX, each document is decomposed into a series of components [12]. Each document $d$ is represented by $d = \mathbb{X} + m + \epsilon$, where $\mathbb{X}$ is a set of document signatures, $m$ is document metadata, and $\epsilon$ is other document information. $X$ should be constructed in such a way that the following conditions are satisfied as best possible: if documents $A$ and $B$ are similar (a binary judgment), then (1) $|\mathbb{X}_A \cap \mathbb{X}_B| \geq 1$; and, by extension, if documents $A$ and $B$ are not similar then, ideally, (2) $|\mathbb{X}_A \cap \mathbb{X}_B| = \varnothing$. (1) serves to ensure that similar documents can be retrieved based on their signatures alone, whereas (2) serves to minimize the number of comparisons made between non-similar documents. SimSeerX can be used with any similarity function that allows for documents to be decomposed this way since the document signatures $\mathbb{X}$ can be used for indexing and retrieval.

Using this document representation, the indexing, querying, and ranking processes are then described by:

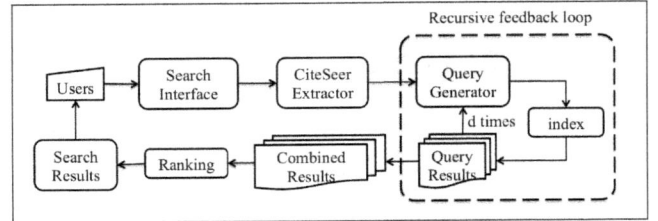

**Figure 2: The SimSeerX workflow.**

**Indexing.** Index every document in C in a standard information retrieval index $I$: $\forall d \in C, index(X, m, \epsilon)$ in $I$.

**Querying.** For a query document $d_q = X + m + \epsilon$, retrieve the set of candidate similar documents $S$ from the index using the document signatures as queries: $S = query(X_{d_q}, I)$.

**Ranking.** Score each document $d$ in $S$ using a scoring function $sim(\cdot)$ that calculates the similarity between $d$ and $d_q$: $\forall d \in S, sim(d, d_q)$, where $sim(\cdot)$ might take into consideration any of $X, m, \epsilon$. Return $S$ sorted by score in descending order.

## 3.3 Indexing Subsystem

The indexing subsystem indexes each document in order to allow for similar files to be retrieved based on document signatures. Each document to be indexed is preprocessed, which involves tokenization, punctuation removal, conversion to lower case and possibly stemming. Signatures are then constructed for each document and indexed in a Lucene index, along with metadata and other information that may be necessary to calculate the full similarity of the documents with a given query document. The only difference between the type of indexing that takes place in most search engines and the indexing that takes place here, is that here the focus is on indexing document signatures for retrieval.

## 3.4 Query Subsystem

The query subsystem encapsulates the SimSeerX workflow, which is shown in Figure 2. The subsystem receives a document as a query and returns a ranked list of similar documents. Querying involves document submission, preprocessing, query signature construction, candidate retrieval, and re-ranking. A document undergoes automatic information extraction when it is submitted, which might involve text extraction if the document is a PDF as well as metadata extraction. SimSeerX makes use of CiteSeerExtractor [14] to perform text and metadata extraction. CiteSeerExtractor provides an API that performs various types of extraction, such as text, header, and citation extraction.

Once the text and metadata have been extracted from the document, queries are automatically constructed and used to query the index along with any query parameters that the user might specify. The Solr instance that SimSeerX is based on has been modified to support custom ranking functions for different types of similarity queries (discussed in Section 4). Thus, documents are retrieved based on their signatures and ranked using an appropriate ranking function. SimSeerX also includes a general ranking function whereby each result can be ranked by its cosine similarity with the original query document. Finally, the ranked results are returned to the user.

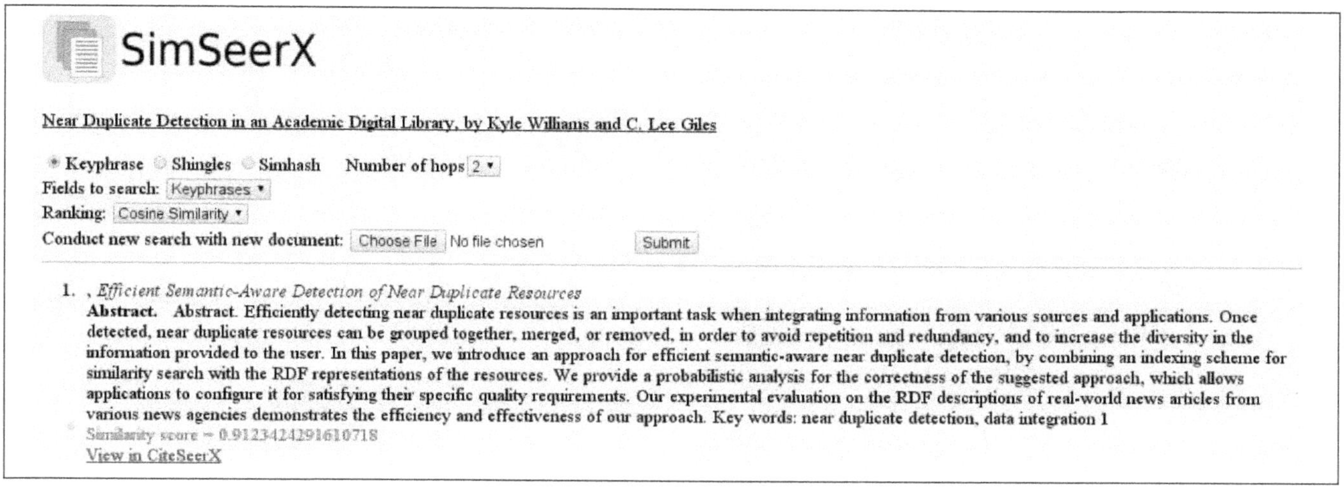

1. , *Efficient Semantic-Aware Detection of Near Duplicate Resources*
**Abstract.** Abstract. Efficiently detecting near duplicate resources is an important task when integrating information from various sources and applications. Once detected, near duplicate resources can be grouped together, merged, or removed, in order to avoid repetition and redundancy, and to increase the diversity in the information provided to the user. In this paper, we introduce an approach for efficient semantic-aware near duplicate detection, by combining an indexing scheme for similarity search with the RDF representations of the resources. We provide a probabilistic analysis for the correctness of the suggested approach, which allows applications to configure it for satisfying their specific quality requirements. Our experimental evaluation on the RDF descriptions of real-world news articles from various news agencies demonstrates the efficiency and effectiveness of our approach. Key words: near duplicate detection, data integration 1
Similarity score = 0.9123424291610718
View in CiteSeerX

Figure 1: The SimSeerX results page.

# 4. SIMILARITY IN SIMSEERX

SimSeerX currently implements three similarity functions that can be used to find similar documents: key phrase-based similarity, shingle similarity and simhash similarity.

## 4.1 Key Phrase Similarity

Key phrases provide high level descriptions of documents and can be used for efficient document retrieval and similarity measures [11]. To generate key phrases, the Maui tool [8] is used and trained on the SemEval 2010 dataset. For each document that is indexed by SimSeerX, the top 10 key phrases are extracted and indexed alongside the document. At search time, the top 10 key phrases are extracted from the query document in the same way. These key phrases can be used to query either the key phrases of the indexed documents or the full text of the indexed documents. In both cases, the query is a phrase and the resulting documents are ranked using the standard Lucene ranking function.

## 4.2 Shingle Similarity

Shingles are sequences of tokens (words) in a document and were first introduced as a means for calculating the similarity of documents [1]. For a shingle length $w$, i.e. a sequence of $w$ words, which is also known as a $w$-shingle, the similarity between two documents can be calculated in terms of the number of shingles that they have in common. Given the $w$-shingles of two documents, $d_1$ and $d_2$, the resemblance $R$ of the two documents is given by:

$$R(d_1, d_2) = \frac{S(d_1) \cap S(d_2)}{S(d_1) \cup S(d_2)}, \qquad (1)$$

where $S(d)$ is the set of shingles in document $d$.

The actual similarity measure is not calculated based on the shingles themselves, but rather on a hash of the shingles. Because it is computationally expensive to calculate the similarity of two documents based on all of their shingles, a fixed number of shingles, which is known as a sketch, are selected from each document and the similarity of the two documents is estimated based on the Jaccard similarity of the shingles in their sketch. The calculation of the sketch of a document is done using a technique known as *minhash*.

For a length $w$, the sequences of tokens whose length is $w$ represent the shingles. Then, each shingle, which is represented by the value of its 64-bit Rabin fingerprint is hashed with $h$ hash functions and track is kept of the minimum hash value found for each hash function. The sketch of each document is then represented by its set of $h$ minimum hash values and the resemblance of two documents can be estimated based on the extent to which their sketches overlap [6].

To select shingles we use 84 hash functions in the form of $h(x) = (Ax + B) \mod p$, where $x$ is the Rabin fingerprint of the shingle, $p$ is a large prime, which we set to $2^{64} - 59$, and $A$ and $B$ are random integers in the range $[1, p]$.

During indexing, the sketch of each document is calculated and the shingles of that sketch are indexed. During retrieval, the sketch of the query document is calculated and used to retrieve documents that have a shingle in common with the query document with the ranking of each document calculated by the Jaccard similarity of their sketches.

## 4.3 Simhash Similarity

Simhash [2] is a state of the art near duplicate detection algorithm. Near duplicate detection is a natural application of SimSeerX, where the goal is to retrieve near duplicates to a query document. For each document, the simhash is calculated as follows. A fingerprint $V$ of size $f$ represents each document. Each token (word) $t$ that appears in a document is hashed using the 64-bit Jenkins hash function. Then, if the $i$-th bit of the hash $F_t$ of token $t$ is 1, then the $i$-th bit of $V$ is increased by 1. Conversely, if the $i$-th bit of $F_t$ is 0, then $V$ is decreased by 1. Once all tokens have been processed, $V$ contains both positive and negative numbers at each of its $f$ locations that are the result of the sums of the weights of all of the tokens. Each of the $f$ locations in $V$ is thresholded to either 0 or 1 to create a final bit-hash for $V$.

In simhash two documents are considered as being near duplicates if their simhash Hamming distances is at most $k$. To retrieve documents that have a Hamming distance of at most $k$, we apply an efficient algorithm [7] that has been modified to work with an inverted index as follows. Once the simhash for each document has been calculated, it is partitioned into $k + 1$ sub-hashes and these sub-hashes are

**Table 1: Average time taken (in seconds) using 10 query documents.**

| Data Size | Time (cold/cached) |
|---|---|
| ~3.5 million | 4.74 (0.52)/1.70 (0.27) |
| 2.5 million | 4.26 (0.49)/1.88 (0.25) |
| 1.5 million | 4.23 (0.61)/1.89 (0.32) |

indexed. At query time, the simhash of the query document is also partitioned into $k + 1$ sub-hashes that are used to query the index and retrieve documents that have at least one sub-hash in common with the query document. This method guarantees that all documents whose simhashes differ from the query simhash by $k$ bits will be found since, in the worst case, the differing bits can only occur in $k$ of the sub-hashes and the final similarity between two documents can then be calculated based on the Hamming distance of their full simhashes.

We have briefly introduced the 3 similarity functions that are currently supported by SimSeerX. It is relatively simple to implement additional similarity functions as long as a document can be decomposed into a set of signatures.

## 5. SCALABILITY

To evaluate the scalability of SimSeerX, a snapshot of the CiteSeer$^X$ dataset containing 3,577,543 documents was used. Evaluation is performed on subsets of this collection of size $S$ with $S = 1.5M, 2.5M, \sim 3.5M$ (M = million). The time taken to search without recursion was measured using key phrases to search over key phrases. Two results are reported: the search time for a cold start whereby the memory buffers are flushed and the Solr instance restarted before every search run; and the search time for a cached search whereby the search is repeated after it completes the first time. The time reported is the wall time to perform search excluding document upload, extraction and result rendering.

Table 1 shows the mean time and standard deviation for both cold start and cached start search runs, where each search run involves searching with 10 papers from the CiteSeer$^X$ collection. As can be seen from the table, the time taken to conduct the search is relatively consistent regardless of the size of the indexed collection thus suggesting that the system can scale well.

## 6. CONCLUSIONS

We present SimSeerX, a query by document search engine for finding similar documents. SimSeerX was designed so as to allow users to submit full documents as queries in order to find which documents in a collection are most similar according to a predefined similarity function. The overall design of SimSeerX is a modular architecture with various pluggable similarity functions. The key difference between SimSeerX and existing query by document systems is that, while other work has tended to focus on specific query and ranking methods, SimSeerX as a framework provides a generic architecture for query by document for any similarity scoring function. Currently, SimSeerX requires users to submit queries for each similarity function separately. Thus, a future feature could involve displaying the results from different similarity functions side by side or combining them into a single ranked list.

## Acknowledgments

We gratefully acknowledge partial support by the National Science Foundation under Grant No. 1143921.

## 7. REFERENCES

[1] A. Broder, S. Glassman, M. Manasse, and G. Zweig. Syntactic clustering of the Web. *Computer Networks and ISDN Systems*, 29(8-13):1157–1166, 1997.

[2] M. Charikar. Similarity estimation techniques from rounding algorithms. In *ACM symposium on Theory of computing*, pages 380–388, 2002.

[3] A. Dasdan, P. D'Alberto, S. Kolay, and C. Drome. Automatic retrieval of similar content using search engine query interface. In *Proceeding of the 18th ACM conference on Information and knowledge management*, pages 701–710, 2009.

[4] B. Gipp and N. Meuschke. Citation pattern matching algorithms for citation-based plagiarism detection. In *Proceedings of the 11th ACM symposium on Document engineering*, pages 249–258, 2011.

[5] V. Govindaraju and K. Ramanathan. Similar Document Search and Recommendation. *Journal of Emerging Technologies in Web Intelligence*, 4(1):84–93, 2012.

[6] M. Henzinger. Finding near-duplicate web pages. In *Proceedings of the 29th international ACM SIGIR conference on research and development in information retrieval*, pages 284–291, 2006.

[7] G. Manku, A. Jain, and A. D. Sarma. Detecting near-duplicates for web crawling. *Proceedings of the 16th international conference on World Wide Web*, pages 141–149, 2007.

[8] O. Medelyan, V. Perrone, and I. H. Witten. Subject Metadata Support Powered by Maui. In *Proceeding of the 10th annual international ACM/IEEE joint conference on Digital libraries*, pages 407–408, 2010.

[9] M. Pera and Y. Ng. Brek12: A book recommender for k-12 users. In *Proceedings of the 35th international ACM SIGIR conference on research and development in information retrieval*, pages 1037–1038, 2012.

[10] A. Pereira and N. Ziviani. Retrieving similar documents from the web. *Journal of Web Engineering*, 2(4):247–261, 2004.

[11] R. Shams and R. E. Mercer. Investigating Keyphrase Indexing with Text Denoising. In *Proceeding of the 12th annual international ACM/IEEE joint conference on Digital libraries*, pages 263–266, 2012.

[12] L. Weng, Z. Li, R. Cai, Y. Zhang, Y. Zhou, L. T. Yang, and L. Zhang. Query by document via a decomposition-based two-level retrieval approach. In *Proceedings of the 34th international ACM SIGIR conference on research and development in information retrieval*, pages 505–514, 2011.

[13] K. Williams and C. L. Giles. Near duplicate detection in an academic digital library. In *Proceedings of the 2013 ACM symposium on Document engineering*, pages 91–94, 2013.

[14] K. Williams, L. Li, M. Khabsa, J. Wu, P. C. Shih, and C. L. Giles. A Web Service for Scholarly Big Data Information Extraction. In *Proceedings of the IEEE International Conference on Web Services*, 2014.

# Pagination: It's What You Say, Not How Long It Takes To Say It

Joshua Hailpern
HP Labs
Palo Alto, CA, USA
joshua.hailpern@hp.com

Niranjan Damera Venkata
HP Labs
Chennai, Tamil Nadu, India
niranjan.damera-venkata@hp.com

Marina Danilevsky
University of Illinois
Urbana, IL, USA
danilev1@illinois.edu

## ABSTRACT

Pagination - the process of determining where to break an article across pages in a multi-article layout - is a common layout challenge for most commercially printed newspapers and magazines. To date, no one has created an algorithm that determines a minimal pagination break point based on the content of the article. Existing approaches for automatic multi-article layout focus exclusively on maximizing content (number of articles) and optimizing aesthetic presentation (e.g., spacing between articles). However, disregarding the semantic information within the article can lead to overly aggressive cutting, thereby eliminating key content and potentially confusing the reader, or setting too generous of a break point, thereby leaving in superfluous content and making automatic layout more difficult. This is one of the remaining challenges on the path from manual layouts to fully automated processes that still ensure article content quality. In this work, we present a new approach to calculating a document minimal break point for the task of pagination. Our approach uses a statistical language model to predict minimal break points based on the semantic content of an article. We then compare 4 novel candidate approaches, and 4 baselines (currently in use by layout algorithms). Results from this experiment show that one of our approaches strongly outperforms the baselines and alternatives. Results from a second study suggest that humans are not able to agree on a single "best" break point. Therefore, this work shows that a semantic-based lower bound break point prediction is necessary for ideal automated document synthesis within a real-world context.

## Categories and Subject Descriptors

I.7.2 [**Document Preparation**]: Desktop Publishing; I.7.4 [**Document and Text Processing**]: Electronic Publishing

## Keywords

Pagination; Truncation; Novelty; Semantic; Cut; SLM

## 1. INTRODUCTION

Traditional document composition is an iterative process involving copy editors and professional publication designers who work in concert to make decisions on what content to include and how to format it for aesthetic presentation. Within the context of newspapers or magazines, each page can contain multiple articles. However, space constraints dictate that the full text of any (or all) given articles can not be presented on a single page. Articles are therefore broken or paginated across a paper. The first portion of an article is presented upfront, while the full text is presented later on, should the reader wish to consume more. Copy editors and designers work to strike a balance between presenting enough content on this front page so readers can understand the article, while maximizing the space constraints and aesthetic presentation of the page as a whole.

Automated document composition algorithms have been introduced to automate this largely manual workflow. Current approaches to automated document synthesis/layout focus extensively on content and aesthetic maximization [17, 18]. These optimization algorithms work with a series of rules and constrains to maximize the presentation within the spatial and visual constraints.

While these approaches have largely been successful at addressing issues of presentation, they do not take into account the content of the articles. This can result in break points being set too aggressively, resulting in missing key content and a potential misrepresentation of the article content, or too late in the article, potentially lowering the flexibility of layout algorithms by requiring more content to be placed on the front page. To combat these problems, many of these layout algorithms enforce minimal content requirements. However, these rules are arbitrary, consisting of static or relative lower bounds (e.g., at least 2 sentences, or at least 20% of the article). Given that these rules are not related to the *actual* article, key content can still be left out, or excess text may still be forced to be included.

The primary contribution of this work is an algorithm that predicts a lower-bound break point for news article pagination based upon the semantic information contained within the article. Our approach not only outperforms existing solutions, but to the authors' knowledge, is also the first such semantic based pagination algorithm.

In this paper we develop four candidate break point algorithms, all of which are based on the semantic information of an article to be paginated. These four approaches are then directly compared against four baselines currently used in both print and digital media. To facilitate these comparisons, we conduct an extensive Mechanical Turk study across 7 subject areas (Sports, US News, Entertainment, etc). Results from this experiment show that one of our approaches strongly outperforms the baselines and alternatives. We also investigate whether an 'ideal' break point could be found for paginating news articles. Results from a large CrowdFlower study strongly suggest that humans can not agree on a single best break point. Therefore, this work shows that a semantic-based lower bound break point prediction is necessary for ideal for automated document synthesis within a real-world context.

## 2. RELATED WORK

The majority of work on pagination - the need to split a document or series of documents over multiple pages - focuses on content maximization and aesthetic presentation. Such approaches aim to create 'high-quality documents,' defined as documents 'without unwanted empty areas' [7]. Within the context of a single document, such as a book or a paper, pagination impacts the layout relationship of text content to related figures or tables [5].

However, the problem complexity greatly increases for automated document layout of newspapers or magazines[12, 17, 18]. In addition to optimizing the placement of figures within text, a given page can also contain content from multiple articles, and all content must fit within a predetermined page count. When determining how to break up articles across multiple pages, the preferred approach is to use constraint-based layout models, in which layout specifications are described by linear constraints imposed on the items within a layout [2, 19, 23, 29, 35]. The focus of these models is on the composition quality [1, 8], and they in no way account for the semantic information contained within the articles themselves.

### 2.1 Automatic Summarization

A similar problem to pagination is that of single document summarization - the process by which the text of an article is reduced either by extraction (lifting sentences from the original text)[24] or abstraction (using natural language processing techniques to generate new sentences)[11]. While these approaches are not used by layout or copy editors, they are relevant to the construction and evaluation of our semantic-based break point techniques.

Corpus summarization uses a large collection of documents to build a model of the topics being discussed (e.g. topic modeling [4, 6], SumBasic[13], KLSum[26]) or opinions rendered (e.g. Opinion Mining [15]). Corpus summarization approaches rely upon a large body of documents (e.g., a collection of tweets [6]) from which patterns about the 'whole' can be derived, and are generally easier and more powerful because they have more data from which to draw summaries. In contrast, single document summarization [22, 21] utilizes only one document to create a summary. Within single document summarization, most algorithms are designed to summarize long (e.g. book)[34], well structured (e.g. chapters or sections) text[9, 30, 33], thus maximizing the amount of text and structural cues from which to derive summaries. The most notable exceptions to single unstructured documents are TextRank[24] and LexRank[10]. Both of these algorithms use a simple graph-based approach, treating each sentence as a node. The summary sentence of the document is calculated by finding the centroid of the graph based on a distance vector. There has been some work specifically with summarizing news articles by extracting the most important facts from the article [20]. Finally, it has shown that using the first n sentences of a news article as the article's summary performs very well [25], which adds motivation to our end goal.

### 2.2 Document Sub-Topic Segmentation

Another tangential, though different, problem space is that of document sub-topic segmentation, most notably Text-Tiling [16, 27]. The main focus of Sub-Topic Segmentation is to divide a document into subtopics, or sections. These sections are not ranked, as to importance or quality, but strive to focus on conceptual shifts in the content being discussed. TextTiling is a straightforward and simplistic [3] method the examines lexical co-occurred of terms between phrases in a document, and identifying sharp changes as breaks or dividers between subtopics. However, because these approaches lack of ranking or quality of each sub-topic shift, their direct application to the pagination problem are limited and a direct comparison of TextTiling with this problem is difficult. However, this work does suggest techniques or broad approaches we can build upon; detecting breaks based on semantic change variation across a document relative to a mean change, using occurrent of vocabulary to signify information/theme [16].

## 3. SCOPING & KEY TERMS

The goal of this work is to create and test a novel algorithm that can use a news article's semantics (rather than layout/spacing optimization) to determine a lower bound where to break an article for pagination. This serves two key purposes: first, if an article is broken too early, the reader may miss key information and potentially be mislead about the article's content; second, if too much of an article's content is forced to be shown, the page layout may not be as flexible because more text would be required to be presented therefore, there may not be space to present as many articles on the front page.

While there are many applications of this technique, this work specifically looks at news articles. Our novel approaches draw on and compare with pagination techniques both in print and digital presentation.

In this context, we define the following terms:

**Topic:** Refers to the use in the english vernacular, such as the topic of a news article (e.g. a specific bomb that goes off in a specific country on a specific day), rather as it is used in the context of Topic Modeling approaches.

**Article:** A piece of written text about a specific topic (e.g. a specific New York Times article about a bomb that went off in a country).

**Break Point:** The location at which you 'break' or stop an article, such that the content before the break point is displayed on the current page, and the content after the break point goes on a different page, or after a 'read more' link.

**Lower Bound Break Point:** The location within a news article denoting that the reader would have, by this time, gained a general understanding about the topic being discussed, but has not yet seen all the details or nuances. Breaking before this lower bound is likely to cause the reader to miss a key concept or aspect of the article, and risk being mislead about the content. However, if more space is available, a layout algorithm can choose to include more text from a given article.

**Pagination:** the task of determining where to break an article across a multi-article, multi-page layout.

**Corpus:** A collection of articles on the same topic (e.g. 100 news articles about a specific bombing event).

**Subject:** An overarching thematic grouping of articles or corpuses (e.g. Sports, Politics)

**Document:** Any set of sentences, which could be a single article, a subset of an article, multiple articles, a Corpus or Subject, etc.

**Semantics:** Refers to the english definition of "semantics," focusing on the *meaning* of words or phrases.

**It should be noted that there is an important distinction between pagination (the focus of this paper) and truncation (not discussed in this paper – see [14]).** Pagination, as used in this context, implies that after the break point, a reader will see more of the given article, usually on a subsequent page. On the contrary, when an article is truncated, the portion of the article which follows the break point will never be presented to the reader in any form. We do *not* deal with truncation tasks in this work. Further, this work does not perform document summarization, or sub-topic identification. These approaches can be used to inform our design, but the functionally address and solve a different problem and their output is not directly comparable to the output of pagination.

In this paper, we first describe the algorithms developed for content-aware pagination, as well as the baselines for comparison. Next, we present our experiment comparing the quality of the suggested break points based on article content. Finally, we briefly explore the challenges of predicting an 'ideal' break point in a document.

## 4. LOWER BOUND ALGORITHMS

The primary goal of this works is to develop and compare algorithms that can predict a lower bound break point for pagination of news articles. This section details the four content-agnostic algorithms that are used as 'current state' baselines, as well as our novel predictive algorithms that directly leverage the semantic content of the articles.

### 4.1 Four Baselines

To facilitate a comparison, we leveraged four baselines that are commonly used as lower-bounds for pagination: the first sentence, the first two sentences, the first paragraph, and the first twenty percent of the article.

#### 4.1.1 One & Two Sentences

Commonly used in online news websites (e.g. Google News, NBCNews.com), the first or first two sentences of a news article are used to 'preview' the full text. Thus, pagination occurs after these sentences, and the reader can consume the full text by clicking a link[1]. We refer to these two techniques as **One Sentence** and **Two Sentences**, respectively.

#### 4.1.2 One Paragraph

While writing, a structurally delimiter between semantic concepts is often the paragraph break. Thus, the first paragraph of an article can be thought of as the first digestible nugget of an article's content and may make a natural break point. This is used at Wall Street Journal's website (wsj.com) for non-subscribers who seek to access subscriber only articles. We will refer to this as **One Paragraph**.

#### 4.1.3 Twenty Percent Rounded Up to Nearest Paragraph

When constructing printable newspapers, many sources use an article length dependent approach. Minimal breakpoints are calculated by the first 20% of a document (measured by character count), then rounded up to the end of the current paragraph. This approach assumes that within the first fifth of a document, key concepts have been presented to the reader, and are roughly bounded by paragraph delimitation. We refer to this technique as **Twenty Percent**.

### 4.2 Keyword Novelty

The first approach we develop is predicated on the idea that as a reader traverses through a document, he or she is exposed to key concepts/words. First exposure to a given key word is enough to make the reader aware of that subject and that it is relevant to the article[2]. To this end, the Keyword Novelty approach attempts to find when the reader has been exposed to 'enough' of these key words that he or she would have a general understanding of the article.

#### 4.2.1 Calculating Keyword Novelty

The first step is determining what are the key words in a document. Following standard IR techniques, we limit a document's text to information-heavy words (nouns), and remove any pluralization through lemmatization. However, not all of the remaining keywords are equally relevant to the document in question. Commonly, term frequency (TF) can be used as a proxy for keyword relevance. However, TF is generally not robust on shorter or sparse data, such as a single newspaper article.

An alternative technique to discovering keyword important is to use Singular Value Decomposition (SVD). SVD is able to filter out the noise in relatively small or sparse data, and is often used for dimensionality reduction. To repurpose SVD to calculate word weight, we represent each sentence as a row in a sentence-word occurrence matrix encompassing $m$ sentences and $n$ unique words, which we will refer to as $\mathbf{M}$ (which can be constructed in O(m)).

SVD decomposes the $m \times n$ matrix $\mathbf{M}$ into a product of three matrices: $\mathbf{M} = \mathbf{U} \, \Sigma \, \mathbf{V}^*$. $\Sigma$ is a diagonal matrix whose values on the diagonal, referred to as $\sigma_i$, are the singular values of M. By identifying the four largest $\sigma_i$ values, which we

---

[1] It should be noted, that some online websites (e.g. New York Times) create custom one or two sentence previews, rather than drawing them directly from the original text. This research does not examine the quality of these custom hand-crafted previews, which are more akin to single-document summaries.

[2] Exactly how the given subject is related to the full text may not be clear until later in the article.

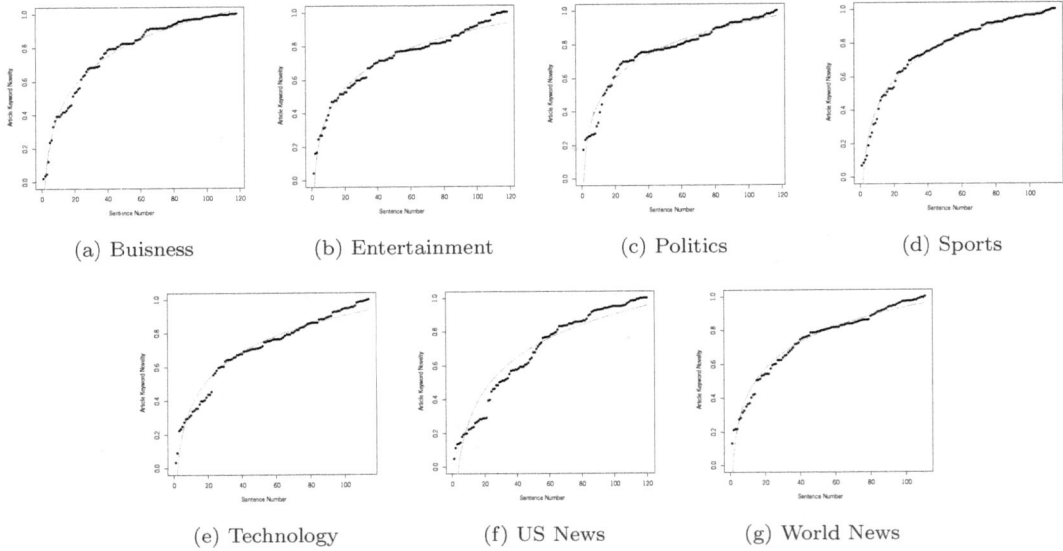

Figure 1: Examples of Article Keyword Novelty Curves
*Points are presented with the resulting regression line in red | Graphs are high resolution best viewed in PDF*

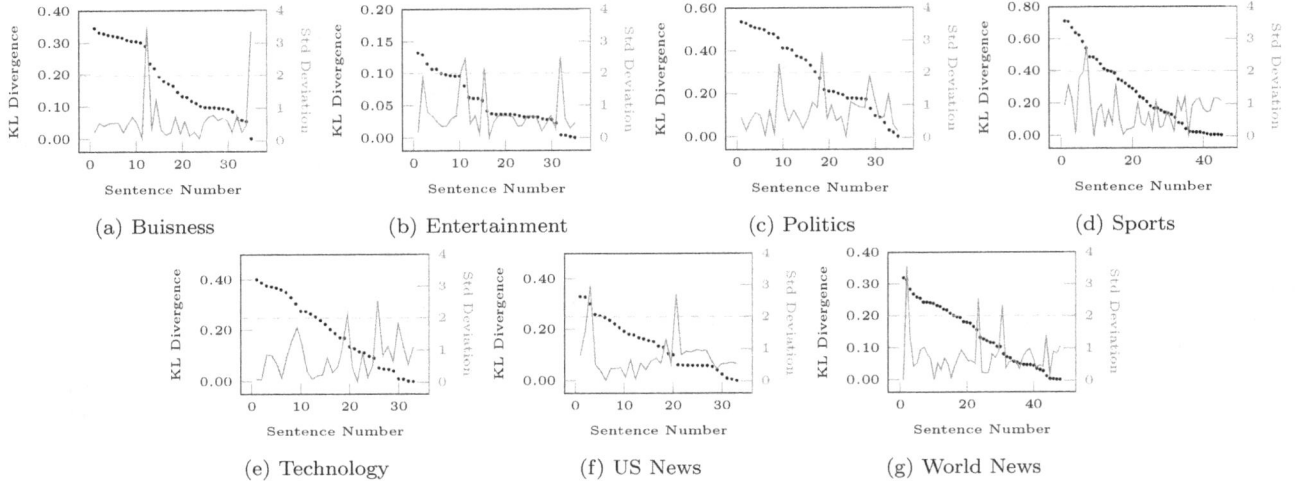

Figure 2: Examples of SLM Article Plots + Std Deviation in Slope Plot
*KL Divergence are Black Points (left axis), Standard Deviations Away in Gray (right axis) | Graphs are high resolution best viewed in PDF*

refer to as $\lambda_1 - \lambda_4$, we are able to take the corresponding top eigenvector columns of V (which is the conjugate transpose of V*), which we refer to as $\xi_1 - \xi_4$. Note that each entry in each of these vectors $\xi_1 - \xi_4$ corresponds to a unique word in **M**.

We then create $\xi'$, a master eigenvector calculated as the weighted average of $\xi_1 - \xi_4$, weighted by $\lambda_1 - \lambda_4$:

$$\xi' = \frac{1}{4} \sum_{i=1}^{4} \lambda_i \xi_i \qquad (1)$$

Thus, $\xi'$ is a vector in which each entry represents a unique word, and the value can be interpreted as the 'centrality' of the word to the given document [34].

Once we have the keyword weights,[3] we iterate over each sentence in a given article. The 'value' of a sentence is the sum of all of the unique keywords' weights seen up to (and including) that sentence. Thus, the weight of a given sentence is a cumulative sum and each keyword only contributes to the overall sum on its first occurrence.

When plotted, the resulting sequence generally fits a logarithmic curve (see Figure 1), allowing us to consider the inflection point as a 'lower bound' break point.[4] The inflection point is an ideal point to paginate in that it is the

---

[3] To reduce noise, we use only the top 500 words from SVD.
[4] To find the inflection point:

1. *Log of the number of sentences (convert to linear)*

2. *Normalize the weights from 0.0 to 1.0*

150

location where the amount of text needed (space) is increasing more than the amount of new concepts (keywords).

### 4.2.2 Article vs. Corpus Novelty

Based on the keyword novelty metric, we created two variations:

- **Article Keyword Novelty:** SVD weights are based on the individual article in question
- **Corpus Keyword Novelty:** SVD weights are based on all articles in a corpus treated as a single document

The corpus approach takes a more holistic view of the topic being discussed, whereas the article approach is more sensitive to the specific issues being addressed in a specific article.

## 4.3 Statistical Language Modeling (SLM)

The second approach we present is based on the idea that there is a probabilistic distribution of words (and their frequencies) that are an 'ideal' we strive to mimic (e.g. the full text of the article, or the distribution of words in a corpus). We use SLM to create a model of the 'ideal' document, and, for a given portion of an article being made visible to the reader, we use an information theoretic measure to discover how closely the model of that article portion comes to the 'ideal' model of the entire document.

An added benefit of the SLM approach is the ability to smooth the keyword frequencies that are to common to the broad subject (in this work we use Dirichlet Prior Smoothing, which has been shown to be effective [36]).

### 4.3.1 Calculating SLM

As in Keyword Novelty, we pre-filter the text in each article to only contain the lemmatized high-information (noun) words.

In order to explain our use of SLM, consider $S$ to be the set of all subjects ($s_0 \dots s_g$) in our dataset. We work with one subject at a time, which we will refer to as $s_i$.

Let $D$ be the set of all articles ($d_0 \dots d_b$) in the given subject $s_i$ and $W$ to be the set of all unique words ($w_0 \dots w_h$) in $s_i$.

Denote the frequency of a given word $w_j$ in a given document $d_k$ as $f(w_j|d_k)$. Then the total count of all words in $d_k$ is calculated as:

$$T(d_k) = \sum_{j=0}^{h} f(w_j|d_k) \qquad (2)$$

and the probability of of a given word ($w_j$) in $d_k$ is:

$$p(w_j|d_k) = \frac{f(w_j|d_k)}{T(d_k)} \qquad (3)$$

This therefore allows us to calculate the probability of a word in a document, using Dirichlet Prior smoothing [36]:

$$q(w_j|d_k) = \frac{f(w_j|d_k) + \mu * p(w_j|s_i)}{T(d_k) + \mu} \qquad (4)$$

where $p(w_j|s_i)$ is the occurrence probability of the word $w_j$ in the entire subject $s_i$:

_____

3. *Create a linear regression with the x-axis to be log of the number of sentences, and y-axis to be normalized sentence weights*

4. *Use the x-axis coefficient (e to the coefficient) as the inflection point*

$$p(w_j|s_i) = \frac{\sum_{d_k \in s_i} f(w_j|d_k)}{\sum_{d_k \in s_i} T(d_k)} \qquad (5)$$

and where the smoothing constant $\mu$ is estimated using [31]:

$$
\begin{aligned}
m_{w_j} &= p(w_j|s_i) \\
B_{w_j} &= \sum_{d_k \in s_i} \left( \left( \frac{f(w_j|d_k)}{T(d_k)} - m_{w_j} \right)^2 \right) \\
\mu &= \frac{\sum_{w_j \in W} \frac{B_j}{m_{w_j} * (1 - m_{w_j})}}{\sum_{w_j \in W} \frac{B_j^2}{m_{w_j}^2 * (1 - m_{w_j})^2}}
\end{aligned} \qquad (6)
$$

As we traverse an article sentence by sentence, we redefine the variable $N$ to refer to the subset of sentences in a given article we have seen. Thus, we calculate the probability of a word in N, using Dirichlet Prior smoothing [36] as:

$$q(w_j|N) = \frac{f(w_j|N) + \mu * p(w_j|s_i)}{T(N) + \mu} \qquad (7)$$

To compare each successive test SLM to the Ideal document, we use the KL-Divergence metric (smaller is better):

$$KLDivergence = \sum_{w_j \in d_k} \left( ln\left( \frac{q(w_j|d_k)}{q(w_j|N)} \right) \right) * q(w_j|d_k) \qquad (8)$$

Thus for each sentence in an article, we can calculate the KLDivergence score, returning another set of distributions. When plotted (x-axis=sentence, y-axis=KLDivergence), these distributions appear relatively linear, with occasional 'jumps' when the models get closer/further apart (for article and corpus respectively). We can detect the first of these 'jumps,' and use it as our break point. To find a jump, we perform the following steps:

1. Calculate the delta in KL-Divergence between having seen $N$ sentences and $N + 1$ sentences, for the entire document.

2. Determine the mean and standard deviation of this set of delta values.

3. if the delta in KL-Divergence between having seen $N$ and $N + 1$ sentences is greater than or equal to 2 standard deviations away from the mean, there a 'jump' after the $N^{th}$ sentence.[5]

### 4.3.2 Variations

As with the keyword novelty metric, we created two variations:

- **Article SLM:** The ideal SLM is generated based upon the full text of the specific article
- **Corpus SLM:** The ideal SLM is generated based on all articles in the Corpus treated as a single document

The corpus approach takes a more holistic view of the topic being discussed, whereas the article approach is more sensitive to the specific issues and phrasing being addressed in a specific article.

_____

[5]We ignore the change between the first and second sentence since, due to many articles having 'low' value first sentences, having almost any content in the second sentence creates a large delta.

| Subject | Total # Corpuses | Total # Articles | $\mu$ Articles per Corpus (sd) |
|---|---|---|---|
| US | 183 | 19429 | 106.17 (52.81) |
| Business | 166 | 19209 | 115.72 (63.45) |
| Politics | 129 | 25094 | 194.53 (122.53) |
| Entertainment | 218 | 30534 | 140.06 (78.70) |
| World | 158 | 20440 | 129.37 (75.59) |
| Sports | 203 | 27463 | 135.29 (65.08) |
| Technology | 232 | 42104 | 181.48 (119.72) |
| All | 1289 | 184273 | 142.96 (90.73) |

Table 1: Data Collected from Google News from 10/13 to 11/13

# 5. MASTER DATASET: ARTICLE COLLECTION

We collected corpuses of news articles by scraping Google News every 8 hours, beginning on October 21 to November 27 2013[6]. Specifically, we collected corpuses from 7 subjects (World News, US News, Entertainment, Business, Technology, Sports and Politics). Corpuses were 'accepted' if they contained at least 50 unique articles. Google News therefore acted as a news aggregator, clustering the articles by topic. From the articles (grouped as a corpus by Google News), we retrieved the source HTML of the original article from the originally hosted website. The body copy of said article was then extracted using CETR [32]. The description of the resulting articles and corpuses can be found in Table 1. To conduct each experiment, we randomly select articles and corpuses from this master dataset.

# 6. EXPERIMENT: MODEL PERFORMANCE

The primary experiment in this paper is to the evaluate ( in terms of break point semantic content) the performance of the 4 baseline lower bound metrics (One Sentence, Two Sentence, One Paragraph, and Twenty Percent) against the 4 lower bound candidate models (Article Keyword Novelty, Corpus Keyword Novelty, Article SLM, Corpus SLM). In this section we introduce the data set, then describe our methods used for comparing the above 8 algorithms for lower bound break point prediction.

## 6.1 Dataset

100 corpuses from each subject were randomly selected from the master dataset, with one article randomly selected from each corpus. This results in 100 articles from each subject, and 700 articles overall. This allows performance to be compared overall, and take into account the varying writing styles and language within each subject area. Summary statistics including Grade Level[7], Reading Level[8], and Fog Index[9] are presented in Table 2.

---

## 6.2 Methods

Amazon Mechanical Turk (MT) HITs were constructed from the 700 articles. A HIT is an individual task given to a person on MT. Each HIT consisted of a brief definition of a break point, the original source text of one article[10] and the 8 candidate break points presented in random order (reducing order effects). Before each sentence in the source text, we inserted the characters '(SX)' where X was the sentence number. We used these indexes to refer to a given break point. For each break point, the participants were asked to respond to the statement *Is (SX) a good Minimal Break Point?* with a 7-point scale (*Too Short - Missing text* (1) to *Balanced* (4) to *Too Long - Extra Text* (7)). Each HIT was completed by 2 Master level Turkers[11], yielding 1400 measures of quality per model (100 articles across 7 areas).

To ensure 'legitimate' HIT completion, one 'sanity check question' was included asking Turkers to find the Nth word in the Mth sentence. In addition, a HIT was rejected if the Turkers' response failed basic logic checks on their responses. First, all responses could not be the same. Second, if a single HIT asked about the same cut point more than once, that specific Turker's response must be the same to both questions (e.g. one Turker rating sentence #4 as a 6 and then rating sentence #4 as a 2 for the same article). Third, ratings must be in chronological order. For example, a sentence early in the document was listed as TOO LONG, and then a sentence later was listed as TOO SHORT, that doesn't make sense. However succeeding break points (in article order) could have the same ranking. If any of the three logic tests or the sanity check are failed, the HIT is rejected and re-posted. Participants were remunerated 30 cents per accepted HIT.

An ANOVA and Student's T-test were used to compare the algorithms' performance. While performing multiple comparisons may suggest statistical adjustment to a more conservative value (i.e., Bonferroni correction), we chose a more transparent method, highlighting multiple thresholds of significance [28]. We further report results and summary statistics broken down by subject area. However, it is outside the scope of this paper to optimize for an individual subject area.

### 6.2.1 Method Limitations

Any evaluation with multiple comparisons has an interaction effect, in that the rating or quality of one break point can be impacted by the other break points offered for comparison. Thus, a break point that might have been rated a 5 (slightly too long) when viewed in isolation, may be pushed 'higher' if there are other, less optimal break points located earlier in the article. Thus, these results must necessarily be viewed in the broader context of the other break points presented.

## 6.3 Results

Cross subject results are presented in Table 3 and results by subject area are in Table 4. ANOVA comparing the 8 algorithms resulted in a highly significant difference p<0.001

---

| | Grade Level | Reading Level | Fog Index | Sentence Count | Word Count | Corpus Size |
|---|---|---|---|---|---|---|
| **Business** | 11.00 (2.68) | 48.54 (8.26) | 7.33 (2.83) | 54.52 (23.96) | 854.57 (151.78) | 112.04 (61.47) |
| **Ent.** | 12.70 (4.18) | 49.60 (13.66) | 10.30 (4.04) | 40.02 (16.27) | 904 (202.95) | 148.71 (82.72) |
| **Politics** | 13.16 (3.03) | 43.64 (10.77) | 9.72 (3.02) | 40.15 (13.61) | 887.93 (148.24) | 187.36 (117.04) |
| **Sports** | 11.00 (7.15) | 58.54 (19.28) | 9.55 (7.39) | 42.11 (13.51) | 875.98 (176.31) | 127.89 (60.35) |
| **Tech.** | 12.23 (4.37) | 49.55 (14.91) | 9.53 (4.19) | 42.31 (15.20) | 903.67 (197.98) | 170.9 (109.85) |
| **US** | 13.14 (3.15) | 45.17 (11.00) | 10.01 (3.12) | 38.83 (12.92) | 893.36 (190.52) | 109.71 (48.98) |
| **World** | 13.97 (3.13) | 40.32 (11.83) | 10.27 (2.95) | 38.93 (12.57) | 925.18 (190.72) | 130.38 (72.28) |
| **All** | 12.46 (4.32) | 47.91 (14.23) | 9.53 (4.30) | 42.41 (16.61) | 892.10 (184.32) | 141.00 (86.56) |

Table 2: Documents Source Statistics
*Mean and Std Values Reported*

| | Algorithm | Mean (sd) | Median |
|---|---|---|---|
| **All Subject Areas** | First Sentence | 1.78 (0.97) | 1.00 |
| | Second Sentence | 2.47 (1.18) | 2.00 |
| | First Paragraph | 2.44 (1.29) | 2.00 |
| | Twenty Percent | 5.19 (1.20) | 5.00 |
| | Novelty Article | 5.83 (1.14) | 6.00 |
| | Novelty Corpus | 5.52 (1.19) | 6.00 |
| | SLM Article | 4.66 (1.76) | 5.00 |
| | SLM Corpus | 4.18 (1.65) | 4.00 |

Table 3: Overall Performance
*Ratings based on a 7-Point scale:*
*(1) "missing information" (4) "balanced" and (7) "excess text."*

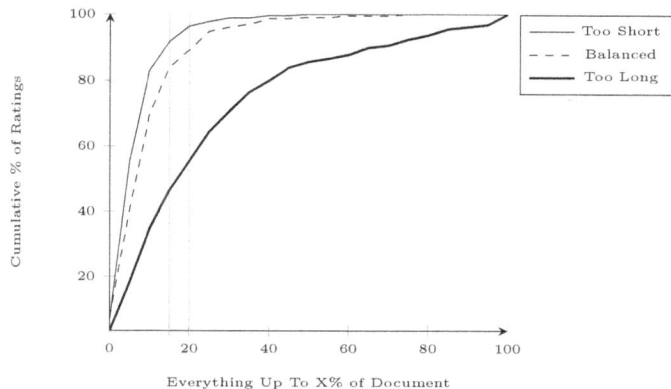

Figure 3: When Failure Occurs
*Gray vertical lines at 15% and 20% for reference*

(F=1977). Pairwise comparative t-tests between algorithms were likewise all highly significant with with p<0.001, the one exception being the comparison between Two Sentences and One Paragraph, which had p=0.264. This similarity may be due to many articles breaking the first paragraph after two sentences.

Overall, the most balanced approach (minimal extra text while retaining enough key content) was SLM Corpus followed closely by SLM Article. The three static baseline approaches (First Sentence, Second Sentence, First Paragraph) were all overly aggressive, cutting too much text and losing key information that was central to the article themselves. The remaining baseline approach (Twenty Percent) and the two Keyword Novelty methods were generally too relaxed with their break point prediction, choosing to break after superfluous text.

### 6.3.1 Results: Correlations

Given the varying readability and length of the articles (Table 2), we wanted to determine if any of those descriptive features influenced the performance of our algorithms. To this end, we tested the performances of each of the 8 algorithms against all readability statistics found in Table 2 using a Spearman's rank test. No correlations were detected for any pairing of algorithm and readability statistic (with Spearman's rho never reaching above 0.2). This suggests that the performances reported in Table 3 & 4 were due to the algorithms themselves, and not the length or readability of the articles.

## 6.4 Discussion: Algorithm Comparison

Overall, the two SLM approaches performed quite well with a mean score of 4.18 and 4.66 for SLM-Corpus and SLM-Article respectively. The improvement in performance between the corpus and article versions is to be expected,

since striving to reach the ideal language model that is the composite of an entire corpus of articles on a topic will smooth out author-specific phrasing, and focus more on the most central key words. However, it is not always realistic to assume that a layout system will have a broader corpus on which to build a more robust language model. Yet SLM Article, which built a language model only from the article, still outperforms the 3 other algorithms with scores above 5 (the two Keyword Novelty approaches, and Twenty Percent).

Given these results, we can also consider First Sentence, Second Sentence, and First Paragraph approaches to be extremely unreasonable for real-world use. When optimizing a document layout, missing key content (score less than 4) is worse than than including extra text (score at or above 4), since by leaving out critical information, the reader can be misinformed.

Thus, using SLM objectively produces minimal break points that are more respectful of the semantic content of the article, preventing over-cutting and misleading the readership. In some situations, these break points are more aggressive than other approaches, potentially saving space while maintaing content readability. Yet overall, whether more or less content is needed for a minimal break point, SLM ensures content readability rather than form (layout) over function (readability).

### 6.4.1 A Closer Look at SLM

Based on the high performance of SLM Corpus, we wanted to determine if there was a group of breakpoints that were

| | Algorithm | Mean (sd) | Median |
|---|---|---|---|
| **Buisness** | First Sentence | 2.12 (1.08) | 2.00 |
| | Second Sentence | 2.83 (1.32) | 3.00 |
| | First Paragraph | 2.78 (1.41) | 3.00 |
| | Twenty Percent | 5.33 (1.23) | 5.00 |
| | Novelty Article | 5.70 (1.11) | 6.00 |
| | Novelty Corpus | 5.61 (1.17) | 6.00 |
| | SLM Article | 4.99 (1.81) | 5.00 |
| | SLM Corpus | 4.47 (1.64) | 5.00 |
| **Entertainment** | First Sentence | 1.43 (0.72) | 1.00 |
| | Second Sentence | 2.08 (0.92) | 2.00 |
| | First Paragraph | 2.24 (1.05) | 2.00 |
| | Twenty Percent | 5.23 (1.10) | 5.00 |
| | Novelty Article | 5.88 (1.03) | 6.00 |
| | Novelty Corpus | 5.42 (1.05) | 6.00 |
| | SLM Article | 4.70 (1.78) | 5.00 |
| | SLM Corpus | 3.82 (1.62) | 3.00 |
| **Politics** | First Sentence | 1.72 (0.93) | 1.00 |
| | Second Sentence | 2.43 (1.17) | 2.00 |
| | First Paragraph | 2.40 (1.31) | 2.00 |
| | Twenty Percent | 5.30 (0.91) | 5.00 |
| | Novelty Article | 5.89 (0.81) | 6.00 |
| | Novelty Corpus | 5.65 (0.94) | 6.00 |
| | SLM Article | 4.79 (1.62) | 5.00 |
| | SLM Corpus | 4.37 (1.48) | 5.00 |
| **Sports** | First Sentence | 1.62 (0.86) | 1.00 |
| | Second Sentence | 2.42 (1.06) | 2.00 |
| | First Paragraph | 2.44 (1.40) | 2.00 |
| | Twenty Percent | 5.40 (1.17) | 6.00 |
| | Novelty Article | 6.12 (1.02) | 6.00 |
| | Novelty Corpus | 5.81 (1.10) | 6.00 |
| | SLM Article | 4.52 (1.65) | 4.00 |
| | SLM Corpus | 4.40 (1.59) | 4.00 |
| **Technology** | First Sentence | 1.82 (0.99) | 1.00 |
| | Second Sentence | 2.50 (1.31) | 2.00 |
| | First Paragraph | 2.47 (1.27) | 2.00 |
| | Twenty Percent | 5.13 (1.33) | 5.00 |
| | Novelty Article | 5.78 (1.32) | 6.00 |
| | Novelty Corpus | 5.27 (1.42) | 6.00 |
| | SLM Article | 4.58 (1.89) | 5.00 |
| | SLM Corpus | 4.10 (1.83) | 4.00 |
| **US News** | First Sentence | 1.74 (0.94) | 1.00 |
| | Second Sentence | 2.39 (1.13) | 2.00 |
| | First Paragraph | 2.27 (1.27) | 2.00 |
| | Twenty Percent | 5.05 (1.17) | 5.00 |
| | Novelty Article | 5.79 (1.15) | 6.00 |
| | Novelty Corpus | 5.50 (1.19) | 6.00 |
| | SLM Article | 4.46 (1.81) | 4.00 |
| | SLM Corpus | 3.90 (1.61) | 4.00 |
| **World News** | First Sentence | 2.02 (1.07) | 2.00 |
| | Second Sentence | 2.64 (1.17) | 2.00 |
| | First Paragraph | 2.49 (1.24) | 2.00 |
| | Twenty Percent | 4.88 (1.33) | 5.00 |
| | Novelty Article | 5.66 (1.39) | 6.00 |
| | Novelty Corpus | 5.37 (1.32) | 6.00 |
| | SLM Article | 4.55 (1.71) | 5.00 |
| | SLM Corpus | 4.20 (1.67) | 4.00 |

Table 4: Performance Per Subject
*Ratings based on a 7-Point scale:*
*(1) "missing information" (4) "balanced" and (7) "excess text."*

indicative of failure, or success. First, we classified the break point ratings as too short (1-3), balanced (4), and too long (5-7). So as to compare across articles (which have varying length), we divided break points into percentage of document intervals (0-5%, 5-10%, etc), and tabulated the number of ratings in each interval for a given class. To compare across the three classes, we must consider the tabulation as a percentage of the total ratings in said class. The results are plotted in Figure 3.

Upon viewing the curves for the three classes, it is worth noting that the 'Too Short' and 'Balanced' curves are almost identical. More specifically, 82% of the failed, 69% of the balanced, and 34% of the too long occur at less than 15% of the document. These results suggest why absolute approaches (e.g. Twenty percent) may not be aggressive enough. Further, these results also indicate that there does not appear to be a universal lower threshold below which we are assured to be 'too short.' Thus, having adaptive algorithms that are dependent upon the semantic content of a document is critical to achieving quality pagination.

## 7. GOLD STANDARD GENERATION

While the above work strove to identify an improved algorithm to better predict a lower bound break point based on semantics, we postulated that there may be a truly 'ideal' break point in each article. This 'ideal' would be the natural place to break the article, and unlike the minimal break point, this ideal could be longer and contain more than just the bare minimum of information. To this end, we attempted to create a 'gold standard' dataset.

### 7.1 Study Design

The goal of this study was to find consensus on an ideal break point for a given article for the construction of a gold standard. We followed the same random selection technique as described in Section 6, pulling 700 unique articles (100 from each subject area). We used CrowdFlower (**CF**) as our crowd-sourced platform. Unlike MT, CF has a premium set of crowd-sourced individuals called the Editorial Crowd. From the CF website:

> *This group of contributors have been tested for a deep understanding of the English language. These contributors have shown that they understand syntax, grammar, punctuation, and other elements of the English language.*

We realize that this task, attempting to find consensus, is a challenge and we therefore opted to use the more expensive CF verified workers with an expertise in English editing to ensure a careful reading and quality consideration of the ideal break point. We will refer to workers on CF as **CFWs**.

CF HITs were constructed from the 700 randomly selected articles. A HIT consisted of a brief definition of a break point and the original source text (using the same sentence numbering as in the above experiment). The text was accompanied by the question, 'What is the best break point in this document?' CFWs were asked to choose one of the sentence numbers as the best break point (indicating everything before that number would be kept, and everything after would be cut). A full definition of an "ideal" break point was included to clear up any ambiguity on the labeling task including the statement *"This should be the shortest document possible without sacrificing key content."* To ensure legitimate HIT completion, one 'sanity check question'

| Sentence Tolerance | No CFW Agree | 2 CFW Agree | 3 CFW Agree | 4 CFW Agree | 5 CFW Agree |
|---|---|---|---|---|---|
| **0 Away** | 361 | 292 | 46 | 1 | 0 |
| **1 Away** | 168 | 345 | 139 | 34 | 15 |
| **2 Away** | 92 | 304 | 201 | 68 | 35 |
| **3 Away** | 42 | 263 | 240 | 95 | 60 |

Table 5: Gold Standard Consensus for 700 Random Articles

*Values represent the number of articles where consensus was at the column level given the row's tolerance. For example, there were 139 articles where 3 CFWs agreed on a break point within a 1 sentence tolerance (those three breakpoints were separated by no more than one sentence.)*

was included asking CFWs to find the Nth word in the Mth sentence. Failed sanity check question HITs were reposted.

The CF infrastructure groups HITs together. Thus, each CFW was required to complete 4 HITs at a time, and was remunerated a total of 40 cents for those 4 HITs. Every HIT was evaluated by 5 unique CFWs, totaling 3500 observations.

Given the subjective nature of these observations, we wished to only accept a break point (and its corresponding article) as a gold standard if a majority (at least 3 of the 5 CFWs) could agree upon an ideal break point, within a tolerance.

## 7.2 Results & Discussion

In a surprising turn of events, we saw an extremely low level of CFW agreement, as illustrated in Table 5. As part of our analysis, we include a range of agreement tolerance values (how many sentences are allowed to separate the break points chosen by k CFWs such that they could still be said to agree?) With the strictest tolerance (break points must exactly match,), only 46 of the 700 articles had 3 out of 5 CFWs agreeing, 1 had 4 CFWs agreeing, and no articles had all 5 CFWS agreeing. This results in only 6.7% of the articles reaching any semblance of consensus. Even at a very generous 3 sentence tolerance (there may be up to 3 sentences between break points chosen by k CFWs, and agreement could still be claimed), only 395 articles (slightly above 50%) reached a consensus at or above 3 CFWs.

Given these low consensus results, the ability to meaningfully construct a gold standard is extremely limited. This suggests that the use of machine learning techniques, which rely upon a training set, would be prohibitive in this context.

Furthermore, this lack of consensus may suggest that there is no single 'ideal' break point in a given article. Beyond finding a minimal 'do not cut before this place' break point, the remaining text of the article (and its importance to the reader) may be too subjective to readily predict, and subsequently, this task may be "too hard for a human." This adds further support to the importance and tractable outcome observed in our minimal break point detection.

## 8. FUTURE WORK

The first area of future work would be to develop a variation of PDM [8, 1] that integrates pagination quality as part of the layout quality metric. Currently these approaches are based on fit of content alone. Subsequently, integrating pagination quality would be a substantial challenge, but a critical next step to testing the impact of pagination break point quality in a existing print publications.

Second, we are examine the applications of pagination break points' application to e-documents. In this context, there is an explicit metric of quality to test layout impact: number of clicks of a "read more" link after the initial document content. This is another exciting application that would require a large amount of structural work to set up an experiment.

One last area of future work is to explore alternative statistical language models, including those that do not accord equal weight to each occurrence of a word. This could further improve SLM performance, especially for the SLM Article context. We still believe that the Keyword Novelty approach has merit; however a more 'aggressive' keyword weighting algorithm may be needed to cause the curves' inflection point to occur earlier in the article.

## 9. CONCLUSION

Automatic document layout is rapidly becoming central to the production of most commercially printed newspapers and magazines. Within this context, pagination is a common layout challenge. However, all existing approaches to automatically calculate article break points for pagination neglect to account for the semantic content of the presented article. Disregarding the semantic information within the document can lead to overly aggressive or overly relaxed cutting, thereby running the risk of either eliminating key content and confusing the reader, or leaving in superfluous content and boring the reader, as well as making automatic layout more difficult.

We seek to directly address this shortcoming in this work. We present the first semantic-based pagination algorithm, to the authors' knowledge, for news article layout. Our approach predicts minimal break points based on the semantic content of an article through the use of a statistical language model. This approach is tested via a multi-subject experiment on 700 documents, comparing our method to 4 currently employed baselines and 3 alternative semantic approaches (also created for this paper). Results from this experiment clearly show that our approach strongly outperforms the baselines and alternatives. To further explore break point detection for pagination, we investigate whether an 'ideal' break point could be found for paginating news articles. Results from a second study suggest that humans are not able to agree on a single best break point, suggesting that it is more practical to define reliable minimal break points for pagination tasks.

This work presents a strong validation that break point detection for pagination tasks can benefit from an examination of the semantic content of the news articles themselves. Within a real-world context, a combination of semantic-based lower bound break point prediction and spacial/aesthetic optimization is ideal for automated document synthesis.

## 10. REFERENCES

[1] I. Ahmadullin and N. Damera-Venkata. Hierarchical probabilistic model for news composition. In *DocEng*, page 141, New York, New York, USA, Sept. 2013. ACM Request Permissions.

[2] G. J. Badros, A. Borning, and P. J. Stuckey. The Cassowary linear arithmetic constraint solving algorithm. *TOCHI*, 8(4 (Dec)):267–306, Dec. 2001.

[3] D. Beeferman, A. Berger, and J. Lafferty. Statistical Models for Text Segmentation. *Machine learning*, 34(1-3):177–210, 1999.

[4] D. M. Blei, A. Y. Ng, and M. I. Jordan. Latent dirichlet allocation. *The Journal of Machine Learning Research*, 3:993–1022, Mar. 2003.

[5] A. Brüggemann-Klein, R. Klein, and S. Wohlfeil. On the pagination of complex documents. *Lecture Notes in Computer Science*, 2598:49–68, 2003.

[6] F. Chua and S. Asur. Automatic Summarization of Events From Social Media. In *ICWSM*, 2013.

[7] P. Ciancarini, A. Di Iorio, L. Furini, and F. Vitali. High-quality pagination for publishing. *Software—Practice & Experience*, 42(6), June 2012.

[8] N. Damera-Venkata, J. Bento, and E. O'Brien-Strain. Probabilistic document model for automated document composition. In *DocEng*, page 3, New York, New York, USA, Sept. 2011. ACM Request Permissions.

[9] H. P. Edmundson. New Methods in Automatic Extracting. *Journal of the ACM (JACM*, 16(2), Apr. 1969.

[10] G. Erkan and D. R. Radev. LexRank: Graph-based lexical centrality as salience in text summarization. *J Artif Intell Res(JAIR)*, 2004.

[11] M. Fiszman, T. C. Rindflesch, and H. Kilicoglu. Abstraction summarization for managing the biomedical research literature. pages 76–83, May 2004.

[12] F. Giannetti. An exploratory mapping strategy for web-driven magazines. In *Proceeding of the eighth ACM symposium*, pages 223–229, New York, New York, USA, 2008. ACM Press.

[13] A. Haghighi and L. Vanderwende. Exploring content models for multi-document summarization. pages 362–370, May 2009.

[14] J. Hailpern, N. Damera Venkata, and M. Danilevsky. Truncation: All the News that Fits WeâĂŹll Print. In *DocENG*. ACM, 2014.

[15] J. Hailpern and B. A. Huberman. Echo: the editor's wisdom with the elegance of a magazine. In *EICS*. ACM Request Permissions, June 2013.

[16] M. A. Hearst. TextTiling: segmenting text into multi-paragraph subtopic passages. *Computational Linguistics*, 23(1), Mar. 1997.

[17] N. Hurst, W. Li, and K. Marriott. Review of automatic document formatting. In *DocEng*, page 99, New York, New York, USA, Sept. 2009. ACM Request Permissions.

[18] C. Jacobs, W. Li, E. Schrier, D. Bargeron, and D. Salesin. Adaptive grid-based document layout. *SIGGRAPH*, 22(3):838–847, July 2003.

[19] N. Jamil, J. Mueller, C. Lutteroth, and G. Weber. Extending Linear Relaxation for User Interface Layout. In *ICTAI*. IEEE Computer Society, Nov. 2012.

[20] I. Kastner and C. Monz. Automatic single-document key fact extraction from newswire articles. In *EACL*. Association for Computational Linguistics, Mar. 2009.

[21] R. Katragadda, P. Pingali, and V. Varma. Sentence position revisited: a robust light-weight update summarization baseline algorithm. pages 46–52, June 2009.

[22] C.-Y. Lin and E. Hovy. Identifying topics by position. In *ANCL*. Association for Computational Linguistics, Mar. 1997.

[23] C. Lutteroth, R. Strandh, and G. Weber. Domain Specific High-Level Constraints for User Interface Layout. *Constraints*, 13(3), Sept. 2008.

[24] R. Mihalcea and P. Tarau. TextRank: Bringing order into texts. In *EMNLP*, 2004.

[25] A. Nenkova. Automatic text summarization of newswire: lessons learned from the document understanding conference. In *AAAI*. AAAI Press, July 2005.

[26] A. Nenkova and L. Vanderwende. The impact of frequency on summarization. Technical Report MSR-TR-2005-101, Microsoft Research, 2005.

[27] L. Pevzner and M. A. Hearst. A critique and improvement of an evaluation metric for text segmentation. *Computational Linguistics*, 2002.

[28] D. A. Savitz and A. F. Olshan. Multiple comparisons and related issues in the interpretation of epidemiologic data. 1995.

[29] A. Scoditti and W. Stuerzlinger. A new layout method for graphical user interfaces. In *TIC-STH*, pages 642–647. IEEE, 2009.

[30] Y. Seki, K. Eguchi, and N. Kando. Compact Summarization for Mobile Phones. *Mobile and Ubiquitous Information Access*, 2954(Chapter 13):172–186, 2004.

[31] J. Seo and W. B. Croft. Unsupervised estimation of dirichlet smoothing parameters. In *SIGIR '10*, pages 759–760, New York, New York, USA, 2010. ACM Press.

[32] T. Weninger, W. H. Hsu, and J. Han. CETR: content extraction via tag ratios. *WWW 2010*, 2010.

[33] C. C. Yang and F. L. Wang. Automatic summarization of financial news delivery on mobile devices. In *WWW'03*, 2003.

[34] C. C. Yang and F. L. Wang. Hierarchical summarization of large documents. *J. of the American Society for Information Science and Technology*, 59(6), Apr. 2008.

[35] C. Zeidler, J. Müller, C. Lutteroth, and G. Weber. Comparing the usability of grid-bag and constraint-based layouts. In *OzCHI*, pages 674–682, New York, New York, USA, Nov. 2012. ACM Request Permissions.

[36] C. Zhai. *Statistical Language Models for Information Retrieval*. Morgan & Claypool Publishers, 2009.

# Extracting Web Content for Personalized Presentation

Rodrigo Chamun, Daniele Pinheiro, Diego Jornada
João Batista S. de Oliveira, Isabel Manssour

Pontifícia Universidade Católica do Rio Grande do Sul — PUCRS
Faculdade de Informática — FACIN
Porto Alegre — Brazil
{rodrigo.chamun, daniele.pinheiro, diego.jornada}@acad.pucrs.br
{joao.souza, isabel.manssour}@pucrs.br

## ABSTRACT

Printing web pages is usually a thankless task as the result is often a document with many badly-used pages and poor layout. Besides the actual content, superfluous web elements like menus and links are often present and in a printed version they are commonly perceived as an annoyance. Therefore, a solution for obtaining cleaner versions for printing is to detect parts of the page that the reader wants to consume, eliminating unnecessary elements and filtering the "true" content of the web page. In addition, the same solution may be used online to present cleaner versions of web pages, discarding any elements that the user wishes to avoid.

In this paper we present a novel approach to implement such filtering. The method is interactive at first: The user samples items that are to be preserved on the page and thereafter everything that is not similar to the samples is removed from the page. This is achieved by comparing the path of all elements on the DOM representation of the page with the path of the elements sampled by the user and preserving only elements that have a path "similar" to the sample. The introduction of a similarity measure adds an important degree of adaptability to the needs of different users and applications.

This approach is quite general and may be applied to any XML tree that has labeled nodes. We use HTML as a case study and present a Google Chrome extension that implements the approach as well as a user study comparing our results with commercial results.

## Categories and Subject Descriptors

H.3.3 [**Information Systems**]: Information Search and Retrieval—*Information Filtering*; H.3.3 [**Information Systems**]: Information Search and Retrieval—*Search process*

*DocEng'14,* September 16–19, 2014, Fort Collins, Colorado, USA.
Copyright 2014 ACM 978-1-4503-2949-1/14/09 ...$15.00.
http://dx.doi.org/10.1145/2644866.2644871.

## Keywords

Web content extraction; Web content filtering; Levenshtein algorithm

## 1. INTRODUCTION

The printed version of a web page is usually a disappointing document: quite often it has poor layout and too many pages. The reason is that the HTML language used to format the pages was not designed for printing (or for obtaining printable versions of the content) and web browsers render pages with unrestricted boundaries, making the conversion of digital content into physically constrained paper unnatural. The way many pages are designed worsens the experience: In most cases, main content is surrounded with elements such as menus, advertisements, comment boxes and others and all these elements are also transferred to the printed version. Even reading the online version of a page may be in many cases annoying because these elements grab the attention and use too much real estate on the screen.

One solution for these problems is to identify the main content of the page (the part that most readers probably wish to consume) and extract these items for cleaner presentation. This technique is known as content extraction. To ease the manipulation, a HTML page may be represented as the Document Object Model (DOM [12]), which translates the HTML text into a tree structure. In this structure, every element is represented as a node in the tree, with the control elements usually being internal nodes and content being leaf nodes. The goal of content extraction is to find out efficiently and precisely what is desired content and what is not.

In this work we propose a method to solve the content extraction problem. This solution starts when the user actively samples elements on the page: The DOM tree is traversed and used to identify the nodes that were selected, and every node in the tree that is considered similar to the sample is identified as possibly interesting content. Similarity is measured by comparing the node types, their level on the tree and their paths from the root. The user also provides a threshold which defines how different a node might be from the sample to be still considered similar to it. The core of our approach is the path comparison between nodes, which is a variation of the Levenshtein algorithm for string edit distances [9]. After samples are selected from a given web page, any information about the selection may be stored and used later for automatic filtering of pages from the same web site. Thus, interactive filter construction is made only once.

The approach is general enough to be used in any tree that has labeled nodes. The main contribution is that with a few clicks the user is able to select from the page only the interesting elements, whereas the threshold used for similarity allows for better customization. The filter produced from the samples may be applied to the web page already on the web browser and immediately all items that were not selected are removed, and it may also be stored for later use.

We present a Google Chrome extension supporting the approach and extended the filtering procedure so that users may apply a filter to several pages from the same web site at once, obtaining a customized view of a set of web pages. This may be presented as a new HTML document or as a PDF document for printing.

This paper is structured as follows: In Section 2 we provide an overview of web content extraction in the academic literature and existing commercial solutions. Section 3 explains in deeper detail how the proposed method works and how it relates to previous works. In Section 4 we describe an application that implements the method as a Google Chrome extension. Section 5 presents user impressions when comparing our results with the results of an existing commercial solution. Finally, in Section 6 we present our conclusions and goals for future research.

## 2. RELATED WORKS

Several approaches have been proposed to tackle the problem of content extraction from HTML pages. Most of these try to find the most interesting content by exploring the DOM representation of the page and assigning some relevance to each node, sometimes using visual cues from the rendered page to help in the task. Other approaches assume a domain context (mainly the news article domain) and explore features unique to this domain.

Cai et. al. [5] presented a hierarchical structure for identifying web content based on the page representation that groups page segments that look alike. Each identified segment of the page is a branch in the DOM hierarchy. Under the same parent there are elements that are thought to be in the same section of the page, thus having a similar semantic context. This branching is done according to visual features on the page such as the font used for text elements (color and size), segments that are placed near each other, background colors and natural page divisors such as the <hr> tag.

A semi-automatic approach is proposed by Line et. al. [10]. It uses visual features to guess the main content of a page and the user is able to modify it at will. The algorithm explores the DOM tree of the page looking for leaf nodes and groups them by similarity. The similarity is measured by element properties such as geometry, position, style and tag types. Groups are clustered into blocks that have their importance measured by a heuristic. The block with the highest importance is returned as the main content of the page. The goal of that work is to start from pages that originally have complex layouts and contain a balanced mixture of text and multimedia content and obtain printed versions without the diversity of elements usually presented on a web page.

The approach proposed by Wang et. al. [14] aims at extracting content from news sites. It takes advantage of the fact that most news pages are based on a static template filled with content. This suggests the creation of a wrapper for a web page (without knowing its original template) based on content and spatial features. It is based on machine learning and the wrapper is learned from a few samples from a single site and extended to extract news content from other sites. This technique consists in finding the best sub-tree of the DOM tree, as presented in [10]. The extracted article has exactly the same visual style as the page and the result may still have some unwanted content.

Reis et. al. [13] proposes an approach that also takes advantage of the templates filled with content that many news pages adopt for their presentation. Web sites are crawled and have their pages gathered and clustered according to the similarity of their tree structures. For each cluster, a template is extracted from elements that do not change among the pages in the cluster. Once the most important content of an input page is desired, it is submitted to a classification process to find which cluster it belongs to, then, its content is retrieved by looking for changes between the page and the template of that cluster.

Another filtering process is proposed in Gupta et. al. [6] to provide a clean version of the web page for screen readers used by visually impaired people. Instead of trying to find the most important content, the algorithm tries to eliminate non-content and assumes that what is left is interesting. The elimination is done by removing elements from the DOM using a series of different filtering techniques and the authors report that the algorithm performs well on pages with large blocks of text, such as news articles.

Also trying to provide a clean printable version of a web page, Luo et. al. [11] approach the problem by grouping text segments that appear to be in the same context (i.e. do not have a line break between them) and identify the set of segments more likely to contain the most relevant information, to make sure only segments that belong to the news story are selected.

There are also commercial solutions developed either as native browser features or as extensions. HP Clipper [7] is a web browser extension to extract content semi-automatically. It tries to find the main content of the page and allows users to fine tune the result by manually removing items. CleanPrint [1] is another extension that works similarly, where users manually select the content they wish to remove. Reading View [3] and Reader [4] are native features for the Internet Explorer and Safari browsers, respectively, that automatically selects the content, but the user cannot add or remove elements and they do not work for every page on the web. Finally, Evernote Clearly [2] works exactly as the Reading View and Reader but as a browser extension.

The above methods have different approaches to the problem of recognizing content: Some are based on template recognition, some on hierarchical structure or item context, others do not disclose their methods as in the case of commercial software. In any case, they seldom ask the most important agent of the whole process, the user has very little say in the selection of items. Even when this is done, as is the case of HP Clipper [7] and CleanPrint [1], this has to be done for each web page and the selection cannot be reused for different pages. In our proposal, the user will be the main agent for selection and his selection will be made only once and produce a filter to be applied over and over.

## 3. PROPOSED METHOD

Our approach for content extraction works on documents represented as a hierarchical structure. In order to identify the most important content of a web page and extract it for later presentation, we use the Document Object Model (DOM) [12]. This representation translates the string of HTML text to a tree structure where every element is turned into a node in the tree, with control elements usually being internal nodes and content being leaf nodes. One naive approach might suggest that all leaves of a given HTML tree are the content, but the superfluous elements are also leaves in the tree and since elements have no semantic information the goal to solve the problem is to find out what is desired content and what is not.

The first developed approach to select content was quite simple: As HTML nodes are sampled from the screen by the user, the HTML path for each of those nodes is stored and the collection of paths represents a selection (or filter) to be used on that web page. When the filtering process runs on another web page it searches for all nodes with exactly the same paths from the root as the sampled ones. Although straightforward, this approach is very restrictive as even the slightest difference in the HTML paths will force relevant nodes to be rejected.

Clearly, such a strict method is not flexible enough to be used with a language as tolerant as HTML, where slight changes in the structure may not affect the visual presentation of content (and thus preserve its logical connection in the interpretation of users). Therefore some kind of tolerance should be inserted into the path analysis, providing for some measure of "closeness" to the nodes originally selected.

In this second approach the process begins when users perform manual sampling of items to be preserved on the web page and associate to each sampled item a threshold representing an acceptable difference between the sample and other candidate elements. With that information each leaf node in the HTML tree has its path compared to the sample. When changes are found, the amount of difference is calculated and if it is less than or equal to the provided threshold, we assume that the nodes are similar and the node is part of the desired content. Clearly, the same approach may be used with any XML tree and is not limited to HTML.

The amount of difference compared with the threshold value is processed as follows: Before comparing paths, a specific weight is assigned to each level of the HTML tree. These weights are used to assure higher penalties to path differences happening closer to the top of the tree and more lenient to differences closer to the bottom of the tree. We define that the tree has total weight 100 assigned to its longest path and distribute that weight across all levels in a way that levels close to the root weight more than deeper levels. This works as follows: For the root node, we divide the total weight assigned to the tree by a damping coefficient, take this value out of the total weight and divide the new value of the total weight by the damping coefficient on the next level. Then we keep doing this process until we reach all levels of the tree. The remaining of the total weight is equally distributed among all levels of the tree. Algorithm 1 describes this process.

For example, Figure 1a shows a HTML tree with the weights of its levels already calculated. In this example the user has selected the node $IMG21$ as the sample node (its path in the tree is shown in Figure 1b) and the nodes to

---

**Algorithm 1** Algorithm that calculates the weights for the tree levels.

> **function** WEIGHTS($tree$: HTML tree)
> $\quad w \leftarrow 100$
> $\quad h \leftarrow tree's\ height$
> $\quad list \leftarrow \emptyset$
> $\quad$**for** $i \leftarrow 0$ **to** $h$ **do**
> $\quad\quad list_i \leftarrow \frac{w}{DAMPING}$
> $\quad\quad w \leftarrow w - list_i$
> $\quad$**end for**
> $\quad rest \leftarrow \frac{w}{h}$
> $\quad$**for** $i \leftarrow 0$ **to** $h$ **do**
> $\quad\quad list_i \leftarrow list_i + rest$
> $\quad$**end for**
> $\quad$**return** $list$
> **end function**

---

be compared to it are $IMG5$ and $IMG18$ (with the paths shown in Figures 1c and 1d respectively).

To quantify the amount of difference between the paths we add the weights of the levels where changes happen. The first test happens between the paths to nodes $IMG21$ and $IMG5$. As presented in Figure 1a, the first difference between $IMG21$ and $IMG5$ occurs on the second level where the weight is 2.61 and the final result of this comparison is 11.66.

The second test happens between the paths to nodes $IMG21$ and $IMG18$. The difference between the paths happens deeper on the tree, on a level of which weight is 1.78 and the final result is significantly smaller, only 4.75.

The threshold provided by the user controls how much one element is allowed to be different from the sample. Following the same example and keeping node $IMG21$ as the sampled node, a threshold value of 5 will make node $IMG18$ be considered similar whereas $IMG5$ will be rejected. A larger value may consider node $IMG5$ similar as well at the risk of including more content that is less similar to $IMG21$.

The changes between paths are detected by a variation of the Levenshtein algorithm [9]. This algorithm is originally used to calculate the minimum amount of operations needed to transform a string of characters $S$ into another string $S'$. The original string operations are character substitution, insertion and deletion and each of these operations adds 1 to the cost of the transformation. Our adaptation to the path comparison problem consists of using this algorithm to find how many operations are needed to transform the path of the current node into the path of the sample, but instead of characters we use node labels and instead of using 1 as the operation cost we use the weight assigned to the level where the operation takes place. This variation of the Levenshtein algorithm is shown in Algorithm 2 below.

### 3.1 Comparison with other approaches

We do not wish to extract content from web pages autonomously, but rather to provide a tool for users to select samples of what they want and provide some measure of adaptability to select other items that may be similar to the samples. This information can be used later to automatically filter pages that share similar structure with the sampled pages, eliminating the need for the user to sample

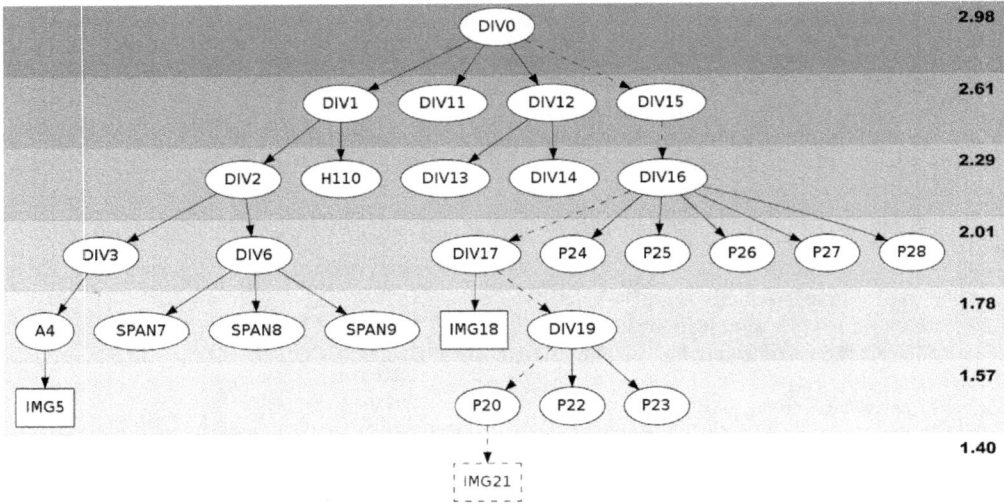

(a) Part of a HTML tree: first levels are shown and the weight of each level is on the right

(b) Path to IMG21 node

(c) Path to IMG5 node

(d) Path to IMG18 node

Figure 1: Example of a HTML tree and the weights for each level and paths to three nodes in that tree.

---

**Algorithm 2** Algorithm to calculate the difference between paths

> **function** CALCULATE($a$, $b$: node path, $w$: list of weights, $i$, $j$: path position)
>     **if** $i < 0$ **then**
>         **return** $\sum_{k=0}^{j} w_k$
>     **end if**
>     **if** $j < 0$ **then**
>         **return** $\sum_{k=0}^{i} w_k$
>     **end if**
>     $cost \leftarrow w_{max}(i, j)$
>
>     **if** $a_i == b_j$ **then**
>         $cost \leftarrow 0$
>     **else**
>         $equal \leftarrow w_{max}(i, j)$
>     **end if**
>     **return** $min(calculate(a, b, w, i - 1, j) + cost,$
>           $calculate(a, b, w, i, j - 1) + cost,$
>           $calculate(a, b, w, i - 1, j - 1) + equal)$
> **end function**

---

elements again in another page from the same domain. This approach should not be exclusive for news or HTML pages, even though we use them as case study. We also implement a proof of concept application as a Google Chrome extension, to be detailed in Section 4.

As several works [6, 10, 14] our approach explores the DOM structure for extracting content from web pages. On the other hand, the proposed method is not limited to news sites [14, 13] and may be applied automatically after a first sampling made by the user, unlike [3, 4, 2].

Two of the related works have similar approaches to ours: Gupta [6] also proposes a filtering approach in which the DOM structure is navigated and a series of heuristics to remove specific nodes are used. Thus it is expected that content will remain on the page while non-content is removed. This approach also requires user interaction because the heuristics are set by the user. Besides the filtering action, this approach is opposite from ours, since our users must select what they want to keep on the page. It also has a drawback since it requires specific rules for specific types of elements and every undesired type must have specific heuristics associated to it. On the other hand, as our method allows users to select what they want on the page any type of element may be selected with no special rule whatsoever.

The approach by Reis [13] is also similar to ours but depends on crawling to get all pages of a web site, process them in sets of similar pages and store this information. Therefore, the approach works only for a web site that was processed, new websites must have all of its pages crawled to have their content extracted. Our approach allows a very simple filter creation in less than a minute for any page the users want. Since users know the pages they visit, they know if they are similar, and the filter information is the only thing that needs to be saved. Finally, the creation of a new filter requires only a few clicks and no need to crawl a entire web site.

## 4. APPLICATION OF THE METHOD

In this section we describe an application that implements our method as an extension to the Google Chrome web browser. The choice of browser was based on its popularity and the availability for several operating systems, but other browsers could have been used as well.

Before content extraction, node sampling is necessary: The user is asked to sample nodes and assign them to several existing node types. Thus, a node assigned to a type called "headline" may be handled differently than a node classified as "text". Similar information could be obtained from the analysis of HTML tags of the nodes, but we chose to avoid that analysis and work with explicit information provided by the user.

For example, to identify all paragraphs of a web page and handle them as normal text later on, the user selects a paragraph element on the page, assigns it to the *text* type, adjusts the threshold and runs the algorithm. Every DOM node similar to the sample is assigned to *text* as well. We provide three default types that categorize most elements on a page: "headline", "text" and "image", but we also provide the option of creating new, personalized types. This personalization allows users to select elements from the page and assign those elements to a new type, as for example date and author. This may be interesting when further processing is to be made on the data obtained from the web page and content may be "tagged" with such types for easier identification.

For node sampling, the user clicks on an element on the page, assigns it to a type and moves a slider to set the threshold as described in Section 3 and the higher it is, less similar a node needs to be from the sample to be selected as similar content. As the slider is changed, all elements that are selected by the algorithm are highlighted on the screen.

Figure 2 shows the extension's menu. The extension works in two modes: The *Clean* and the *Clean All* options. The *Clean* option resets the application and begins to work with samples, so the user may select items to create a new filter for that web page, apply it to the page (and clean it, therefore the name), save the filter or load an existing one. The second option is *Clean All*, where an existing filter can be applied immediately to several links that are selected from the current web page.

Figure 3 illustrates the selection of a sample of text. When the user moves the slider in the extension's menu, the algorithm selects other elements according to the threshold defined by the slider value. Figure 4 depicts the web page after the threshold specification. The process for headline, image and custom elements is the same.

A filter may be applied on the same page used to create it by clicking on the *Apply* button on the extension's interface. When this action is performed, only the elements that match the sampling will remain on the page – thus cleaning the page. Figure 5b presents the results of a filter that keeps only the headline and the paragraphs of the news pages shown on Figure 5a.

Figure 2: Extension's interface

Figure 3: Sampling a piece of text.

The extension also provides the functionality of applying the filter created for a single page to a set of other pages. By clicking on *Clean All*, this may be automated for a number of links on a page. The link selection follows the same approach presented for sampling elements: The user selects a link from the current page as a sample and then moves the slider to select more or less similar links. This is exemplified on Figure 6. Thereafter, clicking at the *Apply* option starts the process: All links that match the sample will be followed and the filter will be applied to them.

The extension receives the results obtained from following the links and sends them to an external tool to create a layout for this content. The tool used in our extension implements the algorithms presented by Oliveira [8] to render

Figure 4: Selected paragraphs of a web page.

(a) Original page.

(b) Filtered page.

Figure 5: A news page before (a) and after (b) content extraction.

pages with columns. The output format is chosen by the user, either as a PDF file or HTML to be rendered by the browser. Figure 7 presents the HTML output of this feature on the browser, with a navigator at the top which paginates the output, a page for each link. Figure 8 shows the PDF output that is downloaded by the user.

Figure 6: Selected links where filters are to be applied.

For a non-news web page, Figure 9a shows the original web page containing a recipe and several other minor elements, including advertising. Figure 9b, on the other hand, shows a much cleaner version of the same web page after filtering, without any ads. It is interesting to notice that in this case we used the existing item types (headline, text, image) and a fourth type was created to select the recipe

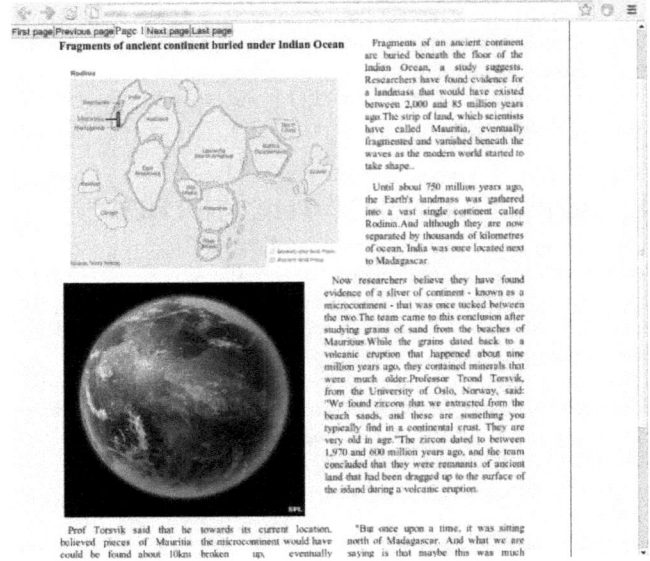

Figure 7: HTML output. Content from http://www.bbc.com.

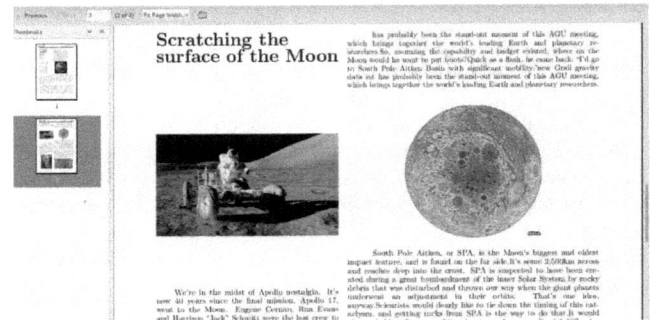

Figure 8: PDF output. Content from http://www.bbc.com.

ingredients. Thus, if further processing was needed these ingredients would be readily recognized in the HTML file.

## 5. USER EVALUATION

This user evaluation was based on interviews to collect user opinions about the extracted content rather than the prototype usability or the final document layout. Users were asked to compare the output from our prototype with the output of Reading View [3] and point out their preference. Two pages from BBC News[1] and one from G1[2] were selected arbitrarily and used in all interviews. Since the concern was on the tool output only, the users were presented with printed versions of each page and printed versions of the results of each tool.

Eighteen people between ages 19 and 30 were interviewed individually. Their background ranged from computer science to psychology and communication. Each interview was performed as follows: a brief explanation about web content extraction was given to the volunteer and then the printouts of each web page were shown in turn. For each page, the

---

[1] http://www.bbc.com/
[2] http://g1.com.br/

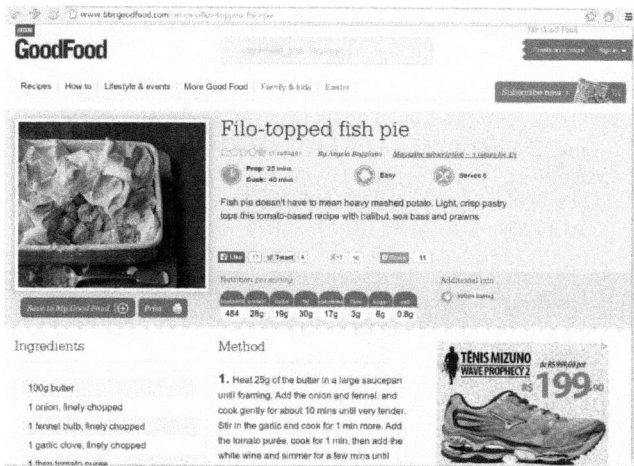

(a) Original web page with a recipe, including several extra items and an advertisement.

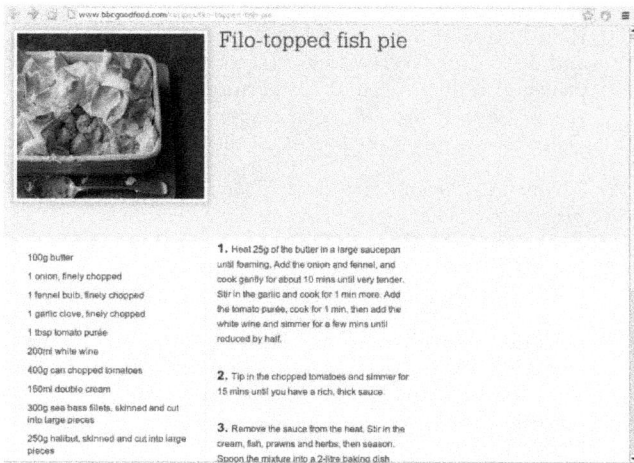

(b) The content from the page, after filtering.

Figure 9: An example of extraction on a non-news web page.

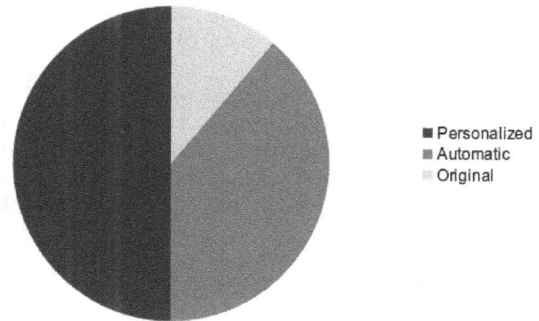

Figure 10: Graph with the interviewee's preference

user was told which printout was the original news page, for the Reading View output the user was told only that a tool generated it automatically, and for the output of our prototype the user was told that another tool generated it with a few clicks. To emphasize that the output could be personalized, two versions of our output (one containing the news headline, text and image and the other with the same content plus the author name and date) were shown as being different outputs of the same tool for the same page. It was never mentioned the name of the application that generated each output and the volunteer was asked to disregard the layouts and evaluate only whether the extracted content interested them in contrast to the original page. After showing all versions of the same news page we asked which one the volunteer preferred and why.

As presented in Figure 10, 9 people preferred the output from our prototype claiming that it is more useful to choose what goes to the output while 7 people preferred Reading View's automatic approach. Only 2 people said they would stay with the original page. These results leads to the thinking that most people are not satisfied with the printing of web pages as they are presented on the screen and wish some degree of adaptation to paper.

At the end of the interview we asked the volunteers whether they would use a personalized content extraction application if it was available to them. From the 18 people, 13 said they would use such an application. Some of them said they would use it only if it was made available for a mobile version.

Most people preferred a clean and customizable version. We believe that there are two reasons for this reaction: first, some people really prefer cleaner pages, whereas a second reason could be that people generally wish to be able to customize stuff, even when they do not do that in practice.

## 6. CONCLUSION

Web pages and specially news pages are in many cases composed by a "main" content usually made of text and images as well as items such as advertisements, menus and others. These may be very distracting to readers and when the page is printed such items usually are sent to the output. This is in most cases a waste of resources since they do not add any value to the content. One solution for this problem is to extract the main content from the page and show it in a cleaner presentation, either on the screen or on paper.

In this work we offer a solution that consists on creating a filter to be applied based on items from the page: Only that content goes through the filter, anything else is blocked and not presented. Users are able to create this filter in a semi-automatic way: They sample elements to be considered relevant and any element similar to the samples is identified and collected by our algorithm. We represent the web pages as the DOM standard, a tree like structure for HTML documents in which each element is a node. Element similarity is measured by comparing their node paths with a variation of the Levenshtein algorithm. Our approach produces a cleaner output containing only elements the users think are interesting.

This approach has the obvious advantage that users provide their own concept of relevance, thus avoiding a possibly complex process of trying to identify relevant items and also allowing for the production of personalized filters better suited to each user.

Also, a filter created for a specific page can be reused for a different page as long as they have a similar structure and the result can be obtained automatically, meaning that the element sampling is a one-time job that may be used extensively for similar pages.

To validate our approach, we implemented it as a Google Chrome extension and validated its output with users by comparing them with the output of a commercial solution. The users preferred our outputs mainly because it was known to be customizable.

Finally, for future works we intend to detach the filtering implementation from the browser so that it can run as a standalone process, implement the approach for mobile devices and to conduct an user evaluation that examines both the users reaction to the results and their experience using our approach.

# 7. ACKNOWLEDGMENTS

This paper was achieved in cooperation with Hewlett-Packard Brasil Ltda. using incentives of Brazilian Informatics Law (Law n. 8.2.48 of 1991).

# References

[1] Clean Print. http://www.formatdynamics.com/cleanprint-4-0/, 2014. [Online; accessed 24-March-2014].

[2] Evernote Clearly. http://evernote.com/clearly/, 2014. [Online; accessed 24-March-2014].

[3] Internet Explorer Reading View. http://msdn.microsoft.com/en-us/library/ie/hh771832(v=vs.85).aspx#reading-view, 2014. [Online; accessed 24-March-2014].

[4] Reader. http://support.apple.com/kb/ht4550, 2014. [Online; accessed 24-March-2014].

[5] Deng Cai, Shipeng Yu, Ji-Rong Wen, and Wei-Ying Ma. Vips: A vision-based page segmentation algorithm. Technical report, Microsoft technical report, MSR-TR-2003-79, 2003.

[6] Suhit Gupta, Gail Kaiser, David Neistadt, and Peter Grimm. Dom-based content extraction of html documents. In *Proceedings of the 12th international conference on World Wide Web*, pages 207–214. ACM, 2003.

[7] HP Clipper. http://www.hpclipper.com/, 2014. [Online; accessed 24-March-2014].

[8] João Batista S. de Oliveira. Two algorithms for automatic document page layout. In *Proceedings of the Eighth ACM Symposium on Document Engineering*, DocEng '08, pages 141–149, New York, NY, USA, 2008. ACM. ISBN 978-1-60558-081-4. doi: 10.1145/1410140.1410170. URL http://doi.acm.org/10.1145/1410140.1410170.

[9] Vladimir I Levenshtein. Binary codes capable of correcting deletions, insertions and reversals. In *Soviet physics doklady*, volume 10, page 707, 1966.

[10] Suk Hwan Lim, Liwei Zheng, Jianming Jin, Huiman Hou, Jian Fan, and Jerry Liu. Automatic selection of print-worthy content for enhanced web page printing experience. In *Proceedings of the 10th ACM symposium on Document engineering*, pages 165–168. ACM, 2010.

[11] Ping Luo, Jian Fan, Sam Liu, Fen Lin, Yuhong Xiong, and Jerry Liu. Web article extraction for web printing: a dom+ visual based approach. In *Proceedings of the 9th ACM symposium on Document engineering*, pages 66–69. ACM, 2009.

[12] J. Marini. *Document Object Model : Processing Structured Documents: Processing Structured Documents*. McGraw-Hill Professional Publishing, 2002. ISBN 9780072228311. URL http://books.google.com.br/books?id=vFXu8D9ml8AC.

[13] Davi de Castro Reis, Paulo Braz Golgher, ASd Silva, and AF Laender. Automatic web news extraction using tree edit distance. In *Proceedings of the 13th international conference on World Wide Web*, pages 502–511. ACM, 2004.

[14] Junfeng Wang, Chun Chen, Can Wang, Jian Pei, Jiajun Bu, Ziyu Guan, and Wei Vivian Zhang. Can we learn a template-independent wrapper for news article extraction from a single training site? In *Proceedings of the 15th ACM SIGKDD international conference on Knowledge discovery and data mining*, pages 1345–1354. ACM, 2009.

# Truncation: All the News that Fits We'll Print*

Joshua Hailpern
HP Labs
Palo Alto, CA, USA
joshua.hailpern@hp.com

Niranjan Damera Venkata
HP Labs
Chennai, Tamil Nadu, India
niranjan.damera-venkata@hp.com

Marina Danilevsky
University of Illinois
Urbana, IL, USA
danilev1@illinois.edu

## ABSTRACT

A news article generally contains a high-level overview of the facts early on, followed by paragraphs of more detailed information. This structure allows copy editors to truncate the latter paragraphs of an article in order to satisfy space limitations without losing critical information. Existing approaches to this problem of automatic multi-article layout focus exclusively on maximizing content and aesthetics. However, no algorithm can determine how "good" a truncation point is based on the semantic content, or article readability. Yet, disregarding the semantic information within the article can lead to either overly aggressive cutting, thereby eliminating key content and potentially confusing the reader; conversely, it may set too generous of a truncation point, thus leaving in superfluous content and making automatic layout more difficult. This is one of the remaining challenges on the path from manual layouts to fully automated processes with high quality output. In this work, we present a new semantic-focused approach to rate the quality of a truncation point. We built models based on results from an extensive user study on over 700 news articles. Further results show that existing techniques over-cut content. We demonstrate the layout impact through a second evaluation that implements our models in the first layout approach that integrates both layout and semantic quality. The primary contribution of this work is the demonstration that semantic-based modeling is critical for high-quality automated document synthesis within a real-world context.

## Categories and Subject Descriptors

I.7.2 [**Document Preparation**]: Desktop Publishing; I.7.4 [**Document and Text Processing**]: Electronic Publishing

## Keywords

Truncation; Pagination; Novelty; Semantic; Cut; SLM

---

*The title is a play on words based on the New York Times tagline, "All the News that's fit to print"

*DocEng'14*, September 16–19, 2014, Fort Collins, Colorado, USA.
Copyright 2014 ACM 978-1-4503-2949-1/14/09 ...$15.00.
http://dx.doi.org/10.1145/2644866.2644869 .

## 1. INTRODUCTION

Within the context of traditional newspapers or magazines, there are a finite amount of space within each issue limiting the amount of content being presented. A news article generally contains a high-level overview of the facts early on, followed by paragraphs of more detailed information [23, 24, 34]. This is done with two aims in mind: First, if the reader does not consume the entire text, "partial reading in that case will not result in partial understanding but only in missing a few, lower-level details.." [34]; Second, because the most relevant and important information is upfront, copy editors have the ability to cut paragraphs from the ends of the articles to make the included characters fit within space limitations without the loss of critical content [34]. Thus, copy editors and designers work to strike a balance between presenting enough detailed content for readability, while also accounting for space constraints and the aesthetic presentation of the page.

Automated document composition algorithms have been introduced to automate this largely manual workflow. Current approaches to automated document synthesis/layout focus extensively on content and aesthetic maximization [18, 19]. These optimization algorithms work with a series of rules to maximize the presentation within the spatial and visual constraints.

While these approaches have largely been successful at addressing issues of layout, they do not take into account the *semantic* content of the articles. This can result in either cutting too aggressively, resulting in missing key information and potentially misrepresenting the article content, or forcing superfluous content to remain potentially lowering the flexibility of layout algorithms.

Thus, the primary contribution of this work is an algorithm that predicts the likelihood that a given cut point is too short (missing key content) or too long (showing excessive details) based on article semantic content and readability. To the authors' knowledge, this is the first such semantic-based truncation algorithm, allowing layout algorithms to prioritize discarding the least critical content, thus maximizing both layout, aesthetics, and readability.

In this paper we performed an extensive user study on over 700 news articles, in which participants rated 8 potential cut points as being too short or too long. Using all data collected, we extracted readability and semantic content features and used them to create two predictive models: one that determines the probability that a given truncation point is too short (and should have a high penalty if cut) and a second that predicts if a cut point is too long (reducing the value of including it in a final layout). These models were then tested within the context of an existing newspaper layout algorithm with promising results.

## 2. RELATED WORK

For journalists who write news articles, truncation of content by layout editors is expected. Thus, articles are structured so that it is possible to truncate and fit them within the confines of a print layout [23, 24, 34]. Though the style and exact structure varies by subject domain [23], journalists construct articles to be overly long so as to provide editors with as much flexibility as possible [34].

For automatic news layout systems, truncation is viewed as a byproduct of the layout system- given spacial constraints, articles are trimmed to reduce their length to maximize content (article count) and aesthetic presentation[1, 9, 3]. Subsequently, determining ideal truncation points beyond overall layout optimization (especially considering the semantic content therein) has not been explored in the related literature.

In this section we highlight three related problem spaces to Truncation from which we can inform our approach.

### 2.1 Pagination

Pagination, unlike truncation, preserves all of an article's content while splitting it over multiple pages. Pagination approaches aim to create 'high-quality documents,' defined as documents 'without unwanted empty areas' [8]. Within the context of a single document, such as a book or a paper, pagination impacts the layout relationship of text content to related figures or tables [6].

However, the problem's complexity increases for automated document layout of newspapers or magazines[13, 18, 19]. In addition to optimizing the placement of figures within text, a given page can also contain content from multiple articles, and all content must fit within a predetermined page count. When determining how to break up articles across multiple pages, the preferred approach is to use constraint-based layout models, in which layout specifications are described by linear constraints imposed on items [2, 20, 25, 31, 38].

### 2.2 Automatic Summarization

A similar problem to truncation is that of single document summarization - the process by which the text of an article is reduced either by extraction (lifting sentences from the original text)[26] or abstraction (using natural language processing techniques to generate new sentences)[12]. While these approaches are not used by layout or copy editors, they are relevant to the construction and evaluation of our semantic-based break point techniques.

Corpus summarization uses a large collection of documents to build a model of the topics being discussed (e.g. topic modeling [5, 7], SumBasic[14], KLSum[28]) or opinions rendered (e.g. Opinion Mining [16]). Corpus summarization approaches rely upon a large body of documents (e.g., a collection of tweets [7]) from which patterns about the 'whole' collection can be derived, and are generally more powerful because they have more data from which to draw summaries. In contrast, single article summarization [23, 22] utilizes only one article to create a summary. Within single article summarization, most algorithms are designed to summarize long (e.g. book)[37], well structured (e.g. chapters or sections) text[10, 32, 36], thus maximizing the amount of se-

mantic and structural cues from which to derive summaries. The most notable exceptions to single unstructured documents are TextRank[26] and LexRank[11]. Both of these algorithms use a simple graph-based approach, treating each sentence as a node. The summary sentence of the article is calculated by finding the centroid of the graph based on a distance vector. There has been some work specifically with summarizing news articles by extracting the most important facts from the article [21]. Finally, it has shown that using the first $n$ sentences of a news article as a summary performs very well [27], which adds motivation for our problem.

### 2.3 Article Sub-Topic Segmentation

Another tangential, though separate problem space is that of article subtopic segmentation, most notably TextTiling [17, 29]. The main focus of subtopic segmentation is to divide a single article into subtopics, or sections. The goal is not to rank the sections on importance or quality, but rather to identify the conceptual shifts in the content. TextTiling is a straightforward and simplistic [4] method that examines lexical co-occurrances of terms between phrases in a document, and identifies sharp changes to be breaks between subtopics. However, the lack of ranking or quality of each subtopic shift means that such approaches' direct application to the truncation problem are limited, and a direct comparison of TextTiling with this problem is difficult. However, this work does suggest broad techniques to build upon, such as detecting breaks based on semantic change variation across an article relative to a mean change, and using vocabulary occurences to signify content themes [17].

## 3. SCOPING & KEY TERMS

The goal of this work is to create and test a novel algorithm that can use a news article's semantic content and readability (rather than only layout/spacing optimization) to determine the probability a given cut point in an article is too short or too long for successful truncation. The challenge is twofold: first truncating an article too early risks eliminating key information and potentially confusing the reader as to the article's content; and second, setting too generous of a truncation point leaves in superfluous content and makes automatic layout less flexible.

While there are many applications of this technique, this work specifically looks at news articles. Our novel approaches draw on and compare with an existing static truncation technique, and two semantic-based pagination techniques [15].

In this paper we first define our vocabulary and project scope. We then describe our article collection, followed by our truncation point evaluation experiment. Based on this data we present our modeling approaches to predict truncation point quality. Finally, we discuss results from applying our findings in a real-world context.

### 3.1 Key Terms

**Topic:** Refers to the use of the word in the English vernacular, such as the topic of a news article (e.g. a specific election in a specific country on a specific day), rather as it is used in the context of Topic Modeling approaches.

**Article:** A piece of written text about a specific topic (e.g., a specific New York Times article about an election in a country).

**Cut Point:** The location at which an article is 'broken', such that the content before the cut point is used, and the content after the cut point is never seen by the reader.

**Minimal or Lower Bound Cut Point:** The first (and thereby minimal) location within a news article which would make an acceptable cut point. In other words, the reader would have, by this time, understood enough about the topic being discussed, but has not yet seen all the details or nuances. Breaking before this lower bound is likely to cause the reader to miss a key concept or aspect of the article, and risk being mislead about the content.

**Truncation:** The task of determining the cut point(s) of an article.

**Corpus:** A collection of articles on the same topic (e.g. 100 news articles about the same specific bombing event).

**Subject:** An overarching thematic grouping of articles or corpuses (e.g. Sports, Politics)

**Document:** A set of sentences (a single article, subset of an article, multiple articles), including related images and their layout on a page(s).

**Semantics:** Refers to the use of the word in the English vernacular, focusing on the *meaning* of words or phrases.

## 3.2 Pagination & Summarization

**It should be noted that there is an important distinction between truncation (the focus of this paper) and pagination (not discussed in this paper - see [15]).** Pagination, as used in this context, implies that after the break point, a reader will see more of the given article, usually on a subsequent page. On the contrary, when an article is truncated, the portion of the article which follows the break point will never be presented to the reader in any form. We do *not* deal with pagination tasks in this work.

Further, this work does not address the task of document summarization or subtopic identification. Within the context of automatic news article layouts, article content is not summarized, and the content is preserved in the order and sentence structures of the journalist. Furthermore, subtopic breaks do not rank or determine which points are of more or less importance. While we do cite relevant summarization, subtopic identification and IR literature, we use these approaches to help inform our feature selection and readability metrics - but they are not directly applicable to solving the task of truncation quality prediction.

## 4. EXPERIMENT: DATA COLLECTION

The primary goal of this work is to develop and test models that can predict if any given cut point would be missing key content (too short) or allows for too large an amount of superfluous content (too long). To this end, we conducted a data collection experiment on Amazon Mechanical Turk (MT) which generated a hand coded dataset of articles with cut point quality ratings. This section details our experimental methods for data collection.

| Subject | Total # Corpuses | Total # Articles | $\mu$ Articles per Corpus (sd) |
|---------|------|------|------|
| **US** | 183 | 19429 | 106.17 (52.81) |
| **Business** | 166 | 19209 | 115.72 (63.45) |
| **Politics** | 129 | 25094 | 194.53 (122.53) |
| **Ent.** | 218 | 30534 | 140.06 (78.70) |
| **World** | 158 | 20440 | 129.37 (75.59) |
| **Sports** | 203 | 27463 | 135.29 (65.08) |
| **Tech** | 232 | 42104 | 181.48 (119.72) |
| **All** | 1289 | 184273 | 142.96 (90.73) |

Table 1: Corpus Summary Statistics
*Data Collected from Google News from 10/13 to 11/13*

## 4.1 Hypotheses

The data collected from this experiment will be used to address four research hypotheses:

H1 A model can be constructed that can predict the likelihood that a truncation cut point is missing key content (too short)

H2 A model can be constructed that can predict the likelihood that a truncation cut point has superfluous content (too long)

H3 A model can be constructed that can determine the minimal truncation point (not too long or too short)

H4 The identification of a good truncation point for an article is functionally different than that of a good pagination point.

All these hypothesis are from the perspective of the reader of a news article (not necessarily a layout editor, copy editor, or journalist).

## 4.2 Article Data Set

We collected corpuses of news articles by scraping Google News every 8 hours, from October 21 to November 27 2013[1]. Corpuses were 'accepted' if they contained at least 50 unique articles (as aggregated by Google News). The source HTML of the original articles from the originally hosted websites were retrieved, allowing the body copy to be extracted using CETR [35]. Because "... paradigmatic discourse structure differs significantly over text genres and subject domains" [23], we collected corpuses from 7 subject areas: World News, US News, Entertainment, Business, Technology, Sports and Politics. Descriptive statistics of the downloaded corpuses can be found in Table 1.

To conduct this experiment, we randomly selected 1 article from 100 randomly selected corpuses from each of 7 subject areas. This ensures a wide variety of topics being discussed. The resulting data set consisted of 700 articles. Descriptive and readability statistics for the randomly selected 700 articles are presented in Table 2.

## 4.3 Mechanical Turk Methods

MT HITs were constructed from the 700 articles. A HIT is an individual task given to a person on MT. HITs were not grouped together (containing more than one article) and presentation order was random (reducing order effects). Each HIT consisted of a brief definition of a cut point, minimal truncation point, the source text and the 8 candidate cut

---

[1]Collection stopped when at least 100 corpuses per subject area were collected.

|  | Grade Level | Reading Level | Fog Index | Sentence Count | Word Count |
|---|---|---|---|---|---|
| **Business** | 11.35 (3.53) | 47.35 (11.29) | 7.63 (3.45) | 56.70 (25.50) | 911.23 (180.56) |
| **Ent** | 13.56 (4.26) | 47.92 (12.91) | 11.29 (4.30) | 36.79 (15.31) | 921.50 (217.30) |
| **Politics** | 13.87 (3.46) | 41.75 (10.71) | 10.42 (3.52) | 37.94 (12.75) | 888.33 (160.91) |
| **Sports** | 10.51 (2.47) | 59.29 (8.63) | 8.93 (2.43) | 40.37 (12.61) | 839.67 (164.86) |
| **Tech** | 12.04 (3.07) | 51.15 (11.33) | 9.58 (2.82) | 41.20 (12.70) | 923.77 (225.70) |
| **US** | 13.06 (3.11) | 45.86 (11.14) | 10.04 (3.03) | 37.72 (10.70) | 881.95 (171.30) |
| **World** | 14.37 (3.61) | 39.06 (12.59) | 10.63 (3.46) | 36.89 (11.67) | 896.77 (182.52) |
| **All** | 12.68 (3.64) | 47.48 (12.84) | 9.79 (3.52) | 41.08 (16.55) | 894.78 (189.57) |

Table 2: Article Source Statistics

*100 Articles for each Subject (700 overall) | Mean and Std Values Reported*

points presented in random order (reducing order effects). Before each sentence in the source text, we inserted the characters '(SX)' where X was the sentence number. We used these indices to refer to a given cut point. For each cut point, the participants were asked to respond to the statement *Is (SX) a good Cut Point?* using a 7-point scale (*Too Short - Missing Content* (1) to *Minimally Acceptable Cut Point* (4) to *Too Long - Extra Details* (7)). Each HIT was completed by 2 Master level Turkers[2], yielding 5600 measures.

To ensure 'legitimate' HIT completion, one 'sanity check question' was included asking Turkers to find the Nth word in the Mth sentence. In addition, a HIT was rejected if the Turkers' response failed basic logic checks on their responses. First, all responses could not be the same (e.g. not all 6s). Second, if a singe HIT asked about the same cut point more than once[3], that individual Turker's response must be the same to both questions (e.g. rating sentence #4 as a 6 then rating sentence #4 as a 2). Third, ratings must be in chronological order. For example, labeling a sentence early in the article as "too long", and then a subsequent sentence as "too short", does not make sense. However succeeding break points (in article order) could have the same ranking. If any of the three logic tests or the sanity check were failed, the HIT was rejected and re-posted. Participants were remunerated 30 cents per accepted HIT.

## 4.4 Eight Candidate Cut Points

Our eight candidate cut points were selected as follows:

**Truncation Baseline** – One of the candidate cut points was set at the first 20% of an article (measured by character count), then rounded up to the end of the current paragraph. This approach (the modus operandi for constructing printable newspapers at Company XYZ) assumes that within the first fifth of an article, key concepts have been presented to the reader, and are roughly bounded by paragraph delimitation. We refer to this technique as **Twenty Percent**.

**Pagination Baseline** – As discussed in our related work, the only semantic based breaking technique was [15], though the focus was on pagination not truncation. We therefore explicitly repurpose their two minimal pagination break point algorithms to answer H4. We will refer to their Novelty Article algorithm as **Novelty**, and their SLM Article algorithm as **SLM**. However, unlike [15], we take a more conservative approach, and will round the Novelty and SLM points up to the end of the current paragraph for any given cut point to reflect the bias that human judgement is more likely to favor a cut point located at the end of a paragraph.

---

[2]Approval Rate above 95% and at least 1000 approved HITs
[3]The three baselines could produce the same cut point

**Random Sample** – The remaining 5 candidate points were randomly selected from the remainder of the article. All random cut points are selected between paragraphs (preserving full paragraphs). If a cut point was already selected by a baseline, we re-select an alternative random cut point.

### 4.4.1 Method Limitations

Any evaluation with multiple comparisons has an interaction effect, in that the rating or quality of one cut point can be impacted by the other cut points offered for comparison. Thus, a cut point that might have been rated a 5 (slightly too long) when viewed in isolation, may be pushed 'higher' if there are other, less optimal cut points located earlier in the article. Thus, these results must necessarily be viewed in the broader context of the other cut points presented.

## 5. RESULTS: DATA COLLECTION

In this section, we describe the results of our data collection experiment. Summary statistics for each response rating are presented across all subjects in Table 3 Based on an examination of these hand-coded responses, we can draw conclusions regarding some of our hypothesis as well as inform how we will predict truncation point quality.

## 5.1 H3: No "ideal" Truncation Point

H3 hypothesized that a model could be constructed to predict a minimally acceptable truncation point in an article. However, when we examine Table 3, a very small percentage of all ratings were a 4 (minimally acceptable truncation point). Moreover, this implies that the granularity tested in this experiment (7-point) was too fine. Subsequently, predicting only one rating (be it 4 or any of the others) would rely upon too small a data set to build an accurate data set and not end up modeling the "noise."

Based on this observation (that H3 should be rejected) our subsequent experiment to predict the truncation point quality collapses all points with rating under 4 as "too short," and all ratings above 4 as "too long." This will focus on broader trends in the data.

## 5.2 Twenty Percent is Too Short

Of the eight candidate cut points, one was Twenty Percent, a "reasonable" lower bound for news article layout. The results for this subset of truncation points is presented in Table 4. Surprisingly, Twenty Percent appears to cut an article's content overly aggressively, with the median value never reaching a score of 3 (which would still be too short). However, when we consider that 20% is a relative value based entirely on the length of the article, it is reasonable to con-

| | User Response | | Sentence Number | | | KLD Score | | | NVL Score | | | Percent of Article | | |
|---|---|---|---|---|---|---|---|---|---|---|---|---|---|---|
| | Rank | % | Mean (sd) | Median | Hist | Mean (sd) | Median | Hist | Mean (sd) | Median | Hist | Mean (sd) | Median | Hist |
| All Subjects | 1 | 17.43 | 7.47 (4.01) | 7.00 | | 0.37 (0.15) | 0.35 | | 0.31 (0.17) | 0.29 | | 0.16 (0.09) | 0.15 | |
| | 2 | 20.45 | 14.02 (7.05) | 12.00 | | 0.28 (0.13) | 0.26 | | 0.46 (0.20) | 0.44 | | 0.31 (0.14) | 0.28 | |
| | 3 | 16.98 | 22.36 (12.26) | 19.00 | | 0.20 (0.14) | 0.18 | | 0.62 (0.24) | 0.62 | | 0.49 (0.25) | 0.43 | |
| | 4 | 9.12 | 21.28 (12.24) | 17.00 | | 0.21 (0.15) | 0.20 | | 0.61 (0.24) | 0.57 | | 0.48 (0.26) | 0.39 | |
| | 5 | 11.39 | 24.27 (10.31) | 22.00 | | 0.18 (0.13) | 0.16 | | 0.67 (0.22) | 0.66 | | 0.55 (0.22) | 0.51 | |
| | 6 | 10.06 | 29.94 (7.74) | 29.00 | | 0.13 (0.10) | 0.10 | | 0.77 (0.18) | 0.79 | | 0.67 (0.17) | 0.68 | |
| | 7 | 14.58 | 40.38 (9.41) | 39.00 | | 0.06 (0.08) | 0.04 | | 0.89 (0.13) | 0.95 | | 0.85 (0.14) | 0.88 | |

Table 3: Summary Statistics for each User Ranking Response
*Ratings based on a 7-Point scale:*
*(1) "missing information" (4) "balanced" and (7) "excess text."*

| | Algorithm | Mean (sd) | Median | Histogram |
|---|---|---|---|---|
| Overall | Twenty Percent | 2.23 (1.11) | 2.00 | |
| | Novelty | 2.90 (1.29) | 3.00 | |
| | SLM | 2.58 (1.83) | 2.00 | |
| BUS. | Twenty Percent | 2.12 (1.08) | 2.00 | |
| | Novelty | 2.78 (1.22) | 2.00 | |
| | SLM | 2.24 (1.52) | 2.00 | |
| ENT. | Twenty Percent | 2.82 (1.37) | 2.50 | |
| | Novelty | 3.30 (1.52) | 3.00 | |
| | SLM | 3.28 (2.04) | 3.00 | |
| POL. | Twenty Percent | 2.27 (1.02) | 2.00 | |
| | Novelty | 2.92 (1.19) | 3.00 | |
| | SLM | 2.89 (1.98) | 2.00 | |
| SPT. | Twenty Percent | 1.96 (0.95) | 2.00 | |
| | Novelty | 2.60 (1.21) | 2.00 | |
| | SLM | 1.99 (1.50) | 1.00 | |
| TECH. | Twenty Percent | 2.21 (1.25) | 2.00 | |
| | Novelty | 2.90 (1.45) | 2.50 | |
| | SLM | 2.49 (1.71) | 2.00 | |
| US | Twenty Percent | 2.16 (0.87) | 2.00 | |
| | Novelty | 2.99 (1.15) | 3.00 | |
| | SLM | 2.74 (1.92) | 2.00 | |
| WLD | Twenty Percent | 2.06 (0.98) | 2.00 | |
| | Novelty | 2.81 (1.15) | 3.00 | |
| | SLM | 2.44 (1.81) | 2.00 | |

Table 4: Lower Bound Prediction Performance
*In Histogram, ratings of 4 are in black*

clude that an article's key content is not based exclusively on a relative percentage of the document. This is backed up by the data in the last column of Table 3; When we examine the percent of an article each user rank is at, there is a large standard deviation. This makes the raw document percentage (be it 20% or any other percentage) an unlikely lone predictor of minimal truncation point. That said, percentage may be useful when combined with other features for predicting quality of a truncation point.

## 5.3 H4: Truncation is not Pagination

While pagination is conceptually different from truncation, there are parallels between the two techniques. In H4 we hypothesized that the cut point at which readers would feel comfortable paginating an article would be different than where an article would be truncated. To test this hypothesis, semantic-based minimal pagination point algorithms [15] to generate two of the eight candidate break points, since their mean performance in a pagination experiment were rated 4.66 and 5.83 (SLM and Novelty respectively). However, readers considered these points to be too short for the truncation task, as seen in Table 4.

Upon reflection, these results make conceptual sense. Readers are more conservative when they know that after the cut, there will be no more content. Therefore, they wish to en-

sure a higher level of detail in the presented article. This confirms H4.

## 6. EXPERIMENT: MODELING

In this section, we detail the features extracted for each cut point, modeling techniques tested, and the methods used to evaluate model performance. To simplify our discussion of features, we divide them into Readability Measures (features that describe the article as a whole), and Incremental Measures (features that describe the current truncation point and change throughout the article). The subsequent section will then highlight the resulting performance results of the models.

### 6.1 Measures: Readability

For each candidate cut point, we associate a set of features based on the readability of the *entire* article. This allows the modeling algorithms to account for the complexity, length, and quality of the article as a whole. Grade Level was calculated using the Flesch-Kincaid grade level, which indicates that a student at that current U.S. school grade should be able to understand said article (7.0 to 8.0 is 'optimal.') Reading Level, or Flesch Reading Ease rates text on a 100 point scale, with higher scores meaning easier to understand (60-70 is 'optimal.') The Fog Index is another measure that indicates the years of education to understand a article in a single reading (8.0 is 'optimal.') Overall sentence count and word count were included as additional features.

It should also be noted that the subject area of the article was also used as a feature, allowing the algorithm to account for changes in writing styles of each article's subject area.

### 6.2 Measures: Incremental

The first feature we developed, **NVL** is predicated on the idea that as a reader traverses an article, he or she is exposed to key concepts/words. The initial exposure to a given key word is enough to make the reader aware that the subject is relevant to the article[4]. To this end, the Keyword Novelty approach attempts to find when the reader has been exposed to 'enough' of these key words so that he or she would have a general understanding of the article.

The second feature, **KLD**, is based on the idea that there is a probabilistic distribution of words (and their frequencies) that are 'ideal,' and we should strive to mimic (e.g. the full text of the article). We use a Statistical Language Model approach (SLM) to create a model of the 'full' article, and, for a given portion of an article being made visible to the reader, we use an information theoretic measure (KL Divergence) to evaluate how closely the model of that ar-

---

[4]Exactly how the given subject is related to the full text may not be clear until later in the article.

ticle portion matches the 'ideal' model of the entire article (implying that the article portion conveys much of the same content). The value of the KL Divergence metric at every sentence can be used as a feature when constructing our models. An added benefit of the SLM approach is the ability to smooth the keyword frequencies that are to common to the broad subject (in this work we use Dirichlet Prior Smoothing, which has been shown to be effective [39]).

In addition to Novelty Score and KL Divergence, we also included non-semantic features such as the number of completed sentences at the current cut point (**SEN**) and the percent of the article (based on word count) at the cut point (**PRC**). While not as complex as NVL of KLD, these measures are seen in much of the related work and therefore may be useful features for truncation point quality prediction.

### 6.2.1  Calculating Keyword Novelty

The first step is determining the article keywords. Following standard IR techniques, we limit an article's text to information-heavy words (nouns), and remove any pluralization through lemmatization. However, not all remaining keywords are equally relevant to the article in question. Commonly, term frequency (TF) can be used as a proxy for keyword relevance. However, TF is generally not robust on short or sparse data, such as a single newspaper article.

An alternative technique to discovering keywords is to use Singular Value Decomposition (SVD). SVD is able to filter out the noisy aspects of relatively small or sparse data, and is often used for dimensionality reduction. To repurpose SVD to calculate word weight, we represent each sentence as a row in a sentence-word occurrence matrix encompassing $m$ sentences and $n$ unique words, which we will refer to as $\mathbf{M}$ (which can be constructed in O($m$)).

SVD decomposes the $m \times n$ matrix $\mathbf{M}$ into a product of three matrices: $\mathbf{M} = \mathbf{U} \, \Sigma \, \mathbf{V^*}$. $\Sigma$ is a diagonal matrix whose values on the diagonal, referred to as $\sigma_i$, are the singular values of M. By identifying the four largest $\sigma_i$ values, which we refer to as $\lambda_1 - \lambda_4$, we are able to take the corresponding top eigenvector columns of V (which is the conjugate transpose of V*), which we refer to as $\xi_1 - \xi_4$. Each entry in each of these vectors $\xi_1 - \xi_4$ corresponds to a unique word in $\mathbf{M}$.

We then create $\xi'$, a master eigenvector calculated as the weighted average of $\xi_1 - \xi_4$, weighted by $\lambda_1 - \lambda_4$:

$$\xi' = \frac{1}{4} \sum_{i=1}^{4} \lambda_i \xi_i \tag{1}$$

Thus, $\xi'$ is a vector in which each entry represents a unique word, and the value can be interpreted as the 'centrality' of the word to the given article [37].

Once we have the keyword weights,[5] we iterate over each sentence in a given article. The 'value' of a sentence is the sum of all of the unique keywords' weights seen up to (and including) that sentence. Thus, the weight of a given sentence is a cumulative sum and each keyword only contributes to the overall sum on its first occurrence.

### 6.2.2  Calculating KL Divergence

As in Keyword Novelty, we pre-filter the text in each article to only contain the lemmatized high-information (noun) words.

---
[5]To reduce noise, we use the top 500 words from SVD [30].

In order to explain our use of SLM, consider $\boldsymbol{S}$ to be the set of all subjects ($s_0 \ldots s_g$) in our dataset. We work with one subject at a time, which we will refer to as $s_i$.

Let $\boldsymbol{D}$ be the set of all articles ($d_0 \ldots d_b$) in the given subject $s_i$ and $\boldsymbol{W}$ to be the set of all unique words ($w_0 \ldots w_h$) in $s_i$.

Denote the frequency of a given word $w_j$ in a given article $d_k$ as $f(w_j|d_k)$. Then the total count of all words in $d_k$ is calculated as:

$$T(d_k) = \sum_{j=0}^{h} f(w_j|d_k) \tag{2}$$

and the probability of a given word ($w_j$) in $d_k$ is:

$$p(w_j|d_k) = \frac{f(w_j|d_k)}{T(d_k)} \tag{3}$$

This therefore allows us to calculate the probability of a word in an article, using Dirichlet Prior smoothing [39]:

$$q(w_j|d_k) = \frac{f(w_j|d_k) + \mu * p(w_j|s_i)}{T(d_k) + \mu} \tag{4}$$

where $p(w_j|s_i)$ is the occurrence probability of the word $w_j$ in the entire subject $s_i$:

$$p(w_j|s_i) = \frac{\sum_{d_k \in s_i} f(w_j|d_k)}{\sum_{d_k \in s_i} T(d_k)} \tag{5}$$

and where the smoothing constant $\mu$ is estimated using [33]:

$$m_j = p(w_j|s_i)$$
$$B_j = \sum_{d_k \in s_i} \left( \left( \frac{f(w_j|d_k)}{T(d_k)} - m_j \right)^2 \right)$$
$$\mu = \frac{\sum\limits_{w_j \in W} \frac{B_j}{m_j * (1 - m_j)}}{\sum\limits_{w_j \in W} \frac{B_j^2}{m_j^2 * (1 - m_j)^2}} \tag{6}$$

As we traverse an article sentence by sentence, we redefine the variable $\boldsymbol{N}$ to refer to the subset of sentences in a given article we have seen. Thus, we calculate the probability of a word in N, using Dirichlet Prior smoothing [39] as:

$$q(w_j|N) = \frac{f(w_j|N) + \mu * p(w_j|s_i)}{T(N) + \mu} \tag{7}$$

To compare each successive test SLM to the Ideal article, we use the KL-Divergence metric (smaller is better):

$$KLDivergence = \sum_{w_j \in d_k} (ln(\frac{q(w_j|d_k)}{q(w_j|N)})) * q(w_j|d_k) \tag{8}$$

Thus for each sentence or paragraph in an article, we can calculate the KLDivergence score and use it as a feature.

## 6.3  Modeling Techniques

In order to predict the probability a truncation cut point was "too short" or "too long," we construct a series of predictive models using Weka:

- Logistic regression (LGST) - used extensively to predict the probability of an event's occurrence

- J48 decision tree (TREE) - a classifier which uses the concept of information gain to build a decision tree from data features

- Random Forest (RFST) - an ensemble classifier, combining multiple concurrently built decision trees

| Rank | Classifier | Measures | TP | TN | FP | FN | Kappa | aroc | Accuracy | Inaccuracy | Sens. | Spec. | Prec. | F1 |
|---|---|---|---|---|---|---|---|---|---|---|---|---|---|---|
| 1 | TREE | NVL\|PRC\|SEN | 4104 | 4624 | 1529 | 959 | 0.557 | 0.808 | 0.778 | 0.222 | **0.811** | 0.752 | 0.729 | 0.767 |
| 2 | TREE | PRC\|SEN | 4056 | 4636 | 1517 | 1007 | 0.550 | 0.803 | 0.775 | 0.225 | **0.801** | 0.753 | 0.728 | 0.763 |
| 3 | TREE | KLD\|SEN | 4053 | 4644 | 1509 | 1010 | 0.550 | 0.822 | 0.775 | 0.225 | **0.801** | 0.755 | 0.729 | 0.763 |
| 4 | TREE | KLD\|NVL\|SEN | 4049 | 4654 | 1499 | 1014 | 0.551 | 0.827 | 0.776 | 0.224 | **0.800** | 0.756 | 0.730 | 0.763 |
| 5 | TREE | KLD\|PRC\|SEN | 4047 | 4639 | 1514 | 1016 | 0.548 | 0.803 | 0.774 | 0.226 | **0.799** | 0.754 | 0.728 | 0.762 |
| 14 | LGST | KLD\|NVL\|SEN | 3601 | 5096 | 1057 | 1462 | 0.543 | 0.853 | 0.775 | 0.225 | **0.711** | 0.828 | 0.773 | 0.741 |
| 32 | RFST | KLD\|SEN | 3182 | 4253 | 1900 | 1881 | 0.320 | 0.793 | 0.663 | 0.337 | **0.628** | 0.691 | 0.626 | 0.627 |
| 46 | SVM | KLD\|NVL\|PRC\|SEN | 2973 | 4405 | 1748 | 2090 | 0.305 | 0.652 | 0.658 | 0.342 | **0.587** | 0.716 | 0.630 | 0.608 |

Table 5: Less Than 4 "Too Short" Top Five Models (Across All Subjects)

*Sorted by Sensitivity | For any classification technique not in the top 5, first occurrence and rank is shown*

| Rank | Classifier | Measures | TP | TN | FP | FN | Kappa | aroc | Accuracy | Inaccuracy | Sens. | Spec. | Prec. | F1 |
|---|---|---|---|---|---|---|---|---|---|---|---|---|---|---|
| 1 | LGST | KLD\|PRC | 6215 | 2720 | 1320 | 961 | 0.550 | 0.879 | 0.797 | 0.203 | 0.866 | 0.673 | 0.825 | **0.845** |
| 2 | LGST | KLD\|PRC\|SEN | 6221 | 2711 | 1329 | 955 | 0.549 | 0.880 | 0.796 | 0.204 | 0.867 | 0.671 | 0.824 | **0.845** |
| 3 | LGST | NVL\|PRC\|SEN | 6215 | 2719 | 1321 | 961 | 0.550 | 0.878 | 0.797 | 0.203 | 0.866 | 0.673 | 0.825 | **0.845** |
| 4 | LGST | PRC\|SEN | 6220 | 2711 | 1329 | 956 | 0.549 | 0.879 | 0.796 | 0.204 | 0.867 | 0.671 | 0.824 | **0.845** |
| 5 | LGST | KLD\|NVL\|PRC | 6207 | 2728 | 1312 | 969 | 0.550 | 0.879 | 0.797 | 0.203 | 0.865 | 0.675 | 0.826 | **0.845** |
| 13 | TREE | NVL\|SEN | 5784 | 3195 | 845 | 1392 | 0.580 | 0.844 | 0.801 | 0.199 | 0.806 | 0.791 | 0.873 | **0.838** |
| 31 | SVM | KLD\|NVL\|PRC\|SEN | 5766 | 2050 | 1990 | 1410 | 0.321 | 0.655 | 0.697 | 0.303 | 0.804 | 0.507 | 0.743 | **0.772** |
| 39 | RFST | KLD | 5513 | 2363 | 1677 | 1663 | 0.353 | 0.805 | 0.702 | 0.298 | 0.768 | 0.585 | 0.767 | **0.768** |

Table 6: Greater Than 4 "Too Long" Top Five Models (Across All Subjects)

*Sorted by F1 | For any classification technique not in the top 5, first occurrence and rank is shown*

- Support Vector Machines (SVM) - supervised learning model that constructs a classifier

To ensure robustness, we performed a 5-way cross validation (training a model on a random 80% of the data points and holding 20% in reserve for accuracy testing).

Each model was built using all readability measures. However, having more features can also mean extra noise and a reduction in quality. We therefore created multiple models using different permutations of our 4 Incremental Features. This allowed us to easily uncover which features are useful, and which are harmful or superfluous (some of the modeling techniques like Decision Tree of Random Forest prune features that are not used as decision points, thus automatically reducing the feature space.)

## 6.4 Modeling Evaluation

There are numerous evaluation metrics for model quality, from sensitivity to kappa. However, choosing the appropriate metric for the specific context of the problem is critical for maximizing the models' performance.

In this regard, for the "too short" model, we chose to maximize **Sensitivity**, the measure that focuses on the true positive rate. In short, by not labeling a truncation point that is too short, critical article content is missed. Thus, we need to ensure that the actual positives are correctly identified.

The "too long" model, however, has a less detrimental outcome if there are false positives or false negatives. For this model, overall performance is key, and thus we used the **F1 Score,** the harmonic mean of precision and sensitivity (thus providing a more holistic performance assessment)[6].

## 7. RESULTS: MODELING

Results from the various "too short" and "too long" modeling techniques are presented in Tables 5 and 6 respectively. While these models were trained on data from all 7 subjects, they take into account the subject area when predicting the quality of the truncation point[7].

Random Forest and SVM both performed surprisingly poorly. Further, the performance for each outcome was largely stratified based on classification technique, rather than features used. Subsequently, the top "too short" models were all variations of J48 Tree, and the top "too long" models were Logistic Regression[8].

Using the J48 Tree and Logistic Regression, we can extrapolate a scalar value that indicates the probability that a given truncation point is either "too short" or "too long." These values can then be used to inform the layout of multiple articles within a document and determining where to cut. For logistic regression, we apply the output of the model to a sigmoid function to get get a probabilistic outcome (probability that the given point is "too long").

For the decision tree, each leaf contains both the outcome and the number of instances of the training data assigned to that leaf, and how many of those instances were incorrectly classified. Thus, we can calculate the probability that a truncation point that reaches a given leaf is "too short" by the following equations: $Not\ Too\ Short = 0 + \frac{incorrectly\ classified}{total\ assigned}$ and $Too\ Short = 1 - \frac{incorrectly\ classified}{total\ assigned}$

The strengths of these two models, as shown in Tables 5 and 6, confirm our hypotheses H1 and H2, showing that we can create predictive models that can determine if a truncation point is too short or too long, based on reader impression. These results indicate that these models generate more complete (from a readability perspective) truncated news articles than existing non-semantic techniques.

## 8. LAYOUT IMPACTS

We now illustrate the utility and application of the content based article truncation algorithms in producing practical document layouts. Specifically, we examine the impact of article truncations on layout quality. As discussed earlier, layout designers strike a balance between what semantic content to keep and how to present it. In general, layout quality focuses on making documents to be more aesthetically pleasing by creating room for images or by ensuring

---

[6]In many situations, accuracy is used as a holistic measure. However, with sparse data, accuracy is a poor measure of performance because always guessing 0, or "not part of classification" can lead to high accuracy but poor performance.

[7]We did create models for each individual subject area, however,

these models were nearly identical to subsets of the global models which took subject area into account. We therefore simplified our entire process by using the global models.

[8]When building models for each subject area, these top modeling techniques were consistently the best performing.

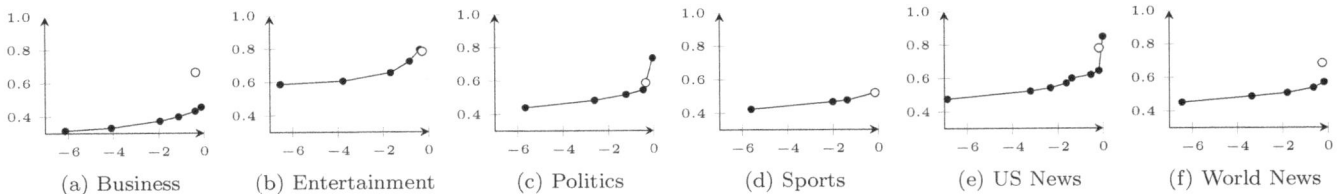

Figure 1: Semantic Content vs. Presentation Tradeoffs

*• Semantic based plots are solid circles | − Semantic efficiency frontier is solid line | ○ Non-Semantic layout is empty circle*
*Y-Axis represent "Probability too Long" | X-Axis represents Layout Quality*

(a) Non-Semantic Truncation  (b) Semantic Truncation

Figure 2: Examples of Article Layouts

*All article text and images used with permission of the Associated Press*

that blank space on a page is filled. This section, to the authors knowledge, is the first automated parallel to the traditional human drive approach that maximizes both layout *and* semantic content.

## 8.1 News Articles & Layout

To illustrate the impact of semantic based layout, we created six different layouts of news content, each taken from one of six content subject areas (Business, Sports, Entertainment, World news, US news and Politics). Articles, along with any corresponding images, were collected from the AP news feed.

Each subject area layout consisted of three long main articles and four short sidebar articles are arranged across two-pages. This allows us to test both "too short" (sidebar articles) and "too long" (main articles) measures.

## 8.2 Measuring Layout Quality

In order to explore the automatic layout improvements of our truncation algorithm, we situated this experiment within the context of the probabilistic document model (PDM) [9, 1] as a measure of document layout quality. PDM explicitly models the dependency between key design choices[9] including what content should be placed on each page, choice of relative arrangements for page elements (what template to use for each page), and template parameters (physical dimensions of page elements like images, whitespace etc.).

---
[9]The coupling between these design variables is explicitly modeled as a Bayesian network.

PDM is a *micro model* for document quality that associates a probability (or log probability quality score) distribution with each conditional design choice made on each page. These probability distributions (e.g. whitespace, template, variance of acceptable whitespace) are specified at design time by a document designer (see [9, 1]). As an example, PDM will give higher probability to the documents that use designer-preferred templates (to enhance use of images) and designer-preferred physical dimensions for page elements (e.g., image and whitespace deviating from preferred "aesthetic" values will be penalized). We use the layout synthesis method described in [1] to generate and score layouts.

## 8.3 Measuring Content: Without Semantics

As a baseline, we create layouts without semantic consideration. A reasonable approach makes the assumption that, since articles are written to be cut from the end [34], longer articles have more superfluous information and can be truncated more aggressively. We iteratively truncate paragraphs from the longest article (given all cuts made up to this point). We then evaluate each possible truncation, and choose the final truncation corresponding to the best layout score achieved. Thus, finding an ideal layout becomes a process of maximizing layout quality, and content quality is only implicitly included in the determination of which content to cut.

## 8.4 Measuring Content: Semantic Truncation

In order to account for the semantic information in each article, our two semantic truncation algorithms are re-calculated for each paragraph, such that, if the article is truncated at the start of that paragraph, the *probability too short* measure gives the probability that the remaining content in an article will be missing key content, and the *probability too long* measure gives the probability that the remaining content in an article will contain superfluous content. Thus, these two measures of semantic quality can be used to compare the content included in a given layout. Given that multi-article layouts combine multiple articles, we compute a content truncation score for all included articles by averaging the corresponding "too short" and "too long" scores.

### 8.4.1 Content vs. Presentation Tradeoffs

Subsequently, any given document is measured by both the layout quality and the content quality. However, to construct the ideal document, we must choose from several possible documents corresponding to various truncation points. For each "truncation" opportunity, we can cut a paragraph from any of the $N$ articles. To limit the number of possible documents to choose from, we set an upper limit on the number of paragraphs to cut, $m$. This results in $N^m$ permutations of possible total truncation points. However, this simplistic approach results in an intractable number of permutations. Even a moderate set of possible cuts and a small number of articles yields a huge number of documents (e.g., 10 cuts and 3 articles yields $3^{10}$=59,049 documents).

Instead of using all possible permutations, we use a sub-optimal but reasonable approach of ordering all paragraphs from all articles in ascending order of "probability too short." This allows us pick from articles that are the least likely to be missing key content. Then, among paragraphs that have the same "probability too short," we sort in descending order according to the "probability too long" measure. Thus articles that are unlikely to be missing key content, and highly likely to have superfluous content, bubble to the top. This creates a well defined sequence of possible truncations that sweeps the content space.

Each possible truncation layout is mapped to a point in 3-D space corresponding to the three measures (2 semantic-based measures described above, and 1 for layout measure). With respect to the layout size, we create two 2-D plots: long main articles (prob. too long vs. layout quality) and short sidebar articles (prob. too short vs. layout quality). In each plot we want to minimize the probability an article is too short/too long while maximizing the layout quality. We can easily eliminate *inefficient* document permutations, those that have both a larger "too short/too long" score and also at the same time a lower layout quality score. The remaining points represent a legitimate *efficient* trade-off between content and presentation. We refer to the set of document points as a pseudo-efficient frontier.[10] The exact truncation to use may be chosen by selecting a frontier point above a layout quality threshold that minimizes the probability too long/short. This gives a natural tradeoff between content and presentation, thus automating this selection.

## 8.5 Results & Discussion

For each of the six subject areas, we extract and plot the frontiers in Figure 1. For the long main articles, the frontiers are curves. By sliding along the frontier, content semantics can be easily traded for presentation quality. Thus, an ideal document layout can be determined.

### 8.5.1 Comparing Semantic & Non-Semantic Layout

For three areas (Business, World, US News) the non-semantic truncation[11] created sub-optimal and *inefficient* layouts[11] showing that the content based approach yields better layouts and less superfluous content in these cases. For example, Figure 2 shows visual comparisons for the Business news case. Notice[12] that the non-semantic truncation includes superfluous content and a twitter link at the end of the Macy's article that is unrelated to the content. In fact the semantic based truncation made space for additional images, increasing layout quality while also minimizing the probability "too long".

For two of the area (Politics, Sports) the non-semantic truncation corresponds exactly to a semantic-based frontier point. For only one area (Entertainment) the non-semantic based truncation outperforms (albeit slightly) the semantic-based method. This non-semantic layout, however, was never considered by the frontier because we cannot explore all possible truncations to get a true *efficient frontier*. However, since we sweep the space in a principled manner, we are never too far from a possible optimal point.

In general the results show that the content-based truncation strategy can automatically harmonize content and presentation, something a skilled content editor, together with a publication designer, had to manually do in the past.

### 8.5.2 SideBar: Extremely Aggressive Truncation

Given the extremely aggressive truncation required to fit 4 short articles into the sidebars, all truncations that fit the content with reasonable quality had the same probability that an article was too short. In other words, our algorithm was quite sure (no variation) that the requisite truncation of the articles were way too short. Thus the frontier was a single point, representing the highest quality layout of the sidebar articles with this aggressive truncation.

This is a byproduct of the users that generated the ratings of truncation point quality. These reviewers were members of the general public, and subsequently were extremely conservative with their minimal acceptable content. This is in stark contrast to layout editors who are more comfortable aggressively cutting content to fit extremely small space constraints. New models could be generated if layout editors were tasked to rate truncation points, or members of the general public were explicitly told that articles needed to be truncated to fit within an extremely small area. We strongly suspect that minimal acceptable truncation points would be lower, and provide discrimination among the various very short truncation points.

## 9. FUTURE WORK

One potential direction of future work is to expand this approach to model expert layout editors and journalists as to their perceived truncation point quality. Given that this work focused exclusively on *readers'* perceived quality, editors and journalists may have a more aggressive or nuanced view as to what is superfluous or necessary.

## 10. CONCLUSION

Creating ideal layouts is a challenge for both human layout editors, and computer systems. Efficient solutions strike

---

[10] Not all possible permutations are explored

[11] Figure 1, non-semantic point is above and to the left of frontier
[12] PDF is high resolution, and can be zoomed in.

a balance between aesthetics and semantic content within articles. Prior to this work, computer layout systems truncated content from articles to create documents based almost exclusively on optimizing aesthetics, at the detriment of any semantic information. In response, we have created the first model of truncation quality (based on the content of the article) and the first layout approach that integrates both layout quality *and* article content quality. These models were built from data collected during an extensive user study, and the resulting document layouts were validated and compared to that of non-semantic based approaches (in a real world context). The semantic+layout quality documents utilized more images while maximizing the articles' semantic information.

# 11. REFERENCES

[1] I. Ahmadullin and N. Damera-Venkata. Hierarchical probabilistic model for news composition. In *DocEng*, page 141, New York, New York, USA, Sept. 2013. ACM Request Permissions.

[2] G. J. Badros, A. Borning, and P. J. Stuckey. The Cassowary linear arithmetic constraint solving algorithm. *TOCHI*, 8(4 (Dec)):267–306, Dec. 2001.

[3] J. Batista and D. Oliverira. Two algorithms for automatic document page layout. In *DocEng*, page 141, New York, New York, USA, Sept. 2008. ACM Request Permissions.

[4] D. Beeferman, A. Berger, and J. Lafferty. Statistical Models for Text Segmentation. *Machine learning*, 34(1-3):177–210, 1999.

[5] D. M. Blei, A. Y. Ng, and M. I. Jordan. Latent dirichlet allocation. *The Journal of Machine Learning Research*, 3:993–1022, Mar. 2003.

[6] A. Brüggemann-Klein, R. Klein, and S. Wohlfeil. On the pagination of complex documents. *Lecture Notes in Computer Science*, 2598:49–68, 2003.

[7] F. Chua and S. Asur. Automatic Summarization of Events From Social Media. In *ICWSM*, 2013.

[8] P. Ciancarini, A. Di Iorio, L. Furini, and F. Vitali. High-quality pagination for publishing. *Software—Practice & Experience*, 42(6), June 2012.

[9] N. Damera-Venkata, J. Bento, and E. O'Brien-Strain. Probabilistic document model for automated document composition. In *DocEng*, page 3, New York, New York, USA, Sept. 2011. ACM Request Permissions.

[10] H. P. Edmundson. New Methods in Automatic Extracting. *Journal of the ACM (JACM*, 16(2), Apr. 1969.

[11] G. Erkan and D. R. Radev. LexRank: Graph-based lexical centrality as salience in text summarization. *J Artif Intell Res(JAIR)*, 2004.

[12] M. Fiszman, T. C. Rindflesch, and H. Kilicoglu. Abstraction summarization for managing the biomedical research literature. pages 76–83, May 2004.

[13] F. Giannetti. An exploratory mapping strategy for web-driven magazines. In *Proceeding of the eighth ACM symposium*, pages 223–229, New York, New York, USA, 2008. ACM Press.

[14] A. Haghighi and L. Vanderwende. Exploring content models for multi-document summarization. pages 362–370, May 2009.

[15] J. Hailpern, N. Damera-Venkata, and M. Danilevsky. Pagination: It's what you say, not how long it takes to say it. In *DocENG*. ACM, 2014.

[16] J. Hailpern and B. A. Huberman. Echo: the editor's wisdom with the elegance of a magazine. In *EICS*. ACM Request Permissions, June 2013.

[17] M. A. Hearst. TextTiling: segmenting text into multi-paragraph subtopic passages. *Computational Linguistics*, 23(1), Mar. 1997.

[18] N. Hurst, W. Li, and K. Marriott. Review of automatic document formatting. In *DocEng*, page 99, New York, New York, USA, Sept. 2009. ACM Request Permissions.

[19] C. Jacobs, W. Li, E. Schrier, D. Bargeron, and D. Salesin. Adaptive grid-based document layout. *SIGGRAPH*, 22(3):838–847, July 2003.

[20] N. Jamil, J. Mueller, C. Lutteroth, and G. Weber. Extending Linear Relaxation for User Interface Layout. In *ICTAI*. IEEE Computer Society, Nov. 2012.

[21] I. Kastner and C. Monz. Automatic single-document key fact extraction from newswire articles. In *EACL*. Association for Computational Linguistics, Mar. 2009.

[22] R. Katragadda, P. Pingali, and V. Varma. Sentence position revisited: a robust light-weight update summarization baseline algorithm. pages 46–52, June 2009.

[23] C.-Y. Lin and E. Hovy. Identifying topics by position. In *ANCL*. Association for Computational Linguistics, Mar. 1997.

[24] J. Liu, E. Wagner, and L. Birnbaum. Compare&contrast: using the web to discover comparable cases for news stories. In *WWW*, page 541, New York, New York, USA, May 2007. ACM.

[25] C. Lutteroth, R. Strandh, and G. Weber. Domain Specific High-Level Constraints for User Interface Layout. *Constraints*, 13(3), Sept. 2008.

[26] R. Mihalcea and P. Tarau. TextRank: Bringing order into texts. In *EMNLP*, 2004.

[27] A. Nenkova. Automatic text summarization of newswire: lessons learned from the document understanding conference. In *AAAI*. AAAI Press, July 2005.

[28] A. Nenkova and L. Vanderwende. The impact of frequency on summarization. Technical Report MSR-TR-2005-101, Microsoft Research, 2005.

[29] L. Pevzner and M. A. Hearst. A critique and improvement of an evaluation metric for text segmentation. *Computational Linguistics*, 2002.

[30] H. Schütze and C. Silverstein. Projections for efficient document clustering. In *SIGIR*, pages 74–81, New York, New York, USA, Dec. 1997. ACM Request Permissions.

[31] A. Scoditti and W. Stuerzlinger. A new layout method for graphical user interfaces. In *TIC-STH*, pages 642–647. IEEE, 2009.

[32] Y. Seki, K. Eguchi, and N. Kando. Compact Summarization for Mobile Phones. *Mobile and Ubiquitous Information Access*, 2954(Chapter 13):172–186, 2004.

[33] J. Seo and W. B. Croft. Unsupervised estimation of dirichlet smoothing parameters. In *SIGIR '10*, pages 759–760, New York, New York, USA, 2010. ACM Press.

[34] T. A. van Dijk. *News as discourse*. Lawrence Erlbaum Associates, Inc, 1988.

[35] T. Weninger, W. H. Hsu, and J. Han. CETR: content extraction via tag ratios. *WWW 2010*, 2010.

[36] C. C. Yang and F. L. Wang. Automatic summarization of financial news delivery on mobile devices. In *WWW'03*, 2003.

[37] C. C. Yang and F. L. Wang. Hierarchical summarization of large documents. *J. of the American Society for Information Science and Technology*, 59(6), Apr. 2008.

[38] C. Zeidler, J. Müller, C. Lutteroth, and G. Weber. Comparing the usability of grid-bag and constraint-based layouts. In *OzCHI*, pages 674–682, New York, New York, USA, Nov. 2012. ACM Request Permissions.

[39] C. Zhai. *Statistical Language Models for Information Retrieval*. Morgan & Claypool Publishers, 2009.

# JAR Tool: Using Document Analysis for Improving the Throughput of High Performance Printing Environments

Mariana Kolberg
UFRGS
Porto Alegre, Brazil
mlkolberg@inf.ufrgs.br

Luiz Gustavo Fernandes
GMAP - FACIN - PUCRS
Porto Alegre, Brazil
luiz.fernandes@pucrs.br

Mateus Raeder
GMAP - FACIN - PUCRS
Porto Alegre, Brazil
mateus.raeder@acad.pucrs.br

Carolina Fonseca
GMAP - FACIN - PUCRS
Porto Alegre, Brazil
carolina.fonseca@acad.pucrs.br

## ABSTRACT

Digital printers have consistently improved their speed in the past years. Meanwhile, the need for document personalization and customization has increased. As a consequence of these two facts, the traditional rasterization process has become a highly demanding computational step in the printing workflow. Moreover, Print Service Providers are now using multiple RIP engines to speed up the whole document rasterization process, and depending on the input document characteristics the rasterization process may not achieve the print-engine speed creating a unwanted bottleneck. In this scenario, we developed a tool called Job Adaptive Router (JAR) aiming at improving the throughput of the rasterization process through a clever load balance among RIP engines which is based on information obtained by the analysis of input documents content. Furthermore, along with this tool we propose some strategies that consider relevant characteristics of documents, such as transparency and reusability of images, to split the job in a more intelligent way. The obtained results confirm that the use of the proposed tool improved the rasterization process performance.

## Categories and Subject Descriptors

I.7 [**Document and Text Processing**]: Document management; I.7.2 [**Document and Text Processing**]: Document Preparation; I.7.4 [**Document and Text Processing**]: Electronic Publishing

## Keywords

Document Analysis; Document profiling; High performance printing; Load balancing

## 1. INTRODUCTION

Digital printers have consistently improved their speed in the past years. Meanwhile, the need for document personalization and customization has increased. As a consequence of these facts, the traditional rasterization process, responsible for transforming documents described in formats that most printers cannot interpret (e.g. *PDF*) in printable formats (e.g. *Bitmap*), has become a highly demanding computational step in the printing workflow. In general, a Print Service Provider (or PSP) uses a set of RIP (*Raster Image Processing*) engines in parallel to achieve the best possible performance considering a queue of $n$ initial jobs to be processed and new jobs being inserted in the queue at any time.

However, a wide variety of PDF documents with different characteristics can be found in the context of PSPs. The presence of each characteristic in a document page has a different impact on the computational time needed to raster it. In this context, the information about documents characteristics might be used to split the document in fragments in a clever way, improving the load balance of documents among RIP engines and leading to a better performance of the rasterization process. This paper presents the development of a tool named Job Adaptive Router (JAR) aiming at balancing the workload among RIP engines and optimizing the rasterization process. JAR uses the metrics proposed in [1, 3] to estimate the job rasterization cost and chooses the most suitable strategy to split the document considering the job characteristics that might have an important influence on the computational time. Our main contribution in this paper can be summarized as (i) the development of a Job Adaptive Router (JAR) to obtain a fair load balance among RIPs and (ii) the definition of 5 different strategies based on document analysis to split the queue in such a way that the workload will be balanced among RIPs.

## 2. JOB ADAPTIVE ROUTER

In general, load balance algorithms for the rasterization process do not consider documents internal content. However, the document content is a key information in PSP scenario and a detailed analysis of the PDF document characteristics may improve the rasterization throughput. The identification of some specific characteristics in each document page allows a more intelligent workload division among RIPs.

We first had to modify the PDF Profiler tool to be able to compute the computational cost of each page of the document. In addition, we developed a tool called PDF Splitter, which breaks the PDF document into several fragments (which will be the tasks to be rasterized). PDF Splitter can be used to break the input document in two ways: individual pages or groups of pages. Note that the least grain of each piece of a fragment is a page.

## 2.1 JAR Architecture

The Job Adaptive Router main goal is to decide during the runtime which developed strategy will be selected for a given job. This decision is based on the document information contained in a XML file provided by PDF Profiler. Based on this information, JAR will split the document generating fragments that will be rasterized. Figure 1 shows an overview of the rasterization process using JAR tool.

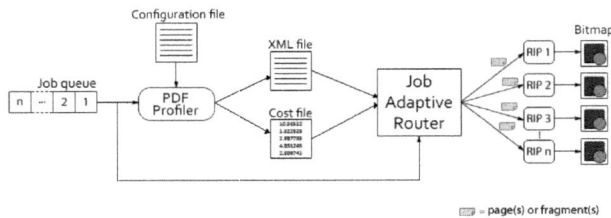

Figure 1: Overview of rasterization process using JAR

The *Job queue* has all jobs (PDF documents) that must be rasterized, and each one of them is sent to PDF Profiler tool. In addition to that, PDF Profiler also receives as input a *Configuration file* which indicates which information must be extracted from the job. Thus, PDF Profiler analyzes the job and generates two files: (i) the file containing the computational cost of each page; (ii) a XML file containing information about each document page (which pages contain text, which contain images, whether these images are opaque, transparent or reusable, etc.). After that, JAR analyzes these files and discovers which strategy should be used for a given job.

Figure 2 presents the JAR internal architecture. JAR is divided into 3 modules: Strategy Identifier, Fragment Organizer and PDF Splitter. Each one of these modules has a specific function and, in order to improve the performance, they run in different concurrent threads. First, the XML and cost files are read by the Strategy Identifier module. This module is mainly responsible for finding out which strategy will be used over the jobs. According to the information obtained from the XML file, Strategy Identifier knows the characteristics of the job, such as the amount of pages with transparency and/or reusability, choosing the best strategy. Strategy Identifier also reads the cost file to create a list of job pages with their characteristics and costs.

After discovering the best strategy, the Strategy Identifier module sends it along with a list of jobs pages characteristics for the next module, the Fragment Organizer. This module is responsible for informing the PDF Splitter module how the job must be split. As mentioned before, the PDF Splitter only divides the job into fragments and needs to known which pages constitute each fragment. Thus, the way fragments will be created depends on the selected strategy. In this context, Fragment Organizer module receives

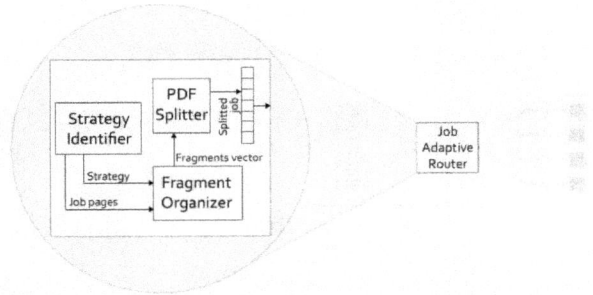

Figure 2: JAR internal architecture

the Strategy Identifier output and then creates a *Fragments vector*, which contains the information of which pages will be grouped to form each fragment. This *Fragments vector* is sent to the PDF Splitter that creates the job fragments and inserts them into another queue of jobs ready to be sent to the available RIPs.

## 2.2 Developed Strategies

This section proposes five strategies to obtain a better load balancing among RIPs, focusing on two job characteristics that might have an important influence on the computational time for rasterizing a job [3]: the amount of reusable objects and transparent images. The computational cost of each page is obtained using PDF Profiler tool.

The first strategy, called *Transparency Strategy*, is suitable for documents which have only transparent images without any reusable images. Since the cost for rasterizing pages with transparent images is high, these pages should not be allocated to a single RIP. This algorithm separates the pages with transparency, ordering them by their computational cost (from the highest to the lowest cost) in a queue of pages. After ordering these pages with transparency, the remaining pages of the job (pages with opaque images and/or text) are also sorted by their computational cost and are inserted individually into the pages queue.

The *Reusability Strategy* deals with documents which have reusable images but no transparent images. The proposed algorithm first combines the pages with reusable objects, creating sets of pages that contains the same image. After that, these sets are inserted into the queue of pages, sorted by their computational cost (from the highest to lowest). The remaining pages are inserted in the same queue individually. Finally, the load distribution is performed creating $n$ fragments (where $n$ is the number of RIPs).

The *More-Transparency-than-Reusability Strategy* is a first mixed strategy and deals with documents that have more pages with transparent images than pages with reusable images. As the most costly pages of a PDF document are that ones that contain transparency, these pages are sorted by their computational cost and inserted in the page queue. After that, pages with reusability are grouped, creating sets of pages that are also inserted in the page queue, always sorted by their computational cost. The remaining pages of the job are inserted individually in the same queue. When all pages are in this queue, the distribution of the pages or sets among the fragments starts.

The *More-Reusability-than-Transparency Strategy* is suitable for PDF documents which combine transparency and reusability but there are more pages with reusability than pages with transparency. Similarly to the *Reusability strategy*, the algorithm groups all pages with the same reusable image, creating different sets. They are then inserted in the page queue according to their computational cost. Pages containing transparency are the next to be inserted in the queue followed by pages with opaque images and/or text. Once all pages/sets are in the queue, they are distributed among the fragments.

Finally, the *No-Transparency, No-Reusability Strategy* was developed to be used in the case where no transparent or reusable object are found. In that case, the algorithm sorts all pages by their computational cost (from the highest to the lowest cost). After that, pages are inserted in the page queue and they are distributed among fragments.

# 3. PERFORMANCE EVALUATION

This section presents the environment setup and input job queues used to run the Job Adaptive Router and discusses the average gain achieved using our tool. Results were obtained using the ImageMagick convert tool, which is an open-source RIP engine. In the tests, PDF documents were rasterized using a 40 dpi resolution.

Aiming at verifying JAR performance, we compared the results with a well known algorithm: Largest Processing Time First (LPT) [2]. Since we need the computational time to use LPT algorithm, it is possible that RIP engines are idle waiting for jobs that are blocked in the queue waiting to be analyzed. To overcome this problem, we made a slight modification in the LPT algorithm: while a thread executes the PDF Profiler step, another thread concurrently sends jobs to the RIPs - even though they were not analyzed by the PDF Profiler tool. This improved version was called Optimized-LPT (O-LPT).

In order to get closer to the reality of the PSPs, we perform tests on a cluster composed of 32 machines connected by a high-speed Gigabit Ethernet network. Each machine consists of two AMD Opteron 246 2.0 GHz, 8 GB of main memory and 1TB hard drive. The operating system of these machines is Linux (Ubuntu 4.2.4-1ubuntu4) version 2.6.24. Each node of this cluster run one RIP engine.

To implement the five previously described strategies, the programming language we used was Java (version 1.6). We also used the Java iText library (version 2.0.7) to create the set of input jobs. The MPJ-Express library was used to enable the communication among processes.

A set of 75 jobs with different characteristics was created to evaluate the JAR Tool and the five developed strategies. The number of pages of each job vary from 60 to 220. These jobs are divided into five groups: PDFs with transparencies, PDFs with reusability, PDFs with more transparency than reusability, PDFs with more reusability than transparency and PDFs that present neither transparency nor reusability.

Moreover, for testing JAR using the five strategies developed, six different queue configurations were created: Queue 1 - 15 PDF documents with transparency; Queue 2 - 15 PDF documents with reusability; Queue 3 - 15 PDF documents with more transparency than reusability; Queue 4 - 15 PDF documents with more reusability than transparency; Queue 5 - 15 PDF documents with no transparency or reusability; Queue 6 - 15 PDF documents with mixed characteristics as follows: 3 with transparency; 3 with reusability; 3 with more

transparency than reusability; 3 with more reusability than transparency; 3 with no transparency or reusability.

## 3.1 JAR Performance Analysis

This section presents the performance analysis of the JAR tool in comparison to the Optimized-LPT algorithm. In this sense, 30 runs were performed over each one of the six queues already described, from which the highest and lowest times were removed, obtaining an average of the other 28 values. For each execution, one process will execute JAR, meaning that to exist RIPs in parallel, the number of processes should not be less than three (one to run JAR and 2 for RIPs). Moreover, the number of processes ranged from 3 to 19.

| Queue 1 | 3 | 4 | 5 | 6 | 7 | 8 | 9 | 10 | 11 |
|---|---|---|---|---|---|---|---|---|---|
| JAR | 447.6 | 312.4 | 305.2 | 220.2 | 190.8 | 170.6 | 146.6 | 131.8 | 126.6 |
| O-LPT | 488.6 | 308.8 | 258.6 | 250.8 | 189.4 | 150.8 | 154.8 | 139.6 | 157.4 |
| | 12 | 13 | 14 | 15 | 16 | 17 | 18 | 19 | |
| JAR | 122.4 | 120.2 | 119.8 | 121.2 | 117.6 | 122.8 | 123.8 | 118.4 | |
| O-LPT | 136.8 | 137.2 | 131.6 | 131.8 | 148.2 | 147.2 | 133.6 | 148.4 | |
| Queue 2 | 3 | 4 | 5 | 6 | 7 | 8 | 9 | 10 | 11 |
| JAR | 758.4 | 537.8 | 515.4 | 422.2 | 337.6 | 300.2 | 292.4 | 274.8 | 261.2 |
| O-LPT | 896.8 | 480.6 | 504.8 | 328.2 | 301.4 | 310.2 | 260.6 | 259.6 | 273.6 |
| | 12 | 13 | 14 | 15 | 16 | 17 | 18 | 19 | |
| JAR | 232.4 | 226.6 | 223.8 | 227.2 | 225.8 | 225.4 | 226.8 | 224.4 | |
| O-LPT | 205.4 | 204.4 | 231.6 | 232.2 | 241.4 | 250.2 | 249.8 | 213.6 | |
| Queue 3 | 3 | 4 | 5 | 6 | 7 | 8 | 9 | 10 | 11 |
| JAR | 467.4 | 333.8 | 292.8 | 240.4 | 181.8 | 151.6 | 134.2 | 129.6 | 128.4 |
| O-LPT | 485.4 | 265.6 | 264.6 | 241.6 | 197.8 | 169.4 | 153.2 | 148.4 | 164.2 |
| | 12 | 13 | 14 | 15 | 16 | 17 | 18 | 19 | |
| JAR | 118.4 | 115.8 | 115.6 | 116.8 | 118.4 | 116.8 | 117.6 | 118.4 | |
| O-LPT | 122.6 | 137.8 | 132.2 | 123.4 | 147.8 | 131.8 | 131.6 | 139.2 | |
| Queue 4 | 3 | 4 | 5 | 6 | 7 | 8 | 9 | 10 | 11 |
| JAR | 408.4 | 325.4 | 234.6 | 213.6 | 179.8 | 141.6 | 129.8 | 114.6 | 111.8 |
| O-LPT | 425.8 | 224.2 | 221.4 | 208.6 | 147.8 | 159.2 | 133.4 | 125.4 | 137.4 |
| | 12 | 13 | 14 | 15 | 16 | 17 | 18 | 19 | |
| JAR | 108.4 | 108.8 | 109.8 | 108.8 | 112.2 | 109.4 | 113.8 | 113.6 | |
| O-LPT | 117.4 | 134.2 | 120.2 | 115.2 | 136.6 | 127.2 | 126.2 | 124.4 | |
| Queue 5 | 3 | 4 | 5 | 6 | 7 | 8 | 9 | 10 | 11 |
| JAR | 381.8 | 285.2 | 259.8 | 196.6 | 166.6 | 150.8 | 146.2 | 122.4 | 120.2 |
| O-LPT | 401.8 | 266.4 | 263.8 | 219.4 | 167.6 | 150.2 | 148.2 | 126.4 | 133.8 |
| | 12 | 13 | 14 | 15 | 16 | 17 | 18 | 19 | |
| JAR | 118.4 | 118.8 | 103.4 | 103.2 | 105.4 | 107.8 | 107.8 | 107.2 | |
| O-LPT | 121.6 | 132.2 | 115.4 | 117.8 | 127.4 | 132.2 | 119.2 | 128.2 | |
| Queue 6 | 3 | 4 | 5 | 6 | 7 | 8 | 9 | 10 | 11 |
| JAR | 408.6 | 350.2 | 285.2 | 233.8 | 213.2 | 167.6 | 159.6 | 145.4 | 147.2 |
| O-LPT | 498.4 | 300.6 | 288.2 | 232.8 | 218.6 | 169.4 | 164.2 | 150.8 | 168.6 |
| | 12 | 13 | 14 | 15 | 16 | 17 | 18 | 19 | |
| JAR | 147.6 | 146.4 | 140.6 | 143.8 | 136.8 | 138.2 | 132.4 | 131.6 | |
| O-LPT | 160.8 | 143.4 | 137.2 | 133.6 | 153.4 | 161.2 | 146.8 | 162.2 | |

Table 1: Execution times (in seconds)

It is possible to see in Table 1 the situation in which the *Transparency* strategy was selected by JAR for Queue 1. This strategy achieved better results in 13 of the 17 processes configurations, and when using 5 process JAR execution time presented a execution time more than 40 seconds faster than Optimized-LPT. The values obtained for *Reusability* strategy are also shown in Table 1. In this case, the Optimized-LPT, in general, presented better performance than JAR selected strategy in 9 of the 17 configurations. The better results of Optimized-LPT over the *Reusability* strategy can be explained by the chosen grain size. It is possible that the gain of grouping pages with reusable images may not compensate the time spent by JAR.

The time obtained using the queue containing documents with more transparency than reusability (Queue 3) can be seen in Table 1. Note that the performance of Optimized-LPT is better than the *More-Transparency-than-Reusability* strategy only in processes 4 and 5, showing that JAR chosen strategy has a better performance in this case. In the case of queue 4 (documents with more reusability than trans-

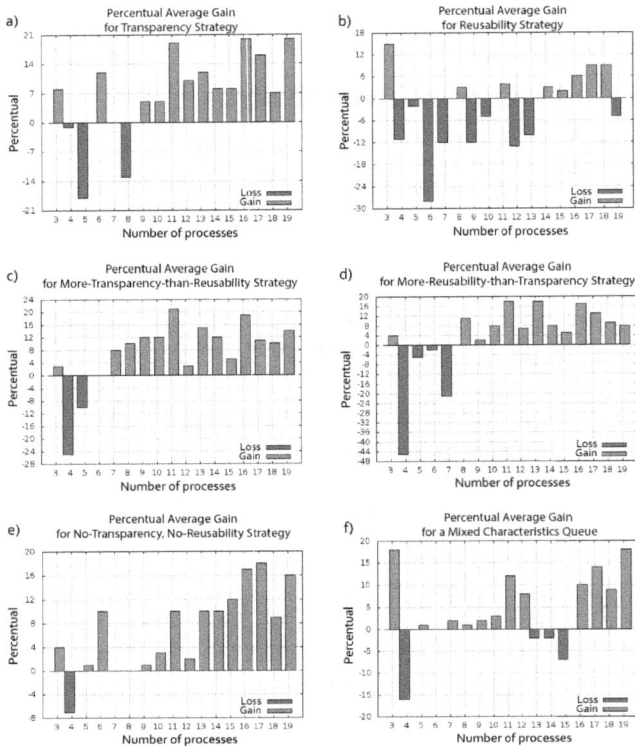

Figure 3: JAR Percentual Average Gain

| Queue | Average of % differences | JAR wins | Highest % gain |
|-------|--------------------------|----------|----------------|
| 1 | 7.22 | 13/17 | 20.64 |
| 2 | -2.79 | 8/17 | 15.43 |
| 3 | 7.50 | 15/17 | 21.80 |
| 4 | 3.60 | 13/17 | 18.93 |
| 5 | 7.17 | 15/17 | 18.47 |
| 6 | 4.38 | 12/17 | 18.87 |

Table 2: *Performance summary*

*More-Transparency-than-Reusability* (Figure 3c) and *No-Transparency, No-Reusability* (Figure 3e) strategies presented worse results than Optimized-LPT only in 2 situations. When a queue of heterogeneous documents was used (Figure 3f), JAR obtained a better performance than Optimized-LPT with an average of percentage differences equals to 4.38%. Only the *Reusability* strategy showed a performance loss in general (Figure 3b), resulting in an average of -2.79%.

## 4. CONCLUSION

This paper presented the Job Adaptive Router tool for achieving a fair load balance among RIPs in the rasterization process of high performance printing environments. JAR architecture uses the information about documents content to decide during runtime which load balance strategy should be used for a given job considering its characteristics. The results obtained using JAR presented a better load balance, resulting in performance gains in comparison to Optimized-LPT. It is important to highlight that PSPs deal with a wide variety of documents with different characteristics, like the scenario of queue 6. As can be seen in Figure 3f, in this situation JAR presents average gains up to 18.87%. This scenario is specially important since it illustrates the JAR ability to dynamically choose the best strategy for each document. Moreover, it is possible to notice that the more processes we use, the better is the average gain of JAR in comparison with Optimized-LPT, which indicates a good scalability. Based on the good results, a further research is needed for investigating the JAR portability for multiprocessor machines, once nowadays clusters are typically multiprocessor machines. In addition, the analysis of the impact of other document characteristics in the rasterization time will be conducted aiming at the creation of new strategies.

## 5. REFERENCES

[1] L. G. Fernandes, T. Nunes, M. Kolberg, F. Giannetti, R. Nemetz, and A. Cabeda. Job profiling and queue management in high performance printing. *Computer Science - Research and Development*, 27(2):147–166, May 2012.

[2] R. L. Graham. Bounds on Multiprocessing Timing Anomalies. *SIAM Journal on Applied Mathematics*, 17(2):416–429, March 1969.

[3] T. Nunes, F. Giannetti, M. Kolberg, R. Nemetz, A. Cabeda, and L. G. Fernandes. Job profiling in high performance printing. In *Proceedings of the 9th ACM symposium on Document engineering*, DocEng '09, pages 109–118, New York, NY, USA, 2009. ACM.

parency), the results obtained with JAR lost in some configurations, but in general JAR presents better performance than Optimized-LPT. For instance, the strategy selected by JAR performed the rasterization process 25.6 seconds faster than Optimized-LPT over 11 processes.

For a queue composed of documents with no transparency nor reusable images, the strategy chosen by JAR wins in 15 of the 17 occasions compared to Optimized-LPT. Only in 2 occasions the performance obtained with Optimized-LPT is better, and in the case of 8 processes the difference is only 0.6 seconds; Finally, the results for the sixth queue (using for each document the suitable strategy, thereby addressing all five strategies) once again show that JAR performs better than Optimized-LPT in most cases (12 out of 17).

### 3.2 JAR Percentual Avarage Gain

This section discusses the percentual average gain for each strategy using JAR. Figure 3 presents six graphs comparing all obtained results between JAR and Optimized-LPT in terms of percentage difference. Moreover, Table 2 contains important information about each queue tested.

As can be seen in Figure 3a, only in 4 situations JAR presented worse results. However, in general the *Transparency* strategy performed better than Optimized-LPT, with an average of percentage difference equals to 7.22%. That also occurs with the *More-Reusability-than-Transparency* strategy (Figure 3d), which lost also in four cases but in most cases obtained a better gain than Optimized-LPT, with an average of the percentage differences equals to 3.60%.

# Humanist-centric Tools for Big Data:
# Berkeley Prosopography Services

Patrick Schmitz
OCIO/Research IT
UC Berkeley
Berkeley, CA
pschmitz@berkeley.edu

Dr. Laurie Pearce
Dept. of Near Eastern Studies
UC Berkeley
Berkeley, CA
lpearce@berkeley.edu

## ABSTRACT

In this paper, we describe Berkeley Prosopography Services (BPS), a new set of tools for prosopography - the identification of individuals and study of their interactions - in support of humanities research. Prosopography is an example of "big data" in the humanities, characterized not by the size of the datasets, but by the way that computational and data-driven methods can transform scholarly workflows. BPS is based upon re-usable infrastructure, supporting generalized web services for corpus management, social network analysis, and visualization. The BPS disambiguation model is a formal implementation of the traditional heuristics used by humanists, and supports plug-in rules for adaptation to a wide range of domain corpora. A workspace model supports exploratory research and collaboration. We contrast the BPS model of configurable heuristic rules to other approaches for automated text analysis, and explain how our model facilitates interpretation by humanist researchers. We describe the significance of the BPS assertion model in which researchers assert conclusions or possibilities, allowing them to override automated inference, to explore ideas in what-if scenarios, and to formally publish and subscribe-to asserted annotations among colleagues, and/or with students. We present an initial evaluation of researchers' experience using the tools to study corpora of cuneiform tablets, and describe plans to expand the application of the tools to a broader range of corpora.

## Categories and Subject Descriptors

H.3.1 [**Information Storage and Retrieval**]: Content Analysis and Indexing – *Linguistic processing*, H.3.5 [**Information Storage and Retrieval**]: Online Information Services–*Web-based services*, D.2.13 [**Software Engineering**]: Reusable software.

## General Terms

Design, Experimentation, Human Factors.

## Keywords

Annotation; Assertions; Big Data; Cyberinfrastructure; Digital Humanities; Prosopography; Social Network Analysis; Web-services.

## 1. INTRODUCTION

A long tradition of data-driven research in the physical and life sciences has made for a relatively straight-forward transition to the techniques of data science and so-called "big data". However, in much of the humanities, traditional scholarship has focused on close examination of texts and the interpretation of associated corpora. While linguistic and other analytic tools have shifted some research more toward data science, the transition to the requisite/accompanying tools has not been a natural one for many humanist scholars.

In both the sciences and the humanities, the promise of big data is that new insights may be garnered through the analysis of datasets that are significantly larger than those that could reasonably be considered before, that new questions may be asked and answered, and that new connections may be found across corpora and domains. In the sciences, the transformative aspect is often understood in terms of the huge increase in data gathering, storage, and processing techniques, and so big data is often associated with measures of scale like petabytes or even exabytes of data. However beyond the popular definitions of big data in terms of the size and processing requirements, the real shift has been in the *practices* of scholarly inquiry [15]. As examples, astronomers have shifted from direct (or indirect) observation to pure data analysis, and with the rapid drop in the cost of genetic sequencing, a whole new data-driven approach has come into practice in life sciences (these new approaches are often distinguished as *computational* biology, etc.).

While the shift in the sciences is associated with large scale data and computation, applying these same measures and notions of scale to the humanities misses the point that the transformative aspect is fundamentally an expansion of a scholarly workflow focused on close reading and interpretation of texts, to one in which analytic tools enable the consideration of larger corpora and the associated relationships among entities, linguistic patterns, etc. Moreover, while numerical and analytic tools comport with the tradition of research in the sciences, many such tools do not fit well with the conceptual models and scholarly workflows of research in the humanities.

As the tools and methods of document engineering are applied to larger and larger corpora, document engineering for big data becomes a more pressing challenge. Just as with the variance across domains, however, the challenge is sometimes one of efficiently managing large quantities of content, and sometimes one of incorporating new workflows into document engineering applications to accommodate the shifts that result in processing and analyzing a new scale of corpus content.

Against this background, we describe Berkeley Prosopography Services (BPS): an interactive tool-kit for analyzing and visualizing prosopographical datasets, available to researchers working in diverse disciplines and operating on a range of data that derives from a variety of text sources and formats. BPS innovates by providing software tools to perform association and computation tasks for name disambiguation, long done by hand, by adding a new model for curation and collaboration, and by connecting Social Network Analysis (SNA) tools and visualizations that reveal patterns and key features in a social network. BPS is built as an automation of the same conceptual models that humanist researchers have used in their analyses, and avoids (or de-emphasizes) abstract mathematical models that are in wider use in machine-learning or purely statistical tools. The BPS tools are developed using current software best practices, which provide a reusable, scalable and more sustainable software base than is commonly implemented by digital humanities research tools. BPS provides novel productivity tools, visualization tools, and workspace support for exploration and collaboration.

## 1.1 Finding Big Data in <500K Clay Tablets

The total number of cuneiform texts cataloged in museums, libraries, and private collections throughout the world is well under 500,000 (cdli.ucla.edu). The number is at once stunningly large and small. These clay and stone documents, composed in one of the world's oldest writing systems, provide the first documentation of three and one-half millennia of human activity—economic, religious, intellectual, and scientific. It is remarkable both that so many have survived and, at the same time, frustrating that the uneven distribution of their number over such a long time span means that the study of various times and places often depends on fragmentary data (Figure 1). Nonetheless, scholars of the ancient Near East, lands and empires that flourished in modern Iraq, parts of Syria, Turkey, and Iran, ask of the available resources questions recognizable from many other humanities disciplines. These scholars are increasingly turning to methodologies and tools from the digital and social science worlds to frame and answer their research agendas.

An exploration of the remarkable embrace of digital tools by practitioners of this recondite specialty deserves more attention than might be expected, particularly in light of the size of text

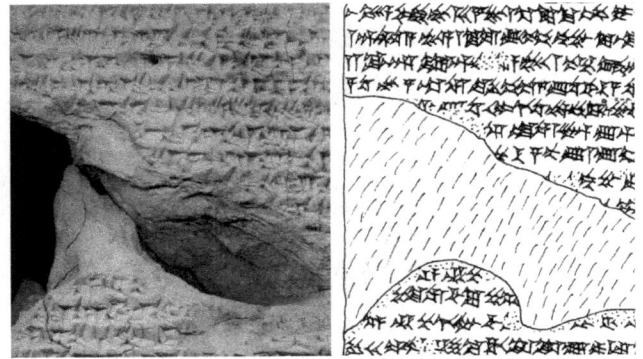

Figure 1: Fragmentary document – photograph and line drawing of a broken cuneiform text passage.

corpora with which researchers are concerned—from several hundred to ±10,000—and the corresponding (small) digital footprint of such data as presented in a standard off-the-shelf database. Nonetheless, the data and the questions researchers are asking of it suggest that even "small data" faces challenges in modeling authority and data review, areas of concern in big data.

BPS is unique as a tool-kit for prosopography: it emulates the workflow—including, and notably, the *uncertainty*—of real scholars grappling with data analysis. While the small cuneiform corpus of some 500 texts from the city of Uruk in the 4th-3rd centuries BCE would seem to consign it irrevocably to the realm of small data, that same size served BPS well as a development corpus as it attempted to capture and replicate in digital tools the human researcher's analytic process(es) of disambiguation of multiple instances of name-sakes into discrete name instances, even as it allowed for a process of modeling authority, scholarly debate and the *communis opinio*.

The central problem in prosopography, and thus, in the social network analysis that draws upon it, is the disambiguation of the many individuals who share the same names. Culturally specific naming practices may simplify or complicate the process: kings of England named Henry are numbered VI, VII, VIII, just as men in

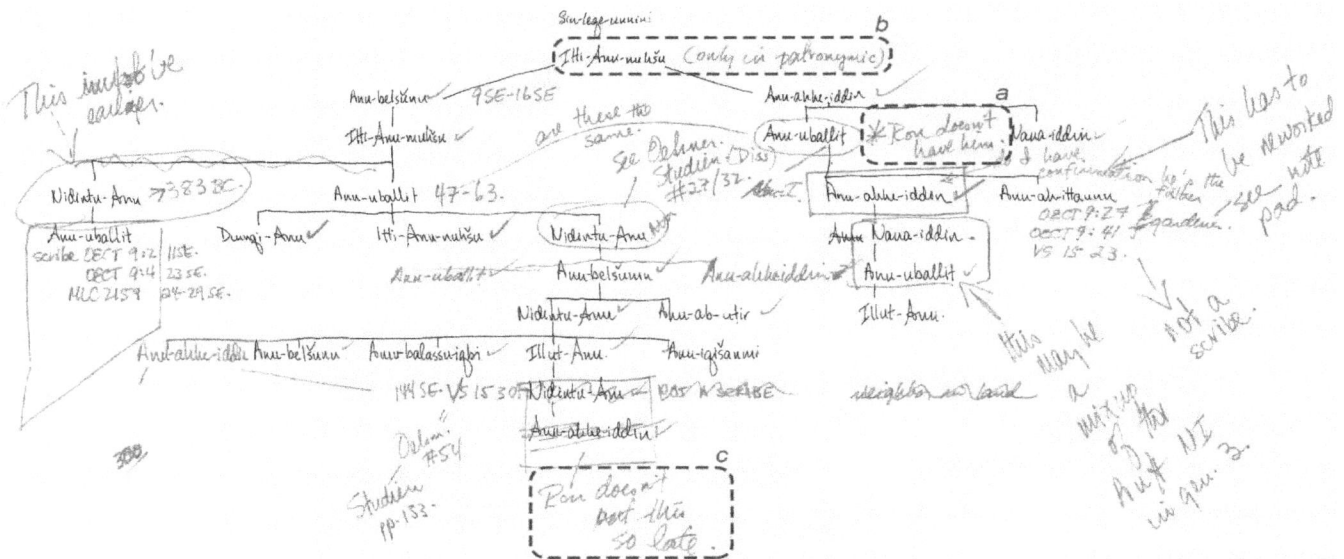

Figure 2: Hand-written Family Tree (a: "Ron doesn't have him"; b: "only in patronymic"; c: "Ron doesn't put this so late")

non-royal families might be called John Sr., John Jr., John III, etc. Disambiguation is made more difficult when, for example, individuals in alternating generations are named for their grandfathers (a practice called papponymy), with the result that a document may record the participation of Anu-uballiṭ, son of Nidintu-Anu, son of Anu-uballiṭ, son of Nidintu-Anu.

The specialist in any corpus knows that clues that inhere in the data and the context in which they appear facilitate disambiguation. Were the specialist asked how he distinguishes between close namesakes, he might claim "intuition", his expertise so ingrained that it obscures the sequential process considering attributes and the likelihood that any one or a collection of those features applies to one, but not the other, of the namesakes. For example, dates in documents that record two transactions occurring seventy-five years apart would, in some social contexts, make it highly unlikely that Anu-uballiṭ(1) is the same individual as Anu-uballiṭ(2). Other attributes do not provide such clear criteria, and different scholars might variously assess the utility of those measures (and/or meta-data) in disambiguation, effectively assigning them different weights in their evaluation. For example: how likely is a buyer of real-estate also to participate in slave sales? Differences in outcomes are chalked up to scholarly debate, which may range on the continuum from friendly to flame. Scholars committed to the exploration of ideas may annotate the differences and note how their procedures and assumptions led to variant outcomes. Examples include: (a) the inclusion or exclusion of data from different researchers' data sets, (b) identification of few attestations, appearing in limited contexts, of data across the corpus, and (c) discrepancies reflecting lacking or corrupted metadata. These are highlighted in Figure 2.

When these differences are small, few in number, and occur in a small number of texts, dissenters or the merely curious can easily retrace the analytic process that brought assertions and facts together to a conclusion. But when a researcher studies a corpus of 10,000 economic records from temples, and tracks the price of the sale of a liter of barley on specified festival days in several months over a thirty year period in three cult centers, in the hopes of determining the economic prowess of similarly-named members of families of cult officiants, he faces a much greater challenge. The research quickly becomes a complex interplay of layers of data (prices, quantities, days, years, and location) associated with relevant individuals who have been disentangled, with varying degrees of likelihood and certainty, from multiple namesakes. The researcher's colleagues may simply choose to accept all of his assertions on the basis of the researcher's reputation and standing in the field. Alternatively, they might dismiss the same results produced at the hand of a relative unknown, perhaps a recent PhD (even if a student of a legendary professor) or by an interested dilettante.

Common notions of scientific exploration include "reproducible results", which carries with it the corollary that the data and research method can be tracked and implemented repeatedly. In order to approach that standard in research fields such as prosopography, where degrees of uncertainty factor into the methodology, tracking of the changes and the researchers who introduced them are a necessary component of responsible practice. A feature of the BPS architecture designed to support probabilistic assertions is the creation of workspaces for individual experimentation, recording of parameters applied in any particular research question, and authority tracking. In this way, BPS engages with one of the questions big data faces, even

as the number of bytes that any BPS researcher may process is small.

## 1.2 Workflows in prosopography

Prosopography is at the core of many humanities research agendas. It enables researchers to identify in text corpora the unique individuals who populated a documented social milieu.

Disambiguation, the initial task in prosopographical research, is fundamentally a probabilistic endeavor. Initially, the prosopographer considers all namesakes in each text and throughout the corpus as references to discrete individuals. As the impact or validity of factors (metadata) — such as life-span, co-occurrences with other individuals, mutually exclusive roles within a transaction-context — are taken into account, multiple name instances may be collapsed or maintained as different individuals. The process may be complicated by the state of preservation, where broken sources (Figure 1) may be reconstructed on the basis of specialized knowledge; different researchers may advocate for variant reconstructions. The implications of different disambiguations carry great importance for the generating of the social networks which articulate the links between individuals, and for the graph visualizations which facilitate their exploration by multiple investigators. It is common, also, for different researchers to assign different weights to parameters resulting in potentially and dramatically differing disambiguations. The uncertainty inherent in all prosopography fosters discussion and, in the most collegial of research environments, promotes advancements in the field of study. Prosopography transforms probabilistic assertions about data into narrative, and provides foundations for additional discovery.

## 1.3 Traditional curation and annotation

A common theme in big data workflows is the amount of time and effort spent cleaning and normalizing datasets in preparation for analysis. In many areas of humanities, these activities directly correspond to *curation*. Martin Mueller [10] describes processes to Complete, Correct, and Connect. Texts must be completed to address content that is missing or illegible due to damage or problems with digital capture. Corrections address OCR errors, incorrect markup produced in transcription, etc. Connection makes texts machine-actionable by adding markup and relations on entities, features, structure, etc. to support subsequent analysis. Especially in the humanities, however, these curation activities are often the subject of discourse and debate. While many annotation models include support for provenance (authorship) of annotations, curation models rarely incorporate this aspect, and annotation models generally do not actually change the underlying text (so that the changes are reflected in further processing workflows).

In addition, despite the emergence of digital curation models (e.g., [9]) that will support "access, use and reuse of digital materials throughout their lifecycle," the workflows to perform these curation activities are still largely human-based; people create the metadata, and commonly assume that it will be interpreted by other people. Aside from the problems of scaling this to larger corpora, the unstructured or semi-structured nature of the resulting documents, curatorial metadata and even many annotations are often ill-suited for the algorithmic processing that underlies many digital humanities tools.

A final challenge is one not uncommon across digital humanities, especially as tools from other big data applications are adapted to humanities corpora and domains: where analytic tools are applied to these new corpora, many of the underlying algorithms are based upon mathematics that is unfamiliar and opaque to most humanists. For certain tools (e.g., algorithms that support SNA visualization) this not an issue, as the researcher will interpret the results and draw her conclusions referencing the corpus directly. However, in many other cases (e.g., supporting name disambiguation), humanists have expressed reluctance to "trust" an algorithm that they cannot (at least conceptually) understand. Inasmuch as the tools support rather than replace scholarly workflows, researchers' willingness to integrate the tools into their reasoning process is essential to adoption and ultimate utility.

## 1.4 BPS approach to infrastructure

The BPS project originated in the context of a larger exploration of cyberinfrastructure in support of humanities research[1]. As such, the requirements included both functional needs of the domain researchers, as well as software architecture and design requirements that the solution be generalized, re-usable across domains, scalable, and sustainable. These technical requirements led to a number of basic design decisions for the infrastructure, and approaches to the implementation of specific functional needs. The core application logic is implemented as a set of RESTful [7] web services, following the principles of Service- (and Resource-) Oriented Architecture (SOA/ROA). Communication between services is loosely coupled, and generally uses standard or abstract XML (or json) payload formats. This facilitates the re-use of individual components or services in other projects. It also makes it easier to replace individual pieces of the underlying infrastructure, since the details of the implementation are abstracted behind a service API. For example, the initial implementation took a lightweight approach to Identity and Access Management (IAM – a.k.a. authentication and authorization), and to corpus content management. To scale up these components, the IAM implementation could be tied into campus IAM infrastructure, and the content management could be tied into common repository services, without requiring changes to the rest of the application.

BPS streamlines prosopography and SNA by offering an integrated and customizable out-of-the-box digital analysis tool-kit and work environment. The tool-kit includes: (1) corpus services to parse TEI [16] and build an internal model of name-citations, etc. in documents, (2) a probabilistic disambiguator that determines the likelihood that two or more name instances refer to the same person, (3) support for assertions that parameterize various tools, and that let a user confirm or override disambiguation results, (4) SNA services that compute features and aspects of the resulting social network, (5) a visualization module that renders interactive visual representations of the networks based on data drawn from the text sources, and (6) workspace support that allows users to manage various corpora and experiment with what-if scenarios for each corpus.

BPS leverages an assertion model that reflects the tradition of discourse among researchers. The BPS productivity tools support the essential disambiguation steps, and also allow the researcher's individual conclusions or conjectures to be modeled explicitly as assertions. These assertions can be published to collaborators, reviewed and accepted (or rejected) by these research peers, maintaining the original provenance.

In order to support a wide range of domains, the disambiguation engine is based upon a plug-in model for abstract rules that influence the disambiguation process. Some rules can be used across many corpora (e.g., if they are based upon document dates), where others may be more domain specific (e.g., in a legal transaction, a named witness cannot be the same person as a named principal, even if the names are the same; a rule can express this constraint). The rules are applied in an automated framework that closely follows the researchers' mental model of the process they traditionally (if laboriously) applied by hand. This ensures that algorithmic results can reasonably be understood and vetted by the humanist researchers. Thus, rather than imposing a foreign paradigm from an engineering or mathematical domain, BPS incorporates the humanists' scholarly workflow into a computational model that can scale up to much larger corpora than were traditionally manageable by hand.

In the following sections we describe work related to aspects of BPS, present details of the BPS models and implementation, and relate our work to the larger context of big data and the humanities.

## 2. RELATED WORK

BPS is unique among existing digital prosopography projects in its corpus-agnostic architecture that ensures reusability of technical components to solve comparable problems across corpora, in its modeling of probabilistic assertions for disambiguation, and in its workspace environments that support and encourage individual and collaborative exploration, authority tracking and reputation building.

Most existing digital prosopography projects superimpose elegant interfaces over relational databases (e.g., PASE[2], CCEd[3], and PBW[4]). These models all present a single editorial view produced by humans, and have no tools for disambiguation, no support for assertions or exploratory research, and limited or no support for SNA and visualization.

In addition to support for online queries in both English and Chinese, the Chinese Biographical Database[5] (CBDB) [8] is one of a very limited number of projects that make their databases accessible via download, in an effort to share digital resources. While downloads support offline visualization of graphs, they do not provide an integrated online environment for research and inquiry. The project has created a tool to help extract information from source documents (the "RegEx Machine"), but lacks a more general disambiguation engine, and has no support for assertions or exploratory workspaces.

Mapping the Republic of Letters[6] provides, under a single banner, analytic and visualization tools to a group of projects grounded in corpora that differ in content. In essence, however, each project remains a standalone presentation of the research results of a single research group, and there is no possibility of actively engaging with the data. There is no support for disambiguation, assertions, workspaces, etc.

---

[1] http://www.projectbamboo.org/

[2] http://pase.ac.uk/

[3] http://theclergydatabase.org.uk/

[4] http://pbw.kcl.ac.uk/

[5] http://isites.harvard.edu/icb/icb.do?keyword=k16229

[6] http://republicofletters.stanford.edu

Mining Social Structures from Genealogical Data[7] (MISS) includes support for disambiguation, leveraging probabilistic machine learning (ML). However, ML approaches are better suited to very large data sources with extensive common patterns upon which a model can be trained; common corpora in humanities domains often number in the hundreds of documents, and so are not well suited to ML approaches. In addition, when the model makes a recommended disambiguation choice, researchers have expressed a desire to see an explanation for the suggestion. An ML model trained to maximize a function over a vector expression of features will be hard for most humanists to understand, whereas the BPS heuristics represent the same mental model they have used in the past – the researchers describe the rules that they used by hand, and BPS implements these formally as algorithms. There is often a temptation to apply tools commonly used in big data applications across other domains, however the needs of researchers in established scholarly workflows contra-indicate ML tools for the central problem of name disambiguation in prosopography.

In [6], a method for deriving social networks from English novels is described, using Natural Language Processing (NLP) to recognize named persons, and when persons are depicted in conversation. This approach has merit for those corpora for which good language models exist and for corpora in which conversations are depicted. For many of the ancient corpora in the BPS applications, no language model exists (nor can one easily be generated given the nature of the corpus), and so many NLP tools are not appropriate. In addition, in many corpora the documents are not narratives with conversation, so the approach (while interesting) cannot be applied.

Explorations in novel visualization for prosopography are described in [12]; however these are not yet integrated into a larger framework for research. Initial experiments with SNA visualization of related corpora [18] yielded a dense, difficult- to-interpret "thicket"; filtering and other query tools are needed for effective prosopographical visualization.

Booth [2] points to the impact of varieties of unstable data, a term seemingly applied to attributes associated with an individual in the BPS model, on the creation of digital prosopographies. The call to use XML markup (BESS) to identify "basic facts" in the construction of biographies and prosopographies resonates with identification and integration of attributes (role, status, active life-span) into the BPS assertion model.

# 3. THE BPS MODEL AND TOOLS

A brief user story clarifies the róle of the main functional components in BPS for prosopography research. The disambiguator performs an activity central to all prosopographical research, regardless of discipline or corpus content: it determines which of multiple name-instances can refer to a single person (discussed in I.A., above). Typically, researchers use criteria of date, provenance, profession or title. Since the data that are relevant and available differ from one text corpus to the next, some disambiguation rules are highly specific, not only to a discipline, but to a particular corpus. Although certain cases may be very clear, in many cases there may remain at least some doubt or margin of error. In order to feed such data into a family tree or into an SNA computation, a decision (even a provisional one) is needed, and may change as the result of the introduction of new

data or different valuation of the criteria. BPS provides the researcher with the possibility of generating and exploring what-if scenarios, and with easy means to redraw graph visualizations to explore the consequences of these changes.

Although SNA is widely used in the social sciences, its penetration in the humanities and in historical studies is relatively low, in spite of early success in diverse implementations: studies of the history of early Islamic intellectuals [1] and the development of the anti-Persian movement among the Neo-Babylonian elite [17] illustrate the utility of SNA for understanding social dynamics. As BPS's integrated disambiguator and visualization service replicate processes the humanist already employs, the tool-kit supports the iterative computational aspect of prosopography and SNA.

## 3.1 BPS Architecture

The architecture is divided into three major areas that correspond to the processing steps[8]:

1. Text Preprocessing

2. Disambiguation and Social Network Analysis

3. Presentation, Visualization, and Reporting.

In Text Preprocessing, a corpus is converted from some native format to TEI (possibly transliterating from, e.g., cuneiform, to a Unicode representation of Akkadian). The TEI markup includes elements denoting the individual documents, activities within each document, and persons that have roles in those activities. This markup may be generated by hand or by some semi-automated processes to recognize names, filiation, roles and activities (this step tends to be domain or even corpus specific, and is considered peripheral to the core of the BPS system). In many big data and text analysis applications, NLP tools are an essential part of the processing workflows. However, there are fundamental challenges with applying traditional NLP tools to many corpora like cuneiform texts. For most ancient languages, no language models exist that enable the immediate application of typical NLP tools. Although the total number of texts under consideration may be large, the individual texts are spread across large geographic regions and considerable time spans (several millennia), making it very difficult to train a reliable language model. Nevertheless, we are exploring the application of simple NLP tools to automatically enrich metadata (markup) in the TEI (e.g., entailment phrases that indicate the role a named person has in an activity). Ongoing work in the current and next phases of the project includes adding services to support a broader range of corpora formats as input (e.g., direct from an existing database).

In Disambiguation and Social Network Analysis, TEI is ingested and parsed by corpus services, and a native data model is built internally. The workspace services share this model, and leverage authentication and authorization components to support login and access controls on corpus and workspace resources. The disambiguation engine incorporates rules that may be generic or may be corpus-specific, and associates the name citations in each document with actual persons depicted in the texts. It includes support for assertions that researchers make to confirm or reject the possibilities suggested by the engine. Finally, GraphML (a standard XML format) is passed to the SNA services to compute significant features of the social networks.

---

[7] http://swarmlab.unimaas.nl

[8] See also Figure 3, BPS Architecture Diagram, below.

The Presentation, Visualization, and Reporting area presents results from various core model and analysis components, including the declared data model in each corpus (names, activities, etc.), assertions that the researcher has made or imported from others, family tree visualizations, as well as interactive network graphs for exploration and understanding.

The following sections describe the major areas of functionality in BPS. The assertions model underlies several areas, but is described in the primary context of making assertions about disambiguation.

## 3.2 Corpus input and management

A set of web services provides basic corpus services, including TEI parsing of a corpus file and conversion to the internal model of documents, activities, and name citations with an associated role.

RESTful APIs provide access to the basic document metadata, activities, roles, and names present in the corpus. We chose to implement the core functionality as REST services both to facilitate re-use of individual components, but as well to enable other applications to more easily integrate with BPS data and services. This has become a common architectural pattern in many applications, even if it is not all that common in digital humanities tools. The RESTful APIs support query and filter options, e.g., to list names that occur in a given role, and/or with specified features (e.g., a given value for gender). The associated web-application functionality provides a UI for these corpus services, as well as for uploading new corpus files, etc. All property values used in the UI, e.g., the list of activities and the list of roles, are derived dynamically from the corpus; the BPS UI need not be rewritten or customized to support different corpora or domains.

## 3.3 Disambiguation support

A central task in prosopography is to associate each name instance to some real-world person. All name instances in a corpus, both within a single document (intra-document) and in documents across the corpus (inter-document), provide evidence for disambiguation. The algorithmic model is based upon the heuristics that researchers have long used, and so is familiar to users. To begin, a unique person is posited for each name instance in each document. Then, the model attempts to *collapse* persons into one another, so that the persons posited for name instances that refer to a given real-world person are collapsed into a single person in the model as well. It does this according to user-configured rules that operate on various features (properties) of each original person.

Filiation (declaration of parents and ancestors) is a primary feature used by the model. Additional features include the *activity* in which each associated name instance is cited, the *roles* that the name-citation had in the activity, the date of the respective activities, etc. In response to interviews with researchers, the disambiguation engine is being expanded to support a more generic model allowing an extensible set of features (e.g., life-role or offices held, titles, etc.).

The rules operate on these features and can have one of three functions:

1.  **Shift** rules shift weight from one person to another.

2.  **Boost** rules magnify the effect of applied shift rules.

3.  **Discount** rules reduce the effect of applied shift rules.

A rule that produces a conclusive match between two person/name instances may shift 100% of the weight from one to the other. A rule that is only *likely* but not certain, may shift less weight. Name-matching rules are generally modeled as *shift* rules. Rules that provide additional evidence for a match are modeled as a *boost*, and tend to leverage features like location (where an activity took place) or type of activity. Rules that provide evidence of counter-indication are modeled as a *discount*; examples include date rules that consider the typical life-span and span of activity, along with the dates of respective activities (if two activities are 30 years apart, there is less likelihood that two person/name instances refer to the same real-world person, and so even if a name matches, a discount reduces the effect of the collapse). The date discount rule is implemented as a modified Gaussian function that accommodates a user parameter for the expected duration of an individual active life span.

Rules may apply only to person/names within a document (intra-document rules), or to persons across the corpus (inter-document rules). Many rules can operate in either model, but function slightly differently in the two contexts.

The end result of applying the rules is a set of probabilities (i.e., a probability distribution) for each name-instance, for the set of real-word persons to which that name instance may correspond (low weight probabilities can be filtered out to remove unlikely matches, and simplify the results).

The model closely follows the approach researchers have traditionally applied "by hand": within each document, the person posited for each name is considered against each other person (with at least a minimally matching name). Researchers consider the roles, filiations, and other features associated to each name-citation, and come to at least a tentative conclusion about whether the two could be the same person. Once all the intra-document collapsing has been considered, researchers look across the corpus to correlate persons among different documents. Again, features such as filiation and roles are considered, but additional rules come into play like the dates of the documents (two persons mentioned 5 years apart are more likely to be the same than persons mentioned 40 years apart), the place in which respective activities took place, etc. BPS formalizes these research workflows as the described classes of rules operating on a probabilistic mathematical representation. The collapser algorithm also has an initial pass over each document to apply intra-document rules, and then a subsequent pass at the corpus level to apply inter-document rules. As each rule is applied, the calculated weight-shifts are normalized to produce a consistent probabilistic distribution; an optional threshold can be specified to filter very low probability matches (after which the distribution is re-normalized).

Each rule is implemented as a plug-in to a standard API, and each can be configured separately as it applies to a given corpus. The API includes methods for the computation of weight shift (or boost, or discount, respectively, for each class of rule). These methods just take two person instances and associated metadata for the respective documents, and return a floating point value for the shift/boost/discount. A second set of methods in the API supports the generation of a configuration UI with which researchers can parameterize the rules. Each rule returns a simple string that describes the impact of the rule ("what it does", in plain language). Each rule also returns any named parameters that can be set (commonly, a confidence weight, but other values can also be described). The generated UI allows a researcher to specify her confidence in a given rule (i.e., the scaling weight in the interval 0

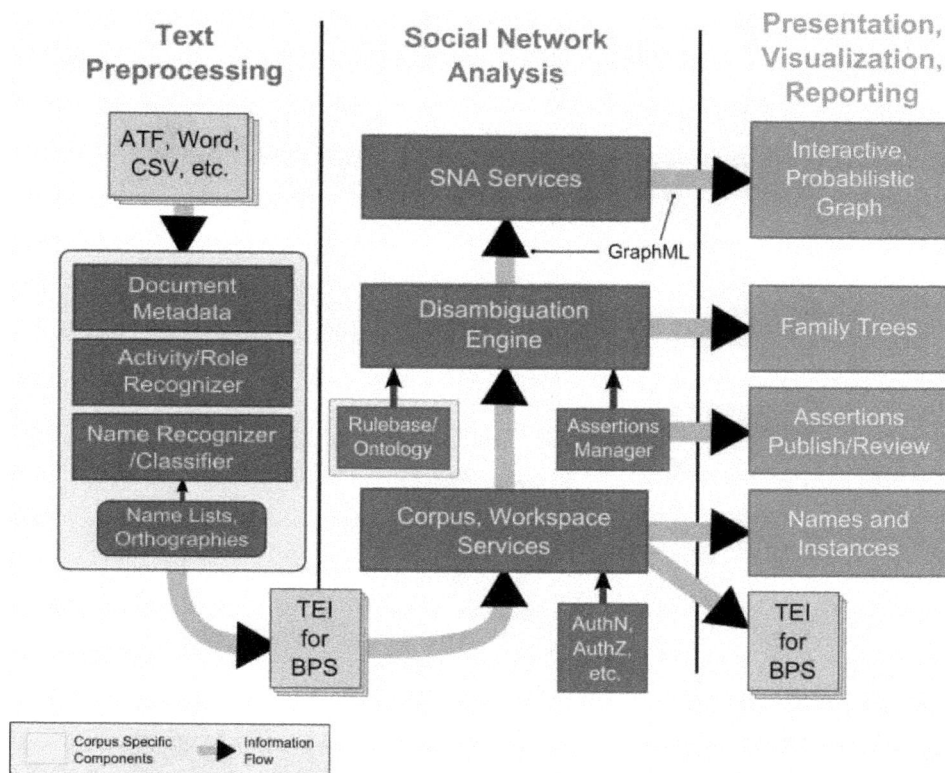

**Figure 3 – BPS Architecture Diagram**

to 1 that is applied to the computed result of the rule; the UI often presents a simplified set of values like "*Never: 0%*", "*Conservative: 30%*", "*Aggressive: 70%*", and "*Always: 100%*"). Each researcher can configure her confidence in each rule that is configured for her corpus, and thereby individually control how the heuristic proceeds. Changing these values in a different workspace (described below, in section 3.3.4) allows researchers to explore *what-if* scenarios.

BPS provides base classes that support common functionality (e.g., serialization, a confidence parameter) for each class of rule. BPS also provides some generic rules (e.g., a discount based upon the dates of two name-citations) that can be re-used without modification in many domains. A more complex but still-generic rule leverages a half-matrix of all the role-names specified in the corpus (discovered when the corpus is parsed). The UI for this is a table of parameters allowing the user to specify which pairs of roles are compatible (or not).

Additional effort is of course required to support the plug-in infrastructure, and the abstraction that supports automated generation of a configuration UI. However, the infrastructure makes BPS much more easily adapted to other domains (where different rules must be defined). The broader applicability and re-use makes BPS a more sustainable project, especially given the relatively small communities in each individual domain.

### 3.3.1 Assertion support

Additional infrastructure supports an assertion model by which researchers can confirm or discard results of the automated disambiguation engine. Assertions are also used internally to model the users' chosen values for rule parameters, etc. More

details of the BPS assertion model are described in [14], but it is worth noting that BPS assertions connect big data algorithms that are necessarily more generic and abstract to small data workflows in which researchers draw their own specific conclusions in a given instance. In addition, by providing provenance tracking in a model that can be shared among researchers, assertions support reproducible research in a manner that is relatively uncommon in the humanities.

An important infrastructure challenge arises for corpora in which the content of individual documents is changing (as curators correct errors, etc.) – maintaining the references for assertions requires a robust linking model. We are refining the serialization and internal support for BPS assertions, and are working to extend the Hypothes.is fuzzy reference model described in [5] to provide a more robust model. Some of this is reflected in the emerging Open Annotation Data Model [13] as well, and we will track its progress at the W3C.

### 3.3.2 SNA support

BPS includes a set of RESTful web services that provide common algorithms from graph theory and social network analysis, including clustering, statistical analysis, and calculation of network distances, flows, and ranking measures (centrality, PageRank, HITS, etc.). The services are implemented as a thin abstraction layer over the Java Universal Network/Graph (JUNG) Framework [11], which implements the actual methods. The BPS services abstract the graph model, and handle translation to and from GraphML [4] for service payloads. We define a graph-context that maps user-level queries and filters on the underlying corpus, persons, features, etc., to database queries to select the

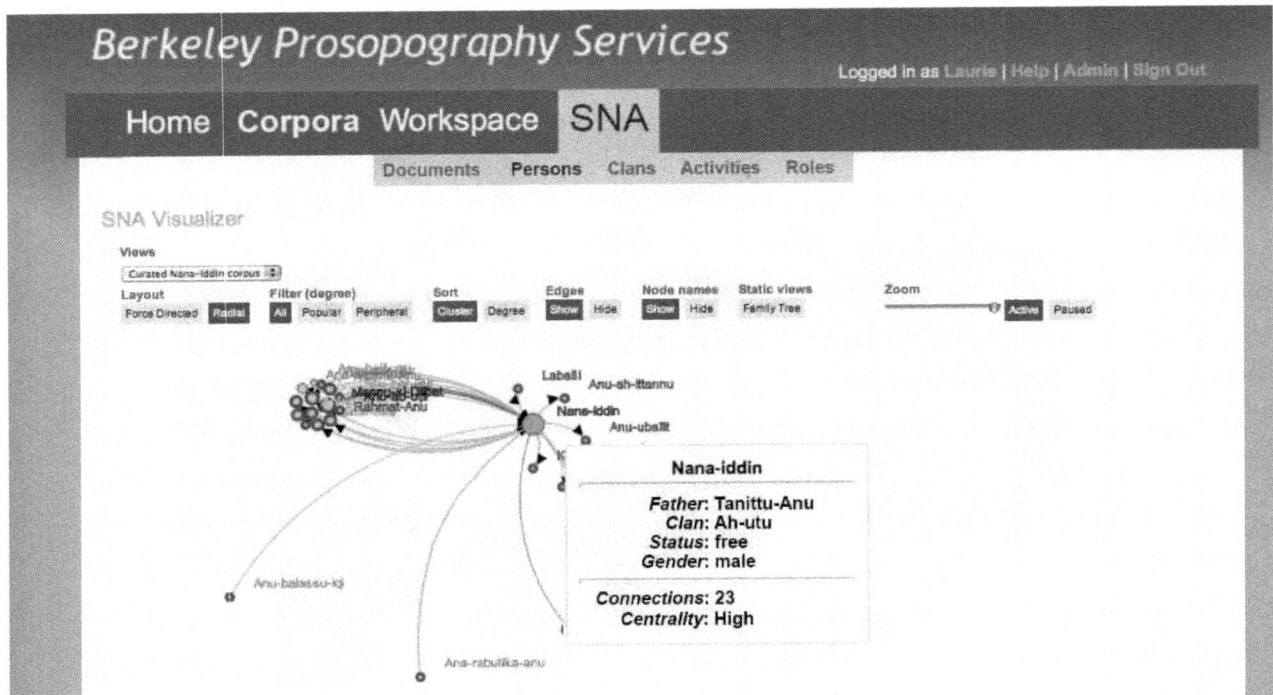

Figure 4 – BPS Screen-shot illustrating SNA diagram focused on details of an individual

nodes of interest, and then produces GraphML for the SNA algorithm services.

The abstractions (e.g., GraphML as a payload format) were chosen to make the BPS SNA services reusable as core cyber-infrastructure across a range of applications. The services provide common functionality as is, and can also be more tightly integrated with other applications by providing a graph context implementation that is specific to the application data model.

## 3.4 Visualization and Workspace support

### 3.4.1 Visualization support

The BPS web application includes a range of visualization supports – lists, tables and reports with query filters and graph visualization support that lets users view family trees, social networks, clusters – that let users explore the corpus and the prosopographical analysis. The visualization support is particularly important to most humanist researchers, who prefer narrative to computation or numerical representations. The challenge has been to provide a seamless model for querying and filtering the corpus and/or persons in both simple report views and in the visualization; naïve application of SNA and visualization to large datasets is often hard to use. BPS includes various filters and queries that narrow in on specific questions and produce more useful visualization. Figure 4 provides a screen-shot of the BPS interface showing the network visualization, and detailed metrics for a given individual.

BPS defines script libraries to manage the data from the services (especially the SNA services), but the visualization support is built upon the D3 script library [3].

### 3.4.2 Workspaces in BPS

The Digital Humanities research environment exposes the functionality of the probabilistic model and assertions in workspaces. Each user can have one or more workspaces for his projects, and can import one or more corpora into each workspace for analysis; each workspace has an independent set of model parameters and curatorial assertions. After setting parameters for disambiguation rules and making specific assertions, a researcher can see the effects on the resulting SNA visualizations. Support for *freezing* a workspace and bookmarking specific visualizations means that results and views of a model can be shared and cited in publication. The current implementation, which supports this workspace model, has been evaluated with current users, who embrace the semblance of the digital workflow to that carried out with the familiar pen-and-paper one. User requests for future expansion include implementation of support for publishing an experimental result as a workspace and shared workspaces that enable collaboration among colleagues. These move humanities research into the realm of big data by inviting both speculative and collaborative investigation and encouraging the study of larger and more complex data sets. Pedagogical use-cases enable students to follow along as a faculty member works through the process of prosopographical research in a corpus, learn the process, and track the judgments of the experienced user, all while being trained in best digital humanities practices.

### 3.4.3 Linked Open Data and BPS

In the realm of prosopographical research, Linked Open Data (LOD) should find immediate reception and application. In traditional prosopographical research, some attributes within any given domain (e.g., toponyms, names of rulers, and generally agreed-upon terms) may readily be assigned unique identifiers. In traditional prosopographical research, the promotion of results of a single-authority disambiguation model may equally prompt the assignment of unique identifiers, in spite of a range of uncertainty that may surround a disambiguation. BPS differs from other prosopography tools and projects in formalizing and integrating the probabilistic heuristics prosopographers naturally apply in their research, and in providing a workspace environment in which individual or collaborating researchers may approach a single corpus with different assertions. Each modification may result in variant disambiguations, which the researcher explores and may accept or reject. In view of the mutability of results that the probabilistic tools may generate, BPS is faced with a challenge with respect to assigning unique identifiers to disambiguated individuals. Recognizing the value of LOD, BPS researchers continue to investigate the application of unique identifiers to the results the tools generate.

## 4. EVALUATION WITH USERS

The merits of data-driven science, social science research, and text-based humanities derive in large measure from the approbation of colleagues qualified to assess the validity of data utilized as well as the methodological underpinnings of the research program. As humanists approach larger text corpora and ask wider-ranging questions of that data, they face increasing computational complexity, regardless of the actual number of bytes they process. Tools that replicate workflows with which they are already familiar are transformative not because of the manner in which they are implemented, but because of the ways they enable the humanist to expand his enquiry.

In early stage workshops, humanists expressed strong support for the BPS model and tools, suggesting that they would result in "aha!" moments, characterized by new research directions and outcomes not previously possible. The assertions-based model and the workspaces in which different parameterizations could find expression and evaluation that would be the catalyst to further discourse and dialogue.

Users confirmed that the disambiguation and assertion models reflect actual workflows, and affirmed the value of assigning attribution provenance and the creation of workspace environments for individual and collaborative research. Users explored the implications of the flexible BPS data model, which allowed them to filter on features of persons and activities in ways that had not been practical before. As they did so, they discovered that BPS allowed them to ask new questions about their corpora. The BPS team and workshop participants compiled and prioritized a list of desired features and tools for, e.g., performing date conversions between different calendars, adding new import models, and supporting multiple workspaces. A subsequent webinar included a real-time demonstration of the implementation of the SNA graph visualization. Response was good, and users endorsed the approach presented in the proof of concept demonstration.

A current effort is providing tools to map name references in a simple database, prepared by scholars working in a different corpus, for import into the BPS framework. The BPS model is mapping well, and the project participants have been positive about the possibility of using the BPS tools.

Additional discussions with scholars in other domains have indicated the potential application for quite different corpora. E.g., researchers in vertebrate zoology are working with archives of field collection notebooks to understand the networks of influence and interaction among collectors and museum staff. We are in discussions to explore how BPS tools can be adapted to support disambiguation and network analysis in this corpus.

Future development phases will expand and refine core functionality, and will also expand upon the evaluation to consider whether and how BPS is changing scholarly workflows.

## 5. CONCLUSIONS AND FUTURE WORK

Big data in the humanities is not about the number of bytes, but rather about the nature of the work and accompanying workflows. BPS is a big data humanities tool-kit that changes workflows by expanding the capacity to ask new questions, to handle larger data sets and to discover features that were previously impractical to identify. Extending the research model means that humanists could: discover the relation of mercantile activity between multiple families in differing locations, assess individuals' wealth accumulation against patterns of seasonal variation in agricultural productivity, and establish the agency of women as principals and witnesses in a social network of economic transactions — questions previously deemed not possible or practical to answer.

Big data applies to humanities research, even when a corpus contains <500K items. Humanists rejoice when archaeological excavations or cataloging projects in libraries turn up masses of new documentation. But at the same time, they may be reluctant or ill-equipped to incorporate the data and metadata from 20,000 new documents into a standing research project. Changes in the size of data-sets on the order of 10-20% (regardless of the absolute number of data items) can best be transformative when tools incorporate the new data easily into an existing workflow.

BPS enables the implementation of big data in humanities research by automating humanist workflows. Tools at home in the disciplines of computer science, natural language processing, and statistics are not part of the historical workflow in this kind of disambiguation and prosopographical analysis, in spite of the fact that the process is probabilistic and computational. A thoughtful, well-engineered tool-kit brings to a field of humanities research tools that serve existing needs and facilitates the answering of new and expanding questions.

A tool-kit such as BPS also facilitates and promotes communication and collaboration in the research process. In the humanities, debate and authority is traditionally expressed and established on static pages of learned journals. The workspace environment of BPS affords researchers the opportunity to engage immediately and intimately in digital "conversations", and to track, through their own, shared, or others' BPS workspaces.

In the next phase of work we will be expanding upon the assertions model, generalizing some of the model for features used in disambiguation, and adding additional workspace support. We plan to conduct a series of formal evaluations to track and quantify the computations implemented by the humanists and correlate those with the self-reported impact that the tools have on the framing of humanities scholarship, with particular focus on the contribution of BPS toward extending the complexity of research agendas and opening viable humanities approaches to the realm of big data.

## 6. ACKNOWLEDGMENTS

The early development of BPS was supported in part by a Digital Humanities Start-Up Grant from the National Endowment for the Humanities. We would also like to acknowledge the Oracc project[9] which provides infrastructure support for cuneiform corpus transliteration, and contributed supporting technology for TEI markup of the corpora. Finally, we would like to acknowledge the contributions of Davide Semenzin, Utrecht University ICS, who implemented a number of key features as part of his Master's final project.

---

[9] http://oracc.org

# 7. REFERENCES

[1] Ahmed, A. 2011. *The Religious Elite of the Early Islamic Ḥijāz : Five Prosopographical Case Studies*. Occasional Publications of the Oxford Unit for Prosopographical Research 14. Oxford: Unit for Prosopographical Research Linacre College University of Oxford.

[2] Booth, A. 2013. Brief Overview of Curating Lives: Museums, Archives, Online Sites, Autobiography, Biography, and Life Writing session, MLA Commons, Jan 5 2013. Available at: http://commons.mla.org/docs/a-brief-synopsis-of-curating-lives-mla-paper-alison-booth/

[3] Bostock, M., et al. 2011. *D3: Data-Driven Documents*, IEEE Trans. Visualization & Comp. Graphics (Proc. InfoVis), 2011.

[4] Brandes, U., et al. 2000. *The GraphML file format.*

[5] Csillag, K. 2013. *Fuzzy anchoring* (blog post, April 22, 2013). Available at: http://hypothes.is/blog/fuzzy-anchoring.

[6] Elson, D., Dames, N., and McKeown, K. 2010, *Extracting Social Networks from Literary Fiction*, Proc. of 48th Annual Meeting of the Association for Computational Linguistics, pages 138–147, Uppsala, Sweden, 11-16 July 2010

[7] Fielding, R., and Taylor, R. 2002. *Principled design of the modern Web architecture.* ACM Trans. Internet Technol. 2,2 (May 2002) DOI=10.1145/514183.514185

[8] Gerritsen, A. 2008. *Prosopography and its Potential for Middle Period Research*, Journal of Song-Yuan Studies Volume 38, 2008 pp. 161-201.

[9] Higgins, S. 2011. *Digital Curation: The Emergence of a New Discipline*, International Journal of Digital Curation, 2011, Vol. 6, No. 2, pp. 78-88, doi:10.2218/ijdc.v6i2.191. http://ijdc.net/index.php/ijdc/article/view/184

[10] Mueller, M. 2011. *Collaboratively Curating Early Modern English Texts*. Contributed essay to Project Bamboo wiki. https://wikihub.berkeley.edu/x/QAdRB. Accessed June 2013.

[11] O'Madadhain, J., et al. 2005. *Analysis and visualization of network data using JUNG.* Journal of Statistical Software 10.2 (2005): 1-35.

[12] Pasin, M. 2012, Exploring Prosopographical Resources Through Novel Tools and Visualizations: a Preliminary Investigation, Digital Humanities 2012, Hamburg.

[13] Sanderson, R, et al. (eds.) *Open Annotation Data Model*, W3C Community Draft, Accessed July 2014. http://www.openannotation.org/spec/core/.

[14] Schmitz, P., and Pearce, L., 2013. *Berkeley Prosopography Services: Ancient Families, Modern Tools*, DH-Case 2013 (workshop), ACM Document Engineering 2013, Florence, Italy.

[15] Szaley, A., 2012. *Data-intensive discoveries in science: the fourth paradigm.* Data-Intensive Distributed Computing 2012 (DIDC '12). DOI=10.1145/2286996.2286998

[16] TEI P5: *Guidelines for Electronic Text Encoding and Interchange, Ch. 13 Names, Dates, People, and Places*, V 2.3.0. Available at: http://www.tei-c.org/release/doc/tei-p5-doc/en/html/ND.html (accessed April 2014).

[17] Waerzeggers, C. 2003-2004. *The Babylonian Revolts Against Xerxes and the 'End of Archives'*, Archiv für Orientforschung 50: 150–173.

[18] Waerzeggers, C. 2013. *Social Network Analysis of Cuneiform Archives: A New Approach.* Proc. of the Second START Conference in Vienna (17-19th July 2008) Too Much Data? Generalizations and Model-building in Ancient Economic History on the Basis of Large Corpora of documentary Evidence, edited by H. D. Baker and Michael Jursa.

# The Impact of Prior Knowledge on Searching in Software Documentation

Klaas Andries de Graaf
VU University Amsterdam
ka.de.graaf@vu.nl

Peng Liang
Wuhan University
liangp@whu.edu.cn

Antony Tang
Swinburne University of
Technology
atang@ict.swin.edu.au

Hans van Vliet
VU University Amsterdam
hans@cs.vu.nl

## ABSTRACT

Software documents are used to capture and communicate knowledge in software projects. It is important that this knowledge can be retrieved efficiently and effectively, to prevent wasted time and errors that negatively affect the quality of software. In this paper we investigate how software professionals search for knowledge in documentation. We studied the search behaviour of professionals in industry. Prior knowledge helps professionals to search software documents efficiently and effectively. However, it can also misguide professionals to an incomplete search.

## Categories and Subject Descriptors

H.3.3 [**Information Search and Retrieval**]: Search process; D.2.7 [**Software Engineering**]: Distribution, Maintenance, and Enhancement—*Documentation*

## Keywords

Software Documentation; Information Retrieval; Search Strategies; Prior Knowledge; Heuristics; Cognitive Bias

## 1. INTRODUCTION

In software industry, it is a common practice to capture information about a software system, its design, and architecture in file-based documents, e.g., in text documents and diagram files. It is important that software professionals can quickly and correctly answer questions from these documents. Otherwise valuable time could be wasted, costly errors could be made, and software may not be built according to specification, which increases the cost of software projects and decreases the quality of software [13].

The organisation of documents by directories, titles, and sections typically does not support all of the questions asked by software professionals [4, 13]. Spelling errors, abbrevia-

tions, and synonyms make keyword searching ineffective and professionals may not know the right keywords to find answers [9]. Exhaustive exploration of all document content is time-consuming and impractical in a large document set.

These issues introduce search uncertainty and make it hard for professionals to find complete and correct answers within reasonable time. Professionals waste time searching for answers in unstructured documentation [13]. The obstacles to finding the right information can be so great that it discourages professionals from trying to search at all [9,10].

In this paper we investigate how software professionals search for knowledge in software documentation. We studied how 26 software professionals in industry retrieved knowledge from documentation to answer architecture-related questions. The software professionals were asked to think aloud while answering questions about software and architectural elements such as subsystems, components, behaviour, requirements, and decisions. We measured how much time was spent on finding answers to the questions and whether answers were complete and correct.

We found that the search behaviour of software professionals is heavily influenced by their prior knowledge about the documentation and the software specified in this documentation. Prior knowledge is used to guide predictions about, e.g., the location of knowledge, which keywords can be used to find knowledge, and whether the knowledge found is correct and complete. Professionals use their prior knowledge as a short-cut to find answers to their questions, i.e. they use a heuristic (or 'experience-based') approach [15, 18] to searching.

Use of prior knowledge helped some of the participants in the study to quickly find the location of correct answers, even when the document organisation did not support the questions asked. The participants preferred to use their prior knowledge instead of exhaustively exploring documentation content.

We however observed that availability and confirmation bias can occur when using prior knowledge, which results in wasted time and incomplete answers. Availability bias and confirmation bias are cognitive biases that cause errors in judgement. Participants made inaccurate predictions about whether documents contained answers and whether searching for certain keywords would lead to answers. Moreover, several participants only looked for confirmation of answers that they said to know from their prior knowledge.

**Table 1: Demographics of Participants in Study**

| Number of participants | Primary role of participants | Average years in role at Océ | Average years in role | Average years working at Océ |
|---|---|---|---|---|
| 6 | Domain architect | 3.60 | 4.77 | 9.92 |
| 5 | Software engineer | 6.47 | 6.81 | 7.47 |
| 5 | Software project manager | 3.83 | 5 | 14 |
| 4 | Product or system test engineer | 9.75 | 11.75 | 11.625 |
| 4 | Workflow architect | 7.25 | 7.25 | 18.75 |
| 1 | Configuration manager | 3 | 10 | 3 |
| 1 | Software designer | 1 | 1 | 1 |

In this paper we first describe how prior knowledge is used by professionals to search knowledge in software documentation. We then evaluate the use of prior knowledge in terms of search efficiency and effectiveness and report cognitive biases that lower this efficiency and effectiveness. These findings provide guidance for software practitioners to make optimal use of their prior knowledge when searching knowledge in software documentation.

We make the following contributions:

1. Report how professionals use prior knowledge to search in software documents.

2. Identify cognitive biases that may occur when using prior knowledge to search in software documents.

3. Report how prior knowledge and cognitive bias affect the efficiency and effectiveness of searching.

Section 2 details on the study design and identification of the search strategies and cognitive process of participants. Section 3 reports and evaluates how prior knowledge is used when applying the search strategies and how cognitive biases may occur. Lessons learnt for document users and writers are described in Section 4 and Section 5 discusses threats to validity. In Section 6 we discuss related work and Section 7 reports our conclusions.

## 2. DESIGN AND ANALYSIS OF SEARCH BEHAVIOUR STUDY

### 2.1 Study Design

We conducted a study to investigate how software professionals search for knowledge in software documents. The study was conducted in a software project at the R&D department of Océ technologies in the Netherlands. Océ applies an agile development methodology to encourage creativity and productivity.

Participants are all software professionals at Océ R&D who are involved in the software development process. Table 1 gives the demographics of the participants.

The architecture documents used are:

- Two Software Architecture Documents (SAD) of 3 and 9 pages, respectively. SADs detail the design of functionality, behaviour, and components. One SAD gives an overview of what knowledge can be found in the other SAD.

- Four Software Behaviour Documents (SBD), ranging in size from 8 to 18 pages. SBDs describe the behaviour of software together with all requirements and settings for that behaviour. One SBD describes all possible settings for behaviour.

- One System Reference Document (Sysref), of 19 pages. The Sysref document details the high level system design and decomposition, in terms of subsystems, components, and interfaces, and gives design decisions and rationale on system design.

- One Design Document containing three UML diagrams that detail on the design of subsystems, components, and interfaces.

These documents are stored in 3 directories. A directory SAD contains the overview SAD and one subdirectory with the other SAD. A directory 'SBD' contains SBDs. A directory 'Sysref' contains the Sysref and design document.

The documents specify the software for a series of document printing machines developed at Océ and are a subset of all documentation used in the project. An Océ professional estimated that there are around 50-75 users of these documents. The documents are written in English, and consist of 79 pages, 1,794 paragraphs, 3,183 lines, and 13,962 words. Participants could search the documents using a file explorer (MS Windows Explorer), document editor (MS Word), and UML editing tool (MagicDraw).

We formulated 7 questions about the knowledge in the documents. Criterion for selection of these questions include that the interpretation of the questions is similar between different participants and that their answers can be quantitatively assessed, i.e., the questions should not be open-ended. Part of the questions have been obfuscated for non-disclosure reasons: 'QQ', 'XX', 'YY', and 'ZZ' replace an actual software entity or concept.

**1A:** *Which settings have an impact on behaviour "History"?*

**1B:** *Which settings have an impact on behaviour "Alert Light"?*

**2:** *Which requirements for behaviour "XX" should be satisfied (realized) by component "Settings Editor"?*

**3A:** *Which decisions have been made about component "Settings Editor"?*

**3B:** *Which decisions have been made on the configuration of behaviour "YY", "ZZ", "History", and "XX"?*

**4A:** *Which subsystem is interface "QQ" part of?*

**4B:** *Which other interfaces are offered by this subsystem?*

13 of the 26 participants answered questions 1A, 1B, and 2 and the other 13 participants answered questions 3A, 3B,

**Table 2: Encoding of search actions from video recordings**

| Search action | Description and criteria for identification |
|---|---|
| **Exploring directories** | |
| Open Dir | Participant opens directory. |
| Inspect Dir | Participant has contents of directory on screen for 3 seconds or more. |
| Open Doc | Participant opens document. |
| Dir keyword search | Participant searches for keyword in the documents in a directory. |
| Inspect Dir search result | Participant inspects the list of documents found by using a keyword search in directory. |
| **Exploring documents** | |
| Scan section | Participant has content of document section or diagram on screen for 3-5 seconds. |
| Detailed scan | Participant has content of document section or diagram on screen for more than 5 seconds. |
| Scroll to section | Participant scrolls to a specific section and does not inspect intermediate sections. |
| Scroll to see section title | Participant scrolls to see the title of section currently being read. |
| View TOC | Participant looks at Table of Contents for 3 seconds or more. |
| Click TOC | Participant clicks on an entry in Table of Contents to navigate to section. |
| Keyword Search | Participant searches for keyword in document. |
| Inspect context of search result | Participant looks at keyword search result and surrounding text for more than 3 seconds. |

4A, and 4B. Answering these questions was part of an experiment reported in [4]. An ontology-based documentation approach was used by participants to answer the remaining questions. For example, the participants that answered questions 1A, 1B, and 2 using file-based documentation would subsequently answer questions 3A, 3B, 4A, and 4B using ontology-based documentation. This use of ontology-based documentation is outside the scope of this paper.

In total 91 answers to the 7 questions were given by 26 participants when using file-based documentation. The researcher conducting the study read the 7 questions aloud to the participants. We asked all participants to search until they were satisfied with the time spent on an answer and its perceived correctness and completeness. Participants were instructed that this satisfaction should reflect their normal way of working.

We measured efficiency by recording how much *time* participants spent on accomplishing each task, namely, searching and providing an answer to a question. Effectiveness was measured by recording the *recall* of participants, i.e. the completeness of their answers, and *precision*, i.e. the correctness of their answers. A complete answer (resulting in perfect recall) to questions 1A, 1B, 2, and 4B inluded multiple knowledge elements, e.g., two settings, three requirements, or four interfaces.

The 'ground truth' for evaluating recall and precision was verified in a pilot with two Océ professionals who did not participate in the study. They were asked whether an answer for a given question was complete and correct. We use "completeness" to refer to recall and "correctness" to refer to precision in the rest of the paper for a better understanding.

The two professionals that participated in the pilot also proposed improvements to the question set. They evaluated whether each question was representative of the questions that software professionals at Océ normally ask and whether each question was relevant to software professionals in different roles. The questions were also evaluated on their representativeness and relevancy by five participants in a questionnaire after the experiment reported in [4]. They evaluated all questions as relevant and representative for their jobs except for question 3A, which one participant evaluated as irrelevant and not representative.

The researcher conducting the study kept track of what participants indicated to be answers to a question. When a participant stopped searching, said s/he found an answer, or said s/he was satisfied, the researcher verified with the participant whether this was the final answer to the question.

We captured the search actions of participants by video recording their monitor screen. We used the think aloud method [19] and asked participants to think aloud when searching and recorded their voice in the video recordings.

## 2.2 Identification of Search Strategies and Prior Knowledge

We identified around 2,500 search actions in over 11 hours of video recordings. Table 2 details the different types of search actions that we identified and encoded from the videos. We collected the search actions used to find 90 of the 91 answers given by the participants. The video record of one participants answering one question was corrupted beyond repair and is thus excluded from our analysis.

Not all participants were talkative, so the think aloud recordings for some questions were more detailed than others. Also, some phrases and parts of sentences said in video recordings of 22 of the 90 answers could not be heard clearly due to low sound recording volume and low volume of participants' voices. We however could often still infer what was said from the context of the search. One researcher spent 8 weeks to encode the search actions and transcribe think-aloud recordings from the videos.

From the identified search actions and think aloud verbalization we constructed Problem Behaviour Graphs (PBG) [11]. The construction of PBGs is a form of protocol analysis [6] which can be used to identify how people use their intelligence to solve problems in complex real-world environments [2]. In [2], Chen and Dhar used PBGs to model and investigate the cognitive process of people engaged in online document-based information retrieval. In our case the problem space consists of finding answers to questions using the document organisation, content, and the search functions of the documentation tools.

A PBG starts with the initial state of knowledge one has about a problem. In our case the initial state of knowledge was the question asked and the existing prior knowledge of participants about the documentation, its content, and the software system and project it specifies.

The initial knowledge state in a PBG changes to other knowledge states as the problem-solving process progresses. Problem-solving progressed when participants executed search

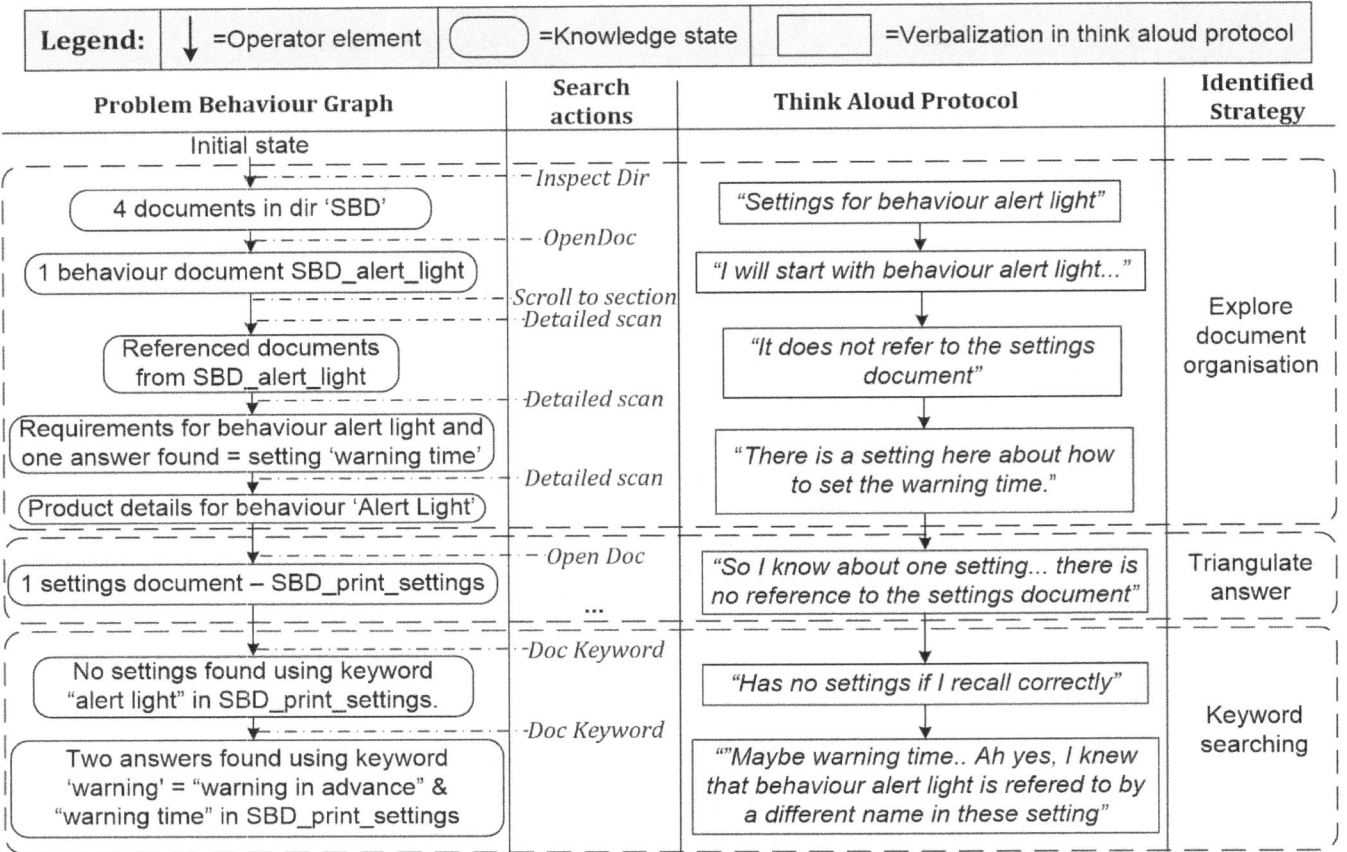

| Legend: | ↓ =Operator element | (⬭) =Knowledge state | ▭ =Verbalization in think aloud protocol |

| Problem Behaviour Graph | Search actions | Think Aloud Protocol | Identified Strategy |
|---|---|---|---|

Initial state

**Explore document organisation**

- Inspect Dir — 4 documents in dir 'SBD' → "Settings for behaviour alert light"
- OpenDoc — 1 behaviour document SBD_alert_light → "I will start with behaviour alert light..."
- Scroll to section / Detailed scan — Referenced documents from SBD_alert_light → "It does not refer to the settings document"
- Detailed scan — Requirements for behaviour alert light and one answer found = setting 'warning time' → "There is a setting here about how to set the warning time."
- Detailed scan — Product details for behaviour 'Alert Light'

**Triangulate answer**

- Open Doc — 1 settings document – SBD_print_settings → "So I know about one setting... there is no reference to the settings document"
- ...

**Keyword searching**

- Doc Keyword — No settings found using keyword "alert light" in SBD_print_settings. → "Has no settings if I recall correctly"
- Doc Keyword — Two answers found using keyword 'warning' = "warning in advance" & "warning time" in SBD_print_settings → ""Maybe warning time.. Ah yes, I knew that behaviour alert light is refered to by a different name in these setting"

Figure 1: Problem Behaviour Graph of participant answering question 1B (*Which settings have an impact on behaviour "Alert Light"?*).

actions in order to obtain new knowledge about the search problem. When a solution is found the problem-solving process ends. In our case the problem-solving ended when an answer to a question was given by a participant.

Figure 1 shows one of the constructed PBGs in which a participant had to find settings for behaviour 'Alert Light' in order to answer question 1B. The time sequence of search actions is from top to bottom in this PBG. The knowledge states are represented by boxes with rounded corners, that each contain the additional knowledge acquired by the participant when searching for knowledge.

We identified four search strategies using PBGs which are detailed below with a concrete example. We could identify to which search strategy each of the 2,500 encoded search actions belonged. In most cases multiple search strategies were used when answering a question.

In the PBG example shown in Figure 1 the first search strategy used by the participant is to **explore the document organisation** in directory *SBD*. The documentation was organized by means of directories, documents, and sections. Part of the information in the contents of document sections was organised by lay-out and text notations, e.g., in the phrase "*REQ_1: users can save login credentials in Comp_3: UI*" which makes a requirement explicit. Information was organized in diagrams by means of UML notations that, e.g., denoted interfaces and interactions.

Figure 1 shows that using this strategy the participant finds document *SBD_Alert_Light* by inspecting the content of directory *SBD*. The title of *SBD_Alert_Light* relates to behaviour '*Alert Light*' in question 1B, which indicates that this document contains information relevant for answering question 1B. The participant then opens *SBD_Alert_Light* and checks if it contains a reference to a dedicated settings document. In the next two search actions the participants scans for requirements and product information related to behaviour '*Alert Light*' and one setting is found.

Exploring document organization is a search strategy that was used when searching for 88% of the answers in the study. Participants that spent time on exploring this document organisation would often quickly gather relevant clues about which locations contained answers to questions. In [4], which is partly based on the data described in this paper, we found that exploration of document organisation was often time-effective for answering the questions. During a subsequent analysis of the study in [4] and its replication we found evidence that the use of document organisation that relates to a question correlates with the time-effectiveness of answering that question.

The organisation of documents does not always fully relate to the questions that document users have to answer. For example, none of the directory and document titles used in the study revealed where the decisions for question 3A and

**Table 3: Overview of prior knowledge, evaluation, and cognitive biases identified in study**

| Prior knowledge | Gain if correct | Loss if incorrect | Cognitive bias and possible underlying reasons |
|---|---|---|---|
| Answer is in location $X$ | large | small | |
| Answer is not in location $X$ | small | large | Availability bias: difficult to recall examples of answers found in unfamiliar location $X$. |
| Keyword $X$ leads to answer | large | large | Availability bias: keywords that are often used for searching are familiar and more easily remembered. |
| Answer can be triangulated | large | small | |
| Answer is already known | small | large | Confirmation bias: focus on confirming known answer. |

3B could be found. Only the section titles inside two documents were explicitly related to these decisions and the documents had to be opened to discover this. Participants could exhaustively explore the document organisation to discover documents and sections that related to a question, however, this took a lot of time for several participants.

Alternatively, participants would directly **search the expected locations of answers** by predicting in which location (directories, documents, and sections) they would most likely find answers to a question. Participants that used this alternative strategy directly navigated to certain locations at the start of a question, without exploring the available document organisation beforehand[1]. Searching the expected location of answers is a search strategy that was used when searching for 29% of the answers.

The third and fifth sentences in the think aloud protocol in Figure 1 show that the participant thinks aloud about another document. After finding an answer in document *SBD_Alert_Light* the participant decides to open the other document *SBD_Print_Settings* so s/he can verify the correctness and completeness of the answers. We named this strategy '**triangulate answer**', as multiple sources are used to verify and improve the answer. This strategy was used by participants when searching for 11% of the answers.

The participant subsequently uses a strategy of **keyword searching** for the name of behaviour '*Alert Light*'. After an unsuccessful keyword search, the participant recalls from prior knowledge that the settings may not be mentioned by the exact name of behaviour '*Alert Light*', and starts to use a different keyword.

The file explorer, document editor, and UML tool used in the study provide keyword search functions that show their users which document titles, text fragments, and UML elements match a given keyword. We identified **keyword searching** as a strategy that participants used when searching for 62% of the answers.

# 3. USING PRIOR KNOWLEDGE TO SEARCH UNDER UNCERTAINTY

In the think aloud recordings the participants voiced that they were uncertain about the correctness and completeness

---

[1] We observed from the search actions and think aloud statements that participants required 3 seconds or more to recognize and explore the document organisation when it was shown on their screen. After 3 seconds or more the participants acted upon the information by exploring the document organisation and they talked about this information, e.g. "*I see a settings document in this directory*". The participants did not actively explore the available document organisation if it was shown on their screen for less than 3 seconds. Instead the participants directly navigated to directories, documents, and sections in which they expected to find answers.

of 34 answers, out of the 90 answers (38%) given in the study . 13 of these 34 answers were actually correct and complete. Participants also voiced for 11 of the 34 answers that in everyday practice they would verify the answer with a colleague.

Typical remarks about this uncertainty are: "*It is difficult to know whether you found everything in the documentation. [I am] 70% sure of [my] answer*", "*Because searching was difficult I am not sure if this is [the] correct [answer].*", "*I think there is a 50% change that I have found all answers*", and "*I have reasonable confidence that I have not missed [any parts of the answer]*".

We observed how participants used their prior knowledge to deal with their uncertainty. Prior knowledge was used to predict which documents might contain answers when the document organisation did not relate to the question. Participants were able to recall from prior knowledge what different spelling variations, synonyms, and acronyms existed for technical terms required in the search, and this enabled them to quickly find answers by keyword searching. Participants also used prior knowledge to recognize answers and to predict whether an answer was correct and complete.

Participants talked about how to use their prior knowledge when applying the search strategies identified in Section 2.2. For example, they voiced which documents might be relevant ("*I think only Sysref contains answers*"), which keywords to search for ("*I know that Alert Light is referred to by a different name*", also see Figure 1), and which answers were complete ("*This setting is the answer. I already knew this setting.*"). Participants acquired this prior knowledge by, e.g., having used the documentation, working on the software system, and by attending meetings, presentations, and conversations with other professionals.

In the next subsection we first describe how participants acquire prior knowledge in the study. In subsections 3.2 to 3.6 we report the different ways in which participants used their prior knowledge to search for answers. We also report cognitive biases that may occur during the use of prior knowledge.

We describe the gain when use of prior knowledge leads to complete and correct answers and the loss when it does not lead to answers. The gain is categorized as 'small' or 'large' in terms of time saved (compared to the average time spent on a question) and whether the use of prior knowledge helped participants to find complete and correct answers. The loss is similarly categorized as 'small' or 'large'. If a large gain means that participants found many answers in little time, then a comparatively large loss is that many answers were missed and much time was wasted.

We have summarized the findings in Table 3. The first column denotes what prior knowledge a searcher may have and the last column denotes what cognitive bias may occur when using this prior knowledge. Column *'Gain if correct'* denotes whether a small or large gain was observed when the prior knowledge was correct and led to answers. Column *'Loss if incorrect'* similarly denotes the loss when the prior knowledge was incorrect and did not lead to answers

## 3.1 Acquiring Prior Knowledge

Several participants voiced that they learn about how knowledge is organised in the documentation when searching. For example, one participant voiced: *"From the previous question I have gained knowledge about behaviour History"* and *"I already have seen that this knowledge is described in SBDs and not in SADs. So I already have an approach that works for [searching] requirements"*. A participant explicitly voiced that this learning process was intentional: *"I would need to build up a kind of model in this environment, in documentation, to find an approach for searching. I need to open a few documents in order to come to that approach."*.

We could observe that participants most often acquired knowledge about documentation by exploring the document organisation (one of the search strategies). Participants visited or ignored locations based on what they had learned from exploring the document organisation during preceding questions. Participants also used keywords that were successful in earlier searches and used keyword spelling variations they found when exploring document organisation.

## 3.2 Predicting Which Locations Contain Answers

Several participants voiced in which locations they expected to find answers. For example, four participants voiced in which locations they expected an answer to the first question 1A before they started to search: *"I will first look in SBD"*, *"I will look in SBD_history, it has standards settings"*, *"Behaviour is in SBDs"*, and *"Then I would look in the requirements."*.

After these statements the participants directly navigated to directories, documents, and sections instead of exploring the available document organisation. They acted on their prior knowledge about the documentation. One participant explicitly voiced this: *"From my knowledge I know I should look in SBD_history and SBD_print_settings. I would not expect something in SBD_docbox ... I however do not claim that this is indeed the case"*. Such experience provides a starting point for the search.

The participants intuitively predicted from prior knowledge that certain locations contained relevant information or an answer because they found (similar) information or answers there before. This is an availability heuristic, described by Tversky and Kahneman in [18], which people use to estimate the probability or frequency of an event by recalling occurrences of similar events from their memory.

Correctly predicting that a location contains an answer resulted in a large gain. Namely, participants that directly navigated to locations found 19 answers to questions in the expected location and spent, on average, 37% less time compared to the average time spent on searching these answers.

Incorrectly predicting that a location contained an answer resulted in a small loss compared to the gain above. Namely, one participant wasted 70 seconds searching for an answer that was not in the expected location. The participant however still spent less time than average to answer this question. After the unsuccessful search in the expected location,

the participant used other search strategies (explore document organisation and keyword searching) and then found the answer. He used an agile search approach by switching to a different search strategy after the initial search strategy did not work.

## 3.3 Predicting Which Locations do not Contain Answers

Prior knowledge was also used to predict that an answer could *not* be found in certain locations, namely, in specific directories and documents. Participants ignored locations, i.e., they did not search in locations where it was unlikely to find an answer. This helped to cut down the search space and thereby save time. However, participants also gave incomplete and incorrect answers to questions because they ignored certain locations.

One of the participants said that a document containing answers to questions 1A and 1B was not related to these questions. During question 1B he voiced: *"SBD_print_settings has nothing to do with [behaviour] 'alert light'. This I know."*. Three participants ignored locations with answers, but gave no explicit reason as to why they ignored the locations. Another participant said that he decided to not open the Sysref document because he was not very familiar with it: *"I cannot do much with the Sysref ... I do not really know the Sysref that well"*.

In [18] Tversky and Kahneman describe how estimating the occurrence of an event is affected by the ease with which one can bring instances of this event to mind from personal experience. Events that are familiar to a person are more easily retrieved from memory than less familiar events, and this biases the use of availability heuristics. The participant that explicitly voiced that he was not familiar with a location had difficulty in recalling examples of answers in this location. The participant chose to visit locations he was more familiar with and not the location that he was less familiar with. This suggests that the participant missed answers because of availability bias.

Correctly predicting that a location can be ignored, i.e. ignoring a location that indeed does not contain answers, resulted in a small gain, namely, time was saved by not having to inspect this location.

Incorrectly predicting that a location can be ignored however resulted in a large loss compared to the gain above. Namely, participants did not find complete answers to 7 questions because they ignored the location containing the answer. Moreover, they wasted time searching for answers in other locations that they did not ignore. When these participants did not find answers they did not reconsider and check the locations they ignored. We asked all participants in the study to search until they were satisfied with the time spent and answer found. In this case the participants decided to stop searching without finding an answer within reasonable time.

## 3.4 Predicting Which Keywords Lead to Answers

The names of certain knowledge elements, e.g. decisions, settings, and subsystems, can be recorded using different spelling variations and acronyms. For example, the component in questions 2 and 3A has three spelling variations in the documents; *'settings editor'*, *'settingseditor'*, and *'setting editor'*, and one acronym; *'SE'*. Keyword searching for only one of these spelling variations does not return all locations that mention this component.

A participant voiced this problem quite clearly after keyword searching for requirements realized by component settings editor (question 2): "*I am not sure if [my answer] is complete. There could be requirements that do not contain the name 'settings editor'. Or [the name] is recorded differently*". Another participant voiced concerns about how to spell the interface fo question 4A: "*IJ-I. I wonder if there are different ways of writing it*". One participant emphasized the importance of prior knowledge in this situation: "*So context, about how we call certain things within Océ, is really needed to search fast*".

Moreover, certain keywords only led to part of the answers, because these keywords were not recorded in all descriptions of these answers. This was often the case for keywords that indicated a type of knowledge. For example, only part of the decisions could be found using keyword 'decision' because several descriptions of decisions did not contain the actual word 'decision'. People used prior knowledge to predict the 'coverage' or 'frequency' of keywords.

We observed that 8 of the 26 participants used part of a name in their keyword search, which allows multiple spelling variations to be covered in one keyword. For example, they used keyword '*editor*' to search for component '*settings editor*' in question 2 and 3A. One participant voiced this use of partial keywords for question 2: "*Maybe I can search for something like 'setting' or 'editor'*". Participants that used partial keywords however found much knowledge that was irrelevant for their question, and this resulted in lower average efficiency than the use of full names when keyword searching.

The participants had a clear preference for using certain keywords over others. They used keyword searching when trying to find 56 of the 90 answers, but in only 7 cases they searched for all the keywords phrased in the question they tried to answer. Participants voiced that they are familiar using certain keywords: "*I do not know how this is always written in the text so I always search for settings editor concatenated and settings editor with a space in between*" and "*Normally I would have to search for keyword 'decision'*". One participant used keyword '*requirement*' to answer questions 1B and 2 because he had successfully used the keyword during preceding question 1A: "*I already have an approach that works for [searching] requirements*".

Several participants in our study voiced that they used certain keywords because they were familiar with using these. They recalled from experience that these keywords could be used to find answers, however, these keywords did not always lead to answers in this study. This selection of keywords based on familiarity suggests an availability bias.

Accurately searching for keywords, i.e. using keywords that lead to descriptions of answers, resulted in a large gain. Namely participants found 34 answers to questions by keyword searching even though they spent 17.7% more time than the average for these questions.

Keyword searching allowed participants to find answers without having to spend a lot of time on exhaustively exploring document content. Several participant voiced this as their motivation: "*I find a lot of text here so I will switch to keyword searching*", "*It is a relatively huge document so what I will do is a keyword search*", and "*I have no other option than to use keyword searching*".

Inaccurately searching for keywords, i.e., using keywords that do not lead to descriptions of answers, resulted in a large loss compared to the gain above. Participants could not find 22 answers to questions via keyword searching and spent 8% more time on these questions than the average time required for these questions. These participants also used other search strategies, however, they gave up searching without finding a complete answer to 15 of these 22 questions. They gave up partially because relatively much time was spent on keyword searching without finding an answer.

## 3.5 Predicting Whether Answers can be Found in Multiple Locations (Triangulation)

After finding an answer in some location, several participants tried to verify whether the answer was complete and correct by searching in other locations. This strategy is called *triangulation*, which we describe in Section 2.2. This strategy is applied when, after a participant finds an answer in one location, s/he navigates to other locations to verify and improve the answer.

Participants predicted from prior knowledge whether they could find the same - possibly more complete - answer in another location. For example, one participant first found an answer to question 4B by searching in document Sysref and then voiced "*there should be a diagram here somewhere*". The participant then visited the UML document to find a more complete answer.

The answers for questions 1A, 1B, 4A, and 4B were described in multiple locations. For example, participants looking for settings whilst answering question 1B often could not find all the settings in *SBD_Alert_Light*. Settings were not very explicit in this SBD and the section titles did not clearly show where an answer could be found. Participants who also looked for an answer in *SBD_Print_Settings* would however find the settings more explicitly recorded.

Accurately triangulating answers, i.e. an answer is improved by searching for the same answer in another location, resulted in a large gain. Participants improved the completeness and correctness of 3 answers by triangulating the answers, even though they spent 95% more time on average (one participant spent 420% of the average time finding 1 of the 3 answers). 16 out of the 90 answers (18%) in this study could have been more complete and correct if the participants had triangulated their answers.

Inaccurately triangulating answers, i.e. searching for the answers in another location but not finding relevant information to improve the answers, resulted in a small loss compared to the gain above. Six participants triangulated one of their answers in another location but did not improve the answer. They spent on average 23.6% more time than other participants that answered the same questions.

## 3.6 Estimating Whether an Answer is Complete and Correct

Most participants had extensive experience using the documents and building the software specified in it. Several of these participants had a good idea what would be the likely answers to the questions. When participants said that they knew an answer from prior knowledge, we instructed them to nevertheless answer the question using the documentation.

Participants used their prior knowledge about possible answers to recognize answers while searching and to estimate the completeness and correctness of the answers they found. This often worked well, however, in some cases the prior knowledge about possible answers was incomplete. We found that 5 out of the 26 participants made a false assumption because of this.

These 5 participants falsely assumed that an answer they knew from prior knowledge was complete and correct, whilst in reality their answer was incomplete. Two of these five participants gave an answer that was both incomplete and incorrect.

For example, one participant voiced: *"I think my answer is right and I am thus satisfied. I however already knew this was the answer"*. Another participant who had to find two settings for question 1B voiced: *"this is indeed the only setting"*. All these participants had the missing parts of their answer on screen for some time but ignored this.

The search behaviour of these 5 participants was affected by confirmation bias [12]. The participants searched for answers that they knew from prior knowledge and confirmed that these answers were recorded in documentation, i.e., they confirmed their prior beliefs. In the process they ignored other answers and information that was inconsistent with these beliefs.

Accurately estimating whether an answer is complete and correct based on prior knowledge resulted in a small gain. 10 participants gave a correct and complete answer that they claimed to already know from prior knowledge. These participants spent, on average, 3% less time to find this answer than other participants.

Inaccurately estimating that an answer is complete and correct based on prior knowledge or prior belief, resulted in a large loss compared to the gain above. Five answers to questions that were assumed to be correct and complete by 5 participants were in fact incomplete and incorrect. The participants answered the five questions in 74% of the average time that other participants spent on these questions. This was because they searched briefly or they stopped searching immediately after finding an answer known from prior knowledge.

## 4. LESSONS LEARNT

### 4.1 Lessons for Documentation Users

Prior knowledge can be used to quickly find correct answers to questions when the document organisation does not support the questions. We found that the use of certain prior knowledge yields larger gains than other prior knowledge. Moreover, there is a difference in losses when incorrect predictions are made based on prior knowledge.

Table 3 shows that it was rewarding for participants to visit the expected location of an answer and to triangulate an answer in multiple locations known from prior knowledge. If this prior knowledge proves to be incorrect the loss is small, and it is therefore relatively safe to use. Using prior knowledge to predict which keywords lead to an answer often yields a large gain, however, incorrect predictions may result in a large loss and this prior knowledge should thus be used with caution. Ignoring certain locations or estimating that an answer is complete and correct from prior knowledge yields a small gain and such cognitive biases increase the chance of a large loss.

Being more aware of cognitive biases can prevent the aforementioned losses. It may be hard to remember examples of answers being recorded in a certain location because one

is not familiar with this location, however, this does not imply that the location indeed contains no answers. Certain keywords are easily remembered because they are often used and familiar. Using these keywords in searching may however be counter-productive. Prior knowledge about the answer to a question may be incorrect, incomplete, or outdated.

Existing prior knowledge can be evaluated and updated, by thoroughly exploring document organisation and content, i.e., conducting empirical investigation and seeking disconfirmatory evidence [15]. This prevents inaccurate predictions and cognitive biases later on. An additional benefit of exploring the document organisation and content is that it can remove search uncertainty and the need for using prior knowledge. A searcher may find document organisation that is fitting for the question asked, and this organisation often leads to complete and correct answers.

### 4.2 Lessons for Documentation Writers

We observed several causes for search uncertainty:

- Document organisation does not relate to a question because document writers do not plan the document organisation to answer all questions that could arise.

- Documents that are not searched might contain answers.

- The same knowledge might be referred to by multiple spelling variations and acronyms.

- The type of knowledge might not be consistently recorded.

- Complementary knowledge might be described in multiple locations.

Consequently, a searcher might only become certain that an answer is correct and complete when all text in the available documentation is read. We observed that none of the participants exhaustively inspected all available document contents. Participants either quickly found answers using document organisation that was fitting for the questions, or they used their prior knowledge to predict which locations and keywords were relevant when searching.

Searchers make predictions from their prior knowledge to deal with search uncertainty. These predictions can however be inaccurate and are prone to cognitive biases. This results in inefficient and ineffective use of documentation, and in turn lowers the incentive to spend resources on producing good documentation, creating a vicious cycle [13]. Moreover, incomplete and incorrect answers are used to build software and may result in costly errors.

Addressing causes for search uncertainty removes the need for searchers to use prior knowledge and lowers the chance that cognitive biases occur. Creating a document organisation that fully relates to commonly asked questions removes much search uncertainty. Introducing spelling conventions and consistently recording what type of knowledge is described makes keyword searching more efficient and less error-prone. Recording the same type of knowledge in one location prevents scattered descriptions of the same knowledge that can become inconsistent over time, and in turn removes the need for searchers to triangulate answers.

These solutions are difficult to realize when writing and maintaining documentation in a linear file-based format with multiple authors. As an alternative, ontology-based documentation can address above issues, whilst it also provides benefits from the use of explicit semantics and nonlinear organization of knowledge. Ontology-based documentation encapsulates relationships between pieces of information, which allows users to traverse and search knowledge more effectively [4]. Participants in our study were also asked to retrieve knowledge from ontology-based documentation, as part of a larger experiment reported in [4]. We found that the use of ontology-based documentation was significantly more efficient and effective for answering the questions as compared to the use of file-based documentation [4].

## 5. THREATS TO VALIDITY

The participants also used ontology-based documentation to answer questions as part of the larger research reported in [4]. We did not find evidence that the use of the ontology-based documentation approach had an influence on how participants used the reported search strategies and their prior knowledge in file-based documentation.

To verify the consistency of the used encoding scheme, described in Section 2.2, two researchers independently applied the scheme to identify search actions from the videos. After applying the scheme they checked if they came up with the same set of search actions.

We constructed PBGs using the format depicted in [2] and Figure 1. We observed that participants acquired new knowledge with each executed search action. For example, one participant voiced: "I have already seen that this knowledge is described in SBDs and not in SADs.". As such the participants did not return to a previous state of knowledge, which is proposed as a PBG modelling construct by Newell and Simon in [11] but not applied in this paper.

The use of SADs, SBDs, Sysref, and design documents, and the search functions of the tools used for searching these documents, can be considered generic documentation practice in industry. This suggest that the identified search strategies are also generalizable to other software projects.

The evaluation in terms of efficiency and effectiveness in this paper is specific to the questions and Océ documentation used in this study. The use of prior knowledge and cognitive biases that may occur are however largely independent of the question asked and documentation searched. The use of prior knowledge and impact of cognitive biases also apply when searching in software documentation in other domains and is therefore generalizable.

## 6. RELATED WORK

How knowledge is used in software documentation is systematically reviewed in [5], and in this section we only discuss related work on using prior knowledge to search software documentation.

Chen and Dhar describe in [2] how prior knowledge is used during online document-based information retrieval and how prior knowledge affects the selection of search strategies. In [14] Shute and Smith identify the use of prior knowledge as 'subject-dependent expertise' for searching bibliographic databases. For example, the 'known-item-instantiation' strategy described in [2] uses subject-dependent expertise. Shute and Smith describe how participants talk

about using their intuition and "gut feeling", which suggests that they use their prior knowledge.

In [3] de Boer and van Vliet describe how software professionals in the same team have similar mental models of documentation. They have a shared understanding of the contents of these documents. Moreover, the development process affects the level of shared understanding within a team. Such mental models of documentation are part of the prior knowledge that we discuss in this paper.

In [9] LaToza et al. describe how developers rely on implicit code knowledge and spend much effort to maintain a mental model of code. Developers recall details, e.g., about the architecture and design of their code, as part of their prior knowledge, i.e., they know code details by heart. Moreover, they often do not consult documentation to check if their mental model is consistent with documentation.

In [17] Tang describes how software design is affected by cognitive biases. Designers use prior beliefs and intuition to make judgements, and cognitive biases may occur because of this. In [1] Calikli et al. investigate how confirmation biases during software testing can be prevented.

In [15] Stacy and Macmillian describe how software professionals develop and use their mental models during software engineering activities and how this is influenced by cognitive biases. For example, code features that are easily remembered by software professionals may be judged to occur more frequently than other features due to availability bias. They suggest that keywords that are very long, occur in recently read documents, or occur in code recently worked on may be more easily remembered than other keywords, and this may cause availability bias. Similarly, we observed that software professional tend to search keywords that are familiar and easily remembered from prior knowledge, and that this may result in availability bias.

In [8] Korkala and Maurer identify communication waste, e.g., outdated and scattered information, in a software project. The software documentation in our study is used to communicate knowledge. As such, the losses during the use of prior knowledge, described in sections 3.2 through 3.6, can be regarded as communication waste. The identified causes for search uncertainty can in turn be regarded as causes for communication waste.

In [16] Su et al. used Information Foraging theory to explain how software professionals search for architectural knowledge in document sections using several foraging styles. Information Foraging theory tries to explain the search behaviour of people in terms of cost and reward when navigating an information topology. The study in [16] however does not evaluate whether the observed search behaviour is time-efficient and does not focus on use of prior knowledge.

In [7] Ko et al. report an exploratory study of how developers seek, relate, and collect relevant information during software maintenance tasks. Their analysis of information seeking behaviour of software developers relates to our work in which software professionals also exhibit information seeking behaviour. However, software maintenance information is searched in source files and on the Internet, whereas in our work software professionals search for knowledge in architecture documents.

## 7. CONCLUSIONS

Software documents are used to capture and communicate knowledge in software projects. It is important that this knowledge can be retrieved efficiently and effectively, to prevent wasted time and errors that negatively affect the quality of software. The organisation of software documentation typically does not support all of the questions asked by software professionals. This introduces search uncertainty and makes it hard for software professionals to find complete and correct answers within reasonable time.

We conducted an industry study to investigate how software professionals search for knowledge in software documentation. We found that professionals use their prior knowledge to find answers when the document organisation did not relate to the questions they had to answer. Prior knowledge was used to make predictions about the location of knowledge, which keywords can be used to search relevant knowledge, and whether the knowledge found is correct and complete.

Using prior knowledge is often time-effective, however, inaccurate predictions and cognitive biases can lead to inefficient and ineffective knowledge retrieval. Availability bias may cause searchers to ignore locations and keywords that they are not familiar with, even though these locations and keywords may lead to answers. Using prior knowledge is also prone to confirmation bias when searchers mainly focus on confirming the answers that they already know from their prior knowledge.

Awareness of these cognitive biases may reduce the likelihood that they occur when searching in software documentation. Searchers can evaluate and update their existing prior knowledge by spending time on exploring the document organisation and content, which further reduces the probability that cognitive biases occur. Addressing causes for search uncertainty when writing documentation removes the need for searchers to use prior knowledge and in turn prevents that cognitive biases occur.

## Acknowledgements

The authors wish to thank René Laan, Wim Couwenberg, Pieter Verduin, Amar Kalloe, and the other good folks at Océ R&D for their support, interest to participate in this research, and excellent insights. This research has been partially sponsored by the Dutch "Regeling Kenniswerkers", project KWR09164, "Stephenson: Architecture knowledge sharing practices in software product lines for print systems" and by the Natural Science Foundation of China (NSFC) project No. 61170025 "KeSRAD: Knowledge-enabled Software Requirements to Architecture Documentation".

## 8. REFERENCES

[1] G. Calikli, A. Bener, and B. Arslan. An analysis of the effects of company culture, education and experience on confirmation bias levels of software developers and testers. In *International Conference on Software Engineering (ICSE)*, pages 187–190. IEEE, 2010.

[2] H. Chen and V. Dhar. Cognitive process as a basis for intelligent retrieval systems design. *Information Processing & Management*, 27(5):405 – 432, 1991.

[3] R. C. de Boer and H. van Vliet. Writing and reading software documentation: How the development process may affect understanding. In *ICSE Workshop on Cooperative and Human Aspects on Software Engineering (CHASE)*, pages 40–47. IEEE, 2009.

[4] K. A. de Graaf, A. Tang, P. Liang, and H. van Vliet. Ontology-based software architecture documentation. In *Joint Working IEEE/IFIP Conference on Software Architecture (WICSA) and European Conference on Software Architecture (ECSA)*, pages 121–130. IEEE, 2012.

[5] W. Ding, P. Liang, A. Tang, and H. van Vliet. Knowledge-based approaches in software documentation: A systematic literature review. *Information and Software Technology*, 56(6):545 – 567, 2014.

[6] K. A. Ericsson and H. A. Simon. *Protocol Analysis: Verbal Reports as Data*. MIT Press, revised edition, 1993.

[7] A. Ko, B. Myers, M. Coblenz, and H. Aung. An exploratory study of how developers seek, relate, and collect relevant information during software maintenance tasks. *IEEE Transactions on Software Engineering*, 32(12):971–987, 2006.

[8] M. Korkala and F. Maurer. Waste identification as the means for improving communication in globally distributed agile software development. *Journal of Systems and Software*, 2014. http://dx.doi.org/10.1016/j.jss.2014.03.080.

[9] T. D. LaToza, G. Venolia, and R. DeLine. Maintaining mental models: A study of developer work habits. In *International Conference on Software Engineering (ICSE)*, pages 492–501. ACM, 2006.

[10] T. C. Lethbridge, J. Singer, and A. Forward. How software engineers use documentation: The state of the practice. *IEEE Software*, 20(6):35–39, 2003.

[11] A. Newell and H. A. Simon. *Human Problem Solving*. Prentice Hall, 1972.

[12] R. S. Nickerson. Confirmation bias: A ubiquitous phenomenon in many guises. *Review of General Psychology*, 2(2):175–220, 1998.

[13] D. L. Parnas. Precise Documentation: The Key to Better Software. In *The Future of Software Engineering*, chapter 8, pages 125–148. Springer, 2011.

[14] S. J. Shute and P. J. Smith. Knowledge-based search tactics. *Information Processing & Management*, 29(1):29 – 45, 1993.

[15] W. Stacy and J. MacMillan. Cognitive bias in software engineering. *Communications of the ACM*, 38(6):57–63, 1995.

[16] M. T. Su, E. Tempero, J. Hosking, and J. Grundy. A study of architectural information foraging in software architecture documents. In *Working IEEE/IFIP Conference on Software Architecture (WICSA) and European Conference on Software Architecture (ECSA)*, pages 141–150. IEEE, 2012.

[17] A. Tang. Software designers, are you biased? In *Proceedings of the 6th International Workshop on SHAring and Reusing Architectural Knowledge, (SHARK)*, pages 1–8. ACM, 2011.

[18] A. Tversky and D. Kahneman. Judgment under uncertainty: Heuristics and biases. *Science*, 185(4157):1124–1131, 1974.

[19] M. W. van Someren, Y. F. Barnard, and J. A. Sandberg. *The Think Aloud Method - A practical guide to modelling cognitive processes*. Academic Press London, 1994.

# What Academics Want When Reading Digitally

Juliane Franze
Faculty of IT
Monash University
Caulfield, Australia

Kim Marriott
Faculty of IT
Monash University
Caulfield, Australia

Michael Wybrow
Faculty of IT
Monash University
Caulfield, Australia

{Juliane.Franze, Kim.Marriott, Michael.Wybrow}@monash.edu

## ABSTRACT

Researchers constantly read and annotate academic documents. While almost all documents are provided digitally, many are still printed and read on paper. We surveyed 162 academics in order to better understand their reading habits and preferences. We were particularly interested in understanding the barriers to digital reading and the features desired by academics for digital reading applications.

## Categories and Subject Descriptors

H.1.2 [**Models and Principles**]: User/Machine Systems—*human factors*; H.5.2 [**Information Interfaces and Presentation**]: User Interfaces—*evaluation/methodology*

## Keywords

Human behaviour; usability; technical reading; digital documents; e-books

## 1. INTRODUCTION

Researchers spend significant amounts of time reading academic documents such as conference papers, journal articles and theses. The time devoted to reading grows as the number of publications and available digital information increases every year [3, 10]. Academic documents are characterised by a consistent logical hierarchy and the use of footnotes, endnotes (references), figures and tables. Hillesund [5] shows that academic documents are read non-linearly, and that annotation plays an important role. Pugh [11] identifies different reading techniques: scanning and searching, in order to locate specific information; skimming, to gain a basic understanding of the text and its structure; and receptive and responsive reading to fully read the text, which includes note taking and annotation.

The majority of academic documents are provided digitally, often as PDF files [9, 10]. PDF documents encode a fixed layout and are therefore presented in the same way, independent of device. Specialised software for reading PDF

files exists for all common devices, and is stable, mature and freely available. It typically provides annotation, dictionary lookup and position syncing between devices. Digital reading used to equate to reading on a desktop computer but now includes reading on eReaders, tablets and smartphones.

Here we present the results of a survey of 162 academics investigating their reading device preferences, reading habits and the features they would like supported by digital reading applications. Such a survey is important because it is several years since the last in this rapidly changing field. We found that paper and desktop computers still dominate academic reading, both being used about equally. Smartphones and eReaders are almost never used for academic reading but tablets are not infrequent.

The most novel and interesting aspect of the survey were questions asking what features respondents desire from a digital reading environment. The answers revealed that many did not want reading on digital devices to replicate that of print but rather to take advantage of new kinds of navigation and layout adaptation. This is in line with Chartier's suggestion from the late 1990s that "digital text inevitably requires new ways of reading" [2]. Of course, as Marshall points out, "to promote the transition to reading on the screen, it is vital to make the experience as good as the experience of reading on paper" [9].

## 2. METHODOLOGY

The survey was designed as an online questionnaire. All participants could complete the survey directly in their web browser at their own pace. The survey was voluntary and no payment or reward was offered. All responses were anonymous. The survey questions and responses were in English.[1] The survey consisted of 18 questions and required approximately 10 minutes to complete. About one-third of the questions were closed-ended and involved selection from predefined responses while the remaining questions were openended.

The invitation for participation was advertised in a weekly newsletter sent to all academic staff and students at Monash University. Additionally, colleagues from the Ludwig Maximilian University of Munich and Fraunhofer institutes in Munich were invited via email lists. The survey was available for three months from December 2013 to February 2014.

We used a coding process [12] to categorise all the responses. For the open-ended questions, all textual responses were read independently by two members of the research

---

[1]One participant responded in German and the responses were translated by a member of the research team.

team who independently chose categories of responses (with surprising consistency). Final categories for each question were decided by discussion between these two team members. One of the research team members performed the coding by reading all responses and recording the matching categories. This matching was checked by another team member who flagged any perceived inconsistencies, which were then discussed by the team to determine the final coding. The entire questionnaire, plus the responses and processed data, are available online.[2]

## 3. ANALYSIS AND DISCUSSION

A total of 162 participant surveys were analysed. The gender distribution was slightly uneven: 58% females to 42% males, with 5 respondents not giving their gender. The sample consists of a diverse range of ages from under 25 to above 65, with 60% under 35, and 41% in the "26 to 35" bracket.

### Device usage

The first survey question asked respondents to indicate how often they read academic papers using: *Print*, *Desktop* (including laptops), *Tablet*, *eReader* and *Smartphone*. Allowed responses were: *Most often*, *Often*, *Occasionally* and *Never*. From the responses we extracted two data sets: Frequency and Preferred. Frequency assigned each device a ranking of *Never*, *Occasionally* or *Often* where *Often* was true if the respondent had indicated either *Most often* or *Often* for that device. Preferred was a boolean indicating if the participant selected that medium as their most often used.

| Device | Preferred | Often | Occ. | Never |
|--------|-----------|-------|------|-------|
| Print | 56% | 71% | 23% | 5% |
| Desktop | 53% | 83% | 14% | 3% |
| Tablet | 8% | 16% | 30% | 54% |
| eReader | 2% | 4% | 12% | 84% |
| Smartphone | 0% | 0% | 27% | 72% |

Print and desktops are by far the most frequently used devices for reading academic papers, followed by tablets. Smartphones and eReaders are rather uncommon. We confirmed that this difference was significant at the 0.05 confidence level using a Kruskal-Wallis $H$ ($\chi^2(4) = 477.3246$, $p < 2.2e-16$). Post-hoc analysis using pairwise comparisons with the Wilcoxon rank sum test using a Bonferroni correction indicated that Print and Desktop were significantly more frequent than eReader, Tablet and Smartphone and that Tablet was significantly more frequent than eReader and Smartphone.

This device preference was supported by the data on most preferred device, i.e., Print and Desktop were used most often for reading academic papers, followed by Tablets. Smartphones and eReaders are very uncommon. We used a $\chi^2$ test with equal probability null hypothesis ($\chi^2(4) = 159.6567$, $p < 2.2e-16$). We used a two-way $\chi^2$ test and Fisher's exact test to examine if gender, age or field of study affected preference for Print or Desktop. We found that participants from BIOMED (life sciences, health, psychology and psychiatry) read on Desktop significantly more often than other fields ($\chi^2(6) = 14.0295$, $0.02931$; Fisher $p = 0.02665$). These results were not significantly affected by gender or age.

To put this in context, Liu [7] evaluated how the reading behaviour in the digital environment has changed between 1993 and 2003. He found that "the digital environment has begun to affect people's reading behaviour" in that more time is spent on browsing and scanning as well as non-linear reading. Notably, he points out that in-depth reading of academic articles is still dominated by paper. Sellen and Harper provide similar evidence in various studies [13]. Tenopir found that more than two-thirds of electronic reading actually involved immediate downloading and printing on to paper [15]. Our findings suggest that some five years later print usage has decreased and that print and reading on digital devices are now equally common.

It is not surprising that smartphones are rarely used. Small screen require users to scroll a lot, especially reading PDF documents which are not reflowable. This causes increased effort and interruption in the reading flow for continuous reading. As a result, in-depth reading is very difficult on such devices. Similarly unsurprising are the results for eReaders. Their shortcomings are well documented: navigation problems finding tables and figures [17]; issues with switching modes as well as annotating, highlighting and bookmarking [16]; non-optimal display of figures and lack of cross-referencing to jump between documents [1]. Our results suggest that Tablets are the small mobile device of choice for reading academic papers.

### Reading habits

Several questions explored the reasons why respondents read academic papers, how they read them, and the environment in which they read. We asked respondents to indicate all the reasons why they typically read an academic paper (multiple-choice). The most common reasons were: finding particular facts or results (82%); skim-reading to check for relevance (81%); detailed reading for full understanding of paper (76%); and learning about an area (72%). Reviewing was also reasonably common: conference/journal review (40%); student paper (31%). Interestingly, 38% of respondents read academic papers for entertainment or interest.

Participants tended to begin reading with the Abstract (84%), the Introduction (15%) or Conclusion (13%). In terms of perceived importance, participants rated the Conclusion (38%), Results (32%), Abstract (28%) and Methods (26%) sections as the most critical.

Another (open-ended) question asked respondents how they typically arranged their work area when reading academic papers. Our coding-based analysis showed that 69% read at their desk, 45% read away from their desk, with some 8% reading while travelling. Without any prompting, more than half of the participants (57%) explicitly mentioned that they keep annotation materials such as pens nearby while reading. This is further evidence that annotation is considered an integral part of the academic reading process.

Many people's responses indicated they chose reading locations free of distractions or interruptions, and some specifically mentioned the use of relaxation aids such as music or coffee. Many of the responses suggest a pre-planned, almost ritualistic aspect to reading where people carefully prepare themselves and their environment for the reading task:

> "I sit at my desk (whether at home or in my office at Uni) with my laptop/PC in front of me (whether I am reading off screen or not, so I can google/look up additional things as I go). I have pens (black and red), highlighters, and post it notes (in matching colours) on the desk. If I

---

[2]http://marvl.infotech.monash.edu/doceng-2014.zip

*have printed articles etc, then I pile all the papers I have not read yet on the left of the computer, and once I have read them I put them in a pile on the right. I always have a drink with me, usually a bottle of water and/or coffee. I also have note/scrap paper available if I need to write notes for myself or for any ideas not appropriate to annotate on the paper itself.*" (#132)

We had two open-ended questions on annotation. The first asked where participants make annotations, notes or corrections when reading a paper and the second enquired how they link these to specific text. Most people annotate the document itself (both PDF and paper, 85%). Some annotate a separate physical document (25%) or a separate digital document/annotation application (19%). This was dependent upon the most frequent reading media, ($\chi^2(2) = 9.2682$, $p = 0.009715$), with those reading Print more likely to annotate the document (95%) vs Desktop (77%) or Tablet (83%). However, even for those who preferred Print many would also annotate on separate physical documents (22%) or separate digital documents (29%).

Annotations were linked to corresponding text in a number of different ways: Linking with lines or arrows (28%); By proximity, i.e., placing nearby notes (25%); Highlighting, underlining or circling text (25%); Using keys such as numbers, asterisks, symbols, or colours (16%); Layout-dependent description, e.g., "Second sentence in column 2 on page 3" (11%); Logical description (including quoting text), e.g., "Section 2, paragraph 3, sentence 2" (9%). There was no indication that this depended upon the reading media.

We asked participants about the kinds of resources they commonly use to source background information when reading a paper (multiple-choice) and how these are accessed (open-ended). Virtually all respondents use on-line resources such as Google Scholar or Wikipedia (97%) and many use physical documents (67%) and colleagues (36%). They access these resources on the same reading device (49%), a nearby computer/laptop (60%), in printed form (19%), or on a mobile device such as tablet or phone (7%).

### Reasons for reading on paper

A key aim of the survey was to better understand why academics still commonly read printed documents. Ease of **annotation** was mentioned by 44% of respondents who frequently cited the convenience, freedom and accuracy of creating annotations on paper. This reaffirms previous results [7, 13] and shows once more that directly annotating the document is very important for academic reading.

**Physical comfort** was the second most common reason given for reading on paper (29%). Respondents mentioned that paper is more comfortable on the eyes and easier to hold and view than an electronic device. Given that many academics spend a lot of their day in front of a computer, switching to another medium for reading is not surprising.

**Portability** (15%), **tangibility** (13%), easier **navigation** (13%) and **better comprehension** (9%) were other reasons given for preferring to read paper. Portability was mentioned as an advantage for reading papers outside of the office, especially when travelling. Battery life and airport security were mentioned as issues for digital reading. The importance of tangibility has been confirmed by previous studies [4, 6, 7, 8]. Physical touch plays an important role in collaborative work on a paper as well as in

proof-reading [14]. Interestingly, age affected the importance of tangibility ($\chi^2(4) = 15.5399, p = 0.003703$; Fisher $p = 0.003648$) with only participants older than 25 mentioning it. In terms of navigation, respondents appreciated "quick random access" (#16), that it is "easier to flip back and forth from page to page" (#112), as well as "shuttling to and from references" (#82).

Habits and personal preferences also play a minor role with several participants stating: "I am a print generation so used to it." (#83); "Habit, and I like the feeling of real paper." (#72).

### Desired features for digital reading

Several questions explored desired features in digital reading software. A multiple-choice question asked participants to select the kinds of adjustable layout options they would like to have for digital reading. We found that adjustable font size is important to 76% of respondents, while varying the font family was much less important (22%). Also fairly unimportant were user adjustment of background colour and text colour (both 19%). Adjustable margins were important to 33% of the respondents, and ability to alter the orientation of the content was important to 54%. Almost half of the respondents (48%) wanted to be able to change the numbers of columns used to display the document and 57% of participants wished to be able to vary the amount of text shown on the screen. 43% of respondents wanted control over placement of figures and tables, while 35% desire adjustable placement for references and footnotes. This shows that the layout options provided by non-technical reading applications like the Kindle are not enough for academic reading and that more flexible layout is required.

We also asked an open-ended question about how a paper should ideally be laid out on digital devices. 23% responded that they would like the same layout as on paper, with many of these people expressing surprise that other layouts would even be possible. 21% of respondents volunteered that they like to have a single column layout with reflowed text. Respondents also said that they would like the layout to adapt to different screens (12%) and that the text should allow continuous scrolling (10%). Interestingly, a few participants wanted more drastic layout changes such as a dedicated stream for just the document text (2%). Others wished to have linked content—such as figures, footnotes, tables—"nearby" (9%).

In terms of navigation within the document, the most frequent requests were for hierarchical navigation (14%) and hyperlinked navigation (15%) where the user could jump to a desired figure, section or paragraph. A few respondents (7%) requested the ability to work with a collection of documents or library, rather than with a single document. Many people (22%) volunteered that they desired better annotation support in general. Additionally, some people requested more space for annotations (8%), annotation syncing (2%), as well as the ability to export annotations and notes (6%).

## 4. CONCLUSIONS

This research aimed to provide better understanding of why so many researchers still read on print and to identify the current barriers to the use of digital devices. It is intended to inform the design of future digital reading environments for academics and other technical professionals.

Our results suggest that future digital reading environments should take into account the following issues.

*Navigation:* The typical academic reading workflow is non-linear. As most academic papers have similar structure, readers know what to expect in particular sections and thus wish to jump to them directly. Reading features requested by participants that correlate with this behaviour were content indexes, hierarchical and hyperlinked navigation.

*Annotation:* Annotation is a key aspect of the academic reading process. The ease of annotating on paper and the relative inflexibility of digital annotation remains a major reason that people still prefer to work with print. There is a clear need for digital reading software to provide more flexible annotation features, including various styles of annotation links, syncing and export of annotations, and improved display of in-place annotations within the document.

*Tablets:* Tablet computers have greatly increased in availability and popularity in recent times. While still not commonly used for academic reading, they have become the mobile device of choice for this purpose. It is important to focus on improving the academic reading experience on such devices to support mobility as many academics wish to read outside the office, especially while travelling.

*Layout:* While some wanted the print and digital version of a document to look identical, many did not. Participants requested reflowable adaptive layout, and even radically different presentation such as a single scrollable text stream. Presentation of references, figures and tables close to their referencing text and the ability to enlarge figures and tables to be full-screen on demand would seem useful features.

*Contextual literature:* Participants requested the ability to work with a collection of documents or library. This is currently not something that most digital reading applications have focussed upon. Unsurprisingly we found that almost all academics use online resources for finding background information and viewing related work while reading. This action usually interrupts continuous reading regardless of whether they are reading on paper or digitally. Through careful design we should be able to allow this to be done faster and less jarringly on digital devices.

*Physicality:* Our study shows there are some aspects of the physical reading experience that cannot be achieved in digital form due to the difference of the mediums. These are things such as the feeling of paper, the physical experience when page flipping, having less distractions, positioning or storing paper in a particular place, as well as being away from digital screens. Our belief is that while we need to be aware of these limitations, by offering well designed and task-specific interfaces and features, digital devices can become the preferred medium for certain modes of technical reading.

## Acknowledgments

We thank Monash University and the Ludwig Maximilian University of Munich for funding Juliane's visit. We thank participants of the DocEng 2013 workshop "Reimagining Digital Publishing for Technical Documents" whose thought-provoking discussions inspired this study.

## 5. REFERENCES

[1] M. Aaltonen, P. Mannonen, S. Nieminen, and M. Nieminen. Usability and compatibility of e-book readers in an academic environment: A collaborative study. *IFLA Journal*, 37(1):16–27, 2011.

[2] R. Chartier. The end of the reign of the book. *SubStance*, 26(1):9–11, 1997.

[3] H. de Ribaupierre and G. Falquet. New trends for reading scientific documents. In *Proceedings of the 4th ACM Workshop on Online Books, Complementary Social Media and Crowdsourcing*, BooksOnline '11, pages 19–24, New York, NY, USA, 2011. ACM.

[4] M. C. Dyson. How do we read text on screen. In H. van Oostendorp, L. Breure, and A. Dillon, editors, *Creation, Use, and Deployment of Digital Information*, pages 279–306. Routledge, 2005.

[5] T. Hillesund. Digital reading spaces: How expert readers handle books, the web and electronic paper. *First Monday*, 15(4), 2010.

[6] D. M. Levy. *Scrolling Forward: Making Sense of Documents in the Digital Age*. Arcade Publishing, 2001.

[7] Z. Liu. Reading behavior in the digital environment: Changes in reading behavior over the past ten years. *Journal of Documentation*, 61(6):700–712, 2005.

[8] A. Mangen. Hypertext fiction reading: Haptics and immersion. *Journal of Research in Reading*, 31(4):404–419, 2008.

[9] C. C. Marshall. Reading and interactivity in the digital library: Creating an experience that transcends paper. In *Proceedings of the CLIR/Kanazawa Institute of Technology Roundtable*, pages 3–4. MIT Press, 2005.

[10] S. Pettifer, P. McDermott, J. Marsh, D. Thorne, A. Villeger, and T. K. Attwood. Ceci n'est pas un hamburger: modelling and representing the scholarly article. *Learned Publishing*, 24(3):207–220, 2011.

[11] A. K. Pugh. *Silent Reading: An Introduction to Its Study and Teaching*. Heinemann, London, UK, 1978.

[12] J. Saldaña. *The coding manual for qualitative researchers*. SAGE, 2012.

[13] A. J. Sellen and R. H. Harper. *The Myth of the Paperless Office*. MIT Press, 2003.

[14] H. Shibata, K. Takano, and K. Omura. Impact of the use of a touch-based digital reading device in immersive reading. *SID Symposium Digest of Technical Papers*, 44(1):45–48, 2013.

[15] C. Tenopir, D. W. King, S. Edwards, and L. Wu. Electronic journals and changes in scholarly article seeking and reading patterns. School of Information Sciences Publications and Other Works, 2009.

[16] A. Thayer, C. P. Lee, L. H. Hwang, H. Sales, P. Sen, and N. Dalal. The imposition and superimposition of digital reading technology: The academic potential of e-readers. In *Proceedings of the SIGCHI Conference on Human Factors in Computing Systems*, CHI '11, pages 2917–2926, New York, NY, USA, 2011. ACM.

[17] J. Young. 6 lessons one campus learned about e-textbooks. *The Chronicle of Higher Education*, 55(39), 2009.

# A Platform for Language Independent Summarization

Luciano Cabral[a,b], Rafael Dueire Lins[a], Rafael Mello[a], Fred Freitas[a], Bruno Ávila[a],
Steven Simske[c], and Marcelo Riss[d]

[a] Federal University of Pernambuco, Recife, Brazil
[b] Federal Institute of Pernambuco, Caruaru, Brazil
[c] Hewlett-Packard Labs., Fort Collins, CO 80528, USA
[d] Hewlett-Packard Brazil, Porto Alegre, Brazil

{lsc4,rdl,rflm,fred,bta}@cin.ufpe.br, {steven.simske,marcelo.riss}@hp.com

## ABSTRACT

The text data available on the Internet is not only huge in volume, but also in diversity of subject, quality and idiom. Such factors make it infeasible to efficiently scavenge useful information from it. Automatic text summarization is a possible solution for efficiently addressing such a problem, because it aims to sieve the relevant information in documents by creating shorter versions of the text. However, most of the techniques and tools available for automatic text summarization are designed only for the English language, which is a severe restriction. There are multilingual platforms that support, at most, 2 languages. This paper proposes a language independent summarization platform that provides corpus acquisition, language classification, translation and text summarization for 25 different languages.

## Categories and Subject Descriptors

I.2.7 [**Artificial Intelligence**]: Natural Language Processing – *Language understanding, Machine translation and Text analysis.*

## General Terms

Measurement, Experimentation and Algorithms.

## Keywords

Multilingual Summarization; Classification; Translation; Platform

## 1. INTRODUCTION

The amount of data available on the web is growing every year. There are millions textual documents published in different languages making of the web an open environment for content dissemination. It is increasingly difficult to efficiently find useful information in the Internet. Thus, it is necessary to use language independent methods to understand, classify and present, clearly and concisely the existing information in different languages, saving users resources and time. Text summarization has been pointed out as a possible solution to the document classification problem and creates a shorter version of a document with its essential content. Most automatic document summarization techniques and tools were developed for the English language. This paper presents a platform for language independent

summarization that combines techniques for language identification, content translation and summarization. The proposed solution first pre-processes the input text to make it treatable by the following modules. Then, language identification is performed followed by translation into English and then summarization or direct summarization. The results are then analyzed to yield the final summary.

Other works found in the technical literature aim to perform multilingual summarization. MEAD, by Radev and his colleagues [1], makes use of only 8 summarization algorithms and was assessed only with the Chinese and English languages. Evans and his collaborators [2] use sentence similarity and clustering, as a summarization strategy and was focused on Arabic and English. Roark and Fisher [3] use Machine Learning to obtain a query-focused sentence ranking (with supervision). In reference [3] they describe an experiment with translated documents which bears some resemblance to the strategy proposed here. However, their work neither explicitly mentions the number of supported languages nor brings the idea of having more than one translation of the same document as a way to compensate the semantic loss of the translation process as introduced here. Litvak, Last and Friedman [4] more recently, use genetic algorithms in the summarization task. Similarly to the aforementioned multi-language summarization algorithms, their work supports only two languages (English and Hebrew). Gupta [5] uses a hybrid algorithm for summarization, supporting Hindi and Punjabi docs.

Unfortunately, none of the multilingual summarization references listed above offer elements for testing their performance in a common data set or corpus making difficult an independent assessment or performance analysis. Despite this, they focus on a disjoint set of languages (Arabic, Chinese, Hebrew, Hindi and Punjabi), while the focus here is on the languages spoken by the European Union. As they address only specific languages: no language identification module is part of their solutions.

## 2. PLIS - ARCHITECTURE DESCRIPTION

This section presents the functionality of the main modules of the Platform for Language Independent Summarization. Figure 1 sketches the PLIS architecture.

The initial task of the platform is text pre-processing in which the input text has all its non-textual parts removed and sentences numbered and organized one sentence per line. Then, the resulting text undergoes the language identification phase. If the text is in English it is submitted to the extractive summarization module, which selects the most significant sentences from the original text after pre-processing using the several sentence scoring methods described in the literature acknowledged as the most efficient ones for extractive summarization. Otherwise, the text is submitted to some language independent summarization algorithms and to several tools that will translate each of the sentences in the original text into English. As the automatic translation process is likely to introduce semantic losses to the original text the use of more than one translation tool may compensate such losses. The several versions of the translated text are submitted to the extractive summarization module yielding for each input a set of numbers, each of them related to the sentences in the original text. The different sets of sentences chosen are analyzed by the Sentence Scoring and Selection Module, which will produce a new set of indices that correspond to the summary, encompassing the chosen sentences in the original text.

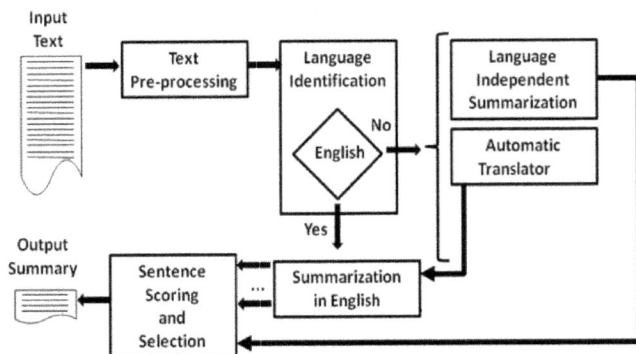

**Figure 1. The PLIS Architecture.**

The following sections detail the functionality of the main modules of the PLIS architecture.

## 2.1 Language classification

This module implements the CALIM language identification algorithm, described in reference [6], which works with all the 25 languages in use in the European Community today. Such algorithm was inspired on the ideas of Dunning [7], Cavnar and Trenkle [8] and Lins and Gonçalves [9], based on language profiles containing the most frequent words ($\cong$250 per language). Beyond your respective relative frequency in a total of 25 languages (English, Portuguese, Spanish, Italian, French, German, Bulgarian, Czech, Danish, Dutch, Estonian, Finnish, Greek, Hungarian, Latvian, Lithuanian, Polish, Romanian, Slovak, Slovenian, Swedish, Arabic, Hebrew, Hindi and Korean.). To help in the profile creation task were used some language databases provided by Lexiteria [10], which is an initiative aiming at understanding various aspects of human language.

Besides that, due to performance reasons, only words with maximum length $\leq 5$ were considered. This choice is justified because, in most languages, the most frequent words like prepositions, personal pronouns, etc. are also the shorter ones. Thus, in case a word is longer than 5 characters, was taken its 5-length suffix to be included in the language profile. Other values were considered for average length in our experiments, but the best performance results were achieved with $length \leq 5$ [11]. The Language Identification Module of PLIS applies a heuristic that contributed to more accurate results in the experiments performed. This heuristic assumes that if a word (or token) comprises very specific n-grams exclusively found in certain language (such as "ão" in Portuguese), then the method assigns a greater value than the normal vote, which is equal to 1. The language with the highest accumulative scoring value will be chosen as the best matching language for the document.

At the end, each token from the input text will be classified in one or more languages. In case of two or more languages ended in a draw, proceeds to with an additional scoring step consisting in multiplying the final score of each token by its confidence rating. It is calculated by the ratio between the token frequency and the sum of all token frequencies for each profile, so this simple heuristic contributed to choose the right language.

The Europarl v7 "full" corpus [12] with about 60,000 documents with a random distribution between documents and the 21 official languages from the European Community was used to test the accuracy of the Language Identification Module and provided an accuracy of 99.992 %. The other four languages implemented (Arabic, Hebrew, Hindi and Korean) use alphabet-based identification yielding 100% recognition accuracy.

## 2.2 Automatic Translation Module

This task performs an intermediate automatic translation process using Microsoft API [13]. Such function is a fundamental contribution, which aggregates to the platform the condition of supporting some languages, making it language independent. Simple to use, this API is free for requests up to 2,500 characters, which generated an initial difficulty, solved by the textual fragmentation before the translation process to proceed with the defragmentation after processing.

**Frame 1. Translation sample. (a) Original.**

```
[1] (CNNMéxico) — El jamaicano Usain Bolt, que consiguió
este domingo su tercera medalla de oro en Moscú,
su octava medalla de oro en campeonatos del mundo y la
décima en total, se dijo orgulloso de sí mismo y anunció
que seguirá trabajando "para dominar tanto tiempo como
sea posible".
[2] "Da gusto vencer", dijo, luego de ganar con el equipo
jamaicano el primer lugar en la carrera de relevos 4x100,
según EFE.
...
[14] En días anteriores, durante las actividades del
Mundial de Atletismo en Moscú, Rusia, Bolt recuperó su
corona en los 100 metros y también se posicionó como el
mejor en los 200.
[15] La última victoria de Bolt, al igual que la de sus
compatriotas, llega como aire fresco para el deporte en
Jamaica, sacudido en los últimos meses por escándalos de
dopaje como el del velocista Asafa Powell.
```

**(b) Performed by Microsoft Translation API.**

```
[1] (CNNMéxico) - the Jamaican Usain Bolt, who won on
Sunday their third gold medal in Moscow, its eighth gold
medal in the World Championships and tenth overall, said
proud of itself and announced that it will continue to
work "to dominate as long as possible".
[2] "It gives taste to beat," he said, after winning
first place with the Jamaican team in the 4 x 100,
according to EFE relay race.
...
[14] In earlier days, during the activities of the
Athletics World Cup in Moscow, Russia, Bolt regained his
Crown in the 100 meters and also ranked as the best in
the 200.
[15] The last victory of Bolt, as well as of their
compatriots, arrives as fresh air for the sport in
Jamaica, shaken in recent months by scandals of doping as
the sprinter Asafa Powell.
```

In fact, despite translation differences, the sentence indices are maintained, which helps in the multi-language summarization strategy, which concerns in: translating the original content to English; to run the summarization process; and finally, with the results, perform a mapping between the sentences of the obtained summary and the original document. It provides at the final, an abstract in original language of the document.

As sentences are individually numbered by the Text Pre-Processing Module and the summarization process chooses the number of a sentence, instead of the sentence itself, the platform will work correctly even if the language does not follow the left-to-right and top-to-bottom way of writing which is the standard for European languages. In Hebrew and Arabic, for instance, two languages that are also in the PLIS architecture, texts are written right-to-left and top-to-bottom.

## 2.3 Summarization

This step aims to automatically create a small version of the original document. It tries to extract the meaning of the text. This work uses only combined extractive methods combined. The choice of the methods to be implemented was directed by the work in reference [14], which evaluates some methods in different corpora. The methods presented better results and processing time were chosen to compose this task, they are:

- *Word Frequency:* The most frequently occurring words in a text have the highest score. In other words, sentences containing the most frequent words in a document stand a higher chance of being selected for the final summary. The assumption is that the higher the frequency of a word in the text, the more likely that it indicates the subject of the text.

- *Sentence Length*: This feature is employed to penalize sentences that are either too short or long. These sentences are not considered an optimal selection. The method considers length as the number of words in a sentence.

- *Sentence Position*: Many approaches use sentence position as a score criterion. According to Abuobieda *et al.* [15], the first sentence in the paragraph is considered an important sentence and a strong candidate to be included in the summary; Grupta [16] says that the first sentences of paragraphs and words in titles and headings are more relevant to summarization. The method proposed in [17] assigns score 1 to the first N sentences and 0 to the others, where N is a given threshold for the number of sentences.

In the processing, each approach compute values for the sentences of the text, these values are aggregated and ranked; the most punctuated sentences are selected for the summary according the threshold provided by user, which may be the sentence quantity (e.g. 6) or percentage of the text size (i.e. if the original contains 20 sentences, 30% corresponds to 6 sentences).

## 3. EXPERIMENTAL RESULTS

This section presents the methodology experimental results and its analysis for assessing the quality of the summaries generated by the PLIS. The experiments used three different corpora, which have different languages: CNN-English, CNN-Spanish and TeMário-Portuguese. The corpora have the following characteristics: news containing only the text, i.e. neither figures nor videos; high quality news text written by professionals; and a gold-standard summary generated by humans.

The ROUGE (Recall-Oriented Understudy for Gisting Evaluation) [18] was used for assessing the quality of the summaries generated by the platform. It is a quantitative method based on *n*-gram statistics and it is highly correlated with human evaluations [19]. This fully automated evaluator essentially measures the content similarity between system-generated summaries and the corresponding gold-standard summaries (generated by humans). The evaluation is performed using the *n*-gram (1,1) setting of ROUGE, because it was found to have the highest correlation with human judgments at a confidence level of 95%.

In the following sections, the experimental results and its analyses are presented separately for each corpus.

## 3.1 CNN-English

The CNN-English corpus developed by Lins and his collaborators [20] contains news articles extracted from the CNN website. The current version of this corpus presents 400 texts assigned to 10 categories: Asia, business, Europe, Latin America, Middle East, US, sports, technology, travel and world news.

The experimental results of ROUGE for the CNN-English dataset are shown in Table 1. For comparison purposes, some of the experimental results obtained by Ferreira and his colleagues reported in reference [14] were used here. They assessed 17 different summarization algorithms, including those used in this work, using the same CNN-English corpus. They labeled their implementations of the word frequency, length and position of the sentence as Alg01, Alg09 and Alg10, respectively.

**Table 1. ROUGE results for CNN-English dataset.**

| Summarizer | Avg Recall | Avg Precision | Avg F-measure |
|---|---|---|---|
| PLIS | **0.71 (±0.24)** | 0.29 (±0.13) | 0.41 (±0.16) |
| Alg01 [14] | 0.71 (±0.19) | 0.35 (±0.13) | 0.46 (±0.15) |
| Alg09 [14] | 0.70 (±0.18) | 0.33 (±0.12) | 0.44 (±0.15) |
| Alg10 [14] | 0.61 (±0.22) | **0.40 (±0.13)** | **0.47 (±0.15)** |

As one may observe in Table 1 the current strategy in the Summarization Module of PLIS achieved the best recall result, similarly to the word frequency scoring strategy (Alg 01) in [14]. Alg10 (sentence position) has the best precision and F-measure. PLIS showed slightly lower values in precision and F-measure than the other summarization algorithms analyzed. Although the platform loses on average precision, it maintains the average recall for the best result (Alg01). The analysis of better tuning strategies of the sentence scoring algorithms to compose results in the Summarization Module of PLIS are under study.

## 3.2 CNN-Spanish

The CNN-Spanish corpus developed in this work followed the same development path of the CNN-English corpus [20]. It contains news articles extracted from the CNN Mexico website. The current version of this corpus presents 400 texts assigned to 08 categories: sports, entertainment, world, national, opinion, technology, travel and health news.

The experimental results of ROUGE for CNN-Spanish dataset are shown in Table 3. Since this corpus is introduced here, then there no experimental results from other summarizers to analyze.

**Table 2. ROUGE results for CNN-Spanish dataset.**

| Summarizer | Avg Recall | Avg Precision | Avg F-measure |
|---|---|---|---|
| PLIS | **0.72 (±0.11)** | 0.11 (±0.03) | 0.20 (±0.05) |

The average recall of PLIS is close to the values achieved by other corpora presented in Sections 3.1 and 3.3. It might indicate that the amount of errors introduced by the intermediate translation step did not affect the overall process. Nevertheless, further experiments are being developed to yield more accurate figures.

## 3.3 TeMário-Portuguese

TeMário test collection [21] contains 100 news articles from the Brazilian newspapers: *Jornal de Brasil* and *Folha de São Paulo*. The documents were selected to cover a variety of domains (e.g. world, politics, foreign affairs, editorials) and an expert in Brazilian Portuguese language produced manual summaries.

The experimental results of ROUGE for the TeMário dataset are shown in Table 2. For comparison purposes, some of the experimental results obtained by Leite and Rino [22] were used here. They used the same TeMário-Portuguese corpus in their experiments aiming to assess the combination of multiple machine learning features for automatic summarization. They used the measure ROUGE-1 with 30% compression rate and the manual summaries were used as gold. However, only the average recall was reported. For a fair comparison, the experiments used the same configuration.

**Table 3. ROUGE results for TeMário-Portuguese dataset.**

| Summarizer | Avg Recall | Summarizer | Avg Recall |
|---|---|---|---|
| PLIS | **0.77** | TextRank [22] | 0.51 |
| SuPor2-LR [22] | 0.53 | BestCN [22] | 0.50 |
| SuPor-2 [22] | 0.52 | Baseline [22] | 0.49 |

The average recall of PLIS is the highest one. This means that translating the text to English and then extracting a summary appears to be a *valid* technique for multilingual summarization.

## 4. CONCLUSIONS

This paper presented a language independent summarization platform that aims to create short versions of documents to help in multilingual content analysis on the web. An architecture using integrated services based on language classification and translation, summarization, where each method was chosen by prior studies according the best results obtained over years. Three different corpora and languages were used to assess the platform.

The main contributions of this paper are: (a) providing an extensible platform to language independent summarization; (b) supporting up to 25 different languages with the translation intermediate process and a summarization-combined method; (c) the evaluation shows compatible results compared other recent works of the similar purpose. In addition, the summarization platform is easily extensible and with differential adding new languages or new summarization methods. Studies to improve the platform are being intensified, aiming to encompass other languages and summarization methods to yield even better results, including in future studies regarding the sensitivity of summarization with respect to translation process.

The strategies used in the Sentence Scoring and Selection Module are in a better tuning process, but depend on having a much larger test corpus. Efforts in such direction are being performed by the authors.

## 5. ACKNOWLEDGMENTS

The research results reported in this paper have been partly funded by a R&D project between Hewlett-Packard-Brazil and UFPE originated from tax exemption (IPI-Law n 8.248, of 1991 and later updates).

## 6. REFERENCES

[1] D. Radev, T. Allison, S. Blair-Goldensohn, J. Blitzer, A. Çelebi, S. Dimitrov, E. Drabek, A. Hakim, W. Lam, D. Liu, J. Otterbacher, H. Qi, H. Saggion, S. Teufel, M. Topper, A. Winkel e Z. Zhu, "MEAD - a platform for multidocument multilingual text summarization.," *Proceedings of LREC 2004*, Lisbon, Portugal, 2004.

[2] D. K. Evans, K. Mckeown e J. L. Klavans, "Similarity-based Multilingual Multi-Document Summarization," *IEEE Transactions on Information Theory*, vol. 49, 2005.

[3] B. Roark e S. Fisher, "OGI/OHSU baseline multilingual multi-document summarization system," *IEEE International Conference on Microelectronic Systems Education*, , USA, 2005.

[4] M. Litvak, M. Last e M. Friedman, "A New Approach to Improving Multilingual Summarization Using a Genetic Algorithm," *48th Annual Meeting of the Assoc for C. Linguistics*, Sweden, 2010.

[5] V. Gupta, "Hybrid Algorithm for Multilingual Summarization of Hindi and Punjabi Documents," *Lecture Notes in Computer Science. Mining Intelligence and Knowledge Exploration*, vol. 8284, pp. 717-727, 2013.

[6] L. Cabral, R. Lins, R. Lima, R. Ferreira, F. Freitas, G. Silva, G. Cavalcanti, S. Simske e L. Favaro, "A Hybrid Algorithm for Automatic Language Detection on Web and Text Documents," *11th IAPR International Workshop on Document Analysis Systems. Tours – Loire Valley, France,* 10 April 2014.

[7] T. Dunning, "Statistical identification of language," Technical Report CRL MCCS-94-273, Computer Research Lab, New Mexico University, New Mexico, 1994.

[8] W. B. Cavnar e J. M. Trenkle, "N-Gram Based Text Categorization.," *Proceedings of the 3rd Annual Symposium on Document Analysis and Information Retrieval*, pp. 161-169, 1994.

[9] R. Lins e P. Gonçalves, "Automatic language identification of written texts," em *Proceedings of the ACM Symposium on Applied Computing (SAC'04)*, New York, NY, USA, 2004.

[10] Lexiteria, "Word Frequency Lists," Lexiteria, 2002. [Online]. Available: http://www.lexiteria.com/. [Acesso em 09 10 2013].

[11] L. Cabral, R. Lins, R. Lima e S. Simske, "A comparative assessment of language identification approaches in textual documents," *IADIS International Conference Applied Computing 2012*, Madrid, 2012.

[12] P. Koehn, "Europarl: A Parallel Corpus for Statistical Machine Translation," *MT Summit 2005*, 2005.

[13] Microsoft Corporation, "Microsoft Translator V2," MSDN, 2014. Available: http://msdn.microsoft.com/en-us/library/ff512423.aspx. [Last acess 10 March 2014].

[14] R. Ferreira, L. Cabral, R. Lins, G. Silva, F. Freitas, G. Cavalcanti, R. Lima, S. Simske e L. Favaro, "Assesing sentence scoring techniques for extrative text summarization," *Expert Systems with Applications*, pp. 5755-5764, 2013.

[15] A. Abuobieda, N. Salim, A. Albaham, A. Osman e Y. Kumar, "Text summarization features selection method using pseudo genetic-based model.," *International Conference on Information Retrieval Knowledge Management (CAMP)*, pp. 193-197, March 2012.

[16] P. Gupta, V. Pendluri e I. Vats, "Summarizing text by ranking text units according to shallow linguistic features," *13th International Conference on Advanced Communication Technology (ICACT)*, pp. 1620-1625, February 2011.

[17] C. N. Satoshi, S. Satoshi, M. Murata, K. Uchimoto, M. Utiyama, H. Isahara e K. Human, "Info-communication: Sentence extraction system assembling multiple evidence.," *Proceedings of 2nd NTCIR Workshop*, pp. 319-324, 2001.

[18] C.-Y. Lin, "Rouge: A package for automatic evaluation of summaries.," em *Text summarization branches out: Proceedings of the ACL-04 workshop*, Barcelona, Spain, Stan Szpakowicz Marie-Francine Moens, 2004, pp. 74-81.

[19] C.-Y. Lin e E. Hovy, "Automatic evaluation of summaries using n-gram co-occurrence statistics," *Proc. of Human Language Technology Conference (HLT-NAACL 2003)*, Canada, 2003.

[20] R. D. Lins, S. J. Simske, L. S. Cabral, G. F. P. Silva, R. J. Lima, R. F. Mello e L. Favaro, "A multi-tool scheme for summarizing textual documents," em *Proceedings of 11st IADIS International Conference WWW/INTERNET*, Madrid, Spain, 2012.

[21] T. Pardo e L. Rino, "TeMario: a corpus for automatic text summarization.," Technical report, NILC-TR-03-09., São Paulo, 2003.

[22] D. Leite e L. Rino, "Combining multiple features for automatic text summarization through Machine Learning," em *Computational Processing of the Portuguese Language: 8th International Conference, PROPOR 2008*, Springer-Verlag , 2008, pp. 122-132.

# Document Changes: Modeling, Detection, Storage and Visualization (DChanges 2014)

Gioele Barabucci
Cologne Center for eHumanities
Universität zu Köln
Cologne, Germany
gioele.barabucci@uni-koeln.de

Angelo Di Iorio
Department of Computer Science
Università di Bologna
Bologna, Italy
diiorio@cs.unibo.it

Uwe M. Borghoff
Institute for Software Technology
Universität der Bundeswehr München
Neubiberg, Germany
uwe.borghoff@unibw.de

Sonja Maier
Institute for Software Technology
Universität der Bundeswehr München
Neubiberg, Germany
sonja.maier@unibw.de

Ethan Munson
University of Wisconsin-Milwaukee
Milwaukee, WI, USA
munson@uwm.edu

## ABSTRACT

With collaborative tools getting more and more widespread, users have started to become accustomized to features like automatic versioning of their documents or the visualization of changes made by other users. The research community, however, sees that the state of the current tools is seriously lack lusting. The second edition of the DChanges workshop focuses on these shortcomings, introducing new ways to produce version-aware documents and merge changes from multiple sources. Other aspects – in particular, the standardization of formats for tracking changes – are discussed, too.

The gathering is also an occasion to follow up on the projects that were discussed or presented during DChanges 2013, and to foster new collaborations among researchers.

## Categories and Subject Descriptors

I.7.1 [**Document and Text Processing**]: Document and Text Editing—*Version control; Document management*

## Keywords

applications; change analysis and interpretation; change detection; change tracking; merging changes

## 1. INTRODUCTION

This is the second edition of DChanges. The goal of this series of events is to share ideas, common issues and principles about models and algorithms for change tracking and detection, versioning, collaborative editing and related topics. Multidisciplinarity and heterogeneity are key aspects of our vision: we want to look at these topics from different perspectives and we want to identify the most common issues and the peculiarities of each domain and each approach.

The first edition of the workshop [1] was very successful and sparkled many discussion threads; this edition shows how these discussions have progressed during the last year. In particular, the workshop will be focused on tracking changes and interpreting them. Last year, several issues were pointed out as still unsolved, and will be discussed: interfaces do not scale very well when dealing with many changes, changes at different levels of abstraction are often not sufficiently taken into account, detection and visualization are often inter-mixed, logs are often detailed but underexploited, and versioning techniques are not very well suited for non-technical people.

Contributions on related topics (for instance, diff and merge algorithms, standardization of change models, . . . ) and from related areas (e.g., software engineering, online collaboration, . . . ) will complete the discussion.

## 2. PROGRAM

The program reflects quite clearly the fact that DChanges 2014 continues the discussions started in the last edition of the workshop, a fact that we appreciate and regard as an initial step towards the creation of a more connected community of researchers.

At the time of preparation of this summary, we have not finalized the program, yet.

We plan to have four main sessions: the initial keynote given by Jean-Yves Vion-Dury, a first series of presentations on research topics, a second series of more practical talks about experiences in implementing collaborative features in word processors, and finally, a round-table discussion.

*DocEng'14,* September 16–19, 2014, Fort Collins, Colorado, USA.
ACM 978-1-4503-2949-1/14/09.
http://dx.doi.org/10.1145/2644866.2644896 .

During the discussion, some space will be given to the presentation and comparison of formats for tracking changes in XML and in WYSIWYG editors.

## 2.1 Invited Talk

The keynote of this year will be delivered by Jean-Yves Vion-Dury, who works at Xerox Research Centre Europe, and who is a long-time contributor to the DocEng conference series.

## 2.2 Research Papers

The main part of the workshop is the session devoted to the presentation and discussion of research papers. We selected four research papers that represent well the topics of DChanges and show where the research is leading.

All the presented papers will be included in the proceedings of the workshop, planned to be published as a volume of the ACM International Conference Proceedings Series (ICPS) [2].

## 2.3 Experiences and Progress Reports

The second series of talks will focus on more practical issues: the main topic will be the gap between theory and practice that must be crossed when implementing collaborative features in editors and word processors that are meant to be used by users. These users do not care about the intricacies of versioning and just want a simple way to understand who did what and to revert unwanted changes. The talks will highlight how wide this gap is, what has been done to close it and what still has to be done, also in the light of last year's keynote [3].

## 2.4 Round-Table Discussion

The workshop will have plenty of room for discussions. The goal is twofold: fostering research collaboration and eliciting topics and suggestions for a third edition of the workshop. The round-table, in particular, will start with a topic suggested by the organizers, but ample space will be given to the ideas brought by the participants. This formula was very successful last year, generating a lively and fruitful discussion.

A summary of the round-table will be published online at `http://diff.cs.unibo.it/dchanges2014/roundtable/` soon after the conclusion of the workshop.

## 3. TOPICS OF INTEREST

The main focus of this year's workshop are *version-aware documents*, i.e., documents created using formats that are able to internally store multiple revisions or a set of changes that the users have performed on them. The related problem of *how to reconcile changes* from multiple versions will be debated as well.

The second topic that will be discussed extensively this year is *change tracking*. There will be multiple presentations on this topic, spanning from the discussion of models for interoperable mechanisms for change tracking to aspects related to the user interfaces that are used to show the tracked changes.

Another important theme of this year's workshop is the use of different *merging strategies* to reconcile changes made at the same time by different users on the same document.

Besides these topics, the usual DChanges themes are touched by the received submissions: *models and algorithms for the analysis of changes, high-level tools for processing changes* and *user interfaces for versioned documents*.

In contrast to the precedent edition, the submissions received this year show that particular attention has been given to office documents and applications. This signals a welcome shift of focus: from the computer science domain (source code, UML diagrams, ontologies) to more general domains (literary documents, spreadsheets).

## 4. PEOPLE

For the 2014 edition, the original group of organizers (Gioele Barabucci, Uwe M. Borghoff, Angelo Di Iorio and Sonja Maier) has been extended to include Ethan Munson, who was the keynote speaker for DChanges 2013.

An international program committee helped the organizers getting in touch with the researchers, selecting the best submissions, and improving them. The organizers thank them all: Serge Autexier (DFKI Bremen), Boris Konev (University of Liverpool), John Lumley, Pascal Molli (Université de Nantes - LINA), Sebastian Rönnau (Zalando AG), Wolfgang Stürzlinger (York University), Yannis Tzitzikas (University of Crete and FORTH-ICS), Fabio Vitali (Università di Bologna), and Jean-Yves Vion-Dury (Xerox Research Centre Europe).

## 5. REFERENCES

[1] BARABUCCI, G., BORGHOFF, U. M., DI IORIO, A., AND MAIER, S. Document changes: modeling; detection; storing and visualization (DChanges). In *ACM Symposium on Document Engineering 2013, DocEng '13, Florence, Italy, September 10-13, 2013* (2013), S. Marinai and K. Marriott, Eds., ACM, pp. 281–282.

[2] BARABUCCI, G., BORGHOFF, U. M., DI IORIO, A., MAIER, S., AND MUNSON, E., Eds. *DChanges 2014: Proceedings of the 2nd International workshop on Document Changes: Modeling, Detection, Storage and Visualization, Fort Collins, CO, USA, September 16, 2014* (2014), ICPS, ACM. 978-1-4503-2964-4.

[3] MUNSON, E. V. Collaborative authoring requires advanced change management. In *DChanges 2013: Proceedings of the International workshop on Document Changes: Modeling, Detection, Storage and Visualization, Florence, Italy, September 10, 2013* (2013), G. Barabucci, U. M. Borghoff, A. Di Iorio, and S. Maier, Eds., vol. 1008 of *CEUR Workshop Proceedings*, CEUR-WS.org.

# Semantic Analysis of Documents Workshop (SemADoc)

Evangelos Milios
Dalhousie University
6050 University Avenue
Halifax, Nova Scotia B3H 1W5
Canada
eem@cs.dal.ca

Carlotta Domeniconi
George Mason University
4400 University Drive
Fairfax, VA 22030
USA
carlotta@cs.gmu.edu

## 1. MOTIVATION AND AIMS

A large number of document management problems would benefit from having the semantics of documents explicitly represented. However, manually assigning semantic descriptions to documents is labour intensive and error prone. At the same time, the manual generation of domain specific taxonomies is not only labour intensive, but it also needs to be repeated often as the domains themselves and their key concepts shift with time.

In this workshop we focus on document content analysis and semantic enrichment to generate a layer of semantic description of documents that is useful for document management tasks, such as semantic information retrieval, conceptual organization and clustering of document collections for sense making, semantic expert profiling, and document recommender systems. The aim of the workshop is to bring together researchers and practitioners, and discuss different perspectives on the problems, challenges encountered in various application scenarios, and potential solutions.

We have invited submissions in all areas of semantic analysis and enrichment of documents, such as automatic tagging, named entity disambiguation, semantic linking, interactive classification and clustering of documents, document summarization, curation and validation of the analysis process, generation of visualizations of document, author and document collection semantics, user engagement in the semantic analysis process via suitable annotation and correction tools, and study of the trade off between accuracy of the results and user effort. Submissions aimed at solving practical problems in specific application domains, including but not limited to digital libraries, legal document management, personalized online learning systems, news media, are especially welcome.

The workshop is timely and relevant to the Document Engineering community, as its focus is on semantically enriching documents and document collections, to make them more accessible to their readers. The task is nontrivial due to the volume of text data and the rate at which text data is accumulated by companies, government, and individuals.

We have encouraged submissions of work in progress, concept papers, and generally material that will stimulate discussion, generate useful feedback to the authors, encourage research collaborations and vigorous exchange of ideas on promising research directions. We will publish online proceedings. Selected papers describing mature work will be invited to a special issue of Computational Intelligence. We are looking forward to a fruitful and stimulating workshop.

*Acknowledgments.*

The idea for this workshop originated in a birds of a feather session at the 13th ACM Symposium on Document Engineering (DocEng 2013), September 10-13, 2013, Florence, Italy. We thank the participants, Alex Constantin, Angelo Di Iorio, Stefano Ferilli, Enrico Francesconi, Hamid Nourashraf, Francesco Poggi, Marian Simko, Axel Soto, for their input.

*Organizers.*

*Evangelos Milios* is a Professor in the Faculty of Computer Science at Dalhousie University. He has published in interactive document clustering, automatic tagging of documents, topic extraction, cluster evolution in dynamic social streams, and Google n-gram based text relatedness. He has served as the Chair of the Computer Science Discovery Grants Evaluation group at the Natural Sciences and Engineering Research Council of Canada, and on the program committees of ACM Hypertext, AAAI, ACL, WIDM. He has conducted collaborative research on text mining with Boeing, IBM, Palomino System Innovations, Innovatia and Oris4. He is co-Editor-in-Chief of Computational Intelligence. More information is available at http://www.cs.dal.ca/~eem.

*Carlotta Domeniconi* is an Associate Professor in the Department of Computer Science at George Mason University. She has published extensively in premier journals and conferences in machine learning and data mining. She was the program co-Chair of SDM (SIAM International Conference on Data Mining) in 2012; she co-organized the Multi-Clust Workshop collocated with KDD 2013, and the 3Clust Workshop collocated with PAKDD 2012. She is also the co-organizer of a Mini-symposium on "Multiple Clusterings, Multi-view Data, and Multi-source Knowledge-driven Clustering" to be held on April 26, 2014 at SDM. More information is available at http://www.cs.gmu.edu/~carlotta.

# DH-CASE II: Collaborative Annotations in Shared Environments: Metadata, Tools and Techniques in the Digital Humanities

Patrick Schmitz
OCIO/Research IT
UC Berkeley
Berkeley, CA
pschmitz@berkeley.edu

Laurie Pearce
Dept. of Near Eastern Studies
UC Berkeley
Berkeley, CA
lpearce@berkeley.edu

Quinn Dombrowski
OCIO/Research IT
UC Berkeley
Berkeley, CA
quinnd@berkeley.edu

## ABSTRACT
The DH-CASE II Workshop, held in conjunction with ACM Document Engineering 2014, focused on the tools and environments that support annotation, broadly defined, including modeling, authoring, analysis, publication and sharing. Participants explored shared challenges and differing approaches, seeking to identify emerging best practices, as well as those approaches that may have potential for wider application or influence.

## Categories and Subject Descriptors
H.3.1 [**Information Storage and Retrieval**]: Content Analysis and Indexing – *Linguistic processing*, H.3.5 [**Information Storage and Retrieval**]: Online Information Services–*Web-based services*, D.2.13 [**Software Engineering**]: Reusable software

## General Terms
Design, Experimentation, Human Factors

## Keywords
Annotation; Metadata; Cyberinfrastructure; Digital Humanities

## 1. INTRODUCTION
Digital humanities is rapidly becoming a central part of humanities research, drawing upon tools and approaches from computer science, information organization, and document engineering to address the challenges of analyzing and annotating the growing number and range of corpora that support humanist scholarship.

From cuneiform tablets, ancient scrolls, and papyri, to contemporary letters, books, and manuscripts, corpora of interest to humanities scholars span the world's cultures and historic range. More and more documents are being transcribed or transliterated, digitized, and made available for study with digital tools. Scholarship ranges from translation to interpretation, from syntactic analysis to multi-corpus synthesis of patterns and ideas. Underlying much of humanities scholarship is the activity of annotation. Annotation of the "aboutness" of documents and entities ranges from linguistic markup, to structural and semantic relations, to subjective commentary; annotation of "activity" around documents and entities includes scholarly workflows, analytic processes, and patterns of influence among a community of scholars. Sharable annotations and collaborative environments support scholarly discourse, facilitating traditional practices and enabling new ones.

The DH-CASE II Workshop built upon the first DH-CASE Workshop [1] held in conjunction with ACM Document Engineering 2013 in Florence, Italy. The first workshop was organized by Professors Francesca Tomasi and Fabio Vitali, of the University of Bologna.

### 1.1 Workshop Organizers
Patrick Schmitz is the Associate Director of Research IT at UC Berkeley. Schmitz is the technical architect for Berkeley Prosopography Services[1], technical lead of the CollectionSpace project[2] (open source museum collections management), and was senior architect on Project Bamboo[3] (cyberinfrastructure for arts and humanities research).

Dr. Laurie Pearce is a lecturer in Assyriology in the Department of Near Eastern Studies, at UC Berkeley. She specializes in the social and economic history of Mesopotamia (modern Iraq) in the late first millennium BCE. The legal texts from Hellenistic Uruk, which serve as the development and demonstrator corpus for Berkeley Prosopography Services, are the core component of her project "Hellenistic Babylonia: Texts, Images and Names"[4], a component of the Open Richly Annotated Cuneiform Corpus.

Quinn Dombrowski is the Digital Humanities Coordinator in Research IT at UC Berkeley. She is the lead developer of the DiRT (Digital Research Tools) directory[5] and the co-founder and technical editor for the DHCommons[6] project / collaborator matching hub. Her projects include a guide to Drupal for humanists, and an ongoing study of graffiti in public areas of university libraries.

*DocEng'14*, September 16–19, 2014, Fort Collins, Colorado, USA.
ACM 978-1-4503-2949-1/14/09.
http://dx.doi.org/10.1145/2644866.2644898.

---

[1] www.berkeleyprosopography.org

[2] www.collectionspace.org

[3] www.projectbamboo.org

[4] oracc.museum.upenn.edu/hbtin

[5] dirtdirectory.org

[6] dhcommons.org

## 2. WORKSHOP CONTRIBUTIONS

Contributions were solicited related to the intersection of theory, design, and implementation, emphasizing a "big-picture" view of architectural, modeling and integration approaches in digital humanities. Participants were encouraged to discuss data and tool reuse, and explore what the most successful levels are for reusing the products of a digital humanities project (complete systems? APIs? plugins/modules? data models?). We noted that submissions discussing an individual project should focus on these larger questions, rather than primarily reporting on the project's activities.

The workshop was a forum in which to consider the connections and influences between digital humanities annotation tools and environments, and the tools and models used in other domains, which may provide new approaches to the challenges we face. It was also a locus for the discussion of emerging standards and practices such as OAC (Open Annotation Collaboration) and Linked Open Data in Libraries, Archives, and Museums (LODLAM).

We received nine submissions, of which we accepted four for inclusion in the proceedings. The remaining authors were encouraged to attend and participate in the workshop discussion. We received additional requests to participate from members of the community who did not submit papers, and we welcomed their participation.

DH-CASE II was a full-day workshop. Authors of accepted papers were given time to present their research/project, followed by a discussion of emerging themes, best practices, and the potential for integration or collaboration. We summarized the workshop and discussion to the broader DocEng community during the conference.

Proceedings will be published via the ACM International Conference Proceedings Series. Workshop organizers will produce and submit a paper to "Digital Humanities Quarterly" (www.digitalhumanities.org/dhq/) summarizing topics that arose in the workshop. We may consider a special issue on workshop topics or key findings to an appropriate journal.

## 3. ACKNOWLEDGMENTS

Our thanks to Research IT at UC Berkeley for sponsoring the workshop, and to the ACM ICPS for publishing support.

See also the workshop website, at:
http://research-it.berkeley.edu/dhcase2014

### 3.1 Program Committee

We would like to thank the program committee members for their help reviewing submissions, and ensuring that the proceedings were of high quality. The PC members were:

Antoine Isaac, Vrije Universiteit Amsterdam
Cerstin Mahlow, University of Stuttgart
Christof Schöch, University of Würzburg
Claus Huitfeld, University of Bergen
Corey Harper, New York University
Elisabeth Burr, University of Leipzig
Fabio Vitelli, University of Bologna
Francesca Tomasi, University of Bologna
Jacco van Ossenbruggen, CWI, Amsterdam
Jody Perkins, Miami University of Ohio
John Bradley, King's College London
Lisa Spiro, Rice University
Michael Piotrowski, Leibniz Institute of European History
Paolo Ciccarese, Harvard University
Paul Spence, King's College London
Ryan Shaw, University of North Carolina
Silvio Peroni, University of Bologna, Italy

## 4. REFERENCES

[1] Tomasi, F., and Vitali, F., 2013. *Collaborative annotations in shared environments: metadata, vocabularies and techniques in the digital humanities (DH-CASE 2013)*. In Proceedings, ACM DocEng 2013.
http://doi.acm.org/10.1145/2494266.2494323

# DOCENG 2014: PDF TUTORIAL

Steven R. Bagley
School of Computer Science
University of Nottingham
Nottingham NG8 1BB, UK

srb@cs.nott.ac.uk

Matthew R. B. Hardy
Adobe Systems Inc.
345 Park Ave
San Jose, CA 95110-2704

mahardy@adobe.com

## ABSTRACT

Many billions of documents are stored in the Portable Document Format (PDF). These documents contain a wealth of information and yet PDF is often seen as an inaccessible format and, for that reason, often gets a very bad press. In this tutorial, we get under the hood of PDF and analyze the poor practices that cause PDF files to be inaccessible. We discuss how to access the text and graphics within a PDF and we identify those features of PDF that can be used to make the information much more accessible. We also discuss some of the new ISO standards that provide profiles for producing Accessible PDF files.

## Categories and Subject Descriptors

I.7.2 [Document and Text Processing]: Document Preparation — *Markup languages*; I.7.4 [Document and Text Processing]: Electronic Publishing. D.3.4 [Programming Languages] Processors — Compilers; Code Generation

## Keywords

PDF; Compilation; Interpretation; Document Format; Page Description Languages

## 1. INTRODUCTION

The Portable Document Format (PDF) was introduced to the world in 1991 and formally published by Adobe Systems as the PDF Reference Manual in 1993 [1]. PDF was created with the intent of being a final form, paginated, fixed-layout format for documents.

Over the years Adobe Systems has published eight versions of PDF, 1.0-1.7, each of them adding new capabilities to the format. PDF became a *de facto* standard before being published as an ISO standard (ISO 32000-1:2008). Indeed, ISO 32000-1:2008 represents PDF 1.7 as an ISO standard. ISO is currently working on producing ISO 32000-2, PDF 2.0.

### 1.1. Features and Capabilities

The initial versions of PDF were primarily aimed at perfect print and display reproduction and device independence. While later versions added support for new image and font formats, better compression technologies and other capabilities aimed at print and display, there were also many additions aimed at adding "structure" to PDF documents.

These non-print capabilities include items such as bookmarks, article threads, hyperlinks, commenting, logical structure, metadata, file attachments, digital signatures and more. Many of these capabilities are commonly supported by many implementations of consuming software for PDF.

While many users are aware of the print-based capabilities of PDF, far fewer are aware of these non-print capabilities. In fact, there is significant misinformation related to PDF – even within academic communities. It is these higher-level features of PDF that make it such a versatile container format for modern documents.

Also, unlike many current document formats, PDF has a unique object model and a file syntax that appears to make the information stored within the document difficult to access. However, by making correct use of all PDF features and by using the right software all the information can be made easily accessible.

## 2. TUTORIAL DETAILS

This tutorial introduces the capabilities of PDF at a high-level paying particular attention to the non-print capabilities that are essential for content re-use, such as logical structure, accessibility, etc.

The ISO standards have produced subsets of the full PDF specification designed for specific tasks, such as PDF for Archival purposes (PDF/A) and for Universal Accessibility (PDF/UA). The details of these subsets will be discussed.

There will be a focus on the use of PDF in the scientific and engineering communities and the capabilities of the format for representing complex and rich data within PDF.

A breakdown of the tutorial is as follows:

## 2.1. An Introduction to PDF

In this section we introduce the audience to what PDF is and what it is not. We will cover the history described earlier in this document and explain how PDF relates to XML, HTML and other common formats.

## 2.2. Inside PDF

In this section, we will look under the hood of a PDF file and see how it is structured internally as a collection of objects structured into several overlapping trees, representing the various features of a PDF, such as the pages.

We will then spend some time looking at how the pages themselves are described and what it is that can make it difficult to extract information from these descriptions. We will also outline best practices that can be used when creating PDFs to reduce these problems (and also to make the PDFs accessible).

## 2.3. Tagged PDF

PDF is often considered an appearance-based format that describes the *appearance* of information and not the information itself. But this is a mistaken view. In this part of the tutorial, we look at how PDF was extended to contain rich logical structure and semantics.

We will also introduce the audience to the requirements for ensuring accurate content extraction and re-usability.

As part of this section, we will consider the different ways a document can be described (by structure, or by appearance) and see why the approaches taken by many common document processing packages (such as LaTeX) are responsible for PDF's perceived problems.

Finally, in this section, we will introduce the audience to PDF/UA, an ISO profile of PDF enabling strong Accessibility within PDF documents.

## 2.4. Extended Capabilities

PDF has the capability to store file attachments and to indicate the nature of those attachments (e.g. that an attached file represents the source that was used to produce the PDF). This section will described how PDF can be used for Archival purposes (PDF/A).

We will also introduce the audience to some of the cryptographic capabilities of PDF and how digital signatures can be applied to prove that content has not been altered or that it came from a specific author.

## 2.5. Manipulating PDF programmatically

In this section we will cover how to write software that can manipulate PDF documents, using both commercial tools [2,3] and software from open-source projects (such as [4,5,6]). We will consider both how to produce and consume PDF files that conform to the capabilities described above, thereby allowing the scientific community to benefit from these features.

## 2.6. Looking to the Future

PDF 2.0 is on the horizon and with it will come new capabilities. Strongly structured hyperlinks, namespaces for custom logical structure and much more are part of the future of PDF.

## 3. TUTORIAL PRESENTERS

Dr. Steven Bagley, from the University of Nottingham, has performed research in the field of document engineering for the last 14 years. He has provided significant research into PDF analysis and content re-use and is considered a PDF authority.

Dr. Matthew Hardy received his Ph.D. in Document Engineering at the University of Nottingham. His research was related to logical structure representation in PDF and XML. He presently works for Adobe Systems in the Adobe Acrobat and Reader organization and represents the United States at the ISO on PDF Standards (PDF, PDF/A, PDF/E and PDF/UA).

## 4. REFERENCES

[1]  Adobe Systems Incorporated, *Portable Document Format Reference Manual,* Addison-Wesley, June 1993.

[2]  *Acrobat Developer Center*, Adobe Systems Inc. Available at http://www.adobe.com/devnet/acrobat.html

[3]  *PDFlib*. PDFlib GmbH. Available at http://www.pdflib.com/

[4]  *Apache PDFBox*. Available at https://pdfbox.apache.org/

[5]  *iText*, iText Group NV. Available at http://itextpdf.com/

[6]  *XPDF: A pdf viewer for X*. Glyph & Cog, 2005. Available at: http://www.foolabs.com/xpdf/

# Author Index